THE
CENTENARY EDITION
OF THE WORKS OF
NATHANIEL HAWTHORNE

Volume XII

THE AMERICAN CLAIMANT
MANUSCRIPTS

EDITORS

General Editors

WILLIAM CHARVAT, 1905–1966

ROY HARVEY PEARCE

CLAUDE M. SIMPSON, 1910–1976

FREDSON BOWERS, *General Textual Editor*

L. NEAL SMITH, *Associate Textual Editor*

JAMES RUBINO, *Assistant Textual Editor*

This volume edited by

EDWARD H. DAVIDSON

CLAUDE M. SIMPSON

L. NEAL SMITH

A PUBLICATION OF

THE OHIO STATE UNIVERSITY CENTER

FOR TEXTUAL STUDIES

NATHANIEL HAWTHORNE

THE
AMERICAN CLAIMANT
MANUSCRIPTS

The Ancestral Footstep
Etherege
Grimshawe

Ohio State University Press

Editorial expenses for this volume have been supported by
grants from the National Endowment for the Humanities
administered through the
Center for Editions of American Authors of the
Modern Language Association

International Standard Book Number 0–8142–0251–9
Library of Congress Catalogue Card Number 77–75175

CLAUDE M. SIMPSON

CLAUDE SIMPSON was a musician, musicologist, folklorist, cultural historian, textual scholar, literary critic—and in all these roles, the committed professional. He had a marvellous eye for details and was ever concerned to get them exactly straight, only then to make sense of them. It was also thus in his life with his students and colleagues—friends all. With him clarity was a necessary condition of charity; and those who worked with him, above all the editors of the Centenary Hawthorne, learned from him that scholarship, pursued with the utmost rigor, must be a necessary condition of humanism. His was a capacious generosity, and he managed somehow to persuade us that, receiving it, we had in fact earned it. Asking much of us, he asked even more of himself; giving to us, he gave always of himself. The minute particulars of his scholarship and understanding, abundantly evident in the Centenary Edition, are but projections of the minute particulars of his life.

R. H. P.

ACKNOWLEDGMENTS

THE EDITORS are grateful for the assistance given by librarians, scholars, and bibliophiles. We are indebted to Jonathan Culler, Selwyn College, Cambridge University; Herbert T. F. Cahoon, the Pierpont Morgan Library; Jeanne Eason, Columbus, Ohio; Elizabeth C. Simpson, Pasadena, California; Lola L. Szladits, the Berg Collection, New York Public Library; and Paul M. Zall, California State University, Los Angeles.

Special acknowledgment is made to James Rubino for his editorial assistance, and our thanks go to Marianne Bailey, Joyce Heter, and Craig Quellhorst for their work also at Ohio State University, and to Carol Hector-Harris.

For permission to edit the manuscript material of *The American Claimant Manuscripts,* we thank the Pierpont Morgan Library, the Henry E. Huntington Library, the Henry W. and Albert A. Berg Collection of the New York Public Library, Astor, Lenox, and Tilden Foundations, and the Massachusetts Historical Society.

We gratefully acknowledge the support of the National Endowment for the Humanities of the National Foundation on the Arts and Humanities, the Henry E. Huntington Library, the Graduate School of the University of Illinois, Urbana, and the following divisions of the Ohio State University: the Department of English, the Graduate School, the University Libraries, and the Research Foundation.

THE EDITORS

CONTENTS

THE AMERICAN CLAIMANT
MANUSCRIPTS

When Hawthorne died in 1864 he left three unfinished manuscripts developing the theme of an American claimant to an English estate. Along with detached memoranda relating to these works, they make up the content of this volume. The first of these untitled manuscripts was published in the "Atlantic Monthly" in 1882–83 as "The Ancestral Footstep" and is identified here as the "Ancestral Footstep" sketch. A heavily edited composite text drawn from the other two manuscripts was published by Julian Hawthorne in late 1882 as "Doctor Grimshawe's Secret." In printing these latter two manuscripts the Centenary editors have arbitrarily used as titles the name of the doctor in each draft—Etherege in the first, Grimshawe in the second. As working papers these three documents reflect varying degrees of revision and polish, including parenthetical notes on contemplated changes (here printed within angle brackets) and more extended interruptions of the narrative to grapple with problems of story management. A historical commentary following the texts discusses the successive stages in Hawthorne's attempt to write an English romance and describes the posthumous treatment of the several documents here reproduced.

THE ANCESTRAL FOOTSTEP

APRIL 1st, 1858. *Thursday*. He had now been searching long in those rich portions of England, where he would most have wished to find the object of his pursuit; and many had been the scenes which he would willingly have identified with that mentioned in the ancient, time-yellowed record which he bore about with him. It is to be observed that, undertaken at first half as the amusement, the unreal object, of a grown man's play-day, it had become more and more real to him with every step of the way that he followed it up; along those green English lanes, it seemed as if every turning would bring him close to the mansion that he sought; every morning, he went on with renewed hopes; nor did the evening, though it brought with it no success, bring with it the gloom and heaviness of a real disappointment. In all his life, including its earliest and happiest days, he had never known such a spring and zest as now filled his veins, and gave lightsomeness to his limbs; this spirit gave to the beautiful country which he trod a still richer beauty than it had ever borne; and he sought his ancient home in it as if he had found his way into Paradise, and were there endeavoring to trace out the signs of Eve's bridal bower, the birth-place of the human race and all its glorious possibilities of happiness and high performance.

In these sweet and delightful moods of mind, varying from one dream to another, he loved indeed the solitude of his way; but likewise he loved the facility which his pursuit afforded him, of coming in contact with many varieties of men; and he took advantage of this facility to an extent which it was not usually his impulse to do. But now, he came forth from all reserves, and offered himself to whomsoever the chances of the way offered to him, with a ready sensibility that made its way through every barrier that even English exclusiveness, in whatever rank of life, could set up. The plastic character of Middleton was perhaps a variety of his American nature, only presenting itself under an individual form; he could throw off the man of our day, and put on a ruder nature, but still it was with a certain fineness that made this only a distinction between it and the central truth. He found less variety of form in the English character than he had been accustomed to see at home; but perhaps this was in consequence of the external nature of his acquaintance with it; for the view of one well accustomed to a people, and of a stranger to them, differs in this—that the latter sees the homogeneity, the one universal character, the groundwork of the whole, while the former sees a thousand little differences, which distinguish the individual men apart, to such a degree that they seem hardly to have any resemblance among themselves.

But, just at the period of his journey when we take him up, Middleton had been for two or three days the companion of an old man who interested him more than most of his wayside companions; the more especially, as he seemed either to be wandering without an object, or with only such a dreamy object as that which led Middleton's own steps onward. He was a plain old man enough, but with a pale, strong-featured face and white hair, a certain picturesqueness and venerableness, which Middleton fancied might have befitted a richer garb than he now wore. In much of their conversation, too, he was sensible that, though the stranger betrayed no acquaintance with literature, nor seemed to have conversed with cultivated minds, yet that the results of such acquaintance and converse were here. Middleton was inclined to think him, however, an old man, one of those itinerants, such as Wordsworth represented in the Excursion, who smooth themselves by the attrition of the world, and gain a knowledge equivalent to, or better than that of books, from the actual intellect of men, awake and active around them.

Often, during the short period since their companionship originated, Middleton had felt impelled to disclose to the old man the object of his journey; and the wild tale by which, after two hundred years, he had been blown, as it were, across the ocean, and drawn onward to commence this search. The old man's ordinary conversation was of a nature to draw forth such a confidence as this; frequently turning on the traditions of the wayside; the reminiscences that lingered on the battlefields of the Roses, or of the Parliament, like flowers nurtured by the blood of the slain, and prolonging their race through the centuries for the wayfarer to pluck them; or the family histories of the castles, manor-houses, and seats, which, of various epochs, had their park-gates along the road-side, and could be seen, with dark gray towers, or ancient gables, or more modern forms of architecture, rising up among clouds of ancient oaks. Middleton watched earnestly to see, if, in any of these tales, there were circumstances resembling those striking and singular ones which he had borne so long in his memory, and on which he was now acting in so strange a manner; but though there was a good deal of variety of incident in them, there never was any combination of incident having the peculiarity of this.

"I suppose," said he to the old man, "the settlers in my country may have carried away with them traditions, long since forgotten in this country, but which might have an interest and connection, and might even piece out the broken relics of family history, which have remained perhaps a mystery for hundreds of years. I can conceive, even, that this might sometimes be of importance in settling the heirships of estates; but which now, only the two insulated parts of the story being known, remain a riddle, although the solution of it is actually in the world; if only those two parts could be united across the sea, like the wires of an electric telegraph."

"It is an impressive idea," said the old man. "Do you know any such traditions as you have hinted at?"

April 13th. Middleton could not but wonder at the singular chance that had established him in such a place, and in such society, so strangely adapted to the purposes with which he had been wandering through England. He had come hither, hoping as it were to find the past still alive and in action; and here it was so, in this one only spot, and these few persons into the midst of whom he had so suddenly been cast. With these reflections, he looked forth from his window into the old-fashioned garden, and at the stone sun-dial, which had numbered all the hours—all the daylight and serene ones, at least—since his mysterious ancestor left the country. Was this, then, he thought to himself, the establishment of which some rumour had been preserved? Was it here that the secret had its hiding place in the old coffer, in the cupboard, in the secret chamber, or whatever was indicated by the apparently idle words of the document which he had preserved? He still smiled at the idea, but it was with a pleasant, mysterious sense that his life had at last got out of the dusty real, and that strangeness had mixed itself up with his daily experience.

With such feelings, he prepared himself to go down to dinner with his host. He found him alone at table, which was placed in a dark old room, modernized with every English comfort; and the pleasant spectacle of a table set with the whitest of napery and the brightest of glass and silver. The friendly old gentleman, as he had found him from the first, became doubly and trebly so in that position which brings out whatever warmth of heart an Englishman has, and gives it to him if he has none. The impressionable and sympathetic character of Middleton answered to the kindness of his host; and by the time the meal was concluded, the two were conversing with almost as much zest and friendliness, as if they were similar in age, were fellow-countrymen, and had known one another all their life-time. Middleton's secret, as may be supposed, came often to the tip of his tongue; but still he kept it within, from a natural repugnance to bring out the one romance of his life. The talk, however, necessarily ran much upon topics among which this one would have come in without any extra attempts to introduce it.

"This decay of old families," said the Master, "is much greater than would appear on the surface of things. We have such a reluctance to part with them, that we are content to see them continued by any fiction, through any indirections, rather than to dispense with old names. In your country, I suppose, there is no such reluctance; you are willing that one generation should blot out all that preceded it, and be itself the newest and only age of the world."

"Not quite so," answered Middleton; "at any rate, if there be such a feeling in the people at large, I doubt whether, even in England, those who fancy themselves possessed of claims to birth, cherish them more as a treasure than we do. It is, of course, a thousand times more difficult for us to keep alive a name amid a thousand difficulties sedulously thrown around it by our institutions, than for you to do, where your institutions are anxiously calculated to promote the contrary purpose. It has occasionally struck me, however, that the direct lineage might often be found in America, for a family which has been compelled to prolong itself here through the female line, and through alien stocks."

"Indeed, my young friend," said the Master, "if that be the case, I should like to speak further with you upon it; for, I can assure you, there are sometimes vicissitudes in old families that make me grieve to think that a man cannot be made for the occasion."

All this while, the young lady at table had remained almost silent; and Middleton had only occasionally been reminded of her by the necessity of performing some of those offices which put people at table under a christian necessity of recognizing one another. He was, to say the truth, somewhat interested in her, yet not strongly attracted by the neutral tint of her dress, and the neutral character of her manners. She did not seem to be handsome, although, with her face full before him, he had not quite made up his mind upon this point.

April 14th. So here was Middleton, now at length seeing indistinctly a thread, to which the thread that he had so long held in his hand—the hereditary thread, that ancestor after ancestor had handed down—might seem ready to join in. He felt as if they were the two points of an electric chain, which being joined, an instantaneous effect must follow. Earnestly as he would have looked forward to this moment, (had he in sober reason, ever put any real weight on the fantasy in pursuit of which he had wandered so far,) he now, that it actually appeared to be realizing itself, paused with a vague sensation of alarm. The mystery was evidently one of sorrow, if not of crime; and he felt as if that sorrow and crime might not have been annihilated even by being buried, out of human sight and remembrance so long. He remembered to have heard or read, how that once an old pit had been dug open, in which were found the remains of persons that, as the shuddering by-standers traditionally remembered, had died of an ancient pestilence; and out of that old grave had come a new plague, that slew the far-off progeny of those who had first died by it. Might not some fatal treasure like this, in a moral view, be brought to light by the search into which he had so strangely been drawn? Such were the fantasies with which he awaited the return of Alice, whose light footstep sounded afar along the passages of the old mansion; and then all was silent.

At length, he heard the sound, a great way off, as he concluded, of her returning footstep, approaching from chamber to chamber, and up the staircases, closing the doors behind her. At first, he paid no great attention to the character of these sounds; but as they drew nearer, he became aware that the footstep was unlike that of Alice; indeed, as unlike as could be, being heavy, regular, slow, yet not firm, so that it seemed to be that of an aged person, sauntering leisurely through the rooms. We have often alluded to Middleton's sensitiveness, and the quick vibrations of his sympathies; and there was something in this slow approach that produced a strange feeling within him; so that he stood breathlessly, looking towards the door by which these slow footsteps were to enter. At last, there appeared in the doorway, a venerable figure clad in a rich, faded dressing-gown, and standing on the threshold looked fixedly at Middleton, at the same time holding up a light in his left hand. In his right was some object that Middleton did not distinctly see. But he saw the figure, and recognized the face. It was the old man, his long since companion on his first journey hitherward.

"So," said the old man, smiling gravely, "you have thought fit, at last, to accept the hospitality which I offered you so long ago. It might have been better for both of us—for all parties—if you had accepted it then!"

"You here!" exclaimed Middleton. "And what can be your connection with all the error, and trouble, and involuntary wrong, through which I have wandered since our last meeting? And is it possible that you even then held the clue which I was seeking?"

"No,—no," replied Rothermel. "I was not conscious, at least, of so doing. And yet had we two sat down there by the wayside, or on that English style which attracted your fancy so much; had we sat down there and shown forth each his own dream—each his own knowledge—it would have saved much, that we must now forever regret. Are you even now ready to confide wholly in me?"

"Alas," said Middleton, with a darkening brow, "there are many reasons, at this moment, which did not exist then, to incline me to hold my peace. And why has not Alice returned?—and what is your connection with her?"

"Let her answer for herself," said Rothermel; and he called her, shouting through that silent house, as if she were at the furthest chamber, and he were in an instant need. "Alice!—Alice!—Alice!—here is one that would know what is the link between a maiden and her father!"

Amid the strange uproar which he made, Alice came flying back, not in alarm, but only in haste, and put her hand within his own. "Hush, father," said she. "It is not time."

Here is an abstract of the plot of this story. The Middleton, who emigrated to America, more than two hundred years ago, had been a dark and moody man; he came with a beautiful, though sad young woman for his wife, and left a family behind him. In this family, a certain heirloom had been preserved, and with it a tradition that grew wilder and stranger with the passing generations. The tradition had lost, if it ever had, some of its connecting links; but it referred to a murder, to the expulsion of a brother from the hereditary house, in some strange way, and to a Bloody Footstep which he had left impressed into the threshold, as he turned about to make a last remonstrance. It was rumored, however, or vaguely understood, that this expelled brother was not altogether an innocent man; but that there had been wrong done, as well as crime committed, insomuch that his reasons were strong that led him, subsequently, to imbibe the most gloomy religious views, and to bury himself in the western wilderness. These reasons he had never fully imparted to his family; but had occasionally made allusions to them, which were treasured up and doubtless enlarged upon. At last, one descendant of the family determines to go to England, with the purpose of searching out whatever ground there may be for these traditions, carrying with him certain ancient documents and other relics; and goes about the country, half in earnest, half in a sport of fancy, in quest of the old family mansion. He makes singular discoveries, all of which bring the book to an ending unexpected by everybody, and not satisfactory to the natural yearnings of novel-readers. In the traditions that he brought over, there was a key to some family secrets that were still unsolved, and that controlled the descents of estates and titles. His influence upon these matters involves him in divers strange and perilous adventures; and at last it turns out that he himself is the rightful heir to the title and estate, that had passed into another name, within the last half-century. But he rejects both, feeling that it is better to take a virgin soil, than to try to make the old name grow in a soil that had been darkened with so much blood and misfortune as this.

April 27th. Tuesday. It was with a delightful feeling of release from ordinary rules, that Middleton found himself brought into this connection with Alice; and he only hoped that this play day of his life might last long enough to rest him from all that he had suffered. In the enjoyment of his position, he almost forgot the pursuit that occupied him, nor might he have remembered for a long space, if, one morning, Alice herself had not alluded to it. "You are wasting precious days," she suddenly said. "Why do not you renew your quest?" "To what do you allude?" said Middleton, in surprise. "What object do you suppose me to have?" Alice smiled; nay laughed outright. "You suppose yourself to be a perfect mystery, no doubt," she replied. "But do not I know you—have not I known you long—as the holder of the talisman; the owner of the mysterious cabinet, that contains the blood-stained secret?" "Nay, Alice, this is certainly a strange coincidence, that you should know even thus much of a foolish secret that makes me employ this little holiday time, which I have stolen out of a weary life, in a wild-goose chase! But, believe me, you allude to matters that are more a mystery to me, than my affairs appear to be to you. Will you explain what you would suggest by this badinage?" Alice shook her head. "You have no claim to know what I know, even if it would be any addition to your own knowledge. I shall not, and must not enlighten you. You must burrow for the secret with your own tools, in your own manner, and in a place of your own choosing. I am bound not to assist you." "Alice, this is wilful, wayward, unjust," cried Middleton, with a flushed cheek. "I have not told you—yet you well know— the deep and real importance which this subject has for me. We have been together as friends, yet, the instant when there comes up an occasion where the slightest friendly feeling would induce you to do me a good office, you assume this altered tone." "My tone is not in the least altered in respect to you," said Alice. "All along, as you know, I have reserved myself on this very point; it being, I candidly tell you, impossible for me to act in your interests in the matter alluded to. If you choose to consider this unfriendly—as being less than the terms, on which you conceive us to have stood, give you a right to demand of me—you must resent it as you please. I shall not the less retain for you the regard due to one who has certainly befriended me in very untoward circumstances."

This conversation confirmed the previous idea of Middleton, that some mystery of a peculiarly dark and evil character was connected with the family secret with which he was himself entangled; but it perplexed him to imagine in what way this, after the lapse of so many years, could continue to be a matter of real importance at the present day. All the actors in the original guilt—if guilt it were—must have been long ago in their graves—some in the church-yard of the village, with those moss-grown letters embossing their names; some in the church itself, with old mural tablets, recording their names, over the family-pew, and one, it might be, far over the sea, where his grave was first made under the forest-leaves, though now a city had grown up around it. Yet here was he, the remote descendant of that family, setting his foot at last in the county, and as secretly as might be; and all at once, his mere presence seemed to revive the buried secret, almost to awake the dead, who partook of that secret and had acted it. There was a vibration from the other world, continued and prolonged into this, the instant that he stept upon that mysterious and haunted ground.

He knew not in what way to proceed. He could not but feel that there was something not exactly within the limits of propriety in being here, disguised—at least, not known in his true character—prying into the secrets of a proud and secluded Englishman. But, then, as he said to himself on his own side of the question, the secret belonged to himself by exactly as ancient a tenure, and by precisely as strong a claim, as to the Englishman. His rights here were just as powerful and well founded as those of his ancestor had been, nearly three centuries ago; and here the same feeling came over him, that he himself was that very personage, returned after all these ages, to see if his foot would fit that bloody footmark left of old upon the threshold. The result of all his cogitations was, as the reader will have foreseen, that he decided to continue his researches, and, his proceedings being pretty defensible, let the result take care of itself.

For this purpose, he went next day to the Hospital, and ringing at the Master's door, was ushered into the old-fashioned, comfortable library, where he had spent that well-remembered evening which threw the first ray of light on the pursuit that now seemed developing into such strange and unexpected consequences. Being admitted, he was desired by the domestic to wait, as his Reverence was at that moment engaged with a gentleman on business. Glancing through the ivy that mantled over the window, Middleton saw that this interview was taking place in the garden, where the Master and his visitor were walking to-and-fro in the avenue of box, discussing some matter, as it seemed to him, with considerable earnestness on both sides. He observed too that there was warmth, passion, a disturbed feeling on the stranger's part; while, on that of the Master, it was a calm, serious, earnest representation of whatever view he was endeavoring to impress on the other. At last, the interview appeared to come towards a climax, the Master addressing some words to his guest, still with undisturbed calmness, to which the latter replied by a violent and even fierce gesture, as it should seem of menace, not towards the Master, but some unknown party; and then hastily turning, he left the garden, and was soon heard riding away. The Master looked after him awhile, and then shaking his white head, returned into the house, and soon entered the parlour.

He looked somewhat surprised, and, as it struck Middleton, a little startled, on finding him there; yet he welcomed him with all his former cordiality—indeed, with a friendliness that thoroughly warmed Middleton's heart even to its coldest corner. "This is strange!" said the old gentleman. "Do you remember our conversation on that evening when I first had the unlooked for pleasure of receiving you as a guest into my house? At that time, I spoke to you of a strange family-story, of which there was no denouement, such as a novel-writer would desire, and which had remained in that unfinished posture for more than two hundred years! Well; perhaps it will gratify you to know that there seems a prospect of that wanting termination being at length supplied!" "Indeed!" said Middleton.

"Yes," replied the Master. "A gentleman has just parted with me, who was indeed the representative of the family concerned in the story. He is the descendant of a younger son of that family, to whom the estate devolved about a century ago, although at the time there was search for the heirs of the elder son, who had disappeared after the bloody incident which I related to you. Now, singular as it may appear, at this late day, a person claiming to be the descendant and heir of that eldest son has appeared; and if I may credit my friend's account, is disposed not only to claim the estate, but the dormant title, which Eldredge himself has been so long preparing to claim for himself. Singularly enough, too, the heir is an American."

May 2ᵈ. Sunday. "I believe," said Middleton, "that many English secrets might find their solution in America, if the two threads of a story could be brought together, disjoined as they have been by time and the ocean. But are you at liberty to tell me the nature of the incidents to which you allude?"

"I do not see any reason to the contrary," answered the Master; "for the story has already come in an imperfect way before the public, and the full and authentic particulars are likely soon to follow. It seems that the younger brother was ejected from the house, on account of a love affair; the elder having married a young woman with whom the younger was in love, and, it is said, the wife disappeared on the bridal night, and was never heard of more. The elder brother remained single during the rest of his life; and dying childless, and there being still no news of the second brother, the inheritance and representation of the family devolved, on the third brother and his posterity. This branch of the family has ever since remained in possession; and latterly the representation has become of more importance, on account of a claim to an old title, which, by the failure of another branch of this ancient family, has devolved upon the branch here settled. Now, just at this juncture, comes another heir from America, pretending that he is the descendant of a marriage between the second son, supposed to have been murdered on the threshold of the manor-house, and the missing bride! Is it not a singular story?"

"It would seem to require very strong evidence to prove it," said Middleton. "And methinks a Republican should care little for the title, however he might value the estate."

"Both—both," said the Master smiling, "would be equally attractive to your countryman. But there are further curious particulars in connection with this claim. You must know, they are a family of singular characteristics, humourists, sometimes developing their queer traits into something like insanity; though oftener, I must say, spending stupid hereditary lives here on their estates, rusting out, and dying without leaving any biography whatever about them. And yet there has always been one queer thing about this generally very common-place family. It is that each father, on his death-bed, has had an interview with his son, at which he has imparted some secret that has evidently had an influence on the character and after life of the son, making him ever after a discontented man, aspiring for something he has never been able to find. Now the American, I am told, pretends that he has the clue which has always been needed to make this secret available; the key whereby the lock may be opened; the something that the lost son of the family carried away with him, and by which through three centuries he has impeded the prosperity of his race. And, wild as the story seems, he does certainly seem to bring something that looks very like proof of what he says."

"And what are those proofs?" inquired Middleton, wonder-stricken at this strange reduplication of his own position and pursuits.

"In the first place," said the Master, "the English marriage certificate by a clergyman of that day in London, after publication of the banns, with a reference to the register of the parish-church, where the marriage is recorded. Then, a certified genealogy of the family in New England, where such matters can be ascertained from town and church records, with at least as much certainty, it would appear, as in this country. He has likewise a manuscript in his ancestor's autograph, containing a brief account of the events which banished him from his own country; the circumstances which favored the idea that he had been slain, and which he himself was willing should be received as a belief; the fortune that led him to America, where he wished to found a new race, wholly disconnected with the past; and, this manuscript he sealed up, with directions that it should not be opened till two hundred years after his death, by which time, as it was probable to conjecture, it would matter little to any mortal whether the story was told or not. Yet see how strangely it turns out. A whole generation has passed since the time when the paper was at last unsealed and read; so long, it had no operation; yet now, at last, here comes the American, to disturb the succession of an ancient family!"

"There is something very strange in all this," said Middleton.

And, indeed, there was something stranger in his view of the matter than he had yet communicated to the Master. For, taking into consideration the relation in which he found himself with the present recognized representative of the family, the thought struck him that his coming hither had dug up, as it were, a buried secret that immediately assumed life and activity, the moment that it was above ground again. For seven generations, the family had vegetated in the quietude of English country gentility, doing nothing to make itself known, passing from the cradle to the tomb amid the same old woods that had waved over it, before his ancestor had impressed the bloody footstep; and, yet, the instant that he came back, an influence seemed to be at work that was likely to renew the old history of the family. He questioned within himself, whether it were not better for him to leave all as it was; to withdraw himself into the secrecy from which he had but half emerged; and leave the family to keep on, to the end of time perhaps, in its rusty innocence; rather than to interfere with his wild American character to distract it. The smell of that rank crime—that brotherly hatred and attempted murder—seemed to breathe out of the ground as he dug it up. Was it not better that it shd remain for ever buried; for what to him was this old English title—what this estate, so far from his own native land, located amidst feelings and manners which could never be his own? It was late, to be sure—yet not yet too late, for him to turn back; the vibration, the jar, which his footsteps had caused, would soon be forgotten, and again the family would subside into peace! Meditating in this way, he took a hasty leave of the kind old Master, promising to see him again at an early opportunity. By chance, or however it was, his footsteps turned to the woods of Cumnor Close, and there he wandered through its glades, deep in thought, yet always with a strange sense that he was treading on the soil where his ancestors had trodden, and where he himself had best right of all men to be. It was just in this state of feeling, that he found his course arrested by a hand laid upon his shoulder.

"What business have you here?" was the question sounded in his ear; and starting he found himself in the grasp, as his blood tingled to know, of a gentleman in a shooting-dress, who looked at him with a wrathful brow. "Are you poacher, or what?"

Be the cause what it might, Middleton's blood boiled at the grasp of that hand, as it never had before done in the course of his impulsive life. He shook himself free, and stood fiercely before his antagonist, confronting him with his uplifted stick, while the other, likewise, appeared to be shaken by a strange wrath.

"Fellow," muttered he—"Yankee blackguard!—imposter—take yourself off these grounds. Quick; or it will be the worse for you!"

Middleton restrained himself. "Mr Eldredge," said he; "for I believe I speak to the man who deems himself owner of this land on which we tread—Mr. Eldredge, you are acting under a strange misapprehension of my character. I have come hither with no sinister purposes; and am entitled, at the hands of a gentleman, to the consideration of an honorable antagonist, even if you deem me one at all. And perhaps, if you think upon the blue chamber, and the ebony cabinet, and the secret connected with it—"

"Villain, no more!" said Eldredge; and utterly mad with rage, he presented his gun at Middleton; but even at the moment of doing so, he partly restrained himself, so far as, instead of shooting him, to raise the butt of the gun, and strike a blow at him. It came down heavily on Middleton's shoulder, though aimed at his head; but the blow was terribly avenged, even by itself, for the jar caused the hammer to come down; the gun went off, sending the bullet downwards through the heart of the unfortunate man, who fell dead upon the ground. Middleton stood stupified, looking at the catastrophe which had so suddenly occurred.

May 3ᵈ. Monday. So here was the secret, suddenly made safe in this so terrible way; its keepers reduced from two parties to one interest; the other, who alone knew of all this age-long mystery and trouble, now carrying it into eternity, where a long line of those who partook of the knowledge, in each successive generation, might now be waiting to inquire of him how he had held his trust. He had kept it well; there was no doubt of it; for there he lay dead upon the ground, having betrayed it to none, though, by a method which none could have foreseen, the whole had come into the possession of him who brought hither but half of it. Middleton looked down in horror upon the form that had just before been so full of life and wrathful vigour—and now lay so quietly. Being wholly unconscious of any purpose to bring about the catastrophe, it had not at first struck him that his own position was in any manner affected by the violent death, under such circumstances, of the unfortunate man. But now it suddenly occurred to him, that there had been a train of incidents all calculated to make him the object of suspicion; and he felt that he could not, under the English administration of law, be suffered to go at large without rendering a strict account of himself and his relations with the deceased. He might, indeed, fly; he might still remain in the vicinity, and possibly escape notice. But was not the risk too great? Was it just, even, to be aware of this event, and not relate fully the manner of it, lest a suspicion of blood-guiltiness should rest upon some innocent head? But while he was thus cogitating, he heard footsteps approaching along the wood-path; and half impulsively, half on purpose, he stept aside into the shrubbery, but still where he could see the dead body and what passed near it.

The footsteps came on; and at the turning of the path, just where Middleton had met Eldrege, the new-comer appeared in sight. It was Hogan, in his usual dress of velveteen, looking now seedy, poverty stricken, and altogether in ill-case, trudging moodily along, with his hat pulled over his brows; so that he did not see the ghastly object before him till his foot absolutely trod upon the dead man's hand. Being thus made aware of the proximity of the corpse, he started back a little, yet evincing such small emotion as did much credit to his English nerve; then uttering a low exclamation —cautiously low, indeed—he stood looking at the corpse a minute or two, apparently in deep consideration. He then drew near, bent down, and without evincing any horror at the touch of death in this horrid shape, he opened the dead man's vest, inspected the wound, satisfied himself that life was extinct, and then nodded his head and smiled grimly. He next proceeded to examine seriatim the dead man's pockets, turning each of them inside out, and taking the contents, when they appeared adapted to his needs;—for instance, a silken purse, through the interstices of which some gold was visible; a watch, which, however, had been injured by the explosion, and had stopt just at the moment—twenty-one minutes past five—when the catastrophe took place. Hogan ascertained, by putting the watch to his ear, that this was the case; then pocketing it, he continued his researches. He likewise secured a note-book, on examining which he found several bank-notes, and some other papers. And having done this, the thief stood considering what to do next; nothing better occurring to him, he thrust the pockets back, gave the corpse as nearly as he could, the same appearance that it had worn when he found it, and hastened away, leaving the horror there on the wood-path.

He had been gone only a few minutes, when another step, a light, woman's step, came with gentle haste along the pathway; and Alice appeared, having on her usual white mantle, straying alone with that fearlessness which characterized her so strongly, and made her seem like one of the denizens of nature. She was singing in a low tone some one of those airs which have become so popular in England as negro melodies; when suddenly, looking before her, she saw the blood-stained body on the grass, the face looking ghastly upward. Alice pressed her hand upon her heart; it was not her habit to scream, not the habit of that strong, wild, self-dependent nature; and the exclamation which broke from her was not for help, but the voice of her heart crying out to herself. For an instant, she hesitated, as not knowing what to do; then approached, and, with her white maiden hand, felt the brow of the dead man, trembling, but yet firm, and satisfied herself that life had wholly departed. She pressed her hand, that had just touched the dead man's, on her own forehead, and gave a moment to thought.

What her decision might have been, we cannot say; for while she stood in this attitude, Middleton stept from his seclusion; and at the rustle of his approach, she turned suddenly round, looking more frightened and agitated than at the moment when she had first seen the dead body. She faced Middleton, however, and looked him quietly in the eye. "You see this!" said she, gazing fixedly at him. "It is not at this moment that you first discover it."

"No," said Middleton, frankly. "It is not. I was present at the catastrophe. In one sense, indeed, I was the cause of it; but Alice, I need not tell you that I am no murderer."

"A murderer?—no," said Alice, still looking at him with the same fixed gaze. "But you and this man were at deadly variance. He would have rejoiced at any chance that would have lain you cold and bloody on the earth, as he lies now; nay, he would most eagerly have seized on any fair-looking pretext that would have given him a chance to stretch you there. The world will scarcely believe, when it knows all about your relations with him, that his blood is not on your hand. Indeed," said she, with a strange smile, "I see some of it there now!"

And, in very truth, so there was; a broad blood-stain that had dried on Middleton's hand. He shuddered at it, but essayed vainly to rub it off.

"You see," said she. "It was foreordained that you should shed this man's blood; foreordained that, by digging into that old pit of pestilence, you should set the contagion loose again. You should have left it buried forever. But now what do you mean to do?"

"To proclaim this catastrophe," replied Middleton. "It is the only honest and manly way. What else can I do?"

"You can and ought to leave him on the wood-path, where he has fallen," said Alice, "and go yourself to take advantage of the state of things which Providence has brought about. Enter the old house, the hereditary house, where—now, at least—you alone have a right to tread. Now is the hour. All is within your grasp. Let the wrong of three hundred years be righted, and come back thus to your own, to these hereditary fields, this quiet, long descended home; to title; to honor."

Yet as the wild maiden spoke thus, there was a sort of mockery in her eyes; on her brow; gleaming through all her face, as if she scorned what she thus pressed upon him, the spoils of the dead man who lay at their feet. Middleton, with his susceptibility, could not but be sensible of a wild and strange charm, as well as a horror in the situation; it seemed such a wonder that here, in formal, orderly, well-governed England, so wild a scene as this should have occurred; that they two should stand here, deciding on the descent of an estate, and the inheritance of a title, holding a court of their own.

"Come then," said he, at length. "Let us leave this poor fallen antagonist in his blood, and go whither you will lead me. I will judge for myself. At all events, I will not leave my hereditary home without knowing what my power is."

"Come," responded Alice; and she turned back; but then returned and threw a handkerchief over the dead man's face, which while they spoke, had assumed that quiet, ecstatic expression of joy, which often is observed to overspread the faces of those who die of gunshot wounds, however fierce the passion in which their spirits took their flight. With this strange, grand, awful joy, did the dead man gaze upward into the very eyes and hearts, as it were, of the two that now bent over him. They looked at one another.

"Whence comes this expression?" said Middleton, thoughtfully. "Alice, methinks he is reconciled to me now; and that we are members of one reconciled family, all of whom are in Heaven but me."

Tuesday. May 4th. "How strange is this whole relation between you and me," said Middleton, as they went up the winding pathway that led towards the house. "Shall I ever understand it? Do you mean ever to explain it to me? That I should find you here with that old man, so mysterious, apparently so poor, yet so powerful! What is his relation to you?"

"A close one," replied Alice sadly. "He was my father!"

"Your father!" repeated Middleton, starting back. "It does but heighten the wonder! Your father! And yet, by all the tokens that birth and breeding, and habits of thought, and native character, can show, you are my countrywoman. That wild, free spirit was never borne in the breast of an English-woman; that slight frame, that slender beauty, that frail envelopment of a quick, piercing, yet stubborn and patient spirit—are those the properties of an English maiden?"

"Perhaps not," replied Alice quietly. "I am your country-woman. My father was an American, and one of whom you have heard—and no good, alas!—for many a year."

"And who then was he?" asked Middleton.

"I know not whether you will hate me for telling you," replied Alice, looking him sadly though firmly in the face. "There was a man—long years since, in your childhood—

whose plotting brain proved the ruin of himself and many another; a man whose great designs made him a sort of potentate, whose schemes became of national importance, and produced results even upon the history of the country in which he acted. That man was my father; a man who sought to do great things, and, like many who have had similar aims, disregarded many small rights, strode over them, in his way to effect a gigantic purpose. Among other men, your father was trampled under foot, ruined, done to death, even, by the effects of his ambition."

"How is it possible," exclaimed Middleton. "Was it Wentworth?"

"Even so," said Alice, still with the same sad calmness, and not withdrawing her steady eyes from his face. "After his ruin; after the catastrophe that overwhelmed him and hundreds more, he took to flight; guilty, perhaps, but guilty as a fallen conqueror is; guilty to such an extent that he ceased to be a cheat, as a conqueror ceases to be a murderer. He came to England. My father had an original nobility of nature; and his life had not been such as to debase it, but rather such as to cherish and heighten that self-esteem which at least keeps the possessor of it from any meaner vices. He took nothing with him; nothing beyond the bare means of flight, with the world before him, although thousands and thousands of gold would not have been missed out of the scattered fragments of ruin that lay around him. He found his way hither, led, as you were, by a desire to re-connect himself with the place whence his family had originated; for he too was of a race that had somewhat to do with that ancient story which has now been brought to a close. Arrived here, there were circumstances that chanced to make his talents and habits of business available to this Mr. Eldredge, a man ignorant and indolent, unknowing how to make the best of the property that was in his hands. By degrees, he took the estate into his management, acquiring necessarily a preponderating influence over such a man."

"And you," said Middleton. "Have you been all along in England? For you must have been little more than an infant, at the time."

"A mere infant," said Alice, "and I remained in our own country, under the care of a relative, who left me much to my own keeping; much to the influences of that wild culture which the freedom of our country gives to its youth. It is only two years that I have been in England."

"This then," said Middleton thoughtfully, "accounts for much that has seemed so strange in the events through which we have passed; for the knowledge of my identity, and my half-defined purpose, which has always glided before me, and thrown so many strange shapes of difficulty in my path. But, whence,—whence came that malevolence which your father's conduct has so unmistakeably shown? I had done him no injury, though I had suffered much."

"I have often thought," replied Alice, "that my father, though retaining a preternatural strength and acuteness of intellect, was really not altogether sane. And, besides, he had made it his business to keep this estate, and all the complicated advantages of the representation of this old family, secure to the person who was deemed to have inherited them. A succession of ages and generations might be supposed to have blotted out your claims from existence; for it is not just that there should be no term of time which can make security for lack of just a few formalities. At all events, he had satisfied himself that his duty was to act as he has done."

"Be it so! I do not seek to throw blame on him," said Middleton. "Besides, Alice, he was your father!"

"Yes," said she, sadly smiling; "let him have what protection that thought may give him, even though I lose what he may gain. And now here we are at the house. At last, come in! It is your own; there is none that can longer forbid you!"

They entered the door of the old mansion, now a farm-house, and there were its old hall, its old chambers, all before them. They ascended the staircase, and stood on the landing-place above; while Middleton had again that feeling that had so often made him dizzy—that sense of being in one dream, and recognizing the scenery and events of a former dream. So overpowering was now this feeling, that he laid his hand on the slender arm of Alice to steady himself; and she comprehended the emotion that agitated him, and looked into his eyes with a tender sympathy, which she had never before permitted to be visible—perhaps never before felt. He steadied himself, and followed her, till they had entered an ancient chamber, but one that was furnished with all the comfortable luxury customary to be seen in English houses.

"Whither have you led me now?" inquired Middleton.

"Look round," said Alice. "Is there nothing here that you ought to recognize?—nothing that you kept the memory of, for long ages?"

He looked round the room again and again; and at last, in a somewhat shadowy corner, he espied an old cabinet, made of ebony and inlaid with pearl; one of those tall, stately, and elaborate pieces of furniture that are rather articles of architecture than upholstery; and on which a higher skill, feeling, and genius, than now is ever employed on such things, was expended. Alice drew near this stately cabinet, and threw wide the doors, which like the portal of a palace, stood between two pillars; it all seemed to be enlaced, showing within some beautiful old pictures on the pannel of the doors, and a mirror, that opened a long succession of mimic halls, reflection upon reflection, extending to an interminable nowhere.

"And what is this?" said Middleton; "—a cabinet? Why do you draw my attention so strongly to it?"

"Look at it well!" said she. "Do you recognize nothing there? Have you forgotten your description? The stately palace, with its architecture, each pillar, with its architecture, those pilasters, that frieze—you ought to know them all. Somewhat less than you imagined in size, perhaps—a fairy reality, inches for yards; that is the only difference! And you have the key!"

And this then was that palace to which tradition, so false at once, and true, had given such magnitude and magnificence in the stories of the Middleton family, around their shifting firesides in America. Looming afar through the mists of time, the little fact had become a gigantic vision. Yes, here it was in miniature, all that he had dreamed of; a palace of four feet high!

"You have the key of this palace," said Alice, "it has waited—that is, its secret and precious chamber has, for you to open it, these three hundred years. Do you know how to find that secret chamber?"

Middleton, still in that dreamy mood, threw open an inner door of the cabinet, and applying the old-fashioned key at his watch-chain to a hole in the mimic pavement within, pressed one of the mosaics, and immediately the whole floor of the apartment sank, and disclosed a receptacle within. Alice had come forward eagerly, and they both looked into the hiding-place, expecting what should be there. It was empty! They looked into one another's faces with blank astonishment. Everything had been so strangely true, and so strangely false, up to this moment, that they could not comprehend this failure at the last moment. It was the strangest, saddest jest! It brought Middleton up with such a sudden revulsion that he grew dizzy, and the room swam round him, and the cabinet dazzled before his eyes. It had been magnified to a palace; it had dwindled down to Lilliputian size; and yet, up till now, it had seemed to contain, in its diminutiveness, all the riches which he had attributed to its magnitude. This last moment

had utterly subverted it; the whole great structure seemed
to vanish.

"See; here are the dust and ashes of it," observed Alice,
taking something that was indeed only a pinch of dust out
of the secret compartment. "There is nothing else."

May 5th. Wednesday. The father of these two sons, an
aged man at the time, took much to heart their enmity; and
after the catastrophe, he never held up his head again. He
was not told that his son had perished, though such was the
belief of the family; but imbibed the opinion that he had
left his home and native land to become a wanderer on the
face of the earth, and that sometime or other he might return.
In this idea he spent the remainder of his days; in this idea
he died. It may be, that the influence of this idea might be
traced in the way in which he spent some of the latter years
of his life, and a portion of the wealth which had become of
little value in his eyes, since it had caused dissension and
bloodshed between the sons of one household. It was a common mode of charity in those days—a common thing for
rich men to do—to found an alms-house or a hospital, and
endow it for the support of a certain number of old and
destitute men or women, generally such as had some claim
of blood upon the founder, or at least were natives of the
parish, the district, or the county, where he dwelt. The
Eldredge Hospital was founded for the benefit of twelve old
men, who should have been wanderers upon the face of
the earth; men, they should be, of some education, but defeated and hopeless, cast off by the world, for misfortune,
but not for crime. And this charity had subsisted, on terms
varying little or nothing from the original ones, from that
day to this; and, at this very time, twelve old men were not
wanting, of various countries, of various fortune, but all
ending finally in ruin, who had centred here, to live on the

poor pittance that had been assigned them, three hundred years ago. What a series of chronicles would it have been, if each of the beneficiaries of this charity, since its foundation, had left a record of the events which finally led him hither. Middleton often, as he talked with these old men, regretted that he himself had no turn for authorship, so rich a volume might he have compiled from the experience, sometimes sunny and triumphant, though always ending in shadow, which he gathered here. They were glad to talk to him; and would have been glad and grateful for any auditor, as they sat on one or another of the stone benches, in the sunshine of the garden; or at evening, round the great fireside or within the chimney-corner, with their pipes and ale.

There was one old man who attracted much of his attention, by the venerableness of his aspect; by something dignified, almost haughty and commanding in his air. Whatever might have been the intentions and expectations of the founder, it certainly had happened, in these latter days, that there was a difficulty in finding persons of education, of good manners, of evident respectability, to put into the places made vacant by deaths of members; whether that the paths of life are surer now than they used to be, and that men so arrange their lives, as not to be left, in any event, quite without resources as they draw near its close; at any rate, there was a little tincture of the vagabond running through most of these twelve quasi gentlemen—through several of them at least. But this old man could not well be mistaken; in his manner, in his tones, in all his natural language and deportment, there was evidence that he had been more than respectable; and viewing him, Middleton could not but wonder what statesman had suddenly vanished out of public life, and taken refuge here; for his head was of the statesman-class, and his demeanor that of one who had exercised influence over large numbers of men.—He sometimes endeavored to set on foot a familiar relation with this old man; but there was ever a sternness in the manner in which he repelled these advances, that gave little encouragement for their renewal. Nor did it seem that his companions of the Hospital were more in his confidence than Middleton himself. They regarded him with a kind of awe, a shyness, and in most cases, with a certain dislike, which denoted an imperfect understanding of him. To say the truth, there was not generally much love lost between any of the members of this family; they had met with too much disappointment in the world to take kindly, now, to one another, or to anything or anybody. I rather suspect that they really had more pleasure in burying one another, when the time came, than in any other offices of mutual kindness and brotherly love, which it was their part to do; not out of hardness of heart, but merely from soured temper, and because, when people have met disappointment and have settled down into final unhappiness, with no more gush and spring of good spirits, there is nothing any longer to create amiability out of.

So the old people were unamiable and cross to one another, and unamiable and cross to old Hammond, yet always with a certain respect; and the result seemed to be such as suited the old man well enough. And thus he moved about among them a mystery; the histories of the others, in the general outline, were well enough known, and perhaps not very uncommon; this old man's story was known to none, except of course to the trustees of the charity, and to the Master of the Hospital, to whom it had necessarily been revealed, before the beneficiary could be admitted as an inmate. It was judged, by the deportment of the Master, that the old man had once held some eminent position in society; for, though bound to treat them all as gentlemen, he was thought to show an especial and solemn courtesy to Hammond.

Yet by the attraction which two strong and cultivated minds inevitably have for one another, there did spring up an acquaintanceship, an intercourse, betwixt Middleton and this old man, which was followed up in many a conversation which they held together on all subjects that were supplied by the news of the day or the history of the past. Middleton used to make the newspaper the opening for much discussion; and it seemed to him that the talk of his companion had much of the character of that of a retired statesman, on matters which perhaps he could look at all the more wisely, because it was impossible he could ever more have a personal agency in them. Their discussions sometimes turned upon the affairs of his own country, and its relations with the rest of the world, especially with England; and Middleton could not help being struck with the accuracy of the old man's knowledge respecting that country, which so few Englishmen know anything about—his shrewd appreciation of the American character, shrewd and caustic, yet not without a good degree of justice; the sagacity of his remarks on the past, and prophecies of what was likely to happen—prophecies which, in one instance, were singularly verified, in regard to a complexity which was then arresting the attention of both countries.

"You must have been in the United States?" said he, one day.

"Certainly; my remarks imply personal knowledge," was the reply. "But it was before the days of steamers."

"And not, I should imagine, for a brief visit," said Middleton. "I only wish the administration of this government could have the benefit to day of your knowledge of my countrymen. It might be the better for both of these two kindred nations."

"Not a whit," said the old man. "England will never understand America; for England never does understand a foreign country, and whatever you may say about kindred, America is as much a foreign country as France itself. These two hundred years of a different climate and circumstances—of life on a broad continent instead of in an island; to say nothing of the endless intermixture of nationalities in every part of the United States, except New England—have created a new and decidedly original type of national character. It is as well for both parties that they should not aim at any very intimate connection. It will never do."

"I should be sorry to think so," said Middleton; "they are at all events two noble breeds of men, and ought to appreciate one another. And America has the breadth of idea to do this for England, whether reciprocated or not."

Thursday. May 6th. Thus Middleton was established, in a singular way, among these old men, in one of the surroundings most unlike anything that was to be found in his own country. So old it was, that it seemed to him the freshest and newest thing that he had ever met with. The residence was made infinitely the more interesting to him by the sense that he was near the place—as all the indications warned him—which he sought; whither his dreams had tended from his childhood; that he could wander each day round the park, within which were seen the old gables of what he believed was his hereditary home. He had never known anything like the dreamy enjoyment of these days; so quiet, such a contrast to the turbulent life from which he had escaped across the sea. And here he set himself, still with that sense of shadowiness in what he saw and in what he did, in making all the researches possible to him, about the neighborhood; visiting every little church, that raised its square, battlemented, Norman tower of gray stone for several miles roundabout; making himself acquainted with each little village and hamlet, that surrounded these churches, clustering about the graves of those who had dwelt in the same cottages aforetime. He visited all the towns within a dozen miles; and probably there were few of the native inhabitants who had so good an acquaintance with the neighborhood, as this native American attained within a few weeks after his coming thither.

In the course of these excursions, he had several times met with a young woman—a young lady, we might term her, but in fact he was in some doubt what rank she might hold, in England—who appeared to be wandering about the country with a singular freedom. She was always alone, always on foot; he would see her sketching some picturesque old church; some ivied ruin; some fine, drooping elm. She was a slight figure, much more so than English women generally are; and though healthy of aspect, had not the ruddy complexion which he was irreverently inclined to call the coarse tint that is reckoned the great charm of English beauty. There was a freedom in her step, air, and whole little womanhood, an elasticity, an irregularity, so to speak, that made her memorable from first sight; and when he had encountered her three or four times, he felt in a certain way acquainted with her. She was very simply dressed, and quite as simple in her deportment; there had been one or two occasions when they had both smiled at the same thing; soon afterwards, a little conversation had taken place between them; and thus, without any introduction, and in a way that somewhat perplexed Middleton himself, they had become acquaintances. It was so unusual that a young English girl should be wandering about the country entirely alone—so much less usual that she should speak to a stranger—that Middleton scarcely knew how to account for it; but meanwhile accepted the fact readily and willingly, for in truth he found this mysterious personage a very lively and entertaining companion. There was a strange quality of boldness in her remarks, almost of brusqueness, that he might have expected to find in a young countrywoman of his own, if bred up among the strong-minded, but was astonished to find in a young English-woman. Somehow or other, she made him think more of home than any other person or thing which he met with; and he could not but feel that she was in strange contrast with everything about her. She was no beauty; very piquant; very pleasing; in some points of view and at some moments pretty; always good-humored, but somewhat too self-possessed for Middleton's taste. It struck him that she had talked with him as if she had some knowledge of him and of the purposes with which he was there; not that this was expressed, but only implied by the fact that, on looking back to what had passed, he found many strange coincidences in what she had said with what he was thinking about.

He perplexed himself much with thinking whence this young woman had come, where she belonged, and what might be her history; when, the next day, he again saw her, not, this time, rambling on foot, but seated in an open barouche, with a young lady. Middleton lifted his hat to her, and she nodded and smiled to him; and it appeared to Middleton that a conversation ensued about him with the young lady, her companion. Now, what still more interested him was the fact that, on the panel of the barouche, was the arms of the family now in possession of the estate of Smithills; so that the young lady, his new acquaintance, or the young lady, her seeming friend, one or the other, was the sister of the present owner of that estate. He was inclined to think that his acquaintance could not be the Miss Eldredge, of whose beauty he had heard many tales among the people of the neighborhood. The other young lady, a tall, reserved, fair-haired maiden, answered the description considerably better. He concluded, therefore, that his acquaintance must be a visitor, perhaps a dependent and companion; though the freedom of her thought, action, and way of life, seemed hardly consistent with that idea. However, this slight incident served to give him a sort of connection with the family, and he could but hope that some further chance might eventually introduce him within what he fondly called his hereditary walls. He had come to think of this as a dream-land; and it seemed even more a dream-land now than before it realized itself into actual substance, an old house of stone and timber, standing within its park, shaded about with its ancestral trees.

But thus, at all events, he was getting himself a little wrought into the net-work of human life around him, secluded as his position had at first seemed to be, in the farm-house where he had taken up his lodgings. For, there was the Hospital and its old inhabitants, in whose monotonous existence he soon came to pass for something, with his liveliness of mind, his experience, his good sense, his patience as a listener, his comparative youth even—his power of adapting himself to these stiff and crusty old characters, a power learned, among other things, in his political life, when he had acquired something of the faculty (good or evil, as might be) of making himself all things to all men. But though he amused himself with them all, there was in truth but one man among them in whom he really felt much interest; and that one, we need hardly say, was Hammond. It was not often that he found this old gentleman in a conversible mood; always courteous, indeed, but generally cool and reserved; often engaged in his one room, to which Middleton had never yet been admitted, though he had more than once sent in his name, when Hammond was not apparent upon the bench which, by common consent of the Hospital, was appropriated to him.

One day, however, understanding that the old gentleman was confined to his room by indisposition, he ventured to inquire at the door, and, considerably to his surprise, was admitted. He found Hammond in an easy chair, at a table with writing-materials before him; and as Middleton entered, the old gentleman looked at him with a stern, fixed regard, which, however, did not seem to infer any particular displeasure towards this visitor, but rather a severe way of contemplating mankind in general. Middleton looked curiously round the small apartment, to see what modification the character of the man had had upon the customary furniture of the Hospital, and how much of individuality he had given to that general type. There was a shelf of books, and a row of them on the mantel-piece; works of political economy, they appeared to be, statistics, and things of that sort; very dry reading, with which, however, Middleton's experience as a politician had made him acquainted. Besides these, there were a few works on local antiquities, a county-history, borrowed from the Master's library, in which Hammond appeared to have been lately reading.

"They are delightful reading," observed Middleton, "these old county-histories, with their great folio volumes, and their minute accounts of the affairs of families and the genealogies, and descents of estates, bestowing as much blessed space on a few hundred acres, as other historians give to a principality. I fear that, in my own country, we shall never have anything of this kind. Our space is so vast, that we shall never come to know and love it inch by inch, as the English antiquarians do the tracts of country with which they deal; and besides, our land is always likely to lack the human interest that belongs to English estates; for when land changes its owner-ship every few years, it does not become imbued with the personalities of the people who live on it. It is but so much grass; so much dirt; where a succession of people have dwelt too little while to make it really their own. But I have found a pleasure that I had no conception of before, in reading some of the English local histories."

"It is not a usual course of reading for a transitory visitor," said Hammond. "What could induce you to undertake it?"

"Simply, the wish, so common and natural with us Americans," said Middleton—"the hope to find out something about my kindred—the local origin of my own family."

"You do not show your wisdom in this," answered his host. "America had better recognize the fact that it has nothing to do with England, and look upon itself, as other nations and people do, as existing on its own hook. I never heard of any people looking back to the country of their remote origin in the way the Anglo-Americans do. For instance, England is made up of many Alien races, German, Danish, Norman, and what not; it has received large accession of population at a later date than the settlement of the United States. Yet these families melt into the great homogeneous mass of Englishmen, and look back no more to any other country. There are in this country many descendants of the French Huguenots; but they care no more for France than for Timbuctoo, reckoning themselves only Englishmen, as if they were descendants of the aboriginal Britons. Let it be so with you."

"So it might be," replied Middleton; "only that our relations with England remain far more numerous than our disconnections, through the bonds of history, of literature, of all that makes up the memories, and most that makes up the present interests of a people. And therefore I must still continue to pore over these old folios, and haunt around these old precincts, spending thus the little idle time I am likely to have in the course of a busy life. Possibly finding little to my purpose; but that is quite a secondary consideration."

"If you choose to tell me precisely what your aims are," said Hammond, "it is possible I might give you some little assistance."

May 7th. Friday. Middleton was in fact more than half ashamed of the dreams which he had cherished before coming to England, and which since, at times, had been very potent with him, assuming a strong tinge of reality as those into which he had strayed. He could not prevail with himself to disclose fully to this severe and, as he thought, cynical old man, how strong within him was the sentiment that impelled him to connect himself with the old life of England; to join on the broken thread of ancestry and descent, and feel every link well established. But it seemed to him that he ought not to lose this fine opportunity of gaining some light on the obscure field of his researches; and he therefore explained to Hammond that he had reason, from old family traditions, to believe that he brought with him a fragment of a history, that, if followed out, might lead to curious results. He told him, in a tone half serious, what he had heard respecting the quarrel of the two brothers, and the Bloody Footstep, the impress of which was said to remain on the threshold of the ancestral mansion, as a lasting memorial of the tragic termination of that enmity. At this point, Hammond interrupted him. He had, indeed, at various points of the narrative, nodded and smiled mysteriously, as if looking into his mind, and seeing something there analogous to what he was listening to. He now spoke.

"This is curious," said he. "Did you know that there is a manor-house in this neighborhood, the family of which prides itself on having such a blood-stained threshold as you have now described?"

"No, indeed!" exclaimed Middleton greatly interested. "Where?"

"It is the old manor house of Smithells," replied Hammond; "one of those old wood and timber mansions which are among the most ancient specimens of domestic architecture in England. The house has now passed into the female line, and by marriage, has been for two or three generations in possession of another family. But the blood of the old inheritors is still in the family. The house itself, or portions of it, are thought to date back quite as far as the Conquest."

"Smithells?" said Middleton. "Why I have seen that old house, from a distance, and have felt no little interest in its antique aspect. And it has a Bloody Footstep! Would it be possible for a stranger to get an opportunity to inspect it?"

"Unquestionably," said Hammond; "nothing easier. It is but a moderate distance from here, and if you can moderate your young footsteps, and your American quick walk, to an old man's pace, I would go there with you some day. In this languor and ennui of my life, I spend some little time in local antiquarianism, and perhaps I might assist you in tracing out how far these traditions of yours may have any connection with reality. It would be curious, would it not, if you had come, after two hundred years, to piece out a story which may have been as much a mystery here in England as there in America."

An engagement was made for a walk to Smithells the ensuing day; and meanwhile Middleton entered more fully into what he had received from family traditions, and what he had thought out for himself, on the matter in question.

"Are you aware," asked Hammond, "that there was formerly a title in this family, now in abeyance, and which the heirs have at various times claimed, and are at this moment claiming? Do you know too—but you can scarcely know it—that it has been surmised by some that there is an insecurity in the title to this estate, and has always been; so that the possessors have lived in some apprehension, from time immemorial, that another heir would appear, and take from them this fair inheritance. It is a singular coincidence?"

"Very strange," exclaimed Middleton. "No; I was not aware of it; and to say the truth, I should not altogether like to come forward in the light of a claimant. But this is a dream surely!"

"I assure you, Sir," continued the old man, "that you come here in a very critical moment; and, singularly enough, there is a perplexity, a difficulty, that has endured from as long a time as when your ancestors emigrated, that is still rampant within the bowels, as I may say, of this family. Of course, it is too like a romance that you should be able to establish any such claim as could have a valid influence on this matter; but still, being here on the spot, it may be worth while, if merely as a matter of amusement, to make some researches into this matter."

"Surely I will," said Middleton with a smile, which concealed more earnestness than he liked to show; "as to the title, a Republican cannot be supposed to think twice of such a bagatelle. The estate!—that might be a more serious consideration."

They continued to talk on the subject; and Middleton learned that the present possessor of the estate was a gentleman, nowise distinguished from hundreds of other English gentlemen; a country Squire, modified in accordance with the type of to-day, a frank, free, friendly sort of a person enough, who had travelled on the Continent, who employed himself much in field sports, who was unmarried, and had a sister, who was reckoned among the beauties of the county.

While the conversation was still going on, to Middleton's astonishment, there came a knock to the door of the room, and without waiting for a response, it was opened, and there appeared at it the same young woman whom he had already met. She came in with perfect freedom and familiarity, and was received quietly by the old gentleman; who, however, by his manner towards Middleton, intimated that he was now to take his leave. He did so, after settling the hour at which their excursion of the next day was to take place. This arranged, he departed, with much to think of, and a light glimmering through the confused labyrinth of thoughts, which had been un-illuminated hitherto.

To say the truth, he questioned within himself whether it were not better to get as quickly as he could out of this vicinity; at any rate, not to put anything of earnest in what had hitherto been nothing more than a romance to him. There was something very dark and sinister in the events of family history, which now assumed a reality that they had never before worn; so much tragedy, so much hatred, had been thrown into that deep pit, and buried under the accumulated debris, the fallen leaves, the rust and dust, of more than two centuries, that it seemed not worth while to dig it up; for perhaps the deadly influences, which it had taken so much time to hide, might still be lurking there, and become potent if he now uncovered them. There was something that startled him in the strange, wild light, which gleamed from the old man's eyes, as he threw out the suggestions which had opened this prospect to him. What real right had he—an American, a Republican, disconnected with this country so long, alien from its habits of thought and life, reverencing none of the things which Englishmen reverenced—what right had he to come, with these musty claims from the dim past, to disturb them in the life that belonged to them? There was a higher and a deeper law than was any connected with any ancestral claims which he could assert; and he had an idea that this law bade him keep to the country which his ancestor had chosen, and to its institutions, and not meddle nor make with England. The roots of his family tree could not reach under the ocean; he was at most but a seedling from the parent-tree. While thus meditating, he found that his footsteps had brought him unawares within sight of the old manor-house of Smithells; and that he was wandering on a path which, if he followed it further, would bring him to an entrance in one of the wings of the mansion. With a sort of shame upon him, he went forward and leaning against a tree, looked at what he now considered the home of his ancestors.

May 9th. Sunday. At the time appointed, the two companions set out on their little expedition, the old man in his Hospital uniform, the long black mantle, with the bear and ragged staff engraved in silver on the breast, and Middleton in the plain costume which he had adopted during these wanderings about the country. On their way, Hammond was not very communicative, occasionally dropping some shrewd remark, with a good deal of acidity in it; now and then too, favoring his companion with some reminiscence of local antiquity; but oftenest silent. Thus they went on, and entered the park of Pemberton Manor by a by-path, over a style, and one of those footways which are always so well worth threading out in England, leading the pedestrian into picturesque and characteristic scenes, when the high road would show him nothing but what is common place and uninteresting. Soon the gables of the old manor-house appeared before them, rising amidst its hereditary woods, which doubtless dated from a time beyond the days which Middleton so fondly recalled, when his ancestors had walked beneath their shade. On each side of them were thickets and covers of fern, amid which they saw the hares peeping out to gaze upon them, occasionally running across the path, and comporting themselves like creatures that felt themselves under some sort of protection from the outrages of man, though they knew too much of his destructive character to trust him too far. Pheasants, too, rose close beside them, and winged but a little way before they alighted; they likewise knew, or seemed to know, that their hour was not yet come. On all sides, in these woods, these wastes, these beasts and birds, there was a character that was neither wild nor tame. Man had laid his grasp on them all, and done enough to redeem them from barbarism, but had stopt short of domesticating them; although Nature, in the wildest thing there, still acknowledged the powerful and pervading influence of cultivation.

Arriving at a side door of the mansion, Hammond rang the bell, and a servant soon appeared. He seemed to know the old man, and immediately acceded to his request to be permitted to show his companion the house; although it was not precisely a show-house, nor was this the hour when strangers were usually admitted. They entered; and the servant did not give himself the trouble to act as a cicerone to the two visitants, but carelessly said to the old gentleman that he knew the rooms which were usually shown, and that he would leave him to discourse to his friend about them. Accordingly, they went into the old hall, a dark, oaken-panelled room, of no great height, with many doors opening into it. There was a fire burning on the hearth; indeed, it was the custom of the house to keep it up from morning to night; and in the damp, chill climate of England, there is seldom a day, in some part of which a fire is not pleasant to feel. Hammond here pointed out a stuffed fox, to which some story of a famous chase was attached; a pair of antlers of enormous size; and some old family pictures, so blackened with time and neglect, that Middleton could not well distinguish their features, though curious to do so, as hoping to see there the lineaments of some with whom he might claim his kindred. It was a venerable apartment, and gave a good foretaste of what they might hope to find in the rest of the mansion.

But when they had inspected it pretty thoroughly, and were ready to proceed, an elderly gentleman entered the hall, and seeing Hammond, addressed him in a kindly, familiar way, not indeed as an equal friend, but with a pleasant and not irksome condescension. "I am glad to see you here again," said he. "What! I have an hour of leisure; for to say the truth, the day hangs rather heavy till the shooting season begins. Come; as you have a friend with you, I will be your cicerone myself about the house, and show you whatever mouldy objects of interest it contains."

He then graciously noticed the old man's companion, but without asking or seeming to expect an introduction; for, after a careless glance at him, he had evidently set him down as a person without social claims, a young man in the rank of life fitted to associate with an inmate of Pemberton's hospital; and it must be noticed that his treatment of Middleton was not on that account the less kind, though certainly far from being so elaborately courteous as if he had met him as an equal. "You have had something of a walk," said he, "and it is a rather hot day. The beer of Pemberton manor has been reckoned good, these hundred years; will you taste it?"

Hammond accepted the offer, and the beer was brought in a foaming tankard; but Middleton declined it; for, in truth, there was a singular emotion in his breast, as if the old enmity, the ancient injuries, were not yet atoned for, and as if he must not accept the hospitality of one who represented his hereditary foe. He felt, too, as if there were some thing unworthy, a certain want of fairness, in entering clandestinely this house, and talking with its occupier under a veil, as it were; and had he seen clearly how to do it, he would perhaps at that moment have fairly told Mr. Eldredge that he brought with him the character of a kinsman, and must be received on that ground or none. But it was not easy to do this, and after all, there was no clear reason why he should do it; so he let the matter pass, merely declining to taste the refreshment, and keeping himself quiet and retired.

Squire Eldredge seemed to be a good, ordinary sort of a gentleman, reasonably well educated, and with few ideas beyond his own estate and neighborhood, though he had once held a seat in Parliament for part of a term. Middleton could not but contrast him, with an inward smile, with the shrewd, alert politicians, their faculties all sharpened to the utmost, whom he had known and consorted with in the American Congress. Hammond had slightly informed him that his companion was an American; and Mr. Eldredge immediately gave proof of the extent of his knowledge of that country by inquiring whether he came from the State of New England, and whether Mr. Webster was still President of the United States; questions to which Middleton returned answers that led to no further conversation. These little preliminaries over, they continued their ramble through the house, going through tortuous passages, up and down little flights of steps, and entering chambers that had all the charm of discoveries of hidden regions; twisting about, in short, in a labyrinth calculated to put the head into a delightful confusion. Some of these rooms contained their time-honored furniture, all in the best possible repair, heavy, dark, polished; beds that had been marriage beds and dying beds, over and over again; chairs, with carved backs; and all manner of old world curiosities; family pictures; samplers and embroidery; fragments of tapestry; an inlaid floor; everything having a story to it, though, to say the truth, the possessor of these curiosities made but a bungling piece of work in telling the legends connected with them. In one or two instances, Hammond corrected him.

By and by they came to what had once been the principal bed-room of the house; though its gloom, and some circumstances of family misfortune, that had happened long ago, had caused it to fall into disrepute, in latter times; and it was now called the Haunted Chamber, or the Ghost's chamber. The furniture of this room, however, was particularly rich in its antique magnificence; and one of the principal objects was a great, black cabinet of ebony and ivory, such as may often be seen in old English houses, and perhaps often in the palaces of Italy, in which country they perhaps originated. This present cabinet was known to have been in the house as long ago as the reign of Queen Elizabeth, and how much longer neither tradition nor record told. Hammond particularly directed Middleton's attention to it.

"There is nothing in this house," said he, "better worth your attention than that cabinet. Consider its plan; it represents a stately mansion, with pillars, an entrance, with a lofty flight of steps, windows, and everything perfect. Examine it well."

There was such an emphasis in the old man's way of speaking, that Middleton turned suddenly round from all that he had been looking at, and fixed his whole attention on the cabinet; and strangely enough, it seemed to be the representation, in small, of something that he had seen in a dream. To confess the truth, if some cunning workman had been employed to copy his idea of the old family mansion, on a scale of half an inch to a yard, and in ebony and ivory instead of stone, he could not have produced a closer representation. Everything was there.

"This is miraculous!" exclaimed he. "I do not understand it."

"Your friend seems to be curious in these matters," said Mr. Eldredge graciously. "Perhaps he is of some trade that makes this sort of manufacture particularly interesting to him. You are quite at liberty, my friend, to open the cabinet, and inspect it as minutely as you wish. It is an article that has a good deal to do with an obscure portion of our family history. Look, here is the key and the mode of opening the outer door of the palace, as we may call it." So saying, he threw open the outer door, and disclosed within the mimic likeness of a stately entrance hall, with a floor checquered of ebony and ivory. There were other doors, that seemed to open to apartments in the interior of the palace; but when Mr. Eldredge threw them likewise wide, they proved to be drawers and secret receptacles, where papers, jewels, money, any thing that it was desirable to store away secretly, might be kept.

"You said, Sir," said Middleton thoughtfully, "that your family history contained matter of interest in reference to this cabinet. Might I inquire what those legends are?"

"Why yes," Mr. Eledrege musing a little. "I see no reason why I should have any idle concealment about this matter, especially to a foreigner, and a man whom I am never likely to see again. You must know then, my friend, that there was once a time when this cabinet was supposed to contain the fate of the estate and its possessors; and if it had held all that it was supposed to hold, I should not now be the lord of Pemberton Manor, nor the claimant of an ancient title. But my father and his father before him, and his father besides, have held the estate, and prospered on it; and I think we may fairly conclude now, that the cabinet contains nothing but what we see."

And he rapidly again threw open one after another all the numerous drawers and receptacles of the cabinet.

"It is an interesting object," said Middleton, after looking very closely and with great attention at it, being pressed thereto, indeed, by the owner's good natured satisfaction in possessing this rare article of vertû. "It is admirable work," repeated he, drawing back. "That mosaic floor, especially, is done with an art and skill that I never saw equaled."

There was something strange and altered in Middleton's tones, that attracted the notice of Mr. Eldredge. Looking at him, he saw that he had grown pale, and had a rather bewildered air.

"Is your friend ill?" said he. "He has not our English ruggedness of look. He would have done better to take a sip of the cool tankard, and a slice of the cold beef. He finds no such food and drink as that in his own country, I warrant."

"His color has come back," responded Hammond briefly. "He does not need any refreshment, I think, except perhaps the open air."

In fact, Middleton, recovering himself, apologized to Mr. Eldredge, and as they had now seen nearly the whole of the house, the two visitants took their leave, with many kindly offers on Mr. Eldredge's part to permit the young man to view the cabinet whenever he wished. As they went out of the house (it was by another door than that which gave them entrance), Hammond laid his hand on Middleton's shoulder, and pointed to a stone in the threshold, on which he was about to set his foot. "Take care!" said he. "It is the Bloody Footstep."

Middleton looked down, and saw something, indeed, very like the shape of a footprint, with a hue very likely that of blood. It was a twilight sort of a place, beneath a porch, which was much overshadowed by trees and shrubbery. It might have been blood; but he rather thought, in his wicked scepticism, that it was a natural, reddish stain in the stone. He measured his own foot, however, in the Bloody Footstep, and went on.

May 10th. Monday. This is the present aspect of the story; —Middleton is the descendant of a family long settled in the United States; his ancestor having emigrated to New England with the Pilgrims; or perhaps, at a still earlier date, to Virginia with Raleigh's colonists. There had been a family dissension— a bitter hostility between two brothers, in England; on account, probably, of a love affair, the two both being attached to the same lady. By the influence of the family on both sides, the young lady had formed an engagement with the elder brother, although her affections had settled on the younger. The marriage was about to take place, when the younger brother and the bride both disappeared, and were never heard of with any certainty afterwards; but it was believed, at the time, that he had been killed, and in proof of it, a bloody footstep remained on the threshold of the ancestral mansion. There were rumors, afterwards, traditionally continued to the present day, that the younger brother and the bride were seen alive, and together, in England; and that some voyager across the sea had found them living together, husband and wife, on the other side of the Atlantic. But the elder brother became a moody and reserved man, never married, and left his inheritance to the children of a third brother, who thus became the representative of the family in England; and the better authenticated story was, that the second brother had really been slain, and that the young lady (for all the parties may have been Catholic) had gone to the Continent, and taken the veil there. Such was the family history, as known or surmised in England, and in the neighborhood of the manor-house, where the Bloody Footstep still remained on the threshold; and the posterity of the third brother still held the estate, and perhaps were claimants of an ancient baronage, long in abeyance.

Now, on the other side of the Atlantic, the second brother and the young lady had really been married, and became the parents of a posterity, still extant, of which the Middleton of the romance is the surviving male. Perhaps he had changed his name; being so much tortured with the evil and wrong that had sprung up in his family, so remorseful, so outraged, that he wished to disconnect himself with all the past, and begin life quite anew, in a new world. But both he and his wife, though happy in one another, had been remorsefully and sadly so; and, with such feelings, they had never again communicated with their respective families, nor had given their children the means of doing so. There must, I think, have been something nearly approaching to guilt, on the second brother's part, and the bride should have broken a solemnly plighted troth to the elder brother, breaking away from him when almost his wife. The elder brother had been known to have been wounded, at the time of the second brother's disappearance; and it had been the surmise that he received this hurt in the personal conflict in which the latter was slain. But, in truth, the second brother had stabbed him in the emergency of being discovered in the act of escaping with the bride; and this was what weighed upon his conscience throughout life, in America. The American family had prolonged itself through various fortune, and all the ups and downs incident to our institutions, until the present day. They had some old family documents, which had been rather carelessly kept; but the present representative, being an educated man, had looked over them, and found one which interested him strongly. It was—what was it?—perhaps a copy of a letter written by his ancestor on his death-bed, telling his real name, and relating the above incidents. These incidents had come down, in a vague, wild way, traditionally in the American family, forming a wondrous and incredible legend, which Middleton had often laughed at, yet been greatly interested in; and the discovery of this document seemed to give a certain aspect of veracity and reality to the tradition. Perhaps, however, the document only related to the change of name, and made reference to certain evidences by which, if any descendant of the family should deem it expedient, he might prove his hereditary identity. The legend must be accounted for by having been gathered from the talk of the first ancestor and his wife. There must be in existence, in the early records of the colony, an authenticated statement of this change of name, and satisfactory proofs that the American family, long known as Middleton, were really a branch of the English family of Eldredge, or whatever. And in the legend, though not in the written document, there must be an account of a certain magnificent, almost palatial residence, which Middleton shall presume to be the ancestral home; and in this palace, there shall be said to be a certain secret chamber, or receptacle, where is reposited a document that shall complete the evidence of the genealogical descent.

Middleton is still a young man, but already a distinguished one in his own country; he has entered early into politics, been sent to Congress, but having met with some disappointment in his ambitious hopes, and being disgusted with the fierceness of political contests in our country, he has come abroad for recreation and rest. His imagination has dwelt much, in his boyhood, on the legendary story of his family; and the discovery of the document has revised these dreams. He determines to search out the family mansion; and thus he arrives, bringing half of a story, being the only part known in America, to join it on the other half, which is known only in England. In an introduction, I must do the best I can to state his side of the matter to the reader; he having communicated it to me, in a friendly way, at the Consulate; as many people have communicated quite as wild pretensions to English genealogies.

He comes to the midland counties of England, where he conceives his claims to lie, and seeks for his ancestral home; but there are difficulties in the way of finding it, the estates having passed into the female line, though still remaining in the blood. By and by, however, he comes to an old town, where there is one of the charitable institutions bearing the name of his family, by whose beneficence it had indeed been founded, in Queen Elizabeth's time. He, of course, becomes interested in this Hospital; he finds it still going on, precisely as it did in the old days; and all the character and life of the establishment must be picturesquely described. Here he gets acquainted with an old man, an inmate of the establishment, who (if the uncontrollable fatality of the story will permit) must have an active influence on the ensuing events. I suppose him to have been an American, but to have fled his country and taken refuge in England; he shall have been a man of the Nicholas Biddle stamp, a mighty speculator, the ruin of whose schemes had crushed hundreds of people, and Middleton's father among the rest. Here, he had quitted the activity of his mind, as well as he could, becoming a local antiquary &c; and he has made himself acquainted with the family history of the Eldredges, knowing more about it than the members of the family themselves do. He had known, in America (from Middleton's father, who was his friend) the legends preserved in that branch of the family, and perhaps had been struck by the way in which they fit into the English legends; at any rate, this strikes him when Middleton tells him his story; and shows the document respecting the change of name. After various conversations together (in which, however, the old man keeps the secret of his own identity, and indeed acts as mysteriously as possible) they go together to visit the ancestral mansion. Perhaps it should not be in their first visit that the cabinet, representing the stately palace, shall be seen. But the Bloody Footstep may; which shall interest Middleton much, both because Hammond has told him the English tradition respecting it, and because the legends of the American family made some obscure allusions to his ancestor having left blood—a bloody footstep—on the ancestral threshold. This is the point to which the story has now been sketched out. Middleton finds a commonplace old English country-gentleman in possession of the estate, where his forefathers have lived in peace for many generations; but there must be circumstances contrived, which shall cause the advent of Middleton to be attended with no end of turmoil and trouble. The old Hospitaller, I suppose, must be the malicious agent in this; and his malice must be motived in some satisfactory way. The more serious question, what shall be the nature of this tragic trouble, and how can it be brought about.

May 11th. Tuesday. How much better would it have been, if this secret, that seemed so golden, had remained in the obscurity in which two hundred years had buried it. That deep, old, grass-grown grave being opened, out from it steamed into the sunshine the old jealousies, the old crimes, the old misfortunes, the old sorrows, that seemed to have departed from the family forever. But it was too late now to close it up; he must follow out the thread that led him on—the thread of fate, if you choose to call it so; but rather the impulse of an evil will, a stubborn self-interest, a desire for certain objects of ambition, which were preferred to what yet were recognized as real goods. Thus reasoned, thus raved Eldredge, as he considered the things that he had done, and still intended to do; nor did these perceptions make the slightest difference in his plans, nor in the activity with which he set about their performance. For this purpose, he sent for his lawyer, and consulted him on the feasibility of the design which he had already vaguely communicated to him respecting Middleton. But the man of law shook his head, and, though deferentially, declined to have any active concern with a matter that threatened to lead him beyond the limits which he allowed himself, into a seductive, but perilous region.

"My dear Sir," said he, with some earnestness, "you had better content yourself with such assistance as I can professionally and consistently give you. Believe, I am ready to do a lawyer's utmost, and to do more would be as unsafe for the client as for the legal adviser."

Thus left without an agent and an instrument, this unfortunate man had to meditate on what means he could use to gain his ends through his own unassisted efforts. In the struggle with himself through which he had passed, he had exhausted pretty much all the feelings that he had to bestow on this matter; and now he was ready to take hold of almost any temptation that might present itself so long as it showed a good prospect of success and a plausible chance of impunity. While he was thus musing, he heard a female voice chanting some song, like a bird, among the pleasant foliage of the trees, and soon he saw at the end of a wood-walk, Alice with her basket on her arm, passing on toward the village. She looked towards him as she passed, but made no pause, nor yet hastened her steps, not seeming to think it worth her while to be influenced by him. He hurried forward and overtook her.

So there was this poor old gentleman, his comfort utterly overthrown, decking his white hair and wrinkled brow with the semblance of a coronet, and only hoping that the reality might crown and bless them before he was laid in the ancestral tomb. It was a real calamity; though by no means the greatest that had been fished up out of the pit of domestic discord that had been opened anew by the advent of the American; and by the use which had been made of it by the cantankerous old man of the Hospital. Middleton, as he looked at these evil consequences, sometimes regretted that he had not listened to those forebodings which had warned him back, on the eve of his enterprise; yet such was the strange entanglement and interest which had wound about him, that oftener he rejoiced that for once he was engaged in something that absorbed him fully, and the zeal for the developement of which made him careless for the result, in respect to its good or evil, but only desirous that it show itself. As for Alice, she seemed to skim lightly through all these matters, whether as a spirit of good or ill, he could not satisfactorily judge. He could not think her wicked; yet her actions seemed unaccountable on the plea that she was otherwise. It was another characteristic thread in the wild web of madness that had spun itself about all the prominent characters of our story. And when Middleton thought of these things, he felt as if it might be his duty (supposing he had the power) to shovel the earth again into the pit that he had been the means of opening; but also felt, that, whether duty or not, he could never perform it.

For you see, on the American's arrival, he had found the estate in the hands of one of the descendants; but some disclosures consequent on his arrival, had thrown it into the hands of another; or at all events, had seemed to make it apparent that justice required that it should be so disposed of. No sooner was the discovery made, than the possessor had

put on a coronet; the new heir had commenced legal proceedings; the sons of the respective branches had come to
blows and blood; and the devil knows what other devilish
consequences had ensued. Besides this, there was much falling in love at cross-purposes, and a general animosity of
everybody against everybody else, in proportion to the close-
ness of their natural ties, and their obligation to love one
another.

The moral, if any moral were to be gathered from these
paltry and wretched circumstances, was, "Let the past alone;
do not seek to renew it; press on to higher and better things—
at all events to other things; and be assured that the right way
can never be that which leads you back to the identical shapes
that you long ago left behind. Onward, onward, onward!"

"What have you to do here?" said Alice. "Your lot is in
another land. You have seen the birthplace of your forefathers, and have gratified your natural yearning for it; now
return, and cast in your lot with your own people, let it be
what it will. I fully believe that it is such a lot as the world
has never yet seen, and that the faults, the weaknesses, the
errors of your countrymen will vanish away, like morning-
mists before the rising sun. You can do nothing better than
to go back."

"This is strange advice, Alice," replied Middleton, gazing
at her and smiling. "Go back, with such a fair prospect before
me; that were strange indeed! It is enough to keep me here,
that here only I shall see you—enough to make me rejoice to
have come, that I have found you here!"

"Do not speak in this foolish way," cried Alice, pouting.
"I am giving you the best advice, and speaking in the wisest
way I am capable of—speaking on good grounds too—and
you turn me aside with a silly compliment. I tell you that
this is no comedy in which we are performers, but a deep,

sad tragedy; and that it depends most upon you, whether or no it shall be pressed to a catastrophe. Think well of it."

"I have thought, Alice," responded the young man; "and I must let things take their course; if, indeed, it depends at all upon me, which I see no present reason to suppose. Yet I wish you would explain to me what you mean."

To take up the story from the point where we left it; by the aid of the American's revelations, some light is thrown upon points of family history, which induce the English possessor of the estate to suppose that the time is come for asserting his claim to a title, which has long been in abeyance. He therefore sets about it, and engages in great expences, besides contracting the enmity of many persons, with whose interests he interferes. A further complication is brought about by the secret interference of the old Hospitaller; and Alice goes singing and dancing through the whole, in a way that makes her seem like a beautiful devil, though finally it will be recognized that she is an angel of light. Middleton, half bewildered, can scarcely tell how much of this is due to his own agency; how much is independent of him, and would have happened had he staid on his own side of the water. By and by, a further and unexpected development presents the singular fact that he himself is the heir to whatever claims there are, whether of property or rank—all centering in him as the representative of the eldest brother. On this discovery, there ensues a tragedy in the death of the present possessor of the estate; who has staked everything upon the issue; and Middleton standing amid the ruin and desolation of which he has been the innocent cause, resigns all the claims which he might now assert, and retires, arm in arm with Alice, who has encouraged him to take this course, and to act up to his character. The estate takes a passage into the female line, and the old name becomes extinct, nor does Middleton seek to continue it by resuming it in place of the one long ago assumed by his ancestor. Thus he and his wife become the Adam and Eve of a new epoch, and the fitting missionaries of a new social faith, of which there must be continual hints through the book.

A knot of characters may be introduced as gathering round Middleton, comprising expatriated Americans of all sorts; the wandering printer who came to me so often at the Consulate, who said that he was a native of Philadelphia, and could not go home, in the thirty years that he had been trying to do so, for lack of the money to pay his passage. The large banker; the consul of Leeds; the woman asserting her claims to half Liverpool; the gifted literary lady, maddened by Shakspeare &c, &c. The Yankee, who had been driven insane by the Queen's notice, slight as it was, of the photographs of his two children which he had sent her. I have not yet struck the true key-note of this Romance, and until I do, and unless I do, I shall write nothing but tediousness and nonsense. I do not wish it to be a picture of life; but a Romance, grim, grotesque, quaint, of which the Hospital might be the fitting scene. It might have so much of the hues of life that the reader should sometimes think it was intended for a picture; yet the atmosphere should be such as to excuse all wildness. In the Introduction, I might disclaim all intention to draw a real picture, but say that the continual meetings I had with Americans bent on such errands, had suggested this wild story. The descriptions of scenery, &c, and of the Hospital, might be correct, but there should be a tinge of the grotesque given to all the characters and events. The tragic, and the gentler pathetic, need not be excluded by this tone and treatment. If I could but write one central scene in this vein, all the rest of the Romance would readily arrange itself around that nucleus. The begging-girl would be another American character; the actress too; the caravan people. It must be a humorous work, or nothing.

May 12th. Wednesday. Middleton found his abode here becoming daily more interesting; and he sometimes thought that it was his sympathies with the place and people, buried under the supergrowth of so many ages, but now coming forth with the life and vigor of a fountain, that, long hidden beneath earth and ruins, gushes out singing into the sunshine, as soon as these are removed. He wandered about the neighborhood with insatiable interest; sometimes, and often, lying on a hillside, and gazing at the gray tower of the church; sometimes coming into the village, clustered round that same church, and looking at the old timber and plaster houses, the same, except that the thatch had probably been often renewed, that they used to be in his ancestor's days. In those old cottages still dwelt the families—the Nortons, the Prices, the Hogsnorts, the Copleys—that had dwelt there when America was a scattered progeny of infant colonies; and in the church yard were the graves of all the generations since—including the dust of those who had seen his ancestor's face before his departure. The graves, outside the church walls indeed, bore no monuments of this antiquity; for it seems not to have been an early practice in England to put stones over such graves; and where it has been done, the climate causes the inscriptions soon to become obliterated and unintelligible. But, within the church, there were rich records of the personages and times, with whom Middleton's musings held so much converse.

But one of his greatest employments and pastimes was to ramble through the grounds of Smithills, making himself as well acquainted with all its wood paths, its glens, its woods, its venerable trees, as if he had been bred up there from infancy. Some of those old oaks his ancestor might have been acquainted with, while they were already sturdy and well grown trees; might have climbed them in boyhood; might have mused beneath them as a lover; might have flung himself at full length on the turf beneath them, in the bitter anguish that must have preceded his departure forever from the home of his forefathers. In order to secure an uninterrupted enjoyment of his rambles here, Middleton had cultivated the goodwill of the gamekeepers and other underlings whom one was likely to meet about the grounds, by giving them a shilling or a half crown; and he was now free to wander where he would, with only the advice, rather than the injunction, to keep out of the way of their old master; for there might be trouble, if he should meet a stranger on the grounds, in any of his tantrums. But, in fact, Mr. Eldredge was not much in the habit of walking about the grounds; and there were hours of every day, during which it was altogether improbable that he would have emerged from his own apartments in the manor house. These were the hours, therefore, when Middleton most frequented the estate; although, to say the truth, he would gladly have so timed his visits as to meet and form an acquaintance with the lonely lord of this beautiful property, his own kinsman, though with so many years of dark oblivion between. For Middleton had not that feeling of infinite distance in the relationship which he would have had, if his branch of the family had continued in England, and had not intermarried with the other branch, through such a long waste of years; he rather felt as if he were the original emigrant, who long resident on a foreign shore, had now returned, with a heart brimful of tenderness, to revisit the scenes of his youth, and renew his tender relations with those who shared his own blood.

There was not, however, much in what he heard of the character of the present possessor of the estate—or indeed in the strong family characteristics that had become hereditary—to encourage him to attempt any advances. It is very probable that the religion of Mr. Eldredge, as a Catholic, may have created a prejudice against him, as it certainly had insulated the family, in a great degree, from the sympathies of the neighborhood. Mr. Eldredge, moreover, had resided long on the Continent; long in Italy; and had come back with habits that little accorded with those of the gentry of the neighborhood; so that, in fact, he was almost as much a stranger, and perhaps quite as little of a real Englishman, as Middleton himself. Be that as it might, Middleton, when he sought to learn something about him, heard the strangest stories of his habits of life, of his temper, and of his employments, from the people with whom he conversed. The old legend, turning upon the monomania of the family, was revived in full force in reference to this poor gentleman; and many a time, Middleton's interlocutors shook their wise heads, saying, with a knowing look, and under their breath, that the old gentleman was looking for the track of the Bloody Footstep. They fabled —or said, for it might not have been a false story—that every descendant of this house had a certain portion of his life, during which he sought the track of that footstep which was left on the threshold of the mansion; that he sought it far and wide, over every foot of the estate; not only on the estate, but throughout the neighborhood; not only in the neighborhood, but all over England; not only throughout England, but over the Continent, and all about the world. It was the belief of the neighborhood—at least of some old men and women in it—that the long period of Mr. Eldredge's absence from England had been spent in this search for some trace of those departing footsteps that had never returned. It is very possible—probable, indeed—that there may have been some ground for this remarkable legend; not that it is to be credited that this family of Eldredge, being reckoned among sane men, could seriously have sought, years and generations after the fact, for the track of those bloody footsteps which the first rain in drippy England must have washed away; to say nothing of the leaves that had fallen, and the growth and decay of so many seasons, that covered all traces of them since. But nothing is more probable than that the continual recurrence to the family genealogy, which had been necessitated by the matter of the dormant peerage, had caused the Eldredges, from father to son, to keep alive an interest in that ancestor who had disappeared, and who had been supposed to carry some of the most important family papers with him. But yet it gave Middleton a strange thrill of pleasure, that had something fearful in it, to think that all through these ages he had been waited for, sought for, anxiously expected, as it were; it seemed as if the merry ghosts of his kindred, a long shadowy line, held forth their dim arms to welcome him; a line stretching back to the ghosts of those who had flourished in the old, old times; the doubletted and be-ruffed knightly shades of Queen Elizabeth's time; a long line, stretching from the medieval ages, and their duskiness, downward, downward, with only one vacant space, that of him who had left the Bloody Footstep. There was an inexpressible pleasure (airy and evanescent, gone in a moment if he dwelt upon it too thoughtfully, but very sweet) to Middleton's imagination in this idea. When he reflected, however, that possibly his revelations, if they had any effect at all, might serve only to quench the hopes of those long expectants, it of course made him hesitate to declare himself.

One afternoon, when he was in the midst of musings such as this, he saw at a distance through the park, in the direction of the manor-house, a person who seemed to be walking slowly and seeking for something upon the ground. He was a long way off, when Middleton first perceived him; and there were two clumps of trees and underbrush, with interspersed tracts of sunny lawn, between them. The person, whoever he was, kept on, and plunged into the first clump of shrubbery, still keeping his eyes on the ground, as if intently searching for something. When he emerged from the concealment of the first clump of shrubbery, Middleton saw that he was a tall, thin person, in a dark dress; and this was the chief observation that the distance enabled him to make, as the figure kept slowly onward, in a somewhat wavering line, and plunged into the second clump of shrubbery. From that, too, he emerged; and now appeared to be a thin, elderly figure, of a dark man with gray hair, bent, as it seemed to Middleton, with infirmity, for his figure still stooped even during the intervals when he did not appear to be tracking the ground. But Middleton could not but be surprised at the singular appearance the figure had of setting its foot, at every step, just where a previous footstep had been made, as if he wanted to measure his whole pathway in the track of somebody who had recently gone over the ground in advance of him. Middleton was sitting at the foot of an oak; and he began to feel some awkwardness in the consideration of what he should do if Mr. Eldredge—for he could not doubt that it was he—were to be led just to this spot, in pursuit of his singular occupation. And even so it proved.

Middleton could not feel it manly to flee and hide himself, like a guilty thing; and, indeed, the hospitality of the English country gentlemen in many cases gives the neighborhood and the stranger a certain degree of freedom in the use of the broad expanse of ground in which they, and their forefathers, have loved to sequester their residences. The figure kept on, showing more and more distinctly, the tall, meagre, not unvenerable form and features of a gentleman in the decline of life, apparently in ill-health; with a dark face, that might once have been full of energy, but now seemed enfeebled by time, passion, and perhaps sorrow. But it was strange to see the earnestness with which he looked on the ground, and the accuracy with which he at last set his foot, apparently adjusting it exactly to some foot-print before him; and Middleton doubted not, that, having studied and re-studied the family records, and the judicial examinations, which described exactly the track that was seen the day after the memorable disappearance of his ancestor, Mr. Eldredge was now, in some freak, or for some purpose best known to himself, practically following it out. And following it out he did, until at last he lifted up his eyes, muttering to himself. "At this point the footsteps wholly disappear!"

Lifting his eyes, as we have said, while thus regretfully and despairingly muttering these words, he saw Middleton leaning against the oak, within three paces of him.

May 13th. Thursday. Mr. Eldredge (for it was he) first kept his eyes fixed full on Middleton's face, with an expression as if he saw him not; but gradually—slowly, at first—he seemed to become aware of his presence; then, with a sudden flush, he took in the idea that he was encountered by a stranger in his secret mood. A flush of anger or shame, perhaps both, reddened over his face; his eyes gleamed, and he spoke hastily and roughly.

"Who are you?" he cried. "How came you here? I allow no intruders in my park. Begone, fellow."

"Really, Sir, I did not mean to intrude upon you," said Middleton blandly. "I am aware that I owe you an apology; but the beauties of your park must plead my excuse; and the usual kindness of English gentlemen, which admits a stranger to the privilege of enjoying as much of the beauty in which he himself dwells, as the stranger's taste permits him to enjoy."

"An artist perhaps," said Mr. Eldredge, somewhat less uncourteously. "I am told that they love to come here to sketch these old oaks, and their virtues, and the old mansion yonder. But you are an intrusive set, you artists, and think that a pencil and a sheet of paper may be your passport anywhere. You are mistaken, Sir. My park is not open to strangers."

"I am sorry, then, to have intruded upon you," said Middleton, still in good humor; for in truth he felt a sort of kindness, a sentiment, ridiculous as it may appear, of kindred, towards the old gentleman, and besides was not unwilling, in any way, to prolong a conversation in which he found a singular interest. "I am sorry; especially as I have not even the excuse you kindly suggest for me. I am not an artist; merely an American, who have strayed hither to enjoy this gentle, cultivated, tamed Nature which I find in English parks, so contrasting with the wild, rugged Nature of my native land. I beg your pardon and will retire."

"An American!" repeated Mr. Eldrege, looking curiously at him. "Ah; you are wild men in that country, I suppose, and cannot conceive that an English gentleman encloses his grounds—or that his ancestors have done it before him—for his own pleasure and convenience, and does not calculate on having it infringed upon by everybody, like your own forests, as you say. It is a curious country that of yours; and in Italy, I have seen curious people from it."

"True, Sir," said Middleton smiling. "We send queer specimens abroad; but Englishmen should consider that we spring from them, and that, after all, we present only a picture of their own characteristics, a little varied by climate and institutions."

Mr. Eldredge looked at him with a certain kind of interest, and it seemed to Middleton that he was not unwilling to continue the conversation, if a fair way to do so could only be opened to him. A secluded man often grasps at any opportunity of communicating with his kind, when it is casually offered to him; and, for the nonce, is surprisingly familiar, running out towards his chance-companion with the gush of a dammed up torrent, suddenly unlocked. As Middleton made a motion to retire, he put out his hand with an air of authority to restrain him.

"Stay," said he. "Now that you are here, the mischief is done, and you cannot repair it by hastening away. You have interrupted me in my mood of thought, and must pay the penalty by suggesting other thoughts. I am a lonely man here, having spent most of my life abroad, and am separated from my neighbors by various circumstances. You seem to be an intelligent man. I should like to ask you a few questions about your country."

He looked at Middleton as he spoke, and seemed to be considering in what rank of life he was to place him; his dress being such as suited a humble rank. He seemed not to have come to any very certain decision on this point.

"I remember," said he, "you have no distinctions of rank in your country; a convenient thing enough, in some respects. When there are no gentlemen, all are gentlemen. So let it be. You speak of being Englishmen; and it has often occurred to me that Englishmen have left this country, and been much missed and sought after, who might perhaps be sought there successfully."

"It is certainly so, Mr. Eldredge," said Middleton, lifting his eyes to his face as he spoke, and then turning them aside. "Many footsteps, the track of which is lost in England, might be found reappearing on the other side of the Atlantic; aye, though it be hundreds of years since the track were lost here."

Middleton, though he had refrained from looking full at Mr. Eldredge as he spoke, was conscious that he gave a great start; and he remained silent for a moment or two, and when he spoke, there was the tremor in his voice of a nerve that had been touched and still vibrated.

"That is a singular idea of yours," he at length said; "not singular in itself, but strangely coincident with something that happened to be occupying my mind. Have you ever heard any such instances as you speak of?"

"Yes;" replied Middleton, "I have had pointed out to me the rightful heir to a Scottish earldom, in the person of an

American farmer, in his shirt sleeves. There are many Americans who believe themselves to hold similar claims. And I have known one family, at least, who had in their possession, and had hid for two centuries, a secret that might have been worth wealth and honors, if known in England. Indeed, being kindred as we are, it cannot but be the case."

Mr. Eldredge appeared to be much struck by these last words, and gazed wistfully, almost wildly, at Middleton, as if debating with himself whether to say more. He made a step or two aside; then returned abruptly, and spoke.

"Can you tell me the name of the family in which this secret was kept?" said he; "and the nature of the secret?"

"The nature of the secret," said Middleton smiling, "was not likely to be entrusted to any one out of the family. The name borne by the family was Middleton. There is no member of it, so far as I am aware, at this time remaining in America."

"And has the secret died with them?" asked Mr. Eldredge.

"They communicated it to none," said Middleton.

"It is a pity! It was a villainous wrong," said Mr. Eldredge. "And so, it may be, some ancient race, in the old country, is defrauded of its rights for want of what might have been obtained from these Yankees, whose democracy has demoralized them to the perception of what is due to the antiquity of descent, and of the bounden duty that there is, in all ranks, to keep up the honor of a family that has had potency enough to preserve itself in distinction for a thousand years."

"Yes," said Middleton quietly, "we have sympathy with what is strong and vivacious to-day; none with what was so yesterday."

The remark seemed not to please Mr. Eldredge; he frowned, and muttered something to himself; but recovering himself, addressed Middleton with more courtesy than at the

commencement of their interview; and, with this gracious-
ness, his face and manner grew very agreeable, almost fascinating; he still haughty, however.

"Well, Sir," said he, "I am not sorry to have met you. I
am a solitary man, as I have said, and a little communication
with a stranger is a refreshment, which I enjoy seldom
enough to be sensible of it. Pray are you staying hereabouts?"

Middleton signified to him that he might probably spend
some little time in the village.

"Then, during your stay," said Mr. Eldredge, "make free
use of the walks in these grounds; and though it is not
probable that you will meet me in them again, you need
apprehend no second questioning of your right to be here.
My house has many points of curiosity that may be of interest to a stranger from a new country. Perhaps you have heard
of some of them."

"I have heard some wild legend about a Bloody Footstep,"
answered Middleton; "indeed, I think I remember hearing
something of it in my own country; and having a fanciful
sort of interest in such things, I took advantage of the hospitable custom which opens the doors of curious old houses
to strangers, to go to see it. It seemed to me, I confess, only a
natural stain in the old stone that forms the door-step."

"Then, Sir," cried Mr. Eldredge, "let me say that you came
to a very foolish conclusion; and so good-bye, Sir!"

And without further ceremony, he cast a glance of anger
at Middleton, who perceived that the old gentleman reckoned
this Bloody Footstep among his ancestral honors, and would
probably have parted with his claim to the peerage almost
as soon as have given up the legend.

Present aspect of the story; Middleton, on his arrival, becomes acquainted with the old Hospitaller, and is familiarized
at the Hospital. He pays a visit in his company to the manor-
house, but merely glimpses at its remarkable things, at this

visit, among others at the old cabinet, which does not, at first view, strike him very strongly. But, on musing about his visit, afterwards, he finds the recollection of this cabinet strangely identifying itself with his previous imaginary picture of the palatial mansion; so that, at last, he begins to conceive the mistake he has made. At this first visit, he does not have a personal interview with the possessor of the estate; but as the Hospitaller and himself go from room to room, he finds that the owner is preceding them, shyly flitting like a ghost, so as to avoid them. Then there is a chapter about the character of the Eldredge of the day, a Catholic, a morbid, shy man, representing all the peculiarities of an old family, and generally thought to be insane. And then comes the interview between him and Middleton, when the latter excites such an interest that he dwells upon the old man's mind, and the latter probably takes pains to obtain further intercourse with him, and perhaps invites him to dinner and spend a night in his house. If so, this second meeting must lead to the examination of the cabinet, and the discovery of some family document in it. Perhaps the cabinet may be in Middleton's sleeping-chamber, and he examines it by himself, before going to bed; and finds out a secret which will perplex him how to deal with it.

May 14th. Friday. We have spoken several times already of a young girl, who was seen, at this period, about the little antiquated village of Smithills; a girl in manners and in aspect unlike those of the cottages amid which she dwelt. Middleton had now so often met her, and in solitary places, that an acquaintance had inevitably established itself between them. He had ascertained that she had lodgings at a farmhouse near by, and that she connected in some way with the old Hospitaller, whose acquaintance had proved of such interest to him; but more than this he could not learn either from her or others. But he was greatly attracted and interested by the free spirit and fearlessness of this young woman; nor could he conceive where, in staid and formal England, she had grown up to be such as she was, so without manners, so without art, yet so capable of doing and thinking for herself. She had no reserve, apparently, yet never seemed to sin against decorum; it never appeared to restrain her, that anything she might wish to do was contrary to custom; she had nothing of what could be called shyness in her intercourse with him, and yet he was conscious of an unapproachableness in Alice. Often, in the old man's presence, she mingled in the conversation that went on between him and Middleton, and with an acuteness that betokened a sphere of thought much beyond what could be customary with young English maidens; and Middleton was often reminded of the theories of those, in our own country, who believe that the amelioration of society depends greatly on the part that women shall hereafter take, according to their individual capacity, in all the varied pursuits of life. These deeper thoughts, these higher qualities, surprised him as they showed themselves, whenever occasion called them forth, under the light, gay, and frivolous exterior which she had at first seemed to present. Middleton often amused himself with surmises in what rank of life Alice could have been bred, being so free of all conventional rule, yet so nice and delicate in her perception of the true proprieties that she never shocked him.

One morning, when they had met in one of Middleton's rambles about the neighborhood, they began to talk of America; and Middleton described to Alice the stir that was being made in behalf of women's rights; and he said that whatever cause was generous and disinterested always, in that country, derived much of its power from the sympathy of woman, and that the advocates of every such cause were in favor of yielding the whole sphere of human effort to be shared equally with women.

"I have been surprised," said he, "in the little that I have seen and know of English women, to discover what a difference there is between them and my own countrywomen."

"I have heard," said Alice with a smile, "that your countrywomen are a far more delicate and fragile race than Englishwomen; pale, feeble, hot-house plants, unfit for the wear and tear of life, without energy of character, or any slightest degree of physical strength to base it upon. If now you had these large framed Englishwomen, you might, I should imagine, with better hopes, set about changing the system of society, so as to allow them to struggle in the strife of politics, or any other strife, hand to hand or side by side with men."

"If any countryman of mine has said this of our women," exclaimed Middleton indignantly, "he is a slanderous villain, unworthy to have been borne by an American mother; if an Englishman has said it—as I know many of them have and do—let it pass as one of the many prejudices, only half believed, with which they strive to console themselves for the inevitable sense that the American race is destined to higher purposes than their own. But pardon me; I forgot that I was speaking to an Englishwoman, for indeed you do not remind me of them. But, I assure you, the world has not seen such women as make up, I had almost said the mass of womanhood in my own country; slight in aspect, slender in frame, as you suggest, but yet capable of bringing forth stalwart men; they themselves being of inexhaustible courage, patience, energy; soft and tender, deep of heart, but high of purpose. Gentle, refined, but bold in every good cause."

"Oh, you have said quite enough," replied Alice, who seemed ready to laugh outright, during this encomium. "I think I see one of these paragons now, in a Bloomer, I think you call it, swaggering along with a Bowie knife at her girdle, smoking a cigar, no doubt, and tippling sherry coblers and mint-juleps. It must be a pleasant life."

"I should think you, at least, might form a more just idea of what women become," said Middleton considerably piqued, "in a country where the rules of conventionalism are somewhat relaxed; where woman, whatever you may think, is far more profoundly educated than in England, where a few ill-taught accomplishments, a little geography, a catechism of science make up the sum, under the superintendence of a governess, the mind being kept entirely inert as to any training for thought. They are cowards, except within certain rules and forms; they spend a life of old proprieties, and die, and if their souls do not die with them, it is Heaven's mercy."

Alice did not appear in the least moved to anger, though considerably to mirth, by this description of the character of English females. She laughed as she replied, "I see there is little danger of your leaving your heart in England." She added more seriously; "and, permit me to say, I trust, Mr. Middleton, that you remain as much American in other respects as in your preference of your own race of women. The American who comes hither, and persuades himself that he is one with Englishmen, it seems to me, makes a great mistake; at least, if he is correct in such an idea, he is not worthy of his own country, and the higher development that awaits it. There is much that is seductive in English life; but I think it is not upon the higher impulses of our nature that such seductions act. I should think ill of the American, who, for any causes of ambition—any hope of wealth or rank—or even for the sake of any of those old, delightful ideas of the past, the associations of ancestry, the loveliness of an age-long home—the old poetry and romance that haunt these ancient villages and estates of England—would give up the chance of acting upon the unmoulded future of America."

"And you, an Englishwoman, speak thus!" exclaimed Middleton. "You perhaps speak truly; and it may be that your words go to a point where they are especially applicable at this moment. But where have you learned these ideas? And how is it that you know how to awake these sympathies, that have slept perhaps too long?"

"Think only if what I have said be truth," replied Alice. "It is no matter who or what I am that speak it."

"Do you speak," asked Middleton from a sudden impulse, "with any secret knowledge respecting a matter now in my mind?"

Alice shook her head, as she turned away; but Middleton could not determine whether the gesture was meant as a negative to his question, or merely as declining to answer it. She left him; and he found himself strangely disturbed with thoughts of his own country, of the life that he ought to be leading there, the struggles in which he ought to be taking part; and, with these emotions in his impressible mind, the motives that had hitherto kept him in England seemed unworthy to influence him.

May 15th. Saturday. It was not long after Middleton's meeting with Mr. Eldredge in the park of Smithills, that he received—what it is precisely the most common thing in the world to receive, in England—an invitation to dine at the manor-house, and spend the night. The note was written with much appearance of cordiality, as well as in a respectful style; and Middleton could not but perceive that Mr. Eldredge must have been making some inquiries as to his social status, in order to feel himself justified in putting him on this footing of equality. He had no hesitation in accepting the invitation, and on the appointed day, was received in the old house of his forefathers as a guest. The owner met him, not quite on the frank and friendly footing expressed in his note, but still with a perfect and polished courtesy, which, however, could not hide from the sensitive perception of Middleton a certain coldness, a something that seemed to him Italian rather than English; a symbol of a condition of things between them, undecided, suspicious, doubtful. Very likely, Middleton's own manner corresponded to that of his host, and they made few advances towards more intimate acquaintance. Middleton was however recompensed for his host's unapproachableness by the society of his daughter, a young lady, born indeed in Italy, but who had been educated in a Catholic family in England; so that here was another relative —the first female one—to whom he had been introduced. She was a quiet, shy, undemonstrative young woman, with a fine bloom, and other charms which she kept as much in the background as possible, with maiden reserve.

< (There is a Catholic priest at table) >

Mr. Eldredge talked chiefly, during dinner, of art, with which his long residence in Italy had made him thoroughly acquainted, and for which he seemed to have a genuine taste and enjoyment. It was a subject on which Middleton knew little; but he felt the interest in it which appears to be not uncharacteristic of Americans, among the earliest of their developements of cultivation; nor had he failed to use such few opportunities as the English public or private galleries afforded him to acquire the rudiments of a taste. He was surprised at the depth of some of Mr. Eldredge's remarks on the topics thus brought up, and at the sensibility which appeared to be disclosed by his delicate appreciation of some of the excellencies of those great old masters, who wrote their epics, their tender sonnets, or their simple ballads, upon canvass; and Middleton conceived a respect for him which he had not hitherto felt, and which possibly Mr. Eldredge did not quite deserve. Taste seems to be a department of moral sense; and yet it is so little identical with it, and so little implies conscience, that some of the worst men in the world have been the most refined.

After Miss Eldredge had retired, the host appeared to desire to make the dinner a little more social than it had hitherto been; he called for a peculiar species of wine from Southern Italy, which he said was the most delicious production of the grape, and had very seldom, if ever before, been imported pure into England. A delicious perfume came from the cradled bottle, and bore an ethereal, evanescent testimony to the truth of what he said; and the taste, though too delicate for wine quaffed in England, was nevertheless delicious, when minutely dwelt upon.

"It gives me pleasure to drink your health, Mr. Middleton," said the host. "We might well meet as friends in England, for I am hardly more an Englishman than yourself; bred up, as I have been, in Italy, and coming back hither, at my age, unaccustomed to the manners of the county, with few friends, and insulated from society by a faith which makes most people regard me as an enemy. I seldom welcome people here, Mr. Middleton; but you are welcome."

"I thank you, Mr. Eldredge, and may fairly say that the circumstances, to which you allude, make me accept your hospitality with a warmer feeling than I otherwise might. Strangers, meeting in a strange land, have a sort of tie in their foreignness to those around them, though there be no positive relation between themselves."

"We are friends then?" said Mr. Eldredge, looking keenly at Middleton, as if to discover exactly how much was meant by the compact. He continued—"You know, I suppose, Mr. Middleton, the situation in which I find myself, on returning to my hereditary estate, which has devolved to me somewhat unexpectedly, by the death of a younger man than myself. There is an old flaw here, as perhaps you have been told, which keeps me out of a property long kept in the guardianship of the crown, and of a barony, one of the oldest in England. There is an idea—a tradition—a legend, founded, however, on evidence of some weight, that there is still in existence the possibility of finding the proof which we need, to confirm our cause."

"I am most happy to hear it, Mr. Eldrege," said Middleton.

"But," continued his host, "I am bound to remember, and to consider, that for several generations, there seems to have been the same idea, and the same expectation; whereas nothing has ever come of it. Now, among other suppositions—perhaps wild ones—it has occurred to me that this testimony, this desirable proof, may exist on your side of the Atlantic; for it has long enough been sought here in vain."

"As I said in our meeting in your park, Mr. Eldredge," replied Mr. Middleton, "such a suggestion may very possibly be true; yet let me point out, that the long lapse of years, and the continual melting and dissolving of family institutions—the consequent scattering of family documents, and the annihilation of traditions from memory, all conspire against its probability."

"And yet, Mr. Middleton," said his host, "when we talked together, at our first singular interview, you made use of an expression—of one remarkable phrase—which dwelt upon my memory, and now recurs to it."

"And what was that, Mr. Eldredge?" asked Middleton.

"You spoke," replied his host, "of the Bloody Footstep reappearing on the threshold of the old palace of Shnnnnn. Now where, let me ask, did you ever hear this strange name which you then spoke, and which I have since spoken?"

"From my father's lips, when a child, in America," responded Middleton.

"It is very strange," said Mr. Eldredge, in a hasty, dissatisfied tone. "I do not see my way through this."

May 16th. Sunday. Middleton had been put into a chamber in the oldest part of the house, the furniture in which was of antique splendor, well befitting to have come down for ages, witnessing the stately hospitality shown noble, and even royal guests. It was the same room, in which, at his first visit to the house, Middleton's attention had been drawn to the cabinet, which he had subsequently remembered as the palatial residence, in which he had harbored so many dreams. It still stood in the chamber, making the principal object in it, indeed; and when Middleton was left alone, he contemplated it not without a certain awe which, at the same time, he felt to be ridiculous. He advanced towards it, and stood contemplating the mimic façade, wondering at the singular fact of this piece of furniture having been preserved in traditionary history, when so much had been forgotten—when even the features and architectural characteristics of the mansion, in which it was merely a piece of furniture, had been forgotten. And, as he gazed at it, he half thought himself an actor in a fairy portal; and would not have been surprised—at least, he would have taken it with the composure of a dream—if the mimic portal had unclosed, and a form of pigmy majesty had appeared within, beckoning him to enter, and find the revelation of what had so long perplexed him. The key of the cabinet was in the lock, and knowing that it was not now the receptacle of anything in the shape of family papers, he threw it open; and there appeared the mosaic floor, the representation of a stately, pillared hall, with the doors on either side, opening, as would seem, into various noble apartments. And here should have stood the visionary figures of his ancestry, waiting to welcome the descendant of their race, who had so long delayed his coming. After looking and musing a considerable time—even till the old clock from the turret of the house told twelve, he turned away with a sigh, and went to bed. The wind moaned through the ancestral trees; the old house creaked as with ghostly footsteps; the curtains of his bed seemed to waver. He was now at home; yes, he had found his home, and was sheltered at last under the ancestral roof, after all those long, long wanderings—after the little log-built hut of the early settlement, after the shingled roof of the American house, after all the many roofs of two hundred years, here he was at last under the one which he had left, on that fatal night, when the Bloody Footstep was so mysteriously impressed on the threshold. As he drew nearer and nearer towards sleep, it seemed more and more to him, as if he were the very individual—the self-same one throughout the whole—who had done, seen, suffered, all these long toils and vicissitudes, and were now come back to rest, and found his weariness so great that there could be no rest.

Nevertheless, he did sleep; and it may be that his dreams went on, and grew vivid, and perhaps became truer in proportion to their vividness. When he awoke, he had a perception, an intuition, that he had been dreaming about the cabinet, which, in his sleeping imagination, had again assumed the magnitude and proportions of a stately mansion, even as he had seen it afar from the other side of the Atlantic. Some dim associations remained lingering behind, the dying shadows of very vivid ones that had just filled his mind; but as he looked at the cabinet, there was some idea that still seemed to come so near his consciousness, that, every moment, he felt on the point of grasping it. During the process of dressing, he still kept his eyes turning involuntarily towards the cabinet; and at last he approached it, and looked within the mimic portal, still endeavoring to recollect what it was that he had heard, or dreamt about it—what half obliterated remembrance from childhood, what fragmentary last night's dream, it was that thus haunted him. It must have been some association of one or the other nature that led him to press his finger on one particular square of the mosaic pavement; and as he did so, the thin plate of polished marble slipt aside. It disclosed, indeed, no hollow receptacle, but only another leaf of marble, in the midst of which appeared to be a key-hole; to this Middleton applied the little antique key to which we have several times alluded, and found it fit precisely. The instant it was turned, the whole mimic floor of the hall arose, by the action of a secret spring, and discovered a shallow recess beneath. Middleton looked eagerly in, and saw that it contained documents, with antique seals of wax appended; he took but one glance at them, and closed the receptacle as it was before.

Why did he do so? He felt that there would be a meanness and wrong in inspecting these family papers, coming to the knowledge of them, as he had, through the opportunities afforded by the hospitality of the owner of the estate; nor, on the other hand, did he feel such confidence in his host, as to make him willing to trust these papers in his hands, with any certainty that they would be put to an honorable use. The case was one demanding consideration, and he put a strong curb upon his impatient curiosity, conscious that, at all events, his first impulsive feeling was that he ought not to examine these papers without the presence of his host or some other authorized witness. Had he exercised any casuistry about the point, however, he might have argued that these papers, according to all appearance, dated from a period to which his own hereditary claims ascended, and to circumstances in which his own rightful interest was as strong as that of Mr. Eldredge. But he had acted on his first impulse, closed the secret receptacle, and hastening his toilet, descended from his room; and it being still too early for breakfast, resolved to ramble about the immediate vicinity of the house. As he passed the little chapel, he heard within the voice of the priest performing mass, and felt how strange was this figure of medieval religion and foreign manners in homely England.

As the story looks now;—Eldredge, bred, and perhaps born in Italy, and a Catholic, with views to the church, before he inherited the estate, has not the English moral sense and simple honor; can scarcely be called an Englishman at all. Dark suspicions of past crime, and of the possibility of future crime, may be thrown around him; an atmosphere of doubt shall envelope him, though as regards manners, he may be highly refined. Middleton shall find in the house a priest;

and, at his first visit, he shall have seen a small chapel, adorned with the richness, as to marbles, pictures, and frescoes, of those that we see in the churches at Rome; and here the Catholic forms of worship shall be kept up. Eldredge shall have had an Italian mother, and shall have the personal characteristics of an Italian. There shall be something sinister about him, the more apparent when Middleton's visit draws to a conclusion; and the latter shall feel convinced that they part in enmity, so far as Eldredge is concerned. He shall not speak of his discovery in the cabinet.

May 17ᵗʰ. Monday. Unquestionably, the appointment of Middleton as minister to one of the minor continental courts must take place in the interval between Eldredge's meeting him in the park, and his inviting him to his house. After Middleton's appointment, the two encounter each other at the Mayor's dinner in St Mary's Hall, and Eldredge, startled at meeting the vagrant, as he deemed him, under such a character, remembers the hints of some secret knowledge of the family history which Middleton had thrown out. He endeavors, both in person and by the priest, to make out what Middleton really is, and what he knows, and what he intends; but Middleton is on his guard, yet cannot help arousing Eledredge's suspicions that he may have views upon the estate and title. It is possible, too, that Middleton may have come to the knowledge of—may have had some knowledge of—some shameful or criminal fact connected with Mr. Eldredge's life on the continent; the old Hospitaller, possibly, may have told him this, from some secret malignity hereafter to be accounted for. Supposing Eldrege to attempt his murder, by poison for instance, bringing back into modern life his old Italian hereditary plots; and into English life a sort of crime which does not belong to it—which did not, at least, although, at this very period, there have been such fresh and numerous instances of it. There might be a scene, in which Middleton and Eldredge come to a fierce and bitter explanation; for in Eldredge's character there must be the English surly boldness as well as the Italian subtlety; and here, Middleton shall tell him what he knows of his past character and life, and also what he knows of his own hereditary claims. Eldredge might have committed a murder in Italy; might have been a patriot, and betrayed his friends to death for a bribe, bearing another name than his own in Italy; indeed, he might have joined them only as an informer. All this, he had tried to hide, when he came to England in the character of a gentleman of ancient name and large estate. But this infamy of his previous character must be foreboded from the first by the manner in which Eledredge is introduced; and it must make his evil designs on Middleton appear natural and probable. It may be, that Middleton has learned Eldredge's previous character, through some Italian patriot who had taken refuge in America, and there become intimate with him; and it should be a piece of secret history, not known to the world in general, so that Middleton might seem to Eldredge the sole depository of the secret then in England. He feels a necessity of getting rid of him; and thenceforth Middleton's path lies always among pitfalls; indeed, the first attempt should follow promptly and immediately on his rupture with Eledredge. The utmost pains must be taken with this incident to give it an air of reality; or else it must be quite removed out of the sphere of reality by an intensified atmosphere of Romance. I think the old Hospitaller must interfere to prevent the success of this attempt, perhaps through the means of Alice.

The result of Eldredge's criminal and treacherous designs is, somehow or other, that he comes to his death; and Middleton and Alice are left to administer on the remains of the story; perhaps, the Mayor being his friend, he may be brought into play here. The foreign ecclesiastic shall likewise come

forward, and he shall prove to be a man of subtile policy perhaps, yet a man of religion and honor; with a Jesuit's principles, but a Jesuit's devotion and self-sacrifice. The old Hospitaller must die in his bed or some other how; or perhaps
not—we shall see. He may just as well be left in the Hospital. Eldredge's attempt on Middleton must be in some way
peculiar to Italy, and which he shall have learned here; and,
by the way, at his dinner-table there shall be a Venice glass,
one of the kind that were supposed to be shattered when
poison was put into them. When Eldredge produces his rare
wine, he shall pour it into this, with a jesting allusion to
the legend. Perhaps the mode of Eldredge's attempt on Middleton's life shall be a reproduction of the attempt made,
two hundred years before; and Middleton's hereditary knowledge of that incident shall be the means of his salvation.
That would be a good idea; in fact, I think it must be done
so, and no otherwise. It is not to be forgotten that there is
a taint of insanity in Eldredge's blood, accounting for much
that is wild and absurd, at the same time that it must be
subtile, in his conduct; one of those perplexing mad people,
whose lunacy you are continually mistaking for wickedness,
or vice versa. This shall be the priest's explanation and apology for him, after his death. I wish I could get hold of the
Newgate Calendar, the older volumes, or any other book of
murders—The Causes Celebres, for instance. The legendary
murder, or attempt at it, will bring its own imaginative probability with it, when repeated by Eldredge; and at the same
time, it will have a dreamlike effect; so that Middleton shall
hardly know whether he is awake or not. This incident is
very essential towards bringing together the past time and
the present, and the two ends of the story.

May 18th. Tuesday. All down through the ages since
Edward had disappeared from home, leaving that bloody
footstep on the threshold, there had been legends and strange
stories of the murder, and the manner of it. These legends

differed very much among themselves. According to some, his brother had awaited him there, and stabbed him on the threshold; according to others, he had been murdered in his chamber, and dragged out. A third story told, that he was escaping with his lady love, when they were overtaken on the threshold, and the young man slain. It was impossible, at this distance of time, to ascertain which of these legends was the true one, or whether either of them had any portion of truth, further than that the young man had actually disappeared from that night, and that it never was certainly known to the public that any intelligence had ever afterwards been received from him. Now, Middleton may have communicated to Eldredge the truth in regard to this matter; as for instance, that he had stabbed him with a certain dagger that was still kept among the curiosities of the manorhouse. Of course, that will not do. It must be some very ingenious and artifically natural thing, an artistic affair in its way, that should strike the fancy of such a man as Eldredge, and appear to him altogether fit, mutatis mutandis, to be adopted for his own requirements and purposes. I do not at present see in the least how this is to be wrought out. There shall be every thing to make Eldredge look with the utmost horror and alarm at any chance that he may be superseded and ousted from his possession of the estate; for he shall only recently have established his claim to it, tracing out his pedigree, when the family was believed to be extinct. And he is come to these comfortable quarters after a life of poverty, uncertainty, difficulty, hanging loose on society; and therefore he shall be willing to risk soul and body both, rather than return to his former state. Perhaps his daughter shall be introduced as a young Italian girl, to whom Middleton shall decide to leave the estate.

On the failure of his design, Eldredge may commit suicide, and be found dead in the wood; at any rate, some suitable end shall be contrived, adapted to his wants. This character must not be so represented as to shut him out completely from the reader's sympathies; he shall have taste, sentiment, even a capacity for affection, nor, I think, ought he to have any hatred or bitter feeling against the man whom he resolves to murder. In the closing scenes, when he thinks the fate of Middleton approaching, there might even be a certain tenderness towards him, a desire to make the last drops of life delightful; if well done, this would produce a certain sort of horror, that I do not remember to have seen effected in literature. Possibly, the ancient emigrant might be supposed to have fallen into an ancient mine, down a precipice, into some pitfall; no, not so. Into a river; into a moat. As Middleton's pretensions to birth are not publicly known, there will be no reason why, at his sudden death, suspicion should fix on Eldredge as the murderer; and it shall be his object so to contrive his death as that it shall appear the effect of accident. Having failed in effecting Middleton's death by this excellent way, he shall perhaps think that he cannot do better than to make his own exit in precisely the same manner. It might be easy, and as delightful as any death could be; no ugliness in it, no blood; for the Bloody Footstep of old times might be the result of the failure of the old plot, not of its success. Poison seems to be the only elegant method; but poison is vulgar, and in many respects unfit for my purpose. It won't do. Whatever it may be, it must not come upon the reader as a sudden and new thing, but as one that might have been foreseen from afar, though he shall not actually have foreseen it till it is about to happen. It must be prevented through the agency of Alice. Alice may have been an artist in Rome, and there have known Eldredge and his daughter, and thus she may have become their guest in England; or he may be patronizing her now— at all events, she shall be a friend of the daughter, and shall have a just appreciation of the father's character. It shall be partly due to her high counsel that Middleton forgoes his claim to the estate, and prefers the life of an American, with its lofty possibilities for himself and his race, to the position of an Englishman of property and title; and she, for her part, shall choose the condition and prospects of woman in America, to the emptiness of the life of a woman of rank in England. So they shall depart, lofty and poor, out of the home which might be their own, if they would stoop to make it so. Possibly the daughter of Eldredge may be a girl, not yet in her teens, for whom Alice has the affection of an elder sister.

It should be a very carefully and highly wrought scene, occurring just before Eldredge's actual attempt on Middleton's life, in which all the brilliancy of his character—which shall before have gleamed upon the reader, shall come out, with pathos, with wit, with insight, with knowledge of life. Middleton shall be inspired by this; and shall vie with him in exhilaration of spirits; but the ecclesiastic shall look on with a singular attention, and some appearance of alarm; and the suspicions of Alice shall likewise be aroused. The old Hospitaller may have gained his situation partly by proving himself a man of the neighborhood, by right of descent; so that he, too, shall have a hereditary claim to be in the romance.

Eldredge's own position, as a foreigner in the midst of English home life, insulated and dreary, shall represent to Middleton, in some degree, what his own would be, were he to accept the estate. But Middleton shall not come to the decision to resign it, without having to repress deep yearnings for that sense of long, long rest in an age-consecrated home, which he had felt so deeply to be the happy lot of Englishmen. But this ought to be rejected, as not belonging to his country, nor to the age, nor any longer possible.

May 19th. Wednesday. The connection of the old Hospitaller with the story is not at all clear. He is an American by birth, but deriving his English origin from the neighbor-

hood of the Hospital where he has finally established himself. Some one of his ancestors may have been somehow connected with the ancient portion of the story. He had been
a friend of Middleton's father, who reposed entire confidence
in him, trusting him with all his fortune, which the Hospitaller risked in his prodigious speculations, and lost it all.
His fame had been great in the financial world. There were
circumstances that made it dangerous for his whereabouts
to be known, and so he had come hither, and found refuge
in this institution, where Middleton finds him, but does not
know who he is. In the vacancy of a mind, formerly so
active, he has taken to the study of local antiquities; and
from his former intimacy with Middleton's father, he has a
knowledge of the American part of the story, which he con-
nects with the English portion, discovered by his researches
here; so that he is quite aware that Middleton has claims to
the estate, which might be urged successfully against those
of the present possessor. He is kindly disposed towards the
son of his friend, whom he had so greatly injured; but he
is now very old, and. ———. Middleton has been directed to
this old man, by a friend in America as one likely to afford
him all possible assistance in his researches; and so he seeks
him out and forms an acquaintance with him, which the
old man encourages to a certain extent, taking an evident
interest in him, but does not disclose himself; nor does Middleton suspect him to be an American. The characteristic life
of the Hospital is brought out, and the individual character
of this old man, vegetating here after an active career, melancholy and miserable; sometimes torpid with the slow approach
of utmost age; sometimes feeble, peevish, wavering; sometimes shining out with a wisdom resulting from originally
bright faculties, ripened by experience. The character must
not be allowed to get vague, but, with gleams of romance,

must yet be kept homely and natural by little touches of his daily life.

As to Alice, I see no necessity for her being anywise related to or connected with the old Hospitaller. As originally conceived, I think she may be an artist—a sculptress—whom Eldredge had known in Rome. No; she might be a granddaughter of the old Hospitaller, born and bred in America, but who had resided two or three years in Rome in the study of her art, and had there acquired a knowledge of Mr Eldredge, and had become fond of the little Italian girl his daughter. She has lodgings in the village, and of course is often at the Hospital, and often at the Hall; she makes busts, and little statues, and is free, wild, tender, proud, domestic, strange, natural, artistic; and has at bottom the characteristics of the American woman, with the principles of the strong-minded sect; and Middleton shall be continually puzzled at meeting such a phenomenon in England. By and by, the internal influence of her sentiments (though there shall be nothing to confirm it in her manner) shall lead him to challenge her with being an American.

Now, as to the arrangement of the Romance;—it begins, as an integral and essential part, with my introduction, giving a pleasant and familiar summary of my life in the Consulate at Liverpool; the strange species of Americans, with strange purposes in England, whom I used to meet there; and, especially, how my countrymen used to be put out of their senses by the idea of inheritances of English property. Then I shall particularly instance one gentleman who called on me, on first coming over; a description of him must be given, with touches that shall puzzle the reader to decide whether it is not an actual portrait. And then this Romance shall be offered, half seriously, as the account of the fortunes that he met with in his search for his hereditary home.

Enough of his ancestral story may be given to explain what is to follow in the Romance; or perhaps this may be left to the scenes of his intercourse with the old Hospitaller.

The Romance proper opens with Middleton's arrival at what he has reason to think is the neighborhood of his ancestral home; and here he makes application to the old Hospitaller. Middleton shall be described as approaching the Hospital, which shall be pretty literally copied after Leicester's, although the surrounding village must be on a much smaller scale of course. Much elaborateness may be given to this portion of the book. Middleton shall have assumed a plain dress, and shall seek to make no acquaintance, except that of the old Hospitaller; the acquaintance of Alice naturally following. The old Hospitaller and he go together to the Hall, where, as they pass through the rooms, they find that the proprietor is flitting like a ghost before them from chamber to chamber; they catch his reflection in a glass &. &. Then, or sooner, come the village rumors respecting his personal character, mixed up with the legendary fantasies and myths about the feuds of the family &c &c. When these have been wrought up sufficiently, shall come the scene in the wood, where Eldredge is seen yielding to the superstitions that he has imbibed, respecting this old secret of the family, on the discovery of which depends the enforcement of his claim to a title. All this while, Middleton has appeared in the character of a man of no note; but now, through some political change not necessarily told, he receives a packet addressed to him as an ambassador, and containing a notice of his appointment to that dignity. A paragraph in the Times confirms the fact, and makes it known in the neighborhood. Middleton immediately becomes an object of attention; the gentry call on him; the mayor of the neighboring county-town invites him to dinner, which shall be described with all its antique formalities. Here he meets

Eldredge, who is surprised, remembering their encounter in the wood; but passes it off, like a man of the world, makes his acquaintance, and invites him to the Hall. Perhaps he may make a visit of some time here, and become intimate, to a certain degree, with all parties; and here things shall ripen themselves for Eldredge's attempt upon his life.

ETHEREGE

THERE DWELT an ancient gentleman, I know not precisely how many years ago, in a house that stood by a grave-yard; and in his household there was a boy, and a girl a few years younger than himself;—neither of whom, as it appeared, had claims on him as their parent.

<Give vivid pictures of the society of the day, symbolized in the street-scenes.>

<(The Doctor shall be held in great odium in the town, and wicked stories shall be told about him; but seeing him nearer, he proves to be a perfectly loveable old gentleman. The monstrous spider must be introduced as soon as possible) No instance on record of a spider having injured anybody.>

<(The great spider had been sent him by his brother. Fanciful theory about its web.)>

This old gentleman (his name was Etherege) was of somewhat peculiar and solitary habits of life; and though all the town knew him by sight, there were hardly two or three persons who knew much more of him than was to be surmised by his kindly, yet shy old face, his brown, square-cut coat and small clothes, of an antique fashion, and his powdered head, some of the snow from which had worked itself into the collar of the coat. When he came abroad, he shuffled through the streets, with a gold headed cane of a rich Indian wood, nodding now and then to an acquaintance, taking off his hat to the ladies; and when occasion was, stopping to hold a little converse, in which there was usually a remarkably genial and pleasant vein; so that people wondered why so agreeable a man was always in such haste to close up his talk and go shuffling on his way again. Sometimes, the boy and girl walked demurely behind him; but oftener, when seen at all, they were sporting together in the grave-yard, making playmates of the tall slate grave-stones, on some of which were sculptured flat nosed cherubs, who seemed to grin in sympathy with their pastimes; on others, stern portraits of puritans, done to a button, a ruff, and a skull-cap, who frowned on these poor little folks, as if death had not made them a whit more genial than they were in life. But the children seemed to be more encouraged by the good-natured little cherubs, than they were abashed by the sour puritans.

This grave yard (we are sorry to have to treat of such a disagreeable piece of ground; but everybody's business centres there, at one time or another) was the most ancient in the town. The dust of the original Englishmen had become incorporated with the soils of those Englishmen whose immediate predecessors had been resolved into the earth about the country churches, the little Norman, square, battlemented stone towers, of the villages in the old land; so that, in this point of view, as holding bones and dust of the first ancestors, this grave yard was more English than anything else in town. There had been hidden from sight many a broad, bluff visage, of husbandmen that had ploughed the rich English soil; there the faces of noted men, now known in history; there many a personage whom tradition told about, making wondrous qualities of strength and courage for him;—all these, mingled with succeeding generations, turned up and battened down again with the sexton's spade;

until every blade of grass was human, more than vegetable; for a hundred and fifty years will do this; and so much time, at least, had elapsed since the first little mound was piled up in the virgin soil. Old tombs there were too, with armorial sculptures on them, and quaint, mossy grave-stones; although all kinds of monumental appendages were of a date more recent than the time of the first settlers, who had been content with wooden memorials, if any, the sculptor's art not having then reached New England. Thus rippled, surged, broke, about the house, this dreary grave-yard, which made the street gloomy; so that people did not like to pass the dark high wooden fence, with its closed gate, that separated it from the street; and this old house was one that cornered upon it, and took up the ground that would otherwise have been sown as thickly with dead as the rest of the lot; so that it seemed hardly possible but that the dead people should get up out of their graves and come in there to warm themselves. But, in truth, I never heard a whisper of its being haunted.

It did not seem to be a very ancient house, after all; not one of the many-peaked, the seven-gabled houses, which were of the earliest creation; although, very probably, it stood on the site of some older mansion, and may have incorporated parts of it in itself. It had a small, old porch with an oval pane of glass on either side, before it, abutting on the street, and in itself it was an angular old, three-story wooden structure, with low, ugly rooms, the most cheerful of which looked out upon the green space of the grave-yard.

Old Doctor Etherege had the reputation of a very learned man, and not impossibly he may have merited it. Unquestionably, he had inherited from his ancestors a larger amount of literary treasures than were usually found in the possession of private persons, in those days; old editions of the classics, both Greek and Latin, bound in parchment, and with the names of famous printers in the title-pages; and the autographs of scholars of his own race in the fly-leaves, from the boyish handwriting of the disciple in Corderius, to the crabbed characters of the old Doctor of Divinity in a folio of the Fathers. This collection had a grievously theological character, to be sure; but then there were rare works of early medical science, old volumes of Philosophical Transactions; and much curious nonsense of that kind; and there too, more truly valuable, was a desultory collection of English writers, both poets and prosers, down to the time of Addison inclusive; but much fuller in the earlier parts than the more modern. Here the Doctor used to sit, with a great folio before him, in an old easy chair, with a clay pipe of interminable stem between his fingers.

Besides this reputation for classic knowledge, he had another for skill in his profession and for scientific lore; indeed, he was known in the medical journals of the day, for a discovery of certain excellent properties in cobwebs, whereby these products of spinning machines, heretofore considered useless, and swept away heedlessly by the housemaid's broom, were found to be the most sedative of medicines. To say the truth, the good Doctor Etherege had the materials for this discovery close at hand, and could not have made one with more convenience; for of all bachelor's houses, this one was the most overrun with spiders; and their dusky webs festooned the old rooms, and were trailed across the windows, and swung and flaunted in the breezes through broken panes; so that, on his own theory, it ought to have been the quietest residence in Christendom, being a very atmosphere of spiders' webs. Spiders dangled down from the cieling; spiders crept upon the tables, and lurked in the corners; and people even said, very probably with truth, that the Doctor procured spiders of various kinds from far and near; and that he even sent to some torrid region or other to obtain a spider such as heretofore had only been seen, dead and dry, in the collections of naturalists, a spider as big in the body as little Elsie's doubled fist, and spreading its multitude of legs over a foot in space, and whose web seemed made of good-sized cordage; for out of this fabric, he hoped to get a proportionable quantity of sedative influence to allay even public turmoils.

At all events, it was the duskiest, gloomiest, cobwebbediest abode to be anywhere found; all overlaid with deadmen's dust; for it is reasonable to suppose, that the dust, which lay on staircase and hall and chamber came from the neighboring grave-yard. The old gentleman lived contentedly in the dust, and breathed it as his natural atmosphere, and clothed himself in cobwebs as a garment; and people said that the inner chambers of his brain were as densely hung with cobwebs as those of his external abode. There he sat at the book-covered, antique table, in his dark old study, and the spiders ran across the leaf on which he wrote his crabbed characters, and walked leisurely over the page of his folio book. Then, too, the book-worm gnawed; that veritable insect of whom everybody has heard, but whom few have seen; a white abomination that seems to have a little cutting instrument with which it makes circular perforations in precious antique pages. The Doctor himself looked like some strange animal, or existence, in his study-cap and gown, like a magician; and, indeed, there were stories of that kind about him which I do not care to repeat, because all that class of matters is worn out and trite; and ghosts are drugs, and witchcraft beneath notice.

All this squalor of the abode served to set off the lightsomeness and brightsomeness of the little girl, who dwelt in it; she was a pale, large-eyed, little thing; and from such appearances, it might have been supposed that the air of the house or the contiguity of the old burial-place had a bad effect upon her health. But I hardly think this could have been the case; for she was of a very airy nature, dancing and sporting through the house, as if melancholy had never been made. She was fond of the old Doctor, and took all kinds of childish liberties with him, and with his pipe, and with everything appertaining to him except his spiders and cobwebs. She loved to be with him in his study; the silent witness of many a strange experiment, the witness, too, of many a solitary mood of grief, regret, all a bachelor's repentances; the witness of the opening of old caskets; nor did the Doctor seem to be disturbed, when he was made aware of this little intimate's presence by catching her eyes of light upon him, with a sympathizing, perhaps, as he thought, intelligent gleam. So Elsie lived between two persons, both of whom had evidently a large share in her affections; the old man, and the young boy.

The latter, as we have already hinted, was not apparently a favorite with his guardian; not that Dr Etherege did not act towards him with even paternal care and consideration; with even more, indeed, than towards the girl. But there was a character of carefulness and study, a lack of spontaneity in this. There were no kindly impulses; all was a well-planned, wise, and kind order of education, independent of feeling, and such as a tutor, if a man of conscience and sagacity, might have instituted for the education of a boy. He was never pettish towards the boy, as sometimes, in the waywardness of old bachelorship, he was towards Elsie. He was just, and kind, but never exactly tender. And yet the boy had all the qualities fitted to excite tenderness in those who had the care of him; in the first and most evident place, on account of his personal beauty, which was very remarkable;—the most intelligent and expressive face that can be conceived, cheering, in those early years, like an April day, and beautiful in all its changes, dark, but of a soft expression, kindling, melting, glowing, laughing—a varied intelligence, which it was as good as a book to read. He was quick in all modes of mental exercise; quick and strong, too, in sensibility; and, very possibly, before the good old Doctor dreamed of such a thing, he enabled the boy to know with sufficient accuracy what was the sort of feeling in his patron's mind for him. The boy had pride, too, as well as sensibility and affection; and he seemed to make no effort to win the demonstrations of tenderness that flowed spontaneously towards Elsie; although, on the other hand, there was no sign that he took amiss the different light in which he was viewed. But, doubtless, he pondered on the reasons for this; though it was scarcely possible that he could have found one.

Doubtless, this coldness, as respected him, in the temper of his patron, was of no real disadvantage to the boy. It gave him, perhaps, an energy which the softness and impressibility of his nature needed. Then, too, the old Doctor was an admirable instructor; and the scholarship of his youth was turned to good account in the tuition he personally gave the boy. He even gave him lessons in the lighter accomplishments, which he himself had learned, forty years before, in a European town. The art of the sword; the old world demeanour of a polished gentleman; these were among the arts that he communicated to the boy; all seeming to look towards a position in life, which, in any other country than ours, the nameless and fortuneless lad would have little opportunity of alluring. So the beautiful boy, under the tuition and example of the queer old Doctor, with his gown smelling of tobacco smoke, put out new graces daily, and looked worthy to be the heir of a princely house.

Thus was it now the fortune of the old bachelor, in his dusky and uninviting house, to have at his unmistressed fireside two children such as few wedded couples in any rank of life could show; growing up like brother and sister, but perhaps, even at that early age, with a strange sweetness in their intercourse of which the fraternal relation is not susceptible—a racy charm that supplies the lack of something that, on the other hand, can be contained in no bond but that of brother and sister.

The old Doctor, as we have already said, was a genealogist, a collector of historical relics, and interested generally in everything that had come down from the past of New England, with which several names of his ancestors were prominently connected. And so his study—a room panelled with wood that had grown absolutely black—was rich in many things that made it almost a museum. Old weapons of strange and whimsical construction; guns of immense length; swords; a cuirass; a steel cap; not arranged in any order, but strewn carelessly about; of each of which, I suppose, the Doctor could have told some story that would have made the visitor look more carefully at it than he would otherwise be disposed to do. Things, too, such as a gray wig,—that had been worn by people who, what was left of them—were now at but a little distance, a few steps within the adjoining grave yard. Growing up among these rusty things perhaps gave the children, with their fresh beauty, a quaint characteristic, as if they were the children of a long past generation, who, by some unaccountable fatality had never grown up.

The boy took especial interest in these things—an interest arising from an imaginative temperament, that brought up before him many suggestions of circumstances, clinging to these things. He, oftener on such points than any other— broke through the reserve in which his perception of the Doctor's coldness kept him, and questioned him about them. The Doctor generally responded with sufficient freedom; partly, doubtless, from a feeling of duty to convey instruction in all ways to the boy, partly also from the pleasure which he took in talking of matters on which his thoughts ran so frequently.

And so the boy's thoughts were led to dwell on by-gone things; on matters of birth and ancestry, and connections of one family with another; and blood running in such intricate currents; sometimes sinking into the ground and disappearing forever; sometimes, after a long hidden course, reappearing, and ascending prominently like the gush of a fountain. And probably it was such meditations as these that led him to think, occasionally, what had been his own origin; whence came that blood that circled through his own veins. I presume there are more people occasionally occupied by such speculations in a democracy, where all claims of birth are nominally annulled, than in any land of nobility and hereditary honors; because, in the former, there is an uncertainty that admits all to claim even royal blood.

A race missing from England, a hundred & fifty years before, recovered now in America; by the disappearance of the English heir, something had been left at odds, which all that time had been waiting, just as when it was then left. Corresponding to this grave in America, there must be a coffin in a tomb in England, within which lies the maiden that turned to ringlets of golden hair.

Perhaps the Old Doctor himself may have been long in quest of this grave, for which the Englishman comes to seek; and he may have hit upon half the secret, while the Englishman brings the other half. But he will not assist him. The original emigrant knew that he was the heir of a title, and brought the proofs of it with him, the missing link, which he treasured during life, and which—from some mysterious records found in England—it was thought were buried with him in the grave. It might appear that he had visited England afterwards, had gone to the home of his ancestry, and there had deposited this proof in the coffin of the lady whom he had loved. This is mere nonsense; perhaps, in the dim distance, it may be so handled as to look less desperately foolish;—perhaps not. The old Doctor shall have heard, in former generations, that there was great inquest for this man's grave, or for any property that he may have left, or the slightest article or writing appertaining to him.

Very few visitors came to the Doctor's house; but, one day, when the three inhabitants were together, as usual, engaged in their ordinary occupations, there came a knock at the door, and Hannah, the long accustomed handmaiden, ushered a stranger into their presence. He was a fresh-colored, middle-aged man, not very elaborately dressed—rather roughly, in fact—and yet he did not seem an awkward man. Of free manners, but yet not rude. The Doctor, with his old-fashioned courtesy, made him as welcome as was possible for an entire stranger to be; and they sat down together to talk across the table on which the old yellow papers, which the Doctor was then studying, lay.

<(He might bring an introduction from the Doctor's brother; perhaps not.)>

"I have come to this country," said the stranger, after some preliminary talk, "on a singular investigation."

"You are not then a countryman of ours?" said the Doctor, in a tone as if he had suspected the fact already. "An Englishman?"

"Yes, an Englishman," said the stranger.

"I am sorry," said the Doctor, not unmindful of his loyal descent, "that we cannot now call ourselves countrymen. But I shall be as happy to serve you as if we were. You have come hither on an investigation, you say."

"Precisely," said Mr Mountford; for so he had given his name; "and as it has a relation to genealogical matters, and circumstances connected with one of the early settlers of this country, I have been directed to you, as a gentleman of deep knowledge on such like points, and more likely than any other to give me such information as may avail me."

"A little knowledge goes a great way with my good fellow citizens," responded Dr. Etherege smiling. "I have, to be sure, rummaged a little among old yellow papers, like these before me—scraped the moss out of a good many grave stones, in this burial ground under my window and elsewhere. It does not amount to much—not much. But what I know, I shall be happy to devote to your service, if available. To what family, may I ask, do your investigations refer? It has not escaped my knowledge that the true heirs of some respectable and honorable English names, perhaps extinct in their native land, might be successfully sought on this side of the water."

"I scarcely think," said Mr. Mountford, "that the family name can have made any great noise on this side of the water. In fact, it is the peculiarity of this case, that I must seek a person of another name, in order to find one whose fortunes had, and strangely continue to have, an adverse influence on the welfare of a distinguished English family. It is a person of the name of Colcord that I am in quest of."

The Doctor got up to arrange a stick of his wood fire, which had rolled down, and came back again; and sitting down, said quietly,

"And how long since might this person have emigrated to America, and what was his rank in life, and his position among us?"

"Not a high one," responded the Englishman. "In fact, his early residence in this country was as a bond-servant, bought at public auction."

"It will indeed be difficult to discover any traces of a person so obscure," said the Doctor.

"But," resumed the stranger, "his birth and origin were not altogether so obscure as might be indicated by the fact referred to. This unfortunate man appears to have been one of the prisoners at the battle of Worcester, whom the Round-head Government transported to America, in a sort of questionable mercy—a sort of halfway measure between pardoning them and sending them out of the world."

"It amounted to very much the same thing, in this case," said the Doctor thoughtfully; "for the fate of those prisoners was singularly hard, & their life among us brief. Whether from bitter thoughts or hard treatment, they perished within a very few years, and have left scarcely any trace among us of their having ever existed."

"I am aware of it," said the Englishman. "And yet, in the present case, we have seen some reason to suppose that it might not be so. It is known that, a century ago—for so long, and longer, has the desirability existed of finding this person—a hundred years ago, a gentleman of the law came across the Atlantic on the same errand which has now partly drawn me hither. The person in question might then have been dead, perhaps, thirty or forty years; and there is reason to suppose that his grave could be—and, in fact, was—pointed out to my predecessor in this business. It is my wish to find out that grave, and investigate it."

"Singular," said the old Doctor, turning his gray eyes upon his visitor. "And what could you expect to find among the dry dust and crumbly bones of a hundred and fifty years ago? For, so long, by your own statement, it would seem to be since this man was buried."

"Many strange secrets are buried in the grave," said the stranger, with a grave smile; "and some of them, if we sought aright, might possibly be recovered. There are certain very curious circumstances which have led me to wish to see the interiour of this grave. There is an old letter, in the repositories of the English family, which refers us hitherward."

The Doctor walked to the window, and looked out upon the waste of snow, that lay upon the graves, covering the whole surface of the burial place with its white, cold purity, beneath which lay, perhaps, the secret of which the stranger spoke, and many another that never would come to the knowledge of men. Was it possible that, out of so old a pit, should come—that in it now lay—any recoverable knowledge that it could suit the purposes of mortal men to dig up?

"There are certain tokens," said the stranger, referring to the memorandum in his hand, "by which this particular grave might be discovered, supposing that other landmarks still exist. For instance, there were three graves, situated precisely east, west, and north, on which there were an engraved hand pointing to this one."

"The ground has been so often dug over," said the Doctor, "that unless peculiar care has been taken, by surviving members of the families, there is great doubt whether those grave stones are now to be found."

"There was a house to the east;" said Mr. Mountford; "and at seventy-five paces from the door of that, the grave would be found."

"It might be this house," said the doctor; "and the door, that which opens into the burial-place. We will try it, after dinner."

So the good Doctor hospitably kept the stranger to dinner, which was served at the primitive hour of one oclock, and was no very choice collation; but the host produced at it some very old wine, the flavors of which had been on the tongues of more than one bon vivant, who had now gone to sleep under that cold covering of snow, at which the Doctor and his guest had just been looking. The Doctor and the Englishman drank it together, and talked much about ancient times, and the affairs of the old family which the guest had come thither to represent. The aged juice might have led to such topics, by the light, warmth, sunshine, and joy, of so long past time as it held entranced within it. The little boy and girl listened to much of this; but as Dr Etherege kept his guest longer than these young people (not partaking of the wine) liked, they stole away from table and went to play in the old study.

Perhaps it was the old-time talk that they had been listening to that suggested to them the sport of representing old characters, the personages of whom the Doctor had told them so much; they looked at the pictures hanging on the walls, and it seemed as if something inspired them with the feelings and conventionalities of those faded prototypes; for there were these children going through a stately scene of ceremony, and courtly respect, as if they were born to it, when the Doctor and his guest, somewhat exhilarated with the good wine of a former century, returned to the study.

The stranger for the first time appeared to notice the two children.

"You are fortunate, my good Sir," said he, "in having your wintry home illuminated by two such cheerers as these. Are they your own?"

"Ah, no; I am a bachelor," returned the Doctor, "as you may have already concluded from the meagre and careless bachelor dinner that you have eaten. No; I chose this way of life in my early days, and must not complain though I find it rather cold and dreary in this latter time. But the children—come hither, my little girl—the children do their part, though other people were at the pains to provide me with them."

"They have not the ruddiness of most English children," said the guest, "but I know not that any lack of health is indicated by their less vivid colouring. This boy!—what an intelligence he has! A certain quickness, alertness, sensibility, which are not often so early developed among the sturdy little folks of my native land. Is it usual for Yankee boys to have faces bright as this?"

"Well; many of them are so," answered the Doctor. "But the lad is well enough. But here is the picture I was mentioning."

He led the stranger, not to any of the beruffed and gold-laced portraits of his ancestors, but to the picture which we have already slightly alluded to, as being strangely out of place in such a gallery; that of the young man in a coarse dress, with the badge of servitude upon his garments. And the stranger's eyes being thus drawn to it, he surveyed it with great interest and attention, drawing back, three or four times, as if about to leave it, and then returning again to pore over the picture.

"It is a very remarkable face," said he, at length; "a very striking face, especially when seen in such a garb as that. It is not often, in my country, at least, that the face of a man is above his station, or that the look of position and cultivation can be taken on, without the born qualities which it implies. Who was this man?"

"That," said the Doctor, "I am unable to tell you. It has been in the possession of my family a great many years:—but there is room for a conjecture, though perhaps a wild one. What if this were the likeness of the very man of whom we have been talking—of whom you are in quest—whose bones we are about to unearth, if we can find them, in yonder grave yard?"

"A conjecture, as you say," replied the stranger, "but with enough of imaginative probability, at least. My fancy, I suppose, deceives me; but I seem to have seen that remarkable face somewhere, and not in this country either. My present pursuit is altogether such a fantastic one, that I suppose it has driven away my cooler judgement altogether."

After some more talk of this kind, the Doctor proposed to go to the Sexton, who, on his part, demurred to opening a grave except in the usual way of his business; when, as he said, he should be happy to open one for either of the gentlemen. Finally, he insisted upon leave from the Selectmen, which being obtained, the trio proceeded to the spot indicated by the instructions of the stranger. They duly measured the paces, and took the landmarks, accordingly. Meanwhile, little Ned and Elsie had come out in the snow, and stood looking on with great earnestness. It turned out that the spot was the very one where they had been accustomed to play, on an old flat stone, without record; but strange to say, this stone was here stood upright, and formed the headstone of a new grave, which (the one bare place from the snow in the whole grave yard) covered the spot which they were seeking.

"Why, what is this?" said the Doctor, sharply. "What have you been about here, Rollins?"

"Only doing my office by a customer," said the Sexton with composure. "If I had known this was the grave you were seeking, I could have saved us all three the trouble of coming here. I know the spot, ever since I was a boy; and my father, who was sexton before me, bade me bury nobody in it till three and forty years from that time."

"Why three and forty years?" asked the stranger.

"I don't know," said the Sexton; "but my father knew well enough, I warrant you; for he was a knowing character. I often used to think that everyone he buried left his wisdom to my father; and, moreover, he knew all about the graves of everybody that was buried, long before his day, and could tell where the least bit of dust was, akin to that he was going to put away. Ah; there was a great deal of wisdom and knowledge buried yonder, when my father himself was put away."

"No doubt," said the Doctor; "and when they put you away, the same will be true. But whom have you buried here?"

"Old Mother Hubbard," said the Sexton; "for, from some thing that her grandmother had told her, she had a curious sort of feeling about this grave; so I thought to gratify her by putting her in it. She lies deep, I tell you."

"Our quest is ended," said Dr Etherege apart to the stranger; "for no doubt, the very bottom of the old grave was found and turned up."

"What did you find, my good man, in the old grave?" asked Mr Mountford.

"Oh, nothing of any account," said the Sexton, carelessly. "Pretty much the same sort of rubbish that I find in every grave—an old bone or two, the skull which I look care to put back, and nothing else that I know on. When the snow melts, you may find a bone or two hereabouts, mayhap; but I think it decent to put such things away."

"It's no use doing more," said Mr. Mountford.

But the little boy and girl had been searching about among the earth, which the Sexton had left; and little Elsie, whose eyes and observation were very acute, now put her slender little fingers into a crevice between the earth and snow, and drew out something which nobody else had detected. The Doctor took it in his own hand, and after knocking away some foreign substance that adhered, perceived it to be a rusty key, of very antique and peculiar form.

"A strange circumstance this!" quoth the Doctor. "Here seems to be the key of the mystery, at all events. Were you in search of anything like this?"

"Not that I am aware," replied Mr. Mountford, perplexed, but looking much interested. "Yet there are locks within my knowledge to which this key (it is of the sixteenth century, at latest) might apply. As there seems to be nothing else to answer my purpose, and requite me for courting trouble, will you allow me to take it?"

<I rather think the boy should keep the key, perhaps finding it the next day.>

The Sexton made some objection but was requited by a silver dollar which the stranger put into his hand; and the party left the burial ground, and returned to the Doctor's study. That good old gentleman made the Englishman's stay so agreeable, that he professed himself sorry to quit his hospitable home the next morning; which, however, he did, taking the dead man's key along with him. One feels a spirt of spite against Sextons, who live so long, and bury the town twice over, and seem to contract a sort of kindred and partnership with Death, and take his part against mankind.

<(The following should come before the stranger's visit.)>

These three fellow-denizens, in the evenings, used to have much instructive talk together; when the Doctor would tell them such as was suited for his young auditors to hear among the varied experiences of his youth. How that he had been a traveller in various parts of the world, and had seen the manners of many people, and had studied in famous old universities; and been to theatres, courts, and to all the places that look most brilliant to young imaginations. He told them about the great capitals of the world, Paris, Rome, Vienna, London; all about purple and sunny Italy; much about foggy England; about old castles and houses, the delightful permanence of things; the ivy, the misletoe.

"Oh, what a sweet place, dear Uncle!" said little Elsie. "I think I should like it better than this place, here by our grave yard; though this is sometimes pleasant enough when Ned and I play there in the sunshine or the snow. But that would be better!"

"Do you feel strongly drawn towards old England, then my child?" said the old Doctor.

"Ah yes indeed, uncle!" said the little girl.

"Well, well; there is a reason for it!" said her Uncle. "And how is it with you, Ned? Have you the same liking for it?"

"Not I, Sir," said little Edward. "And yet I shall go there, some day, to find out a certain thing that I have dreamed of all my life."

"And what may that be, pray?" asked the Doctor.

"A Bloody Footstep!" replied Ned, laughing, and yet somehow with a slight tremor in his voice.

"A Bloody Footstep!" repeated the Doctor.

"A Bloody Footstep!" quavered little Elsie.

"Yes; a Bloody Footstep!" persisted Edward, with a certain gravity and yet a consciousness of absurdity that made a quaint mixture in such a child. "To tell you the truth, Uncle, and Elsie, either my nurse, or my mother told me the story, when I was a baby, or else I dreamt it; but there is in my mind a thought about this Bloody Footstep, that is imprinted somewhere in England, and which no rain will wipe away. When it happened, or where it it, I don't know; but I never think of England without seeing that in my mind's eye; and it seems as if all England was nothing else but the ground sufficient for this great Bloody Footstep to be imprinted in!"

"Dear, how awful!" said little Elsie quite aghast.

"This is a very queer idea, my little fellow," said the Doctor with much gravity. "Is this all you remember of this terrific footstep; nothing about the time, the manner, the cause?"

"Nothing else; this is all," said Edward. "I mean, nothing else that I can tell; but there seem to be things that I can almost get hold of, and think about; but when I am just on the point of seizing them, they start away, like slippery things. In the day-time, the thought looks to myself like great non-sense; but in the twilight, by the fireside, I often see something about it among the burning-coals; and if I awake at night, that is a bad time to think about it."

"Strange!" quoth the Doctor to himself. "How could this idea have got into the boy's head!"

<(Insert this when the stranger comes)>

Ned listened with the greatest interest to the talk of the stranger and the Doctor, without saying a word; only getting closer to them, and seeming to take in every word, and yet not to get quite the word he wanted. At last, in the pause of the conversation, he came and looked in the stranger's face, while his own (for the changes of color in him were always answering to the emotions of the moment) grew very pale.

"Have you ever seen the Bloody Footstep?" asked he.

"The Bloody Footstep!" said Mr Mountford; for it seemed to be everybody's impulse, on first hearing this grim thing mentioned, to repeat it over, as if it were something not understood at first speaking; "no I have never seen it."

"Nor heard of it?" said Edward, shyly; as if he hated to press the subject, but yet were inwardly compelled to.

"No; nor heard of it," said Mr. Mountford. "Yet stay;—it strikes me that some such thing may have sounded in my ears before. A London lawyer hears of many strange things; and something like this may have been among them. There are many bloody foot-tracks through his experience—so many that he cannot remember them."

"Ah; but you would remember this," said little Ned, with an air of disappointment. "This is one great, separate print of a foot in blood, impressed somewhere near an old house in England, and the blood always fresh upon it."

"Why, Ned;" observed the Doctor, "you did not tell us so much of this marvellous footstep before."

"No," said Ned, "but this flashed upon my mind only now, after I began to speak. Something brought it up, at the moment."

"Well, my little friend," said the lawyer. "I will make inquiries about this matter; and if ever you come to London, find out my chambers in the Temple, and I will tell you all about it."

The Doctor lived there among his cobwebs, spending his life apparently in endeavoring to perfect this discovery; for according to him, all science was to be renewed and established on a sure ground by no other means than this. The cobweb was the magic clue by which mankind was to be rescued from all its errors, and guided safety back to the right. And so he cherished spiders above all things, and kept them spinning, spinning away; the only textile factory that existed, at that epoch, in New England. He distinguished the production of each of his ugly friends, and assigned peculiar qualities to each; and he had been for years engaged in writing a work on this new discovery, in reference to which he had already achieved a great deal of folio manuscript, and had unguessed at resources still to come. With this suggestive subject, he interwove all imaginable learning, collected from his own library, rich in works that few others had read, and from that of his beloved University; crabbed with Greek, rich with Latin, drawing into itself, like a whirlpool, all that men had thought hitherto, and combining them anew in such a way that it had all the charm of a racy originality. Then he had projects for the cultivation of cobwebs, to which end, in the good Doctor's opinion, it seemed desirable to devote a certain part of the national income; and, not content with this, all public spirited citizens would probably be induced to devote as much of their times and means as they could, to the same end. According to him, there was no such beautiful festoon and drapery for the halls of princes, as the spinning of this heretofore despised and hated insect; and by due encouragement, it might be hoped that they would flourish, and hang and dangle, and wave triumphant in the breeze, to an extent as yet generally undreamed of. And he lamented much, the destruction that had heretofore been wrought upon this precious fabric by the housemaid's broom, and insisted upon by foolish women who claimed to be good housewives. Indeed, it was the general opinion that the Doctor's celibacy was in great measure due to the impossibility of finding a woman who would pledge herself to cooperate with him in this great ambition of his life—that of reducing the world to a cobweb factory, or who would bind herself to let her own drawing-room be ornamented with this kind of tapestry. But there never was a wife precisely fitted for our friend the Doctor, unless it had been Arachne herself, to whom, if she could again have been restored to her female shape, he would doubtless have lost no time in paying his addresses.

It was, doubtless, the having dwelt too long among the musty and dusty clutter and litter of things gone by that made the Doctor almost a monomaniac on this subject. There were cobwebs in his own brain; and so he saw nothing valuable but cobwebs in the world around him, and deemed that the march of created things, up to this time, had been calculated by foreknowledge to produce them.

Some people supposed that other objects were entangled within these cobwebs of Dr. Etherege's brain; they looked back upon his life, and remembered that he had been a brilliant young man, who had been a distinguished scholar, giving great promise of professional eminence; and that he had gone abroad to put the finishing touches to the education for which the schools of America had already done what was possible. There he had spent several years, and when he returned, all that knew him had expected him to take the high place for which he was so fitted. But instead of that, he had secluded himself in the house at the corner of the grave-yard, living on little and almost in solitude; and all the account that the world had of him was, that he was making discoveries in the medical efficacy of cobwebs. But, of course, this was not the true explanation of the thing. He had met with a misfortune of some kind; or he had committed a crime; and had come hither to brood about it. I disdain to speak of the rumours about the Doctor's alchymick pursuits, which the foolish people of the town busied themselves with circulating. There was not (we need not say the slightest ground) but not the slightest appearance of them; and the good old gentleman collected his cobwebs with as much simplicity as he would have gathered, and did gather, the weeds from his garden and house corners, to brew into decoctions with which he made other medical experiments in corporibus vilis of cats and dogs, rats and mice.

And yet it was strange! Other people took a different view of his seclusion, and fancied we know not what about a certain brother of the Doctor who had gone abroad early, and was said to be making a great figure in Napoleon's service; but whether as a soldier or a statesman was not accurately determined. At any rate, such a brother there had been, and such a one was not now; so far as the knowledge of men extended. But it was said that the Doctor always kept a chamber in the house ready for the occupancy of the brother when he returned; a fire burning, a meal, some say, prepared, a pair of slippers and a night cap by the bed; and this was so evidently for one particular guest, that when, on some rare occasion, there was another claimant of the Doctor's hospitality, a new room had to be prepared for him by our friend Sukey, instead of the obvious resource of putting him into the many years ready one. The poor Doctor! The guests he might once have expected had probably all gone to a long sleep somewhere else; and the Englishman was the first that had come for years. Could he then have been the one that was expected? It scarcely seemed so, from the little or no effect that had resulted from his visit; but yet, if this was not the visit that the Etherege family had expected for so many generations, there was nothing else that could represent it. So that there was a general belief that the visit had been paid, and had been attended with much more momentous consequences than appeared on the surface.

And this was said to have been the custom of the family from time immemorial. Old people—the oldest inhabitant, who, at this time, called himself 103, but was proved by the record to be ninety seven years old—averred that the father, grandfather, and, I think, likewise the great grandfather of the present doctor, had done the same. All the while the Doctor was absent in Europe, the same custom had been kept up —a fire in winter, in the chamber, fresh arrangement every morning through the year, a plate always at the board, for some shadowy guest, who had never yet appeared. He had never yet appeared; for when a guest did come, still he was proved not to be the expected one by there being still a vacant seat, still a plate, a napkin, a glass; nor was he ever installed in the chamber that was always ready. Those who looked at the matter philosophically, said, that this was only one of the old Doctor's symbols—that he meant to express by it, that he, a lonely man, and a bachelor, had never yet met the one person, whether man or woman, who was made for him, and could alone appreciate him; he or she, who could sympathize with him in his love of cobwebs; who could touch the spring of his energies, which, for lack of that spring being touched, had never yet been put in action; so that now he was likely to go to his grave an unrecognized, and what was worse, an inefficient man, and the spiders spin their web over his dusty memory, and hide him from view. And it was in expectation of hearing that step—never yet heard, but yet familiar, whether masculine or a woman's, that the Doctor listened, when he awoke in the morning, and sat late, listening to tread upon the pavement, to crunch in the snow, in the evening. It was the feeling, kept up through life, and acted on, of the young man, of the budding maiden, who looks, on every new day, for the advent of the person who is to be the fate, the golden fate of a life time. But, alas! where was that beautiful maiden, where that heroic youth, in all these years; and if either of them came now, one would be most probably a gouty senior, long ago awakened from the dreams of his youth; the other a fat dowager, or crinkled, thin, vinagrish maiden lady, whom the Doctor would cover himself with a green sod bed quilt rather than encounter.

It was a picturesque and curious affair enough, however; and those who, by rare chance, visited the old man, found themselves singularly affected by it, listening to every step upon the pavement, to every crunching pressure in the snow, as if the long expected one might appear at that very moment when they chanced to be there. There did, likewise, seem good reason to suppose that it was a family custom, originating probably in some domestic incident—the long absence of a son, it may be, who never returned; kept up by love and despair, and transmitted to a posterity who observed the same custom after they had forgotten the origin of it; taking pride to do what the eccentricities of yearning affection had originally prompted. There were a great many legends connected with this custom, which I deem it not worth while here to repeat. The question still remained—who could he originally have been, this expected guest of ages? and, should he come now, would he come in the flesh, in the skeleton, or in the spirit?

(When the London lawyer appears, he mentions that there is a similar custom, in an ancient English family.)

(In regard to this custom, it shall turn out, in the explanation part of the book, that two lovers, we will say, had parted, two hundred years ago, with the expectation of soon meeting again, and that they had agreed that they would expect one another continually till then, and that all preparations should be kept up, as if they were coming the next minute. Some crime had been perpetrated,—the kidnapping of one party and carrying him off to America—which prevented their ever meeting again. The man settles in America, and then writing to the beloved person, he always expects that she will come to him. He has been involved in some guilt of murder or high-treason, or the suspicion of it, which precludes him from returning to England. On her part, she will not believe that he is dead, although no letters are ever received from him; they being intercepted by the guile of those about her. When she dies, she leaves it ordered in her will, that a room in her mansion shall always be kept ready for him, a fire burning, a plate at the board, until he returns; in fact, being half a maniac, her shade of lunacy shows itself in this way. And, thus, when the hero goes to England, and to the old mansion house, he finds a plate, bed, & everything ready for him, and by some chance, he enjoys the benefit of these things, as if he were the person originally expected, as, indeed, he is his representative. Possibly, in back countries, the institution might have become converted into a hospitable provision for any unexpected guest.)

After all, it was the emblem of most lives; for it is not often that what we most expect and count upon, ever comes; and it may be, too, that the expected guest had really made his appearance, at some unlooked for time, and in some unrecognizable guize, and departed without his fitting welcome.

"Doctor," said the boy, one day, awaking to sudden recognition of the strangeness of the custom, which its being customary had heretofore hidden from him, "do other people do as we do? In every house, is there a chamber for some guest that never comes; at every table, a plate for a person who never sits down to eat a mouthful?"

"I know not how that may be, my boy," said the Doctor. "But in most hearts, there is an empty chamber, waiting for a guest."

"Uncle," said the little girl, "I always feel as if there were somebody sitting in that chair, though we do not see him."

"Him; is it a man then, Elsie?" asked the boy.

"So it seems to me," she replied.

"But to me, always, the prettiest of young girls; rather sad in her manner, but still pleasant and sweet."

"To me it seems a young man with a moustache, and a ruff, and a beard on his chin, and a sword hilt glittering behind him. And how does it seem to you, dear Uncle?" said little Elsie.

"I have forgotten," quoth the Doctor sleepily.

There is still a want of something, which I can by no means get at, nor even describe what it is—which, indeed, would be almost equivalent to supplying the want. A deeper life should be given to the Doctor, who thus far has no real connection with the story. He has a brother in England, who has made a great figure in life, and has done great mischief, and is now in retirement; so much the reader shall be given to understand. Perhaps, at this time, the reader shall be led to understand that this brother is in a very distinguished position; but when, at last, he is introduced to him, he shall be surprised to find him only a pensioner of the hospital. He may have been a great railway projector; a man in very high commercial trust, who has become bankrupt for an immense sum. Perhaps the nature of his former business need not be specified; only he has been high, and now is irreparably fallen. There must be much talk of this brother, in the early part of the Romance, and he must be essentially connected therewith. A man of schemes, who can never refrain from putting his hand to whatever is going forward, and has a wonderful tact to manage it by an imperceptible touch. It shall have been one of his schemes to transfer the heirdom of this old English family to the American descendant; and with this view he may have induced his brother, the Doctor, to seek out the young man, educate him, and make him fit for the station and duties of a great English noble. Perhaps he may be induced to this by remorse for having, at some former time, wronged and ruined the youth's father. Thus the position of the parties, at the beginning of the Romance would be accounted for with reasonable romantic sufficiency; the little girl, moreover, being his granddaughter. The old Doctor shall have sought the boy out, and found him in the poorest circumstances; perhaps (but it must only be hinted so) it may have been in the work-house. The brother shall only have made the discovery of the heirdom of this boy, since he went to England; and putting together some old legends, and also some scraps of genealogical lore which he remembers hearing from his brother, he comes to the conclusion that this is the heir; or at least (which is much the same to him) that he may be made to appear as such. It shall be represented to the reader, that a certain train of events which have been arrested in their course for two centuries, again begin to proceed, the moment the American comes upon the stage. The old, cob-webby Doctor must be much deepened and enriched, and spread a weird sort of effect not only over his own part of the Romance, but all the subsequent events; and when the brother is shown up, there must be a sort of family resem-blance; though they are very different men.

The story of the Bloody Footstep must be made wild, shadowy, and mythical, and yet be so handled that the story shall have all the advantage of its effect.

The boy's early, childish remembrances of the alms house shall mingle and confuse themselves, in a strange way, with the legends which he has learnt about his family, in earliest childhood; and both shall be dreamlike to him.

Thus this little family continued to live on together, there by the burial-ground, singularly insulated from the rest of the world, and whole and defined within themselves; and the boy was getting to the latter end of his childhood, and little Elsie was not so very small as when we first knew her. As for the Doctor, he seemed not very well; whether or no his cobwebs were less efficacious than when he first began with them, we cannot tell. His family of spiders grew and pros-pered, and spun more webs than ever; so that seldom has a tapestry chamber of old times been so well festooned as was his study; great, gloomy flauntings, and monsters hanging from the cieling far downward, by invisible lines, and swing-ing with long pendulum vibrations to-and fro. And here the powdery Doctor sat in the midst of his spider friends, who ran across his books, and his hands, and were said even to spin their webs across the orifice of his inkstand; and the great African spider, who was said to be his familiar, came and sat down before him, looking up into his face, in a manner fearful to see. And the old man seemed to be dim and melancholy, and looked mournfully at the two children, who also were melancholy for his sake; nor could they sport so cheerfully as they used, because there was a vague sense of gloom in the house, and the atmosphere of the grave yard seemed to pervade it, and shadows from it to come into the house. And perhaps they wondered whether the sunshine was scanty, everywhere else in the world as it was here. And they wished that they could do anything for their friend, the Doctor; and little Elsie, with a woman's housewifely instinct, wished that at least the room could be swept, and the cielings brushed free from the cobwebs; and especially that the great African spider would not always be sitting, squatting, so like a fiend, close to the poor old man.

Poor old man; he seemed quiet and calm enough, and yet these two young, sensitive natures had a sense that he was ill at ease. So they tried to show that they were ready to comfort him; and the little girl crept close to his knees; and the boy, who was not demonstrative, knew not what to do to show his feelings. The old man now showed, what is often observable in people who have anything the matter with them, a great uneasiness at being looked at; and if sometimes, starting from a reverie, he found the boy's eyes fixed on him, it made him as angry as his placid nature would allow him to be. But, one day, when he caught those young, anxious eyes upon him, he did not frown, but smiled a heavy, kindly melancholy smile.

"Well, Ned, what do you see in me?" he asked.

"Oh, Uncle," said the boy, "I was wondering why you never smiled, now-a days. And I am glad to see you smile."

"My poor children, I wish you had some occasion to smile. But now I wish you to tell me both—have you had a happy childhood?"

"Happy!" cried little Elsie with her usual ardour. "Oh, yes! we have both been the happiest boy and girl in the world. How could we help it, living with such a nice, kind uncle, in this pleasant place."

And Ned, likewise, in a quieter way, expressed his assent to what Elsie had said; and, indeed, looking back through his dreamy childhood—a vista, hung with wild and beautiful visions, made out of his ignorance of what he was, which had given him all the kingdom of possibilities to choose his origin out of—and had made him, if his imagination pleased —the heir of heroes, the progeny of beautiful women—endowing him with all riches of ancestry, because he had really none—he felt that, with all its shadowy gloom, there was a certain richness that made it better, probably, than other boys' lives. Then the gay, little, warm affections of true-hearted and sportive Elsie; then the mild, gracious, genial, though sad, paternity of the old Doctor, who had fostered everything deep, sweet, and high in him, and rooted out, so far as he could, all evil weeds. Yes it had been a good time with him.

"Very happy have we been," said he.

"Happy, my dear children—happy among these spiders and these cobwebs which have entangled me like a great stupid fly! Happy in this gloom and solitude, whence I have shut out the world till it had no longer any wish to enter! Happy in this corner of the grave-yard, and making it your play-ground. Happy in this melancholy old man, who had but the wreck of his life to bestow upon you! If it be so, thank Heaven."

"And then you have taught me so much," continued Ned —"me who came out of such a mystery!"

"Yes, Ned; a mystery!"

Some more conversation passed, in which the Doctor seemed to pour himself out in a way that was not customary for him; and it was later than usual when he trimmed his lamp, and drew his manuscript towards him, all bescribbled over with that crabbed handwriting, so small, so enigmatic, that you conceived of it as treating of strange matters. And the great giant spider, who had been watching him from aloft, and doubtless wondering what was the reason of his patron's long delay, took the hint, and came dangling down the long line of his web, as usual. He squatted down on the table, with his six sprawling legs, and seemed to gaze into his patron's face; a devilish object; but yet there may have been no harm in him for all that.

The Doctor smiled again.

"You see, Ned—you see, my little Elsie—he is jealous of my bestowing too much time on you. From now till midnight, he and I must be alone together. Good night, my darling— good night, dear Ned."

And so the good Doctor returned to his page, and wrote away, doubtless, deep into the night. But, at what hour we know not, there came a period where it had no business to be; and that was in the middle of a sentence. For when the careful Sukey entered the library next morning, she found the Doctor still seated at the table, with his writing before him; but his head had sunk down and he had fallen asleep. Yes; asleep! But there was to be no more waking for him in this world; and he had died, while yet on the hither verge of the communication which he had so long purposed to make about the medical properties of spiders. And above his head, as Sukey opened the door, was swinging that immense monster of a spider who had so long been the terror and fable of the neighborhood. As Sukey approached he went aloft in among the huge cobwebs which he had spun; and there, in the centre of his works, he was seen sitting, and there he seemed to sit motionless, for many days together—until the funeral was over, and all the mortality of the good Doctor consigned to the grave-yard, out upon which he had so long been gazing. Then—and not till then, out of reverence for the dead, it was thought time to use a broom in the Doctor's premises; and sweep away some of the myriads of spiders whom he had nourished. All the rest were made away with; and at last, with much hesitation and some fear on the part of the assailants, it was determined to make an attack on this immense monster, who still sat, in precisely the same attitude, in the centre of his web. But on cautiously approaching, and giving a great blow, with a long handled broom, which brought him down on the floor, a surprising discovery was made;—no less, than the apparent spider was no more than a simulacrum, the apparition of a spider, a gigantic skin, in short, and set of legs, out of which the former monster, who had so long held converse with the doctor, had crept and vanished. And this was taken as confirmation strong, that it was no real spider, but the devil in a spider's shape, who had taken that guise for the purpose of catching the Doctor's soul in the webs in which he had entangled himself, had now gone off with it, and left his skin for the world to wonder and tremble at.

When the will was examined, it was found that he had made provision for the support and education of the boy, in whose welfare he had taken such a charitable interest; but there was no information to be educed respecting the boy's origin and parentage. The remainder of his small property—not so large as the portion already devised—was left to Elsie Lyndhurst, who was designated as the only child of my beloved brother, James, now resident in foreign parts. There were directions as to her being committed to the charge of a certain person, who would see that she was conveyed to this brother James; and the will concluded with an earnestly expressed hope that public aid would be afforded to his community of spiders, on the existence and labors of which such important human interests depended.

I think the first scene, without any preliminary examination, should discover the Doctor and his two young friends in the study. The spiders dangling from wall and ceiling, and spreading their webs over everything; all which should be graphically depicted; and then this great African spider showing great familiarity with the Doctor. The bright, intelligent, beautiful boy; the old-fashioned, but lively girl, more active and springy than the boy; the powdery Doctor himself, amid his books, and philosophical apparatus, all dusty, and with cobwebs over everything. Antiquarian and genealogical lore to be indicated in many ways.

Through the windows, the grave yard is seen.

Then comes in an explanation, so far as it is desirable to give one of the old Doctor's character and way of life, and of the girl and boy; how the girl had befallen him as the child of a younger brother now abroad; how the boy, for some reason best known to himself, had been adopted from the alms-house. His eccentricities must be much insisted on; especially his belief in the curative properties of spider's web, and, to his external character, a certain grimness and queerity must be imparted; while, within his own little circle, he is shown to be a most simple and loveable man; although even here his intimacy with the African spider (to which some oriental pet name shall be assigned) must throw a sort of grotesque awe about him. It shall be considered his demon &c. The children shall speculate together about it, and develope queer ideas.

The brother in England must be dimly shadowed forth, and it shall be made to appear that he is a person of vast abilities and in eminent position. When the Doctor alludes to him, it shall always be in a vein of admiration, as possessing powers which seem to him—a man of simplicity, and worldly ineffectiveness, very wonderful. But yet the impression of something questionable must be conveyed; so that the reader shall be in doubt whether he is a good man or an enormous villain.

In a dim, uncertain way, the boy's unaccountable legends shall be half-shown, about the Bloody Footstep, &c &. And, without pretensions as he is, an alms-house child, he shall have great sensitiveness to the pride of birth; his imagination dwelling on it so much the more because he has all the world, all possibilities to choose his ancestry from. He shall have imaginative and poetic tendencies; but yet young America shall show a promising blossom in him—there shall be a freedom of thought, a carelessness of old forms of things, which shall sometimes shock the Doctor, and contrast oddly with his imaginative conservatism in other respects. The little girl, I think, shall have a similar freedom of thought; and both together shall perplex and startle the old man, amid his cobwebs.

Some way must be found to give a representation of the common place life of a Yankee town, going on around these insulated three;—by means of glimpses from the windows, of occasional calls, of funerals (by the by, the grave-digger might be early introduced,) of the Unitarian clergyman, and all ways that can conveniently be used.

When the story is fully prepared for him, the English lawyer must be introduced; and after his visit, the boy must be a little more evidently brought forward with his legends and traditions, which must vaguely shadow what he will hereafter see in England. The little girl, too, whose infancy was spent in England, shall contribute some indistinct remembrances, which shall work into the desired effect. The boy shall be so indicated as a personage of importance to the story, that it shall be expected that the Doctor's will shall elucidate the mystery; but it shall do nothing of the kind.

Early and forcibly—let the deep, unconquerable interest, which an American feels in England, its people, and institutions, be brought strongly out. This may partly be done by the mysterious child's yearnings towards his unknown ancestry, and having his imagination set entirely free by knowing nothing about them; so that he may, in fancy, trace his origin to the king's palace, if he likes. Then the family legends which cling dimly about his memory, and which he heard from the old woman who was with him in the almshouse, shall have an effect in the same direction. Great stress must be laid on the effect of his vague position in making him imaginative; also, on the freedom which he feels himself to possess, by being connected by blood with nobody, at the same time that he has a dreary sense of solitude.

The Doctor's brother in England; he shall have been a great speculator, a man endowed with great practical ability, yet having in him a certain wildness or madness, which, in the last result, is liable to produce ruin. He shall have almost irresistible influence over those with whom he holds intercourse; because his plans are so splendid and appear so feasible. In early life, he shall have had some brilliant schemes, in America, which shall end in his ruin, and in that of all concerned; among whom is a dear friend, the father of this boy. Having this on his conscience, he asks his brother to rescue the child from the alms-house, and bring him up tenderly and carefully; he having likewise sent to his care a little girl, his own daughter born in England. He launches into daring speculations, which need not be specifically described; but they are connected with Continental politics, and in the event of success, would have placed him on the top of the wheel of fortune. They fail ultimately, and he is reduced to be a pensioner at the hospital, to which he has a claim as being of the blood of the founder, through the female line. His ancestress, indeed, shall have been a sister of the Bloody Footstep family.

Until his residence in England, the speculator shall have known nothing about the family and heirship of the boy, the son of his friend; but while resident there, he shall have formed an acquaintance with the English representative of the family, and shall, led by certain tokens, and by his own connection with the family in the female line, have made an inquisition, and discovered great probability that this boy is the true heir of the estate, and of the title which has long been claimed, but held in abeyance on account of some defective link. His brother's genealogical lore shall have aided him in tracing this claim, so far as the American descent is concerned; but the Doctor shall deem it not advisable to tell him of these gorgeous fantasies; he being, of his own nature and practice, sufficiently disposed to make life a gilded dream. But the Doctor himself shall be possessed with the dream, and shall not always be able to help treating the boy as if he were the heir of noble inheritances. And his researches shall lead him to the discovery of strange, picturesque, romantic circumstances, which, somehow or other— perhaps in the shape of a legend that he tells the children by the fireside—must be brought to the knowledge of the reader. He may tell this legend as belonging to the little girl's and his own family, which the reader will not as yet understand to be connected with that of the boy.

The legend may refer to the first ancestor; his expulsion from the English mansion, his being kidnapped by a plot between a brother and some other person, or a cousin, with a view to his being murdered, but instead of that he was sent across the sea to Virginia, whence he made his way to New England. But he carried with him some secret that was essential to the prosperity of the family; and, in the course of generations, the family come to the knowledge or suspicion that he was not actually murdered, and they send to America in quest of his descendants;—but owing to a change of name, they send in vain. The lawyer, who visits the Doctor, is an emissary of this kind. The kidnapped man should have been engaged to be married to a cousin, who dies a maid, and turns in her coffin to a great mass of such golden ringlets as she was said to have worn in her life-time; and perhaps among those ringlets shall be preserved the link that they want. On her deathbed, she shall have charged that they lock her coffin with a silver key, and send the key to her lover in America; whom she may have been in secret correspondence with. It may have been the imputation of crime—high treason, for instance—that keeps him from returning. This silver key is the one that the boy finds among the earth which the sexton throws up out of the grave. The Doctor may tell the legend, and leave it unfinished and unsatisfactory; but when Etherege comes to England, and to the old estate, he shall meet with a groom or servant, who shall be the last relic of an old family, whose representative, at the time, was concerned in these facts—the magistrate, for instance, by whose warrant the kidnapped man was led away. He shall tell the legend in such a way that it explains the former mysteries.

The narrative must be pitched in such a tone, and enveloped in such an atmosphere, that improbable things shall be accepted; and yet there must be a certain quality of homely, common life diffused through it, so that the reader shall feel a warmth in it.

After some dreary years, the exile may, must, have got married in New England, and begot a family. This would be a sufficient reason for his never going back. His beloved shall remain faithful and die a maid, inheriting the estate; and keeping a place always at the board for him; who never comes. But in New England, he remembers her still, and she having promised to come over, he keeps a place ever at his married board for her. When little Elsie hears this story, she sets a plate at the Doctor's board as if for an expected guest.

The little girl tells the boy stories of her English infancy; she having left that country at five years old. These stories shall refer to the mansion house, and its surroundings, and the old church, and the hospital; and it shall seem to the boy's imagination as if there were something in his memory, or in an anterior memory, like these things. When he finds his way to the estate, he shall remember these dreams, and feel as if he had been there before.

The Doctor's inventiveness shall be perhaps his one Yankee trait, mixed in with and running through all his cobwebby old hereditary nonsense; and it is so inevitable that, having nothing else to act upon, it deals with the cobwebs. It shall also be akin to the speculative tendencies of the brother. The Doctor shall have his absorbing dream of regenerating the world by means of cobweb, and quite restoring it to health; and shall pursue his discovery as an alchymist that of the golden secret; and shall think it within his reach, if he could but live a year, a week, a day longer; nay even to finish the one process that he has now in hand. But, at the last moment, he shall perhaps relinquish it with a kindly, sweet resignation, and without selfish shame acknowledge that he may have been mistaken.

When the hero is re-introduced to the reader, he shall not at first be named, and it shall be left to be discovered that it is the little boy whom we knew; also, it shall not be said that it is in England, but that, too, shall be left to be inferred from the characteristics of the scenery.

At the Doctor's death, he shall have left a great mass of manuscripts, among which are some poems and tales; these shall be given by his will to Etherege, who shall bring some of them to England, with a purpose, if possible, of getting for them the earliest of publication in London.

The Doctor is not the brother of the old pensioner, but merely an admiring friend.

It shall seem as if the great spider's web were a charm, by means of which the Doctor is enthralling his enemies.

<(Slightly introduce the traveller first)>

It was a day of early summer; and surely the sweetest weather that summer ever brought, and to one accustomed to the climate of most parts of America was a new development in the nature of weather; so soft, so warm, so genial it was, and yet without the torrid quality that usually attends the full sun-burst. It seemed, indeed, that the sun was not quite in its full refulgence; it seemed bright; the day seemed cloudless; it looked like noon; and yet there was this mild and softened character, as if something invisible were interposed between earth and the sun, absorbing all the fierceness of regard with which the latter is apt to woo the earth. It was the gentlest, kindliest sunshine; and yet there was a quality of coolness somehow diffused through it, that gave it its most exquisite charm. Yet, it seemed to have the power of the most cherishing sun in producing verdure; for never was there such luxuriance of grass as overspread the gently undulating country through which the traveller was walking; never such full richness of foliage as that which hung upon the elm-trees along the way.

The path on which he trod was of a character that deserves a word or two of description—a well-trodden, rather broad footpath, running just here along the edge of a field, and bordered on one side by a hedge, which in itself contained materials for a lengthened description; so rich was it with varied vegetable life, such a green intricacy, such a beautiful, impenetrable obstacle, and so did nature luxuriate within its limits; and such a Paradise it was for the birds that built their nests there, in an intricacy and labyrinth where they must have thought themselves as safe as in the first Paradise where they sang for Eve. Flowers, pleasant, homely flowers grew in it; and many creeping plants, that were no contemplated part of the hedge, had come of their own accord and dwelt here, beautifying and enriching the hedge by way of repayment for the shelter and support that it afforded them. At intervals, there grew in this line of hedge, great-trunked trees—whether elms or oaks—and the bark of these great, age-long patriarchs was not brown and barren, like the trees we see, but green with a beautifying moss, and in many cases thickly enwreathed with a network of creeping plants, ivy, clambering upward, of old growth; and on one oak there was a plant of magic and historic interest—the misletoe, clinging close with its mystic leaf.

A little further, the path came to a style, which seemed no frail and temporary structure, but an ancient, worn, but yet stalwart structure of stones, which evidently had known for generations the climbing footsteps of passers-by, had afforded rest for the wayfarer, for the farmer on his way from toil, for youth and maid, and had witnessed many pleasant scenes of love.

A bird rose up out of the grass, and a little way upward from earth burst into a melody, as if it had broken into a sweet audible flame with which it burst skyward. The lark, the lark! A moment afterwards, another voice was heard deep away within a wood, saying softly, in a voice flute-like, as if it proceeded from some instrument of wood—Cuckoo— Cuckoo,—and then was still.

The traveller was a man yet young; a slender, but athletic figure, with a kind of agile grace that betokened considerable powers of endurance. His complexion was pale, at least it had little colour, but it did not betoken ill-health; and the spirit within him was evidently lithe and active, gazing out of his eyes and taking note of everything about him with an eager, untiring curiosity, that appeared to be finding something of interest in the most ordinary object that presented itself in the wide landscape, along by-path, or hedge-row, or whatever else. His dress was not indicative of any high station in life, being a coarse gray suit; but yet it was such as a gentleman might wear of a morning; and evidently he was no mean, mechanical churl, but a man of education and refinement, and there was an indefinable air of authority and position about him.

As he walked along—he could not tell exactly where—the path had somewhat lost its distinctness; and it did not seem so much like one that was constantly trodden. It did not exactly grow wild; for it was the character of this scenery that there was no wildness about, everything seeming to have been touched, handled, arranged, at some period or other, by man. But it seemed to be getting remote; the path led him into plashy places where he had to pick his way; and it seemed, he thought, to be on the point of leaving him altogether, when he should be at a distance from habitation. Still; this would be no great hardship or peril, in a neighborhood which man had got so completely within his control, and where the fiercest wild beast that leapt across his path, or sat up at a distance to gaze at him, was a hare; no peril, surely, to him, who had wandered heretofore in wild primeval forests, and had seen the red Indian in his original haunts, and coped both with bear and buffalo. And so he walked cheerily on, finding a sort of nameless charm in this wandering, where having no certain aim, he could not go astray. And we will let him go on, and not follow him, but remain behind listening to what we may hear, sitting on this stone, because there is a foreboding, a sense within us, that this traveller is not going the right way, and that we shall keep ourselves out of the mire, if we refrain from accompanying him.

However that may be, it is certain that he had not been gone a great while before there were some strange sounds coming from the direction which he had taken. There were voices, the sound of a struggle; a shot that might be from some sportsman in the wood, had it been the season of sport; and then silence; but a little while afterwards, two rough, questionable looking men came along the by-path in a direction that must have brought them athwart the traveller, on the narrow path which he had taken. They were talking to one another in low, gruff tones, and kept onward in haste.

<Throw into the first description of the chamber and the old man all possible dreamlike characteristics>

That day, towards evening, a person was discovered in a remote part of a park, who had been subjected to some great bodily harm, and as it pretty evidently appeared by intentional violence. He lay insensible, but breathing, and had apparently been in that condition for some time. Assistance being summoned, he was conveyed to a certain sort of charitable establishment, in the neighborhood, which was the most conveniently suitable for his receiving the requisite aid and care, of any place to be found thereabout; better certainly than the cottage of a labourer, and more suited to the condition of a lonely wayfarer than a gentleman's house; one of which (being Elider Hall) was at no great distance. We shall attach our story to the consciousness of this person, and endeavor to be present with his struggling recollections, when, that evening, he endeavored to make out where he was, and what had happened to him. His wits were scarcely about him; and perhaps there may have been a degree of delirium, which mixed itself up with his sober perceptions, and by this leaven of untruth made the whole untrue.

<(Make him in a feverish dream, that shall mix itself with the scene)>

He found himself, with these dreamlike perceptions, stretched on a narrow bed, in a small chamber panelled with some wood that had grown absolutely black with age. He noted that it was carved in an antique fashion; there being one particular emblem that was repeated in several places; over the mantle piece, over the doors; and likewise that it seemed to be carved on the posts of the bed. This device was an arm extended, and holding the severed head of some animal by the fur, which it clutched; what the animal was, he could not well tell, it being of the heraldic breed, which neither Buffon nor Agassiz have found within the limits of nature. Around this device was a motto, which his swimming eyes could not then decypher; but which we may as well set down as the old English phrase "Hold hard the Head." Over the mantle-piece there was what looked like a very old engraving of some personage in beard, ruff and rich attire of Queen Elizabeth's time or thereabouts. The furniture of the room was not abundant, appearing to have been provided with a view to only one person's convenience; but it was ancient as the aspect of the apartment itself; a curtained bed, with dark woven curtains, having the same device on them; a high back, carved oaken chair, very quaintly wrought, and having the favorite device of the hand and leopard's head both over the back, and in the wrought open work of the same; a table, with several curious legs; an old looking glass. There were diamond shaped panes in the narrow window through a deep embrasure, through which the moon broke with struggling and often obscured beams; and in the deep grate of the old fire-place, summer season as it was, there was a smouldering and languishing fire of coal; for the genial day, with the quick vicissitude of that island climate, had changed to chill and wet; and a shower of rain spattered against the panes almost at the same time with the struggling moonlight.

On the table stood vials of medicine, and other accompaniments of a sick chamber.

There were items and characteristics in this scene, which made the patient think that he was in a delirium, or waking dream, or some strange sort of confusion; because, of these particular things, he had a sort of remembrance, cherished from early youth; and had often, in his boyish romanticism, had these very images in his mind. That leopard's head, for example; its grin was as familiar to him as his own face in the glass; even that stately old personage over the fireplace seemed to be one whom he had seen, and stood in awe of, in his early childhood.

"What a strange, vivid dream!" murmured he, twisting himself uneasily; and then a twinge of pain, the meaning of which he knew not, surprised him into a groan.

At this sound, there was a heavy, though almost noiseless step on the floor, and a figure emerged from a deep niche that looked as if it might have been an oratory, in old times, to hold a crucifix and a cushion for prayer; but where this figure had been sitting, and apparently making some calculation, or notes, by the light of a candle. It was an elderly, and venerable looking man, with a skull cap on his head, beneath which descended some silvery curls and fell upon his shoulders, and this, with a beard long and white, made him resemble an ancient palmer. His dress had a singular correspondence with the antique walls and furniture of the room. Being a long robe of dark stuff, on the breast and sleeve of which were embroidered in red still that same device of the leopard's head. <breeches described> Had the scene of our story been laid three hundred years ago, we need not have changed a particle of the costume of this memorable figure, in order to make him suitable.

When the traveller beheld this quaint and venerable figure, he was still more convinced that he must be in a delirium; and being of a nature, though not without imaginative tendencies, yet strongly tenacious of the actual and the sober, it greatly troubled him to find himself in such a state. He murmured an impatient exclamation of anger against himself.

"Are you in pain?" asked the venerable stranger, approaching the side of the bed.

"No," said the patient, staring vaguely at him, and thinking that he was doing a very foolish thing to answer a fantasy of his own brain. But, in fact, the appearance of this old father was so dignified and impressive, that he could not help showing him as much respect as if he had been a reality. Scarcely had he given his negative, when he became sensible of another twinge, and discovered that, amid the confusion and delirium of his brain, there was really a terribly severe pain, indicating some recent injury. The traveller began to be sensible that some accident had befallen him—even vaguely to remember of what nature it had been—and this latter recollection seemed to him the only reality, showing through the quaint dream of antiquity in which he lay.

"My head will be clearer tomorrow, perhaps," murmured he to himself. "I will close my eyes now."

"Yes close them now," said the old figure, in his grave, impressive voice of authority, not unmixed with a paternal sort of kindness. "Tomorrow you will the better see truth from falsehood. Meanwhile, take this."

He approached him with a cup, out of which, with a strangely shaped old spoon (and still there was a leopard's head on the handle) he presented to his lips some medicine; which had an antique fragrance such as old doctors imparted to their potions, centuries ago. Feeling that he had somehow gone astray into the past, the traveller obediently sipped it, & soon fell into a slumber.

The patient, as we must call him, had a favorable night, and awoke with a much clearer head, the next morning, though still with a haunting fever upon him that made him keep in a visionary state, and wander as it were among the past, bringing back many visions of his youth. His chamber was visited, during the day, by a surgeon, who seemed to be connected with the establishment; not exclusively, but making it a part of a more extensive round of duties. He examined the patient's head, with a grave, official face, put a few questions to him, and noted a slight wildness in his answers, of which the patient himself was conscious even while he was so answering; but could not resist the tendency to be wild. He left him some potion or other, and retired. An old woman, of motherly aspect, looked in every now and then; but the most constant person present was the white bearded palmerlike personage on whom the patient's eyes had first opened the evening before. In the daylight, and sunshine, his aspect was hardly less picturesque, quaint, and venerable, than it had been in the dim lamplight and dusky fireglow.

As the patient's head grew clearer, instead of being less, he was more impressed with the striking character of this old person's face, which might have been worthy to represent a statesman of the old time. It did not seem naturally benign, as its most characteristic expression, though certainly there was great benignity in the regard which he threw upon the traveller; but thoughtful, speculative, commanding, or as if it had been all these, and now, in the decline of life, was warily reflective on what he had done and seen. He sat a little distance from the bed, gazing at the patient with a fixed look, which, when he opened his eyes, made him feel as if it had been fixed upon him for a long while; and it disturbed him, in his weak and impressible state, to be the object of such fixed regard. He felt as if he had been conscious of it all through his sleep, and as if some dream, which he could not now remember, had been influenced by it.

He tried to shake off all the influences that were about him, and to awake; being intolerably impatient of a dream that lasted so long, and was so vivid, and yet seemed more intermingled with a sense of delusion than dreams usually are.

"How long this lasts!" murmured he. "Why cannot I awake?"

"Be at peace yet a little while," said the voice of the old palmer. "You will awake all the more surely at the fitting time."

"Where am I?" said the patient. "Whose dwelling is this antique one, where I lie?"

"The dwelling of misfortune," said the old man. "Have you ever been in one before?"

Here the patient remembered how, in his earliest days, he had indeed been a denizen of a house of misfortune, and had that for his earliest image of life; and he could hardly help thinking that this sage-looking old man, in his inscrutable knowledge, knew something about this. It was a recollection that had sometimes caused him pain; for there was something in his character that made him long for hereditary connections, and the imposing, imaginative associations of the past, beautifying and making venerable the mean life of the present. However, he had prevailed with himself, especially as he was an American and a republican, not to be ashamed of springing from the lowest, but to consider it as giving additional value and merit to every honorable effort and success that he had thus far made, in the struggle of life.

"Yes," said he; "I am a born child of such a house, so far as I know; but it is in a land far from this. What is this symbol that I see about me everywhere; over the mantle-piece, on yonder chair, in the hangings of this bed, on the breast and sleeve of your garment? I have seen this elsewhere, and had it fixed into my imagination and memory. Do I dream it now, or actually see it?"

<(There should be no definite description of the scheme of the Hospital, till hereafter.)>

"Be at peace," said the old man. "You see it. It is the badge
of the old family who built this house, and who, with whatever benevolent intentions, failed not to make known to the
world and to posterity their good deeds. But it was in Catholic
times, and they did it partly that their race might be continually present to the minds of those who dwelt in these
chambers, and incite them to pray for their benefactors. This
whole ancient edifice was founded upon the transgressions
of the builders; the wealth unjustly obtained, in the wars of
the Roses, by rapine and spoil, being devoted, in the old age
of the founder, to this good end. And it was his wish to
acknowledge and atone for his sin, rather than to proclaim
his glory; though perhaps the latter motive may have subtly
mingled itself therewith."

"And you yourself," said the young man, looking at the
venerable speaker. "Are you in authority here?"

"A simple beneficiary of this charity," said he; "a man who
has seen and been a part of many things in this life, and who
is now content to end here. All the claim I have in this house
is this little chamber, which I have given up to you, and a
seat at the board, and a share of the kitchen fire."

"Ah; I am still in my dream," said the young man, at some
allusion in this speech to recollections which it was impossible
should be known here. "I will sleep a little more, and awaken,
I hope, to a reality."

<(All the people must be of the same name.)>

So he again addressed himself to repose; and the fever,
which attended his wound, being on the mending hand, he
slept well, and awoke with a clearer head than he had felt
yet. But still there was a lack of energy and activity; a disposition to resign himself, with strange quietude, to whatever
should come next; a sense of childlike repose even out of a
fitful and stormy life, by this mischance that had so nearly
put him out of life altogether.

He found such a strange charm in this situation—coming in the intervals of anxiety, trouble, strife, excitement of various kinds—that he did not seek to arouse himself, but was willing to see what would come next; especially as quiet was especially enjoined upon him by the surgeon, and the old palmer; and so he lay in a kind of painful luxury, not seeking any longer to put his finger to the evolution of his own fate. It was so sweet to resign himself, for the first time since he was a child; to have nothing to do with himself; to accept everything; not even to imagine forward, but to lie and let half-defined thoughts succeed one another through his mind, and to look at the devices on the walls through half-shut eyes. He did not care about waking-up; this was better; at least, he could wait patiently until a change should come without any agency of his own. This state was not merely the result of bodily weakness, but also it was the rest which a mind that had known hard toil and exertion—which had been worked to a degree beyond what some of its more delicate characteristics ought to have borne—was now taking in this unlooked for situation.

In this state of mind, his wound did well; all the unfavorable symptoms abated, and the surgeon expressed his approbation of his own skill, and also of the good state of body in which the patient must have been in order to enable him to effect so miraculous an improvement. And, indeed, the patient himself began to be sensible that his happy state of indefiniteness was departing from him; that his positive life was returning; and that he should not be able much longer to keep himself contented in this dark, antique chamber, especially without inquiring whereabout he was, and under whose care.

One morning, when he was meditating on the propriety of calling for his clothes and dressing himself, a somewhat louder step than ordinary was heard in the passage approaching his chamber, and a gentleman entered, with a considerable dignity and sense of authority visible in his manner. It was a kindly dignity, however, and even paternal; though his age was not yet advanced; and it was impossible not to see in him those traits of manner, that cast of expression, which, on features however different among themselves, still appertain to the clerical character; an expression, perhaps, that is not so much made from within as from without—an expression which, it would be curious to inquire, whether the clergyman has it in his own face, when he looks in his glass in deepest solitude, or whether it only comes over him when he is conscious of some other eye. It seems possible to lay it aside with the white cravat; and yet it is always there; it is not sanctity. What is it? It is manner; attire;—and, whatever it is, it is nowhere more evident than in the clergy of the Church of England, with whom it has a certain assumption, authority, and forth-puttingness, which impel a sinful and rebellious nature to resist it, although it would require considerable internal strength to do so.

This gentleman was in undress, and seemed not to have come from abroad, having on only a long, loose summer gown, as if he had stept out of a study. The patient, seeing him, began to expect some ghostly advice; although, to say the truth, the genial, pleasant, and comfortable visage of the reverend personage did not indicate that the shrift would be a very severe one. In spite of his authority, his severity, his professional air, there was a certain comfortableness about him which made it not unpleasant to be in his company. He came up to the bedside, and stood looking a moment at the patient, before he spoke; looking him in the face kindly, but without the courtesy that one man may expect from another of similar rank.

"My friend," said he, "I hope you find yourself comfortable!"

It was as kind a voice as could be desired; and a kind expression beamed from out the face in accordance with it; but still the traveller found himself dissatisfied with something in the tone and manner—an undoubting assumption of superiority, it might be—a certain kindly haughtiness, which his previous habits and position in life had not heretofore subjected him to.

"Yes;" said he in reply to the question. "I am much indebted to the kind care and hospitality of this house."

The reverend visitor seemed somewhat surprised at the tone of his voice; and it may be, that by this, as well as some characteristic of intelligence and cultivation in his face, he was favorably impressed, that the stranger was a gentleman.

"I am the Warden of this Hospital," said he, with not less benignity than heretofore, and more courtesy, "and therefore must consider you under my care, although it is one of the pensionaries of the house who has been the active instrument in the matter. Do you feel yourself able now, to give an account of the circumstances which brought you hither?"

"It will be a very unsatisfactory one, at best," said the traveller. "Being a stranger, I was on a pedestrian tour, in this part of England; and having turned aside into a by-path, with a view to seeing an old Hall which I had heard of, I seem to have been shot down, or struck down, without any assignable cause, except with a view to robbery, and without seeing my assailant. If there were any other circumstances connected with the event, my hurt has driven it out of my memory."

"You were robbed, of course," said the visitor;—"but probably to no great amount."

"I know nothing of that," replied the traveller, a little affronted as an American is apt to be, at this implied supposition that he could have had little to lose. "Those who took charge of me may tell better than I what there was about me."

"Pearson," said the reverend gentleman, raising his voice a little, "what funds or other property were found on this unfortunate man?"

The old gentleman must have been sitting on some settle outside of the door; for he immediately entered, and made an obeisance to the Master, though in a stately fashion, and himself had a natural dignity which the shorter figure and trim-faced clergyman could not claim.

"This purse, and this passport case, were in his pockets, together with a few other papers," said he. "The purse contained twenty-three sovereigns, and there is a letter of credit among the papers to a considerable amount."

"You will excuse this necessary examination of your private papers," said the Warden. "We were necessarily the guardians of one who was thrown upon us in such a helpless state. May I ask of Pearson what name is mentioned in the letter of credit?"

"Edward Etherege," read the person alluded to, reading from the letter, "and he is evidently an American."

"An American?" said the Warden, casting over him a look of careless curiosity such as an Englishman has for our countrymen. "I fancied a little peculiarity in your diction; but methinks you have not the uncouthness which I expected. You have been some time, perhaps, in this country?"

"Six weeks," said Mr. Etherege.

"Only six weeks," repeated the Master. "Well; it gives me pleasure that our establishment has been of service to an American gentleman; and I trust you will find there is some benefit in these age-long charities, which distinguish England."

"I am bound to acknowledge it, and be grateful for it," said Etherege.

"I was under a little mistake," continued the Warden, "from the information I had received, respecting your position in life. You are evidently—pardon me for not having recognized it from the first—a gentleman. When you are capable of being moved, it will give me great pleasure to receive you as my guest, in my own peculiar part of this establishment— where you shall be welcome to a bachelor's hospitality. I am afraid I have made too long a visit for your strength, and will now retire."

He withdrew; and Etherege, feeling somewhat wearied with the interview, again sank into the meditations and reveries to which, in the abeyance of his active powers, he had latterly become addicted. But, soon, arousing himself, and perceiving that the old palmer was sitting in his usual niche, he addressed him.

"Who is the gentleman that has just left us?" asked he.

"The reverend Dr. Blathwaite," said the old man, "Warden of this foundation, as being, in the female line, a descendant of the original founder."

"And what is the foundation?" asked the American. "It is alien from anything in my experience, or customary in my country; so that I am at a loss to know where I am."

"In a day or two," replied the old man, "you will be able to accept, if you so please, the Warden's hospitality; and he, if you take an interest in such matters, will show you the old records of the Hospital, and explain its plan, as he loves to do to strangers. You will be interested in seeing it."

"Have you been long here?" asked Etherege, gazing at the old man's face, which was written over, apparently, with experiences, all of which could not well have been gained within these quiet walls.

"Not very many years," said Pearson. "I had tried much of the world before I proved my hereditary claim, and set up my rest here."

"You must have seen and known many things," said Etherege, "before you set up your rest here. Methinks after a varied and stormy life, it is no undesirable harbour to moor in finally. I am young enough to be not yet wearied—not so old as to have given up many of my illusions, though experienced enough to see that they are such;—but, in good truth, it would be a pleasant idea to me to think, that, at worst, I had such a place to spend my age in as this hospital seems to be. I half wish I were of the founder's blood."

"It may be," said the old man. "My genealogical researches have taught me that we are all akin, a few generations off."

"So a very kind and dear old friend of mine (now long dead,) used to say," observed Etherege. "He also was a genealogist, and loved nothing so well as such researches, except to study cobwebs. Heaven bless him; what will he have done without them, where he is gone!"

"I have seen," said the old man, "a great spider in South America that would have gratified your friend. The native Indians thought it a devil, and that by possessing it, and tracing out its web, a man could see what was to be the course of any event."

"How strange!" said Etherege. "The friend I speak of had that same fantasy, and died in a singular way, in accordance with it."

"It is hard to tell, in this strange world, what things are true, what false!" quoth the oracular old palmer.

So saying he retired.

The patient now appeared to have obtained a fair start; and continued to make regular and equable progress towards convalescence. In a few days more, the Warden renewed his friendly invitation, with hospitable earnestness; for the stranger seemed to have made a favorable impression on him, and he was perhaps curious to see what an American was made of. Etherege had little hesitation in availing himself of the good man's kindness, and the more readily as, now that he had discovered that he was in the peculiar premises of the old palmer, he felt that he could not remain there without greatly incommoding his venerable host. He therefore removed himself to the Warden's house as soon as he felt able to descend the stairs; and this same day, there arrived from London some luggage, for which Etherege had written as soon as he found that his stay here was to be some considerable time longer.

The Warden's house was a part of the ancient establishment in which Etherege was so singularly domesticated, being one side of the quadrangle which the buildings occupied; and it was certainly the most comfortable establishment which the American had then ever seen. A drawing-room, a din'g room, a study, furnished with profound attention to comfort, and a ponderous handsomeness, that gave the guest an idea that life, here, was no slight affair, but something permanent, and in a good degree certain; everything seeming so fixed, that mortal man could not deem himself the only shadow. There was a study, too, which reminded Etherege, by contrast, with the darksome old dungeon of his friend, the Doctor; so sumptuously comfortable was this, so provided with all manner of conveniences for study, in the shape of writing and reading-tables, chairs, and books, in rich, grave bindings, and such a learned fragrance there was about the place; it gave Etherege an idea of the Warden's learning, which he had not attained from his personal appearance, which was rather that of a man of the world. But, indeed, there was not anything in the immediate surroundings of the Warden's chair that indicated that he was now engaged on any subject of abstruse research; these consisting of The Times of the preceding day, one or two of the current magazines, the last Quarterly, and, somewhat to Etherege's amazement, the three volumes of a new novel from a London Circulating Library. There was a fragrance of tobacco in the room, the sources of which were perceptible in two or three German or Turkish pipes that occupied the mantle-piece; sufficiently indicating that the Warden had learned to avail himself of one great comfort of the bachelor-state.

A servant, in a livery of the establishment, had ushered Etherege into his room, where he seated himself and was occupied with the Times, when the Warden himself came in, fresh and rosy from a morning's ride. He shook hands heartily with his guest, and seemed really (though not very frigid before) to have developed into a new man, and to be inspired with a fresh warmth, now that he had received the stranger over his threshold, and thus had made himself responsible for his comforts.

"I shall take it greatly amiss," said he, "if you do not gather a little English color. They tell me your countrymen are a paler set than we; but surely you have English blood enough left in you to give you a ruddy tint, by dint of English beef and English ale, and the moist, kindly, wholesome English air."

"Allow me a little time yet," said Etherege, smiling. "You know, I have lost a good deal of what little blood I had, since coming into your country. It is scarcely fair to treat us pale-faces so."

"Only follow my guidance," said the Warden; "and I assure you you shall have back whatever blood we have deprived you of, together with an addition. It is now luncheon-time, and we will begin the process of replenishing your veins."

So they went into a refectory, where were spread upon the board what might have seemed a goodly dinner, to most Americans; though for this Englishman it was but a by-incident, a slight refreshment, to enable him to pass the mid-way stage of life. It is an excellent thing to see the faith of a hearty Englishman in his own stomach, and how well that kindly organ repays his trust; with what devout assimilation he takes himself his kindred beef, loving it, believing in it, making a good use of it, and without any qualms of conscience or prescience as to the result. They surely eat twice as much as we; and probably because of their undoubting faith, it never does them any harm. Dyspepsia is merely a superstition with us. If we would cease to believe in its existence, it would exist no more. Etherege, eating little himself, his wound compelling him to be cautious as to his diet, was secretly delighted to see what sweets the Warden found in a cold round of beef, in a pigeon-pie, and a cut or two of Yorkshire ham; not that he was ravenous, but that his stomach was so healthy.

"You eat little, my friend," said the Warden, pouring out a glass of sherry for Etherege and another for himself. "But you are right, in such a predicament as yours. Spare your stomach while you are weakly, and it will help you when you are strong. This now, is the most enjoyable meal of the day with me. You will not see me play such a knife and fork at dinner; though there, too, especially if I have ridden out in the afternoon, I do pretty well. But, come, now, if (like most of your countrymen, as I have heard) you are a lover of the weed, I can offer you some as delicate Latakia as you are likely to find in England."

"I lack that claim upon your kindness, I am sorry to say," replied Etherege. "I am not a good smoker, though I have occasionally taken a cigar at need."

"Well; when you find yourself growing old, and especially if you chance to be a bachelor, I advise you to cultivate the habit," said the Warden. "A wife is the only real obstacle or objection to a pipe; they can seldom be thoroughly reconciled, and therefore it is well for a man to consider, beforehand, which of the two he can best dispense with. I know not how it might have been once, had the conflicting claims of these two rivals ever been fairly presented to me; but I now should be at no loss to choose the pipe."

They returned to the study; and while Dr. Brathwaite took his pipe, Etherege, considering that, as the guest of this hospitable Englishman, he had no right to continue a stranger, thought it fit to make known to him who he was, and his condition, plans, and purposes. He represented himself as having been liberally educated, bred to the law, but (to his misfortune) having turned aside from that profession to engage in politics. In this pursuit, indeed, his success wore a flattering outside; for he had become distinguished, and though so young, a leader, locally, at least, in the party which he had adopted. He had been, for one biennial term, a member of Congress, after winning some distinction in the legislature of his native state; but some one of those fitful changes, to which American politics are peculiarly liable, had thrown him out, in his candidacy for his second term; and the virulence of party animosity, the abusiveness of the press, had acted so much upon a disposition naturally somewhat too sensitive for the career which he had undertaken, that he had resolved, being now freed from legislative cares, to seize the opportunity for a visit to England, whither he was drawn by feelings which every educated and impressible American feels, in a degree scarcely conceivable by the English themselves. And being here (but he had already too much experience of English self-sufficiency to confess so much) he began to feel the deep yearning which a sensitive American—his mind full of English thoughts, his imagination of English poetry, his heart of English character and feeling—cannot fail to be influenced by, the yearning of the blood within his veins for that from which it has been estranged; the half-fanciful regret that he should ever have been separated from these woods, these fields, these natural features of scenery, to which his nature was moulded, from these men who are still so like himself, from these habits of life and thought which (though he may not have known them for two centuries) he still perceives to have remained, in some mysterious way, latent in the depths of his character, and now to be reassumed, not as a foreigner would do it, but like habits native to him and only suspended for a season. This had been Etherege's state of feeling ever since he landed in England; and every day seemed to make him more at home; so that it seemed as if he were gradually awakening to a former reality.

After lunch, the Master showed a good degree of kind anxiety about his guest, and ensconced him in a most comfortable chair in his study, where he gave him his choice of books old and new, and was somewhat surprised, as well as amused, to see that Etherege seemed most attracted towards a department of the library filled with books of English antiquities and genealogies, and heraldry; the two latter, indeed, having the preference over the others.

"This is very remarkable," said he, smiling. "By what right or reason, by what logic of character, can you, a Democrat, renouncing all advantages of birth—neither priding yourself on family, nor seeking to found one—how therefore can you care for genealogies, or for this fantastic science of heraldry. Having no antiquities, being a people just made, how can you care for them?"

"My dear Sir," said Etherege, "I doubt whether the most devoted antiquarian in England can care so much for an old thing, merely because it is old, as any American just landed on your shores. Age is our novelty; therefore it attracts and absorbs us. And as for genealogies, I know not what necessary repulsion there may be between it and democracy. A line of respectable ancestors, being the harder to preserve where there is nothing in the laws to defend it, is therefore the more precious when we have it really to boast of."

"True," said the Warden. "When a race keeps itself distinguished among the grimy view of your commonalty, all with equal legal rights to place and eminence as itself, it must needs be because there is a force and efficacy in the blood. I doubt not," he said, looking with the free approval of an elder man at the young man's fairly developed face and graceful form, "I doubt not that you can look back upon a line of ancestry, always shining out from the surrounding obscurity of the mob."

Etherege, though ashamed of himself, could not but feel a paltry confusion and embarrassment, as he thought of his unknown origin, and his advent from the alms-house; coming out of that squalid darkness as if he were a thing that had had a spontaneous birth out of poverty, meanness, petty crime; and here, in ancestral England, he felt more keenly than ever before what was his misfortune.

"I must not let you lie under this impression," said he manfully to the Warden. "I have no ancestry; at the very first step, my origin is lost in impenetrable obscurity. I only know that but for the aid of a kind friend—on whose benevolence I seem to have had no claim whatever—my life would probably have been poor, mean, unenlightened."

"Well, well," said the kind Warden—hardly quite feeling, however, the noble sentiment which he expressed; "it is better to be the first noble illustrator of a name than even the worthy heir of a name that has been noble and famous for a thousand years. The highest pride of some of our peers, who have won their rank by their own force, has been to point to the cottage whence they sprung. Your posterity, at all events, will have the advantage of you—they will know their ancestor."

Etherege sighed; for there was truly a great deal of this foolish yearning for a connection with the past about him; his imagination had taken this turn, and the very circumstances of his obscure birth gave it a field to exercise itself.

"I advise you," said the Warden, by way of changing the conversation, "to look over this excellent history of the County which you are now in. There is no reading better,

to my mind, than these County histories; though doubtless
a stranger would hardly feel so much interest in them as
one whose progenitors male or female have strewn their dust
over the whole field of which the history treats. This history
is a fine specimen of the kind."

The work, to which Etherege's attention was thus drawn,
was in two large folio volumes, published about thirty years
before, bound in calf by some famous artist in that line,
illustrated with portraits and views of ruined castles, churches,
a cathedral, the seats of nobility and gentry; <Roman, British, & Saxon remains—painted windows, oak-carving, &c &c
&c> and as for its contents, the author ascended for the
history of the County as far as into the pre-Romanite ages,
before Caesar had ever heard of Britain, and brought it
down, an ever swelling and increasing tale, to his own days;
inclusive of the separate histories, and pedigrees, and hereditary legends and incidents, of all the principal families. In
this latter branch of information, indeed, the work seemed
particularly full, and contained many incidents that would
have worked well into historical romance.

"Aye, aye," said the Warden laughing at some strange incident of this sort, which Etherege read out to him. "My
old friend Gibben, the learned author of this work (he has
been dead this score of years, so he will not mind my saying it) had a little too much the habit of seeking his authorities in the cottage-chimney corners. I mean that an old
woman's were just about as acceptable to him as a recorded
fact; and to say the truth, they are really apt to have ten
times the life in them."

Etherege saw in the volume a full account of the founding of the hospital, its regulations and purposes, its edifices;
all of which he reserved for future reading, being for the
present more attracted by the mouldy gossip of family anec-
dotes, which we have alluded to. Some of these, and not the

least singular, referred to the ancient family which had founded the hospital; and he was attracted by seeing a mention of a Bloody Footstep, which reminded him of the strange old story which good Doctor Inglefield had related by his New England fireside, in those childish days when Edward dwelt with him by the grave yard. On reading it, however, he found that the English legend, if such it could be called, was far less full and explicit than that of New England; indeed, it assigned various origins to the Bloody Footstep—one being, that it was the stamp of the foot of the Saxon Thane, who fought at his own threshold against the assault of the Norman Baron, who seized his mansion at the Conquest; another, that it was the imprint of a fugitive, who had sought shelter from the lady of the house during the wars of the Roses, and was dragged out by her husband, and slain on the door-step; still another, that it was the foostep of a protestant in Bloody Mary's days, who, being sent to prison by the Squire of that epoch, had lifted his hands to Heaven, and stamped his foot, in appeal against the unjust violence with which he was treated, and stamping his foot, it had left this bloody mark. It was hinted, however, that another version, which out of delicacy to the family the author was reluctant to state, assigned the origin of the Bloody Footstep to so late a period as the Wars of the Parliament. And, finally, there was an odious rumour that was called the Bloody Footstep was nothing miraculous, after all, but most probably a natural reddish stain in the stone door-step; but against this heresy the excellent Dr. Gibben set his face most sturdily.

The original legend had made such an impression on Etherege's childish fancy, that he became strangely interested in thus discovering it, or something remotely like it, in England, and being brought by such unsought means to reside so near it. Curious about the family to which it had occurred, he proceeded to examine its records, as given in the County

History. The name was Grantley. Like most English pedigrees, there was an obscurity about a good many of the earlier links; but the line was traced out with reasonable definiteness from the days of Coeur de Lion, and there was said to be a cross-legged ancestor in the village church, who (but the inscription was obliterated) was probably a Grantley, and had fought either with the Lion Heart or in the next Crusade. It was, in subsequent ages, one of the most distinguished families, though there had been turbulent men, in all those turbulent times, hard fighters. In one age, a barony of early creation seemed to have come into the family, and had been, as it were, playing bo-peep with the race for several centuries. Some of them had actually assumed the title; others had given it up for lack of sufficient proof; but still there was such a claim, and up to the time at which this County History was written, it had neither been made out, nor had the hope of doing so been relinquished.

"Have the Grantly family," asked Etherege of his host, "ever yet made out their claim to this title, which has so long been playing the will of the whisp with them?"

"No; not yet," said the Warden, puffing out a volume of smoke from his meerschaum, and watching it curl up to the ceiling. "Their claim has as little substance, in my belief, as yonder vanishing vapor from my pipe. But they still keep up their delusion. I had supposed that the claim would perish with the last squire, who was a childless man—at least, without legitimate heirs—but the estate passed to one whom we can scarcely call an Englishman;—he being a Catholic, the descendant of forefathers who have lived in Italy since the time of George II, and who is moreover a Catholic. We English would not willingly see an ancestral honor in the possession of such a man."

"Is there, do you think, a prospect of his success?"

"I have heard so, but hardly believe it," replied the Warden. "I remember some dozen or fifteen years ago, it was given out that some clue had been found to the only piece of evidence that was wanting. It had been said that there was an emigration—now I think of it—to your own country, above a hundred years ago, and on account of some family feud, the true heir had gone thither and never returned. Now, the point was to prove the extinction of this branch of the family. But, excuse me, I must pay an official visit to my charge here. Will you accompany me, or continue to pore over the County History?"

Etherege felt enough of the elasticity of convalescence to be desirious of accompanying the Warden; and they accordingly crossed the enclosed quadrangle to the entrance of the hospital portion of the large and intricate structure. It was a building of the early Elizabethan age; a plaster and timber structure, like many houses of that period and much earlier. <(I think it shall be built of stone, however)> Around this court, stood the building, of ancient stone, with the date 1437 cut on the front. On each side, a row of gables looked upon the enclosed space, most venerable old gables, with heavy mullioned windows, filled with little diamond panes of glass, and opening on lattices. One two sides there was a cloistered walk, under echoing arches, and in the midst a spacious lawn of the greenest and loveliest grass, such as England only can show, and which there is of perennial verdure and beauty. In the midst stood a stone statue of a venerable man, wrought in the best of mediaeval sculpture, with robe and ruff, and tunic, and venerable beard, resting on a staff, and holding a clasped book in his hand. The English atmosphere, together with the coal smoke, settling down in the space of centuries from the chimneys of the hospital, had roughened and blackened this venerable piece of sculpture, enclosing it as it were in a superficies of decay; but still (and perhaps the more from these tokens of having stood so long among men) the statue had an aspect of venerable life, and of connection with human life, that made it strangely impressive.

"This is the effigy of Sir Humphrey Brathwaite, the founder of the Hospital," said the Warden. "He is a most peaceful and venerable old gentleman in his attire and aspect, as you see; but he was a fierce old fellow in his day, and is said to have founded the Hospital as a means of appeasing Heaven for some particular deed of blood, which he had imposed upon his conscience in the War of the Roses."

"Yes," said Etherege. "I have just read in the County History that the Bloody Footstep was said to have been imprinted in his time. But what is that thing which he holds in his hand?"

"It is a famous heirloom of the Brathwaites," said the Warden, "on the possession of which (as long as they did possess it) they prided themselves, it is said, more than on their ancient manor-house. It was a Saxon ornament, which a certain ancestor was said to have had from Harold, the last Saxon king; but if there ever was any such article, it has been missing from the family museum for two or three hundred years. There is not known to be an antique relic of that description now in existence."

"I remember having seen such an article—yes, precisely of that shape," observed Etherege, "in the possession of a very dear old friend of mine, when I was a boy."

"What! in America?" exclaimed the Warden. "That is very remarkable. The time of its being missed coincides well enough with that of the early settlement of New England. Some Puritan, before his departure, may have thought himself doing God service by filching the old golden gew gaw from the cavalier; for it was said to be pure, ductile gold."

The circumstance struck Etherege with a pleasant wonder; for, indeed, the old statue held the closest possible imitation, in marble, of that strange old glitter of gold which he himself had so often played with, in the Doctor's study; so identical, that he could have fancied that he saw the very thing, changed from metal into stone, even with its bruises and other casual marks in it. As he looked at the old statue, his imagination played with it, and his naturally great impressibility half made him imagine that the old face looked at him with a keen, subtile, wary glance, as if acknowledging that it held some secret, but at the same time defying him to find it out. And then again came that visionary feeling that had so often swept over him, since he had been an inmate of the hospital.

All over this interior front of the building was carved in stone the dragon's head, with wearisome iteration; as if the founder were anxious to imprint his device so numerously, lest—when he produced this edifice as his remuneration to Eternal Justice for many sins—the Omniscient Eye should fail to be reminded that Sir Humphrey Brathwayte had done it. But, at all events, it seemed to Etherege that the ancient knight had purposed a good thing, and, in a measurable degree, had effected it; for here stood the venerable edifice securely founded, bearing the moss of four hundred years upon it; nor had any subsequent age—though wars, and change of dynasties, and religious change, had swept around it, with seemingly destructive potency—yet here had the lodging, the food, the monastic privileges of its brethren been held secure, and were unchanged by all the altering manners of the age. The old fellow, somehow or other, seemed to have struck upon an everlasting rock, and founded his pompous charity there.

They entered an arched door on the left of the quadrangle, and found themselves in a dark old hall with oaken beams;

to say the truth, it was a barn like sort of enclosure, and was now a sort of rubbish-place for the hospital, where they stored away old furniture, and where carpenter's work might be done. And yet, as the Warden assured Etherege, it was once a hall of state, hung with tapestries, carpeted, for aught he knew, with cloth of gold, and set with rich furniture, and a groaning board in the midst. Here, the hereditary patron of the Hospital had once entertained King James the First, who made a Latin speech on the occasion, a copy of which was still preserved in the archives. On the rafters of this old hall there were cobwebs in such abundance that Etherege could not but reflect on the joy which poor old Dr. Gibbins would have had in seeing them, and the health to the human race which he would have hoped to collect and distil from them.

From this great, antique room they crossed the quadrangle and entered the kitchen of the establishment. A hospitable fire was burning there, and there seemed to be a great variety of messes cooking; and the Warden explained to Etherege that there was no general table in the hospital; but that the brethren, at their own will and pleasure, either formed themselves into companies or messes, of any convenient size, or enjoyed a solitary meal by themselves, each in their own apartments. There was a goodly choice of simple, but good and enjoyable food, and a sufficient supply of potent ale, brewed in the vats of the Hospital, which, among its other praiseworthy characteristics, was famous for this; having, indeed, at some epoch, presumed to vie with the famous ale of Trinity, in Cambridge, and the Arch Deacon of Oxford— these having come down to the hospital from a private receipt of Sir Humphrey's butler, which was now lost in the Brathwaite family; nor would the ungrateful hospital give up its secret even out of loyalty to its founder.

"I would use my influence with the brewer," said the Warden, on communicating this little fact to Etherege; "but the present man—the new holder of the estate—is not worthy to have good ale brewed in his house; having himself no taste for anything but Italian wines, wretched fellow that he is. He might make himself an Englishman if he would take heartily to our ale; and with that end in view, I should be glad to give it him."

The kitchen fire blazed merrily, as we have said, and roast and stewed, and boiled were in process of cooking, producing a pleasant fume, while great heaps of wheaten loaves were smoking hot from the ovens, and the master cook and his subordinates were in fume and hiss, like beings that were of a fiery element, and though irritable and scorching, yet were happier here than they could have been in any other situation. The Warden seemed to have an especial interest and delight in this department of the hospital, and spoke apart to the head-cook, on the subject (as Etherege surmised from what he overheard) of some especial delicacy for his own table that day.

"This kitchen is a genial place," said he to Etherege, as they retired. "In the evening, after the cooks have done their work, the brethren have liberty to use it as a sort of common room, and to sit here over their ale, till a reasonable bed time. It would interest you much to make one at such a party; for they have had a varied experience in life, each one for himself, and it would be strange to hear the varied roads by which they have come hither."

"Yes," replied Etherege, "and, I presume, not one of them ever dreamed of coming hither, when he started in life. The only one with whom I am acquainted could hardly have expected it, at all events; for I have seldom been more impressed with a sense of ability—not present, perhaps, but

strewn along past—as by the venerable person to whose hospitality I owe so much. I could fancy his face as worthy of
an aged statesman, whose deeds were written in history."

"Yes, he is a remarkable man; more so than you can as
yet have had an opportunity of knowing," said the Warden.
"I know not his history, for he is not communicative on that
subject, and it was only necessary for him to make out his
proofs of claim to the charity to the satisfaction of the Cura-
tors. But it has often struck me that there must have been
strange and striking events in his life—he must have played
a part in the eyes of the world; though how it could have
been, without his attracting attention and being known, I
cannot say. I have myself often received good counsel from
him in the conduct of the Hospital; and the present owner
of Brathwaite Hall seems to have taken him for his coun-
sellor and confidant, being himself strange to English affairs
and life."

"I should like to call on him, as a matter of more than
courtesy," observed Etherege, "and thank him for his great
kindness."

They accordingly ascended the dark oaken staircase, with
its black balustrade, and approached the old man's chamber;
coming to the door of which, they found it open, and in the
blurred looking-glass, which hung deep within the room,
Etherege was surprised to perceive the young face of a
woman, who seemed to be arranging her head-gear, as women
are always doing. It was but a moment; and then it vanished
like a vision.

"I was not aware," he said, turning to the Warden, "that
there was a feminine side to this establishment."

"Nor is there," said the old bachelor, "else it would not
have held together so many ages as it has. The establishment
has its own wise, monkish regulations; but we cannot prevent the fact, that some of the brethren may have had foolish
relations with the other sex at some previous periods of their

lives. This seems to be the case with our wise old friend of whom we have been speaking—whereby he doubtless became both wiser and sadder. If you have seen a female face here, it is that of a daughter, who resides out of the hospital—a reputable young woman, I believe, who has charge of a school."

While he was speaking, the young lady in question passed out, greeting the warden in a cheerful, respectful way, in which deference to him was well combined with a sense of what was due to herself.

"That," observed the Warden, who had returned her courtesy with a kindly air, betwixt that of gentlemanly courtesy and a superior's acknowledgement—"that is the daughter of our old friend; a young person—a gentlewoman, I may almost call her—who teaches a little school in the village here, and keeps her father's heart warm, no doubt, with her presence. An excellent young woman, I do believe, and very useful and faithful in her station."

On entering the old palmer's apartment, they found him looking over some ancient papers, yellow, and crabbedly written, and on one of these a large old seal; all of which he did up in a bundle, and enclosed in a parchment cover; so that, before they were well in the room, the documents were removed from view.

"Those papers and parchments have a fine old yellow tint, Pearson," said the Warden; "very satisfactory to an antiquary."

"There is nothing in them," said the old man, "of general interest. Some old papers, they are, which came into my possession by inheritance, and some of them relating to the affairs of a friend of my youth; a long past time, and a long past friend," added he, sighing.

"Here is a new friend, at all events," said the kindly Warden, wishing to cheer the old man, "who feels himself greatly indebted to you for your care. And, by the by, I have never quite understood how he came to be so fortunate as to fall into your charge."

"I had been to the Hall, that morning," said the Palmer, "in compliance with a request from Mr. Brathwaite; and on my way home I heard a sort of struggle and cry, in a remote part of the Park, and making to the spot, I found this young gentleman on the ground insensible."

"Did you see or hear nothing more?" asked the Warden.

"There was the tread of a man escaping," said Pearson; "but I am an old man, and not so ready as I might have been once to pursue a ruffian. Besides, this young gentleman required all the care I knew how to give him. I summoned assistance, and as Providence had flung him on my hands, I thought it right to bring him to my own quarters."

Etherege, who was very impressible by character, and often had perception about people which seemed to be conveyed by imperceptible points, had a feeling that the old man was speaking with a certain cautiousness; that perhaps he knew more than he chose to tell. It was possible, he thought, that he might have recognized the assailant and intended robber, but, for reasons of his own—perhaps from an unwillingess to draw the vengeance of a gang of robbers on his head— chose not to betray him. Supposing this to be the case, Etherege felt it to be his part to connive with the old man, who had conferred such an especial favor on him; nor did care so much, it must be confessed, for the justice of England as to desire the annoyance and loss of time which would probably ensue to himself from the discovery of the villain.

The Warden seemed to have observed nothing of this; and indeed, it was perhaps all a fancy of Etherege, who, however, had had a good deal of experience in reading faces and watching expression.

"Well," said he, "I am heartily glad that the villain missed his booty and was debarred of his crime. The police have ever since been in quest of him; but they seem to make no discoveries. For the sake of English hospitality, it would gratify me much to have him meet his deserts; else this American will think we live in a wilder and more lawless state than his own."

There now ensued a conversation among these three persons; and Etherege was impressed by the manners of the old man, who (seeming to consider that the nature of the visit put him on an equality, for the time, with his guests) manifested a stately courtesy and a ready flow of interesting talk, resulting evidently from much and varied knowledge of the world. In particular, he evinced such an acquaintance with the customs, policy, and feelings of his own country, that Etherege could not help suggesting that he had probably been in America.

"Many—very many years ago," said the old man; "and you are so mobile, you change so speedily, that I suppose there are few external things now that I should recognize. The face of your country changes like one of your own sheets of water, under the influence of sun, cloud, and wind; but I suppose there is a depth below that is seldom effectually stirred. It is a great fault of the country, that its sons find it impossible to feel any patriotism for it."

"I do not by any means acknowledge that impossibility," responded Etherege with a smile. "I certainly feel that sentiment very strongly in my own breast; more especially since I have left America three thousand miles behind me."

"Yes; it is only the feeling of self-assertion that rises against the self-complacency of the English," said the old man. "Nothing else; for what else have you besides the subject of this noble weakness of patriotism? You cannot love anything beyond the soil of your own estate; or, in your case, if your heart is very large, you may possibly take in, in a quiet sort of way, the whole of New England. What more is possible?

How can you feel a heart's love for a mere political arrange-ment, like your union? How can you be loyal where per-sonal attachment—the lofty and noble, and unselfish attach-ment of a subject to his prince is out of the question; where your sovereign is felt to be a mere man like yourselves, whose petty struggles, whose ambition—mean, before it grew to be audacious—you have watched, and know him to be just the same now as yesterday, and that tomorrow he will be walking unhonored amongst you again? Your system is too bare and meagre for human nature to love, or to endure it long. These stately degrees of society that have so strong a hold upon us in England, are not to be done away with so lightly as you think. Your experiment is not yet a success, by any means; and you, young man, will live to see it result otherwise than you think."

"This is excellent doctrine!" ejaculated the Warden, with most hearty concurrence.

"It is natural for you Englishmen to feel this," said Ether-ege with a flash of slightly wounded feeling; "although, ever since I set my foot on your shores—forgive me, but you set me the example of free speech—I have had a feeling of com-ing change, among all that you look upon as so permanent, so everlasting; and though your thoughts dwell fondly on things as they are and have been, there is a deep destruction somewhere in this country, that is inevitably impelling it in the path of my own. But I care not for this. I do aver that I love my country, that I am proud of its institutions, that I have a feeling, unknown probably to any but a republican, but which is the proudest thing in me, that there is no man above me—for my ruler is only myself, in the person of an-other, whose office I impose upon him—nor any below me. If you could understand me, I would tell you of the shame I felt when I first, on setting foot in this country, heard a man speaking of his birth as giving him privileges; saw him looking down on a laboring man, as one of an inferior race; and what I can never understand, is the pride which you positively seem to feel in having men and classes of men above you, born to privileges which you can never hope to share. It may be a thing to be endured, but surely not one to be absolutely proud of. And yet an Englishman is so."

"Ah; I see we lack a ground to meet upon," said the Warden. "We can never truly understand each other. What you have last mentioned is one of our inner mysteries. It is not a thing to be reasoned about, but to be felt, to be born within one; and I uphold it to be a generous sentiment, and good for the human heart."

"Forgive me, Sir," said Etherege, "but I would rather be the poorest and lowest man in America than have that sentiment."

"But it might change your feelings, perhaps," suggested the Warden, "if you were one of the privileged class."

"I dare not say that it would not," replied Etherege; "for I know I have a thousand weaknesses, and have doubtless as many more that I have never suspected myself of. But it seems to me, at this moment, impossible that I should ever have such an ambition; because I have a sense of meanness in not starting fair, in beginning the world with advantages that my fellows have not."

"Really, this is not wise," said the Warden, bluntly. "How can the start in life be fair for all? Providence arranges it otherwise. Did you yourself—a gentleman evidently by birth and education—did you start fair in the race of life?"

Etherege remembered what his birth, or rather what his first recollected place had been, and reddened.

"In birth certainly, I had no advantages," said he, and would have explained further but was kept back by an invincible reluctance; feeling that the bare fact of his origin in an almshouse would be accepted, while all the inward assurances and imaginations that had reconciled himself to this ugly fact would go for nothing. "But there were advantages, very early in life," added he, smiling, "which perhaps I ought to have been ashamed to avail myself of."

"An old cobwebby library—an old dwelling by a graveyard —an old Doctor, busied with his own fantasies, entangled in his own cobwebs—and a little girl for a playmate; these were things that you might lawfully avail yourself of," said the old palmer, unheard by the Warden, who, thinking the conversation had lasted long enough, had paid a slight parting courtesy to the old man and was now leaving the room.

"What can you know of these," exclaimed Etherege in astonishment.

"You spoke of many strange things, when you lay on that bed in delirium," replied Pearson; "and so much I may well have gathered. Perhaps more. But do you remain here long?"

"If the Warden's hospitality holds out," said the American, "I shall be glad; for the place interests me greatly."

"No wonder," replied Pearson.

"And wherefore no wonder," said Etherege, impressed that there was something peculiar in the tone of the old man's remark.

"Because," returned the other quietly, "it must be, to an American, especially interesting to see an institution of this kind, whereby one man's benevolence, or penitence, or it may be his mere whim, is made to take the substance and durability of stone, and last for centuries; whereas, in your own country, the solemn decrees and resolutions of millions melt away like vapour, and everything shifts like the pomp of sunset clouds; though it may be as pompous as they. The past is nothing with you; whereas Heaven intended it as a foundation for a present, to keep it from vibrating and being blown away with every breeze."

"There is something in what you say," replied Etherege; "but I would not see in my country, what I see elsewhere—

the Past hanging like a millstone round a country's neck, or incrusted in stony layers over the living form; so that, to all intents and purposes, it is dead."

"Well, well," said Pearson, "we are only talking of this hospital. You will find no more interesting place anywhere. Look at this company of old men, myself among them—what a variety of fortune has brought them hither, from what a variety of starting-places. One has been a soldier, and fought in some of the proudest battles that England ever won; another a sailor, a midshipman under Nelson; there is a poet, too, I assure you; and another that scattered his wealth abroad in his youth, and has been here now these thirty years. And there is another—someday, perhaps, I will point him out to you—who has had a more singular fate and fall than any of the rest; who raised himself to be a power, who almost made himself an empire, who has stood before kings; and who, even, half voluntarily giving up all this, has come here to spend his old age, in the brethren's robe."

"Is there such a one?" said Etherege. "I could half fancy that you are speaking of yourself."

"Ah, I was dreaming," said the old man, with a sad and bitter smile. "There is no such one;—perhaps there never was. Farewell; yet stay amongst us; this is the very heart of England, and if you wish to know the father-land, the place whence you sprung, this is the very spot."

Again Etherege was struck with the impression that there was something marked; something individually addressed to himself in the old man's words; at any rate, it appealed to that primal imaginative vein in him, which had so often, in his own country, allowed itself to dream over the possibilities of his birth. He knew that the feeling was a vague and idle one; he suspected, moreover, that the old man was half insane, and that the contagion was making itself slightly felt on himself, in whom there was indeed a possibility of extravagance, limited, modified, and, in the last result, sternly controlled by a stern New England common sense. But, yet, just at this time, a convalescent, with a little play moment in what had heretofore been a turbulent life, he felt an inclination to follow out this dream, and let it sport with him, and by-and-by to awake to realities, refreshed by a season of unreality. At a firmer and stronger period of life, though Etherege might have indulged his imagination with these dreams, yet he would not have let them interfere with his course of action; but having come hither in utter weariness of active life, it seemed just the thing for him to do—just the fool's Paradise for him to be in.

"Yes, I see how it is," said the old man, looking keenly in his face. "You will not leave us yet."

Etherege returned through the quadrangle to the Warden's house, and there were the brethren, sitting on benches, loitering in the sun, which though warm for England, seemed scarcely enough to keep these old people warm even with their cloth robes. They did not seem unhappy; nor yet happy; —if they were so, it must be with the mere bliss of existence, a sleepy sense of comfort, and quiet dreaminess about things past, leaving out the things to come—of which there was nothing, indeed, in their features, save one day after another, just like this, with beef and ale, and such substantial comforts, and prayers, and idle days again, gatherings by the great kitchen fire, and at last a day when they should not be there, but some other old men in their stead. And Etherege wondered whether, in the extremity of age, he himself would like to be one of the brethren of the Dragon's Head. The old men, he was sorry to see, did not seem very genial towards one another; in fact, there appeared to be a secret enjoyment of one another's infirmities, wherefore it was hard to tell, unless that each individual might fancy himself to possess an advantage over his fellow, which he mistook for a positive strength; and so there was sometimes a sardonic smile, when,

on rising from his seat, the rheumatism was a little evident
in an old fellow's joints; or when the palsy shook another's
fingers so that he could barely fill his pipe; or when a cough,
the gathered spasmodic trouble of thirty years, feebly con-
vulsed another. Then, any two that happened to be sitting
near one another, looked into each other's cold eyes, and
whispered, or suggested merely by a look (for they were
bright to such perceptions), "The old fellow will not outlast
another winter."

Methinks it is not good for old men to be much together.
An old man is a beautiful object in his own place, in the
midst of a circle of young people, going down in various
gradations to infancy, and all looking up to the patriarch with
filial reverence; keeping him warm by their own burning
youth; giving him the freshness of their thought and feeling,
with such natural influx that it seems as if it grew within his
heart; while on them he reacts with an influence that sobers,
tempers, keeps them down. His wisdom, very probably, is
of no great account; he cannot fit to any new state of things;
but, nevertheless, it works its effect. In such a situation, the
old man is kind and genial, mellow, more gentle and generous, and wider minded than ever before. But if left to himself, or wholly to the society of his contemporaries, the ice
gathers about his heart, his hope grows torpid, his love—
having nothing of his own blood to develop it—grows cold;
he becomes selfish, when he has nothing in the present or the
future worth caring about in himself; so that instead of a
beautiful object he is an ugly one, little, mean, and torpid.
I suppose one chief reason to be, that unless he has his own
race about him, he doubts of anybody's love, he feels himself
a stranger in the world, and so becomes unamiable.

A very few days in the Warden's hospitable mansion produced an excellent effect on Etherege's frame; his constitu-

tion being naturally excellent, and a flow of cheerful spirits contributing much to restore him to health; especially as the abode in this old place, which would probably have been intolerably dull to most young Englishmen, had for this young American a charm like the freshness of Paradise. In truth, it had that charm, and besides it another intangible, evanescent, perplexing charm, full of an airy enjoyment, as if he had been here before. What could it be? It could be only the old, very deepest, inherent nature, which the Englishman, his progenitor, carried over the sea with him, nearly three hundred years before, and which had lain buried all that time under heaps of new things, new customs, new institutions, new snows of winter, new layers of forest leaves, until it seemed dead, and was altogether forgotten as if it had never been; but, now, his return had seemed to dissolve or dig away all this incrustation, and the old English nature awoke all fresh, so that he saw the green grass, the hedgerows, the old structures and old manners, the old clouds, the old rain-drops, with a recognition, and yet a newness. Etherege had never been so quietly happy as now. He had, as it were, the quietude of the old men about him, and the freshness of his own still youthful years.

The Warden was evidently very favorably impressed with his transatlantic guest, and he seemed to be in a constant state of surprise to find an American so agreeable a kind of person.

"You are just like an Englishman," he sometimes said. "Are you quite sure that you were not born on this side of the water?"

This is said to be the highest compliment that an Englishman can pay to an American; and doubtless he intends it as such. All the praise and good will that an Englishman ever awards to an American is so far gratifying to the recipient, that it is meant for him individually, and is not to be put down, in the slightest degree, to the score of any regard to his countrymen generally. So far from this, if an Englishman were to meet the whole thirty millions of Americans, and find each individual of them, a pleasant, amiable, well meaning, and well mannered sort of fellow, he would acknowledge this honestly in each individual case, but still would speak of the whole nation as a disagreeable people.

As regards Etherege's being precisely like an Englishman, we cannot but think that the good warden was mistaken. No doubt, there was a common ground; the old progenitor (whose blood, moreover, was mixed with a hundred other streams equally English) was still there, under this young man's shape, but with a vast difference. Climate, sun, cold, heat, soil, institutions, had made a change in him before he was born, and all the life that he had lived since (so unlike any that he could have lived in England) had developed it more strikingly. In manners, I cannot but think that he was better than the generality of Englishmen, and different from the highest mannered men, though most resembling those. His natural sensitiveness, a tincture of reserve, had been counteracted by the frank mixture with men which his political course had made necessary; he was quicker to feel what was right at the moment than an Englishman; more alive; he had a finer grain; his look was more aristocratic than that of a thousand Englishmen of good birth and breeding; he had a faculty of assimilating himself to new manners, which, being his most un-English trait, was what perhaps chiefly made the Warden think him so like an Englishman. When an Englishman is a gentleman, to be sure, it is as deep in him as the marrow of his bones, and the deeper you know him, the more you are aware of it, and that generation after generation has contributed to develope and perfect these unpretending manners, which, at first, may have failed to impress you, under his plain, almost homely exterior. An American often gets as good a surface of manners, in his own progress from youth, through the wear and attrition of a successful life, to some high station in middle age; whereas, a plebeian Englishman, who rises to eminent station, never does credit to it by his manners. Often, you would not know the American ambassador from a duke.—This is often merely external; but in Etherege, having delicate original traits in his character, it was something more; and, we are bold to say, when our countrymen are developed, or any one class of them, as they ought to be, they will show finer traits than have yet been seen. We have more delicate and quicker sensibilities; nerves more easily impressed; and these are surely requisites for perfect manners; and, moreover, the courtesy that proceeds on the ground of perfect equality is better than that which is a gracious and benignant condescension—as is the case with the manners of the aristocracy of England.

An American, be it said, seldom turns his best side outermost, abroad; and an observer, who has had much opportunity of seeing the figure which they make, in a foreign country, does not so much wonder that there should be severe criticism on their manners as a people. I know not exactly why, but all our imputed peculiarities—our nasal pronunciation, our ungraceful idioms, our forthputtingness, our uncouth lack of courtesy—do really seem to exist on a foreign shore; and even, perhaps, to be heightened of malice prepense. The cold, unbelieving eye of Englishmen, expectant of solecisms in manners, contributes to produce the result which it looks for. Then the feeling of hostility and defiance in the American must be allowed for; and partly, too, the real existence of a different code of manners, founded on, and arising from different institutions; and also certain national peculiarities, which may be intrinsically as good as English peculiarities; but being different, and yet the whole result being just too nearly alike, and, moreover, the English manners having the prestige of long establishment, and furthermore our own manners being in a transition estate between those of old monarchies and what is proper to a new Republic, it necessarily follows that the American, though really a man of refinement and delicacy, is not just the kind of gentleman that the English ever fully appreciate. In cases where they do so, their standard being different from ours, they do not always select for their approbation the kind of man or manners whom we should judge the best; we are perhaps apt to be a little too fine, a little too sedulously polished, and of course too conscious of it—a deadly social crime, certainly.

To return from this long discussion, the Warden took kindly, as we have said, to Etherege, and thought him a miraculously good fellow, to have come from the rude American Republic. Hitherto, in the little time that he had been in England, Etherege had received civil and even kind treatment from the English with whom he had come casually in contact; but still—perhaps partly from our Yankee narrowness and reserve—he had felt, in the closest coming together, as if there were a naked sword between the Englishman and him, as between the Arabian prince in the tale and the princess whom he wedded; he felt as if that must be the case, even if he should love an Englishwoman; to such a distance, into such an attitude of self-defence, does English self-complacency and belief in England's superiority throw the stranger. In fact, in a good natured way, John Bull is always doubling his fist in a stranger's face, and though it be good natured, it does not always produce the most amiable feeling.

The worthy Warden, being an Englishman, had doubtless the same kind of feeling; doubtless, too, he thought ours a poor, distracted country, perhaps prosperous for the moment, but as likely as not to be the scene of anarchy five minutes hence; but being of so genial a nature, when he came to see the amiableness of his young guest, and how deeply he was impressed with England, all prejudice died away, and he loved him like a treasure that he had found for himself, and valued him as if there were something of his own in him. And so, the old master's residence had never before been so cheery as it was now; his bachelor-life passed the more pleasantly with this quiet, vivacious, yet not troublesomely restless spirit beside him—this eager, almost childish interest in everything English, and yet this capacity to take independent views of things, and sometimes, it might be, to throw a gleam of light even on things appertaining to England. And so, the better they came to know one another, the greater was their mutual liking.

"I fear I am getting too strong to burthen you much longer," said Etherege, this morning. "I have no pretence to be a patient now."

"Pooh! nonsense!" ejaculated the Warden. "It will not be safe to leave you to yourself for at least a month to come. And I have half a dozen excursions in a neighborhood of twenty miles, in which I mean to show you what old England is, in a way that you would never find out for yourself. Do not speak of going. This day, if you find yourself strong enough, you shall go and look at our old village church."

"With all my heart," said Etherege.

They went, accordingly, walking slowly, in consequence of Etherege's yet imperfect strength, along the high road, which was overshadowed with elms, that grew in beautiful shape and luxuriance, in that part of England, not with the slenderer, drooping picturesque grace of a New England elm, but more luxuriant, fuller of leaf, sturdier in limb. It was a day which the Warden called fine, and which Etherege, at home, would have thought to bode rain; though here he had learned that such weather might continue for weeks together, with only a few raindrops all the time. The road was in the finest condition hard and dry.

They had not long emerged from the gateway of the Hospital—at the venerable front and gables of which Etherege turned to look with a feeling as if it were his home, when they heard the clatter of hoofs behind them; and a gentleman on horseback rode by, paying a courteous salute to the Warden as he passed. A groom in livery followed at a little distance, and both rode casually towards the village whither the Warden and his friends were going.

"Did you observe that man?" asked the Warden.

"Yes," said Etherege. "Is he an Englishman?"

"That is a pertinent question," replied the Warden; "but I scarcely know how to answer it."

In truth, Etherege's question had been suggested by the appearance of the mounted gentleman, who was a dark, thin man, with black hair, and a black moustache and pointed beard setting off his sallow face, in which the eyes had a certain pointed steeliness, which did not look English—whose eyes, methinks, are usually not so hard as those of Americans or foreigners. Etherege, somehow or other, had fancied that these not very pleasant eyes had been fixed in a marked way on himself, a stranger, while, at the same time, his salute was evidently directed towards the Warden.

"An Englishman—why, no," continued the latter. "If you observe, he does not even sit his horse like an Englishman, but in that absurd, stiff Continental way, as if a poker should get on horseback. Neither has he an English face, English manners, nor English religion, nor an English heart; nor, to sum up the whole, had he English birth. Nevertheless, as fate would have it, he is the inheritor of a good old English name, a fine patrimonial estate, and a very probable claim to an old English title. This is Mr. Brathwaite of Brathwaite Hall, who, if he can make his case good (and they say there is good prospect of it) will soon be Lord Hinchbrooke."

"I hardly know why, but I should be sorry for it," said
Etherege. "He certainly is not English; and I have an odd
sort of sympathy which makes me unwilling that English
honors should be enjoyed by foreigners. This, then, is the
gentleman of Italian birth, whom you have mentioned to
me, and of whom there is a slight mention in the County
History."

"Yes," said the Warden. "There have been three descents
of this man's branch in Italy, and only one English mother
in all that time. Positively, I do not see an English trait in
his face, and as little in his manner. His civility is Italian,
such as oftentimes, among his countrymen, has offered a
cup of poison to a guest, or insinuated the stab of a stiletto
into his heart."

"You are particularly bitter against this poor man," said
Etherege, laughing at the Warden's vehemence. "His appearance—and yet he is a handsome man—is certainly not pre-
possessing; but unless it be countersigned by something in
his actual life, I should hardly think it worth while to con-
demn him utterly."

"Well, well; you can forgive a little English prejudice,"
said the Warden, a little ashamed. "But, in good earnest, the
man has few or no good traits, takes no interest in the country, dislikes our sky, our earth, our people, is close and
inhospitable, a hard landlord, and whatever may be his good
qualities, they are not such as flourish in this soil and climate,
or can be appreciated here."

"Has he children?" asked Etherege.

<(Etherege shows how to find, under the surface of the
village-green, an old cross)>

"They say so, a family by an Italian wife, whom some, on
the other hand, pronounce to be no wife at all. His son is
at a Catholic college in Sienna; his daughter in a convent
there."

In talk like this, they were drawing near the little rustic village of Brathwaite, and saw, above a cloud of foliage, the small, low, battlemented tower, the gray stones of which had probably been laid a little after the Norman conquest. Approaching nearer, they passed a thatched cottage or two, very plain and simple edifices, though interesting to Etherege from their antique aspect, which denoted that they were probably older than the settlement of his own country, and might very likely have nursed children who had gone, more than two centuries ago, to found the commonwealth of which he was a citizen. If you considered them in one way, prosaically, they were ugly enough; but then there were the old latticed windows, and there the old thatch, which was verdant with leek, and strange weeds, possessing a whole botanical growth. And birds flew in and out, as if they had their homes there. Then came a row of similar cottages, all joined on together, and each with a little garden before it, divided from its neighbors by a hedge, now in full verdure. Etherege was glad to see some symptoms of natural love of beauty here; for there were plants of box, cut into queer shapes of birds, peacocks &c as if year after year had been spent in bringing these vegetable sculptures to perfection. In one of the gardens, moreover, the ingenious inhabitant had spent his leisure in building grotto-work, of which the English are rather ludicrously fond, on their little bits of lawn, and in building a miniature castle of oyster shells, where were seen turrets, ramparts, a frowning arched gate way, and miniature cannon looking from the embrasures. A pleasanter and better adornment was the homely household flowers; and a pleasant sound, too, was the hum of bees, who had their home in several beehives, and were making their honey among the flowers of the garden, or came from afar, buzzing sunnily through the air, laden with honey that they had found elsewhere. Fruit-trees stood erect, or in some instances,

were flattened out against the walls of cottages, looking somewhat like hawks nailed in terrorem against a barn-door. The
male members of this little community were probably afield,
with the exception of one or two half torpid great grandsires,
who were moving rheumatically about the gardens, and some
children not yet in breeches, who stared with stolid eyes at
the passers-by; but the good dames were busy within doors,
where Etherege had glimpses of their interior with its pavement of stone-flags. Altogether it seemed a comfortable settlement enough.

"Do you see that child yonder," observed the Warden,
"creeping away from the door, and displaying a vista of his
petticoats as he does so? That sturdy boy is the lineal heir of
one of the oldest families in this part of England,—though
now decayed and fallen, as you may judge. So, you see, with
all our contrivances to keep up an aristocracy, there is still
change forever going on."

"Then is not something agreeable, and something otherwise, in the thought," replied Etherege. "What is the name
of this old family, whose representative is in such a case?"

"Mosely," said the Warden. "Their family residence stood
within three miles of Brathwaite Hall, but was taken down
in the last century, and its place supplied by a grand show-
place, built by a Birmingham manufacturer, who also originated here."

"And his name?" asked Etherege.

"Dobbin," said the Warden. "Some of his kin are still
among us, in the original station of their forefathers."

"Dobbin? Mosely?" said Etherege; and he repeated the
names to himself, three or four times over, inquiringly, medi-
tatively, doubtfully. "These are not very ordinary names," he
continued, at last; "but they have a singular familiarity to my
ear. I have heard them at some former period, and in connection with something that interested my imagination a good
deal. Ah! I remember now!"

Etherege was thinking suddenly of that old, legendary story which the good Doctor had told among his cobwebs, and which had then struck him and little Elsie as so strange, and yet so true. He did not, however, think it advisable to impart this childish nonsense to his friend, who would not have understood the charm which it had for him; and perhaps it owed that charm very much to this dreamy state in which Etherege was. It seemed so singular to have so many circumstances, hereabouts, affecting to him as if he had known them before; yet always occurring with an unexpected and inexplicable difference, that bewildered and thrilled him yet more than the similarity.

They kept onward from this outskirt of the village, and soon, passing over a little rising ground, and descending into a hollow, came to the main portion of it, clustered around its gray, Norman church, one side of the tower of which was covered with ivy, that was carefully kept, the Warden said, from climbing to the battlements, on account of some old prophecy that foretold that the tower would fall, if once the ivy mantled over its tip-top. Certainly, however, there seemed little likelihood, that the square, low mass would fall, unless by external violence, in less than as many ages as it had already stood.

Etherege looked at the old tower and little adjoining edifice with an interest that attached itself to every separate, moss-grown stone; but the Warden, like most Englishmen, was at once amused and wearied with the American's enthusiasm for this spot, which to him was uninteresting for the very reason that made it most interesting to Etherege, because it had stood there such a weary while. It was too common an object to excite in his mind, as it did in Etherege's, visions of the long ago time when it was founded, when mass was first said there, and the glimmer of torches at the altar was seen through the vista of that loved browed porch; and of all the procession of villagers that had since gone in and come out during nine hundred years, in their varying costume and fashion, but yet—and this was the strangest and most thrilling part of the idea—all, the very oldest of them, bearing a resemblance of feature, the kindred, the family likeness, to those who died yesterday—to those who still went thither to worship; and that all the grassy and half-obliterated graves around had held those who bore the same traits.

<(A circular seat around the tree.)>

In front of the church was a little green, on which stood a very ancient yew-tree, all the heart of which seemed to have been eaten away by time, so that a man could now creep into the trunk, through a wide opening, and looking upward, see another opening to the sky.

"That tree," observed the Warden, "is well worth the notice of such an enthusiastic lover of old things; though I suppose aged trees may be the one antiquity that you do not value, having them by myriads in your primeval forests. But then the interest of this tree consists greatly in what your trees have not—in its long connection with men, and the doings of men. Some of its companions were made into bows for Harold's archers. This tree is of unreckonable antiquity; so old, that in a record of the time of Edward II it is styled the Yew tree of Brathwaite green. That carries it back to Roman times, surely. It was in comparatively modern times when it served as a gallows for one of James II's blood thirsty judges to hang his victims on, after Monmouth's rebellion."

On one side of this yew was a certain structure which Etherege did not recognize as anything that he had before seen, but soon guessed its purposes; though, from appearances, it seemed to have been very long since it had served that purpose. It was a ponderous old oaken frame-work, six or seven feet high, so contrived that a heavy cross-piece shut down over another, leaving two round holes; in short it was a pair of stocks, in which, I suppose, hundreds of vagrants and petty criminals had sat of old, but which now appeared to be merely a matter of curiosity.

"This excellent old machine," said the Warden, "had been lying in a rubbish chamber of the church tower for at least a century; when the clerk, who is a little of an antiquarian, unearthed it, and I advised him to set it here, where it used to stand;—not with any idea of its being used (though there is as much need of it now as ever) but that the present age may see what comforts it has lost."

They sat down, a few moments, on the circular seat, and looked at the pretty scene of this quiet little village, clustered round the old church as a centre; a collection of houses, mostly thatched, though there were one or two with rather more pretension, that had roofs of red tiles. Some of them were stone cottages, white-washed; but the larger edifices had timber frames, filled in with brick and plaster, which seemed to have been renewed in patches, and to be a frailer and less durable material than the old oak of their skeletons. They were gabled, with lattice windows, and picturesquely set off with projecting stones, and many little patch work additions, such as, in the course of generations, the inhabitants had found themselves to need. There was not much commerce, apparently, in this little village; there seeming to be only one shop, with some gingerbread, penny whistles, ballads, and such matters displayed in the window; and there, too, across the little green, opposite the church, was the village-ale-house, with its bench under the low projecting eaves; with a Teniers scene of two wayfaring yeomen drinking a pot of beer and smoking their pipes.

With Etherege's Yankee feelings, there was something sad to think how the generations had succeeded one another, over and over, in immemorial succession, in this little spot, being born here, living, dying, lying down among their fathers' dust, and forthwith getting up again, as it were, and recommencing the same meaningless round, and really bringing nothing to pass; for probably the generation of to-day, in so secluded and motionless a place as this, had few or no ideas in advance of their ancestors of five centuries ago. It seemed not worth while that more than one generation of them should have existed. Even in dress, with their smock frocks, and breeches, they were just like their fathers. The stirring blood of the new land—where no man dwells in his father's house—where no man thinks of dying in his birth-place—awoke within him, and revolted at the thought; and, as connected with it, revolted at all the hereditary pretensions which, since his stay here, had exercised such an influence over the fanciful part of his nature. In another mood, the village might have seemed a picture of rural peace, which it would have been worth while to give up ambition to enjoy; now, as his newer impulse stirred, it was a weariness to think of. The new American was stronger in him than the hereditary Englishman.

"I should go mad of it!" exclaimed he aloud.

He started up impulsively, to the amazement of his companion, who of course could not comprehend what seemed so to have stung his American friend. As they passed the tree, on the other side of its huge trunk, they saw a young woman sitting on that side of it, and sketching, apparently, the church tower, with the old Elizabethan vicarage that stood near it, with a gate opening into the churchyard, and much embowered and ivy-hung.

"Ah, Miss Cheltenham," said the Warden, "I am glad to see that you have taken the old church in England; for it is one of the prettiest rustic churches in England, and as well worthy as any to be engraved on a sheet of note-paper, or put into a stereoscope. Will you let my friend and me see your sketch?"

The Warden had made his request with rather more freedom than perhaps he would to a lady whom he considered on a level with himself, though with perfect respect, that being considered; and Etherege, looking at the person, saw that it was the same of whose face he had had a glimpse in the looking-glass, in the old Palmer's chamber.

"No, Dr. Gigglethorpe," said the young lady, with a respectful sort of frankness. "You must excuse me. I am no good artist, and am just jotting down the old church because I like it."

"Well, well, as you please," said the Warden, and whispered aside to Etherege; "a girl's sketchbook is seldom worth looking at. But now, Miss Cheltenham, I am about to give my American friend here a lecture on Gargoyles, and other peculiarities of sacred Gothic architecture; and if you will honor me with your attention, I should be glad to find my audience increased by one."

So the young lady arose, and Etherege, considering the Warden's allusion to him as a sort of partial introduction, bowed to her, and she responded with a cold, reserved, yet not unpleasant sort of courtesy. They went towards the church-porch, and looking in at the old stone bust on the east side of the interiour, the Warden showed them the hacks of the swords of the Roundheads, when they took it by storm. Etherege, mindful of the old graveyard on the edge of which he had spent his childhood, began to look at this far more antique receptacle, expecting to find there many ancient tombstones, perhaps of contemporaries or predecessors of the founders of his country. In this, however, he was disappointed, at least in a great measure; for the persons buried in the churchyard were probably, for the most part—their superiors sleeping less enviably in dismal, mouldy, dusty vaults, instead of under the daisies—of a humble rank in life, such as were not so ambitious as to desire a monument of any kind, but were content to let their low earth-mounds subside into the land where their memory had waxed so faint that none among the survivors could point out the spot, or cared any longer about knowing it. While, in other cases where a monument of red free stone, or even of crudely hewn granite had been erected, the English climate had forthwith set to work to gnaw away the inscriptions; so that, in fifty years—in a time that would have left an American tombstone as fresh as if just cut—it was quite impossible to make out the record. Thus Etherege really found less antiquity here, than in the grave yard which might almost be called his natal spot.

When he said something to this effect, the Warden nodded.

"Yes," said he. "And in truth, we have not much need of inscriptions for these poor people. All good families—everyone, almost, with any pretensions to respectable station, has his family or individual recognition within the church, or upon its walls; or some of them, you see, on tombs on the outside. As for our poorer friends, here, they are content, as they may well be, to swell and subside, like little billows of mortality, here on the outside."

"And, for my part," said Etherege, "if there were anything particularly desirable on either side, I should like best to sleep under this lovely green turf, with the daisies strewn over me by Nature herself, and whatever other homely flowers any friend might choose to add."

"And, Dr Gibbleter," said the young woman, "we see by this grave stone that sometimes a person of humble rank may happen to be commemorated, and that Nature—in this instance, at least—seems to take especial pains and pleasure to preserve the record."

She indicated a flat grave stone, near the porch, which time had indeed beautified in a singular way; for there was cut deep into it a name and date, in old English characters, very deep, it must originally have been; and as if in despair of obliterating it, Time had taken the kindlier method of filling up the letters with moss; so that now, high embossed in loveliest green, was seen the name Richard Oglethorpe, 1613; —green and flourishing, and beautiful, like the memory of a good man. The inscription originally seemed to have contained some twenty lines, which might have been poetry, or perhaps a prose eulogy; or perhaps the simple record of the buried person's life; but all this, having been done in fainter and smaller letters, was now so far worn away as to be illegible; nor had they ever been deep enough to be made living in moss, like the rest of the inscription.

"How tantalizing," remarked Etherege, "to see the verdant shine of this name, impressed upon us as something remarkable—and nothing else. I cannot but think that there must be something worth remembering about a man thus distinguished. When two hundred years have taken all these natural pains to illustrate and emblazon 'Richard Oglethorpe 1613.' Ha! I surely recollect that name. It haunts me, somehow, as if it had been familiar of old."

"And me," said the young lady.

"It was an old name, hereabouts," observed the Warden, "but has been long extinct;—a cottage name, not a gentleman's. I doubt not that Oglethorpes sleep in many of these undistinguished graves."

Etherege did not much attend to what his friend said; his attention being attracted to the tone—to something in the tone of the young lady, and also to her coincidence in his remark that the name appealed to some early recollection. He had been taxing his memory to tell him when and how this name had become familiar to him; and he now remembered it that it had occurred in the old Doctor's story of the Bloody Footstep, told to him and Elsie, so long ago. To him and Elsie! It struck him, what if it were possible—but he knew it was not—that the young lady had a remembrance also of this fact, and that she, after so many years, were again mixing her thoughts with his. As this fancy recurred to him, he endeavored to get a glimpse of her face; and while he did so, she turned it upon him. It was a quick, sensitive face, that did not seem altogether English; he would rather have imagined it American; but at all events, he could not recognize it as one that he had seen before, and a thousand fantasies died within him as, in his momentary glance, he took in the volume of its contour.

After the two friends had parted with the young lady, they passed through the village, and entered the Park gate of Brathwaite Hall, pursuing a winding road through its beautiful scenery, which realized all that Etherege had read or dreamed about the perfect beauty of these sylvan creations, with the clumps of trees, or sylvan oaks, picturesquely disposed. To heighten the charm, they saw a herd of deer reposing, who, on their appearance, rose from their recumbent position, and began to gaze warily at the strangers; then tossing their horns, they set off on a career, but only swept round, and settled down not far from where they rose. Etheredge looked with great interest at these deer, who were at once wild and civilized; retaining a kind of free forest citizenship, while yet they were in some sense subject to man. It seemed as if they were a link between wild nature and tame; as if they could look back, in their long recollections, through a vista into the times when England's forests were as wild as those of America, though now they were but a degree more removed from domesticity than cattle, and took their food in winter from the race of man, and in summer reposed upon his lawns. This seemed the last touch of that delightful, conquered and regulated wildness, which English art has laid upon the whole growth of English nature, animal or vegetable.

"There is nothing really wild in your whole island," he observed to the Warden. "I have a sensation as if somebody knew and had cultivated and fostered, and set out in its proper place, every tree that grows; as if somebody had patted the head and played with your wildest animals. It is very delightful to me, for the present; and yet, I think, in the course of time, I should have a madness for something genuine, as it were; something that had not the touch and breath of man upon it. I suppose even your skies are modified by the modes of human life that are going on beneath it. London skies, of course, are so; but the breath of a great people, to say nothing of its furnace vapours and hearth-smokes, must make the sky other than it was a thousand years ago."

"I believe we English have a feeling like this, occasionally," replied the Warden; "and it is from that, party, that we must account for our adventurousness into other regions; especially for our interest in what is wild and new. In your own forests, now, and prairies, I fancy we find a charm that Americans do not. In the sea, too; and therefore we are Yachters. For my part, however, I have grown to like Nature a little smoothed down, and enriched; less gaunt and wolfish than she would be if left to herself."

"Yes; I feel that charm too," said Etherege. "But yet life would be slow and heavy, methinks, to see nothing but English parks."

Continuing their course through among the noble clumps of oaks, they by and by had a vista of the distant hall itself. It was one of the old English timber and plaster houses, many of which are of unkonwn antiquity; as was the case with a portion of this house; although other portions had been renewed, repaired, or added, within a century. It had, originally, the Warden said, stood all round an enclosed court-yard, like the great houses of the Continent; but now one side of this quadrangle had long been removed; and there was only a front, with two wings; the beams of old oak being picked out with black; and three or four gables in a line forming the front; while the wings seemed to be stone. It was the timber-portion that was most ancient. A clock was on the midmost gamble, and pointed now towards one oclock. The whole scene impressed Etherege not as striking, but as an abode of ancient peace, where generation after generation of the same family had lived, each making the most of life, because the life of each successive dweller there was eked out with the lives of all who had hitherto lived there; and had in it equally those lives which were to come afterwards; so that this was a rare and successful contrivance for giving length, fullness, body, substance, to this thin and frail matter of human life. And, as life was so rich in comprehensiveness, the dwellers there made the most of it for the present and future, each generation contriving what it could to add to the cosiness, the comfortableness, the grave, solid respectability, the sylvan beauty, of the house with which they seemed to be connected both before and after death. The family had its home there; not merely the individual. Ancient shapes, that had apparently gone to the family tomb, had yet a right by family hearth and in family hall; nor did they come thither cold and shivering, and diffusing dire ghostly terrors, and repulsive shrinkings, and death in life; but in warm, genial attributes, making this life now passing more dense as it were, by adding all the substance of their own to it. Etherege could not compare this abode, and the feelings that it aroused, to the houses of his own country; poor tents of a day, inns of a night, where nothing was certain, save that the family of him who built it would not dwell here, even if he himself should have the hap to die under the roof, which, with absurdest anticipations, he had built for his posterity. Posterity! An American can have none.

"All this sort of thing is beautiful; the family institution was beautiful in its day," ejaculated he aloud, to himself; not to his companion; "but it is a thing of the past. It is dying out in England; and as for ourselves, we never had it. Something better will come up; but as for this, it is past."

"That is a sad thing to say," observed the Warden, by no means comprehending what was passing in his friend's mind. "But, if you wish to view the interior of the hall, we will go thither; for, harshly as I have spoken of the owner, I suppose he has English feeling enough to give us lunch, and show us the old house of his forefathers."

"Not at present, if you please," replied Etherege. "I am afraid of destroying my delightful visionary idea of the house by coming too near it. Before I leave this part of the county, I should be glad to ramble over the whole of it, but not just now."

While Etherege was still enjoying the frank hospitality of his new friend, a rather marked event occurred in his life; yet not so important reality as it seemed to his English friend. A large letter was delivered to him, bearing the official seal of the United States, and the endorsement of the State Department; a very important looking document, which could not but add to the importance of the recipient in the eyes of any Englishman, accustomed as they are to bow down before any seal of government. Etherege opened it rather coolly, being rather loth to renew any of his political remembrances, now that he was in peace; or to think of the turmoil of modern and democratic politics, here in this quietude of gone-by ages and customs. The contents, however, took him by surprise; nor did he know whether to be pleased or not.

The official package, in short, contained an announcement that he had been appointed by the President, by and with the advice of the Senate, to one of the Continental missions, usually esteemed an object of considerable ambition to any young man in politics; so that, if consistent with his own pleasure, he was now one of the Diplomatic Corps, a Minister, and representative of his Country. On first considering the matter, Etherege was inclined to doubt whether this honor had been obtained for him altogether by friendly aid, though it did happen to have much in it that might suit his half-formed purpose of remaining long abroad; but, with an eye already rendered somewhat oblique by political practice, he suspected that a political rival—a rival, though of his own party, had been exerting himself to provide an inducement for Etherege to leave the local field to him; while he himself should take advantage of the vacant field, and his rival be thus insidiously, though honorably, laid on the shelf, whence (if he should try to remove himself a few years hence) the shifting influences of American politics would be likely enough to thwart him; so that, for the sake of being, a few years, nominally somebody, he might in fine come back to his own country and find himself permanently nobody. But Etherege had already sufficiently begun to suspect that he lacked some qualities that a politician ought to have, and without which, a political life, whether successful or otherwise, is sure to be a most irksome one—some qualities he lacked, others he had, both almost equally an obstacle. When he communicated the offer, therefore, to his friend the Warden, it was with the remark that he believed he should accept it.

"Accept it?" cried the Warden, opening his eyes. "I should think so, indeed! Why it puts you above the level with the highest nobility of the Court to which you are accredited; simple Republican as you are, it gives you rank with the old blood and birth of Europe. Accept it? By all means; and I will come and see you at your court."

"Nothing is more different between England and America," said Etherege, "than the different way in which the citizen of either country looks at official station. To an Englishman, a commission of whatever kind, emanating from his sovereign, brings apparently a gratifying sense of honor; to an American, on the contrary, it offers really nothing of the kind. He ceases to be a sovereign, an atom of sovereignty, at all events—and stoops to be a servant. If I accept this mission, honorable as you think it, I assure you I shall not feel myself quite the man I have hitherto been; although there is no obstacle in the way of party obligations or connections to my taking it, if I please."

"I do not well understand this," quoth the good Warden. "It is one of the promises of Scripture to the wise man, that he shall stand before Kings; and this embassy will enable you to do so. No man—no person—no man of your country, surely—is more worthy to do so; so pray accept."

"I think I shall," said Etherege.

Much as the Warden had seemed to affectionize Etherege hitherto, the latter could not but be sensible, thereafter, of a certain deference in his friend towards him, which he would fain have got rid of, had it been in his power. However, there was still the same heartiness under it all; and after a little, he seemed, in some degree, to take Etherege's own view of the matter—viz. that, being so temporary as these republican distinctions are, they really do not go skin deep, have no reality in them, and that the sterling quality of the man, be it higher or lower, is nowise altered by it;—an apothegm that is true even of a hereditary nobility, and still more so of our own Honorables and Excellencies. However, the good Warden was glad of his friend's dignity, and perhaps, too, a little glad that this high fortune had befallen one whom he chanced to be entertaining under his roof. As it happened, there was an opportunity which might be taken advantage of to celebrate the occasion; at least, to make it known to the English world, so far as the extent of the county.

<—the dinner is given to the pensioners, as well as to the gentry, I think—>

It was an hereditary custom for the Master of Brathwaite Hospital, once a year, to give a grand dinner to the nobility and gentry of the neighborhood; and to this end, a bequest had been made by one of the former squires or lords of Brathwaite, which would of itself suffice to feed forty or fifty Englishmen with reasonable sumptuousness. The present Master, being a gentleman of private fortune, was accustomed to eke the limited income, devoted for this purpose, with such additions from his own resources as brought the rude and hearty hospitality, contemplated by the first founder, on a par with modern refinements of gourmandism. The banquet was annually given in the fine old hall, where James II. had feasted; and on some of these occasions, the Master's table had been honored with illustrious guests; especially when any of them happened to be wanting an opportunity to come before the public in an after dinner speech. Just at present, there was no occasion of that sort; and the good Master fancied that he might give considerable eclat to his hereditary feast, by bringing forward the young American envoy, a distinguished and eloquent man, to speak on the well worn topic of the necessity of friendly relations between England and America.

"You are eloquent, I doubt not, my young friend?" inquired he.

"Why, no," answered Etherege, modestly.

"Ah, yes, I know it," returned the Master. "You have all the natural pre-requisites of eloquence; a quick sensibility, ready thought, apt expression, a good voice—and not making its way into the world through your nose, either, as they say most of your countrymen's voices do. You shall make the crack speech at my dinner; and so strengthen the bonds of good fellowship between our two countries, that there shall be no question of war for at least six months to come."

Accordingly, the preparations for this stately banquet went on with great spirit; and the Warden exhorted Etherege to be thinking of some good topics for his international speech; but the young man laughed it off, and told his friend that he thought the inspiration of the moment, aided by the good old wine which the Warden had told him of, as among the treasures of the Hospital, would perhaps serve him better than any elaborate preparation.

Etherege, being not even yet strong, used to spend much time, when the days chanced to be pleasant (which was oftener than his pre-conceptions of English weather led him to expect) in the garden behind the Master's house. It was an extensive one, and apparently as antique as the foundation of the establishment; and during all these years, it had prob-ably been growing richer and richer. Here were flowers of ancient race, and some that had been merely field or wayside flowers, when first they came into the garden; but by long cultivation, and hereditary care, instead of dying out, they had acquired a new richness and beauty; so that you would scarcely recognize the daisy or the violet. Roses, too, there were, which Dr. Griffin said had been taken from those white and red rose-trees, in the Temple Gardens, whence the parti-zans of York and Lancaster had plucked their fatal badges. With these, there were all the modern and far-fetched flowers from America, the East, and elsewhere; even the prairie flow-ers, and the California blossoms were represented here; for one of the brethren had horticultural tastes, and was permit-ted freely to exercise them there. The antique character of the garden was preserved, likewise, by the allies of box, a part of which had been suffered to remain, and was now grown to a great height and density, so as to make impervious green walls. There were else yew trees clipped into strange shapes of bird and beast, and uncouth heraldic figures, among which of course the wolf's head grinned triumphant; and as for fruit, the high garden wall was lined with pear-trees, spread out flat against it, where they managed to produce a cold, flavorless fruit, a good deal akin to cucumbers.

Here, in these quiet old arbors, Etherege used to recline in the sweet, mild summer weather, basking in the sun, which was seldom too warm to make its full embrace uncomfortable; and it seemed to him, with its formality, with its marks everywhere of the quiet, long bestowed care of man, the sweetest and cosiest seclusion he had ever known; and two or three times a day, when he heard the screech of the railway train, rushing on towards distant London, it impressed him still more with a sense of safe repose here.

Not unfrequently, he here met the white-bearded Palmer, in whose chamber he had found himself, as if conveyed thither by enchantment, when he first come to the Hospital. The old man was not by any means of the garrulous order; and yet he seemed full of thoughts, full of reminiscences, and not disinclined to the company of Etherege. In fact, the latter sometimes flattered himself that a tendency for his society was one of the motives that brought him to the garden; though the amount of their intercourse, after all, was not so great as to warrant the idea of any settled purpose in so doing. Nevertheless, they talked considerably; and Etherege could easily see that the old man had been an extensive traveller, and had perhaps occupied situations far different from his present one, and had perhaps been a struggler in troubled waters, before he was drifted into the retirement where Etherege found him. Among other parts of the world, Etherege was convinced that Pearson had visited America; and not only that, but he appeared to have a familiar acquaintance with it, such as an Englishman is seldom able, even if he condescends to attain. He was in the habit, too, of bringing his English antiquarian lore, and his American practical knowledge, into a singular sort of juxtaposition and bearing on one another. He talked of the emigrants in old times, and of the void that they must have left; he talked of the unsuspected relationship that must now be existing between many families in England, and an unknown consanguinity in the new world, where perhaps, really, the mainstock of the family tree was now existing, and with a new spirit and life, which the representative growth, here in England, had lost by too long continuance in one air, and one mode of life. For he said that history and observation proved, that all people—and the English people by no means less than others—needed to be transplanted, or somehow renewed, every few generations; so that, according to this ancient philosopher's theory, it would be good for the whole people of England, now, if it could at once be transported to America, where its fatness, its sleepiness, its too great beefiness, its preponderant animal character, would be rectified by a different air and soil; and equally good, on the other hand, for the whole American people to be transplanted back to the original island, where their nervousness might be weighted with heavier influences, where their little women might grow bigger, where their thin, dry men might get a burthen of flesh, and good stomachs; where their children might, with the air, draw in a reverence for age, forms, and usage.

Etherege listened with complacency to these speculations, smiling at the thought of such an exodus as would take place, and the reciprocal dissatisfaction which would probably be the result. But he had greater pleasure in drawing out some of the old gentleman's legendary lore, some of which, whether true or not, was very curious. For example, he told for truth (in reference to this early emigration to America) a story of three brothers, who had a deadly quarrel among them, more than two hundred years ago, for the affections of a young lady, their cousin, who gave her reciprocal love to one of them; who immediately became the object of the deadly hatred of the two others. There seemed to be madness in their love; perhaps madness in the love of all three; for the result had been a plot to kidnap this unfortunate young man and convey him to America, where he was sold for a servant. Some said, however, that this was not the way of it; but that a scheming mother had given all three of the sons the idea that the young lady was unworthy of their affection, false, unchaste, impure, and that they all three had resolved to leave their home forever; and one came to America, in humble station. Now, as it happened, the other two brothers did not really leave their country, but after adventures of various kinds, they settled down in life, and became what the world thought respectable people; but it was doubtful whether the emigrant were really ever heard of more. But the two who remained behind both persecuted the young lady for her love; for they had not been long in discovering the wicked arts of their mother. But their addresses were paid in vain; for the young lady had bestowed her virgin affections on the gone brother, and kept them fixed on him forever. Some said that she had letters from him after his disappearance, promising that he would yet return; others that it was only her woman's fidelity; but so it was, that always she waited and watched for him; who returned no more. And she kept a place at her board for him, and in her half madness, left in her will a behest that whoever inherited her estate should do the same. Now, after many years, a repentance came upon one of the two wicked brothers; and on his death-bed, he left a behest that his son, for his father's sake, should take up the quest of his lost cousin, and never give it up as long as he lived, but should find him or his heirs, if any there were. So, it was said one of his sons, did really cross the sea, and moreover did find some traces of this lost heir, but his fortunes had been so strange that it was impossible to bring him to light—him or them—though, it seemed that he had been married, and there was reason to think that he had left children. So, at last, singularly enough, in the search for the lost one, the other brother's race disappeared, and his own existence became almost as mythical as that of the original disappearant. The other brother therefore remained, and in due time, though the youngest, came into possession of the estate; it being taken for granted that both the elders and their posterity were extinct. But by and by, there came up a claim to an ancient title, which the heir of this branch of the house would have assumed; but, on this, the heralds and genealogists objected, and there came such strong rumors of the existence of nearer claimants that it was doubtful whether the claim would succeed. And for several generations this matter had remained in question.

Suppose: there were three brothers, two of them in love with the same woman. The youngest brother was a dark, designing man; he conspired with the elder to have the middle brother murdered, and thence originated the bloody footstep, when he was taken violently out of the old family residence. But he was not murdered, only kidnapped; and it remains a matter of doubt, whether it was with the design and knowledge of the younger brother that this took place, or by the relenting of the instruments whom he employed. He was taken to America, where he lived many years, ultimately married, and died, leaving posterity—but all under an assumed name; although he likewise left a certain document, properly authenticated, revealing what his true name was. The family may have been Catholic, and this brother a protestant; his misfortunes and these crimes against him shall have given a stern and ascetic character to his life, so that he shall despise all worldly things; and his mind shall have been wrought upon to doubt the fidelity of his lady-love, so that he shall have no reason whatever for keeping up any relations with his family.

The lady, however, shall be faithful to him, shall live unmarried for his sake, and die, having his love-gifts buried in her coffin; and among them a broken piece of gold, or some other token that shall correspond with some token that he has possession of. And when she dies, she shall send a messenger with a silver key of her coffin to be conveyed to her lost lover; and a large sum, also, for the messenger to set forth over land and sea, and deliver him the key. The messenger faithfully performs his part, and finds the kidnapped man, finally, at the point of death, and he has the key buried in his coffin; in his cold despair, it being now too late for him to go back to his mistress. But the tokens remaining in his possession, compared with those in the coffer, shall finally turn out to be a very important link in the chain of evidence, settling the identity of Etherege as the heir of the family.

The elder brother, finding himself scorned and rejected by the lady, so that his crime is without fruit, is troubled with remorse; he becomes an ascetic in Catholicism, performs penances, lives single, and dies without an heir. He has some suspicion, however, that his brother was not murdered; and so he likewise sends out a messenger to seek for him, and, moreover, he keeps, as long as he lives, a place at his solitary table for this brother, a fire burning in the hall, and in a bed chamber prepared, down to the minutest items; and this he does during his life, and ordains in his will that the same shall be done by his heirs, as the tenure by which they hold the estate. The messenger whom he sends shall also find out the brother, but shall be corrupted by the youngest brother; so that, returning when the eldest is on his death-bed, he shall never tell him of the existence of an heir. Thus, in default of other apparent heirs, the youngest brother and his posterity shall inherit the estate and represent the name. It shall be his descendant whom Etherege finds in possession. Now, somehow or other, in some preceding generation, it has leaked out that there may be an elder heir in existence, and this shall not only prevent the possessors from feeling easy in their estate, but shall also be a great barrier to their obtaining a certain ancient title which they seek to call out of abeyance. His posterity, therefore, at various times, shall send out messengers to find out what really became of the lost lover; and the traditions, or records, handed down shall have taught them many of the preceding facts; so that they shall often hunt pretty near the right spot.

Now the Doctor and the old Palmer—who are they? They shall be descendants of a younger son of the youngest brother, who was one of the messengers despatched to find out traces of the lost lover, and who settled in America, and had posterity. They find out some particulars of this story in their family papers; but, by this time, the posterity of the lost lover has disappeared, and only turns up again in this little boy in the almshouse, whom the Palmer discovers, and puts into the hands of the Doctor, while he himself goes to England. The Doctor need not be his brother, but only a dear friend. Some tokens and reminiscences shall the little boy have, which indicate him as the heir; and it shall be the Palmer's purpose to do right by re-instating him in the estate and title. The Palmer's mighty projects having come to nothing, he avails himself of his hereditary claims, to obtain a place in the Hospital.

Still there is something wanting to make an action for the story. When Etherege appears, he should set some old business in motion, that had been suspended ever since he was here before. What can that be?—how can it appear as if dead men's business, that had been buried with them, came to life again, and had to be finished now? Truly this is hard;—here's the rub; and yet without it, the story is meagre and barren.

This old man—what could he possibly be? The inheritor of some peculiarity that has been known heretofore in the history of the family, and the possession of which betrays itself in some of his habits, or in his person. What? I can't make it out. Some physical peculiarity?—'twon't do. Some mental or moral peculiarity? How? The art of making gold? A peculiar kind of poison? An acquaintance with wizard-lore? Nothing of this. He is an eater of human flesh—a vampire— a ghoul. He finds it necessary to eat a young child, every year, in order to keep himself alive. He shall have some famous jewel, known for ages in the family annals—pah! He shall have undertaken some investigation, which many members of his family have been deluded into undertaking heretofore, and the nature of which is, to change their natures disastrously—'twon't do. He shall have been to the Cave of Trophonious. He shall have been to Hell—and I wish the Devil had kept him there. He shall have inherited the Great Carbuncle, and shall be forbidden to show it to any mortal. 'Twon't do. On account of some supposed hidden power of his, the owner of the estate shall seek his aid. What, what, what! How, how, how! When the heir was kidnapped to America, he carried this thing with him, which was the grand peculiarity of the family; and ever since there have been traditions about it, and a general secret inquest to find what has become of it. But what is it! Ah, ah! He knows in what part of the castle something lies hidden; it shall be a rumour of a great treasure, a treasure of gold—but on discovery, it shall prove to be only Evelyn's coffin, full of the golden hair into which she has been entirely changed. The story must not be founded at all on remorse or secret guilt—

all that I've worn out. Alas me! Some strange sort of a
dreamer this old man might well be, who has brought down
into this age some folly that belonged characteristically to
that one—alchemy?—'twon't do. Some one of the Marquis
of Worcester's century of inventions? Hardly; but I wish I
knew what they were. The thing, though adorned with deceitful splendour, shall be rather a curse than a blessing. A
mystic of some kind. If I could but develope this rightly, it
would be a good thing. A man aiming, the wrong way, at
some great good for his race. The first emigrant might have
had the same tendency, and suffered for it. A panacea for all
ills. A friend of Swedenborg? A man with Medea's receipt?
There is a latent something lying hereabouts, which, could
I grip it, 'twould be the making of the story. A sort of apostle
—a devoted, good man, but throwing himself away through
some grand mistake! The example of the emigrant was too
much for him. So there shall be something strange and unworldly in the conduct of all who come to the knowledge of
this man—they shall martyr themselves and their affections,
give up the world, behave as if they were mad; though it
shall really be the highest virtue and wisdom. I don't see my
way yet, nor anything like it. But if I could get rid of any
great crime on the part of the family, it would be better.
Here, then, is a meek, patient, unpretending, wise old man,
who developes peculiarities which draw the attention of profound observers upon him; though others see little that is
remarkable in him. This is a better aspect than what I at first
thought of. Follow out this clue stubbornly, stubbornly.

Now this old man; the world has stormed and raged round
him through life; and he has never had any peace until he
finds himself in this ancient seclusion;—what gives it to him
here?—why has he never had it before? He shall have within
his knowledge the circumstances that show Etherege's identity as the heir; but he shall have a great reluctance to bring

them forward. A religious person, who shall have inherited from this ancestor the power of working miracles, accompanied with gifts that involve great pains and responsibilities. What? It seems as if there were something almost within my grasp—not quite. He shall have come into possession of some terrible secret; as where the plague is hidden, that ravaged England when the ancestor departed, and which is liable to be let loose upon the world again, unless he conducts matters with the highest and severest caution. A plain, quiet old man, and yet with some mighty importance and availability attaching to him. How? It must be something independent of the estate and title, which, in connection with it, shall seem morally incidental and trifling; and he must be the moral representative of the first emigrant—the planter of the Bloody Footstep. O, cracky! His foot shall be bloody yet; a token which many of the family have had to share, since then. In the end, it shall be not Etherege, but this simple old man who is the rightful heir; and he shall have been all along aware of it, but shall have quietly determined not to assert or to accept his rights. So this old man shall be the real hero of the story, and the reader shall have been prepared for him from the first; and his dignity and heroism shall be wrought out of peaceful elements, and shall take poverty and contempt for its royal robes. Contrast him with the English clergyman; with the young American politician, with all sorts of self-seekers. He shall at first, in the reader's expectation, be a wild apostle of confusion; so that it shall be a surprise to find him under this peaceful guise; and yet it shall be seen that the two characters are consistent. Shall he be a Quaker—I don't know; if so, not a modern Quaker, but a representative in good earnest of George Fox. There shall be some faith which this man has inherited, and kept all along, through ages. He might, with some embroidery of fancy, be the possessor of the Golden Rule. 'Twon't do. But for some reason, connected

with the traditions of their ancestor, and their own peculiarities of character, all this line of the race shall have been
persecuted among men; and yet innocent, peaceful, beneficent. A martyr in spirit, and often in external circumstances.
Some dissenter and protestant, it must be, from every faith.
He shall be strangely provocative of disputes among individuals, and quarrels among nations, and yet so peaceful in
himself. After his death, they shall find his foot bloody.
What shall it be that has made him and his ancestors anathema for so many ages? Why don't you have oysters? Don't
know; can't tell. Love and interest shall gather about him, as
about his ancestors, as well as bitter enmity and contempt.
Such shall have been his fate through life. Why? On account
of something in his character, and some peculiar tenet which
he lives up to and exemplifies in his dealings with men. This
is the right sow; but I cannot catch him either by ear or tail.
His ancestor shall have left a work in manuscript behind him,
which he, studying continually and making it the rule of his
life, it has made him impracticable for all worldly purposes.
Perhaps, in all things but one, he shall be saintlike; in one
thing mad. If I can but get hold of the principal spring of
this character, all will go on well—if not, not. Still I shall
keep hold of this slippery idea, stubbornly, stubbornly, and
grasp again, and yet again, and seize it wholly at last.

Now, again, this old man—what one habit, or peculiarity,
can he have, not ugly nor monstrous, which can account for
his being lonely, an outcast, a vagrant in the world? This is
hard. Some unvaried rule of life, not yielding to circumstances, he shall have adopted, which always brings him into
trouble. 'Twon't do. It must be something capable of picturesque representation. An inveterate propensity to do what?
What may this man have been in his previous years?—beginning life as a clergyman, he loses his place by dint of this
hereditary peculiarity; then becomes a teacher; then—this

won't do. What purpose to fulfil shall he have wandered about the world?—the purpose of setting right an ancient wrong?—How? Explain—particularize. He might, and perhaps ought, to be a species of Yankee character. How? A philanthropist?—done with. I suppose I shall have to write him into the story before I can make out what he is to be. Well. He must be very un-English;—a spiritual sort of little devil, most hateful and despicable to their way of thinking and feeling. Yet his character must be capable of being delineated in richly picturesque colours. The original emigrant shall have been expelled in disgrace from his family, under the idea that he has done some base and treacherous wrong, and with this stigma he went abroad, and lived in obscurity and shame; the shame clung to his race; and after so many years, it shall be made clear that he was a noble being—the moral being, that the age in which a man lives is capable of great mistakes as to his moral merit. How can this have been? A murderer? A coward? It must be the tradition of some particular crime. This poor creature must exemplify the same sort of thing. I don't in the least see my way. It shall be vaguely understood that the first emigrant was expelled from his family, and lost his love, for some disgraceful cause; the crime not being specified. The county history, and all other records, shall tell the same uncircumstantial tale;—as if it were a shame too great to tell of. For instance, that he was the man in the masque who beheaded Charles I. 'Twon't do. Yet think of it again. The family is Catholic and royalist; this young man is extruded from them because he is a Protestant, and has refused to take up arms in the cause of the King. They, for certain reasons, believe that under a changed name he has fought for the Parliament, and went so far as to behead the King. There may be plausible reasons for this; circumstantial evidence; and as he disappears utterly after the Restoration, these shall remain unrefuted ever since.

This would account better for his quarrel with his family than the love-affair—which, however, shall be incidental. Etherege shall imagine himself the descendant of this person, but shall really not be so, but that of a younger brother. Crown and Anchor Tavern. A fierce and bloody rebel shall have been the lost heir's character; all harsh roundhead traits shall seem to have been collected into his character. Perhaps the family may have had a kind of pride mixed with shame in his character. Then so much the more the contrast of this mild, peaceful enthusiast whom we find in the old man; who possibly may be the founder of a religious sect, and himself his only disciple. That'll not do. Nothing seems to do. But the emigrant must be made out to have been, in that chaos of strange opinions, a man of peace, and a follower and friend of George Fox. Something may possibly come out of this. The knightly imagination of the family shall have conceived all that fierce turmoil for him.

Possibly some good effect may be wrought out of this—the family tradition of the dark and fierce Puritan—with his own hand a king killer, going into the darkness with a track of blood behind him, whereby he is traced adown the centuries, with all sorts of terrible myths gathering about his memory, because there is something in his nature to which they have a real relation—between this grim figure and the mild and gentle reality, which shall be exemplified in the old pensioner, and gradually revealed as his own original and true character. This bloody footstep—yes; it must leave its impression all down from that time. Perhaps it may be somewhat thus in the tradition—he trod in the king's blood, and ever afterwards he has left a bloody track. He comes back to the paternal mansion, and they eject him; his foot leaving its bloody track on the threshold. It is seen in the crowded streets of towns, and in fields, and in churches, as if he had sat there. The Doctor's story may really be made out of this; and very effectively. The track, too, must somehow or other be seen thro' the Romance, yet not obtrusively—yet so as to diffuse a dim awe through it; and, late in the Romance, the real mark shall be seen on the threshold, after we have traced through the old streets and fields of England, and on the forest leaves of America. Finally, it turns out to be the track, not of guilt, but of persecution. The original emigrant must have been the model of a Christian, and therefore misunderstood by everybody—therefore maligned—therefore bitterly hated always. Even if imperfectly developed, I think this idea had better be retained. Let the old Doctor speak of his brother (if it must necessarily be his brother, or at all related to him) as the highest and noblest of men; the boy, with this idea of him in his mind, shall expect to see somebody in high station, and of noble aspect;—the same mistake which the Jews made about the Savior. Then, at the Hospital, introduce this humble, lowly, unpretending man, much battered with the rebuffs he has received in this world, but still loving, hoping, working, for his fellow men. An enthusist but now tamed, yet sweet to the last. The original shall have been a founder of a sect of one, himself his only disciple, teaching himself and growing better all his life. On the old pensioner's death-bed, he shall tell the real truth of his ancestor's history to Etherege. He was on the scaffold to support and comfort the dying monarch, to die for him if possible; everywhere, he was sacrificing himself. The Doctor shall not be the brother of this man, but a friend. I must hit still upon some picturesque peculiarity to distinguish this man, and embody and symbolize his creed; that done, I think I should have hold of the right clew. His foot must be discovered, on his death-bed, if not sooner—sooner, I think, because his connection with the old tradition will make such a strange contrast with the gentleness of his character; so that there may be suspicions and dim horrors about the old man, in the hospital, in the mind of the Warden, and even reaching to the mind of Etherege; as if he had been guilty of some horrid crime. All this he shall endure till his dying moments. Glimpses, glimpses. Not yet "Eureka"; but it will be so. The old man is conscious of being the heir, but chooses quietly, and without eclat, to give up his claim. He knows too of the flaw in Etherege's title.

Begin very much as before, —the old Doctor amid his cobwebs; the little girl and boy. The old pensioner shall have rescued this boy from the alm's house, and put him under the Doctor's care, with funds for his education; he having taken an interest in his father, and perhaps knowing him to be a descendant of his own kindred, one of the hostile brothers who disinherited him. The Doctor speaks in exalted terms, but with a kind of mystery, of his friend. He tells a story of the Bloody Footstep, in which all the fearful traditions of the family are embodied, but with a mystic intimation of error in these—which, however, must not be understood till long afterwards. The boy—being imaginative—takes it into his head that he is an heir of a proud old English family, and resolves, at some future day, to go in quest of his birth-place and ancestry. The visit of the English lawyer confirms his belief, and heightens his idea of the glories to which he is heir. In England, too, the family have a belief that he is the heir. The Doctor dies, as before, and a long interval elapses.

He appears now in England; he has already been in London, and an agent of the present possessor of the estate has warned his master of his presence; and he, being an unprincipled, long-Italianized Englishman resolves upon his murder; and hence the attack upon him, where he is only saved by accident. He is taken up by the old pensioner, as before, who must be drawn with traits of a deep, sad, tenderness, which makes a profound impression on Etherege. It shall be shown, however, that he is an object of vague suspicion and dislike among his associates in the Hospital, and even the Warden shall not have escaped this influence. It spreads, in some degree, over Etherege, in spite of his gratitude to the old man. The Warden takes him into his house, as already narrated; makes a grand dinner for him, at which he meets the holder of the estate. Everything, all this while, should concur to foster Etherege's belief that he is the heir of the estate and title, and he shall come to the conclusion that the old pensioner knows this, and can produce the proofs of it, if he likes. The daughter of the pensioner must be brought forward now, recognized by Etherege; she is the one person who appreciates, admires, and loves her father, knows of his rights, and agrees with him in not wishing to assert them. Etherege begins to fall in love with her; but there is a certain reserve and dignity about her which keeps him at a distance, though still he sometimes fancies she loves him.

From his agent, the holder of the estate has received intelligence which makes him think that the true heir of the estate may be the old pensioner; at all events, he is sure that the heirdom lies between him and Etherege, and he is resolved to get rid of them both;—this time by poison. He asks Etherege to visit him; then, for the first time, he sees the Bloody Footstep, the old pensioner being in his company at the time. The proprietor's character must be so carefully Italianized throughout, and Popishified, that it shall seem an appropriate thing for such a man to do. By the aid of the pensioner's daughter, this plot may be discovered; and in the shame of detection, the It-Englishman takes the poison which he intended for the others, and dies. A daughter of the Italian must be introduced, as a friend of the pensioner's daughter;— possibly a nun-like personage.

There must have been something in the way in which the lost heir was ejected from his family, that shall make his descendant resolve never again to have anything to do with the estate. Some wrong done to his ancestor; or perhaps some thing in the way in which the family gained possession of this patrimony, by wrong, by murder, by obtaining the execution of a rival and getting his estate granted to them during the civil wars. What shall be his distinguishing trait;—merely a conscience, and the inveterate habit of acting on it. This shall be so managed as to make all his peculiarity; and it would be the bitterest satire (if well done) that ever was written. Perhaps the moral may be, that there is nothing so disorganizing—so certain to overthrow everything earthly, if it can only have its own way, as conscience. The old man need not be represented as without error, or moral defect; only he shall have tried to sacrifice everything to conscience. In his early time, he was a subverter of evil by eloquence, by effort of all kinds; as his power declined, he gave up the struggle and retired to this seclusion. Let the weakness of too much conscience be fairly brought out;—the indecision, the incapacity of action that must result from it; the inability for anything but suffering. He shall try to persuade Etherege, I think, to go away from the Hospital.

In connection and contrast with the weakness, it must be contrived to show that strength in the old man which would enable him to go through martyrdom. The holder of the estate must threaten him, must invite him to the Hall, must try to get him to give up some document which he has, or knows of, and which would settle the descent of the estate and title. The old man will not do this, but threatens, or announces his determination, to do something of the very opposite tendency. Something must depend upon his agency, and his death or surrender be absolutely necessary to the purposes of the Italian. So the Italian confines the old man in one of the secret chambers of the old house, and there tries to work upon him—he and the priest. They keep him on bread and water; they mingle poison with his food; they threaten him with knife and halter, things naturally baleful to him. He bears himself quietly, composedly, simply, but cannot be wrought upon by imminent dread of death, or any other consideration; but something high, noble, courageous, sublime, must break out of all the feeblenesses which have hitherto made the reader despise him. He shall wish to die with his identity unrevealed; but circumstances beyond his controul, at his deathbed, shall disclose all; and the pauper, the humble, the meek, the sad, the suspected, shall die Lord Brathwaite in spite of himself. Perhaps this can be done; perhaps not. The old man may be in the habit of going wandering about the country, occasionally; so that his absence from the Hospital will occasion no wonderment; and Etherege may be living at the Hall, at the same time that he is concealed and confined there. There must be great jollity going on in the house; but still a strain, a taint, an odor of something dreadful shall make itself sensible to the guests. A good effect is capable of being produced, by the revelation that the humble pauper is the lord of Brathwaite and representative of this proud family.

As Etherege sat watching the old man in the garden, he could not help being struck by the scrupulous care with which he attended to the plants; it seemed to him that there was a sense of justice—of desiring to do exactly what was right in the mater, not favoring one plant more than another, and doing all he could for each. His progress, in consequence, was so slow, that in an hour while Etherege was off and on looking at him, he had scarcely done anything perceptible. Then he was so minute; and often, when he was on the point of leaving one thing to take up another, some small neglect that he saw or fancied, called him back again, to spend other minutes on the same task. He was so full of scruples. It struck Etherege that this was conscience morbid, sick, a despot in trifles, looking so closely into life that it permitted nothing to be done. The man might once have been strong and able, but by some unhealthy process of his life, he had ceased to be so now. Nor did any happy or satisfactory result appear to come from these painfully wrought efforts, he still seemed to know that he had left something undone in doing too much in another direction.— Here was a lily that had been neglected, while he paid too much attention to a rose; he had set his foot on a violet; he had grubbed up, in his haste, a little plant that he mistook for a weed, but that he now suspected was an herb of grace. Grieved by such reflections as these, he heaved a deep sigh, almost amounting to a groan, and sat down on the little stool that he carried with him in his weeding, resting his face in his hands.

Etherege deemed that he might be doing the old man a good service by interrupting his melancholy labors; so he emerged from the opposite door of the summer-house, and came along the adjoining walk with somewhat heavy foot-steps, in order that the Palmer might have warning of his approach, without any grounds to suppose that he had been watched hitherto. Accordingly, when he turned into the other alley, he found the old man sitting erect on his stool, looking composed, but still sad, as was his general custom.

"After all your wanderings and experience," said he, "I observe that you come back to the original occupation of cultivating a garden;—the innocentest of all."

"Yes; so it should seem," said the old man; "but somehow or other, I do not find peace in this."

"These plants and shrubs," returned Etherege, "seem at all events to recognize the goodness of your rule, so far as it has extended over them. See how joyfully they take the sun; how clear from all these vices that lie scattered round, in the shape of weeds. It is a lovely sight, and I could almost fancy a quiet enjoyment in the plants themselves, which they have no way of making us aware of, except by giving out a fragrance."

"Ah; how infinitely would that idea increase man's responsibility," said the old Palmer, "if, besides man and beast, we should find it necessary to believe that there is also another set of beings dependent for their happiness on our doing, or leaving anything undone, which might affect them."

"I question," said Etherege smiling, "whether their pleasurable or painful experiences can be so keen, that we need trouble our consciences much with regard to what we do, merely as it affects them. So highly cultivated a conscience as that would be a nuisance to one's self and one's fellows."

"You say a terrible thing," rejoined the old man. "Can conscience be too much alive in us; is not everything, however trifling it seems, an item in the great account, which it is of infinite importance therefore to have right? A terrible thing this is that you have said."

"That may be," said Etherege; "but it is none the less certain to me, that the efficient actors—those who mould the world—are the persons in whom something else is developed more strongly than conscience. There must be an invincible determination to effect something; it may be set to work in the right direction, but after that it must go onward, trampling down small obstacles—small considerations of right of wrong—as a great rock, thundering down a hill side, crushes a thousand sweet flowers, and ploughs deep furrows in the innocent hill-side."

As Etherege gave vent to this doctrine, which was not naturally his, but which had been the inculcation of a life hitherto devoted to politics, he was surprised to find how strongly sensible he became of the ugliness and indefensibleness of what he said. He felt as if he were speaking under the eye of omniscience, and as if every word he said were weighed, and its emptiness detected, by an unfailing intelligence. He had thought that he had volumes to say about the necessity of consenting not to do right in all matters minutely, for the sake of getting out an available and valuable right as the whole; but there was something that seemed to tie his tongue. Could it be the quiet gaze of this old man, so unpretending, so humble, so simple in aspect? He could not tell; only that he faultered, and finally left his speech in the midst.

But he was surprised to find how he had to struggle against a certain repulsion within himself to the old man. He seemed so nonsensical, interfering with everybody's right in the world; so mischievous, standing there and shutting out the possibility of action. It seemed well to trample him down; to put him out of the way—no matter how—somehow. It gave him, he thought, an inkling of the way in which this poor old man had made himself odious to his kind, by opposing himself, inevitably to what was bad in men, chiding it by his very presence, accepting nothing false. You must either love him utterly, or hate him utterly; for he could not let you alone. Etherege, being a susceptible man, felt this influence in the strongest way; for it was as if there was a battle within him, one party pulling, wrenching him towards this old man, another wrenching him away; so that, by the agony of the contest, he felt disposed to end it by taking flight, and never seeing the strange individual again. He could well enough conceive how a brutal nature, if capable of receiving his influence at all, might find it so intolerable that it must needs get rid of him by violence—by taking his blood if necessary.

All these feelings were but transitory, however; they swept across him like a wind, and then he looked again at the old man and saw only his simplicity, his unworldliness—saw little more than the worn and feeble individual, in the Hospital garb, leaning on his staff; and then turning again with a gentle sigh to weed in the garden. And then Etherege went away, in a state of disturbance for which he could not account to himself.

<See lower in the paragraph>

Meanwhile, the stately old hall had been in process of cleaning and adapting to the banquet-purposes (of the nineteenth century) which it was accustomed to subserve, in so proud a way, in the sixteenth. It was, in the first place, well swept and cleansed; the painted glass windows were cleansed from dust, and several panes, which had been unfortunately broken and filled with common glass, were filled in with insulated panes, which the Master had picked up somewhere in his antiquarian researches. They were not, to be sure, just what was wanted; a piece of a Saint, from some cathedral window, supplying what was lacking of the gorgeous purple of a mediaeval king; but the general effect was rich and good, whenever the misty English atmosphere supplied sunshine bright enough to pervade it. Tapestry, too, from antique looms, faded, but still gorgeous, was hung upon the walls. Some suits of armor, that hung beneath the festal gallery, were furbished till the old battered helmets and pierced breastplates sent a gleam like that which they had flashed across the battle fields of old. <(This comes first)> High up in the old carved roof, to be sure, the spiders of centuries still hung their flaunting webs with a profusion that old Doctor Gibbleter would have been ravished to see; but even this was to be remedied, for one day, on looking in, Etheredge found the great hall dim with floating dusk, and down through it came great floating masses of cobweb, out of which the old Doctor would have undertaken to regenerate the world; and he saw, dimly aloft, men on ladders sweeping away these accumulations of years, and breaking up the haunts and residences of hereditary spiders.

Etherege often, in the dim weather, when the prophetic intimations of rain were too strong to allow an American to walk abroad with peace of mind, was in the habit of pacing this noble hall, and watching the process of renewal and adornment; or, which suited him still better, of enjoying its great, deep solitude, when the workmen were away. Parties of visitors, curious tourists, sometimes peeped in, took a cursory glimpse at the old hall, and went away; these were the only ordinary disturbances. But, one day, a person entered, looked carelessly round the hall, as if its antiquity had no great charm to him; then he seemed to approach Etherege, who stood far and dim in the remote distance of the great room. The echoing of feet on the stone pavement of the hall had always an impressive sound; and turning his head towards the visitant, Edward stood as if there were an expectance for him in this approach. It was a middle-aged man—rather, a man towards fifty, with an alert, capable air, a man evidently with something to do in life, and not in the habit of throwing away his moments in looking at old halls; a gentlemanly man enough, too. He approached Etherege without hesitation, and, lifting his hat, addressed him in a way that made Edward wonder whether he could be an Englishman. If so, he must have known that Edward was an American, and have been trying to adapt his manners to those of a democratic freedom.

"Mr. Etherege, I believe," said he.

Etherege bowed, with the stiff caution of an Englishman; for, with American mobility, he had learned to be stiff.

"I think I have had the pleasure of knowing—at least, of meeting you—very long ago," said the gentleman. "But I see you do not recollect me."

Etherege confessed that the stranger had the advantage of him in his recollection of a previous acquaintance.

"No wonder," said the other, "for, as I have already hinted, it was many years ago."

"In my own country then, of course," said Etherege.

"In your own country certainly," said the stranger, "and when it would have required a penetrating eye to see the distinguished Mr. Etherege, the representative of American democracy abroad, in the little, pale-faced intelligent boy, dwelling with an old humorist in the corner of a grave-yard."

At these words, Etherege sent back his recollections, and though doubtfully, began to be aware that this must needs be the young Englishman who had come to his guardian on such a singular errand to search an old grave. It must be he; for it could be nobody else; and, in truth, he had a sense of his identity—which, however, did not express itself by anything that he could confidently remember in his look, manner, or voice; yet, if anything, it was most in the voice. But the image which on searching he found in his mind of a fresh colored young Englishman, with light hair and a frank pleasant face, was terribly realized for the worse in this somewhat heavy figure, and coarser face, and heavier eye. In fact, there is a terrible difference between the mature Englishman and the young man, who is not yet quite out of his blossom. His hair, too, was getting speckled and spoiled with gray; and, in short, there were evident marks of his having worked, and succeeded, and failed, and eaten and drunk, and being made largely of beef, ale, port and sherry, and all the solidities of English life.

"I remember you now," said Etherege, extending his hand frankly; and yet Hammond took it in so cold a way that he was immediately sorry that he had done it, and called up an extra portion of reserve to freeze the rest of the interview. He continued, coolly enough, "I remember you, and something of your American errand—which, indeed, has frequently been in my mind since. I hope you found the results of your voyage, in the way of discovery, sufficiently successful to justify so much trouble."

"You will remember," said Hammond, "that the grave proved quite unproductive. Yes, you will not have forgotten it; for I well recollect how eagerly you listened, with that queer little girl, to my talk with the old governor, and how disappointed you seemed, when you found that the grave was not to be opened. And yet, it is very odd. I failed in that mission; and yet there are circumstances that have led me to think that I ought to have succeeded better—that some other person has really succeeded better."

Etherege was silent; but he remembered the strange old silver key, and how he had kept it secret, and the doubts that had troubled his mind, then and long afterwards, whether he ought not to have found means to convey it to the stranger, and ask whether that was what he sought. And, now, here was that same doubt and question coming up again; and he found himself quite as little able to solve it as he had been twenty years ago. Indeed, with the views that had come up since, it behoved him to be cautious, until he knew both the man and the circumstances.

"You are probably aware," continued Hammond, "(for I understand you have been some time in his neighborhood) that there is a pretended claim, a contesting claim, to the present possession of the estate of Brathwaite and a long dormant title. Possibly—who knows—you yourself might have a claim to one or the other. Would not that be a singular coincidence? Have you ever had the curiosity to investigate your parentage with a view to this point?"

"The title," replied Etherege, "ought not to be a very strong consideration with an American. One of us would be ashamed, I verily believe, to assume any distinction except such as may be supposed to indicate personal, not hereditary merit. We have in some measure, I think, lost the feeling of the past, and even of the future, as regards our own lines of descent; and even as to wealth, it seems to me that the idea of heaping up a pile of gold, or accumulating a broad estate for our children and remoter descendants, is dying out. We wish to enjoy the fulness of our success in life ourselves, and leave to those who descend from us the task of providing for themselves. This tendency is seen in our lavish expenditure, and the whole arrangement of our lives; and it is slowly—yet not very slowly, either—effecting a change in the whole economy of American life."

"Still," rejoined Mr. Hammond, with a smile that Etherege fancied was dark and subtile—"still, I should imagine that even an American might recall so much of hereditary prejudice as to be sensible of some earthly advantages in the possession of an ancient title and hereditary estate like this. Personal distinction may suit you better—to be an Ambassador by your own talent; to have a future for yourself, involving the possibility of ranking (though it were only for four years) among the acknowledged sovereigns of the earth;—this is very good. But if the silver key would open the shut up secret, to-day, it might be possible that you would relinquish these advantages."

Before Etherege could reply (and, indeed, there seemed to be an allusion at the close of Hammond's speech, which, whether intended or not, he knew not how to reply to) a young lady entered the hall, whom he was at no loss, though the colored light of a painted window fell upon her, translating out of the common daylight, to recognize as the daughter of the pensioner. She seemed to have come, to give her fanciful superintendence to some of the decorations of the hall; such as required woman's taste, rather than the sturdy English judgment and antiquarian knowledge of the Warden. Slowly following after her, came the pensioner himself, leaning on his staff and looking up at the old roof and around him, with a benign composure, and himself a fitting figure by his antique and venerable appearance to walk in that old hall.

"Ah," said Hammond, to Etherege's surprise, "here is an acquaintance, two acquaintances of mine."

He moved along the hall to accost them; and as he appeared to expect that Etherege would still keep him company, and as the latter had no reason for not doing so, they both advanced to the pensioner who was now leaning on the young woman's arm. The incident, too, was not unacceptable to the American, as promising to bring him into a more available relation with her—whom he half fancied to be his old American acquaintance—than he had yet succeeded in obtaining.

"Well, my old friend," said Hammond, after bowing with a certain measured respect to the young woman, "how wears life with you? Rather, perhaps, it does not wear at all; you being so well suited to the life around you, you grow by it like a lichen on a wall. I could fancy, now, that you have walked here for three hundred years, and remember when King James of blessed memory was entertained in this hall, and could martial out all the ceremonies, just as they were then."

"An old man," said the pensioner, quietly, "grows dreamy as he waxes away; and I, too, am sometimes at a loss to know whether I am living in the past or the present, or whereabouts in time I am—or whether there is any time at all. But I should think it hardly worth while to call up one of my shifting dreams more than another."

"I confess," said Etherege, "I shall find it impossible to call up this scene, any of these scenes hereafter, without the venerable figure of this, whom I may truly call my benefactor, among them. I fancy him among them from their foundation—young then, but keeping just the equal step with their age and decay—and still doing good and hospitable deeds to those who need them."

The old man seemed not to like to hear these remarks and expressions of gratitude from Hammond and the American; at any rate, he moved away with his slow and light motion of infirmity, but then came uneasily back; displaying a certain quiet restlessness, which Etherege was sympathetic enough to perceive. Not so the sturdier, more heavily moulded Englishman, who continued to direct the conversation upon the pensioner, or at least to make him a part of it, thereby bringing out more of his strange characteristics. In truth, it is not quite easy for an Englishman to know how to adapt himself to the fine feelings of those below him in point of station, whatever gentlemanly deference he may have for his equals or superiors.

"I should like, now, father Pearson," said he, "to know how many steps you may have taken in life, before your path lay into this hall, and whence your course started."

"Do not let him speak thus to this old man," said the young woman, in a low, earnest tone to Etherege. He was surprised and startled; it seemed like a voice that had spoken to his boyhood.

This wretched old pensioner keeps recurring to me, insisting that I have not sufficiently provided for him, nor given him motive enough—or any indeed. At present, therefore, the stubborn old devil will not move. Take him at his death-hour, and work backward from that. He has been smitten with death in the old manor-house, surrounded by Etherege, Elsie, the Warden, the Italian Englishman, and other personages of the drama. The scene takes place in the stately hall of the mansion, surrounded by antique associations of armor, furniture, carvings &c. The old man, as his last moment draws on, becomes invested with a strange aspect and port of dignity and majesty. At the same time, the development of the plot is taking place. Up to this hour, the probabilities have seemed to strengthen that Etherege is the heir of the estate and name; but, at the very last, a slight circumstance shall be counterchanged, which shall at once make it evident that the old pensioner is the true heir; and the spirit of his ancestors shall display itself. Going back a step further, it shall appear that he has been poisoned, unquestionably by the Italo-Englishman, who shall have found out that the old man and Etherege, one or other of them, is the heir. There may be likewise a probability, though not a certainty, that the old man was aware of his own rights, but for some reason, never meant to assert them. I want a character to put him into; his bloody foot? no. He must have been persecuted thro' life,—how and why? What early dream might he have had, in which could be condensed all the love, sacrifice, delicate conscience, of his nature? He might have had this estate and title in early life; but then he had given it up through love of a young maiden, who would have been made unhappy by it. Nonsense! No! The old man is first prophetically seen in the old doctor's hints about him; then he appears in England at Etherege's bedside, taking gentlest care of him, and in some way connected with the young woman. Etherege becomes greatly interested in him, observing, questioning, feeling an influence from him; the character needs an exponent—something to represent and symbolize it. He was born in America, and had the spirit of an apostle, and founder of a sect; that's nothing. It must all be incidental to some main incident. Some behest, delivered by his ancestor two hundred years ago, and transmitted from father to son, he shall have kept in his breast, and means to let it die with him; as he has no child. That won't do; it is paltry, and not new. No; there must be something in this old man, that shall put to shame hereditary distinctions, and make the reader feel that he must have stooped from a position of higher dignity, had he taken up the rank he had inherited. It is not possible to work this out; the idea does not take to itself representative form. He may be a sort of reformer, whose principles are entirely against hereditary distinction. The object of the book, to find the treasure-chest, which the silver key, found in the grave-yard by Etherege, will suit. This at last turns out to be the coffin of a young lady, which being opened, it proves to be filled with golden locks of her hair. But this quest must be merely incidental. Under the hair, or upon it, is a roll of obliterated writing. This nonsense must be kept subordinate, however. 'Twon't do. Cranbo. Mary Mumpson. Cunkey. Miss Blagden. Miss Ingersoll. M\u02b3 Roberts.—Marshall Rynders. President Buchanan of dis United States.

He is partially crazed; yet in a benevolent way, and so as to craze all that associate with him; having a great spiritual fever queerly done up with his weakness and folly. I can't get hold of it. I will. Let him have sought all his life to get back to America in vain; at last, he shall have found accidentally, that he has the qualification requisite to make him a pensioner, and so he comes to the Hospital. There shall be one treasure, which he inherited and has kept; one only thing; being a silver key, similar to that which Etherege found, yet, being compared, there proves to be a difference in the rounds. This key is for the double lock of one treasure chest. I must and will keep to his holy character, but he shall have exercised it in a humble way, at death-beds, in preachings by the wayside, in paltry martyrdoms. His whole life shall have been petty in its means, noble, sublime in its spirit. What shall he have got hold of that changes him, marks him out; a power of working a certain miracle; a talisman? A certain property shall attend him wherever he goes; a bloody footstep. Pshaw! He shall have the fatality of causing death, bloodshed, wherever he goes; and this shall symbolize the strife which benevolence inevitably provokes, because it disturbs everything around it. Make this out. 'Twon't do. Oh, Heavens! Some secret mischief he must inevitably do, immense, of bloody consequences, yet consistent with his mild and beautiful nature. A wanderer he must have been, for many years, until he moors in this quiet haven; and what the object of his wandering? Heaven knows. Whatever it be, his innate delicacy of conscience must be combined with the outward representation of his character. A pedler; a pauper; an American, rambling about in quest of his country;—think of this, and see whether it cannot be modified into what I want. He is left destitute in England, whither he has come on some wild-goose mission; he was long ago, or has now become, partially insane; he wanders about a pauper, with a dreamy idea of getting back to his own country. Possibly, it may be one of the objects of his life to find something that is already in Etherege's possession; the silver key, for instance. Can nothing be done with this? He left America for England very long ago—half a century ago—it might be; having for his object something of the same kind that Etherege has,— to find out his family. He had been married before he went; and the young girl is his granddaughter, whom the old doctor has taken charge of from a tender remembrance of early friendship with the grandsire. He must be conscious, I think, that he is the true heir to the title and estate; only there lacks a clew, a link, a something to prove that his ancestor was the man with the bloody footstep; and this clue he spends his life in seeking, till he gets to be insane, as is natural. Although he cannot get the proofs he wants, he gets enough to entitle him to shelter in the Hospital; so there he enters, and spends the remainder of his life in contemplating the hereditary glories which ought to be his own. At last, Ethrerege comes over, unconsciously bringing with him the very link that the pauper had sought for all his life; and when the latter is dying, it is discovered; so that at his last moment it is seen that this is the true nobleman. There is more common sense in this than in the other idea; and there should be a gentle beauty wrought into the character too.

<(The family name had been changed in America)>

Take the old man from his earliest original;—His ancestor was the second son of the old family, and was thrust out of the paternal mansion; there are conflicting testimonies wherefor. One account says that he was a wild and bloody religionist, and with his own hand beheaded the King, and got the Bloody Footstep by treading in a pool of his blood on the scaffold. Another account bears, that he was a Quaker, or somebody on the George Fox principle; and that his bloody footstep came from his being violently and wounded thrust out from his paternal home. Others say, it was of much earlier time. Well; this race turns up in America, with some vague traditions among themselves of their descent; they are not Quakers; at least, have ceased to be so long before the epoch of the story; but still something of the spirit of their peaceful ancestor has remained in them throughout this length of time. They keep up their traditions. At length, there is born an imaginative man, who marries early in life, and loses his wife; his affections being thus baulked, he leaves his son under the charge of a friend (the Doctor) and goes to England to enter upon a quest into his lineage. He becomes slightly insane; and getting more and more engaged in this delusive enterprise, he remains abroad all the rest of his life, in poverty, in solitude; meanwhile, his son has grown up, married, and left a daughter, whom the Doctor has taken charge of. On the Doctor's death, he divides his property between the girl and Etherege; and the girl, as soon as she is at her own disposal, comes abroad in quest of her grandfather, to whom the Doctor's papers have given her a clew.

The Doctor, an old humorous bachelor, had likewise adopted another child; a boy, who struck his fancy in an alm's house, whither he had come, attended by an old woman. He does this partly because the name is that of the family to which his friend really belonged. This boy is really the descendant of the third son of the old family; but he imagines himself to be the descendant of the old Bloody Footstep man, in respect to whom he adopts the wicked version of the story. He also has inherited traditions of noble descent, together with certain documents, which carry proofs of his birth far upward to the original emigrant; who really came over in quest of his lost brother, because he is penitent for his treatment of him; or because, from some family arrangement, it was necessary to find him. But he met with impediments (such as being carried away by the Indians &c) and ultimately settled in Virginia, whence the family emigrated to New England. Before he goes to England (the present representative, I mean) he gets his pedigree authenticated, showing, through all vicissitudes, that he is descended from the second brother. This he holds in his possession, and is ready to display it on occasion.

Meanwhile, the family in England is represented by a descendant of the youngest brother. There have been traditions of other heirs; and messengers, at various times, have been sent over to America in quest of them, and in hope to find that there were none now existing. Also, by the penitence of the family, there is an old custom of keeping a place at the family board, and a bed-chamber ready.

The old man?—yes! I cannot consent to such a degradation of his character as is implied in his seeking the estate & title. He must all along have been conscious that it was his right; but a peculiar philosophy has taught him that he must not take it. No; there must be some specific cause; a curse, for instance, imposed upon his race if they ever assert their right. Why? Something that should have made his name and station hateful to him—that might be—but how might that hatefulness be continued to his descendants; so that they should prefer poverty and obscurity to name and high position? True. This pensioner is the first one, for two centuries, who has known of his descent; the knowledge of it came to him through the Doctor's researches, and he went to England to investigate it—with a desire to know his relatives and hereditary seat, but not to claim them. The Doctor must have a great agency in these doings, both of the Pensioner and Etherege, making tissues of cobweb out of men's life-threads; he must have the air, in the Romance, of a sort of magician, without being called so; and even after his death, his influence must still be felt. Hold on to this. A dark, subtle manager, for the love of managing, like a spider sitting in the centre of his web, which stretches far to east and west. Who is he, then?—What interest had he in this? Some speculative and philosophical interest, if any; and he dies before it is gratified. I doubt whether 'twill do, but his enterprises go on after his death, and produce strange effects without him to controul them. He shall have stretched out his hand to England, and be operating there, making people his puppets who little think they are so. He must have travelled over England in his youth, and there have fallen in love, and been jilted by a lady of this family;— hence his spite against the family, and his determination to ruin it. He shall have sought out with all his might, an heir, and educated Etherege for that purpose. There may be a germ in this—I don't know. Perhaps the Doctor himself might be an English misanthrope, who had a spite against this family. He must be somebody who knows all about the English part of the family; and he has some plot against them in full concoction, calculated to take effect years hence; when he suddenly dies (perhaps of the poison of his great spider) and leaves his plot to operate as it may, by itself. Make his character very weird indeed, and envelope it in dread and mystery, with as much of the grotesque as can be wrought into it. He may himself be a member of the family—possibly their heir. He shall have meant Etherege as his tool, certainly; but in the end, he shall prove to have no ancestry, an American son of nobody, evolving the moral that we are to give up all those prejudices of birth and blood which have been so powerful in past ages; at any rate, there shall be but vague reason to believe that Etherege is of that descent, and it shall be a rebuke to him for giving up the noble principle that a man ought to depend on his own individuality, instead of deriving anything from his ancestors. The pauper must be the true heir. Then why should not the Doctor have made him out to be so? True. He shall have made a mistake, owing to his lack of acquaintance with the traditions of this pauper, with whom they shall have been a family secret; but his interest and imagination shall have been awakened by what the Doctor said; so that he shall have gone to England to investigate the matter. It is a snarled skein, truly; but I half fancy there is a way to unravel the threads, by dint of breaking one or two.

The lady whom the Doctor loved shall have died; the Doctor shall have treasured up a single lock of golden hair, which, Etherege, from some fanciful reason or other brings with him to England. On opening a coffin with the silver key, it shall prove to be quite full of these golden locks, with the same peculiarity as this. The owner of the estate shall have betrayed the Doctor, and won this lady's love from him; so he, brooding along, shall have resolved to avenge himself in this way. The coffin full of golden locks shall be a symbol that there was nothing in this woman, nothing of her, but her golden hair and other external beauty; and that a wise man threw himself away for that emptiness. He may himself (the Doctor) have been the proprietor of the estate. How, why, what sense? He shall have been at deadly enmity with the holder of it, and being a wicked man, and unscrupulous, shall have contemplated these means of avenging himself. Long after his death, Etherege shall have found the papers which seem to him to prove his claim. The great spider shall be an emblem of the Doctor himself; it shall be his craft and wickedness coming into this shape outside of him; and his demon; and I think a great deal may be made out of it. This shall be his venon, which shall have been gathering and swelling for thirty years; for, in all that time, those who knew the spider and the Doctor earlier shall have seen that the one was growing more swollen with spite and the other with venom. It must be an unsuccessful and ill-treated passion that first caused this; he having loved the woman whom Brathwaite won from him and married. He shall have known the family tradition that there was an heir of the estate and title extant in America, and shall set out with the purpose of finding him. Then, when he cannot find out this heir, he bethinks himself that it will be yet sweeter revenge to substitute some nameless child for their long descended heir, and looking about (being an unscrupulous man) he finds this boy, three or four years old, in the alms-house, without parents, of untraceable origin. Him he takes, educates, and the love that there is in him grows to this child and expends itself all on him. Now, as for the girl? Shall she also be a filia nullius?—or his own daughter?—or a grand daughter of the pensioner? We must have her; and she must have a right in the book. Shall she be a niece of his? Well; she need not be very rigidly accounted for, but may have been consigned to his care, as the last remnant of his own family, the child of a younger sister. So he shall have taken her—perhaps not loving her as his wayward nature does the boy, whom he will feel as if he had made with his own art and skill—but still tolerating her in his house. Now the pauper. He may have been, originally, a New England minister, or a religionist of some sort, who had an early dream of founding a sect of his own, deeming himself to have had a revelation. Or, being of a religious nature, he may have held a tradition in his early days, of a person in his family, long ago, who was of a most pious nature; his life and footsteps he shall have sought out, and this search shall lead him in the track of the Bloody Footstep;—following which, he shall be led across the sea, and to the old mansion-house. There shall be a peculiar odour of sanctity for him in the spot where this saint and martyr was born and bred, and so he shall haunt around it, knowing of his claims, but entirely above asserting them—at least, aside from them. All along, he shall have in his possession the one thing that can prove his descent. What can that be? Some traditionary secret, that explains a mystery which has been mysterious for two centuries. The unlocking of some door that had been locked for centuries. Some coffer? Could it not be contrived to have some antique, highly ornamented coffer, treasured up in the old house, under the idea that it contained something of fatal importance to the family? It shall have two keys; one, the pensioner shall have, transmitted from his ancestors; the other shall be the one that Etherege found by the grave. On opening the coffer it shall prove to be full of golden hair; for it was the coffin of a beautiful lady, who, by that strange process, has turned all to that feature by which she lives in the family legend. The New England government shall have persecuted the first emigrant, as being a non-conformist to their creed; possibly, they may have hanged him, though I hardly think so. Yet, if it will produce any good effect, hanged he shall be. What can he have had to do with the key of the lady's coffin? She must have been murdered, then? It shall have been supposed in the family that she disappeared with him; as she disappeared about the same juncture. Well; this mystery might be left to conjecture, without being definitely solved. It shall explain why the lady never appeared again, certainly. The lady had been beloved by two brothers, and had loved the bloody-footstep man; the other one had murdered her, and deposited her in this antique coffer, which was deposited in a secret chamber. At any rate, somehow or other she shall be reposited in an antique coffer, or it may be, in an old stone coffin;—I think, the former, because of the silver key. The lady being murdered, the elder brother, in horror, shall flee. No; perhaps the brother shall mean to murder him, and shall thrust him out of the mansion with that purpose—he, and the younger brother,— and shall leave him for dead, but he shall be conveyed away. The place where his body shall be thrown, shall be the very one where Etherege was shot down, on his first arrival; and he shall afterwards dreamily recognize it by a description in the Doctor's story. There must be discrepant traditions about all these things; the pensioner having one side of the matter; and the Doctor, as derived from the family in England, the other. Perhaps it is after the death of the lady that he turns religionist, gives up his rank, disappears from England, taking the key of the coffer with him, and leaving the dead body reposited there. He may have killed the lady out of jealousy, and gone off, taking their child, a boy, with him, and have spent the rest of his life in penitence and humble strivings for heaven; dying by the executioner in New England, not for his crime, but for his religion. The erring tradition in his family shall have turned aside the truth of his bloody footstep, which shall have been dyed in the blood of his wife. They shall think that he took his wife with him. Here is reason enough for his deserting his home, extinguishing his name, and becoming a wild religionist. But there shall have been kept in the family an ancient document, in his writing, telling of these things, or some of them—telling of his birth; yes, telling of all, by which the pensioner shall know it, and shall know of the coffer, and shall have one of the keys of it; the other being the one that Etheredge has brought. Hammond, the agent of the old doctor, shall be the one to discover, from his intimacy with the doctor, the truth that Etherege is not one of the old family, but a son of nobody, with all the world for his ancestry. Tomorrow, arrange the chain of events.

Open in the old house in Charter-street; describe it and its surroundings in a sombre, grotesque kind of way. The old gentleman in his study, amid his spiders, must be first touched upon; especially the gigantic spider, to which (quietly, and without telling the reader so) ascribe demonic qualities. Relieve the gloom by resting a little upon the beautiful boy and the cheerful girl. An old woman (Hannah Lord, perhaps) must be the only other member of the household. Perhaps, however, an English man-servant. The old gentleman is known as the Doctor by the town, although he never practices physic; only he is thought to be learned, & Scientific, and he has this theory about cobwebs—which it shall be uncertain whether he is not laughing at the world in it. Tell how he has found the boy in the alms-house; for some reason has adopted him—which reason seems to be, that he knows him to be the heir of an old family in England. Without directly telling the boy that he is the heir, he shall be in the habit of telling him stories about this family. He educates him in all gentlemanly qualities, teaches him fencing, gives him thorough classical teaching. He must be represented as acquiring a vast affection for the boy, passionate, engrossing, more than if he were his own son, because of the peculiarity in the way of acquiring this child; it shall seem as if he had made him—he shall combine himself (the boy shall) with his intellectual purpose. Some thing high and noble must be put into the man, together with morbidness and poison. The boy shall get good and evil from him; growing up proud, ambitious, passionate; the girl shall be the redeeming character, and a gentle light in the house, yet not too gentle either. She is a relative of the Doctor, who was brought to him a child of three years old, by an Englishman, who departed immediately—perhaps by somebody who died, & lies buried near the house. Early in the Romance, introduce the legend of the Bloody Footstep. Gather all sorts of picturesqueness about these characters and circumstances, and mystify about the old man and his spider. The reader must see reason to doubt, very early, or to be puzzled, whether or no the boy is the heir; and his mysterious origin must be so handled as to leave it uncertain whether the devil has not something to do with him. The girl's character must be imbued with natural sunshine, which will seem queer, from its being natural.

When the Romance is fully imbued with all this, introduce the visit of the Englishman. He must be an agent and old friend of the Doctor's,—a man of business, an attorney, I think. He must still further mystify the matter. He shall talk about the fears and expectations, in the English family, of an heir; the rumors they have heard; and of some old document that has been discovered, about something that was hidden in the grave of the first emigrant, that contains something necessary to the development. So there shall be the scene of opening the grave, in the winter-time, as before. His demeanour towards the boy, and some words that fall from him, shall stealthily indicate, yet leave in doubt, the Doctor's whole doings in this matter. Some light, too, should be thrown on the Doctor's wrongs, which have induced this curious project of revenge.

Something must be brought to the reader's notice, even earlier than this, about the old pensioner, though I do not see how. Perchance, a religious character shall see the boy and girl together, and bless them, and make some allusion to the family history; being incited to this by the name which the old Doctor has given to the boy. Something in this man's presence—something holy and beautiful, apostolic, religiously noble—shall touch the boy, and remain in his memory through life. Perhaps the old Doctor should be present, and take some part in the conversation; he shall not know the religionist, but something shall pass which shall indicate that the apostle knows something about the family history, though he and the Doctor shall not understand one another.

Matters being sufficiently in train, the Doctor dies unsuddenly, and it is suspected by the bite of his great spider, who, being the Devil, has probably got his soul. His death-scene shall make it appear that he had something on his mind, which he had half a mind to reveal, but yet he could not bear to give up a revengeful purpose of many years; neither, at the moment of death, can he do what remains needful towards carrying it into execution. There is therefore a portentous struggle and uncertainty, which shall much increase the mystification of the plot. It shall be mentioned, however, that his will makes Etherege inherit an amount of property sufficient to educate and establish him in America; there is likewise provision for the girl; and here ensues an interval of perhaps fifteen years. There is, among his papers, much that seems to indicate Etherege's heirships, pedigrees, genealogies, coats of arms, what seem to be authenticated proofs of American descent; but nothing absolutely proved.

The curtain next rises in England. It should be added, to the last preceding part, that more than one messenger came from England, making inquiries which seemed to have reference to the heirship of the estate; for the branch of the family, heretofore in possession, had died, and a new heir had to be looked for, both for the estate and a dormant title. This heir shall have been found in a branch which had emigrated with the Stuarts, and become Italianized. This man, somehow or other—it need not be exactly indicated how— had got notice of Etherege's arrival in England, and shall suppose it is to assert his rights. He procures him to be dogged in his wanderings, and finding that he comes to the estate, he hires (Italian fashion) an assassin to murder him, on the precincts of the estate, in some place that shall have been described by the Doctor in his story. The old pensioner rescues him, or finds him bleeding, conveys him to his apartments, where Etherege vaguely recognizes the holy presence that has never quite died out of his memory. Much suggestive conversation may ensue between them, at various times, mystifying, enlightening. Then the Warden is introduced, and Etherege is taken into his house, as before. From the antiquarian and genealogical disclosures of the Warden, the books in his library, and a variety of ingeniously arranged circumstances, Etherege is more and more confirmed in the idea that he is the heir. Yet various recollections of something ambiguous in the old Doctor's conduct, and of his dying scene, shall make him hesitate to assert himself, and so shall his democratic education and pride. He shall meditate making a confidant of the Warden, but shall hesitate, on account of the latter's position in respect to the family. Hammond, the Doctor's old agent, appears, and his demeanor shall throw Etherege into still greater perplexity; although it is possible that Hammond may more than strongly suspect the Doctor's fraud. Possibly, he may hint that money is necessary. He must startle Etherege with the dread of something dishonorable.

There must be various interviews with the girl, who has come back to England, and is living in respectability on what the Doctor left; in a poor way, perhaps as governess, or lady's gentlewoman. Perhaps the Italian heir is in love with her.

Then ensues the Warden's grand dinner, where Etherege (now made an ambassador) is the principal guest; and here he meets the Italian heir, who recognizes him as perhaps a relative (from his name) and invites him to the hall. Etherege accepts the invitation, and goes thither; and here ensues in the Romance much description and talk about old English dwellings, and the difference between English and American social life, and how we have given up certain delightful possibilities forever, and must content ourselves with other things.

Meanwhile, the Italian shall have made a plot to poison Etherege, believing him to be truly the heir; for perhaps Hammond may have played him false, and betrayed his projects, and it will be policy to murder him before he takes any public steps. Just at that time, poison was as fashionable in England as it had ever been in Italy. This somehow comes to the knowledge of the girl, who tells it to the old pensioner, who interferes to prevent it. He comes to the hall, and is admitted—he being known to the heir as one who has much knowledge of the genealogy—then he takes state upon himself, announces himself as the American heir, so long expected, produces his proofs; at the same time, Hammond appears, with his evidence of the Doctor's revengeful purpose, and Etherege finds himself at once deprived of all kindred, and left in a truly American condition. The Pensioner declines to take advantage of his rights. The Italian is rejected by the girl; she is left to be the consolation of Etherege. Something more tragical than this must be contrived. The death of the Italian, I think; he cannot comprehend the generosity of the pensioner, and drinks off the poison which he has prepared for Etherege; so that the pauper shall be a lord in spite of himself—which he must take very quietly.

I think, before this denouement, the owner and Etherege might be strolling through the house, and come to the great black coffer, about which there must have been traditions. He opens it with the silver key, and finds there the hair. This the more confirms the Italian in the belief that Etherege is the heir.

The girl, I think, shall have a sense of something false and wrong in Etherege's claim to the estate &c., and shall endeavor to persuade him to relinquish it. Some great misfortune shall impress her as having to be the result. The shadow of the old Doctor must be so contrived as to fall over all the subsequent part of the Romance after his death; so that he shall still seem to darkly live and act; though his revenge is baulked.

So now the great day of the Warden's dinner had arrived; and, as may be supposed, there were fiery times in the venerable old kitchen. The cook, according to ancient custom, concocted many antique dishes, such as used to be set before kings and nobles; dainties that might have called the dead out of their graves; combinations of ingredients that had ceased to be put together for centuries; historic dishes, which had long, long ceased to be in the list of meats. Then there was the stalwart English cheer of the sirloin, and the round; there were the vast plum-puddings; the juicy mutton; the venison; there was the game, now just in season, the half-tame wild fowl of English covers; the half-domesticated wild deer of English parks; the heath cock from the far-off hills of Scotland; and one little prairie hen, and some canvas-back ducks—obtained, heaven knows how, in compliment to Etherege—from his native shores. Oh, the old jolly kitchen. How rich the flavored smoke that went up its vast chimney; how inestimable the atmosphere of steam that was diffused through it. How did the old men peep into it; even venture across the threshold, braving the hot wrath of the cook and his assistants, for the sake of imbuing themselves with these rich and delicate flavors, receiving them in as it were spiritually; for, received through the breath and in the atmosphere, it was really a spiritual enjoyment. The ghosts of ancient epicures seemed, on that day and the few preceding ones, seemed to haunt the dim passages, snuffing in with shadowy nostrils the rich vapors, assuming visibility in the congenial medium, almost becoming earthly again in the strength of their earthly longings for one other feast such as they used to enjoy.

Nor is it to be supposed that it was only these antique dainties that the Master provided for his feast. No; if the cook, the cultured and recondite old cook, who had accumulated within himself all that his predecessors knew for centuries—if he lacked any thing of modern fashion and improvement, he had supplied his defect by temporary assistance from a London club; and the bill of fare was provided with dishes that Soyer would not have harshly criticized. The ethereal delicacy of modern taste, the nice adjustment of flavors, the French style of cookery, was richly attended to; and the list was long of dishes with fantastic names, fish, fowl, and flesh; and entremets, and "sweets," as the English call them, and sugared cates, too numerous to think of.

The wines we will not take upon ourselves to enumerate; but the juice, then destined to be quaffed, was in part the precise vintages that had been broached half a century ago, and had been ripening ever since; the rich and dry old port, so unlovely to the natural palate that it requires long English seasoning to get it down; the sherry, imported before these modern days of adulteration; some claret, the Master said, of rarest vintage; some Burgundy, of which it was the quality to warm the blood and genialize existence for three days after it was drunk. Then there was a rich liquid contributed to this department by Etherege himself; for, five weeks since, when the banquet first loomed in the distance, he had (anxious to evince his sense of the Master's kindness) sent across the ocean for some famous Madeira, which he had inherited from the Doctor, and never tasted yet. This, together with some of the western wines of America, had arrived, and was ready to be broached. The Master tested these modern wines, and recognized a new flavor, but gave it only a moderate approbation; for, in truth, an elderly Englishman has not a wide appreciation of wines, nor loves new things in this kind, more than in literature or life. But he tasted the Madeira, too, and underwent an ecstasy, which was only alleviated by the dread of gout, which he had an idea that this wine must bring on—and truly, if it were so splendid a wine as he pronounced it, some pain ought to follow as the shadow of such a pleasure.

As it was a festival of antique date, the dinner-hour had been fixed earlier than is usual at such stately banquets; viz., at six ºclock, which was long before the dusky hour when Englishmen love best to dine. About that period, the carriages drove into the old court yard of the hospital in great abundance; blocking up, too, the ancient portal, and remaining in a line outside. Carriages, they were, with armorial bearings, family coaches, in which came Englishmen in their black coats and white neckcloths, elderly, white-headed, fresh colored, squat; not beautiful, certainly, nor particularly dignified, nor very well dressed, nor with much of an imposing air, but yet, somehow or other, producing an effect of force, respectability, reliableness, trust, which is probably deserved, since it is invariably experienced. Cold they were in deportment, and looked coldly on the stranger, who, on his part, drew himself up with an extra haughtiness and reserve, and felt himself in the midst of his enemies, and more as if he were going to do battle than to sit down to a friendly banquet. The Master introduced him as an American diplomatist to one or two of the gentlemen, who regarded him forbiddingly, as Englishmen do, before dinner.

Not long after Etherege had entered the reception-room, which was but shortly before the hour appointed for the dinner, there was another arrival betokened by the clatter of hoofs and grinding wheels in the court-yard; and then entered a gentleman of different mien from the bluff, ruddy, simple-mannered, yet worldy Englishmen around him. It was a tall, dark man, with a black moustache, and almost olive skin, a slender, lithe figure, a flexible face, quick, flashing, mobile. His deportment was graceful; his dress, though it seemed to differ in little or nothing from that of the gentlemen in the room, had yet a grace and picturesqueness in his mode of wearing it. He advanced to the Master, who received him with distinction, and yet, Etherege fancied, not exactly with cordiality. It seemed to Etherege that the Master looked round, as if with the purpose of presenting Etherege to this gentleman, but he himself, from some latent reluctance, had turned away and entered into conversation with one of the other gentlemen, who said, now, looking at the new comer,

"Are you acquainted with this last arrival?"

"Not at all," said Etherege. "I know Mr. Brathwaite by sight, indeed, but have had no introduction. He is a man, certainly, of distinguished appearance."

"Why, pretty well," said the gentleman, "but un-English, as also are his manners. It is a pity to see an old English family represented by such a person. Neither he, his father, or his grandfather, was born among us; he has far more Italian blood than enough to drown the slender stream of Anglo Saxon and Norman. His modes of life, his prejudices, his tastes, his religion, are unlike our own; and yet here he is in the position of an old English gentleman, possibly to be a peer. You, whose nationality embraces that of all the world, cannot, I suppose, understand this English feeling."

<(Etherege's place is next to that of the proprietor at table.)>

"Pardon me," said Etherege, "I can perfectly understand it. An American, in his feelings towards England, has all the jealousy and exclusiveness of Englishmen themselves—perhaps, indeed, a little exaggerated."

"I beg your pardon," said the Englishman, incredulously. "I think you cannot possibly understand it!"

<(Dwell upon the antique liveried servants somewhat)>

The guests were by this time all assembled; and at the Master's bidding, they moved from the reception room to the dining-hall, in some order and precedence, which Etherege could not exactly discover the principle, though he found that to himself—in his quality, doubtless, of ambassador—there was assigned a pretty high place. A venerable dignitary of the church—a dean, he seemed to be—having asked a blessing, the fair scene of the banquet now lay before the guests, presenting a splendid spectacle, in the high walled, antique, tapestried hall, overhung with the dark, intricate oaken beams, with the high gothic windows, pictured, through one of which the setting sunbeams streamed, and showed the figures of kings and warriors; and the old Brathwaites among them. Beneath and adown the hall, extended the long line of the table, covered with the snow of the damask table-cloth, on which glittered, gleamed, and shone, a great quantity of ancient armorial plate, and an epergne of silver, extending down the middle; also the gleam of golden wine in the decanters; and truly, Etherege thought, that it was a noble spectacle, made so by old and stately associations, which made a noble banquet of what otherwise would be merely a vulgar dinner. The English have this advantage, and know how to make use of it. They bring—in these old, time-honored feasts—all the past to sit down and take the stately refreshment along with them, and they pledge the historic characters in their wine.

A printed bill of fare, in gold letters, lay by each plate; on which Etherege saw the company glancing with great interest. The first dish, of course, was Turtle Soup, of which—as the Mayor of a neighboring town next him told Etherege—it was allowable to take twice. This was accompanied, accord-

ing to one of those rules which one knows not whether they
are arbitrary or founded on some deep reason, by a glass of
punch. Then came the noble turbot, the salmon, the sole,
and divers of fishes, and the dinner fairly set in. The genial
Master seemed to have given liberal orders to the attendants,
for they spared not to offer hock, champagne, sherry, to the
guests, and good bitter ale, foaming in the goblet; and so the
stately banquet went on, with somewhat tedious magnificence; and yet with a fulness of effect, and thoroughness of
sombre life, that made Etherege feel that, so much importance
being assigned to it—it being so much believed in—it was
indeed a feast. The cumbrous courses swept by, one after
another; and Etherege, finding it heavy work, sat idle most of
the time, regarding the hall, the old decaying beams, the
armor hanging beneath the gallerys and these Englishmen
feasting where their fathers had feasted for so many ages,
the same occasion, the same men, probably, in appearance,
though the black coat and the white neckcloth had taken the
place of ruff, embroidered doublet, and the magnificence of
other ages. After all, the English have not such good things
to eat as we in America, and certainly do not know better
how to make them palatable.

<(The rose-water must precede the toasts)>

Well; but by and by the dinner came to a conclusion, as
regarded the eating part; the cloth was withdrawn; a dessert
of fruits fresh and dried, pines, hot-house grapes, and all
candied conserves of the Indies, was put on the long extent
of polished mahogany. There was a tuning up of musicians;
an interrogative drawing of fiddle-bows, and other musical
twangs and puffs; the decanters, opposite the Master and his
vice president—sherry, port, Etherege's Madeira, and claret,
were put in motion along the table, and the guests filled their
glasses for the toast, which, at English dinner tables, is of
course the first to be honored—the Queen. Then the band

struck up the good old anthem, God save the Queen, which the whole company rose to their feet to sing. It was a spectacle both interesting and a little ludicrous to Etherege—being so apart from an American's sympathies—so unlike anything that he has in his life or possibilities—this active and warm sentiment of loyalty, in which love of country centres and assimilates and transforms itself into a passionate affection for a person, in whom they love all their institutions. To say the truth, it seemed a happy notion; nor could the American —while he comforted himself in the pride of his democracy, and that he himself was a sovereign—could he help envying it a little, this childlike love and reverence for a person embodying all their country, their past, their earthly future. He felt that it might be delightful to have a sovereign, provided that sovereign were always a woman,—and perhap a young and fair one. But, indeed, this is not the difficulty, methinks, in English institutions, which the American finds it hardest to deal with. We could endure a born sovereign, especially if made such a mere pageant as the English make of theirs. What we find it hardest to conceive of, is, the satisfaction with which Englishmen think of a race above them, with privileges that they cannot share, entitled to condescend to them, and to have gracious and beautiful manners at their expense, to be kind, simple, unpretending, because these qualities are more available than haughtiness; to be specimens of perfect manhood;—all these advantages in consequence of their position. If the peerage were a mere name, it would be nothing to envy; but it is so much more than a name; it enables men to be really so superior. The poor, the lower classes, might bear this well enough; but the classes that come next to the nobility—the upper middle-classes—how they bear it so lovingly, is what must puzzle the American. But, probably, the advantage of the peerage is the less perceptible the nearer it is looked at.

It must be confessed that Etherege, as he looked at this assembly of peers and gentlemen, thought with some self-gratulation of the probability that he had within his power as old a rank, as desirable a station as the best of them; and that if he were restrained from taking it, it would probably only be by the democratic pride that made him feel that he could not, retaining all his manly sensibility, accept this gew gaw, on which the ages—his own country especially— had passed judgment, while it had been suspended over his head. He felt himself, at any rate, in a higher position, having the option of taking this rank, and forbearing to do so, than if he took it.

<The jollity of the Warden at the feast to be noticed, and afterwards explained that he had drunk nothing>

After this ensued a ceremony which is of antique date, in old English Corporations and Institutions, at their high festivals. It is called the Loving cup. A sort of herald, or Toastmaster, behind the Warden's chair, made proclamation, reciting the names of the principal guests, and announcing to them, "The Warden of the Brathwaite Hospital drinks to you in a Loving Cup"; of which cup, having sipped, or seemed to sip (for Etherege observed that the old drinkers were rather shy of it) a small quantity he sent down the table. Its progress was accompanied with a peculiar entanglement of ceremony; being pretty much as follows. <(One guest stands up while another drinks)> First, each guest receiving it covered from the next above him, the same took from the silver cup its silver cover; the guest drank with a bow to the Warden and company, took the cover from the preceding guest, covered the cup, handed it to the next below him, then again removed the cover, replaced it after the guest had drunk, who on his part, went through the same ceremony. And thus the cup went slowly on its way down the stately table; these ceremonies being, it is said, originally precautions against the risk, in wild times, of being stabbed by the man who was drinking with you or poisoned by one who should fail to be your taster. The cup was a fine, ancient piece of plate, massive, heavy, curiously wrought with armorial bearings, in which the tiger's head appeared. Its contents, so far as Etherege could analyze them by a moderate sip, appeared to be claret, sweetened with spices, and however suited to the peculiarity of antique palates, was not greatly to Etherege's taste.

<(Mention the old silver snuff-box, which saw at the Liverpool Mayor's dinner.)>

Etherege's companion just below him, while the Loving Cup was beginning its march, had just been explaining the origin of the custom as a defence of the drinker in times of deadly feud; when it had reached Lord Brathwaite, who drank and passed it to Etherege covered, and with the usual bow. Etherege looked into his Lordship's Italian eyes and dark face, as he did so; and the thought struck him, that if there could possibly be any use in keeping up this old custom, it might be so now; for, how intimated he could hardly tell, he was sensible in his deepest self of a deadly hostility in this dark, courteous, handsome face. He kept his eyes fixed on his lordship, as he received the cup, and felt that in his own glance there was an acknowledgement of the enmity that he perceived, and a defiance, expressed without visible sign, and felt in the bow with which they greeted one another. When they had both resumed their seats, Etherege chose to make this ceremonial intercourse the occasion of again addressing him.

"I know not whether your Lordship is more accustomed than myself to these stately ceremonials," said he.

"No," said Lord Brathwaite, whose English, at all events, was very good. "But this is a good old ceremony, and an ingenious one; for does it not twine us into knotted links of love—this Loving Cup—like a wreath of Bacchanals whom I have seen surrounding an antique vase? Doubtless it has great efficacy in entwining a company of friendly guests into one affectionate society."

"Yes; it should seem so," replied Etherege, with a smile and again meeting those black eyes, which smiled back on him. "It should seem so; but it appears that the origin of the custom was quite different, and that it was as a safeguard to a man when he drank with his enemy. What a peculiar flavor it must have given to the liquor, when the eyes of two deadly foes met over the brim of the Loving Cup, and the drinker knew that, if he or whoever watched him drink to see if it were poison withdrew it, a dagger would be in his breast."

"Ah," responded his Lordship, "they had strange fashions in those rough old times. Now-a-days, we neither stab, shoot, nor poison. I scarely think we hate, except as interest guides us, without malevolence."

This singular conversation was interrupted by a toast, and the rising of one of the guests to answer it. Several other toasts of routine succeeded; one of which, being to the honor of the old founder of the hospital, Lord Brathwaite, as his representative rose to reply—which he did, in good phrases, in a sort of eloquence unlike that of the Englishmen around him, and sooth to say, comparatively unaccustomed as he must have been to the use of the language, much more handsomely than they. In truth, Etherege was struck and amused with the rudeness, the slovenliness, the inartistic quality of the English speakers, who rather seemed to avoid grace and neatness of set purpose, as if they would be ashamed of it. Nothing could be more ragged than these utterances which they called speeches; so patched, and darned; and yet, somehow or other—though dull and heavy as ale which seemed to inspire them—they had a kind of force. Every man seemed to have the faculty of getting, after some rude fashion, the sense and feeling that was in him; and without glibness, without smoothness, without form or comeliness, still the object with which each one rose to speak was accomplished—and what was more remarkable, it seemed to be accomplished without the speaker's having any particular plan for doing it. He was surprised, too, to observe how loyally every man seemed to think himself bound to speak, and rose to do his best, however unfit his usual habits made him for the task. Observing this—and thinking how many Americans would be taken aback and dumbfoundered by being called on for a dinner-speech, he could not but doubt the correctness of the general opinion that Englishmen are naturally less facile of public speech than our countrymen.

"You surpass your countrymen," said Etherege, when his Lordship resumed his seat amid rapping and loud applause.

"My countrymen? I scarcely know whether you mean the English or Italians," said Lord Brathwaite. "Like yourself, I am a hybrid, with really no country, and ready to take up with any one."

"I have a country—one which I am little inclined to deny," replied Etherege gravely, while a flush (perhaps of conscientious shame) rose to his brow.

His Lordship bowed, with a dark Italian smile; but Etherege's attention was drawn away from the conversation by a toast which the Warden now rose to give, and in which he found himself mainly concerned. With a little preface of kind words (not particularly aptly applied) to the great and kindred country beyond the Atlantic, the worthy Warden proceeded to remark that his board was honored, on this high festival, with a guest from that new world; a gentleman, yet young, but already distinguished in the councils of his country; the bearer, he remarked, of an honored name, which might well claim to be remembered here, and on this occasion, although he had understood from his friend that the American bearers of this name counted kindred with the English ones. This gentleman, he further observed, with considerable flourish and emphasis, had recently been called from his retirement and wanderings into the diplomatic service of his country, which he would say, from his knowledge, the gentleman was well calculated to honor. He drank the health of the Honorable Edward Etherege, Ambassador of the United States to the Court of Hohen Linden.

The English cousins received this toast with the kindest enthusiasm, as they always do any such allusion to our country; it being a festal feeling, not so used except on holidays. They rose, with glass in hand, in honor of the Ambassador; the band struck up Hail Columbia; and our hero, marshalled his thoughts as well as he might, for the necessary response; and when the tumult subsided, he arose.

His quick apprehension had taught something of the difference of taste between an English and American audience at a dinner-table; he felt that there must be a certain looseness and carelessness and roughness, and yet a certain restraint; that he must not seem to aim at speaking well, although, for his own ambition, he was not content to speak ill; that, somehow or other, he must get a heartiness into his speech; that he must not polish, nor be too neat, and must come with a certain rudeness to his good points, as if he blundered on them and were surprised into them. Above all, he must let the good wine and cheer, and all that he knew and really felt of English hospitality, as represented by the kind Warden, do its work upon his heart, and speak up to the extent of what he felt—and if a little more, then no great harm—about his own love for the father-land, and the broader grounds of the relations between the two countries. On this system, Etherege began to speak; and being naturally and habitually eloquent, and of mobile and ready sensibilities—he succeeded, between art and nature, in making a speech that absolutely delighted the company, who made the old hall echo and the banners wave and tremble, and the board shake, and the glasses jingle, with their rapturous applause. What he said—or some shadow of it, and more than he quite liked to own—was reported in the County paper that gave a report of the dinner; but on glancing over it, it seems not worth while to preserve this eloquent effort in our pages, the occasion and topics being of merely temporary interest.

Etherege sat down, and sipped his claret, feeling a little ashamed of himself, as people are so apt to do after a display of this kind.

"You know the way to the English heart better than I do," remarked his Lordship, after a polite compliment to the speech. "Methinks these dull English are being improved in your atmosphere. The English need a change every few centuries—either by immigration of new stock, or transportation of the old—or else they grow too gross and earthly, with their beef, mutton, and ale. I think, now, it might benefit both countries, if your New England population were to be reciprocally exchanged with an equal number of Englishmen. Indeed, Italians might do as well."

"I should regret," said Etherege, "to change the English, heavy as they are."

"You are an admirable Englishman," said his Lordship. "For my part, I cannot say that the people are very much to my taste, any more than their skies and climate, in which I have shivered during the two years that I have spent here."

Here their conversation ceased; and Etherege listened to a long train of speechifying, in the course of which everybody at table, almost, was toasted; everybody present, at all events, and many absent. The Warden's old wine was not spared; the music rang and resounded from the gallery; and everybody seemed to consider it a model feast, although there was no very vivid signs of satisfaction, but a decorous, heavy enjoyment, a dull red heat of pleasure, without flame. Soda and Seltzer-water, and coffee, by and by were circulated; and at a late hour the company began to retire.

Before taking his departure, Lord Brathwaite resumed his conversation with Etheredge, and, as it appeared, with the purpose of making a hospitable proposition.

"I live very much alone," said he; "being insulated from my neighbors by many circumstances—habits, religion, and everything else peculiarly English. If you are curious about Old English Modes of life, I can show you, at least, an English residence little altered within a century past. Pray come and spend a week with me before you leave this part of the country. Besides, I know the Court to which you are accredited, and can give you, perhaps, useful information about it."

Etherege looked at him in some surprise, and with a nameless hesitation; for he did not like his lordship, and had fancied, in truth, that there was a reciprocal antipathy. Nor did he yet feel that he was mistaken in this respect; although his lordship's invitation was given in a tone of frankness, and seemed to have no reserve, except that his eyes did not meet his like Anglo Saxon eyes, and there seemed an Italian looking out from within the man. But Etherege had a sort of repulsion within himself; and he questioned whether it would be fair to his proposed host to accept his hospitality, when he had the secret feeling of hostility and repugnance—which might be well enough accounted for by the knowledge that he secretly entertained hostile interests to this man, and half a purpose of putting them in force. And, besides this—although Etherege was ashamed of the feeling—he had a secret dread, a feeling that it was not just a safe thing to trust himself in this man's power; for he had a sense, sure as death, that he did not wish him well, and had a secret dread of the American. But he laughed within himself at this feeling, and drove it down. Yet it made him feel that there would be no disloyalty in accepting his lordship's invitation, because it was given in as little friendship as it would be accepted.

"I had almost made my arrangements for quitting the neighborhood," said he, after a pause; "nor can I shorten the week longer which I had promised to spend with my very kind friend, the Warden. Yet your lordship's kindness offers me a great temptation, and I would gladly spend the next ensuing week at Brathwaite Hall."

"I shall expect you then," said Lord Brathwaite. "You will find me quite alone, except my chaplain—a scholar, and a man of the world, whom you will not be sorry to know."

He bowed and took his leave, without shaking hands, as an American would have thought it natural to do, after such a hospitable agreement; nor did Etherege make any motion towards it, and was glad that his Lordship had omitted it. On the whole, there was a secret dissatisfaction with himself; a sense that he was not doing quite a frank and true thing in accepting this invitation, and he only made peace with himself on the consideration that Lord Brathwaite was as little cordial in asking the visit, as he in acceding to it.

The guests were now rapidly taking their departure, and the Warden and Etheredge were soon left alone in the antique hall, which now, in its solitude, presented an aspect far different from the gay festivity of an hour before; the duskiness, up in the carved oaken beams, seemed to descend and fill the hall; and the remembrance of the feast was like one of those that had taken place centuries ago, with which this was now numbered, and growing ghostly and faded, and sad, even as they had long been.

"Well; my dear friend," said the Warden, stretching himself and yawning. "It is over. Come into my study with me, and we will have a devilled turkey bone and a pint of sherry, in peace and comfort."

"I fear I can make no figure at such a supper," said Etherege. "But I admire your inexhaustibleness in being ready for midnight refreshment after such a feast."

"Not a glass of good liquor has moistened my lips to night," said the Warden, "save and except such as was supplied by a decanter of water made brown with toast; and such a sip which I took to the health of the Queen, and another to that of the Ambassador to Hohen Linden. It is the only way, when a man has this vast labor of speechifying to do; and, indeed, there is no possibility of keeping up a jolly countenance, for such a length of time, except on toast-water."

<Etheredge was feverish and disturbed with wine>

They accordingly adjourned to the Warden's sanctum, where that worthy dignitary seemed to enjoy himself over his sherry and braised bones, in a degree that he probably had not heretofore, while Etherege, whose potations had been more liberal, tried the effect of a little brandy and soda-water. As often happens, at such midnight symposiums, the two friends found themselves in a more kindly and confidential vein than had happened before, great as had been the kindness and confidence already grown up between them. Etherege told his friend of Lord Brathwaite's invitation, and of his own resolution to accept it.

"Why not? You will do well," said the Warden, "and will find his Lordship an accustomed host, and the old house most interesting. If he knows the secrets of it himself, and will show them, they will be well worth the seeing."

"I have had a scruple in accepting this invitation," said Etherege.

"I cannot see why," said the Warden. "I advise it by all means, since I shall lose nothing by it myself, as it will not lop off any part of your visit to me."

"My dear friend," said Etherege, irresistibly impelled to a confidence which he had not meditated a moment before, "there is a foolish secret which I must tell you, if you will listen to it; and which I have only not revealed to you, because it seems to me foolish and dreamlike; because, too, I am an American, and a democrat; because I am ashamed of myself and laugh at myself."

"Is it a long story?" asked the Warden.

"I can make it of any length, or almost any brevity," said Etherege.

"I will fill my pipe then," answered the Warden, "and listen at my ease; and if as you intimate, there proves to be any folly in it, I will impute it all to the kindly freedom with which you have partaken of our English hospitality, and forget it before tomorrow morning."

He settled himself in his easy-chair, in a most luxurious posture; and Etherege, who felt a strange reluctance to reveal —for the first time in his life—the shadowy hopes, if hopes they were, and purposes, if such they could be called, with which he had amused so many years, began the story from almost the earliest period that he could remember. He told, even, of his earliest recollection, with an old woman, in the alms-house, and how he had been found there by the Doctor, and educated by him, with all the hints and half-revelations that had been made to him. He described the singular character of the Doctor, his scientific pursuits, his evident accomplishments, his great abilities, his morbidness and melancholy, his moodiness, and finally his death, and the singular circumstances that accompanied it. The story took a considerable time to tell; and, after its close, the Warden, who had only interrupted it by now and then a question to make it plainer, continued to smoke his pipe slowly and thoughtfully, for a long while.

"This Doctor of yours was a singular character," said he. "Evidently, from what you tell me as to the accuracy of his local reminiscences, he must have been of this part of the country—of this immediate neighborhood—and such a man could not have grown up here without being known. I, myself—for I am an old fellow now—must have known him, if he lived to manhood hereabouts."

"He seemed old to me when I first knew him," said Etherege. "But children make no distinctions of age. He might have been forty-five, then, as well as I can judge."

"You are now twenty-seven or eight," said the Warden; "and were four years old when you first knew him. He might now be sixty-five. Do you know, my friend, that I have something like a certainty that I know your Doctor?"

"How strange this seems," exclaimed Etherege. "It has never struck me that I should be able to identify this singular personage with any surroundings, or any friends."

The Warden, to requite his friend's story—and without as yet saying a word, good or bad, or his ancestral claims,—proceeded to tell him some of the gossip of the neighborhood—what had been gossip thirty or forty years ago, but was now forgotten, or, at all events, seldom spoken of, and only known to the old, at the present day. He himself remembered it only as a boy, and imperfectly. There had been a gentleman, at that day, a man of landed-estate, who had fallen deeply in love and been betrothed to a young lady of family; he was a young man of more than ordinary cultivation and abilities, and of great promise, though small fortune. It was not well known how, but the match between him and the young lady was broken off, and his place was supplied by the then proprietor of Brathwaite Hall; as it was supposed, by the artifices of her mother. There had been circumstances of peculiar treachery in the matter; and Mr. Archdale had taken it severely to heart; so severely, indeed, that he had left the country, after selling his ancestral property, and had only been vaguely heard of again. Now, from certain circumstances, it had struck the Warden that this might be the mysterious Doctor, of whom Etherege spoke.

"But why," suggested Etherege, "should a man with these wrongs to avenge take such an interest in a descendant of his enemy's family?"

"That is a strong point in favor of my supposition," rejoined the Warden. "There is certainly, and has long been, a degree of probability that the true heir of this family exists in America. If Archdale could discover him, he ousts his enemy from the estate and honors, and substitutes the person whom he has discovered and educated. Most certainly there is revenge in the thing. Should it happen now, however, the triumph would have lost its sweetness, even were Archdale alive to partake of it; for his enemy is dead, leaving no heir, and this foreign branch has come in without Archdale's aid."

The friends remained musing a considerable time, each in his own train of thought, till the Warden suddenly spoke.

"Do you mean to prosecute this apparent claim of yours?"

"I have not intended to do so," said Etherege.

"Of course," said the Warden, "that should depend upon the strength of your ground, and I understand you that there is some link wanting to establish it. Otherwise, I see not how you can hesitate. Is it a little thing to hold a claim to an old English estate and honors?"

"No, it is a very great thing, to an Englishman born, and who need give up no higher birth right to avail himself of it," answered Etherege. "You will laugh at me, my friend; but I cannot help feeling that I, a simple citizen of a Republic, yet with none above me, except those whom I help to place there—and who are my servants, not my superiors—must stoop to take these honors. I leave a set of institutions which are the noblest that the wit and civilization of man has yet conceived, to enlist myself in one that is based on a far lower conception of man, and which therefore lowers every one who shares in it. Besides," said the young man, his eyes kindling with the ambition which had been so active a principle in his life, "what prospects—what rewards for spirited exertion—what a career, only open to an American, should I give up, to become merely a rich and idle Englishman, belonging (as I should) nowhere, without a possibility of struggle, such as a strong man loves, with only a mockery of a title, which in these days really means nothing—hardly more than one of our own Honorables. What has any success in English life to offer (even were it within my reach, which, as a stranger, it would not be) to balance the proud career of an American statesman?"

"True, you might be a President, I suppose," said the Warden, rather contemptuously—"a four years' potentate. It seems to me an office about on a par with that of the Lord Mayor of London. For my part, I would rather be a baron sixteen times transmitted of three or four hundred years' antiquity."

"We talk in vain," said Etherege laughing. "We do not approach one another's ideas in this subject. But—waiving all speculations as to my attempting to avail myself of this claim —do you think I can fairly accept this invitation to visit Lord Brathwaite? There is certainly a possibility that I may arrange myself against his dearest interests. Conscious of this, can I accept his hospitality?"

The Warden paused. "You have not sought access to his house," he observed. "You have no designs, it seems—no settled designs, at all events, against his Lordship—nor is there a probability that they would be forwarded by your accepting this invitation, even if you had any. I do not see but you may go. The only danger is, that his Lordship's engaging qualities may seduce you into dropping your claims out of a chivalrous feeling which I see is among your possibilities. To be sure, it would be more satisfactory if he knew your actual position, and should then renew his invitation."

"I am convinced," said Etherege, looking up from his musing posture, "that he does know them. You are surprised; but in all Lord Brathwaite's manner towards me, there has been an undefinable something that makes me aware that he knows on what terms we stand towards each other. There is nothing inconceivable in this. The family have for generations been suspicious of an American heir, and have more than once sent messengers to try to search out and put a stop to this apprehension. Why should it not have come to their knowledge that there was a person with such claims, and that he is now in England?"

"It certainly is possible," replied the Warden, "and if you are satisfied that his Lordship knows it, or even suspects it, you meet him on fair ground. But I firmly tell you, my good friend, that—his Lordship being a man of unknown principles of honor, outlandish, and an Italian in habit and moral sense—I scarcely like to trust you in his house, he being aware that your existence may be inimical to him. My humble board is the safer of the two."

"Pshaw," said Etherege impatiently. "You Englishmen are so suspicious of anybody not regularly belonging to yourselves. Poison and the dagger haunt your conceptions of all others. In America, you think we slice every third man with the bowie-knife. But, supposing there were any grounds for your suspicion, I would still encounter it. An American is no braver than an Englishman; but still he is not quite so chary of his life as the latter, who never risks it except on the the most imminent necessity, and takes it much amiss if it be put in hazard by design or carelessness. We take such matters easy. In regard to this invitation, I feel that I can honorably accept it, and there are many idle and curious motives that impel me to it. I will go."

"Be it so; but you must come back to me for another week, after finishing your visit," said the Warden. "After all, it was an idle fancy in me that there could be any danger. His Lordship has good English blood in his veins, and it would take oceans and rivers of Italian treachery to wash out the sterling quality of it. And, my good friend, as to these claims of yours, I would not have you trust too much to what is probably a romantic dream; yet were the dream to come true, I should think the British peerage honored by such an accession to its ranks. And now to bed; for we have heard the chimes of midnight, two hours agone."

They accordingly retired; and Etherege was surprised to find what a distinctness his ideas respecting his claim to the Brathwaite honors had assumed, now that he, after so many years, had imparted them to another. Heretofore, though his imagination had played with them so much, they seemed the veriest dreams; now, they had suddenly taken form and hardened into substance; and he became aware, in spite of all the lofty and patriotic sentiments which he had expressed to the Warden, that these prospects had really much importance in his mind.

Etherege, during the few days that he was spared at the Hospital, previous to his visit to Brathwaite Hall, was conscious of a restlessness such as we have all felt, on the eve of some interesting event. He wondered at himself for being so much wrought up by so simple a thing as he was about to do; but it seemed to him like a coming home, after an absence of centuries; it was like an actual prospect of entrance into a castle in the air,—the shadowy threshold of which should assume substance enough to bear his foot, its thin, fantastic walls actually protect him from sun and rain, its halls echo with his footsteps, its hearth warm him. That delicious, thrilling uncertainty between reality and fancy, in which he had often been enwrapt since his arrival in this region, enveloped him more strongly than ever; and with it, too, there came a sort of apprehension, which sometimes shuddered through him like an icy draught, or the touch of cold steel to his heart. He was ashamed, too, to be conscious of something like fear; yet he would not acknowledge it for fear, and indeed there was such an airy, exhilarating, thrilling pleasure linked up with it that it could not really be so.

It was in this state of mind, that, a day or two after the feast, he saw old Pearson sitting on the bench, before the portal of the Hospital, in the sun, which, September though it was, still came warm and bright (for English sunshine) into that sheltered spot; a spot where many generations of old men had warmed their limbs, while they looked down into the life, the torpid life, of the old village that trailed its homely yet picturesque street along by the venerable buildings of the Hospital.

"My good friend," said Etherege, "I am about leaving you, for a time—indeed, with the limited time at my disposal, it is possible that I may not be able to come back hither, except for a brief visit. Before I leave you, I would fain know something more about one whom I must ever consider my benefactor."

"Yes;" said the old man, with his usual benignant quiet, "I saved your life. It is yet to be seen, perhaps, whether thereby I made myself your benefactor. I trust so."

"I feel it so, at least," answered Etherege smiling; "and I assure you life has a new value for me since I came to this place; for I have a deeper hold upon it, as it were, more hope from it, more trust in something good to come out of it."

"This is a good change—or should be so," quoth the old man.

"Do you know," continued Etherege, "how long you have been a figure in my life?"

"I know it," said Pearson; "but I thought that you had forgotten it."

"Not so," said Etherege. "I remember, as if it were this morning, that sunny time in the New England street, when I first saw you, as I walked hand in hand with the little girl; and how you stopt us and spoke words to us that have perplexed me often since; for they seemed to have counsel and warning in them, yet neither were so definite that I could take advantage of them."

"The man, who then led you by the hand," said the Pensioner, "knew the purport of what I said; and that sufficed."

"And he being long dead, and finding you here now, by such a strange coincidence," said Etheredge, "and being myself a man capable of taking your counsel, I would have you repeat it to me; for I assure you that the current of my life runs darkly on, & I would be glad of any light on its future, or even its present course."

"I am not one of those on whom the world waits for counsel," said the pensioner; "and I know not that mine would be advantageous to you in the light which men usually prize. Yet if I were to give any, it would be that you should be gone hence."

"Gone hence!" repeated Etheredge aghast. "I tell you— what I have hardly hitherto told to myself—that all my dreams, all my wishes hitherto, have looked forward to precisely the juncture that seems now to be approaching. My dreaming childhood dreamt of this. If you know anything of me, you know how I sprang out of mystery, akin to none, a thing concocted out of the elements, without visible agency— how, all through my boyhood, I was alone; how I grew up without a root, yet continually longing for one—longing to be connected with somebody—and never feeling myself so.

Yet there was ever a looking forward to this turn on which I now find myself. If my next step were death, yet while the path seemed to lead onward to a certainty of establishing me in connection with my race, I would yet take it. I have tried to keep down this yearning, to stifle it, annihilate it, with making a position for myself, with being my own past, but I cannot overcome this natural horror of being a creature floating in the air, attached to nothing; nor this feeling that there is no reality in the life and fortunes, good or bad, of a being so unconnected. There is not even a grave, not a heap of dry bones, not a pinch of dust, with which I can claim connection, unless I find it here."

"This is sad," said the old man; "this strong yearning, and nothing to gratify it. Yet I warn you, do not seek its gratification here. There are delusions, snares, pitfalls in this life. I warn you, quit the search."

"No," said Etherege, "I will follow the mysterious clue that seems to lead me on; and even now it pulls me one step further on."

"How is that?" asked the old man.

"It leads me onward even as far as to the threshold, across the threshold, of yonder mansion," said Etherege.

"Step not across it; there is a bloody footstep on that threshold," exclaimed the pensioner. "A bloody footstep emerging. Take heed that there be not as bloody one entering in."

"Pshaw!" said Etherege, feeling the ridicule of the emotion into which he had been betrayed, as the old man's wildness of demeanor made him feel that he was talking with a monomaniac. "We are talking idly. I do but go, in the common intercourse of society, to see this old English residence which (such is the unhappy obscurity of my position) I fancy, among a thousand others, may have been that of my ancestors. Nothing is likely to come of it. My foot is not bloody, nor polluted with anything except the mud of this damp English soil."

"Yet do not go in," persisted the old man.

"Yes, I must go," said Etherege determinedly; "and I will."

Ashamed to have been moved to such idle earnestness by anything that the old man could say, Etherege turned away, though he still heard the sad, half-uttered remonstrances of the old man like a moan behind him, and wondered what strange fancy had taken possession of him.

The effect which this strange opposition had upon him made him the more aware how much his heart was set upon this visit to the Hall; how much he had counted upon being domiciliated there; what a wrench it would now be, to tear himself away without going into that mansion, and penetrating all the mysteries wherewith his imagination, exercising itself upon the theme since the days of the old Doctor's fireside talk, had invested it. In his agitation, he wandered forth from the Hospital, and passing through the village-street, found himself in the Park of Brathwaite Hall, where he wandered for a space, until his steps led him to a point whence the venerable Hall appeared, with its lawn and its oaks around it, its look of peace and aged repose, and home-liness; its stately domesticity, so ancient, so beautiful; its mild, sweet majesty; it seemed the ideal of home. The thought thrilled his bosom, that this was his home;—the home of the wild western wanderer, who had gone away centuries ago, and encountered strange chances, and almost forgotten his origin, but still kept a clue to bring him back, and had now come back and found all the original emotions safe within him. It even seemed to him, that by his kindred with those who had gone before—by the line of sensitive blood linking him with that first emigrant, he could remember all these objects,—that tree, hardly more venerable now than then; that clock-tower, still marking the elapsing time; that spire of the old church raising itself beyond. He spread out his arms in a kind of rapture, and exclaimed:—

"Oh home, my home, my forefathers' home! I have come back to thee! The wanderer has come back!"

There was a slight stir near him; and on a mossy seat, that was arranged to take advantage of a peculiarly good point of view of the old hall, he saw Elsie sitting; she had her drawing materials with her, and had probably been taking a sketch. Etheredge was ashamed to have been overheard by any one, giving way to such idle passion as he had been betrayed into; and yet, in another sense, he was glad—glad, at least, that something of his feeling, as yet unspoken to human being, was shared, and shared by her with whom, alone of living beings, he had any sympathies of old date, and whom he often dwelt upon with feelings that drew him irresistibly towards her.

"Elsie," said he, uttering for the first time the old name, "Providence makes you my confidant! We have recognized each other, though no word has passed between us. Let us speak now again with one another. How came you hither? What has brought us together again? Away with this strangeness that lurks between us. Let us meet as those who began life together, and whose life-strings, being so early twisted in unison, cannot now be torn apart."

"You are not wise," said Elsie, in faultering accents, "to break the restraint which we have tacitly imposed upon ourselves. Do not let us speak further on this subject."

"How strangely everything evades me!" exclaimed Etheredge. "I seem to be in a land of enchantment, where I can get hold of nothing that lends me a firm support. There is no medium in my life between the most vulgar realities, and the most vaporous fiction, too thin to breathe. Tell me, Elsie, how come you here? why do you not meet me frankly? What is there to keep you apart from the oldest friend, I am bold to say, you have on earth? Are you an English girl? Are you one of our own New England maidens, with her freedom, and her know-how, and her force, beyond any thing that these demure and decorous maidens can know?"

"This is wild," said Elsie, struggling for composure, yet strangely moved by the recollections that he brought up. "It is best that we should meet as strangers, and so part."

"No, no," cried Etherege. "The long past comes up, with its recollections; and yet it is not so powerful as the powerful present. We have met again; circumstances have shown that Providence has designed a relation in my fate to yours. Elsie; are you lonely as I am?"

"No," she replied, "I have bonds, ties, a life, a duty! I must live that life, and do that duty! You have, likewise, both. Do yours, live your own life, like me."

"Know you, Elsie," he said, "whither that life is now tending?"

"Whither?" said she, turning towards him.

"To yonder hall!" said he.

She started up, in wild excitement, and clasped her hands about his arm.

"No, no," she almost shrieked. "Go not thither! There is blood upon the threshold! Go not thither! Return, return, to those haunts where we erst knew each other. A dreadful fatality awaits you here."

"Come with me, then," said he, "and I yield my purpose."

"It cannot be," said Elsie.

"Then, I, too, tell you, it cannot be," returned Etherge.

The dialogue had reached this point, when there came a step along the wood-path; the branches rustled; and there was the Lord of Brathwaite Hall looking upon the pair, with the ordinary, slightly sarcastic glance with which he gazed at the world.

"A fine morning, fair lady and fair Sir," said he. "We have few such except in Italy."

<What unimaginable nonsense?>

Half of a secret is preserved in England; that is to say, the particular part of the mansion in which an old coffer is hidden; the other part was carried to America. One key of an elaborate lock is retained in England, among some old curiosities of forgotten purpose; the other is the silver key that Etherege found beside the grave. The old pensioner knows of the secret, but has not the key. A treasure of gold is what they expect; they find a treasure of golden locks. This lady, the beloved of the bloody footstep, had been murdered and hidden in the coffer, on account of jealousy. Elsie must know the baselessness of Etheredge's claims, & be loth to tell him, because she sees that he is so much interested in them. She has a paper of the old Doctor's, revealing the whole plot; a death-bed confession; Etheredge having been absent at the time.

We must begin at the source. What was the motive of the original emigrant in leaving his inheritance, coming to America, and secluding his identity from the knowledge of anybody? Well, thus;—before the civil war, this personage was living in great happiness with his young wife, in his ancestral mansion; but being incited to jealousy (whether truly or falsely need not appear) he is supposed to have killed his wife and reposited her in a very curious old coffer, in a hiding-place of the mansion. He retains one lock of her golden hair to remember her by. He takes his boy with him, and goes forth from his mansion, leaving the blood track on the threshold. He goes to New England, and there lives in seclusion, yet must provide, in some way, for the ascertaining of his identity after two hundred years. How? He leaves a narrative in a paper, which is preserved, and gets into the hands of the old Doctor. Meanwhile, the family in England do not know the truth of the story, nor what became of either of husband, wife, or boy; though, in some inscrutable way, a legend is propagated that they fled to America, and that there is left behind a coffer full of gold, buried somewhere about the house.

One of the legends about this first emigrant shall be that adopted by the English family, and related in the Doctor's legend of the Bloody-Footstep. This shall represent him as a blood-thirsty man, whose foot has been wet by his King's blood.

Another shall be that of the pensioner, representing him as a Saint. This shall have so much of truth in it, that he did, in New England, become a wild religionist, found a sect, and suffer death for non-conformity. The pensioner shall have taken up his religion, and become a preacher of it; but it having been adapted to another state of the world, he has no success, and finally comes to the Hospital. There has been handed down to him a tradition that he belongs to this family, and out of a pious reverence for his ancestor, he has sought out the proofs of his descent, and has them with him. The name has been changed; but there shall be an authentic certificate, of old date, as to this change of name, which saves the old pauper's rights.

Etherege, on the other hand, must have a series of seeming proofs, contrived by the Doctor, for the purposes of revenge; they should seem to strengthen at every step, and become indubitable; but, at the very last moment, most unexpectedly, they should crumble into nothings. Etheredge must discover, by means of Elsie, that the Doctor had contrived this plan. He had revealed this on his death-bed, and given her a paper, signed and witnessed, which she was to produce on occasion; but he could not bring himself to blacken his memory with Etheredge, whom he loved so well, by revealing it sooner.

He was in hopes that Etheredge would never really take up the claim. At the last moment, Elsie delivers the paper, of which she herself does not know the contents. It produces a violent effect on Etherege, but he honorably resolves (when the prize seems actually within his grasp) to relinquish it.

The Doctor shall have supposed the genuine race to be extinct; and under this idea, shall have no hesitation in availing himself of proofs of descent which really belong to the pensioner. But Etherege shall see reason to suppose that he is the real man; and shall declare it, and assign over to him the proofs that he has heretofore thought made out his own claim. The old man must have no suspicion, I think, of the truth. The Warden shall have communicated to Etherege, perhaps, the nature of the proof which the old man has made out, in order to entitle him to the benefits of the hospital; up to a certain point, it makes out his claim, and there the old doctor's proofs join on to it, and show him to be the heir. One branch of the American descent had become extinct; this the old Doctor finds out, but is not aware that another branch is represented by the old pensioner.

The life is not yet breathed into this plot, after all my galvanic efforts. Not a spark of passion as yet. How shall it be attained? The Lord of Brathwaite Hall shall be a wretched, dissipated, dishonorable fellow; the estate shall be involved by his debts, and shall be all but done up. He shall (perhaps) be in love with Elsie. Up to his death, he must feel as if this American had come to thwart him and ruin him in every-thing, and shall hate him accordingly, and think he is doing well to kill him if possible. This won't do; some marked character must be given to this fellow, as if he were a fiend, a man sold to the devil, a magician, a poison-breather, a Thug, a pirate, a pickpocket; something that will look strange and outré in that high position; it must have picturesque characteristics, of course. Something that fixes strange and incongruous necessities upon him, making him most miserable under a show of all possible glory and splendour, and grace, and gaiety. Could I but achieve this, I should feel as if the book were plotted; otherwise, not. Something monstrous he must be, yet within nature and Romantic probability—hard conditions. A murderer—'twon't do at all. A Mahometan?— pish. If I could only hit right here, he would be the centre of interest. It will not do to have him a mere lay figure; there might be good and evil in him. Something most abhorrent to the English he might be; as for instance, a partaker in the massacres of India, a man bedaubed all over with the blood of his own countrymen. A moral of the strange things that happen, when the accident of birth puts people into places for which they are most unfit. Nothing mean must he be, but as wicked as you please. Shall he be preternatural?— not without a plausible explanation. What natural horror is there? A monkey? A Faulkenstein? A man of straw? A man without a heart, made by machinery?—one who has to wind himself in order to go through the day? Wicked as he must be, there shall still be relations between him and the pauper Saint. What? Shall there be an influence in the house which is said to make everybody wicked who inherits it?—nonsense. Remorse it must not be. A Resurrection Man? What? What? What? A worshipper of the Sun? A cannibal? A ghoul? A vampire? A man who lives by sucking the blood of the young and beautiful? He has something to do with the old Doctor's spider-theory; the great spider has got him into his web. The Doctor, before he left England, had contrived a plot of which this man is the victim. How? He has been poisoned by a Bologna sausage, and is being gnawed away by an atom at a time. He shall need a young life every five years, to renew his own, and he shall have fixed upon Elsie for his next victim. Now for it! How? At any rate, he must have dreadful designs on Elsie—dreadful, dreadful, dreadful. May it not be that the revenge of the Doctor has fallen on him? No, no. Let the real difference between him and other people be very small—but pile up upon it. Ye Heavens! A man with a mortal disease?—a leprosy?—a eunuch?—a cork leg?—a golden touch?—a dead hand?—a false nose?—a glass eye? The rumors of his devilish attributes may be very great; but the circumstance itself may be comparatively trifling. Some damn'd thing is the matter. The last survivor and inheritor of the secret of an otherwise extinct society of crime. He was initiated in Italy; all his companions have died by the executioner, and he alone escaped. A Rosycrucian? A Cagliostro?

This wretched man!—A crossing-sweeper?—a boot-black? —He comes of a race that is degenerated in a certain way; rotten, yet retaining a brave outside. How? It should be from some cause that had existed in the family for hundreds of years. It can't be. Some irremediable misfortune has got possession of this poor devil, and makes him an object of pity, as well as horrour. He has yielded to some great temptation, which particularly besets the members of this family. The Unpardonable Sin. He has looked into a blue-beard chamber. He had murdered, by slow poison, the former possessor of the estate; he had buried him in a niche. 'Twon't do. His forefather emigrated to the Continent with King James, and settled in Italy, where he lost entirely his nationality, and gave origin to a race of nondescripts. Upon this race was engrafted something that is proper enough to Italians, but becomes monstrous in Englishmen; some one trait there must be, that produces this terrible and weird effect. He might, as one characteristic, have an ice-cold right hand; but this should be only emblematic of something else. He is in the habit of doing something horrible every day, which his previous life has made necessary to him. He might have a scar, which, in circumstances of desperation, grew blood-red. He may have done something, in this generation, which his ancestor had done in a former one. What? This is a very hard pinch. His icy hand; what it may betoken? That, on some occasion, he has done a deed with that right hand, which has driven the genial warmth out of it. The English shall hate this man, apparently because of his foreign birth and peculiarities; but really there must be something repulsive about him. What? The steam of a crime? The silent influence of hateful qualities. What habit can he have? Perhaps that of having a young child, fricaseed, served up to him for break-fast, every morning. Some strange East Indian habit he may have adopted; and his unpopularity shall be an example of English prejudice. Do not stick at any strangeness, or preter-naturality; it can be softened down to any extent, however wild in its first conception. He may have had a taste of blood, and now feel a necessity for it;—having poisoned people, or stabbed them with a poisoned dagger. His crime gives him an atmosphere disagreeable to other people; but he himself does not suffer from it; except as it has made a necessity for him to have the luxury of committing crime still. In his Italian poverty, he was reduced to great extremities, and found it needful to consort with certain great criminals, amongst whom he had a taste of crime, and found it racier and more ravishing than anything that virtue could supply. He was a member of Italian banditti. He was an executioner; being of a cruel nature; so that he served an apprenticeship to Calcraft, or was an amateur assistant of him. He has been reduced to the dregs of life; had lived in a cellar, on offals. Alas me! Virtuous, beautifully behaved, he may be, in all respects except one, which shall throw a devilish aspect over him, and make the whole romance wild and weird. How? how? how? The key of the Romance ought to be here, in this one little peculiarity; so it must have reference to the past. It must be something that he can't help doing; some

one trait of insanity. He drinks blood. He has a person concealed. No; it must be a great trait in his nature, coming
from the past, in his blood. Pshaw.

This wretched man, still;—A great pride of birth he must
have at bottom, vile varlet as he is; and yet he has been raked
from the very kennels of dirty crime. In Italy, he has lived
upon olives, figs, cheese; has wrapt his cloak about him in
those keen Roman winds. Has crept, has sinned, has suffered,
through all that sordidness, till suddenly raised to this delightful position. Once, he had a great temptation to do a horrible
thing. Of course, he yielded. Agreeable, brilliant, witty, but
heartless and worthless; a man of the world. All this amounts
to just nothing. I don't advance a step. He lives a solitary
life; they avoid him. Why? Partly because they don't like
him. Yet he should have companions, methinks. No, only
now and then a fellow as questionable as himself. He is one
of those characters that only opportunity draws out; like the
monsters that came to the surface of society during the
French Revolution; else hidden through the quiet centuries.
What monsters of men have there been? Raised to this high
seat, there must be some vile peculiarity which he has brought
with him, and cannot keep down entirely; it will, once in a
while, have its gratification, though as a general thing, his
manners are unexceptionable. It might be derived from his
Italian blood. If he could only get rid of this propensity, he
would be a perfectly unexceptional man; he struggles for it;
but in vain. Elsie, perhaps, is in his secret, and wishes to help
him. He fails; she fails. A propensity for drink? A tendency
to feed on horse-flesh? A love of toads? A badge of the mud
that has clung to him in the depths of social degradation in
which he has been plunged? Surely, there is some possible
monster who would precisely fit into this vacant niche. The
girl must, some how, have a close relation with him; he shall
love her; be capable of being redeemed by her. She knows

this, and hesitates to let him fall. Finally, she is compelled to do so by the wild surge of his wickedness. Amen. The thing! The thing? Something derived from old times, this peculiarity ought to be, carried to Italy, there fostered into something monstrous, and brought back to England. What? The old bloody footstep business! No; that won't do. But there must be something definite; no vague assemblage of characteristics. Widen the sweep of the net a little. Shall he be an imposter? No! What fantastic, yet real seeming peculiarity can he have? Supposing him to have once tasted blood, and got an appetite for it—how? But that is vulgar. I think the family history must take hold of his evil imagination, and incite him to crime, by the pestilence and contagion of a crime long past, which is dug up again; and pollutes the moral air, as did the bodies dead long ago of the plague pollute it physically. 'Twon't do. The union of British brutality with Italian subtlety has produced a refinement of wickedness; emblematized how?—and how made picturesque? This is despair, sure enough. Miss Mackintosh. McIntosh. James McIntosh, Esq. I can't see it. Nobody knows what his former life had been, though there were dark hints about it; that it had gone very low, into the kennel, even; but if so, nothing of it was perceptible in his manner. His mother was a low Italian woman; she was now dead, though he was still young. He had come forward without any vouchers for his former character, though with ample proofs of his being the heir of the family. He shall have inherited from his mother the old art of poisoning, and shall be in the habit of poisoning people for his private amusement and experimentally. 'Twon't do, of course.—His character must be evinced in the course he takes with Etheredge, after getting him into the house.

So Etherege left the Hospital, where he had spent many weeks of strange and not unhappy life, and went to accept the invitation of the Lord of Brathwaite Hall. It was with a thrill of strange delight, poignant almost to pain, that he found himself driving up to the door of the Hall, and actually passing the threshold of the house. He looked, as he stept over it, for the Bloody Footstep, with which the house had so long been associated in his imagination; but could nowhere see it. The footman ushered him into a hall, which seemed to be in the centre of the building, and where, little as the autumn was advanced, a fire was nevertheless burning and glowing on the hearth; nor was its effect undesirable in the somewhat gloomy room. The servants had evidently received orders respecting the guest; for they ushered him at once to his chamber, which seemed not to be one of those bachelor's rooms, where, in an English mansion, young and single men are forced to be contented with very bare and straightened accommodations; but a large, well, though antiquely and solemnly furnished room, with a curtained bed, and all manner of elaborate contrivances for repose; but the deep embrasures of the windows made it gloomy, with the little light that they admitted through their small panes. There must have been English attendance in this department of the household arrangements, at least; for nothing could exceed the exquisite nicety and finish of everything in the room, the cleanliness, the attention to comfort, amid antique aspects of furniture; the rich, deep preparations for repose.

The servant told Etherege that his master had ridden out; and adding that luncheon would be on the table at two oclock left him, and Etherege sat some time, trying to make out and distinguish the feelings with which he found himself here in realizing a life-long dream. He ran back over all the legends which the Doctor used to tell about this mansion, and wondered whether this old, rich chamber were the one where any of them had taken place; whether the shadows of the dead haunted here. But, indeed, if this were the case, the apartment must have been very much changed, antique though it looked with the second, or third, or whatever other numbered arrangement, since those old days of tapestry hangings and rush-strewed floors. Otherwise, this stately and gloomy chamber was as likely as any other to have been the one where his ancestor and his spouse appeared for the last time, in the paternal mansion; here they might have been, the night before that mysterious Bloody Footstep was left on the threshold; whence had arisen so many wild legends, and since the impression of which nothing certain had ever been known respecting that ill-fated pair;—nothing certain, in England at least, and whose story was left so ragged and questionable even by all that he could add.

Do what he could, Etherege still was not conscious of that deep home-feeling which he had imagined he should experience, when, if ever, he should come back to the old ancestral place; there was strangeness, a struggle within himself to get hold of something that escaped him, an effort to impress on his mind the fact that here he was at last, established in his temporary home in the place that he had so long looked forward to;—and that this was the moment which he would have thought more interesting than any other in his life. He was strangely cold and indifferent, frozen up, as it were, and fancied that he would have cared little had he been to leave the mansion without so much as looking over the remaining part of it.

At last, he became weary of sitting and indulging this fantastic humor of indifference, and emerged from his chamber, with the design of finding his way into the lower part of the house. The mansion had that delightful intricacy which can never be contrived; never be attained by design; but is the happy result of many builders, many designs—many ages, perhaps—having concurred in a structure, each pursuing his own design. Thus it was a house that you could go astray in, as in a city, and come to unexpected places, but never, until after much accustomance, go where you wished; so Etherege, although the great staircase and wide corridor by which he had been led to his room, seemed easy to find, yet soon discovered that he was involved in an unknown labyrinth, where strange little bits of staircases led up not down, and where passages promised much in letting him out, but performed nothing. To be sure, the old English mansion had not much of the stateliness of one of Mrs. Radcliffe's castles, with their suites of rooms opening one into another; but yet its very domesticity—its look as if long ago it had been lived in—made it only the more ghostly; and so Etherege felt the more as if he were wandering through a homely dream. Sensible of the ludicrousness of his position, he once called aloud; but his voice echoed along the passages, sounding unwontedly to his ears, but arousing nobody. It did not seem to him as if he were going afar, but were bewildered round and round, within a very small compass; a predicament in which a man feels very foolish, usually.

As he stood at an old window, stone mullioned, at the end of a passage into which he had twice come, a door near him opened, and a personage looked out whom he had not before seen. It was a face of great keenness and intelligence, and not unpleasant to look at, though dark and sallow. The dress had something which Etherege recognized as clerical, though not exactly pertaining to the church of England; a sort of arrangement of the vest and shirt-collar; and he had knee breeches of black. He did not seem like an English clerical personage, however; for even in this little glimpse of him, Etherege saw a mildness, gentleness, softness, and asking of leave, in his manner, which he had not observed in persons so well assured of their position as the Church of England clergy.

He seemed at once to detect Etheredge's predicament, and came forward with a pleasant smile, speaking in good English, though with a somewhat foreign accent.

"Ah, Sir, you have lost your way. It is a labyrinthine house for its size, this old English Hall; full of perplexity. Shall I show you to any point?"

"Indeed, Sir," said Etheredge, laughing, "I hardly know whither I want to go; being a stranger, and yet knowing nothing of the public places of the house. To the library, perhaps, if you will be good enough to direct me thither."

"Willingly, my dear Sir," said the clerical personage; "the more easily too as my own quarters are close adjacent; the library being my province. Do me the favor to enter here."

So saying, the priest ushered Etheredge into an austere looking yet exceedingly neat study, as it seemed, on one side of which was an oratory, with a crucifix and other accommodations for Catholic devotion. Behind a white curtain, there were glimpses of a bed, which seemed arranged on a principle of conventual austerity, in respect to limits and lack of softness; but still there was in the whole austerity of the premises a certain character of restraint, poise, principle, which Etherege liked. A table was covered with books, some of them folios in an antique binding of parchment, and others were small, thickset volumes, into which antique lore was rammed and compressed. Through an open door, opposite to the one by which he had entered, there was a vista of a larger apartment, with alcoves, a rather dreary looking room, though a little sunshine came through a window at the further end, distained with colored glass.

"Will you sit down in my little home?" said the courteous priest. "I hope we may be better acquainted; so allow me to introduce myself. I am Father Angelo, domestic Chaplain to his lordship. You, I know, are the American diplomatic gentleman, from whom his lordship has been expecting a visit."

Etheredge bowed.

"I am most happy to know you," continued the priest. "Ah; you have a happy country, most Catholic, most recipient of all this outcast on earth. Men of my religion must ever bless it."

"It certainly ought to be remembered to our credit," replied Etheredge, "that we have shown no narrow spirit in this matter, and have not, like other protestant countries, rejected the good that we found in any man, on account of his religious faith. American statesmanship comprises Jew, Catholic, all."

After this pleasant little mutual acknowledgment, there ensued a conversation having some reference to books; for though Etheredge, of late years, had known little of what deserves to be called literature—having found political life as much estranged from it as it is apt to be with politicians—yet he had early snuffed the musty fragrance of the Doctor's books, and had learned to love its atmosphere. At the time he left college, he was just at the point when he might have been a scholar; but the active tendencies of American life had interfered with him, as with thousands of others, and drawn him away from pursuits which might have been better adapted to some of his characteristics than the one he had adopted. The priest gently felt and touched around his pursuits, and finding some remains of classic culture, he kept up a conversation on those points; showing him the possessions of the library in that department, where, indeed, were some treasures that he had discovered, and which seemed to have been collected at least a century ago.

"Generally, however," observed he, as they passed from one dark alcove to another, "the library is of little worth; except to show how much of living truth each generation contributes to the botheration of life, and what a public benefactor a book worm is, after all—there; now;—did you ever happen to see one? Here is one that I have watched at work, sometime past, and have not thought it worth while to stop him."

Etherege as it happened, never had seen one; so he looked at the learned little insect, who was eating a strange sort of circular track into an old book of scholastic Latin, which probably only he had ever devoured—at least no others ever found to their tastes. The insect seemed in excellent condition, fat with learning, having doubtless got the essence of the book into himself. But Etheredge was still more interested in observing in the corner a great spider, which really startled him—not so much for its own terrible aspect, though that was monstrous—as because he seemed to see in it the very great spider which he had known in his boyhood; that same monster that had been the Doctor's familiar, and had been said to have such an influence in his death. He looked so startled that Father Antonio observed it.

"Do not be frightened," said he; "though I allow that a brave man may well be afraid of a spider, and that the bravest of the brave need not blush to shudder at this one. There is a great mystery about this spider. No one knows whence he came; nor how long he has been here. The library was very much shut up during the time of the last inheritor of the estate; and had not been thoroughly examined for some years when I opened it, and swept some of the dust away from its old alcoves. I myself was not aware of this monster until the lapse of some weeks, when I was startled at seeing him, one day, as I was reading an old book here. He dangled down from the cieling, by the cordage of his web, and positively seemed to look into my face."

"He is of the species *conditus* &c," said Etheredge,—"a rare spider, seldom seen out of the tropic regions."

"You are learned, then, in spiders," observed the priest, surprised.

"I could almost make oath, at least, that I had known this ugly specimen of his race," observed Etheredge. "A very dear friend, now deceased, to whom I owed the highest obligations, was studious of spiders, and his chief treasure was one the very image of this."

"How strange!" said the priest. "There has always appeared to me to be something uncanny in spiders. I should be glad to talk further with you on this subject. Several times I have fancied a strange intelligence in this monster; but I have natural horror of him, and therefore refrain from interviews."

"You do wisely, Sir," said Etherege. "His powers and purposes are questionably beneficent, at best."

In truth, the many legged monster made the old library ghostly to him by the associations which it summoned up, and by the idea that it was really the identical one that had seemed so stuffed with poison, in the lifetime of the Doctor, and at that so distant spot. Yet on reflection, it appeared not so strange; for the old Doctor's spider, as he had heard him say, was one of an ancestral race that he had brought from beyond the sea. They might have been preserved, for ages possibly, in this old library, whence the Doctor had perhaps taken his specimen, and where perhaps the one now before him was the sole survivor. It hardly, however, made the monster any the less hideous to suppose that this might be the case; and to fancy the poison of centuries condensed into this animal, who might have sucked the diseases, moral and physical, of all this family into him, and to have made himself their demon. He questioned with himself whether it might not be well to crush him at once, and so perhaps do away with the evil of which he was the emblem.

"I felt a strange disposition to crush this monster on first sight," remarked the priest, as if he knew what Etherege was thinking of—"a feeling that in so doing I should get rid of a mischief; but then he is such a curious monster. You cannot long look at him without coming to the conclusion that he is indestructible."

"Yes; and to think of crushing such a deep-bowelled monster!" said Etheredge shuddering. "It is too great a catastrophe."

During this conversation, in which he was so deeply concerned, the spider withdrew himself, and hand over hand ascended to a remote and dusky corner, where was his hereditary abode.

"Shall I be likely to meet Lord Brathwaite here in the library?" asked Etheredge, when the fiend had withdrawn himself. "I have not yet seen him since my arrival."

"I trust," said the priest, with great courtesy, "that you are aware of some peculiarities in his Lordship's habits, which imply nothing in detriment to the great respect which he pays all his few guests, and which, I know, he is especially desirous to pay to you. I think that we shall meet him at lunch, which though an English institution, his lordship has adopted very readily."

"I should hope," said Etherege, willing to know how far he might be expected to comply with the peculiarities—which might prove to be eccentricities of his host—"that my presence here will not be too greatly at variance with his lordship's habits, whatever they may be. I came hither, indeed, on the pledge that as my host would not stand in my way, so neither would I in his."

"That is the true principle," said the priest; "and here comes his lordship in person to begin the practice of it."

Lord Brathwaite came into the principal door of the library as the priest was speaking, and stood a moment just upon the threshold, looking keenly out of the stronger light into this dull and darksome apartment, as if unable to see perfectly what was within; or rather, as Etherege fancied, trying to discover what was passing between these two. And, indeed, as when a third person comes suddenly upon two who are talking of him, the two generally evince in their manner some consciousness of the fact; so it was in this case, with Etheredge at least; although the priest seemed perfectly undisturbed, either through practice of concealment, or because he had nothing to conceal.

His Lordship, after a moment's pause, came forward, presenting his hand to Etherege, who shook it, and not without a certain cordiality; till he perceived that it was the left hand, when he probably intimated some surprise by the change of manner.

"I am an awkward person," said his Lordship. "The left hand, however, is nearest the heart; so be assured I mean no discourtesy."

"The Signor Ambassador and myself," observed the priest, "have had a most interesting conversation (to me, at least) about books and book-worms, spiders, and other congruous matters; and I find his Excellency has heretofore made acquaintance with a great spider bearing strong resemblance to the hermit of our library."

"Indeed," said his lordship. "I was not aware that America had yet enough of age and the old misfortune, crime, sordidness that accumulates with it, to have produced spiders like this. Had he sucked into himself all the noisomeness of your past?"

Etherege made some slight answer, that the spider was a sort of pet of an old virtuoso, to whom he owed many obligations in his boyhood; and the conversation turned from this subject to others suggested by topics of the day, and place. His Lordship was affable, and Etheredge could not, it must be confessed, see anything to justify the prejudices of the neighbors against him. Indeed, he was inclined to attribute them, in great measure, to the narrowness of the

English view, to those insular prejudices which have always prevented them from fully appreciating what differs from their own habits. At lunch, which was soon announced, the party of three became very pleasant and sociable, his lordship drinking a light Italian red wine, and recommending it to Etherege; who, however, was English enough to prefer some bitter ale, while the priest contented himself with pure water —which is, in truth, a less agreeable drink in chill, moist England than in any country we are acquainted with.

"You must make yourself quite at home here," said his Lordship, as they rose from table. "I am not a good host, nor a very genial man, I believe. I can do little to entertain you; but here is the house and the grounds at your disposal— horses in the stable—guns in the hall—here is Father Antonio, good at chess. There is the library. Pray make the most of them all; and if I can contribute in any way to your pleasure let me know."

All this certainly seemed cordial, and the manner in which it was said seemed in accordance with the spirit of the words; and yet, whether the fault was in anything of morbid sus- picion in Etherege's nature, or whatever it was, it did not have the effect of making him feel welcome, which almost every Englishman has the natural faculty of producing on a guest, when once he has admitted him beneath his roof. It might be in great measure his face, so thin and refined, and intellectual without feeling; his voice, which had melody, but not heartiness; his manners, which were not simple by nature, but by art:—whatever it was, Etheredge found that Lord Brathwaite did not call for his own naturalness and simplicity, but his art, and felt that he, inevitably, was acting a part in his intercourse with him, that he was on his guard, playing a game; and yet he did not wish to do this. But there was a mobility, a subtleness in his nature, an unconscious tact— which the mode of life and of mixing with men in America fosters and perfects—that made this sort of finesse inevitable to him, with any but a natural character; with whom, on the other hand, Etherege could be as frank and natural as any Englishman of them all.

Etheredge spent the time between lunch and dinner in wandering about the grounds, from which he had hitherto felt himself debarred by motives of delicacy. It was a most interesting ramble to him; among trees which his ancestor, who went to America, might have climbed in his boyhood, might have sat beneath, with his lady-love, in his youth; deer there were, the descendants of those which he had seen; old stone slates, which his foot had trodden. The sombre, clouded light of the day fell down upon this scene, which in its verdure, its luxuriance of vegetable life, was purely English, cultivated to the last extent without losing the nature out of a single thing. In the course of his walk, he came to the spot where he had been so mysteriously wounded on his first arrival in this region; and examining the spot, he was struck to see that there was a path leading to the other side of a hedge, and this path, which led to the house, had brought him here.

Musing upon this mysterious circumstance, and how it should have happened in so orderly a country as England, so tamed and subjected to civilization—an incident to happen in an English park, which seemed better suited to the Indian-haunted forests of the wilder parts of his own land—and how no researches which the Warden had instituted had served in the smallest degree to develope the mystery—he clambered over the hedge, and followed the footpath. It plunged into dells, and emerged from them, led through scenes which seemed those of old romances, and at last by these devious ways began to approach the old house, which, with its many grey gables, put on a new aspect from this point of view. Etherege admired its venerableness anew; the ivy that overran parts of it; the marks of age, and wondered at the firmness of the institutions which, through all the changes that come to man, could have kept this house the home of one lineal race for so many centuries; so many, that the absence of his own branch from it seemed but a temporary visit to foreign parts, to which he was now returned, to be again at home by the old hearthstone.

"But what do I mean to do?" said he to himself, stopping short and still looking at the old house. "Am I ready to give up all the actual life before me for the sake of taking up with what I feel to be a less developed state of human life? Would it not be better for me to depart now, to turn my back on this flattering prospect? I am not fit to be here—I so strongly susceptible of a newer, more stirring life than these men lead; I, who feel, that whatever the thought and cultivation of England may be, my own countrymen have gone forward a long, long march beyond them, not intellectually, but in a way that gives them a further start. If I come back hither, with the purpose to make myself an Englishman—especially an Englishman of rank and hereditary estate—then for me America has been discovered in vain, and the great spirit that has been breathed into us is in vain; and I am false to it all!"

But again came silently swelling over him like a flood all that ancient peace, and quietude, and dignity, which looked so stately and beautiful as brooding round this old house; all that blessed order of ranks, that sweet superiority, and yet with no disclaimer of common brotherhood, that existed between the English gentleman and his inferiors; all that delightful intercourse, so sure of pleasure, so safe from rudeness, lowness, unpleasant rubs, that exists between gentleman and gentleman, where, in public affairs, all are essentially of one mind, or seem so to an American politician, accustomed to the fierce conflicts of our embittered parties; where life was made so enticing, so refined, and yet with a sort of homeliness that seemed to show that all its strength was left behind; that seeming taking in of all that was desirable in life, and all its grace and beauty, yet never giving life a hard enamel of over refinement. What could there be in the wild, harsh, ill-concocted American approach to civilization which could compare with this? What to compare with this juiciness and richness? What other men had ever got so much out of life as the polished and wealthy Englishmen of to-day! What higher part was to be acted, than seemed to lie before him, if he willed to accept it?

He resumed his walk, and drawing near the manor-house, found that he was approaching another entrance than that which had at first admitted him; a very pleasant entrance it was, beneath a porch, of antique form, and ivy-clad, hospitable and inviting; and it being the approach from the grounds, it seemed to be more appropriate to the residents of the house than the other one. Drawing near, Etherege saw that a flight of steps ascended within the porch, old looking, much worn; and nothing is more suggestive of long time, than a pair of worn steps; it must have taken so many soles, through so many years, to make an impression. Judging from the make of the outside of the edifice, Etherege thought that he could make out the way from the porch to the hall and library; so he determined to enter this way.

There had been, as was not unusual, a little shower of rain during the afternoon; and as Etherege came close to the steps, they were glistening with the wet. The stone was whitish like marble, and one of them bore on it a token that made him pause, while a thrill like terror ran through his system. For it was the mark of a footstep, very decidedly made out, in red, like blood—the Bloody Footstep—the mark of a foot, which seemed to have been slightly impressed into the rock, as if it had been a soft substance, at the same time sliding a

little, and gushing with blood. The glistening moisture, of
which we have spoken, made it appear as if it were just freshly
stamped there; and it suggested to Etherege's fancy the idea,
that, impressed more than two centuries ago, there was some
doom connected with the mark which kept still fresh, and
would continue to do so to the end of time. It was well that
there was no spectator there; for the American would have
blushed to have it known how much this old traditionary
wonder had affected his imagination. But, indeed, it was as
old as any bugbear of his mind—as any of those bugbears
and private terrors which grow up with people, and make the
dreams and nightmares of childhood, and the fever-images
of maturer years, till they haunt the deliriums of the dying-
bed, and after that, possibly, are either realized or known no
more. The Doctor's strange story vividly recurred to him, and
all the horrors which he had since associated with this trace;
and it seemed to him as if he had now struck upon a bloody
track, and as if there were other tracks of this supernatural foot
which he was bound to search out, removing the dust of ages
that had settled on them, the moss or deep grass that had
grown over them, the forest leaves that might have fallen on
them in America—marking out the pathway, till the pedestrian lay down in his grave.

The foot was issuing from, not entering into the house.
Whoever had impressed it, or on whatever occasion, he had
gone forth, and doubtless to return no more. Etherege was
impelled to place his own foot in the track, and the action,
as it were, suggested in itself strange ideas of what had been
the state of mind of the man who planted it there; and he
felt a strange, vague, yet strong surmise of some agony, some
terror and horror, that had passed here, and would not fade
out of the spot. While he was in these musings, he saw Lord
Brathwaite looking at him through the glass of the porch,
with fixed, curious eyes, and a smile on his face. On perceiv-

ing that Etherege was aware of his presence, he came forth, without appearing in the least disturbed.

"What think you of the Bloody Footstep?" asked he.

"It seems to me, undoubtedly," said Etherege, stooping to examine it more closely, "a good thing to make a legend out of; and like most legendary lore, not capable of bearing close examination. I should decidedly say that the Bloody Footstep is a natural reddish stain in the stone."

"Do you so, indeed?" rejoined his lordship. "It may be; but in that case, if not the record of an actual deed—of a foot stamped down there in guilt and agony, and oozing out with unwipeupable blood—we may consider it as prophetic;— as foreboding, from the time when the stone was squared and smoothed, and laid at this threshold, that a fatal footstep was really to be impressed here."

"It is an ingenious supposition," said Etherege. "But is there any sure knowledge that the prophecy you suppose has yet been fulfilled?"

"If not, it might yet be in the future," said Lord Brathwaite. "But I think there are enough in the records of this family to prove that there did one cross this threshold in a bloody agony, who has since returned no more! Great seekings, I have understood, have been had throughout the world for him, or for any sign of him, but nothing satisfactory has been heard."

"And it is now late to expect it," observed the American.

"Perhaps not," replied the nobleman, with a glance that Etherege thought had peculiar meaning in it. "Ah; it is very curious to see what turnings up there are in this world of old circumstances that seemed buried forever; how things come back, like echoes that have rolled away among the hills and been seemingly hushed forever. We cannot tell when a thing is really dead; it comes to life, perhaps in its old shape, perhaps in a new and unexpected one; so that nothing really vanishes out of the world. I wish it did."

The conversation now ceased, and Etherege entered the house, where he amused himself for some time in looking at the ancient hall, with its gallery, its armour, and its antique fire-place, on the hearth of which burned a genial fire. He wondered whether, in this fire, was the continuance of that custom which the Doctor's legend spoke of, and that the flame had been kept up these two hundred years, in expectation of the wanderer's return. It might be so, although the climate of England made it a natural custom enough, in a large and damp old room, into which many doors opened, both from the exterior and interior of the mansion; but it was pleasant to think the custom a traditionary one, and to fancy that a booted figure, enveloped in a cloak, might still arrive, and fling open the veiling cloak, throw off the sombre and drooping-brimmed hat, and show features that were similar to those seen in pictured faces on the walls. Was he himself—in another guise, as Lord Brathwaite had been saying—that long unexpected one? Was his the echoing tread that had been heard so long through the ages—so far through the wide world—approaching the blood-stained threshold?

With such thoughts, or dreams (for they were hardly sincerely entertained enough to be called thoughts) Etherege spent the day; a strange, delicious day, in spite of the sombre shadows that enveloped it. He fancied himself strangely wonted, already, to the house; as if his every part and peculiarity had at once fitted into its nooks, and corners, and crannies; but, indeed, his mobile nature and active fancy were not entirely to be trusted in this matter; it was perhaps his American faculty of making himself at home anywhere, that he mistook for the feeling of being peculiarly at home here.

Here I come to a stand still! What does his lordship mean to do with Etheredge, having now got him into his house? To poison him? 'Twon't do. To produce some effect on his mind, by means of spiders and bookworms, and works of natural magic? I don't see the modus operandi. There might be an auction in the house; or preparations for one; and so there should be a general rummage; or there might be repairs going on, because parts of the house are ruinous and leaky. In either of these ways, the old cabinet may be found out. Or the priest and he, forming a friendship together (which may be cordial and sincere; or otherwise), the former (who is in all his lordship's secrets, or has discovered some for himself) lets him into one which he has discovered in his own apartment. It is a secret repository, adjoining his room, in which is the cabinet. No; the old pensioner is, on some occasion, brought to the house, where he tells behind a pannel in this room is a secret place, which he points out, and within it is this coffer, made of oak, or bronze, or what not. Well; all that nonsense might be easily enough arranged; but what is his lordship, and what is he to do? He is a member of a secret society in Italy, who have a hold upon him, which they strenuously assert; and he thereby becomes most miserable. 'Twon't do. He has a secret ulcer. Pish. What does he do? He makes a soup for Etherege out of the bones of his long dead ancestors, spiced with the embalming out of the bowels of one of them; and he himself partakes. Very well. Oh, Heavens! I have not the least notion how to get on. I never was in such a sad predicament before. The old family, as far as refers to his lordship's ancestor, was effete; then came a vein of wickedness in, making him cunning and crafty, which he is, beyond the depth of most men. There has been a spider's web woven of old, which enmeshes all who come near it; and the great spider is the emblem of the person who did it. How can this be? The priest finds the spider, and takes up the plot. This spider's web must be a sort of chorus to the drama that is going on, reflecting it; a new spoke and complication of the web continually corresponding with every new developement. From a life of petty meannesses and shifts, he has come into this high position; and he brings one thing with him—one chain attached—which threatens to throttle him, being about his neck. Oh, fie!

Now here. The old Doctor's spider's web must of course have a signification; it signifies a plot in which his art has involved the story and every individual actor; he has caught them all, like so many flies; nor are they set at liberty by the death of the magician who originally enthralled them. This is good, as an unshaped idea; but how is it to be particularized & put in action? Thus, for instance. It must be an ancient story, certainly; something coming down from the days of the Bloody Footstep; some business which was left unsettled by the sudden disappearance of the original emigrant to America. It must relate to property; because nothing else survives in this world. Love grows cold and dies; hatred is pacified by annihilation. It might indeed have reference to the title; perhaps it may. Could there be a document, or record, somewhere in the old house, which each succeeding heir reads; and is immediately smitten with insane desire to achieve, or obtain, something there written and propounded? What? It refers to a treasure of the family buried in a certain spot. That'll not do. No; we must get out of this idea. It awakens an unhallowed ambition, and madness of lust for something that ought not to be—cannot be possessed. It speaks of a great beauty to be won; and she is found in the old coffer. It must be a mere delusion.

The Doctor must then have an agent in England. This is Hammond, who has been taken possession of by the subtlety and force of the Doctor's character, and continues to do his will even after he has been dead twenty years; for he had laid a command upon him. He has therefore a constant agency in all that takes place, or is hereafter to occur, in the

English scene. Hammond must be an attorney in the vicinity of the Manor-house; he is crafty and ingenious, but has not strength of mind, and has been subjected of old by the power of this old man, who knew some peccadillo of his, and took advantage of it thoroughly to subdue him. The Doctor had a deep purpose of revenge to subserve; it being, in part, to substitute another heir in place of the one then in possession. Hammond was to be his coadjutor in this. This man, deeply read in the history and secrets of the family, plays off all the different possessors of the property. Dying, the Doctor leaves this man to be an uncontrolled agent of the mischief which he himself had set on foot. Yet it shall turn out, in the end, that Hammond had unwittingly made a victim of himself as well as the other personages. The representatives of this ancient and noble family had each been led to do some most unworthy things. Could there be, through all these times, some person hidden in the old house? Could the old Doctor himself be hidden there, being only supposed to be dead? I don't see this, at present. The Doctor, by his subtlety, had saved this Hammond from the gallows; he held him in the bonds of love and fear; he had laid his commands on him, before leaving the country, to do continually some one act, the constant repetition of which produces the strangest consequences. He has hidden some person, whom he wished to keep from the knowledge of the world, in a secret place of the old house; and has commanded this old fellow to feed and nourish, and supply him with books, but never to let him out; and, after the old man has been doing it for a few years, of course it is impossible that he should do otherwise. Who is the prisoner? The true heir of the estate? He might have disappeared suddenly, and been supposed to be murdered. On coming into the property and title, the present possessor shall have been made aware of this dreadful secret and shall have adopted the guilt as his own. There shall be no cruelty in the treatment of the person, except just the solitary confinement; he might have committed some crime, to which he shall be justly condemned to this punishment—had it been by a competent jurisdiction. There should be much talk about this person in the Romance, doubts whether he is dead, whether he may not have gone to America; so that the reproduction of him shall not strike the reader altogether unexpectedly. But the absurd impossibility of the thing? Why so? Should it be man or woman? The woman whom the Doctor loved? and who was false to him? This would be too shocking? It should be the man who wronged him, if anybody. The Doctor, by some of his chemical contrivances, had taken from him the power of speech, or paralyzed him in some way, and hidden him here; and he himself goes to America to find out the true heir. This Hammond remains in the house, being a sort of upper servant. An old priest's chamber readily enough supplies the prison-place. This ghastly thing, without people's well knowing why, has made the house horrible, and the man who knows it horrible. The Doctor might have meant to poison him, but only succeeded in paralyzing him to a certain extent. There seems to be something in this ugly idea, which may eventually answer the purpose; but not as I see it now.

One great point must be the power of the old Doctor's character, operating long years after his death, just as when he was alive. The prisoner should have been very wicked, and worthy of his doom; seducing the Doctor's young wife, and taking her home into his mansion. The wife may have committed suicide, and have been deposited in the old coffer, and have there turned to golden hair. The old Doctor was a man of wonderful scientific skill. He had preserved a man that had been hanged, and thus got him under complete subjection to him; the man had been unjustly accused of crime; but he was of a nature strongly impressible by another's force of character. The Doctor had made him, as it were, created him anew, and he never could dream of being released from his authority. This man, by his recommendation, had been received into the Brathwaite family, with which the man of science was intimate. The Doctor had a beautiful wife, who was seduced by Mr. (or Lord) Brathwaite, and was taken by him to the old mansion. The Doctor finds them there; the wife kills herself, and is buried in the coffer. The man is paralyzed, and kept in confinement, under the guardianship of the half-hanged worthy. The Doctor goes abroad, leaving matters in this state. There has been such an arrangement of incidents, that it appears as if the heir had gone abroad, with the Doctor's wife, instead of coming home; that had been his intention, and he had arranged matters with his stewards and agents as if for a long absence. He stays away a long, long time, indeed; nothing is heard of him; he has vanished; and, by and by, another heir possesses the estate after it has gone through a course of law, and been assigned to him. It was at this period, perhaps, that the legal gentleman comes from London to search for the grave. All these things being pre-supposed, the first part of the Romance may stand pretty much as before shadowed out, with such deepening and darkening of the effects as will come from such pre-suppositions. But the lights must be made brighter in proportion.

Then in England:—Etherege arrives, and takes up his abode in the Hospital pretty much as now. The Doctor's adherents must be pretty speedily brought forward, and must feel a strong interest in Etherege, and be greatly moved on knowing (which he may soon know) that the American had known and been the protegé of the Doctor. He must be a very strange person in his habits and manners. The possessor of the estate must be described; an Italian, as already arranged. Since his accession, he has become noted for strange and secluded habits. There must have been an heir previous to this one, who shall have died mad. He was a needy young man, suddenly exalted from the depths of poverty to this station. The old Doctor himself was mad. The Warden must convey to Etheredge (perhaps in the form of a story) the aspect and fortunes of the family, since the Doctor left England—now some thirty years ago.

A striking point may be made, in respect to the simple and kindly, and upright, loyal, obedient nature of the Doctor's adherent.

The possessor of the estate shall have learned, somehow, of the probability that an American heir was coming with proofs that would oust him. He has gone through so much, that he is not inclined to stop at any crime now; so he endeavors to murder him on his first arrival. Afterwards, he invites him to his home, with indefinite purposes; for sometimes he thinks of giving up the estate and the secret into his keeping, and he himself being thus disburthened. He rather thinks he will poison him, or perhaps give the prisoner a companion.

In the Doctor's legend, the existence of this secret chamber must be disclosed. The old pensioner must also speak of it, and perhaps tell a story about it.

Elsie glimmers through the story, and illuminates with a healthy and natural light.

There is the house, with its hidden tenant in it, who throws a gloom all over it, and imbues it with horrors. It is the presence there of a frightful circumstance that does this. There is the old man who has the care of it. A change has taken place in the characters of the two persons who have inherited it; both have been in great pecuniary distress; so that it required superhuman virtue to make the disclosure that would have deprived them of their property. One has hitherto been a retired man; he becomes madly dissipated, a drunkard, and dies in delirious fever occasioned by drink.

Another was an idle gambler, a man of pleasure, a vaurien, a blackguard; this is the Italian, and he adopts recluse habits. The Doctor might have sworn revenge against the whole race; and after destroying them all, he intends to finish the matter by putting a supposititious heir, of his own choosing, into their hereditary property. He is a madman—made mad by injuries—but with all his powers sharpened by injury. He is a man in humble life, resenting the wrongs done by those hereditarily above him. A surgeon of great skill; or methinks he need not have been of any great skill. He has a beautiful wife, who attracts the attention of the young lord of Brathwaite. I must moderate the horror of all this; or it will be absolutely intolerable. The solitary confinement might be softened to the sufferer as much as possible, in a kind of mockery. He might go through various phases; first of stupefaction; then of violence; then of passiveness; then various awakenings of his intellectual powers, and subsiding again; religious impressions. I think he must, by drugs, have produced a paralyzing effect on some of his physical organs;—those of speech, for instance. The modus operandi—the particular medicinal agent—must be shown, if this be the case. Insanity must plead with the reader for the Doctor's pardon in respect to these horrors:—at his death, it shall blaze out in a terrible delirium; but Etherege must not recognize that his whole life has been affected and distorted by it, until the close of the Romance. Now, if this great bleakness and horror is to be underneath the story, there must be a frolic and dance of bacchanals all over the surface; else the effect will be utterly miserable. There may be a steam of horror escaping through safety-valves; but generally the tone must be joyous. He has concocted a medicine from the spider's web that is generally soothing, in small doses; in large ones, it is paralyzing to all effort. This the prisoner is dosed with. Introduce a chapter, early in the book—without saying where the scene is laid—in which the prisoner is represented in his secret room; make it as mysterious as possible. Then, before the close of the American part, another chapter; then after the arrival in England, another chapter; all developing the progressive state of the prisoner. The excellence of the execution must redeem all absurdities of the narrative—and it may. If we can once establish the prisoner in his dungeon, and keep him there a year, it would all be a matter of course that he should stay there; for the thought of going out would become a horror to him. After the Doctor's death, a chapter should be introduced, in which the prisoner should be sensible, three thousand miles away, of the relief; at least, of a change. When the secret chamber is discovered by Etherege and the pensioner, he shall be just at the point of death, and shall die without any explanation; affrighted, partly, by their coming, so that it shakes out a few months of life that might have been left in him. It will be difficult so to emphasize the Doctor's provocation as to justify him in the least to the reader. Something may be done by heaping all sorts of luxury upon the prisoner; this may have been done by subsequent inheritors of the property.

So Etherege was now established in the great house, which had been so long and so singularly an object of interest with him. With his customary impressibility by the influences around him, he began to take in the circumstances, and to understand them by more subtle tokens than he could well explain to himself. There was the steward, or whatever was his precise office; so quiet, so subdued, so nervous, so strange! What had been this man's history? What was now the secret of his daily life? There he was creeping stealthily up and down the staircases, and about the passages of the house; always as if he were afraid of meeting somebody. On seeing Etherege in the house, the latter fancied that the man expressed a kind of interest in his face; but whether pleasure or pain he could not well tell; only he sometimes found that he was contemplating him from a distance, or from the obscurity of the room in which he sat; or from a window, while he smoked his cigar on the lawn. A great part, if not the whole of this, he imputed to his knowledge of Etherege's connexions with the Doctor; but yet this hardly seemed sufficient to account for the pertinacity with which the old man haunted his footsteps,—the poor, nervous old thing—always near him, or often unexpectedly so; and yet, apparently not very willing to hold communication with him; having nothing of importance to say.

"Mr. Hammond," said Etherege to him, a day or two after the commencement of his visit, "how many years have you been in this situation?"

"Oh, Sir, ever since the Doctor's departure for America," said Hammond, "nine and twenty years, five months, and three days."

"A long time," said Etherege smiling, "and you seem to keep the account of it very intricately."

"A very long time, your honor," said Hammond; "so long, that I seem to have had no life before it began, and I cannot think of any life than just what I lead. My life was broken off short in the midst; and what belonged to the earlier part of it was another man's life; this is mine."

"It might be a pleasant life enough, I should think, in this fine old hall," said Etherege; "rather monotonous, however. Would you not like a relaxation of a few days, a pleasure trip, in all these twenty-nine years? You old Englishmen are so sturdily faithful to one thing. You do not resemble my countrymen in that."

"Ah; none of them ever lived in an old mansion house like this," replied Hammond. "They do not know the sort of habits that a man gets here. They do not know my business either, nor my master."

"Is Mr. Brathwaite, then, so difficult a master?" said Etherege.

"Mr. Brathwaite! Who was speaking of him?" said the old man, as if surprised. "Ah; I was thinking of the Doctor. He was my master, you know."

And Etherege was again inconceivably struck with the strength of the impression that was made on the poor old man's mind by the character of the old Doctor; so that, after thirty years of other service, he still felt him to be the master, and could not in the least release himself from those earlier bonds. He remembered the story that the Doctor used to tell of his once recovering a hanged person, and more and more came to the conclusion that this was the man; and that, as the Doctor had said, this hold of a strong mind over a weak one, strengthened by the idea that he had made him, had subjected the man to him in a kind of slavery that embraced the soul.

And then again, the lord of the estate interested him greatly, and not unpleasantly. He compared what he seemed to be now, with what, according to all reports, he had been in the past, and could make nothing of it, nor reconcile the two characters in the least. It seemed as if the estate were possessed by a devil—a foul and melancholy fiend—who resented the attempted possession of others by subjecting them to himself. One had turned from quiet and sober habits to reckless dissipation; another had turned from the mad gaiety of life to recluse habits, and both, apparently, by the same influence; at least, so it appeared to Etherege as he insulated their story from all other circumstances, and looked at them by one light. He even thought that he felt a similar influence come over himself, even in this little time that he had spent here; gradually, should this be his permanent residence—and not so very gradually either—there would come its own individual mode of change over him. That quiet, suggestive mind would gather the moss and lichens of decay. Palsy of its powers would probably be the form it would assume. He looked back through the vanished years to the time which he had spent with the old Doctor, and he felt unaccountably as if the mysterious old man were yet ruling him, as he did in his boyhood; as if his inscrutable, inevitable eye were upon him in all his movements; nay, as if he had guided every step that he took in coming hither, and were stalking mistily before him, leading him onward. He sometimes would gladly have given up all these wild and enticing prospects, these dreams that occupied him so long, if he could only have gone away, and looked back upon the house, its inmates, and his own recollections no more; but these were a fate, and took the shape of the old Doctor's apparition, holding him back.

And then, too, the thought of Elsie had much influence in keeping him quietly here; her natural sunshine was the one thing that, just now, seemed to have a good influence upon the world. She, too, was evidently connected with this place, and with the fate, whatever it might be, that awaited him here. The Doctor, the ruler of his destiny, had provided her as well as all the rest; and from his grave, or wherever he was, he still seemed to bring them together.

So here, in this darkened room he waited for what should come to pass; and daily, when he sat down in the dark old library, it was with the thought that this day might bring to a close the doubt amid which he lived; might give him the impetus to go forward. In such a state, no doubt the witchcraft of the place was really to be recognized, the old witchcraft, too, of the Doctor, which he had escaped by the quick ebullition of youthful spirit, long ago while the Doctor lived; but which had stored up till now, like an influenza that remains latent for years, and then breaks out in active disease. He held himself open for intercourse with the lord of the mansion; and intercourse of a certain nature they certainly had, but not of the kind which Etherege desired. They talked together of politics, of the state of the relations between England and America, of the court to which Etherege was accredited; sometimes Etherege tried to lead the conversation to the family topics, nor, in truth, did Mr. Brathwaite seem to decline his lead; although it was observable that very speedily, it was not well to be discerned how, the conversation would be found turned upon some other subject, to which it had swerved aside by subtle underhand movements. Yet Etherege was not the less determined, and at no distant period, to bring up the subject on which his mind dwelt so much, and have it fairly discussed between them.

He was sometimes a little frightened at the position and circumstances in which he found himself; a great disturbance there was in his being, the causes of which he could not trace. It had an influence on his dreams, through which the Doctor seemed to pass continually, and when he awoke, it was often with the sensation that he had just the moment before been holding conversation with the old man, and that the latter—with that gesture of power that he remembered so well—had been impressing some command upon him; but what that command was, he could not possibly call to mind. He wandered among the dark passages of the house, and up its antique staircases, as if expecting at every turn to meet some one who would have the word of destiny to say to him. When he went forth into the park, it was as if to hold an appointment with one who had promised to meet him there; and he came slowly back, lingering and loitering, because this expected one had not yet made himself visible; yet plucked up a little alacrity as he drew near the house, because the communicant might have arrived in his absence, and be waiting for him in the dim library. It seemed as if he was under a spell; he could neither go away nor rest—nothing but dream troubled dreams. He had ghostly fears, as if some one were near him whom he could not make out; stealing behind him, and starting away when he was impelled to turn round. A nervousness that his healthy temperament had never before permitted him to be the victim of assailed him now. He could not help imputing it partly to the influence of the generations who had left a portion of their individual human nature in the house, which had become magnetic by them and could not rid itself of their presence in one sense, though, in another, they had borne it as far off as to where the grey tower of the village church rose above their remains.

Again, he was frightened to perceive what a hold the place was getting upon him; how the tendrils of the ivy seemed to hold him and would not let him go; how natural and homelike, grim and sombre as they were, the old doorways and apartments were becoming; how, in no place that he had ever known, had he had such a home-like feeling. To be sure, poor fellow, he had no earliest home except the alms-house, where his recollections of a fireside crowded by grim old women and pale, sickly children, of course never allowed him to have the reminiscences of a private, domestic home. But then there was the Doctor's house by the grave-yard, and little Elsie his constant playmate; no, even those recollections did not hold him like this heavy present circumstance. How should he ever draw himself away? No; the proud and vivid and active prospects, that had heretofore spread themselves before him—the striving to come, the struggle, the victory, the defeat, if such it was to be—the experience for good or ill—the life, life, life—all possibility of these was passing from him; all that hearty earnest contest or communion of man with man, and leaving him nothing but this grim sombre shade, this brooding of the old family mansion, with its dreary ancestral hall, its mouldy dignity, its life of the past, its fettering honour, which to accept, must bind him hand and foot, as respects all effort, such as he had trained himself for—such as his own country offered.

It was not any value for these—as it seemed to Etheredge—but a witchcraft, an indefinable spell, a something that he could not define, that enthralled him, and was doing a work on him analogous to, though different from, that which it wrought on Hammond, or all the other inhabitants, high and low, of this old mansion.

He felt greatly interested in the master of the mansion; although perhaps it was not from anything in his nature; but partly because he conceived that he himself had a controlling power over his fortunes, and likewise from the vague perception of this before-mentioned trouble in him. It seemed, whatever it might be, to have converted an ordinary, superficial man of the world into a being that felt and suffered inwardly, had pangs, fears, a conscience, a sense of unseen things. It seemed as if, underneath this manor-house, were the entrance to the cave of Trophonious; one visit to which made a man sad forever after, and that Mr Brathwaite had been there once, or perhaps went nightly, or at any hour. Or the mansion itself was like dark-colored experience, the reality; the point of view where things were seen in their true lights; the true world, all outside of which was delusion, had here—dreamlike as it sometimes seemed—the absolute truth. All those that lived in it were getting to be a brotherhood; and he among them; and perhaps, before the blood stained threshold, would grow up an impassable barrier, which would cause himself to sit down in dreary quiet, like the rest of them.

Etherege had an unavowed—unavowed to himself—suspicion that the master of the house cherished no kindly purpose towards him; he had an indistinct feeling of danger from him; he would not have been surprised to know that he was concocting a plot against his life; and yet he did not think that Mr. Brathwaite had the slightest hostility towards him. It might make the thing more horrible, perhaps; but it has been often seen, in those who poison for the sake of interest, without feelings of personal malevolence, that they do it as kindly as the nature of the thing will permit; they, possibly, may even have a certain degree of affection for their victims, enough to induce them to make the last hours of life sweet and pleasant, to wind up the fever of life with a double supply of enjoyable throbs, to sweeten and delicately flavor the cup of death that they offer to the lips of him whose life is inconsistent with some state-necessity of their own. "Poor victim—dear friend," such a one might say to the friend whom he reluctantly condemned to death, "think not that there is any base malice, any desire of pain to thee, that actuates me in this thing. Heaven knows, I earnestly wish thy good. But I have well considered the matter—more deeply than thou hast—and have found that it is essential that one thing should be, and essential to that thing, that thou my friend should die. Is that a doom which even thou wouldst object to with such an end to be answered? Thou art innocent; thou art not a man of evil life; the worst thing that can come of it, so far as thou art concerned, would be a quiet, endless repose in yonder churchyard, among dust of thy ancestry, with the English violets growing over thee, those and her green sweet grass, which thou wilt not scorn to nourish with thy dissolving elements, remembering that thy forefather owed a debt, for his own birth and growth, to this English soil, and paid it not—consigned himself to that unstoried soil of another clime, under the forest-leaves. Pay it, dear friend, without repining, and leave me to battle a little longer with this troublesome world, and in a few years, to rejoin thee, and talk quietly over this matter which we are now arranging. How slight a favor, then, for one friend to do another, will seem this that I seek of thee."

Etherege smiled to himself, as he thus gave expression to what he really half-fancied were Mr. Brathwaite's feelings and purposes towards him, and he felt them in the kindness and sweetness of his demeanor, and his evident wish to make him happy, combined with his own subtle suspicion of some design with which he had been invited here, or which had grown up since he came.

<Whoever has read Italian history must have seen instances of this—poisoning without malice or personal ill-feeling>

His own pleasant, companionable, perhaps noble traits and qualities had made a favorable impression on Mr. Brathwaite; he perhaps regretted the necessity of acting as he was about to do, but could not therefore weakly relinquish his deliberately formed design. And, on his part, Etherege bore no malice towards Mr. Brathwaite, but felt really a kindly interest in him, and could he have made him happy at any less cost than his own life, or dearest interests, would perhaps have been glad to do so. He sometimes felt inclined to remonstrate with him in a friendly way; to tell him that his intended course was not likely to lead to a good result; that they had better try to arrange the matter on some other basis, and perhaps he would not find the American so unreasonable as he supposed.

All this, it will be understood, were the mere dreamy suppositions of Etherege, in the idleness and languor of this old mansion, letting his mind run at will, and following it into dim caves whither it tended. He did not actually believe anything of all this; unless it be a lawyer or a policeman, or some very vulgar natural order of mind, no man really suspects another of crime. It is the hardest thing in the world for a noble nature—the hardest and the most shocking—to be convinced that a fellow-being is going to do a wrong thing; and the consciousness of one's own inviolability renders it still more difficult to believe that one's self is to be the object of the wrong. What he had been fancying looked to him like a Romance. The strange part of the matter was, what suggested such a Romance in regard to his kind and hospitable host, who seemed to exercise the hospitality of England with a kind of refinement and pleasant piquancy that came from his Italian mixture of blood? Was there no spiritual whisper here?

So the time wore on; and Etherege began to be sensible that he must soon decide upon the course that he was to take; for his diplomatic position waited for him, and he could not loiter many days more away in this half delicious half painful reverie and quiet in the midst of his struggling life. He was yet as undetermined what to do as ever; or, if we may come closer to the truth, he was perhaps loth to acknowledge to himself the determination that he had actually formed.

One day, at dinner, which now came on after candle-light, he and Mr. Brathwaite sat together at table, as usual, while Hammond waited at the sideboard. It was a wild, gusty night, in which an autumnal breeze of later autumn seemed to have gone astray, and come into September intrusively. The two friends—for such we may call them—had spent a pleasant day together, wandering in the grounds, looking at the old house at all points, going to the church, and examining the cross-legged stone statue; they had ridden, too, and taken a great deal of healthful exercise, and had now that pleasant sense of just weariness enough, which it is the boon of the climate of England to incite and permit men to take. Etherege was in one of his most genial moods, and Mr. Brathwaite seemed to be the same; so kindly they were both disposed to one another, that the American felt that he ought not longer to refrain from giving his friend some light upon the character in which he appeared, or in which, at least, he had it at his option to appear. Mr. Brathwaite might, or might not know it already; but at all events, it was his duty to tell him, or to take his leave, having thus far gained nor sought any thing from their connection which would tend to forward his pursuit—should he decide to undertake it.

When the cheerful fire, the rare wine, and the good fare had put them both into a good physical state, Etherege said to Mr. Brathwaite,—

"There is a matter upon which I have been some time intending to speak to you."

Brathwaite nodded.

"A subject," continued he, "of interest to both of us. Has it ever occurred to you, from the identity of name, that I may be really, what we have jokingly assumed me to be— a relative?"

"It has," said Mr. Brathwaite, readily enough. "The family would be proud to acknowledge such a kinsman, whose abilities and political rank would add a public lustre that it has long wanted."

Etherege bowed, and smiled.

"You know, I suppose, the annals of your house," he continued, "and have heard how, two centuries ago, or somewhat less, there was an ancestor who mysteriously disappeared. He was never seen again. There were tales of private murder, out of which a hundred legends have come down to these days, as I have myself found, though most of them in so strange a shape that I should hardly know them, had I not myself a clue."

"I have heard some of these legends," said Mr. Brathwaite.

"But did you ever hear, among them," asked Etherege, "that the lost ancestor did not really die; was not murdered; but lived long, though in another hemisphere—lived long, and left heirs behind him?"

"There is such a legend," said Mr. Brathwaite.

"Left posterity," continued Etherege—"a representative of whom is alive at this day."

"That, I have not known, though I might conjecture some thing like it," said Mr. Brathwaite.

The coolness with which he took this perplexed Etherege. He resolved to make trial at once whether it were possible to move him.

"And I have reason to believe," he added, "that that representative is myself."

"Should that prove to be the case, you are welcome back to your own," said Mr. Brathwaite quietly. "It will be a very remarkable case, if the proofs for two hundred years, or thereabouts, can be so distinctly made out as to nullify the claim of one whose descent is undoubted. Yet it is certainly not impossible. I suppose it would hardly be fair in me to ask what are your proofs, and whether I may see them."

"The documents are in the hands of my agents in London," replied Etherege, "and seem to be ample,—among them being a certified genealogy from the first emigrant downward, without a break. A declaration, of two men of note among the first settlers, certifying that they knew the first emigrant, under a change of name, to be the eldest son of the house of Brathwaite; full proofs, at least, on that head."

"You are a lawyer, I believe," said Mr. Brathwaite, "and know better than I what may be necessary to prove your claim. I will frankly own to you, that I have heard, long ago—as long as when my connection with this hereditary property first began, that there was supposed to be an heir extant for a long course of years, and that there was no proof that that main line of the descent had ever become extinct. If these things had come fairly before me, and been represented to me with whatever force belongs to them, before my accession to the estate—these, and other facts which I have since become acquainted with—I might have deliberated on the expediency of coming to such a doubtful possession. The property, I assure you, is not so desirable that, taking all things into consideration, it has much increased my happiness. But, now, here I am, having paid a price in a certain way—which you will understand, if you ever come into the property—a price of a nature that cannot possibly be refunded. It can hardly be presumed that I shall see your right, a moment sooner than you make it manifest by law."

"I neither expect nor wish it," replied Etherege, "nor, to speak frankly, am I quite sure that you will ever have occasion to defend your title, or to question mine. When I came hither, to be your guest, it was almost with the settled purpose, never to mention my proofs, nor to seek to make them manifest. That purpose is not, I may say, yet relinquished."

"Yet I am to infer from your words that it is shaken?" said Mr. Brathwaite. "You find the estate, then, so delightful—this life of the old manor house so exquisitely agreeable—this air so cheering—this moral atmosphere so invigorating—that your scruples are about coming to an end. You think this life of an Englishman, this fair prospect of a title, so irresistibly enticing as to be worth more than your claim, in behalf of your American birthright, to a possible Presidency."

There was a sort of sneer in this, which Etherege did not well know how to understand; but there was a look on Brathwaite's face, as he said it, that made him think of a condemned soul, who should be dressed in magnificent robes, and surrounded with the mockery of state, splendor, and happiness, who, if he should be congratulated on his fortunate and blissful situation, would probably wear just such a look, and speak in just that tone. He looked a moment in Brathwaite's face.

"No," he replied. "I do not think that there is much happiness in it. A brighter, healthier, more useful, far more satisfactory, though tumultuous life would await me in my own country. But there is about this place a strange, deep, sad, brooding interest, which possesses me, and draws me to it, and will not let me go. I feel as if, in spite of myself, and my most earnest efforts, I were fascinated by something in the spot, and must needs linger here, and make it my home if I can."

"You shall be welcome; the old hereditary chair will be filled at last," said Brathwaite, pointing to the vacant seat. "Come, we will drink to you in a cup of welcome. Take the old chair now."

<In a half-frolic, Etherege takes the chair.>

He called to Hammond to bring a bottle of a particularly exquisite Italian wine, known only to the most deeply skilled in the vintages of that country, and which he said, was oftener heard of than seen—oftener seen than tasted. Hammond put it on the table in its original glass, and Brathwaite filled Etheredge's glass and his own, and raised the latter to his lips, with a frank expression of his mobile countenance.

"May you have a secure possession of your estate," said he, "and live long in the midst of your possessions. To me, on the whole, it seems better than your American prospects."

Etherege thanked him, and drank off the glass of wine, which was not very much to his taste; as new varieties of wine are apt not to be. All the conversation that had passed had been in a free, careless sort of way, without apparently much earnestness in it; for they were both men who knew how to keep their more serious parts within them. But Etherege was glad that the explanation was over, and that he might now remain at Brathwaite's table, under his roof, without that uneasy feeling of treachery which, whether rightly or not, had haunted him hitherto. He felt joyous, and stretched his hand out for the bottle which Brathwaite kept near himself, instead of passing it.

"You do not yourself do justice to your own favorite wine," observed Etheredge, seeing his host's full glass standing before him.

"I have filled again," said Brathwaite carelessly; "but I know not that I shall venture to drink a second glass. It is a wine that does not bear mixture with other vintages,

though of most genial and admirable qualities when taken
by itself. Drink your own, however, for it will be a rare
occasion indeed that would induce me to offer you another
bottle of this rare stock."

Etherege sipped his second glass, endeavoring to find out
what was this subtile and peculiar flavor that hid itself so,
and yet seemed on the point of revealing itself. It had, he
thought, a singlar effect upon his faculties, quickening and
making them active, and causing him to feel as if he were
on the point of penetrating rare mysteries, such as men's
thoughts are always hovering round, and always returning
from. Some strange, vast, sombre, mysterious truth, which
he seemed to have searched for long, appeared to be on the
point of being revealed to him; a sense of something to come;
something to happen that had been waiting long, long to
happen; an opening of doors, a drawing away of veils, a lifting of heavy, magnificent curtains, whose dark folds hung
before a spectacle of awe;—it was like the verge of the grave.
Whether it was the exquisite wine of Brathwaite's, or whatever it might be, the American felt a strange influence upon
him, as if he were passing through the gates of eternity, and
finding on the other side the revelation of some secret that
had greatly perplexed him on the other side. He thought
that Brathwaite's face assumed a strange, subtile smile—not
malicious, yet crafty, triumphal, and at the same time terribly
sad, and with that perception his senses, his life welled away;
and left him in the deep ancestral chair at the board of
Brathwaite House.

<(Etherege lies in a dreamy state, thinking fantastically,
as if he were one of the Seven Sleepers.)> <He does not
yet open his eyes but lies there in a maze.>

When he awoke, or began to awake, he lay for some time
in a maze, not a disagreeable one, but the thoughts were
running to and fro in his mind, all mixed and jumbled to-

gether. Reminiscenses of early days, even those that were pre-Adamite; referring, we mean, to those times in the alms-house, which he could not at ordinary times remember at all, but now there seemed to be visions of old women and men, and pallid girls, and little dirty boys, which could only be referred to that epoch. Also, and most vividly, there was the old Doctor, with his sternness, his fierceness, his mystery; and all that happened since, playing phantasmagoria before his yet closed eyes; nor, so mystified was his state, did he know, when he should unclose those lids, where he should find himself. He was content to let the world go on in this way, as long as it would, and therefore did not hurry, but rather kept back the process of awakening; willing to look at the scenes that were unrolling for his amusement, as it seemed; and willing, too, to keep it uncertain whether he were not back in America, and in his boyhood, and all other subsequent impressions a dream or a prophetic vision. But at length something stirring near him—or whether it stirred, or whether he dreamed it, he could not quite tell— but the uncertainty impelled him, at last, to open his eyes and see whereabouts he was.

Even then, he continued in as much uncertainty as he was before, and lay, with marvellous quietude in it, trying sluggishly to make the mystery out. It was in a dim, twilight place, wherever it might be; a place of half awakeness, where the outlines of things were not well defined; but it seemed to be a chamber antique, and vaulted, narrow, and high, hung round with old tapestry. Whether it were morning or mid-day, he could not tell, such was the character of the light, nor even where it came from; for there appeared to be no windows, and yet it was not apparently artificial light; no light at all, indeed, but a gray dimness. It was so like his own half-awake state that he lay in it a longer time, not incited to finish his awaking, but in a languor, not disagree-

able, yet hanging heavily, heavily upon him, like a dark pall.
It was, in fact, as if he had been asleep for years, or centuries,
or till the last day was dawning, and then was collecting his
thoughts in such slow fashion as would then be likely.

Again that noise; a little, low, quiet sound, as of one
breathing, somewhere near him; and coming more fully to
himself, Etheredge sat up, but immediately his head began
to swim so actively that the whole world seemed going round.
The whole thing was very much like that incident which
introduced him to the Hospital, and his first coming to his
senses there; and he almost fancied that some such accident
must again have happened to him, and that when his sight
cleared, he should again behold the venerable figure of the
Pensioner. With this idea, he let his head steady itself; and
it seemed to him that its dizziness must needs be the result
of very long and deep sleep. What if it were the sleep of a
century! What if all things, that were extant when he went
to sleep, had passed away, and he were waking now in
another epoch of time! Where was America, and the republic in which he hoped for such great things? Where England?
had she stood it better than the republic? Was the old Hospital still in being; although the good Warden must long
since have passed out of his warm and pleasant life? And
himself, how came he to be preserved? In what musty old
nook had he been put away, where Time neglected and
Death forgot him, until now he was to get up, friendless,
nameless—when new heirs had come to the estate he was on
the point of laying claim to—and go onward through what
remained of life? Would it not have been better to have
lived with his contemporaries, and to be now dead and dust
with them? Poor, petty interests of a day, how slight!

Again the noise; a little stir, a sort of quiet moan, or something that he could not quite define; but it seemed, whenever he heard of it, as if some fact thrust itself through the

dream work with which he was circumfused; something alien
to his fantasies, yet not powerful enough to dispel them. It
began to be irksome to him, this little sound of something
near him; and he thought, in the space of another hundred
years, if it continued, he should have to arouse himself and
see what it was. But, indeed, there was something so cheering
in this long repose—this rest from all the troubles of earth,
which it sometimes seems as if only a church-yard nap would
give us—that he wished the noise would let him alone. But
his thoughts were gradually getting too busy for this slumbrous state. He began, perforce, to come nearer actuality!
The strange question recurred to him:—had any time at all
passed? Was he not still sitting at Mr. Brathwaite's table,
having just now quaffed a second glass of that rare and
curious Italian wine? Was it not affecting his head very
strangely; so that he was put out of time, as it were? He
would rally himself, and try to set his head right with another glass.

<He must be still at table; for, now he remembered he
had not gone to bed at all.> <(Etherege must look at the
old man quietly and dreamily, and without surprise, for a
long while)>

Ah, the noise! He could not bear it; he would awake, now,
now—silence it, and then to sleep again. In fact, he started
up; started to his feet, in puzzle and perplexity, and stood
gazing around him, with swimming brain. It was an antique
room, which he did not at all recognize, and, indeed, in that
dim twilight—which how it came, he could not tell—he
could scarcely discern what were its distinguishing marks.
But he seemed to be sensible, that, in a high-backed chair,
at a little distance from him, sat a figure in a long robe; a
figure of a man with snow-white hair and a long beard, who
seemed to be gazing at him, quietly, as if he had been gazing
a hundred years. And Etherege stood on his feet, in amaze-

ment, and a shadowy terror; for I know not what it was, but there was an influence as if this old man belonged to some other age and category of man than he was now amongst. He remembered the old family legend, of the existence of an ancestor two or three centuries in age.

"It is the old family personified," thought he.

"Where am I?" he exclaimed, at length, in a tremulous voice.

The old figure made no answer, but continued to sit gazing at him, in so strangely still a manner that it made Etherege shiver with something that seemed like affright. There was an aspect of long, long time about him; as if he had never been young, or so long ago as when the world was young along with him. He might be the demon of this old house; the representative of all that happened in it, the grief, the long languor and weariness of life, the deaths, gathering them all into himself, and figuring them in furrows, wrinkles, and white hairs; a being that might have been young, when those old Saxon timbers were put together, with the oaks that were saplings when Caesar landed; and was in his maturity when the Conqueror came, and was now lapsing into extreme age when the nineteenth century was elderly. His garb might have been of any time, that long, loose robe that enveloped him. Etherege lay in this way, gazing at this aged figure; at first, without the least wonder, but calmly, as we feel in dreams, when, being in a land of enchantment, we take everything as if it were a matter of course; and feel, by the right of our own marvellous nature, on terms of equal kindred with all other marvels. So it was with him when he first became aware of the old man, sitting there with that age long regard towards him.

But, by degrees, a sense of wonder had its birth and grew, slowly at first, in Etherege's mind; and almost twin-born with it, and growing piece by piece, there was a sense of awful fear, as his waking senses came slowly back to him. In the dreamy state, he felt no fear; but, as a waking man, it was fearful to discover that the shadowy forms did not fly from his awaking eyes. He started at last to his feet from the low couch on which he had all this time been lying.

"What are you?" he exclaimed. "Where am I?"

The old figure made no answer; nor could Etherege be quite sure that his voice had any effect upon it, though he fancied that it was shaken a little, as if his voice came to it from afar. But it continued to gaze at him, or at least to have its aged face turned towards him, in the dim light; and this strange composure, and unapproachableness, was very frightful. As his manhood gathered about his heart, however, the American endeavored to shake off this besetting fear, or awe, or whatever it was; and to bring himself to a sense of waking things—to burst through the mist and delusive shows that bewildered him, and catch hold of a reality. He stamped upon the floor; it was solid stone, the pavement, or oak so old and staunch that it resembled it. There was one firm thing, therefore. But the contrast between this and the slipperiness, the unaccountableness, of the rest of his position, made him only the more sensible of the latter. He made a step towards the old figure; another; another. He was face to face with him, within a yard of distance. He saw the faint movement of the old man's breath; he caught, through the twilight of the room, some glimmer of perception in his eyes.

"Are you a living man?" asked Etherege faintly & doubtfully.

He mumbled—the old figure did—some faint moaning sound, that, if it were language at all, had all the edges and angles worn off it by decay—unintelligible, except that it seemed to signify a faint mournfulness and complainingness of mood; and then held his peace, continuing to gaze as before. Etherege could not bear the awe that filled him, while he kept at a distance, and coming desperately forward, he stood close to the old figure; he touched his robe, to see if it were real; he laid his hand upon the withered hand that held the staff, in which he now recognized the very staff of the Doctor's legend. His fingers touched a real hand, though, bony and dry, as if it had been in the grave.

"Then you are real?" said Etherege doubtfully.

The old figure seemed to have exhausted itself—its energies, what there were of them—in the effort of making the unintelligible communication already vouchsafed. Then he seemed to lapse out of consciousness, and not to know what was passing, or to be sensible that any person was near him. But Etherege was now resuming his firmness and daylight consciousness, even in that dimness. He ran over all that he had heard of the legend of the old house, rapidly considering whether there might not be something of fact in the legend of the undying old man; whether, as told or whispered in the chimney-corners, it might not be an instance of the mysterious—the half-spiritual mode—in which actual truths communicate themselves imperfectly through a medium that gives them the aspect of falsehood. Something in the atmosphere of the house made its inhabitants and neighbors dimly aware that there was a secret resident; it was by a language not audible, but of impression; there could not be such a secret in its recesses, without making itself sensible. This legend of the undying one translated it to vulgar apprehension. He remembered those early legends, told by the Doctor, in his childhood; he seemed imperfectly and doubtfully to see what was their true meaning, and how taken aright, they had a reality, and were the craftily concealed history of his own wrongs, sufferings, and revenge. And this old man! Who was he? He joined the Warden's account of the family to the Doctor's legends. He could not believe, or take thoroughly in, the strange surmise to which they led him; but, by an irresistible impulse, he acted on it.

"Sir Edward Brathwaite!" he exclaimed.

"Ha! who speaks to me?" exclaimed the old man, in a startled voice, like one who hears himself called at an unexpected moment.

"Sir Edward Brathwaite," repeated Etherege, "I bring you news of Norman Hanscough!"

"The villain! the tyrant! Mercy! mercy! save me!" cried the old man, in the most violent emotion of terror and rage intermixed, that shook his old frame, as if it would be shaken asunder. He stood erect the picture of ghastly horror, as if he saw before him that stern face that had thrown a blight over his life, and so fearfully avenged, from youth to age, the crime that he had committed. The effect—the passion, was too much—the terror with which it shook, the rage that accompanied, blazed up for a moment with a fierce flame, then flickered and went out. He stood tottering; Etherege put out his hand to support him; but he sank down in a heap on the floor, as if a thing of dry bones had been suddenly loosened at the joints, and fell in a rattling heap.

Etherege, apparently, had not communicated to his agents in London his change of address, when he left the Warden's residence to avail himself of the hospitality of Brathwaite Hall; for letters arrived for him, from his own country, both private and with the seal of state upon them; one among the rest that bore on the envelope the name of the President of the United States. The good Warden was impressed with great respect for so distinguished a signature, and not knowing but that the welfare of the Republic (for which he had an Englishman's contemptuous interest) might be involved in the early delivery of it to its destination, he determined to ride over to Brathwaite hall, call on his friend, and deliver it with his own hand. With this purpose, he mounted his horse, at the hour of his usual morning ride; and set forth; and before reaching the village, saw a figure before him which he recognized as that of the pensioner.

<Bubbleandsqueak.>

"Soho—wither go you, old friend?" said the Warden, drawing his bridle as he came up with the old man.

"To Brathwaite Hall, Sir," said the Pensioner, who continued to walk diligently on; "and I am glad to see your
honor (if it be so) on the same errand."

"Why so?" asked the Warden. "You seem much in earnest.
Why should my visit to Brathwaite Hall be a special cause
of rejoicing?"

"Nay," said the Pensioner, "your honor is specially interested in this young American, who has gone thither to abide;
and when one is in a strange country he needs some guidance. My mind it not easy about this young man."

"Well," said the Warden smiling to himself at the old
gentleman's idle and senile fears, "I commend your diligence
on behalf of your friend."

He rode on, as he spoke; and deep in one of the woodland
paths, he saw the flutter of a woman's garment; and greatly
to his surprise, overtook Elsie, who seemed to be walking
along with great rapidity, and startled by the approach of
hoofs behind her, looked up at him with a pale cheek.

"Good morning, Miss Elsie," said the Warden. "You are
taking a long walk this morning. I regret to see that I have
frightened you!"

"Pray whither are you going?" said she.

"To the Hall," said the Warden, wondering at the abrupt
question.

"Ah, Sir," exclaimed Elsie, "for Heaven's sake, pray insist
on seeing Mr Etheredge—take no excuse. There are reasons
for it."

"Certainly, fair lady," responded the Warden, wondering
more and more at this injunction from such a source. "And
when I see this fascinating gentleman, pray what message
am I to give him from Miss Alicompane—who, moreover,
seems to be on the eve of visiting him in person?"

"See him!—see him!—only see him!" said Elsie, with passionate earnestness; "and in haste! See him now!"

She waved him onward as she spoke; and the Warden, greatly commoted for the nonce, complied with the maiden's fantasy so far as to ride on at a quicker pace, uneasily marvelling at what could have aroused this usually shy and reserved girl's nervousness to such a pitch. The incident served, at all events, to titillate his English sluggishness; so that he approached the avenue of the old hall with a vague expectation of something that happened there, though he knew not of what nature it could possibly be. However, he rode round to the side entrance, by which horsemen usually entered the house, and a groom approaching to take his bridle, he alighted and approached the door. I know not whether it were anything more than the glistening moisture, common in an English autumnal morning; but so it was, that the trace of the Bloody Footstep seemed fresh, as if it had been that very night imprinted anew, and the crime made all over again, with fresh guilt upon somebody's soul.

When the footman came to the door, responsive to his ring, the Warden inquired for Mr Etheredge, the American gentleman.

"The American gentleman left for London, early this morning," replied the footman, in a matter of fact way.

"Gone!" exclaimed the Warden. "This is sudden; and strange that he should go without saying good-bye. Gone," and then he remembered the old Pensioner's eagerness that the Warden should come here, and Elsie's strange injunction that he should insist on seeing Etheredge. "Pray is Mr. Brathwaite at home?"

"I think, Sir, he is in the library," said the servant, "but will see; pray, Sir, walk in."

He returned in a moment, and ushered the Warden through passages with which he was familiar of old, to the library, where he found Mr. Brathwaite sitting with the London newspaper in his hand. He rose and welcomed his guest with great equanimity.

To the Warden's inquiries after Etheredge, Mʳ Brathwaite replied that his guest had that morning left the house; being called to London by letters from America; but of what nature Mr. Brathwaite was unable to say, except that they seemed to be of urgency and importance. The Warden's further inquiries, which he pushed as far as was decorous, elicited nothing more than this; and he was preparing to take his leave—not seeing any reason for insisting (according to Elsie's desire) on the impossibility of seeing a man who was not there; nor, indeed, any reason for so doing. And yet it seemed very strange that Etherege should have gone so unceremoniously; nor was he half satisfied, though he knew not why he should be otherwise.

"Do you happen to know Mr. Etherege's address in London?" asked the Warden.

"Not at all," said Mr. Brathwaite. "But I presume there is courtesy enough in the American character to impel him to write to one or both of us, within a day or two, telling us of his whereabout and whatabout. Should you hear, I beg you will let me know; for I have really been pleased with this gentleman, and should have been glad could he have favored me with a somewhat longer visit."

There was nothing more to be said; and the Warden took his leave, and was about mounting his horse, when he beheld the pensioner approaching the house, and he remained standing until he should come up.

"You are too late," said he, as the old man drew near. "Our friend has taken French leave."

"Mr. Warden," said the old man solemnly. "Let me pray you not to give him up so easily. Come with me into the presence of Mr. Brathwaite."

The Warden made some objections; but the pensioner's manner was so earnest, that he soon consented; knowing that the strangeness of his sudden return might well enough be put upon the eccentricities of the pensioner, especially as he was so well known to Mr. Brathwaite. He accordingly again rang at the door; which being opened by the same stolid footman, the Warden desired him to announce to Mr. Brathwaite that the Warden and a pensioner desired to see him. The man returned, with a request that they should walk in, and ushered them again to the library, where they found the master of the house, in conversation with Hammond, at one end of the apartment; a whispered conversation, which detained him a moment, after their arrival. The Warden fancied that he saw in old Hammond's countenance a shade more of that mysterious horror which made him such a bug-bear to children; but when Mr. Brathwaite turned from him and approached his visitors, there was no trace of any disturbance, beyond a natural surprise to see his good friend the Warden so soon after his taking leave.

<They found him in the hall, about to go out.>

"I see you are surprised," said the latter. "But you must lay the blame, if any, on our good old friend here, who, for some reason, best known to himself, insisted on having my company here."

Mr Brathwaite looked to the old pensioner, with a questioning look, as good humoredly, yet not as if he cared much about it, asking for an explanation. As Hammond was about leaving the room, having remained till this time with that nervous look which distinguished him, gazing towards the party, the pensioner made him a sign, which he obeyed as if compelled to do so.

"Well, my friend," said the Warden, somewhat impatient of the aspect in which he himself appeared, "I beg of you explain at once to Mr. Brathwaite why you have brought me back in this strange way."

"It is," said the pensioner quietly, "that in your presence I request him to allow us to see Mr. Etheredge."

"Why, my friend," said Mr Brathwaite, "how can I show you a man who has left my house, and whom, in the chances of this life, I am not very likely to see again, though hospitably desirous of so doing?"

Here ensued a laughing sort of a colloquy between the Warden and Mr Brathwaite, in which the former jocosely excused himself for having yielded to the whim of the pensioner, and returned with him on an errand which he well knew to be futile—"I have long been aware," he said apart, in a confidential way, "of something a little awry in our old friend's mental system. You will excuse him, and me for humouring him." "Of course, of course," said Mr. Brathwaite, in the same tone. "I shall not be moved by anything the old fellow can say."

The old pensioner, meanwhile, had been as it were heating up, and gathering himself into a mood of energy which those who saw him had never before witnessed in his usually quiet person. He seemed somehow to grow taller and larger, more impressive. At length, fixing his eyes on Mr. Brathwaite, he spoke again.

"Dark, murderous man," exclaimed he. "Your course has not been unwatched; the secrets of this mansion are not unknown. For two centuries back, they have been better known to those who dwell afar off, than to those resident within the mansion. The foot, that made the Bloody Footstep, has returned from its long wanderings; and it passes on, straight as destiny—sure as an avenging Providence—to the punishment and destruction of those who incur retribution."

"Here is an odd burst of tragedy," said Mr. Brathwaite, with a scornful smile. "Come, my old friend, lay aside this vein, & talk sense."

"Not thus do you escape your penalty, hardened and crafty one!" exclaimed the Pensioner. "I demand of you, before this worthy Warden, access to the secret ways of this mansion, of which thou dost unjustly retain possession. I shall disclose what for centuries has remained hidden; the ghastly secrets that this house hides!"

"Humor him," whispered the Warden; "and hereafter, I will take care that the exuberance of our old friend shall be duly restrained. He shall not trouble you again."

Mr Brathwaite, to say the truth, appeared a little flabbergasted and disturbed by these latter explosions of the old gentleman. He hesitated, turned pale; but at last, recovering his momentary confusion and irresolution, he replied with apparent carelessness:—

"Go wherever you will, old gentleman. The house is open to you for this time. If ever you have another opportunity to disturb it, the fault will be mine."

"Follow, Sir," said the pensioner, turning to the Warden; "follow, Warden! Now shall a great mystery begin to be revealed."

So saying, he led the way before them, passing out of the hall, not by the doorway, but through one of the oaken panels of the wall, which admitted the party into a passage which seemed to pass through the thickness of the wall, and was lighted by interstices through which shone gleams of light. This led them into what looked like a little vestibule, or circular room, which the Warden, though deeming himself many years familiar with the old house, had never seen before, any more than the passage which led to it. To his surprise, this room was not vacant; for in it sat, in a large old chair, Hammond, like a toad in its hole, like some wild, fearful creature in its den, and it was now partly understood how this man had the possibility of suddenly disappearing, so inscrutably, and so in a moment; and when all quest for him was given up, of as suddenly appearing again.

"Ha!" said old Hammond, slowly rising, as at the approach of some event that he had long expected. "Is he coming at last!"

"Poor victim of another's strong inequality," said the pensioner. "Thy release approaches. Rejoice!"

The old man arose, with a sort of trepidation and solemn joy intermixed in his manner, and bowed reverently, as if there were more in what he heard than other ears could understand in it.

"Yes; I have waited long," replied he. "Welcome; if my release is come."

"Well," said Mr. Brathwaite scornfully. "This secret retreat of my house is known to many. It was the priest's secret chamber, when it was dangerous to be of the old and true religion, here in England. There is no longer any use in concealing this place; and the Warden, or any man, might have seen it as any of the curiosities of the old hereditary house, if desirous so to do."

"Aha! son of Belial!" quoth the pensioner. "And this, too!"

He took three paces from a certain point of the wall, which he seemed to know, and stooped to press upon the floor. The Warden looked at Mr. Brathwaite, and saw that he had grown deadly pale. What his change of cheer might bode, he could not guess; but, at the pressure of the old pensioner's finger, the floor, or a segment of it, rose like the lid of a box, and discovered a small darksome pair of stairs, within which burned a lamp, lighting it downward, like the steps that descend into a sepulchre.

"Follow," said he, to those who looked on wondering.

And he began to descend. Mr Brathwaite saw him disappear, then frantically followed, the Warden next, and old Hammond took his place in the rear, like a man following his inevitable destiny. At the bottom of a winding descent, that seemed deep and remote, and far within, they came to a door, which the pensioner pressed with a spring, and passing through the space that disclosed itself, the whole party followed, and found itself in a small, gloomy room. On one side of it was a couch, on which sat Etherege; face to face with him was a white haired figure in a chair.

"You are come!" said Etheredge, solemnly. "But too late!"

"And yonder is the coffer," said the pensioner. "Open but that; and our quest is ended."

"That, if I mistake not, I can do," said Etherege.

He drew forth—what he had kept all this time, as something that might yet reveal to him the mystery of his birth—the silver key that had been found by the grave in far New England; and applying it to the lock, he slowly turned it on the hinges, that had not been turned for two hundred years. All—even Mr. Brathwaite, guilty and shame-stricken as he felt—pressed forward to look upon what was about to be disclosed. What were the wondrous contents? The entire, mysterious coffer was full of golden ringlets, abundant, curling through the whole coffer, and rising with elasticity, so as immediately, as it were, to flow over the sides of the coffer, and rise in large abundance from the long compression. Into this—by a miracle of natural production which has been known likewise in other cases—into this had been resolved the whole bodily substance of that fair and unfortunate being, known so long in the legends of the family as the beauty of the golden locks. As the pensioner looked at this strange sight,—the lustre of the precious and miraculous hair gleaming and glistening, and seeming to add light to the gloomy room—he took from his breast-pocket another lock of hair, in a locket, and compared it before their faces with those that brimmed over from the coffer.

"It is the same!" said he.

"And who are you that know it?" asked Etherege, surprised.

"He whose ancestors taught him the secret—who has had it handed down to him these two centuries, and now only with regret yields to the necessity of making it known."

"You are then the heir!" said Etherege.

In that gloomy room, beside the dead old man, they looked at him, and saw a dignity beaming on him, covering his whole figure, that broke out like a lustre at the close of day.

Try back again;—Raise the curtain, as before, and discover the Doctor's study in the old house at the corner of the Charter-street Burial ground; the Doctor is there, with two children. He himself is a mystery to his neighbors, and the gossips of the town; but he appears to be an Englishman, of learning and science, and is held in much account by those who know him, and believed to be a physician of London. Of studious and retired habits, frequenting only the public library; not going to church or chapel; sometimes walking on the seashore or in the country with the two children. The spiders to be much emphasized; and, very soon, the analogy of a plot to be suggested by the web of the great spider. Indications are early given of a troubled spirit, of a passionate grief, or sense of wrong, cherished and fondled deep within his consciousness, and perhaps affecting his reason. The beauty of the boy; the innocent gaiety and native tenderness of the girl are much dwelt upon; the fact of the boy's having been taken by the Doctor from the alms-house, and being insensed by him with the idea that he comes of high English blood. Letters are mentioned as being sometimes received from England, and the idea must be conveyed that the Doctor is connected with some train of events going on there. Early, the old Pensioner is introduced, preaching or praying in the street, and taking some sort of notice of the two children, and possibly of the old Doctor. The visit of an Englishman occurs, and the search in the burial ground, where the boy finds a key. Finally, the death of the Doctor, who, at his demise, appears troubled in mind, and to be in doubt whether or no to tell the boy some secret; but dies without doing so, leaving to the boy some property which he possessed here in America, and to the girl some hereditary property in England.

Now what has been the motive for this man's leaving England and coming hither, and what was indicated by the spider's web? He had saved an imperfectly hanged person, and made him morally a slave; so far good; and he thus has an instrument ready to assist him in perpetrating any monstrosity. But what? Then he has been deeply wronged by a gentleman in his neighborhood; a man of wealth and rank, against whom he vows and executes a dire revenge. How? He must somehow subjugate that man, and make him a prisoner and a slave in spite of his rank, and in spite of being himself an inhabitant of another country. In what way? Some continual operation on his mind; some constantly repeated impression, that makes him withdraw himself from society, and give himself up to one morbid way of life. What? He broods over a coffer in which his beloved's ashes are enclosed? Pish. He has her concocted into a ring, which pinches his finger, giving him exquisite torment. Ah! Somehow, he is thoroughly blighted by this Doctor's means. Certainly! This half hanged villain serves him as faithfully as man may, obeying all his orders, except in just one apparently unimportant thing—in that one thing, he obeys the Doctor. Very well! He daily, in obedience to the Doctor's instructions, pours a drop of a certain liquid into his wine. Indeed! He subserves some wicked desire of his, to his eternal ruin. Very right! any rich man may have such an attendant. He does not imprison his foe, but induces him to imprison himself. Lack-a-day! Let it be with his own consent, that he inhabits the secret chamber of the old mansion, and sometimes prowls about the neighborhood. Vastly probable. It should be some contrivance by which this man of wealth becomes powerless in his enemy's hands, and for thirty years is constantly tortured, until torture becomes the necessity of his life. So easily said—so impossible to do. Try back! What had this gentleman done? He had seduced the young wife of this man? I don't like that. Or his daughter or sister? not much better, though the sister, a little. Or by his faithlessness, he had brought to the grave the young sister the only thing in life that this abstracted man of Science valued. That might be passably well for the offence. Then he turns all the resources of his art and ingenuity to avenge himself on this man and his whole race. How easy to say such things! This man, whom he saved from hanging, the gentleman thinks him altogether devoted to himself, but in reality he is doing the bidding of the Doctor. The death and ruin of this girl, shall, by the Doctor's contrivance, prove his misery, temporal and eternal. What shall I do? He might have embalmed a member of the family in some new way; so that he shall appear lifelike—to what good end? The Devil knows; I don't. The girl continues to live with him; no, she is dead. Some secret knowledge of the family, he must have, by dint of which he counteracts all their projects for good, and brings about their utter destruction. Pshaw! It ought to be a knowledge of the history of the family, and the character of its successive representatives, that the Doctor perpetrates his mischief. Somehow or other, a representative, long supposed dead, should be discovered to be still alive, either in confinement or strict voluntary seclusion. Etheredge should discover him, as he does now, and be present at his death. The family has been Catholic, and this should be imposed on him—or he may have imposed it on himself—as a penalty for some crime. What crime? It won't do. The Doctor has left his slave here to do mischief,—one peculiar kind of mischief—what? Is the secret chamber affair too absurd? I fear it is;—not only impossible, but in a manner flat & commonplace. Some old family trait must be prolonged into the present day—nothing else. The man whom the doctor leaves behind must act the part of a household demon to the successive heirs; and it may be quite in character for him to do it, as he is a hanged criminal. He is intensely evil, with nothing good in him except his entire devotion to the Doctor —and even that, by the facilities of wickedness which it offers the latter, may be intended to will him onward to Hell. Well; then the Doctor has left an exceedingly wicked man to be the confidential servant of the family; this man must represent a Demon. He fosters all wickedness in the young, and facilitates it in the old. When the Doctor went abroad, he took measures to get this man into the service of Brathwaite, in order to do all the mischief he could, under the Doctor's guidance; and there must have been one peculiar mode of evil which he specially had in view. What? Or perhaps, he only meant him to be a household demon, with general aptitude for any mischief—be it murder, or what not. I do not see the practicability of this. But this had better be the man's character; he shall be as wicked as possible, and dominated by a perception of greater wickedness in the Doctor. He leaves him, with a general understanding that he is to do all possible mischief, and a special injunction to keep doing one particular thing. Well; specify—I can't; the unparticular things I may, or might, could, would, or should. Having always an agent of mischief at hand, there is a good deal of it done, all the evil desires of their hearts become deeds, by and of an obsequious demon. So far good. There might even be a suspicion of absolute demonism on the part of the servant. Let there be a chapter devoted to the introduction of this important character, in which his qualities shall be mystified, exaggerated, idealized; brought as near the preternatural as may be, and then quietly withdrawn almost within the limits of common-place. The general features of the old English serving-man must be preserved, but he be converted into a devil; a butler, he should be—or steward? Bottler, I think. Boteler. A model of faithful service, too. A pander for the young heir, &c &c &c. A great deal of grotesque fancy must be used in drawing this character. Oh, certainly. Ohe, jam satis est. I can't possibly make this out, though it keeps glimmering before me. But he has grown old in the house, with a sort of wicked fidelity, difficult to describe—or to imagine. The moral of this might be—that if a man could have all the desires of his heart executed, there could be no way so sure of bringing him to hell. A man of great skill and resource. Come on! Conceive such a man, established in the family, and wholly devoted to the Doctor, who has sworn eternal vengeance against the family. What is wanted to consummate that revenge? Materials, and an opportunity. The material must be some long standing trouble or hereditary predicament of the family. What? A crime which is bequeathed to each generation, and of which this servant becomes the instrument. It would do magnificently, if it were not an absurdity. What is the crime? Each son murders his father at a certain age; or does each father try to accomplish the impossibility of murdering his successor? This is not the right tack. One of the family to disappear, of his own will, and to remain in seclusion; the story of Wakefield might afford some hint of it. He might do it from jealousy for there should be an ostensible motive. He wishes to watch his beloved and suspected one. This old servant might be in the secret, and it should be done by the Doctor's contrivance. So he should remain, till the American came back and found him. He secludes himself, from a morbid impulse, and finds himself caught, and can never get back again into society; so that he has given up all the opportunities of life by that one act. The Doctor promotes it in the first instance, and makes it next to impossible for him to return into the world, in the next. The old servant is the agent, who makes it impossible for him to get back, by the easiness of his keeping there. Is not this a glimpse? There must be a motive, in the first place, strong enough to keep him secluded a week; then, let him get out if he can. The fact should show that a strange repulsion—as well as a strong attraction—exists among human beings. If we get off, it is almost impossible to get back again. There is a vein of morbid singularity in this old family, of which the Doctor is aware. It is a very common thing—this fact of a man's being caught and made prisoner by himself. When Etheredge comes, he should be led to the chamber, perhaps, by his acquaintance with the chamber, as derived from the Doctor. But there must be a strong original motive; else, however natural, it will appear outrageously absurd. Now, what can be the motive; he has fallen in love with, and tried to seduce, the Doctor's young sister; possibly, he has seduced her, and she has died. There is a strong popular feeling on this point, and he is forced to seclude himself. Or, he may, in the riot of his youthful blood, have committed an offence against the laws, for which it is convenient for him to go into temporary hiding; and he naturally betakes himself to the secret chamber of his own old mansion. The Doctor facilitates this, and makes it easy for him to stay, difficult for him to come forth; so there he is; and he goes to America, leaving him in charge of this devoted servant. By and by, he comes to dread the face of men, and to dread being seen by them; and so he grows from youth to age. I think it should be vengeance for a crime. The seduction and death of the Doctor's sister; the Doctor, a terrible man, threatens vengeance. The Doctor contrives that a dead body shall be found, and taken to be that of Brathwaite. The crime alleged should be that of murder of the girl; but he shall not have meditated anything more than a vicious connection. Each successive inheritor of the estate shall be duly taken into the secret, as before, and made wretched and guilty by it. It shall be something rather affecting the sanity of this old family; and the moral shall be, that old families become insane.

He might have seduced or broken the heart (which would be better) of the Doctor's sister. A quarrel ensues, in which he has reason to suppose that he has killed the Doctor, and that the law will be wreaked on him. He takes refuge in the secret chamber of the mansion, confiding himself to the care of this half-hanged man; who, being a devoted adherent of the Doctor, acts according to his instructions, and so makes him a life-long prisoner. The Doctor, his family being disgraced, his affections outraged, chooses to vanish from life, and departs for America, leaving no record behind him—no knowledge of where he is, except with this servant. He goes abroad, with the purpose of pursuing his revenge upon the whole race of his enemy; with this view, knowing the family history, he determines to raise up a false heir, who shall oust the present possessor.

In the Romance, after the first two or three chapters, describing the Doctor and his surroundings, there must be introduced one, in which this self-imprisoned man must be described—still young, cherishing purposes of coming out into the world, but deferring it till another day; various tokens must be shown, of what, and whereabouts he is, and what his situation; but so to raise conjecture, not to satisfy it; and a connection must be intimated between him and the plot signified by the Doctor's spider's web. The reader, like the prisoner himself, may see no reason to suppose that he will not be at liberty at any moment; indeed, the situation must be so imperfectly defined that he shall seem at liberty now.

Again, at an after period just before the Doctor's death; or possibly just after his death, (His death should be noticed, and an effect of it suggested) and before the opening of the scene in England, the prisoner must be introduced, now some years older; the effect of these imprisoned years must be developed; his growing horror of the world, yet sometimes a passionate yearning to get back into it. Then again, in order to fill up the gap between the two parts of the story, remove the prisoner forward again, ten years more. Show him with the marks of coming age, and his faculties growing torpid through disuse. Still have allusions to the Doctor and the spider &c. It must not be indicated, as yet, where the prisoner is, nor, perhaps, must it yet be quite certain, that he is only self-confined.

Again, after Etheredge has arrived in England, there must be another chapter, showing the prisoner as he now is. There may be strong indications, now, that the prisoner is confined in the mansion-house; and perhaps one of the Warden's stories may have led the reader to conjecture that it is a former possessor of the house. It must be so arranged as to make the house awful.

Finally, at whatever expense of absurdity, Etherege must meet the man in his prison, as already seen. The surprise, disturbance, fear of men that has grown upon him, probably shakes the life out of the poor old cuss, after thirty years of confinement. His mind, I think, should at all times be full of the Doctor—haunted by some impression of him. But, except in this one fact of his self-confinement, there must be no insanity. He may be a young man of an exceedingly sensitive nature, who has fallen into one fault, sin, crime; yet he might have been the flower of all the race, under happier circumstances; a poetic nature; able to console himself with imaginative reveries. Sometimes, a dreadful glimpse of the way in which he is spending life. A lack of animal spirits, of active energy. He has books, and writing materials. Possibly, there might be two motives for seclusion; one disappointed love, a passion hopeless, wrecked, the other a sense of crime. The girl, whom alone his shy nature ever loved, is dead; he thinks that he has murdered her brother. So he secludes himself, at once afraid and aweary of this world. The devil becomes the turnkey at the prison-gate, and he is inevitably shut in; except for one brief time when he goes forth. Throughout life, still a purpose to emerge.

This runs through the Romance like the vertebrae of the back-bone. There should be a reference to it in everything, grave or gay. Now the girl; she has been sent out from England by the servant. Can she be the daughter of the Doctor's sister? That would make her too old. Well; merely a female relative, the only one of his race. Or could she belong to the old Pensioner, a niece of his? Only, in that case, how came she ever to be under the Doctor's charge? True. Might she be the daughter of this sister; or might this be left in doubt, and only suggested by the fact of his taking charge of her, and feeling evidently a great interest in her, and yet one connected with grief and apparent shame; so that he has no comfort in her? This seems best. What is her situation, when Etherege finds her in England? Can she have been brought back by the Pensioner? Or, can she have come back to the protection of a person who had taken care of her, until she was sent over to the Doctor in America? The old servant is the only person who has heretofore had any thing to do with her. The Doctor has left her sufficient for her support, in a moderate way; only, she wants a position, it seems to me. Could she possibly be made a resident of the house? I think not; for it is requisite to give her a certain respectability of external position. An actress? A rope-dancer? An appurtenance of a wandering show? It must be kept in mind that Etherege is to marry her, which he can hardly do if she sinks below the line of respectability. She must be an artist—or may. A schoolmistress; a sempstress. None of these. It is so desirable to connect her with the Pensioner, that I don't well see how to do anything else. He had met with her in America, and taken a great interest in her; she being still a child, and when he came to England had brought her with him; or had come for that very purpose among others. Perhaps he had had an interview with the old Doctor, shortly before the death of the latter, in which interesting matters had past; and perhaps it was what he had learnt in this interview that the Doctor was ineffectually moved to communicate to Etherege, in his last moments. The pensioner might have satisfied the Doctor that he was the representative of the elder line. He confides her to him, and he takes charge of her. But, of course, the Doctor did not leave her dependent on the Pensioner, while he was making Etherege independent of the world? But, somehow, the Pensioner took charge of her and brought her to England, and she was to him as a daughter. Her property had been embezzled, perhaps, and she was left to support herself as she could; and the New England air had quickened her capacity in this respect. She has some peculiar little handiwork, which enables her to get a living; something that she had learnt in America. Indian manufactures, with beads? No. She sells Indian meal, done up in neat packages, for washing hands. Oh, the devil! It shall not be told, at the close of the American part, that the girl is taken charge of by the Pensioner, but so it shall prove to be. Well; she can be received in England by an old maiden relative, where she may live in a narrow way, sketching, and otherwise idly employing herself, and longing for the wide sphere that America opens to women. The owner of Brathwaite Hall has seen her and fallen in love with her, and perchance tried to ruin her; but she rejects him. She comes often to see the Pensioner at the Hospital, and must be mixed up somehow with the story. The Brathwaite man might even have sought her for a wife; and it might be his jealousy that partly prompts to murder Etherege; as he intends, though the fidelity of the serving-man to the old Doctor induces him only to administer a sleeping potion and so introduce him to the hidden inhabitant of the Hall. This girl must be cheerful, natural, reasonable, beautiful, spirited, to make up for the deficiencies of almost everybody else. Something of wildness in her, intimating an origin not exactly normal, but yet nothing extravagant or unwomanly. The Indian beadwork may do.

Now for the old pensioner—his origin, pursuit, biography. He is the descendant of the eldest branch of the family, and its representative. According to his theory matter, early in the King's troubles with Parliament, his ancestor, being of a religious temperament, became a preacher of a reformed doctrine, very much like those of George Fox; on this account the family, who were then Catholics, rejected him, and thrust him violently forth, some say wounded, so that the track of a bloody footstep was left behind him on the threshold. He disappears, going to America, where again he is persecuted by the Puritans, but founds a race who keep up his own faith, some of his traditions, his unworldliness; the name was changed (perhaps for that of his mother) on his first being thrust out from his father's family.

On the other hand (showing the unreliability of tradition) the family at home have a legend that this person was a fierce and violent religionist, that he fought outrageously against the king, and was even so devilishly inimical that he was the masqued executioner who beheaded him. Always, afterwards, his foot was liable to make a bloody track; as was evidenced, among other cases, by the extant bloody footprint on the threshold, where he was thrust forth from his father's house by his horror-stricken family. They also say that he emigrated to America, and made bloody tracks on the forest-leaves.

Rumors of his existence, and of a family springing from him, remain in England almost to the present day. Messengers, from age to age, are sent in quest of him; for, if he left a still surviving race, they would now be at the head of the family, with claims to the estate, and an ancient barony that has since fallen in; for the children of the eldest son are extinct, though there is a lineage through two younger sons. This has given rise to the Doctor's substitution of Etherege.

Well; the Pensioner inherits the religious spirit of his ancestor; a mild, gentle, sweet, unyieldingness of character, which has always distinguished this branch of the family. An apostolic character. The spirit of his fathers blossoms out in him more strenuously than in several preceding generations, and he is moved to preach, but his doctrines have not enough quackery and humbug about them to make any mark in the world; for he merely preaches the purest christianity. So, he is not successful; rather feeble, he may be pronounced by his auditors. At this period, he encounters the Doctor and the two children; the Doctor is interested in him, asks him to his house, and talks with him. He reappears a little before the Doctor's death. In his first visit to the Doctor, he shall betray a knowledge of some of the traditions of the family.

He has made no impression on the world, being of too mild and meek a spirit, though he has the possibility of a martyr in him, as his forefather had. Perhaps his forefather was hanged by the Puritans—I think so. At last, the little girl being committed to his charge, he takes her back to England; and finding the hospital there, and being in a position to prove his claims, he takes up residence there. He knows his rights to represent the family; but being unworldly, having modelled himself on the character of his martyred ancestor, he will not accept worldly honours. Besides, there is a certain want of the practical in his nature, that hinders such claims on his part; and he has no family—nothing to induce him. Perhaps he sometimes goes out preaching in England; though this is probably frowned upon by the Warden. Take the character of Cowper for this man; melancholic, gentle, shy, conscientious, censorious—therefore not acceptable to his neighbours, though amiable. These little traits will give versimilitude to the character. Weak, ineffectual, with bursts of great force at need. A want of the practical element in his nature.

He shall be conscious of something strange existent in the mansion-house; a delicacy of nature, coming from his freer life, shall have taught him this. Possibly, the wicked servant may have made some communications to him; knowing that he has been in communication with the Doctor, and reverencing, too, the holiness of his character. It is possible he may have met the self-imprisoned, once when he was straying abroad; but I think not. There ought to be some scene contrived, in which his conscientiousness should be very severely tested. Perchance, he discovers the secret, and Brathwaite tried to frighten him into silence by threats of death; or the unhanged villain might do it, but should finally let him go, with the secret in his possession, influenced by holiness of his character making itself felt. The scene might take place in the woods. This is worth working out.

He might be a Fifth Monarchy Man; that is to say, obedient to the higher law within himself, and rejecting human law when it interfered. In figure, Mr. Alcott.

There is—or there was, now many years ago, and a few years also, it was still extant—a chamber, which when I think of, it seems to me like entering a deep recess of my own consciousness, a deep cave of my nature; so much have I thought of it and its inmate, through a considerable period of my life. After I had seen it long in fancy, then I saw it in reality, with my waking eyes; and questioned with myself whether I was really awake.

<(Compare it with Spenser's Cave of Despair. Put instruments of suicide there.)>

Not that it was a picturesque or stately chamber; not in the least. It was dim, dim as a melancholy mood; so dim, to come to particulars, that till you were accustomed to that twilight medium, the print of a book looked all blurred; a pin was an indistinguishable object; the face of your familiar friend, or your dearest beloved one, would be unrecognizable across it, and the figures, so warm and radiant with life and heart, would seem like the faint gray shadows of our thoughts, brooding in age over youthful images of joy and love. Nevertheless, the chamber, though so difficult to see across, was small. You detected that it was within very narrow boundaries, though you could not precisely see them; only you felt yourself shut in, compressed, impeded, in the deep center of something; and you longed for a breath of freer air. Some articles of furniture there seemed to be; but in this dim medium, to which we are unaccustomed, it is not well to try to make out what they were, or anything else,—now at least—about the chamber. Only one thing; small as the light was, it was rather wonderful how there came to be any; for no windows were apparent; no communication with the outward day.

Looking into this chamber, in fancy, (to us that come out of the broad sunny daylight of the world) it is some time before we discover that it has an inmate. Yes; there is some one within; but where? We know it; but do not precisely see him, only a presence is impressed upon us. Is it in that corner;

no, not there, only a heap of duskiness and an antique coffer, that as we look closely at it seems to be made of carved wood. Ah; he is in that other dim corner; and now that we steal closer to him, we see him; a young man, pale, flung upon a sort of mattress-couch. He seems in alarm, at something or other. He trembles, he listens, as if for noises. It must be a great peril, indeed, that can haunt him thus and make him feel afraid in such a seclusion as you feel this to be; but there he is, tremulous, and so pale that really his face is almost visible in this gloomy twilight. How came he here? Who is he? What does he tremble at? In this duskiness we cannot tell. Only that he is a young man, in a state of nervous excitement and alarm. Looking about him, starting to his feet, sometimes standing and staring about him.

Has he been long here? Apparently not; for see, he has a pair of large riding boots on, coming up to the knees; they are splashed with mud, as if he had ridden hastily through foul ways; the spurs are on the heels. A riding dress upon him. Ha! is that blood upon the hand which he clasps to his forehead?

What more do we perceive? Nothing; the light is so dim; but we wonder where is the door; and whence the light comes. There is a strange abundance of spiders, too, we perceive; spinning their webs here, as if they would entrammel everything in them. A mouse has run across the floor, apparently, but it is too dim to detect him, or to detect anything, beyond the limits of a very vague guess. We do not even know whether what we seem to have seen is really so; whether the man is young, or old—or what his surroundings are; and there is something so disagreeable in this seclusion, this stifled atmosphere; that we should be loth to remain here long enough to make ourselves certain of what is now a mystery. Let us forth into the broad, genial daylight; for there is magic, there is a devilish, subtile influence in this chamber, which, I have reason to believe, makes it dangerous to remain here. There is a spell on the threshold. Heaven keep us safe from it.

Hark, has a door unclosed! Is there another human being in the room! We have now become so accustomed to the dim medium that we distinguish a man of mean exterior, with a look of habitual subservience that seems like that of an English serving-man, or in some menial situation; decent, quiet, neat, softly spoken, but yet with a certain hard and questionable manner, which we would not well like to have near us in the room.

"Am I safe?" asks the inmate of the prison-chamber.

"Sir, there has been a search."

"Leave the pistols," said the voice.

<(Once, in looking at the mansion, Etherege is struck by the appearance of a marble inserted into the wall, and kept clear of lichens)>

Again, after this time, a long time extending to years, let us look back into that dim chamber, wherever in the world it was, into which we had a glimpse, and where we saw apparently a fugitive. How looks it now? Still dim—perhap as dim as ever—but our eyes, or our imagination, have gained an acquaintance, a customariness, with the medium; so that we can discern things, now, a little more distinctly than of old. Possibly, there may have been something cleared away that obstructed the light; at any rate we see now the whereabouts better than we did. It is an oblong room, lofty but narrow, and some ten paces in length; its floor is heavily carpeted, so that the tread makes no sound; it is hung with old tapestry, or carpet, wrought with the hand, long ago, and still retaining much of their ancient colours, where there was no sunshine to fade them; so there they are some tapestried story, done by catholic hands, of saints or devils, looking each equally grim and unhumanly. The light, whence comes it? There is no window; but it seems to come through a stone, or something like it, a dull gray medium, that makes noonday look like evening twilight. Though, sometimes, there is an effect as if sunshine were striving to melt itself through this dull medium and—never making a shadow—yet to produce the effect of a cloud gathering thickly over the sun. There is a chimney, yes; a little grate, on which burns a coal-fire, a dim smouldering fire. It might be an illumination, if that were desirable.

What is the furniture? An antique chair; one chair, no more. A table; heavy-footed, of dark wood; it holds writing materials; a book, too on its face, with the dust gathered on its back. There is, moreover, a sort of antique box, or coffer, of some dark wood that seems to have been wrought or carved with skill, wondrous skill, of some period when the art of carving wainscoat with arms and devices was much practised; so that on this coffer—some six feet long it is, and two or three broad—most richly wrought, you see faces in relief of knight and dame, lords, heraldic animals, some story, very lively told, almost revelling in Gothic sculpture of wood which we have seen on the marble sarcophagi of the old Greeks. It has, too, a lock, elaborately ornamented and inlaid with silver.

What else; only the spider's webs spinning strangely over everything; over that light which comes into the room through the stone; over everything. And now we see, in a corner, a strange, great spider, curiously variegated. The ugly, terrible, seemingly poisonous thing makes us shudder.

<(Describe, in rich poetry, all shapes of deadly things)>

What, else! There are pistols; they lie on the coffer! There is a curiously shaped Indian dagger, of the kind which in a groove, has poison that makes its wound mortal. On the old mantel piece, over the fire-place, there is a vial that perhaps contains poison. It would seem as if some one had meditated suicide; <there is a halter, ready noosed> or else that the foul fiend had put all sorts of implements of self destruction in his way; so that, in some frenzied moment, he might kill himself.

But the inmate! There he is; but the frenzied alarm in which we last saw him seems to have changed its character. No throb, now; no passion; no frenzy of fear or despair. He sits dull and motionless. See; his cheek is very pale; his hair long and dishevelled. His beard has grown, and curls round his face. He has on a dressing-gown, a long robe as of one who abides within doors, and has nothing to do with outward elements; a pair of slippers. A dull, dreamy reverie seems to have possessed him. Hark; there is again a stealthy step on the floor; and the serving man is here again. There is a peering, anxious curiosity in his face, as he starts towards him, a sort of enjoyment, one would say, in the way in which he looks at this strange case.

"I am here, your honor," he says, at length, after feasting his eyes for some time on the spectacle.

"I hear you!" says the young man, in a dull, indifferent tone.

"Will not your Honour walk out to-day?" says the man. "It is long now since your Honour has taken the air."

"Very long," says the master, "but I will not go out to-day. What weather is it?"

"Sunny, bright, a summer day," says the man. "But you would never know it in these damp walls. The last winter's chill is here yet. Had not your honor better go forth?"

It might seem that there was a sort of sneer, deeply hidden under respect and obeisance in the man's words and craftily respectful tone; deeply hidden, but conveying a more subtile power on that account. At all events the master seemed aroused from his state of dull indifference, and writhed as with poignant anguish—an infused poison in his veins—as the man spoke.

"Have you procured me that new drug I spoke of?" asked the master.

"Here it is," said the man, putting a small package on the table.

"Is it effectual?"

"So said the apothecary;" answered the man, "and I tried it on a dog. He sat quietly a quarter of an hour; then had a spasm or two, and was dead. But, your honor, the dead carcass swelled horribly."

"Hush, villain! Have there—have there been inquiries for me—mention of me!"

"Oh, none, Sir—none, Sir. Affairs go on bravely in the new time. The world fills up. The gap is not vacant. There is no mention of you. Marry, at the ale house, I heard some idle topers talking of a murder that took place some few years since, and saying that Heaven's vengeance would come for it yet."

"Silence, villain, there is no such thing," said the young man; and with a laugh that seemed like scorn he relapsed into his state of sullen indifference; during which this servant stole away, after looking at him some time, as if to take all possible note of his aspect. The man did not seem so much to enjoy it himself, as he did to do these things in a kind of formal and matter of course way, as if he were performing a set duty; as if he were a subordinate fiend, and were doing the duty of a superior one, without any individual malice of his own, though a general satisfaction in doing what would accrue to the agglomeration of deadly mischief. He stole away, and the master was left to himself.

By and by, by what impulse or cause, it is impossible to say, he started upon his feet in a sudden frenzy of rage and despair. It seemed as if a consciousness of some strange, wild, miserable fate that had befallen him had come upon him all at once; how that he was a prisoner to a devilish influence, to some wizard might, that bound him hand and foot with spider's web. So he stamped; so he half-shrieked, yet stopped himself in the midst, so that his cry was stifled and smothered. Then he snatched up the poisoned dagger and looked at it; the noose and put it about his neck; evil instrument of death, but laid it down again. And there was a voice at the door. "Quietly, quietly, your honor, or they will hear you!" And at that voice, he sank into sullen indifference again.

GRIMSHAWE

EARLY IN THIS present century, in a town with which I used to be familiarly acquainted, there dwelt an elderly person of grim aspect, known by the name and title of Doctor Ormskirk, whose household consisted of a remarkably pretty and vivacious boy, a perfect rosebud of a blonde girl two or three years younger than he, and an old maid of all work, crusty in temper and wonderfully sluttish in attire. It might be partly owing to this handmaiden's characteristic lack of neatness (though, primarily, no doubt to the grim Doctor's antipathy to broom, brush, and dusting-cloth) that the house—at least, in such portions of it as any casual visitor caught a glimpse of—was so overlaid with dust that in lack of a visiting card you might write your name with a forefinger upon the tables, and so hung with cobwebs that they assumed the appearance of dusky upholstery. It grieves me to add an additional touch or two to the reader's disagreeable impression of Doctor Ormskirk's residence, by confessing that it stood in a shabby by-street, and cornered on a grave-yard, with which the house communicated by a back door; so that, with a hop, skip, and jump, from the threshold across a flat tombstone, the two children were in the daily habit of using the dismal cemetery as their play ground. In their graver moods, they spelled out the names and learned by heart doleful verses on the headstones; and in their merrier ones (which were much the most frequent) they chased butterflies, and gathered dandelions, played hide and seek behind the slate and marble, and running half tumbled laughing over the grassy mounds which were too eminent for the short legs to bestride. On the whole, they were the better for the grave yard, and its legitimate inmates slept none the worse for the two children's gambols and shrill merriment over head.

<(Insert sentence at the end of the next paragraph.)>

<(Crusty Hannah is a mixture of Indian and Negro, & as some say, Monkey.)>

<Early introduce Doctor Grim as a smoker & drinker.>

<(It is understood, from the first, that the children are not brother and sister.)>

<The townspeople are at war with the Doctor.>

<The spiders are affected by the weather, and serve as barometers.>

This grave yard (about which we shall say not a word more than may sooner or later be needful) was the most ancient in the town. The clay of the original settlers had been incorporated with the soil; those stalwart Englishmen of the Puritan epoch, the substance of whose immediate ancestors had been planted forth with succulent grass and daisies for the sustenance of the parson's cow, around the low, battlemented Norman church-towers, in the villages of the father-land, had here contributed their rich Saxon mould to tame and christianize the wild forest-earth of the new world. In this point of view—as holding the bones and dust of the primeval ancestors—the cemetery was more English than anything else in the neighborhood, and might probably have nourished English oaks, and English elms, and whatever else is of English growth, without that tendency to spindle upward and lose their sturdy breadth, which is said to be the ordinary characteristic both of human and vegetable productions, when transplanted hither. Here, at all events, used to be some specimens of common English garden flowers, which could not be accounted for, unless they perhaps had sprung out of some English maiden's heart, where the intense love of those homely things, and regret of them in this foreign land, had conspired together to keep their vivifying principle, and cause its growth after the poor girl was buried. Be that as it might, in this grave-yard had been hidden from sight many a broad, bluff visage of husbandmen who had been taught to plough among the hereditary furrows that had been ameliorated by the crumble of ages; much had these sturdy laborers grumbled at the great roots that obstructed their toil in these fresh acres. Here, too, the sods had covered the faces of men known to history, and reverenced when not a pinch of distinguishable dust remained of them, personages whom tradition told about; there, mixed up with successive crops of native-born Americans, had been minister, captain, matron, virgin, good and evil, tough and tender, turned up and battened down by the sexton's spade, over and over again, until every blade of grass had its relations with the human brotherhood of that old town. A hundred and fifty years was sufficient to do this; and so much time, at least, had elapsed since the first hole was dug among the difficult roots of the forest trees, and the first little hillock of all those green beds was piled up. And here were old brick tombs, with curious sculptures on them, and quaint grave-stones, some of which bore puffy little cherubs, and one or two others, the effigies of eminent Puritans, wrought out to a button, a fold of the ruff, and a wrinkle of the skull cap; and these frowned upon the two children, as if death had not made them a whit more genial than they were in life; but the children were of a temper to be more encouraged by the good-natured smiles of the puffy cherubs, than frightened or abashed by the sour Puritans.

<Describe the children with really childish traits, quarreling, being naughty &c &c>

<The result of Crusty Hannah's strangely mixed breed should be shown in some strange way.>

Thus rippled and surged, with its hundreds of little billows, the old grave yard about the house which cornered upon it; it made the street gloomy both at noontide and nightfal, so that people did not altogether like to pass along the high wooden fence that shut it in; and the old house itself, covering ground which else would have been sown thickly with buried bones, partook of its dreariness, because it seemed hardly possible that the dead people should not get up out their graves, and steal in to warm themselves at the convenient fireside. But I never heard that any of them did so; nor were the children ever startled by spectacles of dim horror in the night-time, but were as cheerful and fearless as if no grave had ever yet been dug. They were of that class of children whose material seems fresh, not taken at second hand, full of disease, conceits, whims, weaknesses, that have already served many people's turns, and moulded up, with some little change of combination, to serve the turn of some poor spirit that could not get a better case.

So far as ever came to the present writer's knowledge, there was no whisper of Doctor Ormskirk's house being haunted; a fact on which both writer and reader may congratulate themselves, the ghostly chord having been played upon, in these days, until it has become as wearisome as the familiar tune of a barrel organ. The house itself, moreover, except for the convenience of its position, close to the above described cemetery, was hardly worthy to be haunted. As I remember it (and, for aught I know, it still exists in the same guise) it did not appear to be an ancient structure, nor one that could ever have been the abode of a very wealthy or prominent family; a three-story wooden house perhaps a century old, low studded, with a square front, standing right upon the street, and a small enclosed porch, containing the main entrance affording a glimpse up and down the street through an oval window on each side; its characteristic was a decent respectability, not sinking below the boundary of the genteel. It has often perplexed my mind to conjecture what sort of man he could have been, who, having the means to build a pretty spacious and comfortable residence, should have chosen to lay its foundation on the brink of so many graves; each tenant of these narrow houses crying out, as it were, against the absurdity of bestowing much time or pains in preparing any earthly tabernacle save such as theirs. But deceased people see matters from an erroneous, at least a too exclusive point of view; a comfortable grave is an excellent possession for those who need it but a comfortable house has likewise its merits and temporary advantages. The founder of the house in question seemed sensible of this truth, and had therefore been careful to lay out a sufficient number of rooms and chambers, low, ill-lighted, ugly, but not unsusceptible of warmth and comfort; the sunniest and cheerfullest of which were on the side that looked into the grave yard. Of these, the one most spacious and convenient had been selected by Doctor Ormskirk as a study, and fitted up with book shelves, and various machines and contrivances, electrical, chemical, and distillatory, wherewith he might pursue such researches as were wont to engage his attention. The great result of the grim Doctor's labors, so far as known to the public, was a certain preparation or extract of cobwebs, which, out of a great abundance of material, he was able to produce in any desirable quantity, by the administration of which he professed to cure diseases of the inflammatory class and to work very wonderful effects upon the human system. It is a great pity (for the good of mankind, and the advantages of his own fortunes) that he did not put forth this medicine, in pill-boxes or bottles, and then, as it were, by some captivating title, inveigle the public into his spider's cobweb, and suck out its golden substance and himself wax fat as he sat in the central intricacy.

But grim Doctor Ormskirk, though his aim in life might be no very exalted one, seemed singularly destitute of the impulse to better his fortunes by the exercise of his wits; it might even have been supposed indeed that he had a conscientious principle, or a religious scruple—only, he was by no means a religious man—against reaping profit from this particular nostrum which he was said to have invented. He never sold it; never prescribed it, unless in cases selected upon some principle that nobody could detect or explain. The grim Doctor, it must be observed, was not generally acknowledged by the profession, with whom, in truth, he had never claimed a fellowship, nor had ever assumed, of his own accord, the medical title by which the public chose to know him. His professional practise seemed, in a sort, forced upon him; it grew pretty extensive, partly because it was understood to be a matter of favor and difficulty, dependent on a capricious will, to obtain his services at all. There was unquestionably an odor of quackery about him, but by no means of an ordinary kind. A sort of mystery—yet which, perhaps, need not have been a mystery, had anyone thought it worth while to make systematic inquiry—in reference to his previous life, his education, even his native land, assisted the impression which his peculiarities were calculated to make. He was evidently not a New Englander; not a native of any part of these western shores. His speech was apt to be oddly and uncouthly idiomatic, and even when classical in its form, was emitted with a strange, rough depth of utterance, that came from recesses of the lungs which we Yankees seldom put to any use. In person, he did not look like one of us; a broad, rather short personage, with a projecting forehead, red irregular face, and a squab nose; eyes that looked dull enough in their ordinary state, but had a faculty, in conjunction with the other features, of putting on an expression which those who had ever seen it described as especially ugly and awful. As regarded dress, Doctor Ormskirk had a rough and careless exterior, and altogether a shaggy kind of aspect, the effect of which was much increased by a reddish beard which, contrary to the custom of the day, he allowed to grow profusely, and the wiry perversity of which seemed to know as little of the comb as of the razor.

We began with calling the grim Doctor an elderly personage; but, in so doing, we looked at him through the eyes of the two children who were his intimates, and who had not learnt to decypher the purport and nature of his wrinkles and furrows and corrugations, whether as indicating age or a different kind of wear and tear. Possibly, he appeared so vigorous, and had such latent heat and fire to throw out, when occasion called, he might scarcely have seen middle age; though here again we hesitate, finding him so stiffened into his own way, so little fluid, so incrusted with fables and traditions that he must have left his youth very far behind him, if indeed he ever had any.

<The Doctor should occasionally beat Ned, in course of instruction.>

The patients, or whatever other visitors were ever admitted into the Doctor's study, carried abroad strange accounts of the squalor of dust and cobwebs in which this learned and scientific person lived; and the dust, they averred, was all the more disagreeable, because it could not well be other than dead men's almost intangible atoms, resurrected from the adjoining grave-yard. As for the cobwebs, they were no tokens of housewifely neglect on the part of crusty Hannah, the handmaiden, but the Doctor's scientific material carefully encouraged and preserved, each filmy thread more valuable to him than so much golden wire. Of all barbarous haunts in Christendom or elsewhere, this study was the one most over-run with spiders. They dangled from the cieling, crept upon the tables, lurked in the corners, and wove the intricacy of their webs from point to point, wherever they could hitch the end across the window panes, and even across the upper part of the doorway; in the chimney-place; it seemed impossible to move without breaking some of those mystic threads. Spiders crept familiarly towards you, and walked leisurely across your hands; these were their precincts, and you only an intruder. If you saw none about your person, yet you had an odious sense of one crawling up your spine, or spinning cobwebs in your brain, so pervaded was the atmosphere of this place with spider-life. What they fed upon (for all the flies for miles roundabout would not have sufficed them) was a secret known only to the Doctor. Whence they came was another riddle; though, from certain inquiries and transactions of Doctor Ormskirk's with some of the ship masters of the port, who followed the East or West Indian, the African, or the South American trade, it was supposed that this odd philosopher was in the habit of importing choice monstrosities in the spider kind from all those tropic regions.

<It shall always be a moot point whether or no the Doctor believed in cobwebs, or was laughing at the credulous.>

All the above description, exaggerated as it may seem, is merely preliminary to the introduction of one single, enormous spider, the biggest and the ugliest ever seen, the pride of the grim Doctor's heart, his treasure, his glory, the pearl of his soul, and, as many people said, the demon to whom he had sold his salvation, on condition of possessing the web of this foul creature for a certain number of years. The grim Doctor, according to this theory, was but a great fly which this

spider had subtly entangled in his web. But, in truth, naturalists are acquainted with this spider, though it be a rare one;
the British Museum has a specimen, and, doubtless, so have
many other scientific institutions. It is found in South America,
its most hideous spread of legs covering a space nearly as
large as a dinner plate, and radiating from a body as big as
a door knob, which one conceives to be an agglomeration of
sucked up poison, which the creature treasures through life,
probably, to expend it all, and life itself, on some worthy foe.
Its colors were variegated, in a sort of ugly and inauspicious
splendor distributed over its vast bulk in great spots, some of
which glistened like gems. It was a horror to think of this
thing living; still more a horror to think of the foul catastrophe,
the crushed out and wasted poison, that would follow the
casual setting a foot upon him.

No doubt, the lapse of time, since the Doctor and his
spider lived, has already been sufficient to cause a traditionary
wonderment to gather over them both; and especially this
image of a spider dangles down to us from the dusky cieling of
the past, swollen into somewhat huger and uglier monstrosity
than he actually possessed. Nevertheless, the creature had a
real existence, and has left kindred, like himself; and as for
the Doctor, nothing could exceed the value which he seemed
to put upon him, the sacrifices which he made for the creature's convenience, or the readiness with which he adapted
his whole mode of life, apparently, so that the spider might
enjoy the conditions best suited to his tastes, habits, health.
And yet there were sometimes tokens that made people
imagine that he hated the infernal creature as much as everybody else who caught a glimpse of him.

<(Read the whole paragraph before copying any of it.)>
Considering that Doctor Grimshawe when we first look
upon him had dwelt only a very few years in the house by
the grave yard, it is wonderful what an appearance he and

his furniture, and his cobwebs, and their unweariable spinners, and crusty old Hannah, all had, of having permanently attached themselves to the locality. For a century, at least, it might be fancied that the study, in particular, had existed just as it was now, with those dusky festoons of spider-silk hanging along the walls, those book-cases, with volumes turning their parchment or black leather backs upon you, those machines and engines, that table, and at it, the Doctor in a very faded and shabby dressing gown, smoking a long clay pipe, the powerful fume of which dwelt continually in his reddish and grisly beard, and made him fragrant wherever he went. This sense of fixedness, stony intractability, seems to belong to people who, instead of hope, which exhales everything into an airy, gaseous exhilaration, have a fixed and dogged purpose, around which everything congeals and crystallizes. Even the sunshine, dim through the dustiness of the two casements that looked upon the graves, seemed an old and musty beam that had perhaps lost even its gold, by lying there so long-tarnished. The smoke, as it came warm out of Doctor Grimshawe's mouth, seemed already stale. But if the two children, or either of them, happened to be in the study— if they ran to open a door at the knock—if they came scampering and peeped down over the bannisters—the sordid and rusty gloom was apt to vanish quite away. The sunbeam itself looked like a golden rule that had been flung down long ago, and lain there till it was dusty and tarnished. They were cheery little imps, who sucked up fragrance and pleasantness out of their surroundings, dreary as these looked, even as a flower can find its proper fragrance in any soil where its seed happens to fall. The great spider, hanging by its cordage over the Doctor's head, and waving slowly like a pendulum in a blast from the crack of the door, must have made millions and millions of precisely such vibrations there. They were new, and made over every morning, with yesterday's weariness left out.

The little girl, however, was the merriest of the two. It was quite unintelligible, in view of the little care that crusty Hannah took of her, and, moreover, that she was none of your prim and dainty children, how daintily she kept herself amid all this dust; how the spider's webs never clung to her; and how, when without being solicited, she clambered into the Doctor's arms and kissed him, she bore away no smoky reminiscences of the pipe that he kissed continually. She had a free, mellow, natural laughter, that seemed the ripened fruit of the smile that was generally on her little face, and to be shaken off and scattered about by any breeze that came along. Little Elsie made playthings of everything, even of the grim Doctor, though against his will, and though, moreover, there were tokens now and then, that the sight of this bright little creature was not a pleasure to him, but, on the contrary a positive pain; a pain, nevertheless, indicating a profound interest, hardly less deep than if Elsie had been his daughter. Elsie did not play with the great spider, but she moved among the whole host of spiders as if she saw them not, and being endowed with other senses than those allied to these things, might coexist with them and not be sensible of their presence. Yet the child, I suppose, had her crying fits and her pouting fits, and naughtiness enough to entitle her to live on earth; at least, crusty Hannah often said so, and often made grievous complaint of disobedience, mischief, breakage, attributable to little Elsie, to which the grim Doctor seldom responded by anything more intelligible than a puff of tobacco smoke, and sometimes an imprecation, which, however, hit crusty Hannah instead of the child. Where the child got the tenderness which a child needs to live upon is a mystery to me; perhaps from some aged or dead mother, or in her dreams; perhaps some small measure of it, such as boys have, from the little boy. Perhaps from a Persian kitten, which had grown to be a cat in her arms, and slept in her little bed, and now assumed grave and protective airs towards her former playmate.

<Crusty Hannah teaches Elsie curious needlework &c &c &c>

The boy, as we have said, was two or three years Elsie's elder, and might now be about six years old. He was a healthy and cheerful child, yet of a graver mood than the little girl, appearing to lay a more forcible grasp on the circumstances about him, and to tread with a heavier footstep on the actual earth; yet perhaps not more so than was the necessary difference between a man-blossom, quite conscious of coming things, and a mere baby, with whom there was neither past nor future. Ned, as he was named, was subject very early to fits of musing, the subject of which—if they had any definite object, or were more than vague reverie—it was impossible to guess; they were of those states of mind, probably, which are beyond the sphere of human language, and would necessarily lose their essence in the attempt to communicate or record them. The little girl, perhaps, had some mode of sympathy with these unuttered thoughts or reveries, which grown people had ceased to have; at all events, she early learned to respect them, and, at other times as free and playful as her Persian kitten, never ventured on any greater freedom, in such circumstances, than to sit down quietly beside him, and endeavor to look as thoughtful as the boy himself.

Once, slowly emerging from one of these waking dreams, little Ned gazed about him, and saw Elsie sitting with this pretty pretence of thoughtfulness and dreaminess, in her little chair, close beside him; now and then peeping under her eyelashes to see what changes might come over his face. After looking at her a moment or two, he quietly arose and taking her willing and warm little hand in his own, led her up to the Doctor.

<Describe the boy's dress, with a little sword by his side, feather in his hat, &c &c>

The groupe, methinks, was a picturesque one, and made up of several apparently discordant elements, each of which happened to be so combined as to make a more effective whole; the beautiful, grave boy of a brown cast, slender, with his white brow, and dark, thoughtful eyes, so earnest upon some mysterious theme; the prettiest little girl, a blond, round, rosey, so truly sympathetic with her companion's mood, yet unconsciously turning all into sport by her attempt to assume one similar; these two, standing at the grim Doctor's footstool. He, meanwhile, black, wild-bearded, heavy-browed, red-eyed, wrapped in his faded dressing-gown, puffing out volumes of vapor from his long pipe, and, making, just at that instant, application to a tumbler, which, we regret to say, was generally at his elbow, with some dark-colored potation in it, which required to be frequently replenished from a neighboring black bottle. Half, at least, of the fluids in the grim Doctor's system must have derived from that same black bottle, so constant was his familiarity with its contents; and yet his eyes were never redder at one time than another, nor his utterance thicker, nor his wits less available, nor his mood perceptibly the brighter or the darker for all his conviviality. It is true, when once the bottle happened to be quite empty for a whole day together, Doctor Ormskirk was observed by crusty Hanna, and attentively by the children, to be considerably fiercer than usual; so that probably, by some maladjustment of consequences, his intemperance was only to be found in refraining from brandy.

<(The Doctor deposits some papers in a secret cupboard)>

We must not forget, in attempting to convey the effect of these two beautiful children in such a sombre room, looking on the graveyard, and contrasted with the grim Doctor's aspect of heavy and smouldering fierceness, that over his head, at this very moment, dangled the portentous spider, who seemed to have come down from his web aloft for the very purpose of hearing what the two young people could have to say to his patron.

"Grim Doctor," said Ned, after looking up into the Doctor's face, as a sensitive child inevitably does, to see whether the occasion was favorable, yet determined to proceed with his purpose, whether so or not, "grim Doctor, I want you to answer me a question."

"Here's to your good health, Ned!" quoth the Doctor, eyeing the pair intently, as he often did, when they were unconscious. "So; you want to ask me a question? As many as you please, my fine fellow; and I shall answer as many, and as much, and as truly, as may please myself."

"Ah, grim Doctor," said the little girl, now letting go of Ned's hand and climbing upon the Doctor's knee, "'ou shall answer as many as Ned please to ask, because to please him and me."

"Well, child," said Doctor Grimshawe, "little Ned will have his rights, at least, at my hands, if not other people's rights likewise; and, if it be right, I shall answer his question. Only, let him ask it at once; for I want to be busy thinking about something else."

"Then, Doctor Grim," said little Ned, "tell me, in the first place, where I came from, and how you came to have me."

The Doctor looked at the little man, so seriously and earnestly putting this demand, with a perplexed, and at first, it might almost seem, a startled aspect.

"That is a question, indeed, my friend Ned!" ejaculated he, putting forth a whiff of smoke, and imbibing a sip of his tumbler, before he spoke. "Whence did you come? Whence did any of us come? Out of the darkness and mystery, out of nothingness, out of a kingdom of shadows; out of dust, clay, impure mud, I think, and to return to it again. Out of a former state of being, whence we have brought a good many shadowy recollections, purporting that it was no very pleasant one. Out of a former life, of which this present one is the hell! And why are you come? Faith, Ned, he must be a wiser man than Doctor Grim who can tell why you, or any

other mortal came hither; only, one thing I am well aware
of, it was not to be happy. To toil, and moil, and hope, and
fear, and to love in a shadowy, doubtful sort of way, and to
hate in bitter earnest—that is what you came for!"

<He answers, as many thoughtful and secret people do,
letting out his secret mood to the child, because he knows
he will not be understood.>

"Ah, Doctor Grim, this is very naughty," said Elsie. "You
are making fun of little Ned, when he is in earnest?"

"Fun," quoth the Doctor, bursting into a laugh peculiar to
him, very loud and obstreperous. "I am glad you find it so,
my little woman! Well; and so you bid me tell absolutely
where he came from."

Elsie nodded her bright, little head.

"And you, friend Ned, insist upon knowing," continued
the Doctor.

"That I do, Doctor Grim," answered Ned. His white,
childish brow had gathered into a frown, such was the earnestness of his determination; and he stamped his foot on
the floor, as if ready to follow up his demand by an appeal
to the little tin sword which hung by his side. The Doctor
looked at him with a kind of smile, not a very pleasant one;
for it was a not very amiable characteristic of his temper,
that a display of spirit even in a child, was apt to arouse his
immense combativeness, and make him aim a blow, without
much consideration how heavily it might fall, or on how
unequal an antagonist.

"If you insist upon an answer, Master Ned, you shall have
it," replied he. "You were taken by me, boy, a foundling,
from the alms-house; and if ever hereafter you desire to know
your kindred, you may take your choice of the first man you
meet. He is as likely to be your father as another."

The child's eyes flashed, and his brow grew as red as fire;
it was but a momentary fierceness; the next instant, he
clasped his hands over his face, and wept in a violent

convulsion of grief and shame. Little Elsie clasped her arms about him, kissing his brow and chin, which were all that her lips could touch under his clasped hands; but Ned turned away, uncomforted, and was blindly making his way towards the door.

"Ned, my little fellow, come back," said Dr. Grim, who had very attentively watched the cruel effect produced by his communication.

As the boy did not reply, and was still tending towards the door, the grim Doctor vouchsafed to lay aside his pipe, get up from his arm-chair (a thing he seldom did between supper and bedtime) and shuffle after the two children in his slippers. He caught them on the threshold, brought little Ned back, by main force, (for he was a rough man, even in his tenderness) and sitting down again, and taking him on his knee, pulled away his hands from before his face. Never was a more pitiful sight than that pale countenance, so infantile still, and yet looking old and experienced already, with a sense of disgrace, with a feeling of loneliness; so beautiful, nevertheless, that it seemed to possess all the characteristics which fine hereditary traits, and culture in many forefathers, could do in refining a human stock. And this, then, was a nameless weed, sprouting from the chance seed by the dusty wayside!

"Ned, my dear old boy," said Doctor Grim; and he kissed that pale, tearful face, the first and the last time, to the best of my belief, that he was ever betrayed into that tenderness, "forget what I have said! Yes; remember, if you like, that you came from an alms-house; but, remember, too, what your friend Doctor Grim is ready to affirm and make oath of;— that he can trace your kindred and race through that sordid experience, and back, back, for a hundred and fifty years, into an old English line. Come, little Ned, and look at this picture!"

<The Doctor thinks the picture looks fierce & wicked; the boy and girl think it mild, sweet, sad.>

He led the boy by the hand into a corner of the room, where hung upon the wall a portrait, which Ned had often looked at. It seemed an old picture, but the Doctor had had it cleaned and varnished, so that it looked dim and dark; and yet it seemed to be the representation of a man of no mark, or such rank in life as would naturally leave his features to be transmitted for the interest of another generation; for he was clad in a mean dress, of old fashion, a leather jerkin, it appeared to be; and round his neck, moreover, was a noose of rope, as if he might have been on the point of being hanged. But the face of the portrait, nevertheless, was beautiful, noble, though sad, with a great developement of sensibility, a look of suffering and endurance, amounting to triumph; a peace through all.

"Look at this," continued the Doctor. "If you must go on dreaming about your race, dream that you come of the blood of this being; for, mean as his station looks, he comes of an ancient and noble race, and was the noblest of them all. Let me alone, Ned; and I shall spin out the web that must link you with that race. The grim Doctor can do it."

The grim Doctor's face looked fierce with the earnestness with which he said these words. You would have said that he was taking an oath to overthrow, and annihilate a race, rather than to build one up, by bringing forward the infant heir out of obscurity, and making plain the links, the filaments, which connected that feeble childish life, in a far country, with the great tide of a noble life, embracing great strands of kindred, which had come down like a chain from antiquity, in old England. Having said these words, the grim Doctor appeared ashamed both of the heat and tenderness into which he had been betrayed (for rude and rough as his nature was, there was a kind of decorum in it, too, that kept him within limits of his own) so he went back to his chair, his pipe, and his tumbler, and was gruffer and more taciturn than ever, for the rest of the evening. And, after the children went to bed, he leaned back in his chair, and looked up at the vast tropic spider, who was particularly busy in adding to the intricacies of his web; until he fell asleep with his eyes fixed in that direction, and the extinguished pipe in one hand, and the empty tumbler in the other.

Doctor Grimshawe, after the foregone scene, began a practice of conversing more with the children than formerly; directing his discourse chiefly to Ned, although Elsie's vivacity and more outspoken and demonstrative character, made her take quite as large a part in the conversation as he. The Doctor's communications referred chiefly to a village, or neighborhood, or locality, in England, which he chose to call Newham; although he told the children that this was not the real name, which, for reasons best known to himself, he chose to conceal. Whatever the name were, he seemed to know the place so intimately, that the children, as a matter of course, adopted the conclusion that it was his birth-place, and the spot where he had spent his school-boy days, and had lived until some inscrutable reason impelled him to quit its ivy grown antiquity, all the aged beauty and strength that he spoke of, and cross the sea. He used to tell of an old church, far unlike the brick or pine-built meeting-houses, with which they were familiar; a church, the stones of which were laid, every one of them, before the world knew of the country in which he was then speaking; and how it had a spire, the lower part of which was mantled with ivy, and up which, towards its very top, the ivy was still creeping; and how there was a tradition, that, if the ivy ever reached the top, the spire would fall upon the roof of the old gray church, and crush it all down among its surrounding tombstones.

And so, as this misfortune would be so heavy a one, there seemed to be a miracle wrought from year to year, by which the ivy, though always flourishing, could never grow beyond a certain point; so that the spire and church had stood unharmed for thirty years; though the wise old people were constantly foretelling that the passing year must be the very last one that it could stand.

He told, too, of a kind of place that made little Ned blush, and cast down his eyes, to hide the tears of shame and anger at he knew not what, which would irresistibly spring into them; for it reminded him of the almshouse where, as the cruel Doctor had said, Ned himself had had his earliest home. And yet, after all, it had scarcely a feature of resemblance; and there was this great point of difference, that, whereas in Ned's wretched abode, a large unsightly brick house, there were many wretched infants, like himself, as well as helpless people of all ages, widows, decayed drunkards, people of feeble wit, and all kinds of imbecility, it being a haven for those who could not contend with the hard, eager, pitiless struggle of life, in the place that the Doctor spoke of, a noble, Gothic, mossy structure, there were none but aged men, who had drifted into this quiet harbor to end their days in a sort of humble yet stately ease and decorous abundance. And this shelter, the grim Doctor said, was the gift of a man who died hundreds and hundreds of years ago; and being a great sinner in his lifetime, and having drawn lands, manors, a great mass of wealth into his clutches, by violent and unfair means, this man had thought to get his pardon by founding this hospital, as it was called, in which thirteen poor old men should always reside, and he hoped they would spend their time in praying for his soul.

"Doctor Grim," said little Elsie, "I am glad he did it; and I hope the poor old men never forgot to pray for him, and that it did good to the poor wicked man's soul."

"Well, child," said Doctor Grimshawe, with a scowl into vacancy, as if he saw the dead man of a past century now before him, and a kind of wicked leer of merriment, at the same time, "I happen to be no lover of this man's race, and I hate him for the sake of one of his descendants. I don't think he succeeded in bribing the devil to let him go, or God to save him."

"Doctor Grim, you are very naughty," said Elsie, looking shocked.

"It is fair enough," said Ned, "to hate your enemy to the very brink of the grave, but then to leave him to get what mercy he can."

"After shoving him in," quoth the Doctor.

Doctor Grimshawe made no response to either of these criticisms, which seemed, indeed, to affect him very little, if he even listened to them; for he was a man of singularly imperfect moral culture; insomuch that nothing was so remarkable about him as that—being a man of a good deal of intellectual ability made available by much reading and experience, he was so very dark on the moral side, as if he needed the natural perceptions that should have enabled him to acquire that better wisdom. Such a phenomenon often meets us in life; oftener than we recognize, because a certain tact and exterior decency generally shades the moral deficiency; but often there is a mind well polished, and a conscience and natural passions left as they were in childhood, except that they have sprouted up into wild and poisonous weeds, richly blossoming, with strong-smelling flowers or seeds which it scatters by a sort of impulse, as the Doctor was now half-consciously throwing seeds of his evil passions into the minds of these children. He was himself a grown-up child, with the exception of lost simplicity and innocence, and ripened evil; all the ranker for a native heat that was in him, still active, and that might have nourished good things, as it did evil. Indeed, it did cherish by chance, a root or two of good, the fragrance of which was sometimes perceptible amidst all this rank growth of poisonous weeds. A grown-up child he was—that was all.

After a short silence, the Doctor went on to describe an old country-seat, which stood near this village and the ancient Hospital, which he had been telling about, and which was formerly the residence of the wicked man (a knight, and a brave one, well known in the Lancastrian wars) who had founded the latter. It was a venerable old mansion, which began to be built by a Saxon thane, more than a thousand years ago, the old English oak, that he built into his frame, being still visible in the ancient skeleton of its roof, sturdy and strong as if put up yesterday. And the descendants of the man that built it through the female line (for a Norman baron wedded the daughter and heiress of the Saxon) dwelt there yet; and in each century, they had done something for the old hall, building a tower, adding a suite of rooms, strengthening what was already built, putting in a painted window, making it more spacious and convenient; till it seemed as if Time itself employed himself in thinking what could be done for the old house; and as fast as any part decayed, they renewed it, building on something new with such simple art that it complied, as it were, and fitted itself to the old; so that it seemed as if the house had never been finished till just that thing was added.

For many an age, the possessors went on adding strength to strength; digging out the moat to a greater depth; piercing the walls with holes for archers to shoot through, building a turret to keep watch upon; but, at last, all necessity for such precautions passed away; and then they thought of convenience, and comfort, adding something for every generation to these; and, by-and-by, they thought of beauty, too, and in this time helped them, with its weather stains, and the ivy that grew over the walls and the grassy depth of the dried up moat, and the abundant shade that grew up everywhere, where naked strength would have been ugly.

"One curious thing in the old house," said the Doctor lowering his voice, yet with a look of triumph, and that old scowl, too, at the children, "they built a secret chamber—a very secret one."

"A secret chamber!" cried little Ned. "Who lived in it? A ghost?"

"There was often use for it," said Doctor Grim, "hiding people that had fought on the losing side, or Catholic priests, or criminals, or perhaps—who knows—enemies that they wanted to put out of the way, troublesome folks. Ah, it was often of use, that secret chamber, and is so still."

The Doctor paused, a long while, and leaned back in his chair, slowly puffing long whiffs from his pipe, looking up at the great spider-demon that hung over his head, and, as it seemed to the children, by the expression of his face, looking into the dim secret chamber, which he had spoken of, and which, by something in his mode of alluding to it, assumed such a weird, spectral aspect to their imaginations, that they never wished to hear of it again. Coming back, at length, out of his reverie—returning, perhaps, out of some weird, ghostly, secret chamber of his memory, of which the one in the old house was but the less horrible emblem—he resumed his tale. He said that, a long time ago, a war broke out in the old country, between King and Parliament; at that period, there were several brothers of this old family, which had adhered to the Catholic religion, and these chose the side of the King, instead of that of the Puritan parliament— all but one, whom the family hated, because he took the Parliament side, and became a soldier, and fought against his own brothers; and it was said among them, that so inveterate was he, that he went on the scaffold masqued, and was the very man who struck off the king's head, and that his foot trod in the king's blood; and that always afterwards, he made a bloody track wherever he went. And there was a legend, that his brethren once caught this renegade and imprisoned him in his own birth-place—perhap—

"In the secret chamber?" interrupted Ned.

"No doubt," said the Doctor, nodding, "though I never heard so."

<(Put into the Doctor's character a continual enmity against somebody, breaking out in curses, of which nobody can understand the application.)>

They imprisoned him, but he made his escape and fled; and, in the morning, his prison-place, wherever it was, was empty; but on the threshold of the door of the old manor-house, there was the print of a bloody footstep; and no trouble that the house-maids took, no rain of all the years that have passed since, no sunshine has made it fade, no wear and trample of feet since passing over it, have availed to erase it.

"I have seen it myself," quoth the Doctor, "and know this to be true!"

"Doctor Grim, now you are laughing at us," said Ned, trying to look brave.

And Elsie hid her face on the grim Doctor's knee; there being something that affected the vivid little girl with peculiar horror in the idea of this red footstep always glistening on the door-step, and wetting, as she fancied, every innocent foot of child or grown people, that had since passed over it.

"It is true," reiterated the grim Doctor, "for, man and boy, I have seen it a thousand times."

He continued his family-history, or tradition, or fantastic legend, whatever it might be, telling his young auditors that the Puritan, the renegade son of the family, was afterwards, by the contrivances of his brethren, sent to Virginia and sold as a bond slave, and how he had vanished from that quarter, and come to New England, where he was supposed to have left children. And, by and by, two elder brothers died, and this missing brother became the heir to the old estate and to a title; and then the family tried to track his bloody footstep, and sought it far and near; through the green country-paths and old streets of London, but in vain. Then they sent messengers to see if any traces of one stepping in blood could be found on the forest leaves of America; but still in vain. But still the idea prevailed that he would come back, and it was said they keep a bed-chamber ready for him, yet, in the old house. But, much as they pretended to regret the loss of him and his children, it would be a thing that would make them curse their stars were one of them to return now; for the children of a younger son were in possession of the old estate, and doing as much evil as ever their forefathers did; and if the true heir stood on the threshold, they would, if they might but do it secretly, stain the whole door-step as red as the Bloody Footstep had stained one little portion of it.

"Do you think he will ever come back?" asked little Ned.

"Stranger things have happened, my little man," said Doctor Grimshawe, "than that the posterity of this man should come back, and turn these usurpers out of his rightful inheritance; and sometimes, as I sit here smoking my pipe, and drinking my glass, and looking up at the cunning plot that the spider is weaving yonder, above my head, and thinking of this fine old family, and some little matters that there have been between one of them and me—I fancy that it may be so! We shall see! Stranger things have happened."

And Doctor Grimshawe drank off his tumbler, winking at little Ned, in a strange way, that seemed to be a kind of playfulness, but which did not affect the children pleasantly; insomuch that little Elsie put both her hands on Doctor Grim's knees and begged him not to do so any more.

<They find a grave stone with something like a foot on it.>

The children, after this conversation, often introduced the old English mansion into their little dreams and romances, which all imaginative children are continually mixing up with their lives, making the common-place day of grown people a rich, misty, gleaming sort of fairy-land to themselves. Ned, forgetting or not realizing the long lapse of time, used to fancy the true heir, wandering all this time in America, and leaving a long track of bloody footsteps behind him; until the period when, his sins being expiated, whatever they might be, he should turn back upon his steps, and return to his old, native home. And sometimes the child used to look along the streets of the town where he dwelt, bending his thoughtful eyes on the ground, thinking that perhaps he should see the bloody footstep there, betraying that the wanderer had just gone by that way. As for little Elsie, it was her fancy that the hero of the legend still remained imprisoned in that dreadful secret chamber, which had made a most dismal impression on her mind, and that there he was, forgotten all this time, waiting, like a naughty child shut up in a closet, until someone should come to unlock the door. In the pitifulness of her disposition, she once proposed to little Ned, that, as soon as they grew big enough, they should set out in quest of the old house, and find their way into it, and find the secret chamber, and let the poor prisoner out. So they lived a good deal of the time in a half waking dream, partly conscious of the fantastic nature of their ideas, yet with these ideas almost as real to them as the facts of the natural world, which are at first transparent and unsubstantial to children.

The Doctor appeared to have a pleasure, or a purpose, in keeping his legend forcibly in their memories; he often recurred to the subject of the old English family, and was continually giving new details about its history, the scenery, the neighborhood, the aspect of the mansion house, indicating a very intense interest in the subject in his own mind, of which this much talk seemed to be partly an involuntary overflowing. There was, however, no affection mingled with the sentiment. It appeared to be his unfortunate necessity, to let his thoughts dwell very constantly upon a subject that was hateful to him, with which this old English estate, and manor-house, and family, was somehow connected; the awe belonged to his race; the hatred to himself individually; and, moreover, had he spoken thus to elder and more experienced auditors, they might have detected in the manner and matter of his talk, a certain hereditary reverence and awe, the growth of ages, mixed up with a newer hatred that impelled him to deface and destroy what, at the same time, his deepest impulse was to bow before. It was the feeling of a man lowly born, when he contracts a hostility to his hereditary superior; in one way, being of a powerful, passionate nature, gifted with forces and ability far superior to that of the aristocrat, he might scorn him and feel able to trample on him; in another, he had the same awe as a simple country boy feels of the magnate who flings him a sixpence, or shakes his horsewhip at him. Had the grim Doctor been an American, he might have had the vast antipathy to rank, without the sense of awe that made it so much more malignant; it required a low-born Englishman to feel the two together. What made the hatred so fiendish was a something that, in the natural course of things, would have been loyalty, inherited affection, devoted self-sacrifice to a superior. Whatever it might be, it served, at times, (when his potations took deeper effect than ordinary) almost to drive the grim Doctor mad; for he would burst forth in wild diatribes and anathemas, having a strange, rough force of expression, and a depth of utterance, as if his words came from a bottomless pit within himself, where burned an everlasting fire, and where the furies had their home, and plans of dire revenge were welded into shape in the heat of a furnace. After the two poor children had been affrighted by paroxysms of this kind, the strange being would break out into one of his wild roars of laughter, that seemed to shake the house, and, at all events, caused the cobwebs and spiders, suspended from the cieling, to swing and vibrate with the motion of the volumes of cachinnatory breath which he thus expelled from his capacious lungs. Then, catching up little Elsie upon one knee, and Ned on the other, he would become gentler than in his usual mood, and, by the powerful magnetism of his character, cause them to think him as tender and sweet an old fellow as a child could desire for a playmate. Upon the whole, strange as it may appear, they loved the grim Doctor dearly; there was a loadstone within him that drew them close to him and kept them there, in spite of the horror of many things which he said and did. One thing that wrought mightily towards their mutually suiting each other, slight as it seemed, was, that no amount of racket, hubbub, shouting, laughter, noisy mischief, which the two children could perpetrate, ever disturbed the Doctor's studies, meditations, or employments of whatever kind. He had a hardy set of nerves, not refined by careful treatment in himself or his ancestors, but probably accustomed, from of old, to be drummed by harsh voices, rude sounds, the clatter and clamor of household life among homely, uncultivated, strongly animal people.

As the two children grew apace, it behoved their strange guardian to take some thought for their education. So far as little Elsie was concerned, however, he seemed utterly indifferent to her having any instruction, having imbibed no modern ideas respecting feminine capacities and privileges, but regarding woman, whether in the bud or blossom, as the plaything of man's idler moments; the helpmate, but in a

humble capacity, of his daily life. He sometimes bade her
go to the kitchen and take lessons of crusty Hannah, in bread-
making, sweeping, dusting, washing, the coarser needlework,
and such other things as she would require to know, when
she came to be a woman; but carelessly allowed her to gather
up the crumbs of such instruction as he bestowed on her
playmate, Ned, and thus learn to read, write, and cypher—
which, to say the truth, in the way of scholarship, was about
as far as little Elsie cared to go.

But towards little Ned, the grim Doctor adopted a far
different system. No sooner had he reached the age when the
soft and tender little intellect of the child became capable
of retaining impressions, than he took him vigorously in
hand, assigning him such tasks as were fit for him, and
cursorily investigating what were the force and character of
the powers with which the child grasped them. Not that the
Doctor pressed him forward unduly; indeed, there was no
need of it; for the boy manifested a remarkable docility for
instruction, and singular quickness in mastering the preliminary steps that lead to science; a subtle instinct, indeed, that
it seemed wonderful a child should possess for anything so
artificial as systems of grammar and arithmetic. A remarkable
boy, in truth, he was, to have been found by chance in an
alms-house; except that, such being his origin, we are at
liberty to suppose for him whatever long cultivation and
gentility we may think necessary, in his parentages of either
side, such as was indicated by his graceful and refined beauty
of person. He showed, indeed, even before he knew how to
read at all, an instinctive attraction towards books, and a love
for and interest in even the material form of knowledge, the
plates, the print, the binding of the Doctor's volumes, and
even in a book-worm, which he once found in an old volume,
where it had eaten a circular furrow. But the boy had too
quick a spirit of life to be in danger of becoming a book-

worm himself; he had this side of the intellect, but his impulse would be to mix with men, and catch something fresher from their intercourse than books could give him, though these would give him what they might.

In the grim Doctor, rough and uncultivated as he seemed, this budding intelligence found no inadequate instructor. Doctor Grimshawe proved himself a far more thorough scholar in the classics and mathematics than was ever after to be found in our country. He himself must have had rigid and faithful instruction at an early period of life, though probably not in his boyhood; for, though the culture had been bestowed, yet his mind was left in so singularly rough a state, that it seemed as if the refinement of classical study could not have been begun very early; or, possibly, the mind and nature was incapable of polish, or he may have had a coarse and sordid domestic life around him, in his infancy & youth. It was not a gem of that kind, but a coarser texture. An American, with a like education, would more likely have gained a certain fineness and grace, and it would have been difficult to distinguish him from one who had been born to culture and refinement; this sturdy Englishman, after all that had been done for his mind, and though it had been well done, was still but another ploughman of a long race of such, with a few scratchings of refinement on his hard exterior. His son, if he left one, might be a little less of the ploughman; his grandson, provided the female element were well chosen, might approach to refinement. Three generations—a century, at least—would be required for the slow toil of hewing, chiselling, and polishing a gentleman out of this ponderous old block, now rough from the great quarry of human nature. But, in the meantime, he evidently possessed, in an unusual degree, the sort of learning which refines other minds—the critical acquaintance with the great poets and historians of antiquity, and apparently an appreciation of their merits and power to teach their beauty. So the boy had an able tutor, capable it should seem, of showing him the way to graces which he did not himself possess; besides helping the growth of the strength without which refinement is but sickly and disgusting.

Another sort of culture, which it seemed odd that this rude man should undertake, was that of manners; but, in fact, rude as the grim Doctor's own manners were, he was one of the nicest and severest censors, in this department, whom I ever knew. It is difficult to account for this; although it is almost invariably found that persons, in a low rank of life, servants, laborers, will detect the false pretender to the character of a gentleman, with at least as sure an instinct as the class into which they seek to thrust themselves. Perhaps they recognize something akin to their own vulgarity, rather than appreciate what is unlike themselves. The Doctor possessed a peculiar power of rich, rough humor, on this subject, and used to deliver lectures, as it were, to little Ned, illustrated with sketches of living individuals, in the town where they dwelt, by unscrupulous use of whom he sought to teach the boy what to avoid in manners, if he sought to be a gentleman. But it must be confessed, he spared himself as little as other people; and often wound up with this compendious injunction;—"Be everything in your behavior that Doctor Grim is not."—His pupil, very probably, profited somewhat by these instructions; for there are specialities and arbitrary rules of behavior which do not come by nature; but these are few; and beautiful and noble and genial manners may almost be called a natural gift; and these, however he inherited them, soon proved to be an inherent possession of little Ned. He had a kind of inherent refinement, which nothing coarse can soil, or offend; it seemed, by some magic or other, absolutely to keep him from the knowledge of much of the grim Doctor's rude and sordid exterior, and to render what was around him beautiful, by a sort of reflection from that quality in himself gleaming its white light upon it. The Doctor himself was puzzled, and apparently both startled and delighted, at the perception of these characteristics; sometimes he would make a low, uncouth bow, after his fashion, to the little fellow, saying "Allow me to kiss your hand, my lord"; and little Ned, not quite knowing what the grim Doctor meant, yet allowed the favor he asked, with a grave and gracious condescension that seemed much to delight the suitor. This refusal to recognize or suspect that the Doctor might be laughing at him was a sure token, at any rate, of the lack of one vulgar characteristic in little Ned.

In order to afford every advantage to these natural gifts, Doctor Grimsworth failed not to provide the best attainable instructor, for such positive points of a polite education as his own fierce criticism, being destructive rather than generative, could not suffice for. There was a Frenchman in the town—an M. de Grand but secretly calling himself a Count —who taught the little people, and indeed, some of their elders, the Parisian pronunciation of his own language, and likewise dancing, (in which he was more an adept and more successful than in the former branch) and fencing, in which, after looking at a lesson or two, the grim Doctor was satisfied of his skill. Under his instruction, with the stimulus of the Doctor's praise and criticism, Ned soon grew to be the pride of the Frenchman's school, in both the active departments; and the Doctor himself added a third gymnastic requirement, (not absolutely necessary, he said, to a gentleman's education, but very desirable for a man perfect at all points) by teaching him cudgel-playing. <He teaches him pugilism, too> In short, in everything that related to accomplishments, whether of mind or body, no pains were spared with little Ned; but of the utilitarian turn of education, then almost exclusively given, and especially desirable in a fortuneless boy, like Ned, dependent on a man not wealthy, there was little given.

At first, too, the Doctor paid little attention to the moral and religious nurture of his pupil, nor did he ever make a system of it; but, one evening, I know not how, he was betrayed into speaking on this point; and a sort of inspiration seized him. But, by-and-by, though with a singular reluctance and kind of bashfulness, he began to extend his care to these matters; being drawn into them, unawares, and possibly perceiving and learning what he taught, as he went along. The vista opened before him; handling an immortal spirit, he began to know its requisitions, in a degree far beyond what he had conceived them when his great task was undertaken. So, sometimes, his voice grew deep and had a strange impressive pathos in it; his talk became eloquent with depth of meaning and feeling, as he told the boy of the moral dangers of the world for which he was seeking to educate him; and said that life presented what looked like great triumphs, and yet were the greatest and saddest of defeats. He told him that many things, that seemed nearest and dearest to the heart of man, were destructive, eating and gnawing away, and corroding what was best in him; and what a high, noble, re-creating triumph it was, when these dark impulses were resisted and overthrown, and how, from that epoch, the soul took a new start. He withered the selfish greed of gold, lawless passion, revenge; and here the grim Doctor broke out into a strange passion and zeal of anathema against this deadly sin, making a dreadful picture of the ruin that it creates in the heart where it establishes itself; and how it makes a corrosive acid of the genial juices. Then he told the boy, that the condition of all good was in the first place, Truth; then Courage; then Justice; then Mercy; out of which principles, operating upon one another, would come all brave, noble, high, unselfish actions, and the scorn of all mean ones; and how that, from such a nature all hatred would fall away and all affections be ennobled. I know not at what point it was precisely, in these ethical instructions, that an insight seemed to strike the grim Doctor that something more— vastly more—was needed than all that he had said; and he began doubtfully to speak of man's spiritual nature, and its demands, and the emptiness of everything which a sense of these demands did not pervade, and condense and weighten into realities; and going on in this strain, he soared out of himself, and astonished the two children who stood gazing at him, wondering whether it were the grim Doctor that was speaking thus; until some interrupting circumstance seemed to bring him back to himself, and he burst into one of his great roars of laughter; the inspiration, the strange light passed out of his face, whereby he had been transfigured; and there was the uncouth, wild-bearded, rough, earthy, passionate man, whom they called Doctor Grim, looking ashamed of himself, and trying to turn the whole matter into a jest.

<(It must have somewhat of the characteristics of the catechism, & simple cottage devotion.)>

It was a sad pity that he should have been interrupted, and brought into this mocking mood, just when he seemed to have broken away from the sinfulness of his hot, evil nature, and have soared into a region where, with all his native characteristics transfigured, he seemed to have become an angel in his own likeness. Crusty Hannah, who had been drawn to the door of the study by the unusual tones of his voice, a kind of piercing sweetness in it, always averred that she saw the gigantic spider swinging about his head in great crafty circles, and clutching, as it were, at his brain with its great claws; but it was the old woman's absurb idea that this hideous insect was the devil, in that ugly guise—a superstition which deserves absolutely no countenance.

Nevertheless, though this paroxysm of devotional feeling and insight returned no more to the grim Doctor, it was ever after a memorable occasion to the two children. It touched that religious chord in both their hearts, which there was no mother to touch; but now it vibrated long, and never ceased so long as they remained together, nor perhap after they were parted from each other, and from the grim Doctor;—even then, in those after years, the strange music that had then been awakened was continued, as it were an echo from harps on high. Now, at all events, they made little prayers for themselves, and said them at bedtime, generally in secret, sometimes in unison; and they read in an old dusty bible, which lay among the grim Doctor's books, and from little Heathens, they became Christian children. Doctor Grimshawe was perhaps conscious of this result of his involuntary preachment; but he never directly noticed it, and did nothing either to efface or deepen the impression.

It was very singular, however, that, in both the children's minds, this one gush of irresistible religious sentiment, breaking out of the grim Doctor's inner depths, like a sort of holy lava from a volcano that usually emitted quite other matter, hot, melted wrath and scorn, quite threw out of sight, then and always afterwards, his darker characteristics. They remembered him, with faith and love, as a religious man, and forgot—what perhaps had made no impression on their innocent hearts—all the characteristics that other people might have called devilish. To them, the grim Doctor was a Saint, even during his lifetime and constant intercourse with them, and canonized forever afterwards. There is, almost always, to be sure, this profound faith in childhood with respect to those whom they love; but perhaps, in this instance, the children really had a depth of insight that grown people lacked, and saw a profound recognition at the bottom of this strange man's nature, which was of such stuff as martyrs and heroic saints might have been made of, though here it had been wrought miserably amiss. At any rate, his face with the holy awe upon it was what they saw, and remembered, when they thought of their friend Doctor Grim.

One effect of his zealous and analytic instruction of the boy was very perceptible. Heretofore, though enduring him, and occasionally making a plaything of him, it may be doubted whether the grim Doctor had really any strong affection for the child; it rather seemed a self-imposed task, which, with his strong will, he forced himself to undertake, and carry sedulously forward. All that he had done—his rescuing the bright child from poverty, and nameless degradation, ignorance, sordid life, hopeless of better fortune, and opening to him the whole realm of mighty possibilities, in an American life—did not imply any love for the little individual whom he thus benefitted. It had some other motive.

But, now approaching the child in this close, intimate, and helpful way, his interest, it was most evident, took a tenderer character; there was everything in the boy, that a boy could possess, to attract affection; he would have been a father's pride and joy. Doctor Grimshawe, indeed, was not his father; but to a person of his character, this was perhaps no cause of lesser love than if there had been the whole of that holy claim of kindred between them. We speak of the natural force of blood; we speak of the paternal relation as if it were productive of more earnest affection than can exist between two persons, one protective but unrelated; but there are wild, forcible, unrestricted characters, on whom the necessity and even duty of loving their own child is a sort of barrier to love. They perhaps do not love their own traits, which they recognize in their children; they shrink from their own features in the reflection presented by those little mirrors. A certain strangeness and unlikeness (such as gives poignancy to the love between the sexes) would excite a livelier affection. Be this as it may, it is not probable that Doctor Grimshawe would have loved a child of his own blood, with the coarse characteristics that he knew both in his race and himself, with nearly such fervor as this beautiful, slender, yet strenuous, intelligent, refined boy, with such a high bred air, handling common things with so refined a touch, yet grasping them so firmly; throwing a natural grace on all he did. Was he not his father? he that took him out of the sordid mud in which this fair blossom must soon have withered and perished. Was not this beautiful strangeness, which he so wondered at, the result of his care!

And little Elsie? Did the grim Doctor love her as well? Perhaps not; for, in the first place, there was a natural tie, though not the nearest, between her and Doctor Grimshawe, which made him feel that she was cast upon his love, a burthen which he acknowledged himself bound to undertake. Then, too, there were unutterably painful reminiscenses—thoughts that made him gasp for breath—that turned his blood sour—that tormented his dreams with night-mares and hellish phantoms—all of which were connected with this innocent and happy child; so that cheerful and pleasant as she was, there was to the grim Doctor a little fiend playing about his floor and throwing a lurid light on the wall, as the shadow of this sun-flickering child. It is certain that there was always a pain and horror mingled with his feeling towards Elsie; he had to forget himself, as it were, and all that was connected with the causes why she came to be, before he could love Elsie. Amid his fondness, when he was caressing her upon his knee, pressing her to his rough bosom, as he never took the freedom to press Ned, came these hateful reminiscences, compelling him to set her down, and corrugate his heavy brows, as with a pang of fiercely resented, strongly borne pain. Still, the child no doubt, had contrived to find her way into the great, gloomy cavern of the grim Doctor's heart, and stole constantly farther and farther in, carrying a ray of sunshine in her hand, as a taper to light her way and illuminate the rude, dark pit into which she so fearlessly went.

<Make the following scene emblematic of the world's treatment of a dissenter.>

Doctor Grim had the English faith in open air and daily acquaintance with the weather, whatever it might be; and it was his habit not only to send the two children to play, for lack of a better place, in the graveyard, but to take them himself on long rambles, of which the vicinity of the town afforded a rich variety. It may be that the Doctor's excursions had the wider scope, because both he and the children were objects of curiosity in the town, and very much the subject of its gossip; so that always, in its streets and lanes, the people turned to gaze and came to their windows, and to the doors of shops, to see this grim, bearded figure leading along the beautiful children each by a hand, with a surly aspect, like a bull-dog. Their remarks might not be intended to reach the ears of the party; but certainly were not so cautiously whispered but they occasionally might. The male remarks, indeed, generally died away in the depths of the throats that uttered them; a circumstance that doubtless often saved the utterer from some very rough rejoinder at the hands of the Doctor, who had grown up in the habit of a very ready and free recourse to his fists, which had a way of doubling themselves up, seemingly of their own accord. But the shrill feminine voices sometimes sent their remarks from window to window, without dread of any such repartee on the part of the subject of them.

"There he goes, the Old Spider-minder," quoth one shrill woman, "with those two poor babes that he has caught in his cobweb, and is going to feed upon, poor little tender things. The bloody Englishman makes free with the dead bodies of our friends, and the living ones of our children."

"How red his nose is," quoth another, "he has pulled at the brandy-bottle pretty stoutly to-day, early as it is! Pretty habits those children will learn, between the devil in the shape of the great spider, and this devilish fellow in his own shape. It were well that our townsmen tarred and feathered the old British wizard!"

And as he got farther off, two or three little blackguard, barefoot boys shouted shrilly after him, "Doctor Grim, Doctor Grim! The devil wove a web for him!" being a nonsensical couplet which had been made for the grim Doctor's benefit, and was often cried in the streets and under his own windows. Hearing such remarks, and insults, the Doctor would glare round at them with red eyes, especially if the brandy bottle had happened to be much in request that day. Indeed, poor Doctor Grim had met with a fortune which befals many a man with less cause than drew the public attention on this odd humorist; for dwelling in a town that was as yet but a large village, where everybody knew everybody, and claimed the privilege to know and discuss their characters, and where there were few topics of public interest to take off the attention, a very considerable portion of town-talk and criticism fell upon him. The old town had a certain provincialism, which is less the characteristic of towns in these days when society circulates so freely, than then; besides, it was a very rude epoch, just when the country had come through the war of the Revolution, and while the surges of that commotion were still seething and swelling, and while the habits and morals of every individual in the community still felt its influence; and, especially, the contest was too recent for an Englishman to be in very good odor, unless he should cease to be English, and become more American then the Americans themselves in repudiating British prejudices or principles, habits, modes of thought, and everything that distinguishes Britons at home or abroad. As Doctor Grim did not see fit to do this—and, as moreover, he was a very doubtful, questionable, morose, unamiable old fellow, not seeking to make himself liked, nor deserving to be so—he was a very unpopular person in the town where he had chosen to reside. Nobody thought very well of him; the respectable people had heard of his pipe and brandy-bottle; the religious community knew that he never showed himself at church or meeting; so that he had not that very desirable strength, in a society split up into many sects, of being able to rely upon the party-sympathies of any one of them; the mob hated him with the blind sentiment that makes one surly cur hostile to another surly cur. He was the most insulated individual to be found anywhere, and being so unsupported, everybody was his enemy.

The town, as it happened, had been pleased to interest itself much in this matter of Doctor Grim and the two children, inasmuch as he neither sent them to school, nor came with them to meeting of any kind, but was breeding them up ignorant Heathen, to all appearances; and, as many believed, was devoting them in some way to the great spider, to whom he had bartered his own soul. It had been mooted among the selectmen, the fathers of the town, whether their duty did not require them to put the children under more suitable guardianship; a measure which, it may be, was chiefly hindered by the consideration that, in that case, the cost of supporting them would probably be transferred from the grim Doctor's shoulders to those of the community. Nevertheless, they did what they could. Maidenly ladies, prim and starched, one or two instances, called upon the Doctor (the two children were in the graveyard) to give him Christian advice as to the management of his charges; perhaps, too, instigated by a natural feminine desire to see the interior of a place about which they had heard much, with its spiders' webs, its strange machines and confusing tools; so much contrary to crusty Hannah's advice, they persisted in entering. But, to confess the truth, the Doctor's reception of these fair missionaries was not extremely courteous. Crusty Hannah listened at the door; and it was curious to see the delighted smile which came over her dry old visage, as the Doctor's rough growling voice, often an abrupt question or two, and a reply in a thin voice on the part of the maiden ladies, grew louder, and louder; till the door opened, and forth came the benevolent pair in great discomposure; Crusty Hannah averred, with their caps much rumpled, but this part of the story was questioned; though it were certain that the Doctor called after them, down stairs, that had they been younger and prettier, they should have fared worse. A male emissary who was admitted on the supposition of being a patient, on the same errand, did really fare worse; for (the grim Doctor having been particularly intimate with the black bottle, that afternoon) there was, about ten minutes after the visitor's entrance, a sudden fierce upraising of the Doctor's growl; then a struggle that shook the house, and finally a terrible rumbling down the stairs, which proved to be caused by the precipitate descent of the hapless visitor, who, if he need no assistance of the grim Doctor on his entrance, certainly would have been the better for a plaister or two after his departure.

Such were the terms on which Doctor Grimshawe now stood with his adopted townspeople; and if we consider the idle and dull little town to be full of exaggerated stories about the Doctor's oddities, many of them forged, all retailed in an unfriendly spirit; the horrid suspicions, too, countenanced by his abode in the corner of the grave-yard, affording the terrible Doctor such facilities for making free, like a ghoul as he was, with the relics of mortality from the earliest progenitor to the man killed by the Doctor's own drugs yesterday; misconceptions of a character which was sufficiently amenable to censure, in its best and most candidly interpreted aspects; surmises, taken for certainties; superstitions, the genuine hereditary growth of the frame of public mind which produced the witchcraft delusion; national prejudice; pure mischief— all fermenting together, and all this evil and uncharitableness taking the delusive hue of benevolent interest in two helpless children, we may partly judge what was the odium in which the grim Doctor dwelt, and amid which he walked. He had heretofore contented himself, at most, with occasionally shaking his stick at his assailants; but, this day, the black bottle had imparted, it may be, a little more than ordinary fire to his blood; and, besides, an unlucky urchin happened to take particularly good aim with a mud ball, which took effect right in the midst of the Doctor's bushy beard, and, being of soft consistency, forthwith became incorporated with it; and at this intolerable provocation, the grim Doctor pursued the little villain, amid a shower of similar missles from the boy's playmates, caught him as he was escaping into a back yard, and, with his stick, proceeded to give him merited chastisement.

<He drags into the middle of the street.>

But, hereupon, it was astonishing how sudden a commotion flashed up like gunpowder along the street, which, just before, was so quiet except for the petty shrieks and laughter of a few children. Forth out of every window in those dusky, mean wooden houses, were thrust heads of women, old and young; forth out of every door, and other avenue, and as if they started up from the middle of the street, or out of the unpaved sidewalks, rushed fierce, avenging powers threatening at full yell to take vengeance on the grim Doctor, who still, with that fierce, dark face of his, his muddy beard all strung abroad, stiff and foul, his hat fallen off, his red eyes flashing fire, was belaboring the poor hinder end of the unhappy urchin, paying off upon that one part of one boy's person the whole score which he had to settle with the crude boys of the town; giving him, at once, the whole whipping which he had deserved every day of his life, and not a stroke of which he had yet received. Need enough there was, no doubt, that somebody should interfere with such grim and immitigable justice; and certainly the interference was prompt and promised to be effectual.

"Down with the old rascal! Thrash him! Hang him. Tar and feather the infernal Tory. The wizard! The body-snatcher! Kill him! Kill him."

<One man is in the delirium tremens; another mad.>

It is unaccountable where all this mischievous thirsty multitude came from—how they came into that quietness—in such a moment of time! What had they been about heretofore? Were they waiting in readiness for this crisis, and keeping themselves free from other employment till it should come to pass? Had they been created for the moment; or were they fiends, sent by Satan in the likeness of a blackguard population? There you might see the off-scourings of the recently finished war, old soldiers, rusty, wooden-legged; there sailors, ripe for any kind of mischief; there the drunken populace of a neighboring grog-shop, staggering helter skelter to the scene, and tumbling over one another at the Doctor's feet; there came the father of the punished urchin, who had never shown heretofore any care for his street-bred progeny, but now came pale with rage, armed with a pair of tongs, and with him the mother, flying like a fury, with her cap awry, and clutching a broomstick, as if she were a witch just alighted; up they rose out of cellar-doors, and dropt down from chamber-windows; all rushing upon the Doctor, but overrunning and thwarting themselves by their very multitude; for as good Doctor Grim levelled the first that came within reach of his fist, two or three of the others tumbled over him and lay grovelling at his feet; the Doctor meanwhile having retreated into the angle between two houses. Little Ned, with a valor that did him the more credit inasmuch as it was exercised in spite of a good deal of childish trepidation, as his pale face indicated, brandished his little fists by the Doctor's side, and little Elsie did what any woman may— that is, screeched in Doctor Grim's behalf, with full stretch of lungs. Meanwhile the street-boys kept up a shower of mud-balls, many of which hit the Doctor, while the rest were distributed among his assailants, heightening their ferocity.

"Seize the old scoundrel! the villain! the tory! the rascally Englishman; hang him in the web of his own devilish spider —it's big enough. Tar and feather him! Tar and feather him!"

<(A brother physician sees him and is greatly tickled.)>

It was certainly one of those crises that show a man how few real friends there are, and the sad tendency of mankind to stand aside, at least, and let a poor devil fight his own troubles, if not assist them in their attack. You might have seen a decorous, powdered, ruffle-shirted dignitary, one of the weighty men of the town, standing at a neighboring corner to see what would come of it. "He is not a respectable man, I understand, this Quack Doctor Grimshawe;—a quack —always in these intemperate scuffles; let him get out as he may." And there comes a deacon of one of the churches, and several church-members, who, hearing a noise, come decorously and gravely to see what was going forward in a Christian community. "Ah it is that irreligious and profane Grimshawe who never goes to meeting. We wash our hands of it." And one of the selectmen saw it and observed— "Certainly this common brawler ought not to have the care of those two innocent children. Something must be done about it; and when the man is sober, he must be talked to." Alas! It is a hard case with a man who lives on his own bottom and responsibility, making himself no allies, sewing himself on to nobody's skirts, insulating himself; sad, when his trouble comes, and so poor Doctor Grimshawe was like to find it.

<(Yankee characteristics should be shown in the schoolmaster's manners)>

He had succeeded, by dint of good skill and some previous practice at quarter-staff, in keeping his assailants at bay, though not without some danger on his own part; but their number, their fierceness, and the more skilled assault of some among them, must almost immediately have been successful, when the Doctor's part was strengthened by one unexpected ally. It was a person of a tall, slight figure, who without lifting up his hands to take part in the contest, thrust himself before him, and turned towards the assailants, crying— "Christian men, what would you do! Peace! Peace!" His well-intended exhortation took effect, indeed, in a certain way, but not precisely as might have been wished; for a blow, aimed at Doctor Grim, took effect on the head of this man, who seemed to have no sort of skill or alacrity at defending himself, any more than making an assault; for he never lifted his hands, but took the blow as unresistingly as if it had been kindly meant; and it levelled him senseless on the ground.

Had the mob been really enraged for any strenuous cause, this incident would have operated merely as a preliminary whet to stimulate them for further bloodshed; but as they were mostly actuated only by a natural desire for mischief, they were about as well satisfied with what had been done, as if the Doctor himself were the victim; and, besides, the fathers and respectabilities of the town, who had seen this mishap from afar, now began to push forward, crying out, "Keep the peace! Keep the peace! A riot! A riot!" and other such cries, as suited the nonce; and the crowd vanished even more speedily than it congregated, leaving the Doctor and the two children alone beside the fallen victim of a quarrel not his own. Not to dwell too long on the incident, the Doctor, laying hold on the last of his enemies, after the rest had taken to their heels, ordered him sternly to stay and help him bear the man, whom he had helped to murder, to his house. "It concerns you, friend; for if he dies, you hang, to a dead certainty." And this was done accordingly.

About an hour thereafter, there lay on a couch that had been hastily prepared, a person of singularly impressive presence; a thin, mild looking man, with a peculiar look of delicacy and natural refinement about him, although he scarcely appeared to be, technically and in worldy position, what we call a gentleman; plain in dress, and simple in manner; not giving the idea of remarkable intellectual gifts, but with a kind of spiritual aspect, fair, clear complexion, gentle eyes, still somewhat clouded and obscured by the syncope into which a blow on the head had thrown him. He looked middle-aged, and yet there was a kind of childlike, simple expression, which, unless you looked at him for the very purpose of seeing the traces of time in his face, would make you suppose him much younger.

"And how do you find yourself now, my good fellow?" asked Doctor Grimshawe, putting forth his hand to grasp that of the stranger, and giving it a good warm shake. "None the worse, I should hope!"

<He had a sense of horror of violence, and of the strangeness that it should be done to him; this affected him more than the blow.>

"Not much the worse," answered the stranger; "not at all, it may be. There is a pleasant dimness and uncertainty in my mode of being. I am taken off my feet, as it were, and float in air, with a delightful mistiness in my sensations, a faint delight in my members. The grossness, the roughness, the too great angularity of the actual is removed from me. It is a state that I like much. It may be, this is the way that the dead feel, when they awake in another state of being, with a dim pleasure, after passing through the brief darkness of death. It is very pleasant."

He answered dreamily and sluggishly, reluctantly; as if there were a sense of repose in him which he disliked to break by any effort of putting his sensations into words. His voice had a remarkable sweetness and gentleness, though lacking in depth of melody.

"Here, take this," said the Doctor, who had been preparing some kind of potion in a tea-spoon; it may have been a dose of his famous preparation of spider's web, for aught I know, the operation of which was said to be of a soothing, ameliorating influence, causing a delightful silkiness of sensation; but I know not whether it was considered good for concussions of the brain, such as it is to be supposed the present patient had undergone. "Take this; it will do you good; and here I drink your very good health in something that will do me good."

So saying, the grim Doctor quaffed off a tumbler of brandy and water.

"How sweet a contrast," murmured the stranger, "between that scene of strife and this great peace that has come over me. It is so as when one can say, I have fought the good fight."

"You are right," said the Doctor, with what would have been one of his deep laughs, but which he modified a little, however, in consideration of his patient's tenderness of brain. "We both of us fought a good fight; for though you struck no actual stroke, you took them as unflinchingly as ever I saw a man, and so turned the fortune of the battle better than if you had smote with a sledge hammer. Two things puzzle me, in this affair. First, whence came my assailants, all in that moment of time, unless Satan let loose out of the infernal regions a squad of fiends, hoping thus to get a triumph over me. And secondly, whence came you, my preserver, unless you are an angel and dropt down from the sky."

"No," answered the stranger, with quiet simplicity. "I was passing through the street to my little school, when I saw your peril, and felt it my duty to expostulate with the people."

"Well," said the grim Doctor, "come whence you will, you did an angel's office for me; and I shall do what an earthly man may to requite it. There; we will talk no more for the present."

He hushed up the children, who were already, of their own accord, walking on tiptoe and whispering; and he himself even went so far as to refrain from the usual incense of his pipe, having observed that the stranger, who seemed to be of a very delicate organization, had seemed sensible of its disagreeable effects on the atmosphere of the room. The restraint lasted, however, only till Crusty Hannah had fitted up a little bed-room, on the opposite side of the entry to which she and the grim Doctor removed the stranger, who, though tall, they observed was of no great weight and substance—the lightest man, the Doctor averred, for his size, that ever he had handled. Every possible care was taken of him, and, in a day or two, he was able to walk into the study again, where he sat gazing at the sordidness and unneatness of the apartment, the strange festoons and drapery of spider's web, the gigantic spider himself, and at the grim Doctor, so shaggy, grisly, and uncouth, in the midst of these surroundings, with a perceptible sense of something very strange in it all. His mild, gentle regard dwelt, too, on the two beautiful children, evidently with a sense of quiet wonder how they should be here, and altogether, a sense of their unfitness; they, meanwhile, stood a little apart, looking at him, somewhat disturbed and awed, as children usually are, by a sense that the stranger was not perfectly well, that he had been injured, and so set apart from the rest of the world.

"Will you come to me, little one?" said he, holding out a delicate hand to Elsie.

Elsie came to his knee, without any hesitation, though without any of the rush that accompanied her advent to those whom she affected. "And you, my little man!" added the stranger, quietly, and beckoning to Ned, who likewise willingly approached, and shaking him by the offered hand, let it go again, but continued standing by his side.

"Do you know, my little friends," said the stranger, "that it is my business in life to instruct such little people as you?"

"Do they obey you well, Sir?" asked Ned; perhaps conscious of a want of force in the person whom he addressed.

The stranger smiled faintly. "Not too well," said he. "That has been my difficulty; for I have moral and religious objections and also a great horror to the use of the rod, and I have not been gifted with a harsh voice and a stern brow; so that, after a while, my little people sometimes get the better of me. The present generation of men is too gross for gentle treatment."

"You are quite right," quoth Doctor Grimshawe, who had been observing this little scene, and trying to make out from the mutual deportment of the stranger and the two children what sort of man this fair, quiet stranger was, with his gentleness and weakness; characteristics that were not attractive to himself, yet in which he acknowledged, as he saw them here, a certain charm; nor did he know, scarcely, whether to despise the man in whom he saw them, or to yield to a strange sense of reverence. So he watched the children, with an indistinct idea of being guided by them. "You are quite right, the world now—and always before, so far as I ever heard—requires a great deal of brute force, a great deal of animal food and brandy, in the man that is to make an impression on it."

The convalescence of the stranger—he gave his name as Seymour—proceeded favorably; for the Doctor remarked that, delicate as his system was, it had a certain purity, a simple healthfulness that did not run into disease as stronger constitutions might; it did not apparently require much to crush down such a being as he—not much unkindly breath to blow out the taper of his life—and yet, if not absolutely killed, there was a certain aptness to keep alive in him, not readily to be overcome. No sooner was he in a condition so to do, than he went forth to look after the little school that he had spoken of, but soon came back, announcing in a very quiet and undisturbed way, that, during his withdrawal from duty, the scholars had been distributed to other instructors, and consequently he was without place or occupation.

<Jokes, occasionally, about the Schoolmaster's thinness and lightness; how he might suspend himself from the spider's web, and swing &c.>

"A hard case!" said the Doctor, flinging a gruff curse at those who had so readily deserted the poor Schoolmaster.

"Not so hard," replied Seymour. "Those little fellows were an unruly set, born of parents who have lived rough lives— born in war time, too, with the spirit of battle in them— therefore rude and contentious, beyond my power to cope with them. I have been taught, long ago," he added, with a peaceful smile, "that my business in life does not lie with grownup and consolidated men and women; and so, not to be useless in my day, and to gain the little that my sustenance requires, I have thought to deal with children. But even for this I lack force."

"I dare say," said the Doctor, with a modified laugh. "Little devils they are, harder to deal with than men. Well; I am glad of your failure for one reason, and of your being thrown out of business, because we shall have the benefit of you the longer. Here is this boy to be instructed. I have made some attempts myself; but, having no art of teaching, no skill, no temper, I suppose I make but an indifferent hand of it; and, besides, I have other business that occupies my thoughts. Take him in hand, if you like; and the girl for company. No matter whether you teach her anything; unless you happen to be acquainted with needlework."

"I will talk with the children," said Seymour, "and see if I am likely to do good with him. The lad, I see, has a singular spirit of aspiration and pride—no ungentle pride, but still hard to cope with. I will see. The little girl is a most comfortable child."

"You have read the boy, as if you had his heart in your hand," said the Doctor, rather surprised. "I could not have done it better myself, though I have known him all but from the egg."

Accordingly, the stranger, who had been thrust so providentially into this odd and insulated little community, abode with them, without more words being spoken on the subject, for it seemed to all concerned a natural arrangement; although, on both parts, they were mutually sensible of something strange in the companionship thus brought about. To say the truth, it was not easy to imagine two persons apparently less adapted to one another's society than the rough, crude, animal Doctor, so sturdily a hater, so hotly impulsive, whose faith was in his own right arm, so full of the Old Adam as he was, so deep, subtle, crooked, so obstructed by his animal nature, so given to his pipe and black bottle, so wrathful and pugnacious, and wicked; and this mild, spiritual creature, so milky, with so unforceful a grasp; and it was singular to see how they stood apart and eyed each other, each tacitly acknowledging a certain merit or kind of power, though not well able to appreciate its value. The grim Doctor's kindness, however, and gratitude had been so thoroughly awakened, that he did not feel the disgust that he probably otherwise might at what seemed the mawkishness of Seymour's character; his want, morally speaking, of bone and muscle; his fastidiousness of character, the essence of which, it seemed to be to have no stain upon it; otherwise it must die.

<(The Doctor and the schoolmaster should have much talk about England)>

On Seymour's part, there was a good deal of evidence to be detected by a nice observer, that he found it difficult to put up with the Doctor's coarse peculiarities, whether physical or moral; his animal indulgences of appetites struck him with wonder and horror; his coarse expressions; his free indulgence of wrath; his sordid and unclean habits; the dust, the cobwebs, the monster that dangled from the ceiling; his pipe, diffusing its fragrance through the house, and showing, by the plainest and simplest proof, how we all breathe one another's breath, nice and proud as we may be, kings and daintiest ladies breathing the air that has already served to inflate a beggar's lungs. He shrank, too, from the rude manhood of the Doctor's character, with its human warmth; an element which he seemed not to possess in his own character. He was capable only of gentle and mild regard, that was his warmest affection; and the warmest, too, that he was capable of exciting in others; so that he was doomed, as much apparently as the Doctor himself, to be a lonely creature, without any very deep companionship in the world, though not incapable, when he, by some rare chance, met a soul distinctly akin, of holding a certain high spiritual communion. With the children however he succeeded in establishing some good and available relations; his simple and passionless character coincided with their simplicity, and their as yet unawakened passions; they appeared to understand him better than the Doctor ever succeeded in doing. He touched springs and elements in the nature of both, that had never been touched till now, and that sometimes made a sweet, high music. But this was rarely; and, as far as the general duties of an instructor went, they did seem to be very successfully performed; something was cultivated, the spiritual germ grew, it might be; but the children, and especially Ned, were intuitively conscious of a certain want of substance in the instructor, a something of earthly bulk, a too etherealness. But his connection with our story does not lie in any excellence or lack of excellence that he showed as an instructor; and we merely mention these things as illustrating more or less his characteristics.

The grim Doctor's curiosity was somewhat piqued by what he could see of the schoolmaster's character; and he was desirous of finding out what sort of life such a man could have led in the world which he himself had found so rough a one; through what difficulties he had reached middle-age, without absolutely vanishing away in his contact with more positive substances than himself; how the world had given him a subsistence, if indeed, like a certain people whom Pliny mentions in Africa, he required anything more dense than fragrance; a point, in fact, which the grim Doctor denied, his performance at table being inappreciable, and confined, at least, almost entirely to a dish of boiled rice, which Crusty Hannah set before him, preparing it, it might be, with a sympathy of her East Indian part towards him. Well; Doctor Grimshawe easily got at what seemed to be all of the facts of Seymour's life; how that he was a New Englander, the descendant of an ancient race of settlers, the last of them; for, once pretty numerous in their quarter of the country, they seemed to have been dying out, exhaling from the earth, and passing to some other region.

<(The children were at play in the grave yard)>

"No wonder," said the Doctor bluffly. "You have been letting slip the vital principle, if you are a fair specimen of the race. You do not clothe yourself in substance. Your souls are not cased sufficiently. Beef and ale would have saved you. You have exhaled for lack of them."

The schoolmaster shook his head, and probably thought his earthly salvation and continuance not worth buying at such a cost. The remainder of his history was not tangible enough to afford a narrative. There seemed, from what he said, to have been always a certain kind of refinement in his race, a nicety of conscience, a nicety of habit, which either was in itself a want of force, or was necessarily connected with it; and which, the Doctor silently thought, had culminated in the person before him.

"It was always in us," continued Seymour, with a certain pride which people generally feel in their ancestral characteristics, be they good or evil. "We had a tradition among us of our first emigrant, and the causes that brought him to the New World; and it was said that he had suffered so much, before quitting his native shores,—so painful had been his track—that always afterwards, on the forest-leaves of this land, his foot left a print of blood wherever it trod."

< (He mentions that he was probably buried in the grave yard there) >

"A print of blood!" said the grim Doctor, breaking his pipe-stem by some sudden spasm in his gripe of it. "Pah. The Devil take the pipe! A very strange story that! Pray how was it?"

< (Perhap put this narratively, not as spoken.) >

"Nay, it is but a very dim legend," answered the Schoolmaster; "although there were old, yellow papers and parchments, I remember, in my father's possession that had some reference to this man, too; though there was nothing in them about the bloody footprint. But our family legend is, that this man was of a good race, in the time of Charles First, inhabiting an old hall in England; there were four sons of them, all of whom were originally papists; but one of them— the second son, our legend says, was of a milder, sweeter cast than the rest, who were fierce and bloody men, of a headstrong nature, but he partook most of his mother's character. This son had been one of the earliest Quakers converted by George Fox; and moreover, there had been love between him and a young lady of great beauty, and an heiress, whom likewise the eldest son of the house had designed to make his wife. And these brothers, cruel men, caught their innocent brother, and kept him in confinement long in his own native home."

"How?" asked the Doctor. "Why did not he appeal to the laws?"

"Our legend says," replied the Schoolmaster, "only that he was kept in a chamber that was forgotten."

"Very strange that!" quoth the Doctor.

<He was privately married to the heiress, if she were an heiress.>

<He was sold by his brethren>

<They meant to kill him in the wood, but by contrivance he was kidnapped>

The Schoolmaster went on, to tell, with much shuddering, how a Jesuit priest had been mixed up with this wretched business, and there had been a scheme at once religious and political to wrest the estate and the lovely lady from the fortunate heir; and how this grim Italian priest had instigated them to use a certain kind of torture with the poor heir; and how he had suffered from this; but, one night, when they left him senseless, he contrived to make his escape from that cruel home, bleeding as he went, and how, by some action of his imagination—his sense of the cruelty and hideousness of such treatment at his brethren's hand, and in the holy name of his religion, his foot, which had been crushed by their cruelty, bleeding as he went, that blood had never been staunched. And thus he had come to America, and after many wanderings, and much track of blood along rough ways, to New England.

<They were privately married.>

"And what became of his beloved?" asked the grim Doctor, who was puffing away at a fresh pipe, and with a very queer aspect.

"She died in England," replied the Schoolmaster. "And before her death, by some means or other, they say that she found means to send to him a child, the offspring of their marriage, and from that child our race descended. And they say, too, that she sent him a key to a coffer, in which was locked up a great treasure. But we have not the key. But he never went back to his own country, and being heart-broken, and sick and weary of the world, and its pomps and vanities, he died here, after suffering much persecution likewise from the Puritans. For his peaceful religion was accepted nowhere."

"Of all legends—all foolish legends," quoth the Doctor wrathfully, with a face of a dark blood-red color, so much was his anger and contempt—"and of all absurd heroes of a legend, I never heard the like of this. Have you the key?"

"No; nor have I ever heard of it," answered the Schoolmaster.

"But you have some papers?"

"They existed once; perhaps are still recoverable, by search," said the schoolmaster. "My father knew of them."

"A foolish legend," reiterated the Doctor.

<It is strange how human folly strings itself on to human folly, as a story originally false and foolish grows older.>

He got up and walked about the room with hasty and irregular strides, and a prodigious swinging of his ragged dressing-gown, which swept away as many cobwebs, as it would take a week to reproduce. After a few turns, as if to change the subject, the Doctor asked the schoolmaster if he had any taste for pictures, and drew his attention to the portrait which has been already mentioned; the figure in antique, sordid garb, with a halter round its neck, and the expression in its face which the Doctor and the two children had interpreted so differently. Seymour, who probably knew nothing of pictures, looked at it at first merely from the gentle and cool complaisance of his character, but becoming absorbed in the contemplation, stood long without speaking, until the Doctor looking in his face, perceived that his eyes were streaming with tears.

"What are you crying about?" said he gruffly.

"I don't know," said the schoolmaster, quietly. "But there is something in this picture that affects me inexpressibly; so that, not being a man passionate by nature, I have hardly ever been so moved as now!"

"Very foolish," muttered the Doctor, resuming his strides about the room. "I am ashamed of a grown man that can cry at a picture, and can't tell the reason why."

After a few more turns, he resumed his easy chair, and his tumbler, and looking upward, beckoned to his pet spider, which came dangling downward—great parti-colored monster that it was—and swung about his master's head in hideous conference it seemed; a sight that so distressed the schoolmaster, or shocked his delicate taste, that he went out, and called the two children to take a walk with him, with the purpose of breathing air that was neither infected with spiders nor graves.

After his departure, Doctor Grimshawe seemed even more disturbed than during his presence; again he strode about the study; then sat down with his hands on his knees, looking straight into the fire, as if it imaged the seething element of his inner man, where burned hot projects, smoke, heat, blackness, ashes, a smouldering of old thoughts, a blazing up of new; casting in the gold of his mind, as Aaron did that of the Israelites, and waiting to see what sort of a thing would come out of the furnace. The children coming in from their play, he spoke harshly to them, and eyed little Ned with a sort of savageness, as if he meant to eat him up, or do some other dreadful deed; and when little Elsie came with her usual frankness to his knee, he repelled her in such a way that she shook her little head at him, saying, "Naughty Doctor Grim! What has come to you!" Through all that day, by some subtle means or other, the whole house knew that something was amiss, and nobody was comfortable in it. It was like a spell of weather; like the east-wind; like an epidemic in the air, that would not let anything be comfortable or contented, this pervading temper of the Doctor. Crusty Hannah knew it in the kitchen; even those who passed the house must have known it, some how or other, and have felt a chill, an irritation, an influence on the nerves as they passed. The spiders knew it, and acted as they were wont to do in stormy weather. The schoolmaster, when he returned from his walk, seemed likewise to know it, and made himself secure and secret, keeping in his own room, except, at dinner, when he ate his rice in silence, without looking towards the Doctor, and appeared before him no more till evening, when the grim Doctor summoned him into the study, after sending the two children to bed.

"Sir," began the Doctor. "You have spoken of some old documents in your possession, relating to the English descent of your ancestors. I have a curiosity to see those documents. Where are they?"

<Old descriptive letters, referring to localities as they then existed.>

"I have them about my person," said the schoolmaster; and he produced from his pocket a bundle of old yellow papers, done up in a parchment cover, tied with a piece of whipcord; and presented them to Doctor Grimshawe, who looked over them with interest. They seemed to consist of letters, genealogical lists, certified copies of entries in registers, things which must have been made out by somebody who knew more of business than this ethereal person in whose possession they now were. The Doctor looked at them with considerable attention, and at last did them hastily up in the bundle again, and returned them to their owner.

"Have you any idea what is now the condition of the family to whom these papers refer?" asked he.

"None whatever—none for almost a hundred years," said the schoolmaster. "About that time ago, I have heard a vague story that one of my ancestors went to the old country and

saw the place. But, you see, the change of name has effectively covered us from view; and I feel that our true name
is that which my ancestor assumed when he was driven forth
from the home of his fathers, and that I have nothing to do
with any other. I have no views on the estate; none whatever. I am not so foolish and dreamy."

"Very right," said the Doctor. "Nothing is more foolish
than to follow up such a pursuit as this; against all the
vested interests of two hundred years, which of themselves
also have built up an impenetrable strong objection against
you; they harden into stone, in England, these years, and
become indestructible, instead of melting away, as they do
in this happy country."

"It is not a matter of interest with me," replied the schoolmaster.

"Very right! very right," repeated the grim Doctor.

But something was evidently amiss with him, this evening.
It was impossible to feel easy and comfortable in contact
with him; if you looked in his face, there was the red, lurid
glare of his eyes, meeting you fiercely and craftily as ever;
sometimes he bit his lip; he frowned in an awful manner.
Once, he burst out into an awful fit of cursing, for no good
reason, or any reason whatever, that he explained, or that
anybody could tell. Again, for no more scrutable reason, he
uplifted his stalwart arm, and smote a heavy blow with his
fist on the oak table, making his tumbler and black bottle
leap up, and damaging, one would think, his own knuckles.
Then he rose up and resumed his strides about the room. He
paused before the portrait before mentioned; then resumed
his heavy, quick irregular tread; swearing under his breath;
and you could imagine from what you heard, that all his
thoughts and the movement of his mind was a blasphemy.
Then, again—but this was only once—he heaved a deep,
ponderous sigh, that seemed to come up in spite of him out
of his depths, an exhalation of deep suffering, as if some

convulsion had given it a passage to upper air, instead of its being hidden, as it generally was, by accumulated rubbish of later time heaped above it.

This latter sound appealed to something within the simple schoolmaster, who had sat witnessing the demeanor of the Doctor, like a being looking from another sphere into the troubles of the mortal one; a being incapable of passion observing the mute, hard struggle of one in its grasp.

"Friend," said he, at length, "thou hast something on thy mind."

"Ay," said the grim Doctor, coming to a stand before his chair. "You see that! Can you see as well what it is?"

"Some stir and writhe of something in the past that troubles you; as if you had kept a snake for many years in your bosom, and stupefied it with brandy, and now it awakes again and troubles you with bites and stings."

"What sort of a man do you think me?" asked the Doctor.

"I cannot tell," said the schoolmaster. "The sympathies of my nature are not those that should give me knowledge of such men."

"Am I, think you," continued the grim Doctor, "a man capable of great crime?"

"A great one, if any," said Seymour. "A great good likewise, it might be."

"What would I be likely to do," asked Doctor Grim, "supposing I had a darling purpose, to the accomplishment of which I had given my soul—yes, my soul—my hopes in life, my days and nights of thought, my years of time; dwelling upon it, pledging myself to it; until, at last, I had grown to love the hideous, to bed it, and not to regret my own degradation. I, a man of strongest will. What would I do, if this were to be resisted?"

"I do not conceive of the force of will, shaping out my ways," said the schoolmaster. "I walk gently along, and take the path that opens before me."

"Ha! ha! ha!" shouted the grim Doctor, with one of his portentous laughs. "So do we all, in spite of ourselves; and sometimes the path comes to a sudden ending," and he resumed his drinking.

The schoolmaster looked at him with wonder, and a kind of shuddering at something so unlike himself; but probably he very imperfectly estimated the forces that were at work within this strange being, and how dangerous it made him. He imputed it, in great part, to the brandy, which he had kept drinking in such inordinate quantities; whereas, it is probable that this had a soothing and emollient effect, as far as it went, on the Doctor's emotions; a sort of like to like that he instinctively felt to be a remedy. But, in truth, it was difficult to see those two human natures together, without feeling their incompatibility; without having a sense that one must be hostile to the other. The schoolmaster, through his finer instincts, doubtless had a sense of this, and sat gazing at the livid, wrathful figure of the Doctor, in a sort of trance and fascination; not able to stir; bewitched by the sight of the great spider and other surroundings, and this strange, uncouth fiend; who had always been abhorrent to him; not in the way of hatred; but something as far apart from himself as the range of human nature would permit him to be. It was all like a dream to him; he had a kind of curiosity in it, waited to see what would come of it, but felt it to be an unnatural state to him. And again the grim Doctor came and stood before him, prepared to make another of those strange utterances with which he had already so perplexed him.

That night—that midnight—it was rumored through the town, that one of the inhabitants going home, late, along the street that led by the grave yard, saw the grim Doctor standing by the open window of the study behind the elm-tree, chill as was the night, in his old dressing-gown, and flinging his arms abroad wildly into the night, and muttering like the growling of a tempest, with occasional vociferations that grew ever shrill with passion. The listener, though affrighted, could not resist an impulse to pause, and attempt overhearing something that might let him into the secret counsels of this strange, wild man, whom the town held in such awe and antipathy; to learn, perhaps, what was the great spider, and whether he was summoning the dead out of their graves. However, he could make nothing out of what he overheard, except it were fragmentary curses, of a dreadful character, which the Doctor brought up with might and main out of the depths of his soul, and flung them forth, burning hot, aimed at what, and why, and to what practical end, it was impossible to say, but as necessarily as a volcano, in a state of eruption, sends forth boiling lava, scorching and scintillating stones, and a sulphurous atmosphere, indicative of its inward state. It had a very frightful effect, it must be owned, this idea of a man cherishing emotions in his breast of so horrible a nature that he could neither tell them to any human being, nor keep them in their plenitude and intensity within the breast where they had their germ, and so was forced to fling them forth upon the night, to pollute and put fear into the atmosphere, so that people should breathe in somewhat of horror from an unknown source, and be affected with night-mares, and dreams in which they were startled at their own wickedness. Dreading lest some one of these ponderous anathemas should alight, reason or none, on his own head, the man crept away, and whispered the story to his cronies, from whom, it was communicated to the townspeople at large, and so became one of many stories circulating in reference to our grim hero, which, if not true to the facts, had undoubtedly a degree of appositeness to his character, of which they were the legitimate flowers and symbols. If the anathemas took no other effect, they seemed to have produced a very remarkable one on the unfortunate elm tree, through the naked branches of which the Doctor discharged this fiendish shot; for, the next spring, when April came on, no tender leaves budded forth, no life awakened there; and never again, on that old elm, richly as its roots were embedded among the dead of many years, was there rustling bough in the summer time or the elm's early golden boughs in September; and, after waiting till another spring to give it a fair chance of reviving, it was cut down and made into coffins, and burnt on the Sexton's hearth. The general opinion was, that the grim Doctor's awful profanity had blasted that tree, fostered, as it had been, on pious mould of Puritans. In Lancashire they tell of a similar anathema.

<(There should be symbols and tokens, pointing at the schoolmaster's disappearance, from the first opening of the scene)>

At the breakfast-table, the next morning, however, appeared Doctor Grimshawe, wearing very much the same aspect of an uncombed, unshorn, unbrushed odd sort of a Pagan as at other times, and making no difference in his breakfast, except that he poured a pretty large dose of brandy into his cup of tea; a thing, however, by no means unexampled or very unusual in his history. There were also the two children, fresher than the morning itself, rosy creatures, with newly scrubbed cheeks, creatures made over again for the new day, though the old one had left no dust upon them, laughing with one another, flinging their little jokes about the table—they had got up in remarkably good case, that morning—and expecting that the Doctor might, as was often his wont, set some ponderous old English joke a-trundling round among the breakfast cups; eating the corn-cakes, which crusty Hannah, with the aboriginal part of her, had a knack of making in a peculiar and exquisite fashion. But there was one empty chair at table; one cup, one little jug of milk, and another of pure water, with no guest to partake of them.

"Where is the schoolmaster?" said Ned, pausing as he was going to take his seat.

"Yes, Doctor Grim," said little Elsie.

"He has overslept himself for once," quoth Doctor Grim gruffly;—"a strange thing, too, for a man whose victuals and drink are so light as the schoolmaster's. The fiend take me, if I thought he had mortal mould enough in him ever to go to sleep at all; though he is but a kind of dream-stuff, in his widest awake state. Hannah, you bronze jade, call the schoolmaster to come to breakfast."

Hannah departed on her errand, and was heard knocking at the door of the schoolmaster's chamber, several times, till the Doctor shouted to her, wrathfully, to cease her clatter and open the door at once; which she appeared to do, and speedily came back.

"He no there, massa! Schoolmaster melted away."

"Vanished like a bubble!" quoth the Doctor.

"The great spider caught him like a fly," quoth crusty Hannah, chuckling with a sense of mischief that seemed very pleasant to her strange combination.

"He has taken a morning-walk," said little Ned. "Don't you think so, Doctor Grim?"

"Yes," said the grim Doctor. "Go on with your breakfast, little monkey; the walk may be a long one! Or he is so slight a weight, that the wind may blow him overboard."

A very long walk it proved; or it might be that some wind, whether evil or good, had blown him, as the Doctor suggested, into parts unknown; for, from that time forth, the Yankee schoolmaster returned no more. It was a singular disappearance. The bed did not appear to have been slept in; there was a bundle, in a clean handkerchief, containing two shirts, two pocket handkerchiefs, two pairs of cotton socks, a Testament, and that was all. Had he intended to go away, why did he not take this little luggage in his hand, being all he had, and of a kind not easily dispensed with? The

Doctor made small question about it, however; he had seemed surprised, at first, yet gave certainly no energetic token of it; and when Ned, who began to have notions of things, proposed to advertise him in the newspaper, or send the town crier round, the Doctor ridiculed the idea unmercifully.

"Lost, a thin Yankee schoolmaster," quoth he, uplifting his voice after the manner of the town crier; "supposed to have been blown out of Doctor Grim's window, or perhaps to have ridden off astride of a bumble-bee."

"It is not pretty to laugh in that way, Doctor Grim," said little Elsie, looking into his face, with a grave shake of her head.

"And why not, you saucy little witch?" said the Doctor.

"It is not the way to laugh, Doctor Grim!" persisted the child, but either could not or would not assign any reason for her disapprobation; although what she said appeared to produce a noticeable effect on Doctor Grimshawe, who relapsed into a rough, harsh manner, that seemed to satisfy Elsie better. Crusty Hanna, meanwhile, seemed to dance about the house with a certain singular alacrity, a wonderful friskiness, indeed, as if the diabolical result of the mixture in her nature was particularly pleased with something; so she went, with queer gesticulations, moppings, contortions, friskings, evidently in a very mirthful state; until, being asked by her master what was the matter, she replied—"Massa, me know what become of the schoolmaster. Great spider catch in his web, and eat him!"

Whether that were the mode of his disappearance, or some other, certainly the schoolmaster was gone; and the children were left in great bewilderment at the sudden vacancy in his place. They had not contracted a very yearning affection for him; and yet his impression had been individual and real, and they felt that something was gone out of their lives, now that he was no longer there. Something strange in their circumstances made itself felt by them; they were more sensible of the grim Doctor's uncouthness, his strange, reprehensible habits, his dark, mysterious life, in looking at them, these things, and the spiders, the grave-yard, their insulation from the world, through the crystal medium of this stranger's character, in remembering him in connection with these things; a certain seemly beauty in him showed strikingly the unfitness, the terrible and tarnished colour, the outrèness, of the rest of their lot. Little Elsie perhaps felt the loss of him more than her playmate, although both had been interested by him. But now things returned pretty much to their old fashion; although, as is inevitably the case, whenever persons or things have been taken suddenly or unaccountably out of our sphere, without telling us whither and why they have disappeared, the children could not, for a long while, bring themselves to feel that he had really gone. Perhaps in imitation of the custom in that old English house, of which the Doctor had told them, little Elsie insisted that his place should still be kept at the table; and so, whenever crusty Hannah neglected to do so, she herself would fetch a plate, and a little pitcher of water, and set it beside a vacant chair; and, sometimes, so like a shadow had he been, this pale, slender creature, it almost might have been thought that he was sitting with them. But Crusty Hanna shook her head, and grinned. "The spider know where he is. We never see him more!"

His abode in the house had been of only two or three weeks; and in the natural course of things, had he come and gone in an ordinary way, his recollection would have grown dim and faded out in two or three weeks more; but the speculations, the expectations, the watchings for his reappearance, served to cut and grave the recollection of him into the children's hearts, so that it remained a life-long thing with them—a sense that he was something that had been lost out of their life too soon, and that was bound, sooner or later, to reappear, and finish what business he had with them. Sometimes they prattled around the Doctor's chair about him; and they could perceive, sometimes, that he appeared to be listening, and would chime in with some remark; but he never expressed either wonder or regret; only telling Ned, once, that he had no reason to be sorry for his disappearance.

"Why, Doctor Grim?" asked the boy.

The Doctor mused, and smoked his pipe, as if he himself were thinking why, and at last he answered, "He was a dangerous fellow, my old boy."

"Why?" said Ned again.

"He would have taken the beef out of you," said the Doctor.

I know not how long it was before any other visitor (except such as brought their shattered constitutions there, in hopes that the Doctor could make the worn out machinery as good as new) came to the lonely little household on the corner of the grave-yard. The intercourse between themselves and the rest of the town remained as scanty as ever. Still the grim, shaggy Doctor was seen, setting doggedly forth in all seasons and all weathers, at a certain hour of the day, with the two children, going for long walks on the sea shore, or into the country, miles away, and coming back, hours afterwards, with plants and herbs, that had perhaps virtue in them, or flowers that had certainly beauty; even, in their season, the fragrant magnolias that grow only in spots, the seeds having been apparently dropt by some happy accident, leaving a trail of fragrance after them where those proper to the climate were distributed. Shells, there were, also, in the baskets that they carried, minerals, rare things, that a magic touch seemed to have created out of the rude and common things that others find in a homely and ordinary region. The boy was growing taller, and had got out of the merely infantile age; agile, he

was, bright, but still with a remarkable thoughtfulness, or
gravity, or I know not what to call it; but it was a shadow, no
doubt, falling upon him from something sombre in his way
of life, which the impressibility of his age and nature so far
acknowledged as to be a little pale, and grave, without positive unhappiness; and when a playful moment came, as they
often did to these two healthy children, it seemed all a mistake that you had ever thought either of them too grave for
their age. But little Elsie was still the merriest. They were
still children, although they quarrelled seldomer than of
yore, and kissed seldom, and had ceased altogether to complain of one another to the Doctor; perhaps the time, when
Nature saw these bickerings to be necessary to the growth
of some of their faculties was nearly gone. When they did
have a quarrel, the boy stood upon his dignity, and visited
Elsie with a whole day, sometimes, of silent and stately displeasure, which she was accustomed to bear sometimes with
an assumption of cold indifference, sometimes with liveliness,
mirth in double quantity, laughter almost as good as riot;
little arts which showed themselves in her, as naturally as
the gift of tears and smiles. In fact, having no advantage of
female intercourse, she could not well have learnt them,
unless from crusty Hannah, who was such an anomaly of a
creature, with all her mixtures of race, that she struck you as
having lost all sex as one result of it. Yet this little girl was
truly feminine, and had all the manners, and praiseworthy
or criticizeable tenets, proper to women at her early age.

She had made respectable advancement in study; that is,
she had taught herself to write, with even greater mechanical
facility than Ned; and other knowledge had fallen upon her,
as it were, by a reflected light from him, or, to use another
simile, had been spattered upon her, by the full stream which
the Doctor poured into the vessel of the boy's intellect; so
that she had even some knowledge of the rudiments of Latin,

and geometry, and algebra; inaccurate enough, but yet with such a briskness, that she was sometimes able to assist Ned in studies in which he was far more deeply grounded than herself. All this, however, was more by sympathy than by any natural taste for such things; being kindly, and sympathetic, and impressible, she took the color of what was nearest to her, and especially when it came from a beloved object, so that it was difficult to discover that it was not really one of her native tastes. The only thing, perhaps, altogether suited to her idiosyncrasy (because it was truly feminine, calculated for dainty fingers, and a nice little subtlety) was that kind of embroidery, twisting, needle work, on textile fabric, which, as we have before said, she learnt from crusty Hannah, and which was emblematic, perhaps, of that creature's strange mixture of races. Elsie seemed not only to have caught this art, in its original spirit, but to have improved upon it, creating strange, fanciful, and graceful devices, which grew beneath her finger as naturally as the variegated hues grow in a flower, as it opens; so that the homeliest material assumed a grace and strangeness as she wove it, whether it were grass, twigs, shells, or what not. Never was anything seen, that so combined a wild barbarian freedom with cultivated grace; and the grim Doctor himself, little open to the impressions of the beautiful, used to hold some of her productions in his hand, gazing at them with deep intentness, and at last, perhaps, breaking out into one of his deep roars of laughter; for it seemed to suggest thoughts to him that the children could not penetrate. This one feature of strangeness and wild faculty in the otherwise sweet and natural and homely character of Elsie had a singular effect; it was like a wreath of wild flowers in her hair, like something that set her a little way apart from the rest of the world, and had an even more striking effect than if she were altogether strange.

<(The stranger may be the future Master of the Hospital)>

Thus were the little family going on; the Doctor, I regret to say, growing more morose, self-involved, and unattainable since the disappearance of the schoolmaster than before; more given up to his one plaything, the great spider; less frequently even, than before, coming out of the grim seclusion of his moodiness to play with the children, though they would often be sensible of his fierce eyes fixed upon them, and start, and feel incommoded, by the intensity of his regard;—thus things were going on, when one day there was really again a visitor, and not a dilapidated patient, to the grim Doctor's study. Crusty Hannah brought up his name as Mr Mountford, and the Doctor—filling his everlasting pipe, meanwhile, and ordering Hannah to give him a coal (perhap this was the circumstance that made people say he had imps to bring him coals from Tophet,) ordered him to be shown up.

<Describe the winter-day—>

A fresh-colored rather young man entered the study, a person of rather cold and ungraceful manners, yet <(describe him as clerical)> genial-looking enough; at least, not repulsive. He was dressed in rather a rough, serviceable travelling-dress, and except for a nicely brushed hat, and unmistakeably white linen, was rather careless in attire. You would have thought twice, perhaps, before deciding him to be a gentleman, but finally would have decided that he was; one great token being, that the singular aspect of the room into which he was ushered, the spider festoonery and other strange accompaniments, the grim aspect of the Doctor himself, and the beauty and intelligence of his two companions, and even that horrific weaver, the great dangling spider,—neither one or all of these called any expression of surprise to the stranger's face.

"Your name is Mountford?" began the grim Doctor, with his usual sparseness of ornamental courtesy.

<—Represent him as refined, agreeable, genial young man, of frank, kindly, gentlemanly manners—>

The stranger bowed.

"An Englishman, I see," continued the Doctor; but nowise intimating that the fact of being a countryman was any recommendation in his eyes.

"Yes, an Englishman," replied Mountford; "a briefless barrister, in fact, of Lincoln's Inn, who having little or nothing to detain him at home, has come to spend a few idle months in seeing the new Republic which has been made out of English substance."

"And what," continued Doctor Grim, not a whit relaxing the repulsiveness of his manner, and scowling askance at the stranger, "what may have drawn on me the good fortune of being compelled to make my time idle, because yours is so?"

The stranger's cheek flushed a little; but he smiled to himself, as if saying that here was a grim, rude kind of humourist, who had lost the sense of his own peculiarity, and had no idea that he was rude at all.

"I came to America, as I told you," said he, "chiefly because I was idle, and wished to turn my enforced idleness to what profit I could, in the way of seeing men, manners, governments, and problems which I hope to have time to study, by and by. But I also had an errand, entrusted to me, and of a singular nature; and making inquiry in this little town (where my mission must be performed, if at all) I have been directed to you by your townspeople as to the person not unlikely to be able to assist me in it."

"My townspeople, since you choose to call them so," answered the grim Doctor, "ought to know, by this time, that I am not the sort of man likely to assist any person, or in any way."

"Yet this is so singular an affair," said the stranger, still with mild courtesy, "that at least it may excite your curiosity. I have come here in search of a grave."

"To find a grave!" said Doctor Grim, giving way to a grim sense of humor, and relaxing just enough to let out a joke, the tameness of which was a little redeemed, to his taste, by its grimness. "I might help you there to be sure, since it is all in the way of business. Like others of my profession, I have helped many people to find their graves, no doubt, and shall be happy to do the same for you. You have hit upon the one thing, in which my services are ready."

"I thank you, my dear Sir," said the young stranger, having tact enough to laugh at Doctor Grim's joke, and thereby mollifying him a little; "but, as far as I am personally concerned, I prefer to wait a little before making the discovery of that little spot in Mother Earth which I am destined to occupy. It is a grave which has been occupied as such for at least a century and a half, which I am in quest of; and it is as antiquarian, a genealogist, a person who has had dealings with the dead of long ago, not as a professional man, engaged in adding to their number, that I ask your aid."

"Ah, ahah!" said the Doctor, laying down his pipe, and looking earnestly at the stranger; not kindly nor genially, but rather with a lurid glance of suspicion out of those red eyes of his, but no longer with a desire to escape an intruder; rather, as one who meant to clutch him. "Explain your meaning, Sir, at once."

"Then here it is," said Mr. Mountford. "There is an old English family, one of the members of which, very long ago, emigrated to this part of America, then, a wilderness, and long afterwards, a British colony. <He was on ill-terms with his family.> There is reason to believe that documents, deeds, titular proofs, or some other thing valuable to the family, was buried in the grave of this emigrant; and there have been various attempts, within a century, to find this grave, and, if possible, some living descendant of the man, or both; under the idea that either of these cases might influence the disputed descent of the property, and enable the family to prove its claims to an ancient title. Now, rather as a matter of curiosity, than with any real hope of success— and being slightly connected with the family—I have taken what seems to myself a wild-goose chase—making it merely incidental, you will understand, not by any means the main purpose of my voyage to America."

"What is the name of this family?" asked the Doctor abruptly.

"The man whose grave I seek," said the stranger, "lived and died, in this country, under the assumed name of Colcord."

"How do you expect to succeed in this ridiculous quest," asked the Doctor; "and what marks, signs, directions have you to guide your search? And, moreover, how have you come to any knowledge whatever about the matter, even that the emigrant ever assumed this name of Colcord, and that he was buried anywhere, and that his place of burial, after more than a century, is of the slightest importance?"

"All this was ascertained by a messenger on a similar errand with my own, only undertaken nearly a century ago, and more in earnest than I can pretend to be," replied the Englishman. "At that period, however, there was probably a desire to find nothing that might take the hereditary possessions of the family out of the branch which still held them; and there is strong reason to suspect that the information acquired was purposely kept secret by the person in England into whose hands it came. The thing is differently situated now; the possessor of the estate is recently dead; and the discovery of an American heir would not be unacceptable to many. At all events, any knowledge gained here would throw light on a somewhat doubtful matter."

"Where, as nearly as you can judge," said the Doctor, after a turn or two through the study, "was this man buried?"

"He spent the last years of his life, certainly, in this town," said Mountford, "and very probably may be found, if at all, among the dead of that period."

"And they—their miserable dust, at least, which is all that still exists of them—were buried in the grave yard under these windows," said the Doctor. "What marks, I say,—for you might as well seek a vanished wave of the sea, as a grave that surged upward so long ago."

"On the grave-stone," said Mountford—"a slate one, there was rudely sculptured, traced out, the impress of a foot. What it signifies, I cannot conjecture, except it had some reference to a certain legend of a bloody footstep, which is currently told, and some token of which yet remains, on one of the thresholds of the ancient mansion-house."

Ned and Elsie had withdrawn from the immediate vicinity of the fireside, and were playing at fox and geese in a corner near the window. But little Elsie, having very quick ears, and a faculty of attending to more affairs than one, now called out:—

"Doctor Grim, Ned and I know where that grave stone is!"

"Hush, Elsie," whispered Ned, earnestly.

"Come forward here, both of you," cried Doctor Grimshawe.

The two children approached, and stood before the Doctor and his guest, the latter of whom had not hitherto taken particular notice of them. He now looked from one to the other, with the pleasant, genial expression of a person gifted with a natural liking for children, and the free-masonry requisite to bring him acquainted with them; and it lighted up his face with a pleasant surprise to see two such beautiful specimens of boyhood and girlhood, in this dismal, spider haunted house, and under the guardianship of such a savage lout as the grim Doctor. He seemed particularly struck by the intelligence and sensibility of Ned's face, and met his eyes with a glance that Ned long afterwards remembered; but yet he seemed quite as much interested by Elsie, and gazed at her face with a perplexed, inquiring glance.

"These are fine children," said he. "May I ask if they are your own—pardon me if I ask amiss," added he, seeing a frown on the Doctor's brow.

"Ask nothing about the brats," replied he grimly. "Thank Heaven, they are not my children; so your question is answered."

"I again ask pardon," said Mr. Mountford. "I am fond of children; and the boy has a singularly fine countenance; not in the least English. The true American face, no doubt. As to this sweet little girl, she impresses me with a vague resemblance to some person I have seen. Hers I should deem an English face."

"These children are not our topic," said the grim Doctor with gruff impatience. "If they are to be so, our conversation is ended. Ned, what do you know of this grave-stone with the bloody foot on it?"

"It is not a bloody foot, Doctor Grim," said Ned; "and I am not sure that it is a foot at all; only Elsie and I chose to fancy so, because of a story that we used to play at. But, we were children then. The grave-stone lies on the ground, within a little bit of a walk of our door; but this snow has covered it all over; else we might go out and see it."

"We will go out at any rate," said the Doctor, "and if the Englishman chooses to come to America, he must take our snows as he finds them. Take your shovel, Ned; and, if necessary, we will uncover the grave-stone."

They accordingly muffled themselves in their warmest, and plunged forth through a back door into Ned and Elsie's playground, as the grim Doctor was wont to call it. The snow, except in one spot, close at hand, lay deep, like cold oblivion, over the surging graves, and piled itself in drifted heaps against every stone that raised itself above the level; it filled curiously the letters of the inscriptions, enveloping all the dead in one great winding-sheet, whiter and colder than those which they had individually worn. The dreary space was pathless; not a footstep had tracked through the heavy snow; for it must be warm affection, indeed, that could so melt this wintry impression as to penetrate through the snow and frozen earth, and establish any warm thrills with the dead beneath; daisies, grass, genial earth, these allow of the magnetism of such sentiments; but winter sends them shivering back to the baffled heart.

"Well, Ned!" said the Doctor impatiently.

Ned looked about him, somewhat bewildered, and then pointed to a spot, within not more than ten paces of the threshold which they had just crossed; and there appeared, not a grave-stone, but a new grave (if any grave could be called new, in that often dug soil, made up of old mortality) an open hole, with the freshly dug earth piled up beside it. A little snow (for there had been a gust or two, since morning) appeared, as they peeped over the edge, to have fallen into it; but not enough to prevent a coffin from finding fit room and accommodation in it. But it was evident, that the grave had been dug that very day.

"The head-stone, with the foot on it, was just here," said Ned, in much perplexity, "and as far as I can judge, the old sunken grave exactly marked out the space of this new one."

<Make the old grave digger a laudator temporis acti— especially as to burial customs.>

"It is a shame," said Elsie, much shocked at the indecorum, "that the new person should be thrust here; for the old one was a friend of ours."

"But what has become of the headstone!" exclaimed the young English stranger.

During their perplexity, a person had approached the group, wading through the snow from the gate-way giving entrance from the street; a gaunt figure, with stooping shoulders, over one of which was a spade and some other tool fit for delving in the earth; and in his face there was the sort of keen, humorous twinkle that grave-diggers somehow seem to get, as if the dolorous character of their business necessitated something unlike itself by an inevitable reaction.

"Well, Doctor," cried he, with a shrewd wink in his face, "are you looking for one of your patients? The man, who is to be put to bed here, was never caught in your spider's web."

"No;" said Doctor Grimshawe, "when my patients have done with me, I leave them to you and the old Nick, and never trouble myself about them more. What I want to know is, why you have taken upon you to steal a man's grave, after he has had immemorial passage of it? By what right have you dug up this bed, undoing the work of a predecessor of yours, who has long since slept in one of his own furrows?"

"Why, Doctor," said the grave-digger, looking quietly into the ominous pit which he had hollowed, "it is against common sense that a dead man should think to keep a grave to himself, longer than till you can take up his substance in a shovel. It would be a strange thing enough, if, when living families are turned out of their homes twice or thrice in a generation (as they are likely to be in our new government) a dead man should think he must sleep in one spot till the day of judgement. No; turn about, I say to these old fellows. As long as they can decently be called dead men, I let them lie; when they are nothing but dust, I just take leave to stir them on occasion. This is the way we do things under the Republic, whatever your customs be in the old country."

"Matters are very much the same in any old English churchyard," said the English stranger. "But, my good friend, I have come three thousand miles, partly to find this grave, and am a little disappointed to find my labor lost."

"Ah; and you are the man my father was looking for," said the grave digger, nodding his head at Mr. Mountford. "My father who was a grave digger afore me died four and thirty years ago, when we were under the King; and says he, 'Ebenezer, do not you turn up a sod in this spot, till you have turned up every other in the ground.' And I have always obeyed him."

"And what was the reason of such a singular prohibition?" asked Mountford.

"My father knew," said the grave-digger; "and he told me the reason too; but since we are under the republic, we have given up remembering these old-world legends, as we used to. The newspapers keep us from talking in the chimney-corner; and so things go out of our minds. An old man, with his stories of what he has seen, and what his great grandfather saw before him, is of little account since newspapers came up. Stop—I remember—no, I forget—it was something about the grave holding a witness, who had been sought before, and might be again."

"And that is all you know about it?" said Mountford.

"All—every mite," said the old grave digger. "But my father knew, and would have been glad to tell you the whole story. There was a great deal of wisdom and knowledge, about graves especially, buried out yonder, where my old father was put away, before the Stamp Act was thought of. But it is no great matter, I suppose. People don't care about old graves in these times. They just live, & put the dead out of sight and out of mind."

"Well; but what have you done with the headstone?" said the Doctor. "You can't have eaten it up?"

"No, no, Doctor," said the grave digger, laughing, "it would crack better teeth than mine, old and crumbly as it is. And yet I meant to do something with it that is akin to eating; for my oven needs a new floor, and I thought to take this stone, which would stand the fire well. But here," continued he, scaping away the snow with his shovel, a task in which little Ned gave his assistance, "here is the head-stone, just as I have always seen it; and as my father saw it before me."

The ancient memorial being cleared of snow, proved to be a slab of freestone, with some rude traces of carving in bas-relief around the border, now much effaced, and an impression which seemed to be as much like a human foot as anything else, sunk into the slab; but this device was wrought in a much more clumsy way than the ornamented border and evidently by an unskilful hand. Beneath was an inscription, over which the hard, flat lichens had grown, and done their best to obliterate it, although the following words might be written or guessed.

"Here lyeth the Mortal Part of Thomas Colcord, an upright man, of tender and devout soul, who departed this troublous life September ye Nineteenth, 1687, aged 57 years and nine months. Happier in his death than in his lifetime. Let his bones be."

The name, Colcord, was somewhat defaced; it was impossible, in the general disintegration of the stone, to tell whether wantonly, or with a purpose of altering and correcting some error in the spelling, or, as occurred to Mountford, to change the name entirely.

"This is very unsatisfactory," said Mountford; "but very curious, too. But this is certainly the impress of what was meant for a human foot, and coincides strongly with the legend of the Bloody Footstep—the mark of the foot that trode in the blessed King Charles's blood."

"For that matter," said the grave-digger, "it comes into my mind, that my father used to call it the stamp of Satan's foot, because he claimed the dead man for his own. It is plain to see that there was a deep cleft between two of the toes."

"There are two ways of telling that legend," remarked the Doctor. "But did you find nothing in the grave, Hewen?"

"Oh, yes,—a bone or two; as much as could be expected after above a hundred years," said the grave-digger. "I tossed them aside; and if you are curious about them, you will find them when the snow melts. That was all; and it would have been unreasonable in old Colcord—especially in these republican times—to have wanted to keep his grave any longer, when there was so little of him left."

"I must drop the matter here, then," said Mountford, with a sigh. "Here, my friend, is a trifle for your trouble."

"No trouble," said the grave-digger; "and, in these republican times, we can't take anything for nothing, because it won't do for a poor man to take off his hat and say thank you." Nevertheless, he did take the silver, and winked a sort of acknowledgment.

The Doctor, with unwonted hospitality, invited the English stranger to dine in his house; and though there was no pretense of cordiality in the invitation, Mr. Mountford accepted it, being probably influenced by curiosity to make out some definite idea of the strange household in which he found himself. Doctor Grimshawe having taken it upon him to be host—for, up to this time, the stranger stood upon his responsibility, and having voluntarily presented himself to the Doctor, had only himself to thank for any scant courtesy he might meet—but now the grim Doctor became genial after his own fashion. At dinner, he produced a bottle of port which made the young Englishman almost fancy himself on the other side of the water; and he entered into a conversation, which I fancy was the chief object which the grim Doctor had in view in showing himself in so amiable delight; for, in the course of it, the stranger was insensibly led to disclose many things, as it were of his own accord, relating to the part of England whence he came, and especially to the estate and family which have been before mentioned; the present state of that family, together with other things that he seemed to himself to pour out naturally; for, at last, he drew himself up, and attempted an excuse.

"Your good wine," said he, "or the unexpected accident of meeting a countryman, has made me unusually talkative, and on subjects, I fear, which have not a particular interest for you."

"I have not quite succeeded in shaking off my country, as you see," said Doctor Grimshawe, "though I neither expect nor wish ever to see it again."

There was something rather ungracious in the grim Doctor's response; and, as they now adjourned to his study, and the Doctor betook himself to his pipe and tumbler, the young Englishman sought to increase his acquaintance with the two children, both of whom showed themselves graciously inclined towards him; more warmly so than they had been to the schoolmaster, who was the only other guest whom they had ever met.

"Would you like to see England, my little fellow?" he inquired of Ned.

"Oh, very much! more than anything else in the world," replied the boy; his eyes gleaming and his cheeks flushing with the earnestness of his response; for, indeed, the question stirred up all the dreams and reveries which the child had cherished, far back into the dim regions of his memory. After what the Doctor had told him of his origin, he had never felt any home-feeling here; it seemed to him that he was wandering web, which the wind had blown from afar; somehow, or other, from many circumstances which he put together and seethed in his childish imagination, it seemed to him that he was to go back to that far, old country, and there wander among the green, ivy-grown, venerable scenes; the older he grew, the more his mind took depth, the stronger was this fancy in him; though even to Elsie he had scarcely breathed it.

"So strong a desire," said the stranger, smiling at his earnestness, "will be sure to work out its own accomplishment. I shall meet you in England, my young friend, one day or another. And you, my little girl, are you as anxious to see England as your brother?"

"Ned is not my brother," said little Elsie.

The Doctor here interposed some remark on a different subject; for it was observable that he never liked to have the conversation turn on these children, their parentage, or relations to each other or himself. The children were sent to bed; and the young Englishman, finding the conversation lag, and his host becoming gruffer and less communicative than he thought quite courteous, retired. Just before he went, however, he could not refrain from making a remark on the gigantic spider, which was swinging like a pendulum above the Doctor's head.

"What a singular pet!" said he; for indeed, the nervous part of him had latterly been getting uppermost, so that it disturbed him—in fact, the spider above and the grim man below equally disturbed him. "Are you a naturalist? Have you noted his habits?"

"Yes," said the Doctor, "I have learned from his web how to weave a plot, and how to catch my victim and devour him!"

"Thank God," said the Englishman, as he issued forth into the cold grey night, "I have escaped the grim fellow's web, at all events. How strange a group—those two sweet children, that grim old man!"

As regards this matter of the ancient grave, it remains to be recorded, that, when the snow melted, little Ned and Elsie went to look at the spot, where, by this time, there was a little hillock, with the brown sods laid duly upon it, which the coming spring would make green. By the side of it, they saw, with more curiosity than repugnance, a few fragments of old, crumbly bones, which they plausibly conjectured to be appertaining to some part of the framework of the ancient Colcord, wherewith he had walked through the troublous life of which his grave-stone spoke. And little Elsie, whose eyes were very sharp, and her observant qualities of the quickest, found something which Ned at first pronounced to be only a bit of old iron, incrusted with earth; but Elsie persisted to knock off some of the earth that seemed to have incrusted it, and discovered a key. The children ran with their prize to the grim Doctor, who took it between his thumb and finger, turned it over and over, and then proceeded to rub it with a chemical substance, which soon made it bright. It proved to be a silver key, of antique and curious workmanship.

"Perhaps this is what Mr. Mountford was in search of," said Ned. "What a pity he is gone. Perhaps we can send it after him."

"Nonsense," said the gruff Doctor.

And attaching the key to a chain, which he took from a drawer, and which seemed to be gold, he hung it round Ned's neck.

"When you find a lock for this key," said he, "open it, and consider yourself heir of whatever treasure is revealed there!"

Little Ned continued that sad, fatal habit of growing out of childhood, as boys will, until he was now about ten years old, and little Elsie as much as six or seven. He looked healthy, but pale; something there was, in the character and influences of his life, that made him look as if he was growing up in a shadow, with less sunshine than he needed for a robust and exuberant development, though enough to make his intellectual growth tend towards a subtle luxuriance in some directions. He was likely to turn out a fanciful, perhaps a poetic youth; young as he was, there had been already discoveries, on the grim doctor's part, of certain blotted and clumsily scrawled scraps of paper, the chirography on which was arrayed in marshalled lines, of unequal length, and each commanded by a capital letter, and marching onward on from six to ten lame feet. Doctor Grim inspected these things curiously, and, to say the truth, most scornfully, before he took them to light his pipe withal; but they told him little as regarded this boy's internal state, being mere echoes, and very lugubrious ones, of poetic strains that were floating about in the atmosphere of that day, long before any now remembered bard had begun to sing. But, there were the rudiments of a poetic and singular mind within the boy, if its subsequent culture should be such as the growth of that delicate flower requires; a brooding habit taking outward things into itself, and imbuing them with its own essence, until, after they had lain there awhile, they assumed a relation both to truth and to himself, and became mediums to affect other minds with the magnetism of his own. He lived far too much an inward life for healthfulness, at his age; the peculiarity of his situation, a child of mystery, with certain reaches and vistas that seemed to promise a bright solution of his mystery, keeping his imagination always awake and strong. That castle in the air—so much more vivid than other castles, because it had perhaps a real substance of ancient, ivy grown, hewn stone somewhere—that visionary hall, in England, with its surrounding woods and fine lawns, and the beckoning shadows at the ancient windows, and that fearful threshold, with the blood still glistening on it—he dwelt and wandered so much here, that he had no real life in the sombre house on the corner of the grave-yard; except that the loneliness of the latter, and the grim Doctor, with his grotesque surroundings, and even the great ugly spider, and that odd, inhuman mixture of Crusty Hannah, all served to remove him out of the influences of common life. Little Elsie was all that he had to keep life real, and substantial; and she, a child so much younger than he, was influenced by the same circumstances, and still more by himself, so that, as far as he could impart himself to her, he led her hand in hand through the same dream-scenery amid which he strayed himself. They knew not another child in town; the grim Doctor was their only friend. As for Ned, this seclusion had its customary and normal effect upon him; it had made him think ridiculously high of his own gifts, powers, attainments, and at the same time doubt whether they could pass with those of others; it made him despise all flesh, as if he were of a superior race, and yet have an idle and weak fear of coming in contract with them, from a dread of his incompetency to cope with them; so he at once depreciated and exalted, to an absurd degree, both himself and others.

"Ned," said the Doctor to him one day, in his gruffest tone, "you are not turning out to be the boy I looked for, and want to make you. I have given you sturdy English instruction, and solidly grounded you in matters that the poor superficial people and time merely skim over; I looked to see the rudiments of a man in you, by this time; and you begin to mope, and pule, as if your babyhood were coming back on you. You seem to think more than a boy of your years should; and yet it is not manly thought, nor ever will be so. What do you mean, boy, by making all my care of you come to nothing, in this way?"

"I do my best, Doctor Grim," said Ned, with sullen dignity. "What you teach me, I learn. What more can I do?"

"I'll tell you what, my fine fellow," quoth Doctor Grim, getting rude, as was his habit. "You disappoint me, and I'll not bear it. I want you to be a man; and I'll have you a man or nothing. If I had foreboded such a fellow as you turn out to be, I never would have taken you from the place where, as I once told you, I found you—the alms-house!"

"Oh, Doctor Grim, Doctor Grim," cried little Elsie, in a tone of grief and bitter reproach.

Ned had risen slowly, as the Doctor uttered those last words, turning as white as a sheet, and stood gazing at him, with large eyes, in which there was a calm upbraiding; a strange dignity was in his childish aspect, which was no longer childish, but seemed to have grown older, all in a moment.

"There is nonsense that ought to be whipt out of you, Sir," added the Doctor, incensed at the boy's aspect.

"You have said enough, Sir," said the boy. "Would to God you had left me where you found me! <He aims a blow, perhaps with his pipe, at the boy, which Ned wards off> It was not my fault that you took me from the alms house. But it will be my fault if I ever eat another bit of your bread, or stay under your roof an hour longer."

He was moving towards the door, but little Elsie sprang upon him and caught him round the neck, although he repelled her with Roman dignity; and Doctor Grimshawe, after looking at the group in which a bitter sort of mirth and mischief struggled with a better and kindlier sentiment, at last flung his pipe into the chimney, hastily quaffed the remnant of a tumbler, and shuffled after Ned, kicking off his old slippers in his hurry. He caught the boy just by the door.

"Ned, Ned, my boy, I'm sorry for what I said," cried he. "I am a guzzling old blockhead, and don't know how to treat a gentleman when he honors me with his company. It is not in my blood nor breeding to have such knowledge. Ned, you will make a man, and I lied if I said otherwise. Come, I'm sorry, I'm sorry."

The boy was easily touched, at those years, as a boy ought to be; and though he had not yet forgiven the grim Doctor, the tears, to his especial shame, gushed out of his eyes in a torrent, and his whole frame shook with sobs. The Doctor caught him in his arms, and hugged him to his old tobacco-fragrant dressing-gown, hugged him like a bear, as he was; so that poor Ned hardly knew whether he were embracing him with his love, or squeezing him to death in his wrath.

"Ned," said he, "I'm not going to live a great while longer. I seem an eternal nuisance to you, I know; but it's not so. I'm mortal, and I feel myself breaking up. Let us be friends while I live; for believe me, Ned, I've done as well by you as I knew, and care for nothing, love nothing, so much as you. Little Elsie here, yes. I love her too. But that's different. You are a boy, and will be a man; and a man whom I destine to do for me what it has been the object of my life to achieve. Let us be friends. We will—we must be friends; and when old Doctor Grim, worthless wretch that he is, sleeps in his grave, you shall not have the pang of having parted from him in unkindness. Forgive me, Ned; and not only that, but love me better than ever; for though I am a nasty old wretch, I am not altogether evil as regards you!"

I know not whether the Doctor would have said all this, if the day had not been pretty well advanced, and if his potations had not been many; but, at any rate, he spoke no more than he felt, and his emotions thrilled through the sensitive system of the boy, and quite melted him down. He forgave Doctor Grim, and, as he asked, loved him better than ever, and so did Elsie. Then it was so sweet, so good, to have had this one outgush of affection; he, poor child, who had no memory of mother's kisses, or of being cared for out of tenderness, and whose heart had been hungry, all his life, for some such thing; and probably Doctor Grim, in his way, had the same kind of enjoyment of this passionate crisis; so that though, the next day, they all three looked at one another a little ashamed, yet it had some remote analogy to that delicious embarrassment of two lovers, at their first meeting after they know all.

It is very remarkable that Ned had so much good in him as we find there; in the first place, born as he seemed to be of a wild vagrant stock, a seedling sown by the breezes, and falling among the rocks or sands; then growing up without a mother, to cultivate his tenderness with kisses and the inestimable, inevitable love of love breaking out on all little occasions, without reference to merit or demerit, unfailing whether or no, mother's faith in excellences, the buds which were yet invisible to all other eyes, but to which her warm faith was the genial sunshine necessary to their growth; mother's generous interpretation of all that was doubtful in him, and which might turn out good or bad, according as should be believed of it; mother's pride in whatever the boy accomplished, and unfailing excuses, explanations, apologies, so satisfactory, for all his failures; mother's deep, intuitive insight, which should see the permanent good beneath all the appearance of temporary evil, being wiser through her love than the wisest sage could be—the dullest, homeliest mother than the wisest sage; the Creator, apparently, had set a little of his own infinite wisdom and love (which are one) in a mother's heart; so that no child, in the common course of things, should grow up without some heavenly instruction; instead of all this, and the vast deal more that mothers do for children, there had been only the gruff, passionate Doctor, without sense of religion, with only a fitful tenderness, with years' length between the fits, so fiercely critical, so wholly unradiant of hope, misanthropic, savagely morbid. Yes; there was little Elsie too; it must have been that she was the boy's preserver, being childhood, sisterhood, womanhood; all that there had been for him of human life, and enough—he being internally of such good stuff— to keep him good. He had lost much, but not all; he was not nearly what he might have been, under better auspices—

flaws and imperfections there were, in abundance, great, uncultivated wastes and wildernesses in his moral nature, tangled wilds where there might have been stately venerable religious groves; but there was no rank growth of evil. That unknown mother, that had no opportunity to nurse her boy, must have had gentle and noblest qualities to endow him with; a noble father, too, a long, unstained descent, one would have thought. Was this an alm's house child?

Doctor Grim knew, very probably, that there was all this on the womanly side that was wanting to Ned's occasion; and very probably, too, being a man not without insight, he was aware that tender treatment, as a mother bestows it, tends likewise to foster strength and manliness of character, as well as softer developments; but all this he could not have supplied, and now as little as ever. But there was something else which Ned ought to have, and might have; and this was, intercourse with his kind, free circulation, free air, instead of the stived up house, with the breeze from the grave-yard blowing over it; to be drawn out of himself, and made to share the life of many; to be introduced, at one remove, to the world with which he was to contend. To this end, shortly after the scene of passion and reconciliation above described, the Doctor took the resolution of sending Ned to an Academy, famous in that day, and still extant. Accordingly, they all three—the grim Doctor, Ned, and Elsie—set forth, one day of spring, leaving the house to Crusty Hannah and the great spider, in a carryall, being the only excursion, involving a night's absence, that either of the two children remembered from the house by the grave-yard; as at night-fall, they saw the modest pine-built edifice, with its cupola and bell, where Ned was to be initiated into the school-boy. The Doctor, remembering perhaps days spent in some gray, stately, legendary great school of England, instinct with the boyhood of men afterwards great, puffed forth a deprecatory curse upon it; but nevertheless made all arrangements for Ned's behoof, and, next morning, prepared to leave him there.

"Ned, my son, goodbye," cried he, shaking the little fellow's hand as he stood tearful and wistful beside the chaise, shivering at the loneliness which he felt settling around him—a new loneliness to him—the loneliness of a crowd.—"Do not be cast down, my boy. Face the world; grasp the thistle strongly, and it will sting you the less. Have faith in your own fist! Fear no man! Have no secret plot! Never do what you think wrong! If, hereafter, you come to know that Doctor Grim was a bad man, forgive him, and be a better one yourself. Good bye; and if my blessing be good for anything—in God's name, I invoke it upon you heartily."

Little Elsie was sobbing, and flung her arms about Ned's neck, and he about hers; so that they parted without a word. As they drove away, a singular sort of presentiment came over the boy, as he stood looking after them.

"It is all over—all over," said he to himself. "Doctor Grim and little Elsie are gone out of my life. They leave me, and will never come back—not they to me, not I to them. Oh, how cold the world is! Would we three—the Doctor, and Elsie, and I—could have lain down in a row, in the old grave yard close under the eaves of the house—and let the grass grow over us. The world is cold; and I am an almshouse child."

The house by the grave yard seemed dismal now, no doubt, to little Elsie, who, being of a cheerful nature herself, had grown up with the idea that it was the most delightful spot in the world—feminine natures often having this delusion about a home; the place fullest of pleasant play, and of household love (because her own love welled over out of her heart, like a spring in a barrel); the place where everybody was kind and good; the world beyond its threshold appearing, perhaps, strange, sombre; the spot where it was pleasantest to be, for its own lone sake; the dim, old, homely place, so warm and cozy in winter, so cool in summer; who else was fortunate enough to have such a home; with that nice, kind, beautiful Ned; and that dear, kind, gentle old Doctor Grim, with his sweet ways, so wise, so upright, so good, beyond all other men. Oh, happy girl that she was, to have grown up in such a home. Was there ever any other house with such cozy nooks in it? Such, probably, were the feelings of good little Elsie about this place, which has seemed to us so dismal; for the home-feeling in the child's heart, her warm, cheerful, affectionate nature, was a magic, so far as she herself was concerned, and made all the house and its inmates over, after her own fashion. But now that little Ned was gone, there came a change. She moped about the house, and, for the first time, suspected it was dismal.

As for the grim Doctor, there did not appear to be much alteration in that hard old character; perhaps he drank a little more, though that was doubtful, because it is difficult to see where he could find niches to stick in more frequent drinks. Nor did he more frequently breathe through the pipe. He fell into desuetude, however, of his daily walk, and sent Elsie to play by herself in the grave yard (a dreary business enough for the poor child) <no longer could play at quarter-staff with Ned.> instead of taking her to country or seaside himself. He was more savage and blasphemous, sometimes, than he had been heretofore known to be; but on the other hand, he was sometimes softer, with a kind of weary con- senting to circumstances, intervals of helpless resignation, when he no longer fought and struggled in his heart. He did not seem to be alive, all the time; but on the other hand, he was sometimes a great deal too much alive and could not bear his potations as well as he used to do; and was overheard blaspheming at himself for being so weakly, and having a brain that could not bear a thimbleful, and growing to be a milksop like Seymour, as he said. This person, of whom the Doctor and his young people had had such a brief experience, appeared nevertheless to hang upon his remembrance in a singular way—the more singular as there was little resemblance between them, or apparent possibility of sympathy. Little Elsie was startled to hear Doctor Grim sometimes, call out Seymour, Seymour, as if he were summoning a spirit from some secret place. He muttered, sitting by himself, long, indistinct masses of talk, in which this name was discernible, and other names; going on, remembering, by the hour together, great masses of vague trouble, in which, if it only could have been unravelled and put in order, no doubt all the secrets of his life, secrets of wrath, guilt, vengeance, love, hatred, all beaten up together, and the best quite spoiled by the worst, might have been found. His mind evidently wandered. Sometimes, he seemed to be holding a conversation with unseen interlocutors, and almost invariably, so far as could be gathered, he was bitter, and threatened, immitigable, pouring out wrath and terror, domineering, tyrannical, speaking as to something that lay at his foot, <referring to places and people in England, the bloody footstep sometimes &c &c &c &c> but which he would not spare. Then suddenly, he would start, look round the dark old study, upward to the dangling spider overhead, and then at the quiet little girl, who, try as she might, could not keep her affrighted looks from his face, and always met his eyes with a loyal frankness, and unyielded faith in him.

<Talks that seemed to indicate that he was walking in an English park, or hearing the prayers in an English church &c>

"Oh, you little jade, what have you been overhearing?"

"Nothing, Doctor Grim;—nothing that I could make out."

"Make out as much as you can," he said. "I am not afraid of you."

"Afraid of little Elsie, dear Doctor Grim?"

"Neither of you, nor of the devil," murmured the Doctor— "of nobody but little Ned, and that milksop Seymour. If I have wronged anybody, it is they. As for the rest, let the day of judgment come. Dr. Grim is ready to fling down his burden at the judgment-seat and have it sorted there."

Then he would lie back in his chair, and look up at the great spider, who (or else it was Elsie's fancy) seemed to be making great haste in these days, filling out his web, as if he had less time than was desirable for such a piece of work.

One morning, the Doctor arose as usual, and after break-fast (at which he ate nothing, and, even after filling his coffee cup half with brandy, half with coffee, left it un-touched, save sipping a little out of a tea spoon) he went to the study (with a rather unsteady gait, chiefly remarkable, because it was so early in the day) and there established himself with his pipe, as usual, and his medical books and machines, and his manuscript. But, he seemed troubled, irresolute, weak; and at last, he blew out a volley of oaths, with no apparent appropriateness, and then seemed to be communing with himself.

"It is of no use to carry this on any further," said he, fiercely, in a decided tone, as if he had taken a resolution. "Elsie, my girl, come and kiss me."

So Elsie kissed him, amid all the tobacco smoke which was curling out of his mouth, as if there were a half extinguished furnace in his inside.

"Elsie, my little girl, I mean to die to-day," said the old man.

"To die, dear Doctor Grim!—Oh no, Oh no."

"Oh, yes, Elsie," said the Doctor, in a very positive tone. "I have kept myself alive by main force, these three weeks; and I find it hardly worth the trouble. It requires too much ex-ercise of will; and I am weary, weary. The pipe does not taste good; the brandy bewilders me; Ned is gone, too;—I have nothing else to do. I have wrought this many a year for an object, and now, taking all things into consideration, I don't know whether to execute it or no. Ned is gone; there is nobody but my little Elsie—a good child, but not quite enough to live for. I will let myself die, therefore, before sunset."

"Oh no, Doctor Grim. Let us send for Ned, and you will think it worth the trouble of living."

"No, Elsie, I want no one round my death-bed; when I have finished a little business, you must go out of the room, and I will turn my face to the wall, and say good night. But first send Crusty Hannah for Mr. Pickering."

This was a lawyer of the town, a man of classical and antiquarian tastes, as well as legal acquirement, and some of whose pursuits had brought him and Doctor Grim occasionally together. Beside calling this gentleman, Crusty Hannah (of her own motive, but whether out of good will to the poor Doctor Grim, or from a tendency to mischief inherent in such unnatural mixtures as hers) summoned, likewise, in all haste, a medical man—and as it happened, the one who had taken a most decidedly hostile part to our Doctor—and a clergyman, who had often devoted our poor friend to the infernal regions, almost by name, in his sermons; a kindness, to say the truth, which the Doctor had fully reciprocated in many anathemas against the clergyman. These two worthies, arriving simultaneously, and in great haste, were forthwith ushered to where the Doctor lay half reclining in his study; and upon showing their heads, the Doctor flew into an awful rage, threatening, in his customary improper way, when angry, to make them smell the infernal regions, and proceeding to put his threat into execution by flinging his odorous tobacco pipe in the face of the medical man, and re-baptizing the clergyman with a half emptied tumbler of brandy and water, and sending a terrible vociferation of oaths after them both, as they clattered hastily down the stairs. Really, that Crusty Hannah must have been the devil—for she stood grinning and chuckling, at the foot of the stairs, courtseying grotesquely.

"He terrible man, our old Doctor Grim," quoth crusty Hannah. "He drive us all to the wicked place before him."

This, however, was the final outbreak of poor Doctor Grim. Indeed, he almost went off at once, in the exhaustion that succeeded. The lawyer arrived shortly after, and was shut up with him for a considerable space, after which Crusty Hannah was summoned, and desired to call two indifferent persons from the street as witnesses to a will; and this document was duly executed, and given into the possession of the lawyer. This done, and the lawyer having taken his leave, the grim Doctor desired, and indeed commanded imperatively, that crusty Hannah should quit the room, having first—we are sorry to say—placed the brandy bottle within reach of his hand, and leaving him propt up in his armchair, in which he leaned back, gazing up at the great spider who was dangling over head. As the door closed behind crusty Hannah's grinning, and yet strangely interested face, the Doctor caught a glimpse of little Elsie in the passage, bathed in tears, and lingering, and looking earnestly into the chamber. Seeing the poor little girl, the Doctor cried out to her, half-wrathfully, half tenderly, "Don't cry, you little wretch! Come and kiss me once more." So Elsie, restraining her grief with a great effort, ran to him, and gave him a last kiss.

"Tell Ned," said the Doctor solemnly, "to think no more of the Old English Hall, or of the Bloody Footstep, or of the Silver Key, or any of all that nonsense. Good-by, my dear!" Then he said, with his thundrous and imperative air, "Let no one come near me till tomorrow morning."

So that parting was over; but still the poor little desolate child hovered by the study-door, all day long, afraid to enter, afraid to disobey, but unable to go. Some times, she heard the

Doctor muttering, as was his wont; once she fancied he was praying, and dropping on her knees, she also prayed fervently, and perhaps acceptably; then, all at once, the Doctor called out in a loud voice.

"No, Ned, no. Drop it—drop it!"

And then there was an utter silence, unbroken, forevermore, by the lips that had uttered so many objectionable things.

And, finally, after an interval which had been prescribed by the grim Doctor, a messenger was sent by the lawyer to our friend Ned, to inform him of this sad event, and to bring him back temporarily to town, for the purpose of hearing what were his prospects, and what disposition was now to be made of him. We shall not attempt to describe the grief, astonishment, and almost incredulity of Ned, on discovering that a person so mixed up with and built into his whole life, as the stalwart Doctor Grimshawe, had vanished out of it thus unexpectedly, like something thin as a vapour, like a red flame, that one instant is very bright in its lurid way, and then is nothing at all, amid the darkness. To the poor boy's still further grief and astonishment, he found, on reaching the spot that he called home that little Elsie (as the lawyer gave him to understand by the express orders of the Doctor, and for reasons of great weight) had been conveyed away by a person under whose guardianship she was placed, and that Ned could not be informed of the place. Even crusty Hannah had been provided for, and disposed of, and was no longer to be found. Mr Pickering explained to Ned the dispositions in his favor, which had been made by his deceased friend, who, out of a moderate property, had left him the means of obtaining as complete an education as the country would afford, and of supporting himself, until his own exertions would be likely to give him the success which his abilities were calculated to win. The remainder of his property (a less sum than that disposed of) was given to little Elsie, with the exception of a small provision to Crusty Hannah, with a recommendation from the Doctor that she should retire and spend the remainder of her life among her own people. There was likewise a certain sum left for the purpose of editing and printing (with a dedication to the Medical Society of the State) an account of the process of distilling balm from cobwebs; the bequest being worded in so singular a way, that it was just as impossible as it had ever been to discover whether the Grim Doctor was in earnest or no.

What disappointed the boy, in a greater degree than we shall try to express, was the lack of anything in reference to those dreams and castles of the air; any explanation of his birth; so that he was left with no trace of it, except just so far as the alms-house whence the Doctor had taken him. There all traces of his name and descent vanished, just as if he had been made out of the air, as an aerolite seems to be, before it tumbles on the earth with its mysterious iron.

The poor boy, in his bewilderment, had not yet come to feel what his grief was; it was not to be conceived, in a few days, that he was deprived of every person, thing, or thought that had hitherto kept his heart warm. He tried to make himself feel it, yearning for this grief as for his sole friend. Being, for the present, domiciled with the lawyer, he obtained the key of his former home, and went through the desolate house that he knew so well, and which now had such a silent, cold, familiar strangeness, with none in it, though the ghosts of the grim Doctor, of laughing little Elsie, of crusty Hannah,— dead and alive alike,—were all there, and his own ghost among them; for he himself was dead, that is, his former self, which he recognized as himself, had passed away, as they were. In the study everything looked as formerly, yet with a sort of unreality, as if it would dissolve and vanish on being touched; and, indeed, it partly proved so; for over the Doctor's chair seemed still to hang the great spider, but on looking closer at it, and finally touching it with the end of the Doctor's stick, Ned discovered that it was merely the skin, shell, apparition, of the real spider, the reality of whom, it is to be supposed, had followed the grim Doctor, whithersoever he had gone.

A thought struck Ned while he was here; he remembered the secret niche in the wall, where he had once seen the Doctor deposit some papers. He looked, and there they were. Who was the heir of those papers, if not he? If there were anything wrong in appropriating them, it was not perceptible to him in the desolation, anxiety, bewilderment, and despair, of that moment. He grasped the papers, and hurried from the room and down the stairs, afraid to look back, and half expecting to hear the gruff voice of Doctor Grim thundering after him to bring them back.

Then Ned went out of the back-door, and found his way to the Doctor's new grave, which, as it happened, was dug close beside that one which occupied the place of the one which the stranger had come to seek; and as if to spite the Doctor's professional antipathies, it lay beside a grave of an old physician and surgeon, one Doctor Swinnerton, who used to help diseases and kill patients, above a hundred years ago. But Doctor Grim was undisturbed by these neighbors, and apparently not more by the grief of poor little Ned, who hid his face in the crumbly earth of the grave, and the sods that had not begun to grow, and wept as if his heart would break.

But the heart never breaks on the first grave; and, after many graves, it gets so obtuse that nothing can break it.

And now let the mists settle down over the trail of our story, hiding it utterly in its onward course, for a long way to come, until, after many years, they may disperse, and discover something which, were it worth while to follow it through all that obscurity, would prove to be the very same

track which that boy was treading when we last saw him—
though it may have lain over land and sea, since then; but
the footsteps that trod there, are treading here.

Notes.   A great deal must be made out of the spiders, and
their gloomy, dusky, flaunting tapestry. A web across the orifice of his inkstand, every morning; everywhere, indeed, except
across the snout of his brandy bottle.

Depict the Doctor in his old dressing-gown, and a strange
sort of a cap, like a wizard's.

The two children are witnesses of many strange experiments in the study; they see all his moods, too.

The Doctor is supposed to be writing a work on the Natural
History of Spiders. Perhaps he used this as a blind for his real
project, and used to bamboozle the learned, with pretending to
read them passages, in which great learning seemed to be
elaborately worked up; crabbed with Greek and Latin; as if
the topic drew into itself like a whirlpool, all that men
thought and knew; plans to cultivate cobwebs on a large
scale. Sometimes, after overwhelming them with astonishment in this way, he would burst into one of his laughs.
Schemes to make the world a cobweb factory &c &c. Cobwebs
in his own brain.

Crusty Hannah such a mixture of persons and races as could
be found only at a seaport. There was a rumor that the Doctor
had murdered a former maid, for having, with housewifely
instinct, swept away the cobwebs; some said that he had her
skeleton in a closet. Some said that he had strangled a wife
with web of the great spider.

Read the description of Poulton Hall, the garden, lawn
&c August 8th 53.

Bebbington church & church yard, August 29th 53.

The Doctor is able to love—able to hate; two great and
rare abilities, now-a-days.

Introduce two pine-trees, ivy grown, as at Lowwood Hotel, July 16th 55.

The family name might be Redcliffe.

Thatched cottages, June 22d '55.

Early introduce the mention of the cognizance of the family—the Leopard's Head, for instance—in the first part of the Romance; the Doctor may have possessed engraved as crest of a coat of arms, in a book.

The Doctor shall show Ned, perhaps, a drawing or engraving of the Hospital, with figures of the pensioners in the quadrangle, fitly dressed; and this picture and the figures shall impress themselves strongly on his memory.

A traveller, with a knapsack on his shoulders, comes out of the duskiness of vague unchronicled time, throwing his shadow before him in the morning sunshine, along a well trodden, though solitary path.

It was early summer, or perhaps latter spring, and the most genial weather that either spring or summer ever brought, possessing a character, indeed, as if both seasons had contrived their best qualities to create an atmosphere and temperature most suitable for the enjoyment and exercise of life. To one accustomed to a climate where there is seldom a medium between heat too fierce and cold too deadly, it was a new development in the nature of weather; so genial it was, so full of all comfortable influences, and yet, somehow or other, void of the torrid characteristic that inevitably burns in our full sun-bursts. The traveller thought, in fact, that the sun was at less than his brightest glow; for though it was bright—though the day seemed cloudless—though it appeared to be the clear transparent morning that preceeds an unshadowed noon—still, there was a mild and softened character, not so perceptible when he directly sought to see it, but as if now some veil were interposed between the earth and sky, and absorbed the passionate qualities out of the former, and leaving only the kindly ones. Warmth was in abundance, and, yet, all through it, and strangely akin to it, there was a half suspected coolness that gave the atmosphere its rare, most thrilling and delicious charm. It was good for human life, as the traveller felt throughout all his being; good, likewise, for vegetable life, as was seen in the depth and richness of verdure over the gently undulating landscape, and the luxuriance of foliage, wherever there was tree or shrub to put forth leaves.

The path, on which the traveller was moving, deserved at least a word or two of description; it was a well trodden footpath, running just here along the edge of a field of grass, and bordered on one side by a hedge, which contained materials within itself for varied and minute researches in natural history; so thickly luxuriant was it with its diverse vegetable life, such a green intricacy did it form, so impenetrable, and so beautiful, and such a Paradise it was for the birds that built their nests there, in a labyrinth of little boughs and twigs, unseen and inaccessible, while close beside the human race to which they attach themselves, that they must have felt themselves as safe as when they first sang to Eve. Homely flowers likewise grew in it; and many creeping and twining plants, that were no original part of the hedge, had come of their own accord and dwelt here, beautifying and enriching this verdant fence by way of repayment for the shelter and support which it afforded them. At intervals, trees of vast trunk and mighty spread of foliage, whether elms or oaks, grew in the line of the hedge, and the bark of those gigantic, age-long patriarchs, was not gray and naked, like the trees which the traveller had been accustomed to see, but verdant with moss, or, in many cases, richly enwreathed with a net work of creeping plants, and oftenest the ivy, of old growth, clambering upward, and making its own twisted stem almost of one substance with the supporting tree. On one venerable oak there was a plant of mystic leaf which the traveller knew by instinct, and plucked a bough of it with a certain reverence for the sake of the Druids and Christmas kisses and of the poetry in which it was rooted from of old.

The path on which he walked, rustic as it was, and made merely by the feet that pressed it down, was one of the ancientest of ways; older than the oak that bore the misletoe, older than the villages between which it passed, older perhaps than the Roman road which the traveler had crossed that morning; old as the times when people first debarred themselves from wandering freely and widely, wherever a vagrant impulse led them. The footpath, therefore, still retains some of the characteristics of a woodland walk, taken at random, by a lover of nature, not pressed for time, nor restrained by artificial barriers; it swerves and lingers along, and finds pretty little dells and nooks of delightful scenery, and picturesque glimpses of halls or cottages, in the same neighborhood where a high-road would disclose only a tiresome blank. They run into one another, too, for miles and miles together, and traverse rigidly guarded parks and domains, not as a matter of favor, but as a right; so that the poorest man thus retains a kind of property and privilege in the oldest inheritance of the richest. The high road sees only the outside; the footpath leads down into the heart of the country.

A pleasant feature of the foot-path was the stile, between two fields; no frail and temporary structure, but betokening the permanence of this rustic way, the ancient solidity of the stone steps, worn into cavities by the hobnailed shoes that had pressed upon them; here, not only the climbing foot had passed, for ages, but here had sat the maiden with her milk pail, the rustic on his way afield or homeward; here had been love-makings, cheerful chance chats, songs as natural as bird note, a thousand pretty scenes of rustic manners. It was curious to see the traveller pause, to contemplate so simple a thing as this old style of a few stone-steps; antique as an old castle; simple and rustic as the gap in a rail-fence; and while he sat on one of the steps, making himself pleasantly sensible of his whereabout, like one who should handle a dream and find it tangible and real, he heard a sound that bewitched him with still another dreamy delight. A bird rose out of the grassy field, and, still soaring aloft, made a cheery melody, rapturous music, as if the whole soul and substance of the winged creature had been distilled into this melody, as it vanished skyward.

"The lark! The lark!" exclaimed the traveller, recognizing the note (though never heard before) as if his childhood had known it.

A moment afterwards, another bird was audible in the shadow of two neighboring trees, or some other inscrutable hiding-place, saying softly, in a flute-like note, as if blown through an instrument of wood—"Cuckroo, Cuckroo"—only twice, and then a stillness.

"How familiar these rustic sounds!" he exclaimed. "Surely I was born here!"

The person who thus enjoyed these sounds, as if they were at once familiar and strange, was a young man, tall, and rather slenderly built; and though we have called him young, there were the traces of thought, struggle, and even of experience, in his marked brow, and somewhat pale face; but the spirit within him was evidently still that of a youth, lithe and active, gazing out of his dark eyes and taking note of things about him, with an eager, untiring interest, that seemed to be unusually awake at the present moment, enabling him to find a rare enjoyment, as we have seen, in by-path, hedge-row, rustic style, lark and cuckoo, and even the familiar grass and clover-blossoms. It could be but a few

years since he first called himself a man; but they must have
been thickly studded with events, turbulent with action,
spent amidst circumstances that called for resources of energy
not often so early developed; and thus his youth might have
been kept in abeyance until now, when, in this simple rural
scene, he grew almost a boy again. As for his station in life,
his coarse gray suit being worn thin, and the knapsack on his
shoulders, did not indicate a very high one; yet it was such
as a gentleman might wear, of a morning, or on a pedestrian
ramble, and was worn in a way that made it seem of a better
fashion than it really was. It was as if he had long been shut
in a sick chamber or a prison; or, at least, within the iron cage
of busy life, that had allowed him but few glimpses of natural
things through its bars; or else this was another kind of
nature than he had heretofore known.

As he walked along (through a kind of dream, though he
seemed so minutely observant of many of the trifling things
around him) he failed to notice that the path grew somewhat
less distinctly marked, overarched, more infringed upon by
grass, more shut in by shrubbery; he had deviated into a side
track, and in fact, a certain painted board, nailed against a
tree, had escaped his notice, warning off intruders, with inhospitable threats of prosecution. He began to suspect that
he must have gone astray, when the path led over plashy
ground, with a still fainter trail of preceding footsteps, and
plunged into shrubbery, and seemed on the point of deserting
him altogether, after having beguiled him thus far. The spot
was an entanglement of boughs, and yet did not give him
the impression of wildness; for it was the stranger's idea that
everything, in this long cultivated region, had been touched
and influenced by man's care, every oak, every bush, every
sod, that man knew them all, and that they knew him, and by
that mutual knowledge had become far other than they were
in the first freedom of growth, such as may be found in an

American forest. Nay, the wildest denizens of this sylvan neighborhood were removed in the same degree from their primeval character; for hares sat on their hind-legs to gaze at the approaching traveller, and hardly thought it worth their while to leap away among some ferns, as he drew nearer; two pheasants looked at him from a bough, a little inward among the brush; and, to complete the wonder, he became aware of the antlers and brown muzzle of a deer, protruded among the shrubbery, and, though, immediately, there ensued a great rush and rustling of the herd, it seemed evidently to come from a certain lingering shyness, an instinct that had lost its purpose and object, and only mimicked a dread of man whose neighborhood and familiarity had tamed the wild deer almost into a domestic creature. Remembering his experience of true woodland life, the traveller fancied that it might be possible to want freer life, freer air, less often used for human breath, than was to be found anywhere among these woods.

But then the sweet, calm sense of safety that was here! The certainty that, with the wild element that, centuries ago, had passed out of this scene, had gone all the perils of wild men and savage beasts, precipices, swamps, potholes, leaving nature, not effete, but only disarmed of those rougher, deadlier characteristics, that cruel rawness, which make primeval Nature the deadly enemy even of her own children. Here was consolation, doubtless; so we sit down on the stone step of the last stile that he had crossed, and listen to the footsteps of the traveller, and the distant rustle among the shrubbery, as he goes deeper and deeper into the seclusion, having by this time lost the deceitful track. No matter if he go astray; even were it after nightfall instead of noontime, a will o the whisp, or Puck himself, would not lead him into worse harm in this solitude than to drench him in some mossy pool, the depths of which the truant schoolboys had known for ages.

Nevertheless, some little time after his disappearance, there was the report of a shot, that echoed sharp and loud, startling the pheasants from their boughs, and sending the hares and deer a scampering in good earnest.

We next find our friend, from whom we parted on the footpath, in a situation of which he himself was but very imperfectly aware; for, indeed, he had been in a state of unconsciousness, lasting until it was now late towards the sunset of that same day. He was endeavoring to make out where he was, and how he came thither, or what had happened; or whether, indeed, anything had happened, unless to have fallen asleep, and to be still enveloped in the fragments of some vivid and almost tangible dream, the more confused because so vivid. His wits did not come so readily about him as usual; there may have been a slight delusion, which mingled itself with his sober perceptions, and by its leaven of extravagance made the whole substance of the scene untrue. Thus it happened, that, as it were at the same instant, he fancied himself years back in life, thousands of miles away, in a gloomy cobwebbed room, looking out upon a grave-yard, while yet, neither more nor less distinctly, he was conscious of being in a small chamber, panelled with oak, and furnished in an antique style. He was doubtful, too, whether or no there was a grim bearded figure in a shabby dressing-gown, and in an old velvet cap, sitting in the dusk of the room, smoking a pipe that diffused no scent of tobacco —quaffing a deep-hued liquor out of a tumbler—looking upwards at a spider that hung above. Was there, too, a child sitting in a little chair at his footstool! In his earnestness to see this apparition more distinctly, he opened his eyes wider, and stirred, and ceased to see it at all.

But, though that other dusky, squalid, cobwebbed scene quite vanished, and along with it the two figures, old and young, grim and childish, of whose visible portraits it had been the framework, still there were the features in the old, oaken panelled chamber that seemed to belong rather to his dream. The panels were ornamented, here and there, with antique carving, representing over and over again an identical device, being a bare arm, holding the torn off head of some savage beast which the stranger could not know by species, any more than Agassiz himself could have read its type or kindred; because it was that kind of natural history of which heraldry alone keeps the menagerie. But it was just as familiar to his recollection as that of the cat which he had fondled in his childhood. There was likewise a mantle piece, heavily wrought of oak, quite black with smoke and age, in the center of which, more prominent than elsewhere, was that same leopard's head that seemed to thrust itself everywhere into sight, as if typifying some great mystery which human nature would never be at rest with till it had solved; and below, in a cavernous hollow, there was a smouldering fire of coal; for the genial day had thus suddenly grown chill, and a shower of rain spattered against the small window panes, almost at the same time with the struggling sunshine. And over the mantle-piece, where the light of the declining day came strongest from the window, there was a larger and more highly relieved carving of this same device, and underneath it a legend, in old English letters, which, though his eyes could not precisely trace, at that distance, he knew to be this—"Hold hard the Head." Otherwise, the aspect of the room bewildered him by not being known, since this one circumstance was so familiar; a narrow precinct it was, with one window, full of old-fashioned diamond-shaped panes of glass; a small chest, standing on many feet; two or three high backed chairs, on the top of each of which was carved that same crest of the fabulous brute's head, which the carver's fancy seemed to have clutched so strongly that he could not let it go; in another part of the room, a very old engraving, rude and strong, representing some ruffed personage, which the stranger only tried to make out with a sort of idle curiosity, because it was strange he should dream so distinctly. Very soon, it became intolerably irritating that these two dreams, both purposeless, should have knotted and entangled themselves in his mind. He made a nervous and petulant motion, intending to rouse himself fully; and immediately a sharp pang of physical pain took him by surprise, and made him groan aloud.

<(Let the old man have a beard as part of the costume.)>

Immediately, there was an almost noiseless step on the floor; and a watcher emerged from a deep niche that looked as if it might once have been an oratory, in ancient times, and the figure, too, might have been supposed to possess the devout and sanctified character of those who knelt in the oratories of ancient times. It was an elderly man, tall, thin, and pale, and wearing a long, dark tunic, cut in a peculiar fashion, which—like almost everything else about him—the stranger seemed to have a confused remembrance of; this venerable person had a benign and pitiful aspect, and approached the bedside with such an evident good will and desire to do the sufferer good that the latter felt soothed, at least, by his very presence. He lay, a moment, gazing up at the old man's face, without caring to exert himself to say a word, but sensible, as it were, of a mild, soft influence from him, cooling to a fever which seemed to burn in his veins.

"Do you suffer much pain?" asked the old man, gently.

<Compare him to a palmer>

"None at all," said the stranger; but again a slight motion caused him to find a burning twinge in his shoulder. "Yes; there was a throb of strange anguish. Why should I feel pain! Where am I?"

"In safety, and with those who desire to be your friends," said the old man. "You have met with accident; but do not inquire about it now. Quiet is what you need."

Still the traveller gazed at him; and the old man's figure seemed to enter into his dream, or delirium, whichever it might be, as if the peaceful presence were but a shadow, so quaint was his address, so unlike real life, in that dark robe, with a velvet skull cap on his head, beneath which his hair made a silvery border; and looking more closely, the stranger saw embroidered on the breast of the tunic that same device, the arm and the leopard's head, which was visible in the carving of the room. Yes; this must still be a dream, which, under the unknown laws which govern such psychical states, had brought out thus vividly figures, devices, words, forgotten since his boyish days. Though of an imaginative tendency, the stranger was nevertheless strongly tenacious of the actual, and had a natural horror at the idea of being seriously at odds, in beliefs, perceptions, conclusions, with the real world about him; so that a tremor ran through him, as if he saw the substance of the world shimmering before his eyes like a mere vaporous consistency.

"Are you real?" said he to the antique presence,—"or a spirit? or a fantasy?"

The old man laid his thin, cool palm on the stranger's burning forehead, and smiled benignantly, keeping it there an instant.

"If flesh and blood are real, I am so," said he; "a spirit, too, I may claim to be, made thin by fantasy. Again—do not perplex yourself with such things. Tomorrow, you may find denser substance in me. Drink this composing draught, and close your eyes to those things that disturb you."

"Your features, too, and your voice," said the stranger, in a resigned tone, as if he were giving up a riddle the solution of which he could not find, "have an image and echo somewhere in my memory. It is all an entanglement. I will drink, and shut my eyes."

He drank from a little, old fashioned silver cup, which his venerable guardian presented to his lips; but, in so doing, he was still perplexed and tremulously disturbed with seeing that same weary old device, the leopard's head, engraved on the side; and shut his eyes to escape it, for it seemed to irritate a certain portion of his brain with vague, feverish, elusive ideas. So he sighed and spoke no more. The medicine, whatever it might be, had the merit, rare in doctor's stuff, of being pleasant to take, assuasive of thirst, and imbued with a hardly perceptible fragrance, that was so ethereal that it also seemed to enter into his dream and modify it. He kept his eyes closed, and fell into a misty state, in which he wondered whether this could be the panacea or medicament which old Doctor Grimshawe used to distil from cobwebs, and of which the fragrance seemed to breathe through all the waste of years since then. He wondered, too, who was this benign, saint-like old man, and where, in what former state of being, he could have known him, to have him thus, as no strange thing, and yet so strange, be attending at his bedside, with all this ancient garniture. But it was best to dismiss all things, he being so weak, to resign himself; all this had happened before, and had passed away, prosperously or unprosperously; it would pass away in this case, likewise; and, in the morning, whatever might be delusive would have disappeared.

<Describe him as delirious, and the scene is adopted into his delirium>

The patient had a favorable night, and awoke with a much clearer head, though still considerably feverish, and in a state of great exhaustion from loss of blood which kept down the fever. The events of the preceding day shimmered as it were and shifted illusively in his recollection; nor could he yet account for the situation in which he found himself, the antique chamber, the old man of mediæval garb, nor even for the wound which seemed to have been the occasion of bringing him thither. One moment, so far as he remembered, he had been straying along a solitary footpath, through rich shrubbery, with the antlered deer peeping at him, listening to the lark and the cuckoo; the next, he lay helpless in the oak panelled chamber, surrounded with objects that appealed to some fantastic shadow of recollection, which could have had no reality.

<(Make this whole scene very dreamlike, & feverish.)>

To say the truth, the traveller perhaps wilfully kept hold of this strange illusiveness, and kept his thoughts from too harshly analyzing his situation, and solving the riddle in which he found himself involved. In his present weakness, his mind sympathizing with the sinking down of his physical powers, it was delightful to let all go; to relinquish all control, and let himself drift vaguely into whatever region of improbabilities there exists around the dull commonplace of life. Weak, stricken down, given over to influences which had taken possession of him during an interval of insensibility, he was no longer responsible; let these delusions, if they were such, linger as long as they would, and depart of their own accord at last. He, meanwhile, would willingly accept the idea, that some spell had transported him out of an epoch, in which he had led a brief trouble, of battle, mental strife, success, failure, all equally feverish and unsatisfactory, into some past century, where the business was to rest; to drag on dreamy days, looking at things through half-shut eyes; into a limbo where things were put away; shows of what had once been, now somehow parted, and still maintaining a sort of half-existence, a serious mockery; a state likely enough to exist just a little apart from the actual world, if we only know how to find our way into it. Scenes and events that have once stained themselves, in deep colours, on the curtain that Time hangs around us, to shut us in from eternity, cannot be quite effaced by the succeeding phantasmagoria, and sometimes, by a palimpsest, show more strongly than they.

In the course of the morning, however, he was a little too feelingly made sensible of realities, by the visit of a surgeon, who proceeded to examine the wound in his shoulder, removing the bandages which he himself seemed to have put upon this mysterious hurt. The traveller closed his eyes, and submitted to the manipulations of the professional person, painful as they were, assisted by the gentler touch of the old palmer; and there was something in the way in which he resigned himself, that met the approbation of the surgeon.

"A very quiet and well behaved patient in spite of a little fever, and slight delirium, too, to judge by his eye," said he to the palmer. "Unless I greatly mistake, he has been under a surgeon's hand for a similar hurt ere now. He has learnt under great discipline how to take such a thing easily. Yes, yes; see, here is a mark where a bullet went in some time ago—4 or 5 years since, when he could have been little more than a boy. A wild fellow this, I doubt."

<There should be a light wildness in the patient's remark to the surgeon, which he cannot prevent, though he is conscious of it.>

"It was an Indian bullet," said the patient, still fancying himself gone astray into the past, "shot at me in battle, two or three hundred years hereafter."

"Ah; he has served in the East Indies," said the surgeon. "I thought this sun-burned cheek had taken its hue elsewhere than in England."

The patient did not care to take the trouble which would have been involved in correcting the surgeon's surmise; so he let it pass, and patiently awaited the end of the examination, with only a moan or two, which seemed rather pleasing and desirable than otherwise to the surgeon's ear.

"He has vitality enough for his needs," said he, nodding to the palmer. "These groans betoken a good degree of pain; though the young fellow is evidently a self-contained sort of nature, and does not let us know all he feels. It promises well, however. Keep him in bed, and quiet, and within a day or two, we shall see."

He wrote a recipe, or two or three, perhaps, (for, in those days, the medical fraternity had faith in their own art) and took his leave.

The white-bearded palmer withdrew into the half concealment of the oratory, which we have already mentioned, and there, putting on a pair of spectacles, betook himself to the perusal of an old folio volume, the leaves of which he turned over so gently that not the slightest sound could possibly disturb the patient. All his manifestations were gentle, and soft, but of a simplicity most unlike the feline softliness which we are apt to associate with a noiseless tread and movement in the male sex. The sunshine came through the ivy and glimmered upon his great book, however, with an effect which a little disturbed the patient's nerves; besides, he desired to have a fuller view of his benign guardian.

"Will you sit nearer the bedside?" said he. "I wish to look at you."

Weakness, the relaxation of nerves, and the state of dependence on another's care—very long unfelt—had made him show what we must call childishness; and it was perceptible in the low, half-complaining tone in which he spoke, indicating a consciousness of kindness in the other, a little plaintiveness in himself; of which, the next instant, weak and wandering as he was, he was ashamed, and essayed to express it.

<Notice the peculiar depth and intelligence of his eyes, on account of his pain and sickness.>

"You must deem me very poor-spirited," said he, "not to bear this trifling hurt with a firmer mind. But perhaps it is not entirely that I am so weak, but I feel you to be so benign."

"Be weak and be the stronger for it," said the old man, with a grave smile. "It is not in the pride of our strength that we are best or stronger. To be made anew, the man must be again a little child, and consent to be enwrapt quietly in the arms of Providence, as a child in its mother's arms."

"I never knew a mother's care," replied the traveller, in a low, regretful tone, being weak to the incoming of all soft feelings, in his present state. "And since my boyhood, I have lived among harsh men—a life of struggle and hard rivalry. It is good to find myself here in the long past, as in a sheltered harbour."

And here he smiled, by way of showing to the old palmer that he saw though the slight infirmity of mind that impelled him to say such things as the above; that he was not its dupe, though he had not strength, just now, to resist its impulse. After this, he dozed off softly, but felt, through all his sleep, some twinges of his wound, bringing him back, as it were, to the conscious surface of the great deep of slumber, into which he might otherwise have sunk. At all such brief intervals, half unclosing his eyes, (like a child, when his mother sits by his bed, and he fears that she will steal away if he falls quite asleep, and leave him in the dark solitude) he still beheld the white bearded, kindly old man, of saintly aspect, sitting near him, and turning over the pages of his folio volume, so softly that not the faintest rustle did it make; the picture at length got so fully into his idea, that he seemed to see it even through his closed eyelids. After a while, however, the slumbrous tendency left him more entirely, and, without having been conscious of being awake, he found himself contemplating the old man with wide-open eyes. The venerable personage seemed soon to feel his gaze, and ceasing to look at the folio, he turned his eyes with quiet inquiry to meet those of the stranger.

<Perhaps the recognition of the pensioner should not be so decided. Redclyffe thinks it is he, but thinks it as in a dream, without wonder or inquiry; and the pensioner does not quite acknowledge it.>

"What great volume is that?" asked the latter.

"It is a book of English chronicles," said the old man, "mostly relating to the part of the island where you now are, and to times previous to the Stuarts."

"Ah; it is to you, a contemporary, what reading the newspaper is to other men," said the stranger; then with a smile of self-reproach, "I shall conquer this idle mood. I am not so imbecile as you must think me. But there is one thing that strangely haunts me—where, in what state of being—can I have seen your face before? There is nothing in it that I distinctly remember; but some impression, some character, some look, with which I have been long ago familiar, haunts me, and brings back all old scenes. Do you know me?"

The old man smiled. "I knew, long ago, a very bright and impressible boy," said he.

"And his name?" said the stranger.

"It was Edward Redcliffe," said the old man.

"Ah; I remember you now," said the traveller, not too earnestly, but with a soft, gratified feeling, as the riddle thus far solved itself. "You are my old kindly instructor. You are Colcord! That is it. I remember you disappeared. You shall tell me, when I am quite myself, what was that mystery—and whether it is your real self, or only a part of my dream, and going to vanish when I quite awake. Now I shall sleep, and dream more of it."

One more waking interval he had that day, and again

essayed to enter into conversation with the old man, who had thus strangely again become connected with his life, after having so long vanished from his path.

<(The patient, as he gets better, listens to the feet of old people moving in the corridor; to the ringing of a bell at stated periods; to old tremulous voices talking in the quadrangle &c &c &c)>

"Where am I?" asked Edward Redclyffe.

"In the home of misfortune!" said Colcord.

"Ah; then I have a right to be here!" said he. "I was born in such a home. Do you remember it?"

"I know your story," said Colcord.

"Yes; from Doctor Grim," said Edward. "People whispered he had made away with you. I never believed it; but finding you here, in this strange way, and myself having been shot, perhaps to death, it seems not so strange. Pooh! I wander again, and ought to sleep a little more. And this is the home of misfortune; but not like the squalid place of rage, idiocy, imbecility, drunkenness, where I was born! How many times I have blushed to remember that native home. But not of late! I have struggled; I have fought; I have triumphed! The unknown boy has come to be no undistinguished man! His ancestry, should he ever reveal himself to them, need not blush for the poor foundling."

"Hush!" said the quiet watcher. "Your fever burns you. Take this draught, and sleep a little longer."

Another day or two found Edward Redclyffe almost a convalescent. The singular lack of impatience that characterized his present mood—the repose of spirit into which he had lapsed—had much to do with the favorable progress of his cure. After strife, anxiety, great mental exertion, and excitement of various kinds, which had harassed him ever since he grew to be a man, had come this opportunity of perfect rest; this dream in the midst of which he lay, while its magic boundaries involved him, and kept far the contact of actual life, so that its sounds and tumults seemed remote; its cares could not fret him, its ambitions, objects good or evil, were shut out from him; the electric wires, that had connected him with the battery of life, were broken for the time, and he did not feel the unquiet influence that kept everybody else in galvanic action. So, under the benign influence of the old palmer, he lay in slumbrous luxury, undisturbed save by some twinges of no intolerable pain, which, however, he almost was glad of, because it made him sensible that this deep luxury of quiet was essential to his cure, however idle it might seem. For the first time since he was a child, he resigned himself not to put a finger to the evolution of his fortune; he determined to accept all things that might happen, good or evil; he would not even imagine an event beyond to-day, but would let one spontaneous and half-definite thought loiter after another, through his mind, to listen to the spattering shower, the gusts of shut out wind and look with half-shut eyes at the sunshine glimmering through the ivy-twigs, and illuminating those old devices on the wall; at the gathering twilight; at the dim lamp; at the creeping upward of another day, and with it, the lark singing so far away that the thrill of its delicious song could not disturb him with an impulse to awake. Sweet as its carol was, he could almost have been content to miss the lark; sweet and clear, it was too like a fairy trumpet-call, summoning to awake, and struggle again with eager combatants, for new victories, the best of which were not worth this deep repose.

The old palmer did his best to prolong a mood so beneficial to the wounded young man. The surgeon also nodded approval, and attributed this happy state of the patient's mind, and all the physical advantages growing out of it, to his own consummate skill; nor, indeed, was he undeserving of credit not often to be awarded to medical men, for having done nothing to impede the good which kind Nature was willing to bring about. She was doing the patient more good, indeed, than either the surgeon or the palmer could fully estimate, in taking this opportunity to recreate a mind that had too early known stirring impulses, and that had been worked to a degree beyond what its organization (in some respects singularly delicate) ought to have borne. Once in a long while, the weary actors in this headlong drama of life must have such repose, or else go mad or die.

<(When the machinery of human life has once been stopped, by sickness or other impediment, it often needs an impulse to set it going again, even after it is newly wound up.)>

But it could not last forever. The influx of new life into his veins began to have a poignancy that would not let him lie so quietly, lapped in the past, in gone-by centuries, and waited on by quiet Age, in the person of the old palmer; he began to feel again that he was young, and must live in the time when his lot was cast. He began to say to himself, that it was not well to be any longer passive, but that he was again to take the troublesome burthen of his own life on his own shoulders. He thought of this necessity, this duty, throughout one whole day, and determined that the morrow he would reach the first step towards terminating his inaction; which he now began to be half impatient of, at the same time that he clutched it still, for the sake of the deliciousness that it had had.

"Tomorrow, I hope to be clothed and in my right mind," said he to the old palmer, "and very soon I must thank you, with my whole heart, for your kind care, and go. It is a shame that I burthen the hospitality of this house so long."

"No shame, whatever," replied the old man, "but, on the contrary, the fittest thing that could have chanced. You are dependent on no private benevolence, nor on the good offices of any man now living, or who has lived these last three hundred years. This ancient establishment is for the support of poverty, misfortune, and age; and according to the word of the founder, it serves him who was indebted to the beneficiaries, not they to him; for in behalf of his temporal bequests, he asked their prayers for his soul's welfare. He needed them, could they avail him; for this ponderous structure was built upon the founder's mortal transgressions, and even, I may say, out of the actual substance of them. Sir Edward Redclyffe was a fierce fighter in the Wars of the Roses, and amassed much wealth by spoil, rapine, confiscation, and all violent and evil ways that those disturbed times opened to him; and, on his death-bed, he founded this hospital for twelve men, who should be able to prove kindred of his race, to dwell here with a stipend, and pray for him; and likewise provision for a sick stranger, until he should be able to go on his way again."

"I shall pray for him willingly," said Edward, moved by the piety which awaits any softened state of our natures to steal into our hearts. "Though no Catholic, I will pray for his soul. And that is his crest, which you wear embroidered on your garment."

"It is," said the old man. "You will see it carved, painted, embroidered, everywhere about the establishment; but let us give it the better and more reasonable interpretation;— not that he sought to proclaim his own pride of ancestry and rank, but to acknowledge his sins the more manifestly, by stamping the emblem of his race on this structure of his penitence."

"And are you," said Redclyffe, impressed anew by the quiet dignity of the venerable speaker, "in authority in the establishment?"

"A simple beneficiary of the charity," said the palmer; "one of the twelve poor brethren and kinsmen of the founder.

Slighter proofs of kindred are now, of necessity, received, since, in the natural course of things, the race has long been growing scant. But I had it in my power to make out a sufficient claim."

"Singular!" exclaimed Redclyffe, "you being an American."

"You remember me, then," said the old man, quietly.

"From the first," said Edward, "although your image took the fantastic aspect of the bewilderment in which I then was; and now that I am in another state of mind, it seems yet stranger that you should be here. We two children thought you translated, and people, I remember, whispered dark hints about your fate."

"There was nothing wonderful in my disappearance," said the old man. "There were causes, an impulse, an intuition, that made me feel, one particular night, that I might meet harm, whether from myself or others, by not withdrawing from a place with which I had the most casual connection. But I never, so long as I remained in America, quite lost sight of you; and Doctor Grimshawe, before his death, had knowledge of where I was, and gave me in charge a duty which I faithfully endeavored to perform. Singular man that he was! Much evil, much good in him. Both, it may be, will live after him!"

Redclyffe, when the conversation had reached this point, felt a vast desire to reveal to the old man all that the grim Doctor had instilled into his childish mind, all that he himself, in subsequent years, had wrought more definitely out of it, all his accompanying doubts, respecting the secret of his birth, and some supposed claims which he might assert, and which, only half acknowledging the purpose, had availed to bring him, a republican, hither as to an ancestral centre. He even fancied that the benign old man seemed to expect and await such a confidence; but that very idea contributed to make it impossible for him to speak.

"Another time," he said to himself. "Perhaps never. It is a fantastic folly; and, with what the work-house foundling has since achieved, he would give up too many hopes to take the representation of a mouldy old English family."

"I find my head still very weak," said he, by way of cutting short the conversation. "I n.ust try to sleep again."

The next day, he called for his clothes, and, with the assistance of the pensioner, managed to be dressed, and awaited the arrival of the surgeon, sitting in a great easy-chair, with not much except his pale, thin cheeks, faded thoughtful eyes, and his arm in a sling to show the pain and danger through which he had passed. Soon after the departure of the professional gentleman, a step somewhat louder than ordinary was heard on the staircase, and in the corridor leading to the sick chamber; the step (so Redclyffe's perceptions, nicely attempered by his weakness, assured him) of a man in perfect and robust health, and of station and authority. A moment afterwards, a gentleman of middle age or a little beyond, appeared in the door way, in a dress that seemed clerical, yet not very decidedly so; he had a frank, kindly, yet authoritative bearing, and a face that might also be said to beam with geniality, when as now, the benevolence of his nature was aroused and ready to express itself.

"My friend," said he, "Dr Portingale tells me you are much better; and I am most happy to hear it."

There was something brusque and unceremonious in his manner, which a little jarred against Redclyffe's sensitiveness which had become morbid in sympathy with his weakness. He felt that the new-comer had not precisely the right idea as to his own position in life; he was addressing him most kindly, indeed, but as an inferior.

"I am much better, Sir," he replied, gravely, and with reserve; "so nearly well, that I shall very soon be able to bid farewell to my kind nurse here, and to this ancient establishment, to which I owe so much."

The visitor seemed struck by Redclyffe's tone, and finely modulated voice, and glanced at his face, and thence over his dress and figure, as if to gather from them some reliable data as to his station.

"I am the Warden of this Hospital," said he, with not less benignity than heretofore and greater courtesy, "and, in that capacity, must consider you under my care—my guest, in fact—although owing to my casual absence one of the brethren of the house has been the active instrument in attending you. I am most happy to find you so far recovered. Do you feel yourself in a condition to give any account of the accident which has befallen you?"

"It will be a very unsatisfactory one, at best," said Redclyffe, trying to discern some definite point in his misty reminiscences. "I am a stranger to this country, and was on a pedestrian tour with the purpose of making myself acquainted with the aspects of English scenery and life. I had turned into a footpath, being told that it would lead me within view of an old Hall, which, from certain early associations, I was very desirous of seeing. I think I went astray; at all events, the path became indistinct; and, so far as I can recollect, I had just turned to retrace my steps—in fact, that is the last thing in my memory."

"You had almost fallen a sacrifice," said the Warden, "to the old preference which our English gentry have inherited from their Norman ancestors, of game to man. You had come unintentionally as an intruder into a rich preserve much hunted by poachers, and exposed yourself to the deadly muzzle of a spring-gun, which had not the wit to distinguish between a harmless traveller and a poacher. At least, such is our conclusion; for our old friend here (who luckily for you is a great rambler in the woods) when the report drew him to the spot, found you insensible, and the gun discharged."

"A gun has so little discretion," said Redclyffe, smiling, "that it seems a pity to trust entirely to its judgment, in a matter of life and death. But, to confess the truth, I had come this morning to the suspicion that there was a direct human agency in the matter; for I find missing a little pocket-book which I carried."

"Aha!" cried the Warden;—"that certainly gives a new aspect to the affair. Was it of value?"

"Of none whatever," said Redclyffe—"merely containing pencil memoranda, and bills of a traveller's little expenses. I had papers about me, of far more value, and a moderate sum of money, a letter of credit, which have escaped. I do not, however, feel inclined, on such grounds, to transfer the guilt decidedly from the spring-gun to any more responsible criminal; for it is very possible that the pocket book, being carelessly carried, might have beeen lost on the way. I had not used it since the preceding day."

"Much more probable, indeed," said the Warden. "The discharged gun is strong evidence against itself. Mr Colcord," continued he, raising his voice, "how long was the interval between the discharge of the gun and your arrival on the spot?"

"Five minutes, or less," said the old man; "for I was not far off, and made what haste I could, it being borne in on my spirit that mischief had chanced."

"Did you hear two reports?" asked the Warden.

"Only one," replied Colcord.

It is a plain case against the spring-gun," said the Warden; "and, as you tell me you are a stranger, I trust you will not suppose that our peaceful English woods and parks are the haunt of banditti. We must try to give you a better idea of us. May I ask, are you an American, and recently come among us?"

"I believe, a letter of credit is considered as decisive as most modes of introduction," said Redclyffe, observing that the good Warden was desirous of knowing with some precision, who and what he was, and feeling that, in the circumstances, he had a right to such knowledge. "Here is mine on a respectable house in London."

The Warden took it, and glanced it over with a slight apologetic bow; it was a credit for a handsome amount in favor of the Honorable Edward Redclyffe, a title that did not fail to impress the Englishman rather favorably towards his new acquaintance, although he happened to know something of their abundance, even so early in the Republic, among the men branded sons of equality. But, at all events, it showed no ordinary ability and energy, for so young a man to have held such position as this title denoted in fiercely contested political struggles of the new democracy.

"Do you know, Mr Redclyffe, that this name is familiar to us, hereabouts?" asked he, with a kindly bow and recognition —"that it is, in fact, the principal name in this neighborhood, and that a family of your name still posseses Oakland Hall— and that this very hospital, where you have happily found shelter, was founded by former representatives of your name? Perhaps you count yourself among their kindred."

"My countrymen are apt to advance claims to kinship with distinguished English families on such slight grounds as to make it ridiculous," said Redclyffe coloring. "I should not choose to follow so absurd an example."

"Well, well, perhaps not," said the Warden, laughing frankly. "I have been amongst you republicans myself, a long while ago, and saw that your countrymen have no adequate idea of the sacredness of pedigrees, and heraldic distinctions, and would change their own names, at pleasure, and vaunt kindred with an English duke on the strength of the assumed one. But I am happy to meet an American gentleman, who looks upon this matter as Englishmen necessarily must. I met with great kindness in your country, Mr Redclyffe, and shall be truly happy if you will allow me an opportunity of returning some small part of the obligation. You are now in a condition for removal to my own quarters, across the quadrangle. I will give orders to prepare an apartment, and you must transfer yourself there by dinner-time."

With this hospitable proposal, so decisively expressed, the Warden took his leave; and Edward Redclyffe had hardly yet recovered sufficient independent force to reject an invitation so put, even were he inclined; but, in truth, the proposal suited well with his views, such as they were, and was moreover backed, it is singular to say, by another by those dreamlike recognitions which had so perplexed him, ever since he found himself in the Hospital. In some previous state of being, the Warden and he had talked together before.

"What is the Warden's name?" he inquired of the old pensioner.

"Hammond," said the old man; "he is a kinsman of the Redclyffe family, himself a man of fortune, and spends more than the income of his Wardenship in beautifying and keeping up the glory of the establishment. He takes great pride in it."

"And he has been in America," said Redclyffe. "How strange! I knew him there. Never was anything so singular as this discovery of old acquaintances where I had reason to suppose myself unknowing and unknown. Unless dear Doctor Grim, or dear little Elsie were to start up and greet me, I know not what may chance next."

Redclyffe took up his quarters in the Warden's house, the next day, and was installed into an apartment that made a picture, such as he had not before seen, of English household comfort. That evening arrived some luggage for which, as soon as he was able to think upon such matters, he had written to order from his agents in London. He was thus established under the good Warden's roof, and, being very attractive of most people's sympathies, soon began to grow greatly in favor with that kindly personage.

When Edward Redclyffe removed from the old pensioner's narrow quarters to the far ampler accommodations of the Warden's house, the latter gentleman was taking his morning exercise on horseback. A servant, however, in a grave livery, ushered him to an apartment, where the new guest was surprised to see some luggage which, two or three days before, Edward had ordered from London, on finding that his stay in this part of the country was likely to be much longer than he had originally contemplated. The sight of these things— the sense which they conveyed that he was an expected and welcome guest—tended to raise the spirits of the solitary wanderer, and made him—

The Warden's abode was an original part of the ancient Hospital, being nearly an entire side of the quadrangle which the whole edifice surrounded; and, for the establishment of a bachelor (such was his new friend's condition) it seemed to Edward Redclyffe abundantly spacious and enviably comfortable. His own chamber had a grave, rich depth, as it were, of serene and time-long garniture, for purposes of repose, convenience, daily and nightly comfort, that it was soothing even to look at. Long accustomed, as Redclyffe had been, to the hasty and rude accommodations, if so they were to be called, of log-huts and pretty, pine-built houses, in the western states of America, life, its daily habits, its passing accommodations, seemed to assume an importance, under these aspects, which it had not worn before; those deep, down beds, those antique chairs, the heavy carpet, the tester and curtains, the stateliness of the old room—they had a charm, as compared with the thin preparation of an American bed chamber, such as Redcliffe had chiefly known them, in the ruder parts of the country, that really seemed to give a more substantial value to life; so much pains had been taken with its modes and appliances, that it looked more solid than before. Nevertheless, there was something in that stately, curtained bed, with the deep gloom within its drapery, so ancient as it was; and suggestions of slumberers there who had long since slumbered elsewhere.

The old servant, whose grave circumspect courtesy was a matter quite beyond Redclyffe's experience, soon knocked at the chamber door, and suggested that the guest might choose to await the Warden's arrival in the library, which was the customary sitting room. Redclyffe assenting, he was ushered into a spacious apartment, lighted by various gothic windows & surrounded with old oaken cases, in which were ranged volumes, most or many which seemed to be coeval with the foundation of the hospital; <rich old bindings> and opening one of them, Redclyffe saw for the first time in his life a genuine book-worm, that ancient form of creature living upon literature; it had gnawed a circular hole, penetrating through perhaps a score of pages of the seldom opened volume, and was still at his musty feast. There was a fragrance of old learning, in this ancient library; a soothing influence, as the American felt, of time-honored ideas, where the strife, novelties, uneasy agitation, conflict, attrition, of unsettled theories, fresh-springing thought, did not attain; a good place to spend a life which should not be agitated with the disturbing element; so quiet, so peaceful; how slowly, without a little wear, would the years pass here. How unlike what he had hitherto known, and was destined to know; the quick, violent struggle of his native country, which had traced lines in his young brow already! How much would be saved, by taking his former existence, not as dealing with things yet malleable, but with fossils, things that had had their life, and now were unchangeable, and recorded here.

At an end of this large room, there was one embowed window, the space near which was curtained off from the rest of the library; and the window being filled with stained glass (most of which seemed old, though there were restorations evidently of modern and much inferior handiwork) there was a rich medium of light, or you might call it a rich glow, according to your mood of mind. Redclyffe soon perceived that this curtained recess was the especial study of his friend, the Warden, and as such was provided with all that modern times had contrived for making an enjoyment out of the perusal of old books; a study table, with every convenience of multifarious devices, a great inkstand, pens; a luxurious study-chair, where thought might merge into repose. To say the truth, there was not, in this retired and thoughtful nook, anything that indicated to Redclyffe that the Warden had been recently engaged in consultation of learned authorities, or in abstruse labor, whether moral, metaphysical, or historic; there was a volume of translations of Mother Goose's melodies into Greek and Latin, printed for private circulation, and with the Warden's name in the title-page; a London newspaper of the preceding day; Lillibulero, Chevy Chase, and other old political ballads; and, what no little amused Redclyffe, the three volumes of a novel from a circulating library; so that Redclyffe came to the conclusion that the good Warden, like many educated men, whose early scholarlike propensities are backed up by the best of opportunities, and all desirable faculties and surroundings, still content themselves with gathering a flower or two instead of attempting the hard toil requisite to raise a crop.

It must not be omitted, that there was a fragrance in the room, which, unlike as the scene was, brought back, through so many years, to Redclyffe's mind, a most vivid reminiscence of poor old Doctor Grim's squalid chamber, with his wild, bearded presence in the midst of it, puffing his everlasting cloud; for here was the same smell of tobacco, and on the mantel piece of a chimney lay a German pipe, and an old silver tobacco-box, into which was wrought the tiger's head and an inscription in black-letter. The Warden had evidently availed himself of one of the chief bachelor sources of comfort. Redclyffe, whose destiny had hitherto, and up to a very recent period, been, to pass a feverishly active life, was greatly impressed by all these tokens of learned ease, a degree of self-indulgence combined with duties enough to quiet an otherwise uneasy conscience, by the consideration that the performer acted a good part in a world where none is entitled to be an unprofitable labourer. He thought within himself, that perhaps his own galvanized country, that seemed to him, a few years since, to offer such a career for an adventurous young man, conscious of native power, had nothing so enticing as such a nook as this, a quiet recess of unchangeable old time, around which the turbulent tide of war eddied, and rushed, but could not disturb it. Here, to be sure, hope, love, ambition, came not; progress came not; but here was—what, just now, the early wearied American could appreciate better than aught else—here was rest.

The fantasy took Edward to imitate the useful labors of the learned Warden, and to make proof whether his own classical erudition—the results of Doctor Grim's tuition, and subsequently that of an American college—had utterly deserted him, by attempting a translation of a few verses of Yankee Doodle; and he was making hopeful progress, when the Warden came in, fresh and rosy from a morning's ride in a keen east wind. He shook hands heartily with his guest, and, though by no means frigid at their former interview, seemed to have developed at once into a kindlier man, now that he had suffered the stranger to cross his threshold and had thus made himself responsible for his comfort.

"I shall take it greatly amiss," said he, "if you do not pick up fast under my roof, and gather a little English ruddiness, moreover, on the walks and rides that I mean to take you. Your countrymen as I saw them are a sallow set; but I think you must have English blood enough in your veins to eke out a ruddy tint, with the help of good English beef and ale, and daily draughts of wholesome English air."

"My cheeks would not have been so very pale," said Etherege laughing, "if an English shot had not deprived me of a good deal of my American blood."

ANCILLARY DOCUMENTS

Note: The following studies are detached memoranda which Hawthorne wrote before or during his composition of the "Ancestral Footstep" sketch and the "Etherege" and "Grimshawe" drafts. For identification they are labeled 1 through 7 (plus a Handlist), but the ordering is not meant to imply that a sequential relationship can be demonstrated. The first four studies may, however, relate to the "Footstep" stage of development for reasons suggested on page 498 below. Study 5 and that portion of the Handlist from "Mrs Ainsworth's . . ." through "Yearnings . . . off." are reproduced from Julian Hawthorne's 1882 transcripts, the originals having apparently not survived.

A paragraph appearing in the English notebooks under date of April 12, 1855, contains such close verbal parallels with the third paragraph of Study 1 that it deserves place here as embodying part of the same embryonic state of the American claimant theme:

> In my Romance, the original emigrant to America may have carried away with him a family secret, whereby it was in his power (had he so chosen) to have brought about the ruin of the family. This secret he transmits to his American progeny, by whom it is inherited throughout

all the intervening generations. At last, the hero of the Romance comes to England, and finds that, by means of this secret, he still has it in his power to procure the downfal of the family. It would be something similar to the story of Meleager, whose fate depended on the firebrand that his mother had snatched out of the flames: (MS, Morgan Library).

Study 1

An American comes over to England, to search after his ancestry; there has been a family history of interest in the new world; and there are traditions with respect to the family in England, at the distance of more than two centuries, which are very dim and interesting. These look wild and strange. Endeavor to give the effect of a man's leaving England 200 years ago, and coming back to see it so changed. The American shall be a person of high rank, who has reached eminence early: a Governor; a congressman, a gentleman; give him the characteristics and imperfections of an American gentleman. He shall, I think, be unmarried. He searches for relatives, burrows in books of records, consults heralds; for there is a misty idea, as in so many cases, that a great estate and perhaps title is due to him. Bring out the American strongly among old English scenes and manners; make all that he sees objective, as it seems to a new American. There must be a young lady, an Englishwoman—to whom, unflinchingly, give English characteristics, as contrasted with the American. She shall turn out to be one of his relatives; he shall find another in a factory person; another descendant of an old family in a groom; another in a rich merchant. There shall be a vein of wildness and romance in the American, at which the English shall smile and be puzzled; and this, too, shall be characteristic of his country. His researches shall produce effects, by bringing to light facts, which neither he himself nor anyone else expected.

Among the personages introduced shall be an American defalcator, or other criminal, of some years ago, who shall be living here in England, either with his family, or in solitude —the latter, I think. Take Schuyler for a model of this figure. One nobleman must likewise be introduced;—yes—a member of the family. The American's researches must bring about results, unexpected by himself, and not such as he had at all aimed at—overturning whatever seemed fixed. The nobleman's title and estate, for instance.

The first emigrant to America (200 years ago) shall have carried with him a family secret, which shall have been retained in the American branch, though latterly it shall have been looked on as an idle tradition. The English heir shall have lost this secret. At the time of the American's appearance in England, the family shall be at some crisis; and by means of this secret, the American shall find himself empowered to influence the result. He shall keep himself unknown to the family—at least, till the denouement. Perhaps he shall decide to let the old family go to ruin; perhaps otherwise.

The scene of an old gentleman walking through the streets, in a state of mania.

STUDY 2

Thus around this American of to-day will be made to diffuse itself a romantic, if not a preternatural interest; and the feelings of the Democrat and Aristocrat will be brought out in all the stronger contrast. There shall have been a wonderment of ages as to what has become of the lost heir of the family; and all sorts of stories shall be told at the firesides about him; and it shall seem, after awhile, as if he had re-appeared in the person of this American—who, also, shall have the feeling that he is the identical one. A murder shall have been committed; a blood-stain, that keeps freshening out of the floor yet, at due times. But then the family secret, partially lost, but to which the American brings the lost part; —what can that be? Something, I am afraid, that has reference to property; no this secret must typify the hereditary disposition of the family. It shall seem as if dead men still were active agents. How? how? how? I don't know, really. Horror!—horror! Mrs Stowe; authoress of "Uncle Tom's Cabin." The American is of course a lawyer, and might too have been a soldier in the Mexican War;—yes, he shall. And since a politician, and governor of a state; and still quite a young man; therefore capable in affairs. He shall by and by feel himself the master of this nobleman's fate; who shall have confided in him what he would not have confided to a countryman of his own. The great gist of the story ought to be the natural hatred of men—and the particular hatred of Americans—to an Aristocracy; at the same time doing a good degree of justice to the aristocratic system by depicting its grand, beautiful, and noble characteristics. At last, I think, the American must have it in his power to put an end to the nobility of the race; and shall do so, not without reluctance and pain. He shall have proof of something, long ago, that shall have given him this power. The scene need not be entirely in England; it can be carried to the Continent;— perhaps back to America. The present nobleman—there shall be something in the past that may have impelled him to a present crime or meanness, unworthy of his rank; and which he shall daily feel. He must die in some way, most probably by suicide. No; there may be some tremendous error, but no petty vice or meanness in his character. I think he should be drawn with a natural generosity and nobleness, doing credit to the best influences of his position; but some misfortune must unavoidably grow out of his position, and ruin him, through the means of the American, who must make amends to the reader's feelings by marrying an Englishwoman, with every prospect of happiness. How'll that do? It may be his daughter that the American marries;—but how shall she be drawn? She can hardly be made the type of the English maiden. The end must be the ruin of the nobleman, at all events, the absorption of his property, the cancelment of his title. Perhaps he shall all along have had a secret knowledge that he is, as a peer, a humbug. I don't make this out.

Study 3

The English and American ideas to be brought strikingly into contrast and contact. The American comes back to England, somewhat with the sense of a wronged person; for there shall have been a tradition of his ancestors' having been driven away with wrong and contumely. He returns to find them in a state of apparently greater prosperity than ever, but yet on the verge of a crisis, which he perhaps discovers through his researches into old records, and estimates by his legal knowledge. There shall, on the other hand, be a tradition in the English family of a vanished heir, who, if he were alive, would take all the land and estates; and this on comparison, shall coincide with the American tradition. It shall be a story told in the castle, as far back as James I'sts reign, with all the mediaeval romance to it; and the American may learn it, at the family-seat, which is a modern mansion built upon the foundation and taking in some of the walls of an old castle. Feeling himself the heir, the American shall consider himself entitled to dispose as he pleases of the estate and houses, and so shall, in exercise of his judgment, let the title and estate pass away. Some terrific action must, at this time, be going on in the English family; greatly in debt; an hereditary madness in the English branch; a gambler, a man on the turf. It must be shown, I think, throughout, that there is an essential difference between English and American character, and that the former must assimilate itself to the latter, if there is to be any union. Throw it into more extravagant romance, and make the coloring deep and sombre, in order to bear it out;—there may be scenes and passages of the strongest reality interspersed. The noble must have some mark upon him; some fatality; something inherited, which shall represent the craft, the bloody force, the wrong, by which the honors of his race have been obtained. The difficulty is, in this state of non-adventurousness, to introduce any crime. I must think and seek for one such as a gentleman and a nobleman can commit.

The nobleman, what is his condition? He has something on his conscience—what? Something that nullifies all his advantages; and it must be something in the common course of things, only made to seem strange by the imaginative associations that I shall cluster about it. A noble outside, but something mean within. With all his grandeur and state, there must be some mean thing that he does, or some mean tendency. I think he should be of one of the old Catholic families of Lancashire. He must do something strange and grotesque, that nobody would expect a noble to do; go as a scissor-grinder about the country; operate as a horse-doctor; in short, live in two entirely different characters at once. There must be some thing in this nobleman's heart, that shall prick him into the wildest extravagances,—he shall walk on the verge of lunacy, and at last step over. Some thing in the state of his affairs that shall compel him to do these things; or else some malignant influence impelling him. Some thing that tends towards murder. But that is an old story. No; there shall be a terrible ridicule and satire in what this nobleman is compelled to do and suffer, that shall become tragic by its grotesque aptitude.

STUDY 4

The ancestor of Chatsworth emigrated to America 200 years ago, being an outlaw from his family, and desiring to conceal his existence from them. He carried with him certain family heirlooms, records, traditions, and especially some fragment of a thing. The first emigrant was a younger son of a noble family; but by the extinction of the elder branch, his descendants have become, at this time, in reality, the heir to the estate and title. In the long lapse of years, however, this looks dreamlike and fabulous; so that, when Chatsworth comes over, he does not really expect anything. He finds his vouchers, his traditions, his hereditary descriptions of the estate, the title &c singularly agreeing with the reality; and, in fact, satisfies himself that he is really the rightful heir. Meanwhile, he has established an acquaintance, or at least, has obtained the facility of looking into the family, of the nobleman. Here will be ample opportunity of giving all the good and picturesque points of English ancestral homes, English rank, and high society; with the American view of them. By and by, through his close and earnest inspection of the family affairs, Chatsworth discovers a secret connected with them—a secret, to which he has the clue by his ancestral traditions—it has lasted all this time, ulcerating into the heart of the family, and the present nobleman, a man of high honor and admirable qualities, is as much distressed by it as any of his ancestors have been. Now here is the rub; and it seems impossible to get over it. It cannot well be something shameful that has happened long ago—a hereditary insanity—a murder—a blue-beard closet—perhaps what was a mere trifle, in the American's traditions, has come in course of ages to be a terrible impending calamity. Some debt then contracted, and never paid off; some claim, the clue of which the American ancestor carried off. Oh, how strange!

A hospital for poor travelers to have been endowed by the family in ancestral times; and Chatsworth, on his first visit to the family home, gets admittance as a poor traveller into this hospital; and there meets with other personages of the story. Here, too, some member of the family might see and talk with him—the heroine, for instance—while visiting the poor people.

STUDY 5

The heirdom is in the wrong line, the American being the right heir. There must have been some frightful family quarrel to have brought about this result.

Traits of family likeness shall be visible in the two branches, but with the differences resulting from the country and education. The Earl shall be familiar with the facts of the family quarrel, but shall deem the lost heir and his descendants long ago extinct; so that he shall be greatly startled by this apparition of a claimant, after 200 years, bringing proofs of his identity, morally satisfactory.

The American family may have passed through all vicissitudes in their two hundred years; he himself shall be a boy of the workhouse perhaps, at any rate a self-made man, and yet the sense of high birth and long descent shall be clear within him. He shall be the rightful heir, but still the gist of the story shall be not to install him in possession of the property.

Study 6

The story opens at Salem; the old house in Charter-street, on the edge of the grave-yard. There dwells an old gentleman, a scholar, a peculiar sort of man, marked by mild eccentricities. He has a young girl in his gloomy old house; and for some unknown reason, he has noticed a boy, the son of poor and obscure parents, and is instructing him in the languages, paying attention to his morals and manners, and bringing out the graces of a fine and noble character, which seem to exist in him. The life in this gloomy old house, of these three persons, should be strikingly presented; with occasional glimpses, out of a window as it were, of the New England life of the little town; done in a homely, vivid way.

The old gentleman is not to be rich, but it is seen in him that he comes of gentle and genial blood; and, in a remarkable way, he shall draw out similar tokens in the boy.

The little girl shall be elvish and sprite-like; but yet the reader's prevailing impression of her shall be of a sweet and kindly creature; she shall be sportive, though the shadow of that old house and at something dark in her lot shall be upon her. She must not be too strongly defined; rather, she starts ever and anon, in a vivid presentment, out of a surrounding vagueness and obscurity. Her relationship or connection with the old gentleman shall not be defined, though he shall often manifest affection and pity for her.

A youthful Arcadian life, bright and sweet, though curtained round by gloom, shall be led by this boy and girl, in the gloomy old house; sporting in the grave yard; hand-in-hand with ghosts.

The old gentleman's chief business shall seem to be of an antiquarian nature, and to hunt up old genealogies, for his own pleasure; and he shall often show a certain family pride, his own family having a historic name, and having been loyalists and sacrificed thereto a large part of their property. In pursuit of this taste, as well as by inheritance, he shall have gathered around him a great deal of curious colonial lore, and also a large variety of articles, interesting from some connection with noted individuals. The effect of all this must be to gather a certain grim atmosphere of mystery round the kindly and genial individual. It is well to present him to the reader as seen through the observations and conjectures of an imaginative boy. He shall also practice experiments in natural science, and shall have a tincture of medical knowledge from having been originally intended for a doctor. This quaint and queer household shall, in the narrative, be continually brought into relief by contrasts with the practical, modern life about them.

It shall be surmised, from casual observations, and from certain incidents, that the young girl is not a native of New England; perhaps there may be room to suppose that she was born in Old England. Some dim reminiscences she shall have of other modes of life; other scenery; of old, ivy-grown edifices; and there shall be a vague pride in her character, such as the English have of themselves; a looking down upon the Americans, a holding herself above them.

The boy shall appear to be a dependant in the bounty of the old gentleman; yet, whenever he seeks to express his gratitude, the latter shall decline, seeming to feel pain at such expressions.

In this early part of the Romance hints must be given of the family history on which the Romance hinges; and the boy shall have a strong passion to go to England to search out certain riddles that propound themselves to him.

When a sufficient impression on the reader has been made, and a good deal of mystery compelled into a cloud, the old gentleman shall suddenly die; and the other two characters shall vanish for a term of years.

This part of the Romance closes, & after an interval of many years, the story is resumed. A gentleman is introduced as rambling in England, scarcely a gentleman he might seem; being in very humble guise. But the reader shall be suffered to perceive that this is the boy whom he already knows. In the interim, he has gone through great vicissitudes; the old gentleman left him the means of obtaining an education, and he began life as a political adventurer, and met with great success. Still a very young man, he has been in Congress, has displayed brilliant eloquence, has been disappointed in some aspiration, and has thrown up public life in disgust with the abuse, the brutal violence with which it is carried on.

Under these circumstances, in the idleness and collapse after great excitement, he has remembered the old gentleman's brief hints and vague expressions, and has come to England, he hardly knows for what—to search out the family-abode. He is giving rein to the imaginative tendency which he used to indulge in his boyhood, with the more enjoyment because the hard, hot practical life of America has so long made his life arid & dusty. And so he goes wandering about England on foot, guided by the wildest signs, which he will not acknowledge to himself as being his guiding signals. In this way, he by and by comes to an old town, where there is a hospital; but he is robbed about this time, and left for dead, and taken into the hospital; where several people, who are of use in the succeeding parts of the Romance, immediately group themselves around him.

In the first place, however, I think he should be removed into the Warden's house, who proves to be a clergyman of the church of England, a little stiff at first, but genial and gentlemanly, living in comfort, a bachelor. Of him, he learns much about the constitution of the hospital; and when he gets well enough to go out, he becomes acquainted with one of the pensioners, a reserved, stately sort of an old man, who has evidently seen better days.

Before leaving the old house by the grave-yard, it must be mentioned that, one day, two strangers—apparently from foreign parts—come, and are very earnest to find a certain ancient grave. They seek for it, apply to the old gentleman for information; he seems not exactly surprised to meet them. They retire, at last, and as it should seem, without success. Afterwards, the boy meets one or both (if there be more than one) of these men, in England.

Among the old gentleman's pictures, is one of a man of striking appearance, but in the habit of a bond-servant—coarse, and perhaps with some badge of servitude upon him. Afterwards, in England, the boy finds the same face, but in an old family-portrait gallery, and splendidly apparelled. He inquires about this latter portrait, and finds the original had mysteriously disappeared. Perhaps his guardian tells him the servitor's portrait is the likeness of an ancestor of his. It might afterwards come out, that he had been transported after the battle of Worcester.

The brother of the American old gentleman was a man of great ability, whose financial operations had been on a vast scale; so that even national events had depended on his action. Possibly, the action of the story may be thrown back fifty years; and he be a partaker in Burr's treasonable projects. Having had the direction of great affairs, here he is in this seclusion; and in his forced idleness, he takes upon himself to influence everything in a secret manner; by a touch as it were with the remnants of his faculty; and in this way, he intermeddles with our hero's fortunes; more especially as he once ruined his father in America. He shall have made a great impression of sagacity on the Warden, and on all that come in contact with him. As of a man who knew the world and how to guide it, though now so retired and fallow. Or he may have been a wild political reformer, having run into all extravagances of Pantisocracy, & now ending his days in dependence on this queer incident of feudal and old-world customs.

Study 7

The old hereditary Hospital for poor people—to be described from a real scene. Etheridge has the tradition of it dimly in his memory, and he finds it, perhaps, more perfectly realized than any other of his traditionary reminiscences. He is taken ill here; and, being temporarily without resources, he obtains admission into the hospital. Here, perhaps, he has his first interview with the heroine. Possibly, he may already have become known to his relatives by rumor, and may be an object of interest to them. But, at all events, this opening may enable him to get acquainted with the localities and persons of the family, in a way he otherwise could not, and thus he shall see them in a picturesque, and in some sense remote, at the same time as in an intimate way; wandering all round their domicile, sometimes admitted into it, but still as of an alien order. The gentleman may perhaps be seen occasionally through his disguise. Sometimes he may surprise the inhabitants by his knowledge of circumstances respecting the family supposed to be known only to themselves, or by his explanation of what had been immemorially a mystery to those most interested in it. In this way, I think he shall become acquainted with the nobleman himself. Afterwards, they shall meet in society, the American in his own distinguished position. Perhaps he may revisit the ancestral seat, as a guest, or possibly there may be a coolness between him and the nobleman. Etheredge must of course be distant and haughty, and their intercourse will be embarrassed by the terms on which they first met, and by what then passed between them.

Etheredge, after his introduction to the family through his hospital experience, might be represented as searching into old records at Chester;—at the chapter house in the Cathedral there;—or wherever deeds are registered. The American must, in his own consciousness, and also in the conviction of the nobleman, be the rightful heir of the estate and the earliest title; but his democracy, and his generosity, and a feeling of shame, must prevail with him not to claim his rights. The general tenor of the book must illustrate the sympathy and the difference between Americans & Englishmen.

Perhaps his second meeting with the nobleman may be at a Mayor's, or other public dinner, where the American is called up to speak to a toast, as a distinguished politician.

A Handlist

NOTE: With the exception of two references to 1838 passages in his American notebooks, Hawthorne keyed this list to dates and occasional page references to entries in his English journals of 1853–1857. The subjects can be followed out in Randall Stewart's edition of *The English Notebooks* (New York and London, 1941), where page numbering of the several manuscript volumes is inserted.

Hawthorne made errors in his jottings, and the handlist is here emended by corrections entered in square brackets; such corrections preceded by an asterisk are from the transcript by Julian Hawthorne, where errors may represent his misreadings or his father's slips.

Description of City Plate—March 26th [25]   '56
A thatched cottage, June 17th   "
Vagabond Musicians &c. June 20th   '54
Growth of hair in the grave, page 164   '54
Woman in hand-wagon Novr 14th   [53] '54
The profane swearer in Lancashire, whose horrible fit
    of swearing caused a plane-tree before his house to
    wither away.
Paralytic old lady. Page 257 [258]—May 22d   '57
Southport Police Station   March 1st   '57
Character of Mr. Scarisbrooke.
                March 1st [para. preceding]   '57
Coroner's office   Page 200 ——   57
Inspector of Nuisances—page 194   [56] '57
Warwick & Hospital &c   October 30   '57
Whitnash Church   Novr 8th   '57
The Bloody Footstep. August 25th   '55
Kirk Braddon, August 10th   '54
Judge Platt. August 21   '54
St John's Church   August 24   54
Rhuddlan Castle, Sept 20th   '54
Welsh Cottage — do.   do.
Fat women   Sept 26th   54
    (Mem. Look for an earlier passage on this subject)
Capt Gibson—October 19th   54
Crazy old man in the street Novr 14th   54
Tranmere Hall—March 7th [4]   '55
Mrs Ainsworth's Bloody Footstep April 7th   [*55] 1858

William D[*awson]'s grave clothes

                     Aug. 18th [*May 15, '55]   '58

Origin of latter.

Magistracy	June 2nd	1855
Font of Bebbington Church	June 11th	55
Boy with accordion	do.	do.
Whitnash Church	do 24th	do
St Mary's Hall (& elsewhere)	July 1st	do.
Leicester Hospital etc.	do 2nd	do

Little dog snuffer   Aug. 11th [*para. preceding]   1838

Beggar buried, and dug up for his belt of treasure   1838

Yearnings of an Anglo-American to mix his race
again with the old stream from which he has
branched off.

American lady in Liverpool almshouse unknown, Septr 12th
'53

Man with the plague burying himself Octr 22^d '53

Claimants of Booth estate—royal blood Decr 31st '53

Eastham church-yard April 3^d '54

Hospital, May 20th '54. Do. Novr 16th '55

Length of English day, June 17th '54

Musicians June 20th '54

English stone-walls, & parasitical growth, July 13th '55

English eating, March 6th '56

Loving cup, March 25th '56

Pew in Battle Church April 1st '56

Rusty arrow-head, dug up in the church yard of
Radford Semele July 2^d '55

EDITORIAL APPENDIXES

HISTORICAL COMMENTARY

ALMOST from the day in 1853 when he took up
English residence as the American consul at Liverpool, Hawthorne had the idea of writing a narrative
concerning the relations of America with England. Within
two months of his arrival he was seeking his own ancestral
roots, and asked James T. Fields, his Boston publisher, to
find out "what part of England the original William Hawthorne came from. . . . Of all things, I should like to find a
grave-stone in one of those old churchyards, with my own
name on it; although, for myself, I should wish to be buried
in America. The graves are too devilish damp here."[1]

Hawthorne's quest was unsuccessful, but his imagination
nourished the fantasy of an American inspired by traditionary
accounts of his English forebears to seek out his ancestral
home, to which he might now prove to be the heir. The
central motivating force in the fictions known as *The Ancestral Footstep* and *Doctor Grimshawe's Secret* was the theme
of the American claimant, its archetypal character reinforced
by Hawthorne's consular encounters with compatriots impelled by just such a dream. And his own experience suggested an inescapable sense of continuity in both history and
geography:

[1] September 16, 1853, MS, Huntington Library.

My ancestor left England in 1635. I return in 1853. I sometimes feel as if I myself had been absent those two hundred and eighteen years—leaving England just emerging from the feudal system, and finding it on the verge of Republicanism. It brings the two far separated points of time very closely together, to view the matter thus.[2]

Hawthorne's original impulse may have been to write a narrative which would emphasize the common ground between England and America. But the longer he lived abroad, the more he came to resent English condescension, though never himself its victim. The press and the people, he realized, took delight in ridiculing American manners, American speech, and even American achievements. Not unnaturally his defenses took the form of critical comment mingled with sensitive appreciation, and he considered the institutions that preserved English cathedrals and other monuments of the past "musty." "The spirit of my Puritan ancestors was mighty in me," he wrote at York on Easter Sunday, 1857, "and I did not wonder at their being out of patience with all this mummery."[3] He was regularly distressed by the social inequalities he saw in a country prospering in trade and finance. England would some day have to face the issue of her centuries-old demarcations between worker and aristocrat, slum-dweller and businessman, pauper and lord of the manor. "The time will come, sooner or later," he wrote to W. D. Ticknor, "when the old fellow [John Bull] will look to us for his salvation."[4]

He filled his journals with such comments and judgments, intending them "for the side-scenes, and back-grounds, and exterior adornment, of a work of fiction."[5] By early 1855 he was meditating an English romance, which would be "all the

[2] *The English Notebooks by Nathaniel Hawthorne,* ed. Randall Stewart (New York and London, 1941), p. 92.

[3] Ibid., p. 451.

[4] February 16, 1855, MS, Berg Collection, New York Public Library.

[5] Nathaniel Hawthorne, *Our Old Home* (Centenary Edition, 1970), pp. 3–4.

better for ripening slowly." [6] In April of that year he set
down a tentative outline:

> In my Romance, the original emigrant to America may
> have carried away with him a family secret, whereby it
> was in his power (had he so chosen) to have brought about
> the ruin of the family. This secret he transmits to his
> American progeny, by whom it is inherited throughout
> all the intervening generations. At last, the hero of the
> Romance comes to England, and finds that, by means of
> this secret, he still has it in his power to procure the downfal
> of the family. It would be something similar to the story
> of Meleager, whose fate depended on the firebrand that
> his mother had snatched out of the flames. [7]

Defining the secret and surrounding it with plausibly moti-
vated action would pose great difficulty for Hawthorne when
he attempted to draft his English romance. Meanwhile, during that same April of 1855 he was struck by a suggestion
that eventually helped him to focus his ideas about the past
and the present, England and America, and even his rumina-
tions on his own family heritage. He dined at the home of
Liverpool friends, Mr. and Mrs. J. P. Heywood, where he
met Mr. and Mrs. Peter Ainsworth of Smithills Hall near
Bolton-le-Moors. At some point in the dinner-table conversation Mrs. Ainsworth told a legend connected with Smithills:

> The tradition is that a certain martyr, in Bloody Mary's
> time, being examined before the then occupant of the
> Hall, and committed to prison, stamped his foot in earnest
> protest against the injustice with which he was treated.
> Blood issued from his foot, which slid along the stone
> pavement of the hall, leaving a long footmark printed in
> blood; and there it has remained ever since, in spite of the
> scrubbings of all after generations. [8]

[6] Hawthorne to Ticknor, January 19, 1855, MS, Berg Collection, New
York Public Library.
[7] *English Notebooks*, p. 107.
[8] Ibid., p. 106.

The following evening Hawthorne, trying to verify the legend, read in a county history of Lancashire that "the footstep is not a bloody one, but is a slight cavity or inequality in the surface of the stone, somewhat in the shape of a man's foot with a peaked shoe." The martyr was George Marsh, a Nonconformist curate who had been examined at Smithills for heresy, tried, condemned, and burned at the stake in April, 1555, just three hundred years earlier.[9]

On the Ainsworths' invitation, Hawthorne went in August to visit Smithills Hall. His host conducted him around the grounds and through the manor house. At one of the rear entrances Hawthorne stopped to examine a flagstone. "This miraculous footprint is still extant," he noted. "It is . . . a stone two or three feet square, set among similar ones, that seem to have been worn by the tread of many generations. The footprint is a dark-brown stain in the smooth gray surface of the flag-stone." Aware that the stone might have come from the earth bearing that discoloration—the bloodstain was to him "all a humbug"—he concluded: "At any rate, the legend is a good one."[10] Indeed, it laid such a spell on Hawthorne that he built the several versions of his American-claimant narrative around the motif and introduced it incidentally into the two other unfinished romances.

Meantime, although he did not consider himself a good sightseer, he continued to fill his journals with minute accounts of his travels about England, observing the countryside in all its spring and summer loveliness, shrewdly assessing the many varieties of English character he encountered.

9 Ibid. The substance of Hawthorne's description along with the "peaked shoe" detail establishes the source as Edward Baines, *The History of the County Palatine and Duchy of Lancashire* (London, 1836), III, 46.

More than a decade before, Hawthorne had recorded a story idea exploiting roughly the same motif: "The print in blood of a naked foot to be traced through the street of a town" (*The American Notebooks* [Centenary Edition, 1973], p. 239).

10 *English Notebooks*, pp. 194–95.

He tried vainly to capture the impressiveness of cathedral architecture but was more immediately struck by parish churches in decay, their surrounding tombstones overgrown with lichens and moss. If he became impatient in art galleries, he was responsive to ritual surviving from medieval times in civic banquets and festivals. He visited an orphanage and went twice to Leicester's Hospital, an almshouse where old men dozed in the sunshine. At the British Museum he saw a spider as large as a saucer. Much trivia, but also many important perceptions, edged with skepticism, lay ready for him in his notebooks when he should turn to them.

But that would not be immediately, for at the end of 1857 when Hawthorne and his family were preparing to journey to Italy he bundled up his notebooks and entrusted them to his young friend Henry Bright for safekeeping during his absence.[11] Even without his journals at hand, however, his English romance was vividly shaping itself so that before he had been three months in Rome he began to sketch a narrative. We cannot be sure precisely how he proceeded, but the untitled documents that have survived include a manuscript written in April and May, 1858, which his daughter and son-in-law published as *The Ancestral Footstep;* and two longer drafts of a related treatment, written in Concord probably in 1861 and edited by Julian Hawthorne into a composite text that he titled *Doctor Grimshawe's Secret.*[12] In addition, there are eight detached memoranda of a leaf or two each which cannot be precisely dated: seven studies written before or during the composition of the three fic-

[11] Julian Hawthorne, *Nathaniel Hawthorne and His Wife* (Boston, 1884), II, 168–69; James T. Fields, *Yesterdays with Authors* (Boston, 1872), pp. 81–82.

[12] To distinguish the three manuscripts from their published versions, the Centenary editors have adopted as identifying titles "The Ancestral Footstep," "Etherege," and "Grimshawe"—the two latter named for the doctor in the respective drafts. Although the choice of Etherege-Redclyffe—the names of the American claimant—might be more appropriate, it has seemed justifiable not to cast off all linkage with the long-familiar *Grimshawe* title.

tional manuscripts and a Handlist of matters keyed to the English notebooks.

The studies, here labeled 1 through 7 for identification and ordered by the Centenary editors on the basis of inconclusive internal evidence, emphasize the English scenes of the romance. Hitherto they have all been associated with the 1861 manuscripts, but there is nothing in Studies 1 through 4 that could not relate equally well to the "Ancestral Footstep" sketch. The fact that Studies 1 and 2 were written on paper bearing Liverpool watermarks (plus a watermark date of 1853 on one leaf) invites speculation that Hawthorne might have begun to prepare his memoranda in England. There are enough verbal similarities between the April, 1855, notebook plot outline quoted just above and the third paragraph of Study 1 (page 474) to suggest that Hawthorne almost surely wrote this study with the journal open before him (as the Handlist required). This supports its possible composition in England and rules out its composition in Italy when the English notebooks were in Henry Bright's custody. The other studies Hawthorne might have written in Italy, and all of them could date from after his return to America in 1860. None of these possibilities can be dismissed, although affinities with the structure of "The Ancestral Footstep," particularly the assumption of an English setting throughout, may strengthen the case for early composition of Studies 1 and 2, and perhaps Studies 3 and 4 as well.[13]

What we do know is that shortly after Hawthorne brought his household to Rome he wrote "The Ancestral Footstep"

[13] An argument against associating the Liverpool-paper studies with the 1850s is that in the middle of Study 2 there appears the name of Harriet Beecher Stowe, who was a fellow passenger on the ship that brought the Hawthornes back to America in June, 1860. But Hawthorne's bare reference to her as "authoress of 'Uncle Tom's Cabin'" seems to imply no more than all the world knew, unless it were to suggest some connection between that book and the motif of continued influence of the dead that the context supplied.

as a series of diary entries in a copybook reserved for that purpose. The initial segment is dated April 1, 1858, but the opening sentence contains transition words that imply an earlier beginning, as does the fact that the first two leaves of the notebook have been cut out. The next entries are dated April 13, 14, and 27. Finally on May 2 he got under way in earnest and wrote daily (except for May 8) until May 19, when he recapitulated the plot he had been sketching but did not bring it to a clear conclusion.[14] By this time he was about to quit Rome for the more healthful summer climate of Florence and necessarily laid aside his manuscript. Moreover, his imagination had been quickened some weeks earlier by seeing the Faun of Praxiteles in the sculpture gallery of the Capitol; he noted its story possibilities at once and during the summer he spent several weeks working out the first stages of *The Marble Faun*, perhaps in a form resembling that of the "Ancestral Footstep" manuscript.[15] In any event, before returning to Rome in the autumn he wrote Fields that he had planned two romances, "one or both of which I could have ready for the press in a few months if I were either in England or America." [16] Italy was not, he felt, a good place to work, but despite the distractions of Rome and the family's anxiety over daughter Una's severe illness, Hawthorne wrote steadily through the winter of 1858–59. He did not return to his English romance but instead prepared a draft of the *Faun* story, which he put in final form during the following fall in England.

With the genesis of *The Marble Faun* in mind, we can look upon the "Ancestral Footstep" sketch as especially sig-

[14] On days when he worked at the romance Hawthorne continued brief daily entries in his pocket diary but suspended his discursive Italian journal except on April 27 and May 9 and 12, when he made entries in both journal and copybook. Neither the journal nor the pocket diary contains any reference to the romance.

[15] See *The Marble Faun* (Centenary Edition, 1968), pp. xxi–xxii. None of the initial *Faun* sketching is known to have survived.

[16] September 3, 1858, MS, Huntington Library.

nificant, for it is the only surviving document that illustrates a stage in composition between brief studies—chiefly plot skeletons—and fully developed drafts. Something of comparable length must have emerged from his six weeks' work in Florence, and we can only speculate whether Hawthorne's earlier romances had followed the same gestation pattern. What we have in the "Footstep" manuscript shows that a generation before Mark Twain, Hawthorne was exploring the theme of the American claimant that he would embody more elaborately in the later "Etherege" and "Grimshawe" drafts. Here, however, he was only beginning to discover some of his major problems of motivation and resolution.[17]

The opening sentence plunges us into the midst of Middleton's quest for his family roots: "He had now been searching long in those rich portions of England, where he would most have wished to find the object of his pursuit." He is accompanied by an old man, successively named Rothermel, Wentworth, and Hammond, who proves to be a link between past and present—the knowledgeable guide possessed of

[17] The plot outline common to all three stages of development follows the form of the embryonic 1855 journal entry and the slightly amplified statements in Studies 1 and 2: the American claimant discovering his ancestral roots in England, establishing his right to inherit, and exposing the villainy of a false proprietor. Study 1 assembles the chief personages and sketches a few plot details, but Hawthorne has not yet decided whether the American will bring the "old family . . . to ruin." Study 2 particularizes the American's legal and political career, stresses the thematic importance of the contrast between democratic and aristocratic traditions, and introduces the "blood-stain" without elaboration. The nobleman is to lose his estate and title. To assuage "the reader's feelings," the American will marry an Englishwoman, perhaps the nobleman's daughter, but she must not be "unflinchingly" English as Study 1 prescribed. Throughout these memoranda Hawthorne is perplexed to define the family secret by which the American can control events. Study 3 also explores further the contrasts between American and British civilization, and Study 4 introduces the hospital or almshouse. From this point on, the studies contain details reflected in the "Etherege" and "Grimshawe" drafts but not in the "Footstep" sketch, such as the hero's workhouse background (Study 5), a Salem starting point for the story, with a doctor to dominate the American scenes (Study 6), and fixing on the name "Etheredge" for the claimant (Study 7).

mysterious affinities to America yet perhaps English also, as is his daughter Alice. Add the manor house with a bloody footstep on one of its thresholds and a sinister proprietor in residence, and we have the principal ingredients that Hawthorne manipulates as the story takes form. Pemberton Manor becomes Smithills Hall, the property that may rightfully belong to Middleton. The occupant Squire Eldredge is a simple English bully who dies accidentally by his own hand early in the story, after which Hawthorne recasts his role as a continuing central figure, emphasizing an Italianate personality, alien, devious, coolly vengeful. And the action is punctuated by dialogues on the common ground between England and America versus their cultural incompatibility.

The basic plot brings Middleton to the spot from which his ancestors had emigrated to America. His twofold concern is then to determine whether he can prove that he is the true heir and, if so, whether he shall wish to forsake his American freedoms and become an Englishman or return home with Alice as a new Adam and Eve. Because Hawthorne was in process of working out many details of his story line, it is not surprising that he should interrupt his narrative with memoranda such as "abstract of the plot" in the April 14 segment. On four other occasions he summarized "Present aspect of the story" or "As the story looks now," in each instance trying to devise plot details and define character traits that would advance the action plausibly.[18] Tone, too, combining the tragic and "the gentler pathetic," he recognized was an important key: "If I could but write one central scene in this vein, all the rest of the Romance would readily arrange itself around that nucleus." Particularly troublesome was the nature of a family secret Middleton was to discover and thereby establish his claim to the estate; Hawthorne groped for a solution here and continued to

[18] The five meditative passages in "The Ancestral Footstep" occur on pages 10–11, 49–53, 57–58, 68–69, 79–89.

worry the problem as long as he struggled over the American claimant theme.

He terminated his sketching on May 17, 18, and 19, with several pages of plot notations: Eldredge to discover Middleton's rivalry and to die in trying to dispatch him; events somehow to duplicate those of two centuries earlier; Middleton to inherit and renounce the estate; Hammond to act as catalyst; and so on. In contemplating an introduction for his story he noted that he could draw on his consular experiences for a picture of Americans obsessed with a fantasy of inheriting English property. One such claimant he should single out and describe "with touches that shall puzzle the reader to decide whether it is not an actual portrait." Then the Romance itself should follow, presented "half seriously" as the adventure of a young American in search of his hereditary home. A final paragraph rehearsed the whole plot up to the point at which "things shall ripen themselves" for Eldredge's attempt on Middleton's life. The sketch stops short of a resolution except for Hawthorne's earlier hint at a victory for American values and a renunciation of the English inheritance.

For all its skeletal quality, the "Ancestral Footstep" sketch contains almost every element of the English portion of the subsequent drafts, together with hints for the yet unsketched American scenes. Of equal importance, Hawthorne had already begun to discover the difficulties of motivating the action. He was anxiously seeking an organic role for the bloody footstep and was experimenting with several possible relationships between the old pensioner Hammond and the lord of the manor. When he took up the story again after returning to Concord in 1860, he would alter the proportions and reconstitute the cast of characters but the central plot core would remain.

II

We can assign no certain dates to Hawthorne's new attempt to produce his English romance, but the likeliest period is a time span between July 24, 1860, when he finished an essay on Burns for the *Atlantic,* and about a year later, when he wrote a second article "Near Oxford" in the series eventually gathered into *Our Old Home.* During the autumn of 1860 he was distracted by carpenters busily enlarging the Wayside. "I have at present no leisure, opportunity, nor seclusion, for literary pursuits; having turned myself almost out of doors for the sake of repairing my house," he wrote on October 16.[19] The construction of the tower room that was to be his study was prolonged till the end of the year. "I have been very idle since my return to America," he wrote to his London friend Francis Bennoch on December 17, "but am now meditating a new Romance, which ought to be the most elevated of my productions, since I shall write it in the sky-parlour of my new tower."[20] During this period, if not earlier, Hawthorne probably set down some of the detached memoranda, particularly Study 6, which introduces the figure of the (unnamed) doctor and outlines a new opening section against a Salem background, and Study 7, in which the American claimant's name Etheredge-Etheridge first appears.

By February 16, he resumed his old winter work routine and confided to Ticknor; "I spend two or three hours a day in my sky-parlor, and duly spread a quire of paper on my desk, but no very important result has followed, thus far." His familiar tone of self-deprecation carried over into the next

[19] Hawthorne to J. R. Gilmore, MS, John Hopkins University.
[20] MS, University of Virginia.

sentence: "Perhaps, however, I shall have a new Romance ready, by the time New England becomes a separate nation—a consummation I rather hope for than otherwise."[21] It is possible to support that at this time Hawthorne had written about half the first draft of his story, if one assumes that a reference on page 220 to James Buchanan as President was penned before Lincoln's inauguration on March 4, 1861. What we do know is that over the next few months Hawthorne worked successively at the "Etherege" and "Grimshawe" drafts, abandoning the latter not far from the midpoint of the plot. We also know that by the autumn of 1861 he had turned his attention to the immortality theme and was preparing to write *Septimius*. Thus, although he left very few direct clues, the wisps of evidence suggest that "Etherege" and "Grimshawe" occupied him principally during the first six or eight months of 1861.

The two drafts represent a marked expansion of the "Ancestral Footstep" sketch, with an opening American section set in the childhood of the protagonist and characters' names changed. Also new is an elderly doctor who would provide an imperfectly developed link between nineteenth-century America and seventeenth-century England. The first draft begins, as in Study 6, with old Dr. Etherege and his wards Ned and Elsie, who live in a gloomy, cobwebby house overlooking a Salem graveyard. Their backgrounds and relationships are shadowy, though the boy seems to be a foundling (Study 5) and the girl a niece; the doctor is somehow exiled from an English family connection, and Ned's dreams are haunted by fantasies of England and a bloody footstep. The doctor may possess a secret that bears upon a hereditary title and estate, a mystery heightened by the visit of Mountford, a London lawyer.

After only a few pages Hawthorne faced fundamental plot problems and he interrupted his narrative to record possible

[21] MS, Berg Collection, New York Public Library.

solutions, much as he had done in "The Ancestral Footstep."
Nine times he did so in the "Etherege" draft—three such
interruptions occurring before the doctor's death ended the
American section of the story. His colloquies were brief but
not conclusive, and in the third of them his bewilderment
was evident: "There is still a want of something, which I
can by no means get at"—a note he was to sound more poig-
nantly as he proceeded.

The story resumes some years after Dr. Etherege's death;
Ned Etherege has come to England in search of family connections that the doctor's papers contained hints of, and after
an accident he finds himself lodged in an almshouse for
elderly pensioners. From this point the action follows the
Middleton-Alice-Eldredge plot of "The Ancestral Footstep"
with considerable variation of scenes involving virtually no
recopying, and with a shadowy conclusion. Etherege makes
the acquaintance of the villainous Brathwaite, whose estate
may be Etherege's by rights. He visits Brathwaite Hall, is
honored at a banquet, is kidnapped, and, through the agency
of Elsie and the old pensioner, is released in a confused scene
that reveals the pensioner as the true heir.[22]

Between the American and English sections of the story
Hawthorne had stopped to write some 2,200 words fleshing
out the entire plot. This was the fourth meditative passage,
the most extensive up to that point, and on five later occasions
he interrupted the narrative for even longer recapitulations,
peppered with questions to which he seldon found answers.

[22] Hawthorne drew up a Handlist of English notebook passages with
the second half of his story evidently in mind, but he found use for only
a handful of items—thatched cottage, growth of hair in a grave, Whitnash
church, the bloody footstep, Leicester Hospital, the Lancashire swearer, the
loving-cup ceremony. He did, however, mine the notebooks for small
touches not included in his list—comments, for instance, on English fruit,
county histories, public speakers, an old yew with hollow trunk, "Honorable" as a title, ivy encircling a church spire. The list was not significantly
used for the essays comprising *Our Old Home*, aside from three or four
topics common to both books. The same may be said for *Septimius Felton*,
with which G. P. Lathrop associated the list (*Complete Works*, 1883,
VII, 408).

His attempts to account for the doctor or the Italianate villain or the old pensioner or the goals of Ned's quest erupted into skepticism bordering on despair. "All this amounts to just nothing. I don't advance a step." "I can't possibly make this out, though it keeps glimmering before me." " 'Twont do. Oh, heavens!" "What unimaginable nonsense!" More than a quarter of the draft was made up of his soliloquies on plot management, in addition to numerous brief suggestions interpolated in margins and at paragraph ends.[23]

"Try back again" had more than once been Hawthorne's command to himself at an impasse, and he made just such a fresh start in a second draft, the bulk of which expanded the American scenes and pointed up the role of the doctor. He had scarcely begun to rework the English episodes when he broke off, whether from loss of interest or because he wished to pursue the new *Septimius* theme cannot be determined. That he was uneasy and often dissatisfied with the revision is evidenced by the fact that it contains sixty-nine of Hawthorne's interpolated notes to himself (as against forty-six in the first draft). The handwriting is more cramped and careless than before, and alterations were unusually frequent—cancels, interlineations, new phraseology superimposed on wiped-out matter, plus directions for rearranging sentences, paragraphs, or larger units.

Again he shifted names of persons and places. Dr. Etherege was now Ormskirk, giving way to Grimshawe after a few pages. Ned when fully identified became Edward Redclyffe. A new character, the schoolmaster Seymour, later assumed the name of Colcord. Elsie and Mr. Mountford continued unchanged, and so did Hannah except for the adjective "crusty" now usually applied to her. The name Hammond

23 The nine meditative passages in the "Etherege" draft appear on pages 98–99, 114–15, 115–17, 122–28, 195–208, 218–34, 262–69, 285–93, 323–35. The "Grimshawe" draft contains only one such extended memorandum, on pages 440–41.

· 504 ·

appeared in the "Footstep" sketch and in both "Etherege" and "Grimshawe" drafts but was associated with a different character in each: first a hospitaller (the name having evolved from Rothermel and Wentworth), then an English agent of Dr. Etherege, and finally the warden of the old men's home. The estate to which the American is drawn was Pemberton Manor and Smithills Hall initially, and in the two latter drafts successively Brathwaite and Oakland Hall.[24]

The doctor's house pictured the Peabody home in Salem adjacent to the Charter Street cemetery, although the doctor is not modeled after Hawthorne's father-in-law but probably after a minor English painter, Seymour Kirkup, whose studio Hawthorne visited in Florence and there found material for a long notebook entry on the strange domicile that included a little girl whom the old man called his daughter. The spiders owed something to a visit to the British Museum, but perhaps more to those that abounded at Montauto, the Hawthorne's 1858 Florentine villa.[25] Edward Etherege-Redclyffe (the name Chatsworth appears only in Study 4) evolved from an English workhouse boyhood that Hawthorne proposed in Study 5,[26] and in Study 6 he outlined the education

[24] Several names here are reminiscent. Ormskirk was a village to which Hawthorne once walked when the family was living at Southport in 1856–57; Smithills Hall was the Ainsworths' estate associated with the legend of the bloody footstep; Mountford recalls a Unitarian clergyman of that name whom Hawthorne knew in Liverpool; Middleton, Pemberton, Radcliffe, and Grimshaw were Lancashire place or personal names, and Pemberton was also the middle name of John P. Heywood, in whose home the Hawthornes dined with Henry Bright, the Heywoods' nephew. Hannah may owe something to Hannah Lord, a distant relative who was a family servant in Hawthorne's youth. And Etherege was a surname which Hawthorne had used in an 1838 sketch, "Sylph Etherege."

[25] Lathrop, "History of Hawthorne's Last Romance," p. 454; *English Notebooks,* p. 610; Rose H. Lathrop, *Memories of Hawthorne* (Boston, 1897), pp. 403–4.

[26] He might have been recalling "a wretched, pale, half-torpid little thing" whom he had taken into his arms at the West Derby Workhouse (*English Notebooks,* pp. 275–76), but he described the experience in such distasteful terms that the child bears no relation to the gifted Ned of his romance.

and nurture of the youngster in the doctor's house, his adult
career in public life, his withdrawal in disappointment. The
motifs are never much particularized, but they very loosely
parallel the career of his friend Franklin Pierce, who achieved
political success including the presidency, only to be repu-
diated for renomination and cast aside by his own party.

Despite the linkages with real life, however, the tale
Hawthorne wished to tell receded into the shadows. Instead
of exploring the differences between democratic America and
class-bound England as he had originally intended, it became
an old-fashioned gothic romance filled with creaky machinery
that he could never manage. The story line was never satisfactory, no matter how often he rehearsed it: the compelling
quality of a moral center that could give unity to *The Scarlet
Letter* or animate *The House of the Seven Gables* was lacking here. It was his search for an elusive core of meaning
that left Hawthorne baffled and ultimately defeated. After
his three attempts he laid the manuscripts aside.[27] The
paradoxes of contemporary England he found he could treat
in familiar essays, and the successful creative work of his last
years is largely embodied in *Our Old Home*.

III

Sometime after Hawthorne's death, his widow Sophia
turned her attention to the unfinished fictional narratives.
Her glosses in the "Ancestral Footstep" manuscript show that
she had examined it in detail, but if she went further no evidence is known to have survived. She seems to have divided
the labor of copying the "Etherege" and "Grimshawe" material. She herself undertook the first draft and transcribed five

[27] In the preface to *Our Old Home*, p. 4, he described the "abortive
project" and confessed his failure .

manuscript leaves, to "mankind." (Centenary, p. 107).[28] Her son Julian began to copy the second draft. His surviving transcript, so smoothly inscribed that it probably represents a recopying of an initial effort, covered the first third of the draft from the "Second Chapter," as he called it (Centenary, p. 351), to "was done accordingly" (p. 386). The heading on his initial page "Chapter First" is followed by a bracketed note "This chapter is missing. J. H." Julian left gaps for words or phrases he could not deciper, some of which his mother entered in the transcript; a few supplied words appear to be in another hand and some gaps remain unfilled.[29]

The two transcripts were most probably prepared between October, 1868, and August, 1870, while Mrs. Hawthorne and her children were living in Dresden. During his stay Julian attended lectures at the Polytechnic Institute in preparation for a career in engineering; he returned to America in 1870. Mrs. Hawthorne and the girls settled in England the same year, and Mrs. Hawthorne died there in March, 1871. Her fragment cannot be dated with certainty but was doubtless the work of moments snatched from her preparation of her husband's European notebooks and her own *Notes in England and Italy* that occupied the last three years of her life. The Dresden stay provides the limits of time within which Julian made his partial transcript in a locally bought note-

28 The manuscript is in the Morgan Library. Sophia at first omitted Hawthorne's interpolations and asides, but then entered them in pencil at approximately the place they occupied in the manuscript, or put them on the blank versos of her copy.

29 The manuscript, in the Berg Collection, New York Public Library, is inscribed in a red leather notebook trimmed with gold and bearing the stamp of Edouard Pahlman, a Dresden stationer. The chapter rubrics, which are Julian's arbitrary additions, are in the same hand and ink as the transcript itself. Without having had prior access to the opening pages of his father's draft, Julian could not have assumed that a second episode began precisely at the top of Hawthorne's page 5 where Julian's "Second Chapter" takes up. One supposes, then, that Julian had mislaid a previously transcribed first episode. That segment appears in the back of the notebook in a later form of his handwriting.

book, and his mother put her hand to his manuscript in difficult spots.

Whatever the immediate publication hopes may have been, nothing came of the partial transcripts and they play no part in the further history of the work. Eventually in 1882 Julian conflated printer's copy out of his father's two drafts for an edition to which he gave the title *Doctor Grimshawe's Secret*. But until the summer of that year, when the volume was announced as in preparation, the only public knowledge of Hawthorne's preoccupation with the American claimant theme came from a 700-word paragraph in an 1872 *Atlantic* essay by George Parsons Lathrop, who had married Rose in London soon after her mother's death. Lathrop had been able to examine Hawthorne's literary remains bequeathed to the children, and his article reviewing Una's edition of *Septimius Felton* discussed it within the context of the several unfinished manuscripts, all of which seemed to Lathrop abortive efforts of Hawthorne to write the English romance he had meditated from consular days. One of the fragments he described is recognizable as the "Grimshawe" draft; nothing would suggest that he had seen the earlier "Etherege" version.[30] Four years later Lathrop incorporated this account almost verbatim in *A Study of Hawthorne*, the first full critical survey of Hawthorne's literary achievement.[31]

[30] "History of Hawthorne's Last Romance," *Atlantic Monthly*, XXX (October, 1872), 453–55. In Lathrop's account, distinctive motifs found only in the second draft include references to Grimshawe as the "grim doctor" and to his fondness for brandy-and-water. Moreover, it is this draft that breaks off soon after the scene shifts from America to England, as Lathrop's summary states. Although he named no characters and suggested no title, his command of circumstantial detail is reasonably precise. It is curious that he should describe the American and English parts (p. 454) as two "chapters, for they hardly exceed the limit of such"; in actuality they comprise almost fifty thousand words, of which about three-fourths make up the American section, far more than a conventional chapter in extent. He could not have been describing Julian's partial transcript, which had not progressed to English scenes.

[31] *A Study of Hawthorne* (Boston, 1876), pp. 277–79. Of only oblique relation to *Grimshawe* was Julian's public quarrel with Lathrop over the

Meantime, in 1874 Julian moved to England, and in that year, according to his *Grimshawe* preface, the manuscript (Julian consistently referred to it in the singular) came into his hands from the Lathrops. It was, wrote Julian, subsequently stored in a London warehouse and did not reappear until the summer of 1882, after his return to New York.[32] In point of fact, he reached America sometime in the spring and unearthed the *Grimshawe* documents no later than April, for on May 3, 1882, he signed an agreement with the Boston publisher J. R. Osgood & Co. for the publication of *Grimshawe* and a biography of his parents, with an advance of $1,000 on the romance, payable in installments.[33] By July he was being pressed for *Grimshawe* copy and on July 26 wrote Osgood that he could not set a date for delivering the manuscript but hoped it could be published in the autumn; he also evidently gave Osgood information for the publicity campaign that began soon afterward.[34]

A paragraph in the August 9 *New York Tribune,* echoing language in Osgood's advertising, announced "an entirely new romance . . . long overlooked and but recently discovered . . . one of Hawthorne's most powerful and characteristic works." A fuller account appearing three days later in the *New York Times* sketched the story line, asserted that "the plot is carried out and the work is practically finished," and went on to declare that Hawthorne was such a "wretched penman" that his wife prepared his manuscripts from his dictation or transcribed his drafts. Only when Julian "began to

---

Study, aired in the *New York Tribune* of July 8 and 15, 1876. Although Julian objected to Lathrop's use of family papers, his concern was chiefly for what he conceived to be a violation of biographical privacy (a point Lathrop tactfully contested), and did not extend to Lathrop's description of the unpublished romances.

[32] *Doctor Grimshawe's Secret* (Boston, 1883), pp. xii–xiii.

[33] MS, Berg Collection, New York Public Library.

[34] Partially quoted in catalogue of Stephen H. Wakeman Sale, American Art Association, April 28, 1924, Lot 359.

decipher patiently" did the value of the *Grimshawe* story become apparent. Immediately Rose denied that "a new and complete romance" was to be found among Hawthorne's unpublished manuscripts. "A fragmentary and unfinished sketch, vaguely introducing some of the features assigned to this promised publication, has perhaps furnished the basis of the rumor." The work had been described in her husband's *Atlantic* article of 1872, and, she insisted, "cannot be truthfully published as anything more than an experimental fragment." Nor was it true that her father's handwriting had required her mother to act as amanuensis during his lifetime.[35]

The contradictions invited various interpretations, such as that Julian "fished" *Grimshawe* "out of his father's papers and edited it into a story" or that it had been "long overlooked and but recently discovered."[36] Other gossip must have been blunter, for Rose found that her letter to the papers had been construed as charging Julian with forgery. He wrote her in obvious distress at being placed in a false light, saying that he had at hand "ninety thousand words" of their father's manuscript and urging her to speak out in his defense. Within a few days Rose publicly declared that she had never intimated forgery; she also noted, however, that Julian had conceded "that the MS. was not a complete romance."[37]

[35] *New York Tribune*, August 9, 1882, 6:1; *New York Times*, August 12, 1882, 1:4, crediting the *Boston Daily Advertiser*. Osgood's advertisement ran, among other places, in *Publishers' Weekly*, XXII (August 19, 1882), 204. Rose's letter of August 13 to the *Advertiser* appeared also in the *New York Tribune*, August 16, 1882, 5:1, and was the subject of a story in the *New York Times*, August 15, 1882, 5:4, which also drew on an interview with Lathrop in the *Boston Traveler*. In his *Athenaeum* review cited in note 43, Henry A. Bright summarized the *Advertiser* stories and charged Julian with responsibility for misinformation in the *Grimshawe* publicity.

[36] *New York Times*, August 14, 1882, 3:5. The last of these passages is Osgood's advertising language.

[37] Julian's letter, August 28, 1882, is partially quoted in Theodore Maynard, *A Fire Was Lighted* (Milwaukee, 1948), pp. 194–95. Rose's statement, which appeared in the *New York Tribune*, September 9, 1882,

How far Julian's old hostility was mollified by Rose's response is open to question, but he was evidently stung by recurrent doubts that he was publishing an authentic work, and his preface displays an often defensive tone. Moreover, Osgood took the precaution of inserting facsimiles of Hawthorne's manuscript pages in the edition and advertising a display of the original to satisfy the public interest.[38]

Meantime, Julian had extracted the meditative passages from the *Grimshawe* first draft and offered them to *Century Magazine,* where they appeared simultaneously with book publication. By October 12 he had received $500 for this contribution but two days later recorded cryptically in his diary that he had written the editors "impeaching the legitimacy of their conduct in relation to the Grimshawe studies" —perhaps for their unwillingness to publish them complete.

6:1, cited an interview with Julian in the *Boston Daily Advertiser* (August 16) as corroborating her earlier description of an incomplete *Grimshawe.* The *Literary World,* XIII (September 9, 1882), 296, quoted from the latter source Julian's imprecise allusions to "fragmentary notes . . . and . . . the elaborate work itself" containing "only a small break in the middle." Julian was less cautious—and less accurate—in his preface (p. x): "The story, as a story, is complete as it stands; it has a beginning, a middle, and an end. There is no break in the narrative, and the legitimate conclusion is reached."

[38] *New York Tribune,* December 18, 1882, 6:3, and other New York and Boston papers of the same date ran Osgood's basic advertisement. The facsimiles were not chosen at random, as editor and publisher asserted; they represent pages 5 and 6 of Hawthorne's second draft, on which the name "Grimshawe" first appears.

Uneasiness stirred also in England, where Keningale Cook, a lawyer, dramatist, magazine editor, and friend of Julian wrote to assure readers of the *Athenaeum* (No. 2878 [December 23, 1882], 848–49) that *Grimshawe* was a genuine Hawthorne work. Cook recalled reading Julian's partial transcript in a red leather notebook "something over four years ago" and wishing for the whole story, but Julian explained that his father's manuscript had been "mislaid." In 1879 Julian had inquired whether Cook still had the red notebook. Cook, who had written appreciatively of Hawthorne, recognized in *Grimshawe* the hand of the master and his testimony in effect absolved Julian of concocting a spurious work. Julian dedicated the English edition to Cook.

The diary indicates, without details, a further exchange of letters with *Century* during the month.[39]

Subsequent diary entries show a quickening of pace toward book publication. On October 27 an agent for Longmans offered £150 advance against a ten percent royalty on sales of an English edition. On October 31 Julian lunched with Osgood in New York: "We discussed the Grimshawe Romance, and I took home with me the transcript to correct"— a tantalizing statement, for one wonders what he could have been asked to modify aside from illegible penmanship, unless Osgood had wanted emendations for clarity, including inconspicuous treatment of Hawthorne's briefer asides. Whatever was demanded, Julian worked at it all day on November 9 and 10, and again on November 17, when he sent off the last of printer's copy and turned to proofreading during the next few days. The preface followed on November 26. On November 27 he sent the bulk of his father's manuscript to Osgood, a sheet of it to the Longmans agent and another to *Century*, but the diary does not say whether his action was prompted by the need for authentication, publicity, or reproduction in the book.

When Julian undertook his edition he was faced with a need to make a continuous text for a general audience and he could not simply print what Hawthorne had written. Instead, he adopted the revised draft as far as it went, and

[39] Diary, 1880–83, MS, Julian Hawthorne Collection, Bancroft Library, University of California, Berkeley; entries for 1882 begin with October 13 and are intermittent. The *Grimshawe* by-product appeared as "A Look into Hawthorne's Workshop. Being Notes for a Posthumous Romance," *Century*, XXV (January, 1883), 433–48. Of the nine meditative passages in Hawthorne's first draft, only the last four are there printed. Julian had evidently offered a full transcript to R. W. Gilder, whose headnote indicated that "the very interesting first half" was being passed over except for two passages quoted in his headnote from "an early part of the notes." The quotations are actually from Studies 2 and 3, and Gilder alluded to the Salem setting in the language of Study 6; it therefore seems likely that Julian had included transcripts of all the studies in his submission, an assumption perhaps strengthened by his having copied them all into a notebook under date of August 19, 1882 (Morgan).

grafted onto it the remainder of the story from the first draft. When he came to its concluding episode, a kind of dream-vision, he moved it back into the revised draft as a bridge between the American and English sections.[40] He also provided chapter divisions, he regularized personal names in accordance with Hawthorne's last intentions, and he withdrew almost all of Hawthorne's notes and ruminative passages, as we have seen. Not surprisingly, he took many verbal liberties with prose that he knew his father would have rewritten.[41]

Ever since her mother's death Rose had possessed the "Ancestral Footstep" manuscript but had made no move to publish it. Her husband George Lathrop in his 1872 *Atlantic* article (p. 453) and again in his 1876 *Study* (pp. 276–77) had described it as a preliminary stage in the evolution of Hawthorne's English romance, not a realized work in form

[40] The relationship of Julian's 1883 *Grimshawe* text to Hawthorne's first (I) and second (II) drafts and to Centenary pagination is shown in the following tabulation (which does not take account of Julian's omissions):

	1883	MSS	Centenary
American setting	chaps. I–X pp. 1–129	II pp. 1–36	pp. 343–440
Quasi-fantasy	chap. XI pp. 130–38	I fols. 73–74	pp. 335–42
English setting	chaps. XII– mid–XIV pp. 139–77	II pp. 37–47	pp. 441–71
English setting continued	chaps. mid–XIV– XXV pp. 177–343	I fols. 18–67	pp. 145–323

Julian's decision to insert the quasi-fantasy episode between the American and British chapters was doubtless prompted by Hawthorne's suggestion in the meditative passage immediately preceding it in the first draft (Centenary, p. 329).

[41] Although Julian inadequately and even confusingly described his editorial procedures, he did not wholly conceal the fact that he was working with two manuscript drafts. His appendix contains almost all of Hawthorne's second-draft notes (seldom more than a sentence) along with the briefer ones from the portion of the first draft used in his edition; a few he incorporated into the body of the text.

or content. Its status changed with the announcement of Julian's edition of *Grimshawe,* and *The Ancestral Footstep* was serialized in the *Atlantic,* in order, said Lathrop's prefatory note, "that the two documents may be examined together." The first of three installments appeared in the issue of December, 1882, which came out about November 20, a month in advance of *Grimshawe.* One cannot know how the strained relations between Julian and the Lathrops had been affected by the recent skirmish over *Grimshawe;* but even if Rose had succeeded in mollifying her brother, he may not have welcomed this rivalry for public attention. Nonetheless, Julian's diary entry for November 27 notes that he had offered to dedicate *Grimshawe* to Rose and George, but that the couple were in disagreement over it. Twice Julian exchanged letters with George on the subject, and finally on December 2, barely two weeks before publication, George telegraphed their acceptance. The dedication "To Mr. and Mrs. George Parsons Lathrop, The Son-in-Law and Daughter of Nathaniel Hawthorne" appears to have been a genuine conciliatory gesture; were the correspondence extant it might tell us the reasons for touchiness, but not necessarily how to assess blame. Shortly afterward, Lathrop published a penetrating essay that surveyed the four unfinished romances and related the "Etherege" and "Grimshawe" documents to those that came before and after, justifying their publication not as great works but as "a great illustration of an artist's workings" in an evenhanded way calculated to reassure Julian. And although the Lathrops' marriage soon foundered, both George and Rose enjoyed improved rapport with Julian from this time forward.[42]

Doctor Grimshawe's Secret was published by Osgood on December 18, 1882, postdated 1883. A first printing of 5,000

[42] "The Hawthorne Manuscripts," *Atlantic Monthly,* LI (March, 1883), 363-75; Maurice Bassan, *Hawthorne's Son* (Columbus 1970), p. 160.

copies was followed by a second of 500 copies in March, 1883. A few months later the same plates were used for a Library Edition of 500 copies, selling at $2.00, an advance of $.50 over the price of the basic trade edition; similarly derived was a $6.00 deluxe impression of 250 numbered copies (270 printed), with added vignette title pages to make it uniform with the large-paper issue of Houghton, Mifflin's Riverside Hawthorne. A further printing of 1,000 copies in standard format was ordered at the end of October, with title-page date changed to 1884. Subsequently the work became volume XIII of the trade Riverside, and the indexes of that edition which originally concluded volume XII were transferred to the end of the *Grimshawe* volume. A true second edition of Julian's text is represented by a new typesetting for volume XV of the 1900 Autograph Edition and derivative "editions" manufactured from its plates.[43] *The Ancestral Footstep* was not issued separately but during 1883 was included in the Riverside as an appendix to volume XI and in the Little Classic as part of volume XXIV; in the 1900 Autograph it concludes volume XIV.[44]

IV

Reviewers gave relatively little attention to *The Ancestral Footstep,* usually commenting on it in paragraphs detail-

[43] Publication date is established from advertisements in December 18 issues of the *New York Times* and *New York World,* and in the *Boston Transcript* of December 16. Information on the several printings is found in Cost Books of Ticknor & Fields and successors, MSS, Houghton Library, Harvard University. An Osgood advertisement in *Publishers' Weekly,* XXIV (September 22, 1883), 387, linked the large-paper *Grimshawe* with "the similar edition of Hawthorne's works" but without mentioning Houghton, Mifflin.

[44] According to Ellen B. Ballou, *The Building of the House* (Boston, 1970), pp. 287–88, Houghton, Mifflin considered separate publication of *The Ancestral Footstep* in 1883 but decided against it.

ing the contents of current *Atlantic* issues.[45] The *New York Times* devoted more than two columns to the first installment and quoted approvingly a number of passages illustrating Hawthorne's genius. The *New York World* struck a typical note in calling it a less important "contribution to literature than to literary history and methods," and though conceding that any Hawthorne "is exceedingly refreshing reading," felt that the sketch was justifiably abandoned. To the *Nation* reviewer the fragment suggested the "fossil remains" of a story "exhumed and reconstructed after the lapse of a geological period, for some literary museum. Part of its fascination to many lovers of Hawthorne will lie in the musty, antique flavor which it has."

The *Times* gave nearly half a column to the second installment, mostly quotation; the notice questioned the "wisdom" of any posthumous publication but welcomed these fragments for giving an insight into the "tragic sense" of Hawthorne's art. The *Nation* observed that "we see the block in the rough, but the final shape which the artist would have given it we do not know." The last section generated slight attention, although the *Times* quoted at some length.

Meanwhile, soon after mid-December the critics had before them not only the second part of the *Ancestral Footstep* serialization but also Julian's edition of *Doctor Grimshawe's Secret*[46] and the *Century* "Workshop" passages that Julian had

45 This discussion draws on the following notices of *The Ancestral Footstep*: *Nation*, XXXV (November 30, December 28, 1882), 465, 553; ibid., XXXVI (January 25, 1883), 84; *New York Times*, November 19, 1882, 13:1–3, December 25, 1882, 3:5–6, January 21, 1883, 10:1–2; *New York World*, November 25, 1882, 4:5, December 25, 1882, 6:5. Those written in December and January usually refer also to the *Century* article, "A Look into Hawthorne's Workshop." The latter is specifically the subject of a piece in the *New York World*, December 21, 1882, 4:4.

46 This discussion draws on the following reviews and notices: Richard F. Littledale, *Academy*, XXII (December 30, 1882), 466; William Roscoe Thayer, *American*, V (January 27, 1883), 250-51; [Henry A. Bright], *Athenæum*, No. 2880 (January 6, 1883), 9–11; *Atlantic Monthly*, LI (February, 1883), 286; James Herbert Morse, "Nathaniel Hawthorne

withdrawn from the first draft of the romance. Consequently, the notices began to relate the works to each other, and comparisons became common. The *Times*, for instance, judged the *Century* Hawthorne more interesting than the *Atlantic*: to see the author "in the very throes of literary creation" was "an entirely unique chapter in literary history." The *Dial* agreed that "here the author is revealed," adding that readers were more interested in his personality than his plots. Later the *Times*, reporting on the final section of *The Ancestral Footstep*, recognized the similarity of meditative passages here and in the *Century* memoranda, and found them to possess "quite the same interest." The most severe reaction, based on one or perhaps two installments of *The Ancestral Footstep*, was the *Athenæum* view that despite "beautiful little touches—for Hawthorne wrote it—. . . it is so utterly fragmentary and incoherent as to be scarcely interesting. It is literally without head or tail, and the only bits of value may be found in a better form in 'Dr. Grimshawe's Secret.' "

Grimshawe itself generated a wide variety of critical response. The essential genuineness of the work was not seriously questioned, for Hawthornean preoccupations and turns of language were recognizable despite the imperfections; indeed, said the *New York World*, even if the "manuscript had been found in the catacombs" there could be no doubt

Again," *Century Magazine*, XXVI (June, 1883), 309–11; Miriam P. Mason, "Hawthorne Agonistes," *Dial*, III (February, 1883), 222–24; *Harper's New Monthly Magazine*, LXVI (March, 1883), 629–31 [George P. Curtis], 640; *Lippincott's Magazine*, XXXI (March, 1883), 318–19; *Literary World*, XIV (January 13, 1883), 3–4; *Nation*, XXXVI (January 18, 1883), 66; John Addison Porter, *New Englander*, XLII (May, 1883), 339–53; *New York Herald*, December 15, 1882, 5:1–2; *New York Tribune*, December 31, 1882, 8:1–2; *New York World*, December 18, 1882, 5:1–2; *San Francisco Chronicle*, January 7, 1883, 6:4; *Saturday Review*, LV (January 6, 1883), 25–26; *Spectator*, LV (December 30, 1882), 1686–87; *Westminster Review*, CXIX (April 1, 1883), 595–97. The quotations attributed to Whittier and Holmes are in "Literary Notes," *New York Tribune*, December 23, 1882, 6:1.

of its authorship. The recent public display of friction among the Hawthornes led reviewers to wonder how heavily Julian had imposed his hand, and his preface seemed unhappily evasive. The *Nation* felt that a reader could justly withhold interest in the book, "at least until he knows more precisely what the limits of the editor's labors were." The *New Englander* too wished that Julian had explained his editing more fully and clearly. In criticizing the "somewhat thrifty plan" of publishing the non-narrative portions of *Grimshawe* in *Century*, the *New York Herald* joined with the *World* and the *Nation* in asking that all the *Grimshawe* materials be reassembled so that one might see Hawthorne's creative imagination as it grappled with specific problems. The "workshop" insights were praised by critics who accepted *Grimshawe* as an unfinished romance, but *Lippincott's* was saddened by "the bad contrivances of a misleading fancy" and declared that "it must be art of a low kind in which the sight of difficulties encountered is a stimulus to the spectator's enjoyment."

An anonymous *Harper's* reviewer, on the other hand, emphasized Hawthorne's success: "No other artist has blended as subtly . . . the real and the unreal, the imaginary and the concrete, the weird and the natural." A few pages earlier George W. Curtis, writing in the *Harper's* Easy Chair column, accepted Hawthorne's world as "half-spectral" but thought the psychological possibilities only partially realized— "melodrama constantly overpowered the story, and this fact may very well explain Hawthorne's dissatisfaction." Curtis agreed with his colleague that Dr. Grimshawe was "clearly and strongly drawn"; he went further to praise Hawthorne's skill in treating the two children and called the "breezy British warden" "an admirable study." Others considered Grimshawe the only developed character, but the *Literary World* countered that he was "too brutal and profane to be interesting."

Whereas the *New York World* saw the bloody footstep as a "central mystery" that effectively "binds together nearly a dozen others," the *Spectator* considered the "secret" to be "rubbish" though it liked "the spidery-part of the story." *Lippincott's* scorned the gothic machinery altogether, as "commonplace" and "worn-out." Regardless of the trappings, many reviewers found the first half greatly superior. "It is here almost entirely," said the *Literary World*, "that the Hawthorne whom we know shows forth in anything of his ancient power and majesty." To the *Spectator*, "the remainder of the tale might have come from a very ordinary pen." Henry Bright seconded these judgments in the *Athenæum*: "The first part is written in Hawthorne's most careful style, though even there we find much that needs correction and revision. The second part is full of inconsistencies and extravagances. We fail to see the middle of the story, and there is no end at all."[47] It remained for John A. Porter to explain the difference in quality between the two halves. In a knowledgeable essay in the *New Englander* he deduced from Julian's preface and notes that *Grimshawe* was a conflation of two drafts and that the revise occupied only the first half of the volume.

The international aspects of the romance drew mixed comments. With a show of impartiality the *New York World* saw the contrast between American and English culture as exemplifying "the spiritualized influences of the two greatest civilizations of modern times." William Roscoe Thayer in the *American* praised Hawthorne's "outspoken, yet calm, just and impartial, criticism . . . which has aroused the hostility of the British press." The English verdict on the dialogues between the American and the Warden was variously ex-

[47] Although unsigned, the review is clearly by Bright, for it reflects special knowledge of the *Marble Faun* manuscript (which Hawthorne had presented to him) and of the Heywood family seats in Liverpool and London. Most decisive is his quoting a passage from "The Ghost of Doctor Harris," a piece that Hawthorne had inscribed in "the album of an English friend" (i.e., Mrs. John P. Heywood, Bright's aunt) and that remained unpublished until 1900.

pressed: the *Athenæum* called them "dull political conversation," the *Academy* thought they took up "far too much space," the *Spectator* and *Westminster Review* ignored them. The *New York World* complained of their platitudes, and *Lippincott's* added that Hawthorne's views were out of date. Curtis was unconvinced by "the shadowy and perfunctory Americanism of the young American."

Grimshawe inevitably recalled *Denis Duval* and *Edwin Drood,* unfinished works by Thackeray and Dickens. Written at the ends of great writers' lives, all three bore marks of struggle and incompleteness characteristic of geniuses who sought to resolve more than they could express. But *Grimshawe,* said the *American,* "although roughly sketched from beginning to end," was "in no particular as complete as any chapter" of the other two. The *Academy* held that the loss in not having a finished work was far greater with *Denis Duval* than with *Grimshawe.*

Two old friends produced statements for the press that, without committing them noticeably, sounded well as gestures of tribal loyalty toward Hawthorne. J. G. Whittier declared that *Grimshawe* was "one of his weird, unmistakable creations —a creation not fully rounded, chaotic, peopled with strange shapes, like our planet in its first discovery." Oliver Wendell Holmes may well have summarized the prevailing view that held Hawthorne in high esteem even in his ineffectuality and failure: "I feel as one might have felt who had been admitted to Rembrandt's studio. I have been closeted with a magician and admitted within his mysterious circle." Subsequent critics and biographers have usually been content to remain silent or to approach *Grimshawe* diffidently as one of the unfinished works that darkened the closing years of Hawthorne's career.

Although Julian had announced in his 1883 *Grimshawe* notes that the passages printed in *Century* or otherwise omitted from his edition would later be added, he did not carry out his plan. It remained for Edward H. Davidson, using Julian's title, to publish a complete genetic text of Hawthorne's first and second drafts, along with the studies and Handlist, in essentially unedited form, incorporating into the text Hawthorne's alterations and errors.[48] The Centenary Edition, based on a thorough reexamination of the manuscripts, presents a text with several hundred new readings, supplemented by an editorial appendix that records all Centenary emendations as well as Hawthorne's own alterations.

E. H. D.

C. M. S.

---

[48] *Hawthorne's Doctor Grimshawe's Secret* (Cambridge, 1954). Davidson had earlier discussed the genesis of the work and reproduced the then-known studies in *Hawthorne's Last Phase* (New Haven, 1949), where he also treated the manuscripts underlying *The Ancestral Footstep, Septimius Felton,* and *The Dolliver Romance.*

TEXTUAL COMMENTARY

Manuscript Copy-Texts for the Centenary Edition

T HE UNTITLED MANUSCRIPT of the sketch published as *The Ancestral Footstep* is a paper-bound notebook containing forty-four leaves of faintly ruled white wove paper measuring 9⅞ by 7½ inches, inscribed in black ink and paged by Hawthorne 1 through 88 (Morgan).

The notebook was originally four gatherings of 12s. Two leaves are now missing from the beginning and one from the end of the first gathering, as is the last leaf of the final gathering. The leaf of pages 17–18 is taped to the following sheet, and the leaf of pages 67–68, whose counterpart is the missing final leaf of the notebook, is also secured by tape. Given the abrupt beginning, there is reason to infer that Hawthorne discarded an earlier start when he took up the story on April 1, 1858, and numbered the recto of the original third leaf "1". The fact that there is no break in the narrative between pages 18 and 19 indicates that the last leaf of the first gathering was gone before Hawthorne's inscription reached that point. Although the sketch appears to have concluded at the foot of page 88, there is no knowing whether the missing last leaf contained anything germane to the story.

The work which Julian Hawthorne published as *Doctor Grimshawe's Secret* is a composite of two untitled manuscript drafts. They are here reproduced in full, with supplied titles drawn from the name of the doctor in each draft—Etherege in the first, Grimshawe in the second. Two brief segments now excised from the second draft are represented by text from Julian's first edition described below. Duplications in foliation of the first draft and pagination of the second are indicated here (but not in Hawthorne's manuscripts) by superscripts preceding folio or page number.

First Draft: On 72 leaves of white laid paper, 9¾ by 7¾ inches, with an oval blindstamp of a locomotive and tender above "P & P". Foliated irregularly 1–73, inscribed in black ink on rectos and versos except for blank 43ᵛ. Two leaves are numbered 22, two numbered 50. There is no leaf 51, but fol. ²50 shows a correction of number to 51 in a faint hand perhaps not Hawthorne's. The verso of 67 is numbered 68 by Hawthorne. Folio 69 is nonexistent or lost. An unnumbered final leaf [74] is a half sheet of the same paper, measuring 7¾ by 4⅞ inches. The division of the draft among three libraries is as follows: fols. 1–6, 9–18, 32–35, 39–43, 52–53, 70–73 (Huntington); fols. 19–¹22, ²22–31, 36–38, 44–¹50, ²50, 54–67 (Morgan); fols. 7–8, [74] (Berg).

Second Draft: Twenty-five leaves, paged irregularly 1–47. The first eight leaves are of white laid paper, 8¾ by 7¼ inches, with oval blindstamp of an eagle centered in the legend "London Superfine"; paged 1–16, inscribed in black ink. Leaves 9 through 25 are of white laid paper with oval blindstamp of a locomotive and tender above "P & P"; inscribed in black ink and paged 17–¹34, ¹35–²34, ²35–47, [48] blank (Morgan).

Ancillary Documents: Associated with Hawthorne's attempts at an English romance are seven brief memoranda, here labeled 1 through 7 for identification. It should be stressed that this ordering carries no authorial sanction, nor do the contents of the respective notes permit more than an arbitrarily arranged sequence. The one objective basis for grouping is that the first four studies may relate to either the "Ancestral Footstep" sketch or the "Etherege" and "Grimshawe" drafts, while the other three contain details pertinent to the two drafts alone. A further document (identified here as Handlist) indexes matters in the English journals on which Hawthorne drew for "Etherege" and "Grimshawe" and subsequently—using chiefly the same few items—for the *Septimius* drafts and certain essays in *Our Old Home*. Julian Hawthorne made reasonably accurate transcripts of all seven studies plus the Handlist (Morgan); and for Study 5 and part of the Handlist, his text is the only one now known.[1]

Study 1: A single leaf, 8 by 5 inches, of white laid paper with vertical chain lines approximately 1 inch apart. The partially shorn watermark reads "RQUODALE"—identifying the supplier, George McCorquodale[2]—and beneath it in two lines "ERPOOL / 1853". The number "2" centered at the top of the recto appears not to be in Hawthorne's hand. The bottom third of the verso, inverted, contains arithmetical calculations related to others found on the verso of the Handlist, but not necessarily written at the time either document was inscribed (Huntington).

Study 2: A single leaf, $7^{15}\!/_{16}$ by 4⅞ inches, of faded blue paper, cut unevenly along the left recto. A partial watermark

---

[1] Julian titled his transcripts "Grimshawe Fragments. Aug. 19. 82" but included *Dolliver* studies as numbers 3), 4), 5), and 11), apparently without recognizing them as such. His ordering, which may have been completely fortuitous, arranges the studies as indicated by his numbering, compared with the Centenary arrangement and that of Davidson in 1954:

CENTENARY	DAVIDSON 1954	JH MS 1882	
1	A [first half]	9)	
2	B	7)	[preceded by 4]
3	A [second half]	8)	
4	C	7)	[followed by 2]
5	B1	1)	
6	D	6)	
7	E	2)	
Handlist	F	10)	

[2] *Gore's Directory of Liverpool* for 1849 lists "George McCorquodale & Co. Wholesale stationers, printers, and account-book manufacturers. 38, Castle Street."

in three lines "G McCOR/LIVE/18" indicates the same supplier as for Study 1. The recto is number "1" in top center (perhaps not by Hawthorne), although the opening word "Thus" implies a continuation. Along the left edge of the opening paragraph are nine ink dots opposite the questions (Huntington).

Study 3: A single leaf, 8¼₆ by 4¹⁵⁄₁₆ inches, of faded blue paper without watermark, perhaps from the same stock as Study 2; written over the recto and half the verso. The number "3" centered in top recto appears not to be in Hawthorne's hand (Huntington).

Study 4: A single leaf, 8 by 5⅛ inches, of blue paper from slightly heavier stock than that of Studies 2 and 3. The "I" centered in top recto is presumably a roman numeral, but its significance is not apparent (Huntington).

Study 5: No Hawthorne original known. Text is a transcript by Julian Hawthorne copied into one of his notebooks under date of August 19, 1882 (Morgan).

Study 6: Two leaves of white laid paper: the first, 7¾ by 4⅞ inches, with vertical chain lines 1 inch apart, is watermarked with a fleur de lis; the second, 8 by 5 inches, with horizontal chain lines 1¼ inches apart, bears no watermark; its recto is numbered "2" in top center, probably by Hawthorne (Huntington).

Study 7: A single leaf of blue wove, 8 by 5 inches, inscribed on recto and upper half of verso. According to an accompanying letter of July 3, 1867, from Ada Shepard Badger to a Mrs. Leland, the author's autograph signature was pasted onto the verso of the study by Sophia Hawthorne, who sent the leaf to Mrs. Badger, a former governess of the Hawthorne children; she in turn gave it to Mrs. Leland for an autograph collecting friend (Massachusetts Historical Society).

Handlist: A single leaf, 5⅜ by 5⅛ inches, of white wove unwatermarked paper, ruled on the verso with now faded blue lines ⅜ inch apart; perhaps torn from a notebook, as the rough left edge of the recto would imply. Horizontal creases suggest that the paper was folded in thirds, and that the bottom third was cut and torn from a sheet that was originally about 8 inches in length. Separation slightly below the second fold has preserved the tops of several ascenders from the first line of the discarded portion (Huntington).

Julian Hawthorne's 1882 transcript of this Handlist in his notebook reflects the contents of the Huntington leaf, plus additional matter falling between the end of the Huntington recto and the beginning of the verso. Whether the original sheet was still intact in 1882 is not to be determined; the bottom third may already have been detached but in any event seems not to have survived except in Julian's transcript. Although his accuracy cannot be vouched for, the added content is sufficiently authentic to warrant interpolation as the source of entries from "Mrs Ainsworth's . . ." through "Yearnings . . . off" (Morgan).

Printed Copy-Text for the Centenary Edition

In the second or "Grimshawe" draft the bottom third of the leaf containing pages ²35—36 was cut off and lost after Julian had transcribed it. The missing passages "tumbles . . . anxiety," (438.18–439.12) and "The Doctor . . . memory." (441.9–12) are supplied in the Centenary text from the first edition of *Doctor Grimshawe's Secret*, 1883, pp. 127–28, 354.

A Note on Editorial Practices

This edition of the "Ancestral Footstep" sketch and its further development in the "Etherege" and "Grimshawe" drafts reproduces Hawthorne's unfinished working papers with as close an approach to a clear text as is possible. We have, however, used angle brackets to set off his intercalary notes and directions to himself, describing the manuscript position of each in an Alterations entry. Most frequently he inserted such passages between paragraphs and they are so placed here; those written along margins or interlined within paragraphs are inserted in the Centenary text at the point dictated by the logic of the context. An exception is made of those notes heading the first page of the "Etherege" and "Grimshawe" drafts, where for considerations of Centenary format the bracketed notes follow rather than precede the first paragraph. Hawthorne's directions for rearranging narrative elements we have removed from the text to an Alterations entry that describes the change and cites the authority for it; if reordering cannot be carried out because it would entail rewriting, Hawthorne's directions are retained in the text.

Emendations are made only of inadvertent errors that could create confusion and of misspellings resulting from careless inscription; acceptable variants and inconsistencies in compounding or capitalization have been retained. Except for silent elimination of variant spacing in contractions, all Centenary changes are recorded in the list of Editorial Emendations.

Emendation of Substantives. These include (1) additions necessary to sense: "I no" becomes Centenary "I had no", "to reminded" becomes "to be reminded", "proof the extent" becomes "proof of the extent", "belong it" becomes "belong to it"; (2) elimination of dittography: "then then" becomes "then"; (3) correction of a patently miswritten word, such as "indepent", "utilititarian", "insteading", or carelessly inscribed forms such as "phenonenon", "herafter", "feelling"; (4) correction of a miswritten construction, such as "would be ever be", "a agent", "on the each"; (5) the completion of words divided at MS line-end and left unfinished: "be-|" emended to "being", or the converse, "|ish" emended to "boyish", and the normalization of such anomalies as "here-| fore", "delight-|ted", "cont-|ued"; (6) the correction of a speaker's name, as "Warden" for "pensioner". All such changes are recorded in the list of Editorial Emendations.

Emendation of accidentals. The following emendations of punctuation are recorded in the list of Editorial Emendations: the addition of a missing element in pairs of parentheses (as at 49.1, 212.24); the addition or deletion of punctuation (as at 161.16, 357.30); and the replacement of one mark by another (as at 331.18).

Inconsistencies and Anomalies Preserved. These include personal or place names which Hawthorne changed within or between drafts ("Dr. Etherege" | "Inglefield" | "Gibbins"; "Father Angelo" | "Antonio"; "Edward Etherege" | "Etheredge" | "Redclyffe"; "Pemberton Manor" | Smithills Hall" | "Brathwaite Hall" | "Oakland Hall"). Such acceptable variant spellings as "ceiling" | "cieling", "panel" | "pannel", "gray" | "grey", or "centre" | "center" are retained, as are inconsistencies in compounding ("graveyard" | "grave-yard" | "grave yard"), inaccurate accent marks ("outrèness"), and Hawthorne's anomalous "oclock." In "The Ancestral Footstep" is preserved a "nonword" for the name of an old palace (for which "Sheen" might be conjectured), which Hawthorne inscribed clearly as "Shnnnnn" (76.19); also kept in the same text is a long dash (86.20) apparently indicating an addition he intended to supply.

Reordering of passages. Hawthorne revised the "Etherege" and "Grimshawe" drafts heavily, the latter even more than the former. In addition to his usual habit of writing over wiped-out words, he often inserted a revision above or following a cancelled passage. Sometimes he interlined substitute readings without cancelling the superseded language. The two drafts reflect additional modes of revision: on occasion Hawthorne directed that the order of two passages be changed, using such rubrics as "Insert the following paragraph at the end of the one next preceding," also sometimes marking with arrowhead pointers the beginning and end of affected passages; he used other transpositional signs—vertical lines, diagonal lines, two- or three-tiered carets—with or without verbal rubrics. Revisions thus directed or implied have been made in the Centenary text, and entries in the Alterations list set out the authorial sanction for all such changes; verbal rubrics are then reproduced in the list and not retained in the text.[3]

At several points the Centenary text stands unaltered because Hawthorne only partially indicated changes. Passages at 309.6–8, 311.7–8, 456.13–457.12, 467.1–10 have been lightly crossed as if to cancel, but they remain integral with the context and Hawthorne provided no revision. The passage 107.6–108.26 should come before Mountford's arrival, as the text directs, but to make this change would require unauthorized rewriting or excision on pages 97–98. Similarly, directions at 453.23–28 point to revision not fully worked out.

A particularly vexing paragraph (351–52) is manifestly disordered as it stands, and because Hawthorne marked it

---

[3] See Alterations entries for 132.14–16, 347.30–33, 350.11–25, 363.27–364.3, 364.4–5, 376.15–377.12, 381.25–31, 382.22–383.1, 383.29–31, 403.16–404.12, 419.14–19, 436.22–437.7, 444.31–445.11, 448.11–20.

off into eight segments by seven sets of three or four vertical lines, it is apparent that he intended some rearrange-
ment. His transpositional symbols do not, however, suggest
what new sequence of parts he visualized, nor has he indicated whether any of the later segments may be intended as
substitutes for earlier. The paragraph therefore remains unchanged in the Centenary text. It is possible to suggest more
reasonable orderings, but no solution can be more than speculative. First the passage in its original form, with the vertical
lines inserted:

Considering that Doctor Grimshawe when we first look
upon him had dwelt only a very few years in the house
by the grave yard, it is wonderful what an appearance he
and his furniture, and his cobwebs, and their unweariable
spinners, and crusty old Hannah, all had, of having permanently attached themselves to the locality. For a century,
at least, it might be fancied that the study, in particular,
had existed just as it was now, with those dusky festoons
of spider-silk hanging along the walls, those book-cases,
with volumes turning their parchment or black leather
backs upon you, those machines and engines, that table, and
at it, the Doctor in a very faded and shabby dressing gown,
smoking a long clay pipe, the powerful fume of which
dwelt continually in his reddish and grisly beard, and made
him fragrant wherever he went.||| This sense of fixedness,
stony intractability, seems to belong to people who, instead
of hope, which exhales everything into an airy, gaseous
exhilaration, have a fixed and dogged purpose, around
which everything congeals and crystallizes.|||| Even the
sunshine, dim through the dustiness of the two casements
that looked upon the graves, seemed an old and musty
beam that had perhaps lost even its gold, by lying there
so long-tarnished. The smoke, as it came warm out of
Doctor Grimshawe's mouth, seemed already stale.|||| But
if the two children, or either of them, happened to be in
the study—if they ran to open a door at the knock—if they
came scampering and peeped down over the bannisters—
the sordid and rusty gloom was apt to vanish quite away.|||

The sunbeam itself looked like a golden rule that had been flung down long ago, and lain there till it was dusty and tarnished.||| They were cheery little imps, who sucked up fragrance and pleasantness out of their surroundings, dreary as these looked, even as a flower can find its proper fragrance in any soil where its seed happens to fall.|||| The great spider, hanging by its cordage over the Doctor's head, and waving slowly like a pendulum in a blast from the crack of the door, must have made millions and millions of precisely such vibrations there.||| They were new, and made over every morning, with yesterday's weariness left out.

The transpositional problems become apparent at once. The second segment, beginning "This sense of fixedness," seems to be more closely attached to the preceding sentences than to any of the later segments that might be inserted before it. Were it to be moved, it could well follow the first sentence, but Hawthorne put no transposition marks after "locality." The third segment, beginning "Even the sunshine", was considerably revised with interlineations that cannot be read with complete confidence, and it may be that Hawthorne was not satisfied with his tarnished-gold conceit, for "The sunbeam" sentence of the fifth segment seems to be further recasting of the same idea, perhaps intended to replace the earlier sentence. The fourth, sixth, and eighth segments relate to the children and logically belong together to conclude the paragraph. That leaves the seventh segment on "The great spider . . . " to be placed if a referent can be found for "such vibrations"; the most nearly satisfactory is "unweariable spinners" at the beginning of the paragraph, but again Hawthorne gave no signal for an insertion following the first sentence. If, however, we take such a liberty here and then rearrange the rest according to a rough logic, replacing the "Even the sunshine" sentence but performing no other surgery, we can contemplate several possible orderings of which this is one—at best only suggestive of Hawthorne's final intentions and lacking authority that would justify its replacing the received text:

Considering that Doctor Grimshawe when we first look upon him had dwelt only a very few years in the house by the grave yard, it is wonderful what an appearance he and his furniture, and his cobwebs, and their unweariable spinners, and crusty old Hannah, all had, of having permanently attached themselves to the locality. The great spider, hanging by its cordage over the Doctor's head, and waving slowly like a pendulum in a blast from the crack of the door, must have made millions and millions of precisely such vibrations there. For a century, at least, it might be fancied that the study, in particular, had existed just as it was now, with those dusky festoons of spider-silk hanging along the walls, those book-cases, with volumes turning their parchment or black leather backs upon you, those machines and engines, that table, and at it, the Doctor in a very faded and shabby dressing gown, smoking a long clay pipe, the powerful fume of which dwelt continually in his reddish and grisly beard, and made him fragrant wherever he went. This sense of fixedness, stony intractability, seems to belong to people who, instead of hope, which exhales everything into an airy, gaseous exhilaration, have a fixed and dogged purpose, around which everything congeals and crystallizes. The sunbeam itself looked like a golden rule that had been flung down long ago, and lain there till it was dusty and tarnished. The smoke, as it came warm out of Doctor Grimshawe's mouth, seemed already stale. But if the two children, or either of them, happened to be in the study—if they ran to open a door at the knock— if they came scampering and peeped down over the bannisters—the sordid and rusty gloom was apt to vanish quite away. They were cheery little imps, who sucked up fragrance and pleasantness out of their surroundings, dreary as these looked, even as a flower can find its proper fragrance in any soil where its seed happens to fall. They were new, and made over every morning, with yesterday's weariness left out.

Physical Division within Manuscripts. In "The Ancestral Footstep" Hawthorne's divisions take the form of date entries, usually with single or double underscoring, here uniformly italicized. He made no systematic divisions within either the "Etherege" or the "Grimshawe" draft, marking only an occasional break (duly noted in the Alterations list); for convenience of reading, the editors have spaced between scenes in the spirit of chapter divisions in Hawthorne's completed romances.

C. M. S.

EDITORIAL EMENDATIONS IN THE COPY-TEXT

Every editorial change from copy-text is listed here. For each entry, the Centenary reading is at the left of the bracket and the rejected reading follows the bracket. An asterisk * indicates that an accepted emendation appears in the manuscript but was not made by Hawthorne; the list of Alterations in the Manuscripts contains an entry giving details. A vertical stroke | indicates the end of a manuscript line. In recording punctuation emendation, a wavy dash ~ represents a word before the bracket and a caret ʌ indicates the absence of a punctuation mark in the manuscript.

THE ANCESTRAL FOOTSTEP

3.1	April 1st, 1858.] *italic*
3.4	scenes] scene
3.21	there] their
4.15	a distinction] distinction
5.6	Excursion] excursion
5.30	though] *omit*
5.35	country] county
6.11	at?] ~.
7.10	similar] similiar
7.17	families,] ~ʌ

7.34	direct] dirent
8.2	stocks."] ~ₐ"
8.4	speak] *omit*
8.6	grieve] greive
8.13	strongly] stronly
8.17	point.] ~ₐ
8.22	of] of of
8.26	far,] ~ₐ
9.35	meeting?] ~.
10.2	seeking?] ~.
10.9	me?] ~.
10.16	furthest] furtherst
10.17	"Alice!—Alice!—] "~! ~ —
10.21	"Hush] '~
10.22	Middleton] Midleton
10.26	heirloom] heir loom
10.34	expelled] expelld
11.11	country] county
11.19	him] *omit*
12.7	"Nay] ₐ~
12.14	if] *omit*
12.18	you.] ~?
12.25	not in] not in in
13.22	was] *omit*
13.33	cogitations] cogations
14.22	violent] vio-| ent
15.1	house?] ~.
15.21	*May 2ᵈ. Sunday.]* above entry; first period omitted
15.26	allude?] ~.
15.28	"for] ₐ~
16.9	this] ~,
16.18	countryman.] ~."
16.19	particulars] particu-|
16.22	though] thoug
17.5	proofs?] ~,
17.7	pursuits.] ~,"
17.30	this,] ~ₐ

19.12	imposter] impotor
19.19	purposes] puposes
19.33	Middleton] Eldredge
20.11–12	looked down in] looked in down in
20.29	shrubbery] shrubbbery
21.16	a] *omit*
21.31	came] coming
22.9	an] *omit*
22.23	frankly.] ~,
22.24	catastrophe.] ~,
23.23	susceptibility] susceptibity
23.23	but] *omit*
23.27	two] too
23.30	"Let] ∧~
23.34	back; but] ~; (~
24.7	another.] ~∧
24.9	Alice,] ~∧
24.14	"Shall] ∧~
24.17	is] *omit*
24.20	father!"] ~!∧
24.33	face] ~,
24.34	"There] ∧~
25.11	Wentworth?"] ~?∧
25.14	"After] '~
26.1	acquiring] accquiring
26.3	you,] ~∧
26.5	time."] ~.∧
26.6	"A] '~
26.19	"I] '~
26.19	thought,"] ~,'
26.25	ages] age's
26.32	'let] '~
27.1	old] ~,
27.12	followed] follow
27.16	round,] ~∧
27.18	ages?] ~.
27.19	last] least
27.35	description?] ~.

28.6	And] "~
28.16	chamber?] ~.
28.31	Lilliputian] Lillipu- | putian
29.5	else."] ~·ᴧ
29.18	bloodshed] bloodᴧ | shed
31.1	sternness] sterness
32.21	States?"] ~?ᴧ
32.28	nations."] ~ᴧ"
32.32	country] county
33.21	quiet] qui- | iet
33.26	every] ever
34.9	complexion] complexi- | ion
34.13	irregularity] irreg- | larity
36.5	wrought] wroght
37.11	Middleton] Hammond
37.26	had] *omit*
37.29	could induce you] could you induce you
37.29	it?"] ~·ᴧ
38.11	Timbuctoo] Timbutoo
38.24	are,] ~ᴧ
38.32	cynical] cyn- | cal
39.8	in] *omit*
39.12	Hammond] Hammon
39.15	analogous] analogus
39.20	described?"] ~·ᴧ
39.21	Middleton] Hammond
39.23	house] House
39.23	Smithells,] ~ᴧ
39.24	"one] ᴧ~
40.1	Unquestionably,] ~ᴧ
40.9	piece] peiece
40.11	America."] ~ᴧᴧ
40.25	Middleton] Hamilton
41.3	matter] mater
41.13	country] county
42.8	uncovered] uncoverd
42.16	them?] ~.
43.5	reminiscence] reminenscene

43.15	shade.] ~,
43.30	cultivation.] ~∧
43.31	Hammond] Hamond
44.27	shooting] shoting
44.29	whatever] what-| er
45.25	of] of of
45.31	proof of the] proof the
46.5	calculated] caleculated
46.25	originated] orignated
46.28	Hammond] Hammon
46.30	"There] ∧~
46.33	Examine] Examined
47.11	"This] '~
47.11	miraculous!"] ~!∧
48.8	cabinet] Cabinet
48.12	It is an] It an
48.17	equaled.] ~∧
48.21	air.] ~."
48.22	ill?] ~,
48.30	Eldredge] Hammond
49.1	entrance),] ~∧,
49.3	he.] ~∧
49.9	scepticism] scepticsm
51.3	carelessly] carlessly
51.8	vague] vage
51.11	discovery] discovey
51.12	veracity] veraci- | ity
51.15	should] shoud
52.18	Elizabeth's] Elizabeths
52.18	course] couse
52.22	with an old] with old
53.12	because the] because hi the
53.22	must be the] must the
53.26	11th.] ~∧
54.10	deferentially,] ~∧
54.14	Sir,"] ~,'
54.26	showed] should
55.18	lightly] lighty

55.22	otherwise.] $\sim_\wedge$
55.27	he] *omit*
55.31	thrown] throne
56.15	here?] $\sim,$
56.19	will.] $\sim_\wedge$
56.20	has] as
56.24	strange] stranger
56.28	here!"] $\sim!_\wedge$
56.29	way,] $\sim_\wedge$
57.2	it."] $\sim_{\wedge\wedge}$
57.6	mean."] $\sim_\wedge$"
57.19	this is due] this due
57.22	development] devolpment
57.25	brother.] $\sim_\wedge$
57.26	the present] the the present
57.33	seek] seeek
58.14	&c.] $\sim_\wedge$
58.19	Romance] Roman
58.27	story.] $\sim_\wedge$
58.30	treatment.] $\sim_\wedge$
59.13	days.] $\sim_\wedge$
59.24	unintelligible.] $\sim_\wedge$
59.30	bred] bread
62.27–28	was a long] was long
62.29	interspersed] interspered
62.30	them] him
62.33	something.] $\sim_\wedge$
63.14	of him] him
63.24	sequester] sequster
64.20	Sir,] $\sim,$"
64.20	you,"] $\sim,$'
64.25	stranger's] strangers
65.26	him.] $\sim_\wedge$
66.32	of?] $\sim.$
67.8	wistfully, almost wildly,] $\sim_\wedge \sim \sim_\wedge$
67.11	"Can] $_\wedge\sim$
67.26	of descent] of of descent
67.28	distinction] distincetion

68.7	hereabouts?"] ~·∧
68.18	answered] answerd
68.19	a] an
69.6	first visit,] first,
70.32	were] was
71.12	to hand] to had
71.15	by an] by a
71.26	inexhaustible] inexhaustable
72.11	souls] soulds
72.14	replied,] ~∧
72.34	applicable] applica- | be
73.7	mind?] ~.
73.27	received] recived
74.15	in] into
74.25	conceived] coneived
75.2	evanescent] evanscent
75.7	England,] ~∧
75.18	around] aroud
75.22	continued] con- | tued
75.24	somewhat] some∧ | what
75.27	me] *omit*
76.21	spoken?] ~.
76.33	dreams.] ~∧
77.8	piece] pieice
77.15	not] *omit*
78.15	cabinet] Cabinet
79.11	curb] cub
79.24	priest] prest
80.32	to] *omit*
80.33	been] *omit*
82.26	probability] probabity
82.32	since] since since
82.33	leaving that] leaving on that
83.7	ascertain] as- | ertain
83.14	he] *omit*
83.19	mutandis,] ~∧
84.7	last] laste
86.8	whereabouts] wherabouts

86.10	where] wher
86.15	discovered] discoverd
86.30	peevish,] ~∧
87.6	granddaughter] grandaughter
87.17	phenomenon] phenonenon
88.7	Hospitaller] Hospitaler
88.8	copied] copeied
88.9	Leicester's] Leicesters

ETHEREGE

92.19	haunted.] ~∧
92.25	side,] ~∧
*92.30	merited it.] merited.
93.6	then] then then
*93.29	been] *omit*
95.3	melancholy] melancoly
95.34	an] a
96.13	though] thought
96.33	uninviting] uninvting
96.34	couples] couple
97.5	contained] containained
97.14	swords;] ~,
99.12	their] the
99.21	not.)] ~.∧
99.25	already.] ~,
99.27	Englishman,] ~∧
99.28	loyal] loyual
99.32	for] "~
100.6	citizens,"] ~";
100.12	refer?] ~.
*100.15	successfully] successful
100.30	as] *omit*
100.32	"It] '~
100.33	obscure,] ~∧

101.1	This] "~
101.25	ago?] ~.
101.29	"and] ∧~
102.6	up?] ~.
102.12	one.] ~∧
102.13	"The] ∧~
102.14	"that] ∧~
102.17	"There] ∧~
102.17	"and] ∧~
102.20	"It] ∧~
102.20	"and] ∧~
103.10	if] *omit*
104.6	drawn] draw
104.35	paces] spaces
105.27	doubt,] ∧~
105.28	here?"] ~.∧
105.33	"Our] ∧~
106.9	Mountford] Hammond
106.13	fingers] figures
106.20	this?] ~.
106.22	"Yet] ∧~
106.26	it?] ~.
106.27	I] "~
107.32	"A] ∧~
*108.6	in] *omit*
108.12	in!"] ~!'
108.16	cause?"] ~?'
108.17	"Nothing] ∧~
108.17	mean,] ~;
108.24	it."] ~.∧
108.31	wanted.] ~∧
109.3	everybody's] every's body's
109.12	foot-tracks] footracks
109.18	"you] ∧~
109.20	Ned,] ~∧
110.22	flourish] flouish
111.19	instead] in instead
111.27	alchymick] achymick

111.28	foolish] foolishe
113.3	vacant] vacan
113.12	energies] eneregies
113.27	probably] proably
114.12	skeleton] skelton
114.16	it] in
114.28	England] America
114.29	although] although though
115.10	too,] ~∧
115.18	boy,] ~∧
115.26	sweet."] ~·∧
115.27	"To] ∧~
115.32	There] (~
116.1	almost] almot
116.16	therewith] there with
116.19	schemes] shemes
118.2	inkstand] instand
119.3	childhood?] ~∧
119.24	children—] ~ —"
119.31	Heaven.] ~∧
120.6	conceived] conceved
120.20	doubtless] doutless
120.24	writing] wr- | ing
121.20	had taken] have taken
121.24	he] he he
122.10	the old-fashioned] ~, ~ — ~
122.14	ways.] ~∧
125.12	account] accont
126.27	accepted] a- | cepted
127.5	guest.] ~∧
128.3	earliest] ealiest
128.5	friend.] ~∧
128.33	intricacy] intricacey
129.1	within] within in
129.3	intricacy] intricacey
129.21	generations] generation
130.4	be] *omit*
130.10	mechanical] mechancal

132.5	absolutely] absoluty
132.12	breed] breeed
132.15	not] nott
132.23	them;] ⁓∧
132.25	leopard's] leopards
133.7	his boyish] his (MS page break) ish
133.24	shoulders,] ⁓∧
133.25	palmer.] ⁓∧
133.32	suitable.] ⁓∧
134.6–7	thinking that] thinking but that
134.7	thing] *omit*
134.19	perhaps,] ⁓∧
134.28	which had an] which an
135.24	life, was] life, and now was
136.23	springing] spring
136.30	garment?] ⁓.
136.32	it?] ⁓.
136.34	hereafter.)] ⁓.∧
137.1	man. "You] ⁓, ∧⁓
137.16	here? ⁓.
137.17	beneficiary] beneficary
137.24	"I] ∧⁓
137.25	reality."] ⁓.∧
137.28	attended] attend- | ded
139.26	severity,] severtity∧
139.31–32	from another] from one another
140.1	It] "⁓
140.11	as well as some] as well some
140.21	stranger,] ⁓∧
140.33	"Those] ∧⁓
140.35	me.] ⁓?
141.1	"Pearson] '⁓
141.1	voice] voce
141.10	"The] ∧⁓
141.22	"I] '⁓
141.31	grateful] gratefu
142.2	receive] reieve
142.11	perceiving] perceving

142.13	us?] ~,
142.19	country] county
142.24	interested] intereted
144.21	manner of conveniences] manner conveniences
144.25	learning] learing
144.30	The] the The
145.4	livery] l livery
146.7	cautious] caustous
146.13	of] of of
146.34	to choose] to to choose
147.18	undertaken] under- | ken
148.15	heraldry] heraldy
149.21	"it] ∧~
149.21–22	better to] *omit*
149.32	obscure] obscue
149.32	field] fied
149.34	"to] ∧~
150.2	interest] inteerest
150.3	progenitors] progentors
150.5	kind."] ~.∧
151.15	and was dragged] and dragged
151.30	Etherege's] Etheregee's
151.32	means] meanes
152.4	of Coeur] of of Coeur
152.5	be] *omit*
152.22	meerschaum] meerschum
153.1	it,] ~∧
153.23	two] too
154.29	"That] ∧~
155.20	be] *omit*
156.1–2	was now a] was now served a
156.5	tapestries] tapestryes
156.27	characteristics] characterics
157.11	loaves] loves
158.3	history."] ~∧"
158.25	perceive] peceive
159.2	whereby] wherby
159.28	them," . . . "of] ~,∧ . . . ∧~

159.29	are,] ~∧
159.34	man, "who] ~∧ ∧~
160.6	making to] making | ing to
160.15	character] characters
160.21	from an] from a
161.9	guests)] ~,
161.16	ago,] ~∧
161.30	besides] *omit*
161.31	patriotism?] ~.
162.15	think.] ~∧
162.24	deep] ~,
163.1	down on a] down a
163.15	sentiment."] ~.∧
163.23	world] word
164.13	astonishment.] ~∧
164.18	greatly."] ~.∧
164.19	wonder,] ~∧
164.26	made] madle
164.28	resolutions] reso- | tions
165.31	idle] ildle
165.35	limited] limiteed
166.22	features] feature
167.2	another's] anothe's
167.14	keeping him warm] keeping warm
167.17	with an] with a
167.28	ugly] ogly
167.29	his] *omit*
168.7	evanescent] eevanescent
168.27	not]*omit*
169.18	though] thogh
170.23	courtesy—] ~∧
170.25	Englishmen] Englishman
172.7	independent] indepent
172.26	England] New England
172.28	leaf,] ~∧
172.30	have] *omit*
173.6	at] *omit*
173.10	Yes,] ~∧

173.11	"That] ∧~
173.27	religion,] ~∧
175.20	were] was
176.5	who were moving] who moving
176.13	so?] ~.
176.16	is] *omit*
176.19	thought] thoght
176.20	in such] such in
176.28	in] "~
176.35	deal.] ~∧
177.12	similarity.] ~∧
178.8	tree.)] ~.∧
178.14	"is well] ∧~ ~
178.26	Monmouth's] Monmouths
178.29	not] *omit*
179.3	curiosity.] ~∧
179.4	"had] ∧~
179.7	set it here] set here
179.11	circular] ci- | cular
179.19	skeletons] skelleton
179.20	windows] window
179.30	pipes.] ~∧
180.30	see that you] see you that you
180.34	sketch?] ~.
181.4	Etherege,] ~∧
181.25	Etherege] Ether- | ge
181.31	part—] ~,
181.33	daisies—] ~∧
182.1	were content to] were to content to
182.21	here] hee
182.22	Etherege,] ~∧
183.18–19	'Richard Oglethorpe 1613.'] " ~ ~ 1619."
183.22	hereabouts] herabouts
183.27	attention] atte∧ | tion
183.28	lady] la |
183.34	struck him,] struck,
184.19	position] possion
184.34	vegetable.] ~∧

185.2	a] *omit*
185.8	had] *omit*
185.24	too,] ~∧
185.32	been] *omit*
185.33	said] *omit*
186.2	only a front] only front
186.29	country] county
189.6	contrary] country
189.7	ceases to be a] ceases to a
189.16	do so.] do.
189.20	but] *omit*
189.24	Etherege's] Etheregege's
189.25	temporary] temprary
190.21	speech] speach
190.32	requisites] requisite
191.1	voices] voies
191.12	preparation.] prepration∧
192.12	sweetest] sweetiest
193.5	on] *omit*
193.18	America] England
194.15	country] county
194.19	who] *omit*
195.7	brother's] brothers
197.27	indicate] indicaete
198.28	been] *omit*
199.2	man] *omit*
201.2	been] *omit*
201.9	anathema] an anthem	
201.11	can't] Can't
201.21	can] cannot
201.31	what?] ~.
202.9	delineated] dilineated
202.31	went] went went
203.31	eject] ejeect
205.25	elapses.] ~∧
205.27	an agent] a agent
206.9	can] *omit*
208.5	feeblenesses] feeeblenesses

208.28	done] *omit*
209.1	morbid,] ~∧
209.29	this.] ~∧
210.4	responsibility,] responsibilty∧
210.8	affect them] affect on them
210.9	"I] ∧~
210.11	trouble] troble
211.7	aspect?] ~.
211.12	nonsensical,] ~∧
211.14	possibility] possibiliy
211.22	as] *omit*
211.31	swept] sweept
212.4	himself.] ~∧
212.20	gorgeous,] ~∧
212.24	(This] ∧~
213.1	prophetic] phrophetic
213.15	turning] turing
213.21	addressed] address
214.3	when] whent
214.18	heavy] heavey
215.3	recollect] recolect
215.6	failed] faild
216.1	accumulating] accumating
216.29	than] *omit*
217.14	you?] ~.
217.22	whereabouts] wherabouts
217.26	confess,] ~∧
218.11	"to] ∧~
220.3	last] least
220.10	States.] ~∧
220.16	requisite] resu-	site
221.24	insane] insanee
221.33	gentle] gentlle
222.5	wherefor] wherfor
222.6	hand] *omit*
223.3	the wicked] the the wicked
223.8	because] becuse
223.10	&c)] ~,

223.28	specific] specfic
224.14	'twill] 't'will
225.25	avenge] avenege
226.3	outside] outs- | side
227.1	most] mot
227.16	family?] ~.
227.17	keys] locks
227.18	Etherege] Etherge
228.19	boy,] ~ₐ
229.12	however,] ~ₐ
229.23	thorough] through
230.11	seem] *omit*
230.15	a man] an man
231.20	is] are
231.32	not] *omit*
232.13	Etherege] Ethereges
232.19	Hammond] Hammon
233.23	left to be] left be
234.4	having] being
235.3	strength] strengh
235.12	from a] from the a
235.21	that had been] that been
236.11	viz.,] ~ₐ,
236.18	neckcloths] necklouths
236.23	it is] it is is
236.28	as . . . diplomatist to] to as . . . diplomatist
237.22	us] his
239.18	neckcloth] neckloth
239.29	an] a
240.4	American's] Americans'
240.5	possibilities] possibties
240.6	country] county
240.30	classes] classs
241.21	Cup";] ~ₐ;
241.30	guest,] ~ₐ
241.33–34	stately table;] stately;
242.11	dinner.)] ~.ₐ

242.29	him] them
242.31	he.] ~‸
242.34	links] link
243.2	vase?] ~.
243.2	has] is has
243.12	whoever] who
243.18	malevolence.] ~‸
244.1	Every man] Everyman
244.4	which] *omit*
244.18	Italians,"] ~,‸
244.23	shame)] ~,
245.4	emphasis,] ~‸
245.8	health of the] health the
245.9	Linden] Lende
246.1	sensibilities] sensibities
246.10	interest] intrest
247.10	circumstances] circumstance
247.15	Besides,] ~‸
248.6	accepted.] ~‸
249.1	have] *omit*
249.4	inexhaustibleness] inexhaustbleness
249.19	heretofore,] ~.
249.21	soda-water.] ~ — ~‸
250.7	laugh] laught
250.7	myself] yourself
250.9	it] *omit*
250.15	morning."] moring.‸
250.22	an] a
251.7	hereabouts.] ~‸
251.8	him,] ~‸
251.11	"You] ‸~
251.14	Doctor?] ~.
251.26–27	of family] of of family
251.29	known] know
252.22	so,] ~?
254.11	American] America
254.15	England?] ~.
255.12	ranks.] ~‸

256.7	be conscious] be of conscious
256.9	exhilarating] exhilirating
256.13	which,] ~∧
259.3	do] *omit*
259.13	would now be] would be now be
260.28	subject.] ~∧
261.5	know?] ~.
261.11	present.] ~∧
261.17	Elsie,"] ~,∧
261.26	here."] ~∧"
262.4	Half] (~
262.22	anybody?] ~.
264.17	proofs] proof
264.23	attained?] ~.
265.5	probability] pobability
267.30	devilish] devilsh
268.3	Pshaw.] ~∧
268.14	Why?] ~.
268.31	plunged?] ~.
268.33	some how] some or how
269.16	do.] ~∧
269.17	subtlety] sublety
270.9	nevertheless] neverthels
270.12	guest] guests
271.1	case] casee
271.23	interesting] intersting
271.34	having] have
272.25	look at,] look,
272.32	asking of] ~ – ~
273.6	point?] ~.
273.10	thither."]~.∧
273.13	here."] ~.∧
273.14	saying,] ~∧
273.26	entered] entred
274.3	country] county
274.6	It certainly] It is certainly
274.30	as] "~
275.7	no others] *omit*

275.31   "a] ∧~

276.32–33   first sight," remarked] first [*page break*] re-
            marked

277.2   coming] com'g |

277.10   abode.] ~."

277.29   it."] ~·∧

278.2   who] *omit*

278.8   moment's] momen's

278.16   "The] '~

278.32   confessed,] ~∧

279.11   Lordship,] ~;

279.14   Antonio,] ~∧

279.30   was] *omit*

280.15   losing] *omit*

280.27   no] now

281.8   do?] ~,

281.11   life?] ~.

281.13   prospect?] ~,

281.19   myself an] myself a

281.29   English] Englishsh

282.7   this?] ~.

282.7   richness?] ~.

282.14   admitted him;] admitted;

282.21   taken] *omit*

282.27   the] MS *torn away*

282.34   time] *omit*

283.9   affected] affeted

284.6   most] mot

284.12   prophetic] phropetic

284.17   prophecy] prhropesy

284.18   fulfilled?] ~.

285.7   kept] *omit*

285.26   peculiarity] peculiarty

285.33   Here] (~

286.9   otherwise),] ~)∧

286.9   the former (who] the the former, who

286.12   repository] repostory

286.27   refers] referes

287.6	here.] ~;
287.6	Doctor's] Doctor
287.18	annihilation] annilation
287.22	refers] referes
287.31	and force] and of force
288.19	subtlety] sublety
289.16	being] be- |
289.34	strongly] stronly
292.30	generally] generaly
293.3	close] cloe
293.17	difficult so] difficult to so
293.17	emphasize] emphasive
293.24	customary] cutory
293.25	circumstances] circumtances
294.15	situation?] ~.
294.17	"nine] ∧~
294.19	time,] ~∧
294.20	intricately.] ~∧
294.22	began] begins
294.27	hall,"] ~,∧
294.29	years?] ~.
294.32	"Ah] ∧~
294.33	this,] ~∧
295.1	"Is] ∧~
295.1	master?] ~,
295.3	him?] ~,
295.6	Etherege] Etherge
295.15	strengthened] strengt- | ened
295.26	reckless] recklss
296.1	be] *omit*
296.30	like] till
296.30	influenza] influena
297.1	politics,] ~∧
297.5	seem] seemed
297.6	discerned] discered
297.11	them.] ~∧
298.8	it] *omit*
298.21	no,] ~∧

298.23	away?] way.
298.25	to come] $\sim$ - $\sim$
299.4	to] too
299.8	although] althought
299.34	him.] $\sim_\wedge$
300.18	answered?] $\sim$.
302.24	examining] examing
303.1	his duty] his *omitted*
303.8	"There] '$\sim$
303.8	time] *omit*
303.9	you."] $\sim\cdot_\wedge$
303.20	"You] '$\sim$
303.28	Brathwaite.] $\sim_\wedge$
303.32	him?] $\sim$.
303.34	"Left] $_\wedge\sim$
304.2	it,] $\sim_\wedge$
304.11	distinctly] distintly
305.11	relinquished."] $\sim$.'
306.5	Come,] $\sim_\wedge$
306.5	welcome.] $\sim_\wedge$
307.25	time] *omit*
307.28	House.] $\sim_\wedge$
307.32	When he awoke] When awoke
307.33	disagreeable] disgreable
308.8	since] sense
308.9	closed] unclosed
308.17	prophetic] phrophetic
308.21	whereabouts] wherabouts
308.24	twilight] twlight
309.1	upon him,] upon,
309.20	things?] $\sim$.
309.21	republic?] $\sim$.
309.29	life?] $\sim$.
310.27	at] *omit*
311.5	three] *omit*
312.26	perception] peception
312.27	doubtfully]doubfully
312.31	unintelligible] unintellgble

313.2	hand] *omit*
313.5	if] *omit*
313.24	itself] its
314.34	pensioner.] ∼ˏ
315.7	so?] ∼,
315.25	she.] ∼ˏ
316.1	"See] '∼
316.15	than the] the the
316.25	"This] '∼
316.29	"Pray] '∼
316.31	"I] ˏ∼
316.31	servant,] ∼.
317.6	what] *omit*
317.8	Warden's] Warden
317.17–18	London?] ∼,
317.22	whereabout] wherabout
318.32	"Mr.] '∼.
318.14	countenance] *omit*
319.13	will excuse] will you excuse
320.16	Follow,] ∼ˏ
321.1	"Ha!"] ˏ∼ˏ"
321.8	more] *omit*
321.10	replied he.] replied.
321.29	wondering.] ∼ˏ
322.10	do,"] ∼ˏ"
322.18	contents?] ∼.
322.23	been] *omit*
323.4	known."] ∼ˏ"
323.19	spiders] spider's
324.8	property] poperty
324.11	web?] ∼.
324.13	perpetrating] perpetrate
325.8	done?] ∼.
325.15	race] races
326.18	mischief] mishcief
326.21	to be] be be
326.30	a] *omit*
328.10–11	as well] as as well

328.14	a] *omit*
329.28	purposes] purpoes
330.20	perhaps] pe-|haps
330.32	sensitive] senstive
331.5	disappointed] disa- | pointed
331.5	hopeless,] $\sim_\wedge$
331.18	his?] $\sim$.
332.1	appurtenance] appertenance
332.3	do] too
333.2	to see] to to see
333.12	but] by
333.23	disappears] dis- | pears
333.27	father's] father
333.28	unreliability] unreliablity
334.11	are] is
335.9	therefore] therfre
336.4	seen it long] seen long
336.16	seem] *omit*
336.26–27	light was] light it was
337.1	no,] $\sim_\wedge$
337.14	sometimes] someting
337.18	heels] heel
337.20	forehead?] $\sim$.
337.21	perceive] perceve
337.23	perceive] peceive
337.25	everything] everthing
338.9	softly spoken,] softly,
338.9	questionable] quesionable
338.13	search.] $\sim$?
338.14	pistols,] $\sim_\wedge$
339.11	furniture?] $\sim$.
339.29	us] *omit*
340.19	"I] $_\wedge\sim$
340.22	tone.] $\sim_\wedge$
340.26	weather] weathe
340.26	it?] $\sim$.
340.27	"But] $_\wedge\sim$
341.2	spoke.] $\sim_\wedge$

341.3   "Have] ∧~
341.18   since] hence
341.26   performing] perforing

GRIMSHAWE

343.3   person] ~,
343.3   aspect,] ~∧
343.5–6   of a blonde girl] of blonde girl
343.13   write] wright
343.21   threshold] theshold
344.2   played] *omit*
344.3   and running] and and running
344.10   (Crusty] ∧~
344.22   of whose] whose
344.23   had been] had had
344.26   -land] -hand
344.33   sturdy] study
344.33–345.1   is said] is is said
345.2   vegetable productions] vegetable growth, pro-
               ductions
345.4   they] *omit*
345.5   out of some] out some
345.23   sufficient] suficient
346.7   billows,] ~∧
346.12   would] *omit*
346.22   people's] peoples
346.23   could] *omit*
347.3   old,] ~∧
347.15   erroneous,] ~∧
347.26   and various] and a various
347.30   cobwebs,] ~∧
347.31   produce] produced
347.32   quantity,] ~∧
348.3   title,] ~∧
348.11   principle] principal

349.2	forehead,] $\sim_\wedge$
349.16	the purport] the his purport
350.1	handmaiden,] $\sim_\wedge$
350.2	preserved,] $\sim_\wedge$
350.3	Of] or Of
350.5	spiders.] $\sim_\wedge$
350.18	secret] secet
350.20	Ormskirk's] Ormskirks
351.7	knob,] $\sim_\wedge$
351.8	creature] creatures
351.17	lived,] $\sim_\wedge$
351.24	to] *omit*
351.24	creature's] creatures
351.27	tastes,] $\sim_\wedge$
352.6	volumes] $\sim$,
352.25	like] *omit*
352.26	till it was] till was
352.32	made] *omit*
353.21	coexist] coexsit
353.24	grievous] grevious
353.26	responded] Responded
354.23	himself.] $\sim_\wedge$
355.4	blond,] $\sim_\wedge$
355.8	red-eyed,] $\sim$ - $\sim_\wedge$
355.19	conviviality.] $\sim_\wedge$
356.10	myself."] $\sim_\wedge$"
356.12	'ou] $_\wedge$uo
356.27	Whence did you] whence did you
356.32	recollections] recolections
357.1	am] *omit*
357.8	Grim,] $\sim$,"
357.8	"You] $_\wedge\sim$
357.9	earnest.] $\sim$?
357.11	"I] $_\wedge\sim$
357.12	me] *omit*
357.13	from."] $\sim\cdot_\wedge$
357.16	Doctor.] $\sim_\wedge$
357.17	Ned.] $\sim$,

357.21	sword] shord
357.28	"If] ∧~
357.30	alms-house;] ~ - ~;"
357.30	hereafter] herafter
357.32	is] is is
357.33	his] ~,
358.10	Doctor] *omit*
358.33	Ned,] ~∧
359.7	be] *omit*
359.33	been] *omit*
360.2	taciturn] tactern
360.6	fell] feell
360.9	Grimshawe, after] ~∧ After
360.20	was his birth-place] was birth-place
360.22	to] *omit*
360.27	them,] ~∧
360.32	of] *omit*
361.11	him] ~,
361.15	house,] ~∧
361.21	structure,] ~∧
361.30	and] and and
361.32	Elsie,] ~∧
361.33	for] *omit*
362.2	of a past] of past
362.3	him,] ~∧
362.13	¶"After] *no* ¶
362.13	in] ~∧
362.24	decency generally hides] decency hides generally hides
363.13	skeleton] skeloten
363.18	suite] suiet
363.21	if] *omit*
363.23	renewed it,] ~, ~,
363.23	new] knew
363.24	it were] it it were
363.33	by-and-by] ~∧ ~ - ~
364.2	everywhere] ~∧	~
364.6	children,] ~∧

364.10	it,] ~∧
364.10	"hiding] ∧~
365.5	perhap—] ~∧
365.7	"though] ∧~
365.8	so.] ~∧
365.12	imprisoned him,] imprisoned,
365.17	fade,] ~∧
365.32–33	that the] that the the
367.14	bending] bend-	
367.22	someone] some
368.1	scenery,] ~∧
368.3	interest] intererest
368.4	an] a
368.10	individually;] ~∧
368.18	passionate] ~,
368.34	came] *omit*
369.8	cachinnatory] cachinatory
369.9	Then,] ~∧
369.10	other,] ~∧
370.3	needlework,] ~∧
370.18	of] *omit*
370.26	think] thing
370.29–30	love for and] love and
371.2	something] some
371.15	polish,] ~.
371.17	texture.] ~,
371.19	gained] be-	gained
371.32	the sort] the the sort
372.1	able] abable
372.12	servants,] ~;
372.28	noble] nobble
372.30	be] *omit*
373.20	language] languge
373.21	he] *omit*
373.26	Frenchman's] frenchman's
373.28	(not] ∧~
373.33	utilitarian] utilititarian
374.3	pupil,] ~.

375.7	pervade] pevade
375.13	laughter;] ~,
375.15	earthy,] ~‸
375.26	by] *omit*
375.27	always averred] always she averred
375.31	devil] devvil
375.33	paroxysm] paroxyism
376.2	to] *omit*
376.35	Grim.] ~‸
378.23	Elsie.] ~‸
379.20	recourse] resource
379.20	had a way] had a had a way
379.25	"There] ‸~
379.25	Spider-minder,] ~ – ~‸
379.30	his] is
380.2	him,] ~‸
380.3	Grim!] ~‸
380.5	cried] *omit*
380.14	topics] topic
380.15	portion of] portion to
380.24	should] should should
380.34	religious] reglious
381.2	strength] strenght
381.8	enemy.] ~‸
381.16	selectmen] slectmen
381.23–24	(the . . . graveyard)] ‸~ . . . ~‸
381.25	charges;] ~‸
381.29	entering. But] ~; but
381.30	Doctor's] Doctors
381.31	courteous.] ~‸
381.32	delighted] delight- | ted
382.1	ladies,] ~;
382.21	the] The
382.26	yesterday;] ~. &c &
382.27	was] *omit*
383.5	blood;] ~,
383.25	off,] ~‸
383.29	town;] ~.

384.10	pass?] ~.
384.12	population?] ~.
384.24	overrunning] overuning
384.31	as his pale] as pale
385.5	tickled.)] ~._∧
385.13	Quack] Quak
386.1	unexpected] unexpted
386.4	assailants] assailanst
386.8	took] toof
386.15	operated merely as] operated as merely as
386.26	own.] ~_∧
386.31	certainty."] ~_∧"
387.2	appeared] ~,
387.9	unless] unlss
387.19	"not] _∧~
387.22	sensations,] ~.
387.23	members.] ~_∧
387.25	much.] ~."
387.35	have been a] have a
388.8	good."] ~._∧
388.10	water.] ~_∧
388.11	"How] '~
388.23	out of the] out the
388.26	sky.] ~;
389.5	organization,] organazation_∧
389.22	apart] part
390.10	me] them
390.30	being as he—] being as—
391.13	too,] ~_∧
391.25	instructed.] ~,
391.29	Take] Taek
392.6	him] *omit*
392.7	egg."] ~._∧
392.16	hater,] ~_∧
392.16	impulsive,] ~_∧
392.27	Seymour's] Seymours
392.28	speaking,] ~_∧
392.33	of] *omit*

393.7	breathe] breath
393.21	character] ~,
393.26	till now,] till,
393.30	were] was
394.4	schoolmaster's] school‸	master's
394.10	indeed,] ~‸
394.11	Africa,] ~‸
394.15–16	might be,] might,
394.30	buying] bying
395.6	a] a a
395.11	trod."] ~.‸
395.20	"although] ‸~
396.2	home."] ~‸ "—
396.3	How?"] ~?‸
397.1	descended.] ~."
397.8	"Of] '~
397.10	contempt] contempted
397.12	Schoolmaster] Doctor
397.21	irregular] irreguar
397.31	absorbed] aborbed
398.22	thoughts,] ~‸
398.34	comfortable] comfortatble
399.20	person,"] ~,'
399.28	were] wheer
400.20	as] at
401.22	crime?] ~.
401.32	resisted?] ~.
401.34	"I] ‸~
401.35	me."] ~.‸
402.1	of] omit
402.15	incompatibility] incompatibley
403.10	which the Doctor] which Doctor
403.22	should] sheould
404.24	cheeks] cheeeks
404.25	left] omit
404.27	—they] ‸They
404.28	morning—] ~.
404.33	table] tabe

405.13	shouted] should
405.19	seemed] seecked
405.20	combination.] ~∧
405.22	Grim?"] ~.∧
406.3	to have] *omit*
406.5	ridiculed] ridiculd
406.8	Doctor Grim's] Doctor's Grims
406.13	witch?] ~,
406.32	his] *omit*
408.10	answered,] answerd
408.12	Why?] ~∧
408.13	Doctor.] ~∧
408.26	spots] spot
410.14	creature's] creatures
410.21	grass,] ~∧
410.22	cultivated] cultivaed
412.17	so?] ~.
412.25	have time] have no time
412.31	"My] ∧~
413.4	"To] '~
413.4	grave!"] ~!'
413.12	"I] '~
413.16	occupy] ocupy
413.29	English family, one] English one
413.30	wilderness,] ~∧
414.4	descent] decent
414.18	search?] ~.
414.22	importance?] ~.
414.26	"At] ∧~
415.2	buried?] ~.
415.4	may] *omit*
415.12	out,] ~∧
415.22	is!"] ~!'
415.23	"Hush] ∧~
415.31	lighted] light
415.33	girlhood] girlhoood
416.15	seen.] ~∧
416.18	conversation] converstation

416.20	it?"] ~.ᴧ
416.25	this snow] this is snow
416.33–34	snow, . . . hand,] ~ᴧ . . . ~ᴧ
417.7	that could so] that so so
417.13	Well,] ~ᴧ
417.14	Ned] "~
417.20	two] too
417.22	into it;] into;
417.26	far as I] far I
417.31	thrust] thrust in
418.11	never caught] never you caught
418.18	furrows?] ~.
418.27	I] "~
419.5	'Ebenezer] "~
419.6	ground.'] ~,'
419.8	prohibition?"] ~?ᴧ
419.9	Mountford] Mounfford
419.18	been] *omit*
419.23–24	knowledge, . . . especially,] ~ᴧ . . . ~ᴧ
419.26	suppose.] ~ᴧ
419.30	"You] ᴧ~
419.33	with it that] with that
420.3	just as I] just I
420.5	be] *omit*
420.12	flat] ~,
420.23	as] has
420.29	King] King's
420.29	Charles's] Charle's
420.30	"it] '~
420.33	two] too
421.2	Hewen?] ~.
421.4	years,"] ~.ᴧ
421.11	friend,] ~ᴧ
421.11	trouble."] ~.ᴧ
421.30	fancy] fay
422.7	has] have
422.18	him] them

422.25	question] questioned
423.19	indeed] ineed
423.20–21	it disturbed] it distured
423.31	recorded] recoded
424.22	"When] '∼
424.23	there!"] ∼!'
425.3	arrayed] array
425.21	vistas] vista
426.31	"You] ∧∼
427.3	had] has
427.9	whipt out of] whipt of
427.11	"You] '∼
427.20	looking at the] looking the
427.23	tumbler] tumb-|bler
427.29–30	Come, I'm] Come, Im
428.4	"Ned] ∧∼
428.4	'I'm] '∼
428.4	longer.] ∼∧
428.17	wretch] wrethch
429.26	years'] yeares'
430.10	womanly] womanley
430.15	little as ever] little ever
430.31	initiated] intiated
431.4	wistful beside] wistful at beside
431.13	invoke it upon you] invoke upon it upon
431.15	arms] arm's
431.16	hers] her's
431.30–31	world— . . . home;] ∼; . . . ∼∧
432.8	home.] ∼∧
432.9	it?] ∼.
432.25	instead] insteading
433.10	discernible] discernable
433.19	threatened] threated
433.22	would not] woud not
433.28	seemed to indicate] seemed indicate
433.35	"Afraid] ∧∼
433.35	Grim?"] ∼·∧
434.1	"Neither] ∧∼

434.5	there."] ~‸"
434.12	coffee,] ~)
434.13	spoon)] ~;
435.20	decidedly] decidedy
435.23	to say] to the say
436.5	him."] ~‸‸
436.8	succeeded.] ~‸
436.16	placed] paced
436.22	chamber.] chamber; and kissed his hand to her, and laughed [MS laghed] feebly; and that was the last that she or any body, the last glimpse they had of Doctor Grimshawe alive.
436.24	cry,] ~‸
436.26	kiss.] ~‸
436.28–29	the Silver] the the Silver
436.30–31	"Let . . . morning."] ‸let . . . . ~·‸
437.3	acceptably] acceptibly
437.18	one instant is] one is
437.30	country] county
438.2	provision] provi-|ion
438.9	discover] discovered
438.10	no.] ~‸
439.18	close] closee
439.23	ago.] ~‸
439.26	face] faith
439.32	discover] decover
440.4	A] a
440.9	wizard's] wizards
440.30	53.] ~‸
441.2,4	55.] ~‸
441.8	book.] ~‸
442.5	was] was was
442.16	its] it
442.25	hedge] edge
442.26	way] *omit*
443.2	of] of of
443.3	and] and and
443.20	high-road] hiagh-road

443.29	solidity] stolidy
443.30	hobnailed] hobnaild
443.33	afield] a field
444.6	whereabout] where bout
444.8	delight.] ~∧
444.31	moment,] ~.
445.2	turbulent] ~,
445.11	was.] ~∧ —
445.11	long been shut] long shut
445.29	stranger's] strangers
446.2	neighborhood] neigh-|bord
446.10	herd] heard
446.13	whose] who
446.29	seclusion,] secclusion∧
446.31	will-o'-the-whisp] will-o the whisp
446.33	solitude] solitued
447.6	himself] him
447.8	unconsciousness] un-|sciousness
447.30	distinctly] distincly
448.13	elsewhere] elsewere
448.14	leopard's] leopards
448.16	with] *omit*
448.20	And] and
448.30	chest,] ~∧
449.16	who] as
449.16	oratories] orartories
449.22	bedside] beside
450.6	if the peaceful] if peaceful
450.20	shimmering] shimering
450.23	fantasy?"] fantasty?∧
450.27	he;] ~∧
450.28	Again] "~
450.32	too,] ~∧
450.34	could not find] could find
451.6	leopard's] leopar's
451.9	more.] ~∧
451.9	medicine,] ~∧
451.24	would] woud

451.27	Describe] Decribe
452.23	long as they] long they
453.5	palimpsest] palampsis
453.18	hurt ere now] hurt now
454.13	half] haf
454.29	show] *omit*
455.13	since] "Since
455.19	things as the above] things above
455.34	of being awake] of awake
456.14	self-reproach,] ~ – ~.
456.19	remember] rememberber
456.22	smiled.] ~ᴧ
456.23	boy,] ~?
456.23	he.] ~ᴧ
457.8	&c)] &)
457.10	"In] ᴧ~
457.26	"Your] ᴧ~
457.33	harassed] harrassed
458.1	to be] to to be
458.26	its] it
458.33	happy state] happy state of the happy state
459.17	lie] *omit*
459.22	again to take] again take
459.25	inaction] action
459.30	palmer; "and] ~ᴧ ᴧ~
460.2	is] *omit*
460.5	temporal] tempororal
460.22	your] his
460.23	"You] '~
460.31	authority in the] authority the
460.31	establishment?] ~.
461.7	"From] ᴧ~
461.9	another] anthother
461.11	remember] remembeed
461.16	not] *omit*
462.1	"Another] ᴧ~
462.15	so Redclyffe's] so the Redclyffe's
462.16	him)] ~,

462.25	and] "~
463.5	by Redclyffe's] by the Redclyffe's
463.10	heretofore] here-|tore
463.14	recovered.] recoverd∧
463.22	that it would] that would
463.28	Warden,] ~∧
464.13	value?] ~!
464.17	credit,] ~∧
464.21	way.] ~."
464.22	used it since] used since
464.27	spot?] ~.
464.28	less,] ~∧
464.32	one,] ~∧
465.4	us?"] ~?'
465.6	introduction,"] ~,'
465.8	who and] who and and
465.21	know,] ~∧
465.21	Redclyffe,] ~∧
466.3	an] a
466.20	Warden and he] Warden he
466.33	next."] ~∧"
467.4	comfort.] ~;
467.24	quadrangle] quadrange
467.26	friend's] friends
468.18	Warden's] Wardens
469.19	inkstand] instand
469.25	a] *omit*
469.26	Latin,] ~∧
469.29	ballads;] ~∧
470.6	Grim's] Grims
470.10–11	head and an] heand an
470.20	that perhaps his] that his perhaps his
471.4	developed at once into] developed into at once into
471.13	air."] ~∧∧
471.14	"My] '~
471.15	Etherege] Etherge
471.16	blood."] ~∧∧

Ancillary Documents

474.28	been] *omit*
475.3	feeling] feelling
476.7	drawn?] ∼.
477.18	condition?] ∼.
480.16	of a window] of window
480.26	starts] start
481.11–12	effect of all] effect all
481.13	is] *omit*
481.22	is] *omit*
481.23	may] *omit*
482.19	on.] ∼∧
483.24	of an ancestor] of ancestor
486.8	Vagabond] Vagabon
487.76	Battle] Battel

WORD-DIVISION

1. *End-of-the-Line Hyphenation in the Centenary Edition*

Possible compounds hyphenated at the end of a line in the
Centenary text are listed here if they are hyphenated within the
line in the copy-text. Exclusion from this list means that a possible compound appears as one unhyphenated word in the copy-
text. Also excluded are hyphenated compounds in which both
elements are capitalized.

14.4	old-fashioned	91.15	good-natured
14.5	well-remembered	99.12	middle-aged
17.5	wonder-stricken	99.15	old-fashioned
27.1	farm-house	104.1	gold-laced
27.3	landing-place	110.32	drawing-room
28.22	hiding-place	124.11	alms-house
34.30	strong-minded	145.2	bachelor-state
36.6	farm-house	145.25	luncheon-time
54.29	wood-walk	145.30	by-incident
65.21	morning-mists	147.29	half-fanciful
68.33	manor-house	168.17	hedge-rows
69.30	farm-house	176.23	show-place
72.5	ill-taught	177.25	moss-grown
72.28	age-long	179.27	village-|ale-house
83.15	manor-house	197.1	death-bed

200.25	self-seekers	339.8	coal-fire
218.21	death-hour	343.10	dusting-cloth
224.6	life-threads	365.14	manor-house
234.19	half-tame	370.2	bread-making
234.22	canvas-back	370.34	book-worm
237.1	simple-mannered	381.3	party-sympathies
238.26	time-honored	384.2	body-snatcher
241.2	self-gratulation	395.14	pipe-stem
249.13	toast-water	411.22	travelling-dress
259.18	village-street	420.6	bas-relief
266.34	blood-red	427.35	tobacco-fragrant
280.25	Indian-haunted	432.24	quarter-staff
283.13	dying-bed	481.1	hand- | in-hand
298.16	alms-house	482.23	family-abode
301.7	ill-feeling		
308.2	alms-house		
331.34	rope-dancer		
333.6	serving-man		

2. End-of-the-Line Hyphenation in the Copy-Text

The following possible compounds are hyphenated at the ends of lines in the copy-text. The form adopted in the Centenary Edition, as listed below, represents Hawthorne's predominant usage as ascertained by other appearances within the copy-texts.

6.21	daylight	66.20	footsteps
25.21	self-esteem	102.18	seventy-five
34.30	countrywoman	110.26	housemaid's
39.18	manor-house	119.18	true-hearted
44.19	foretaste	119.28	grave-yard
49.11	Footstep	124.27	alms-house
53.14	footstep	129.21	footsteps
53.29	grass-grown	131.10	by-path
60.4	gamekeepers	132.35	moonlight
61.26	footsteps	145.1	mantle-piece

158.24	looking-glass	389.2	tiptoe
169.26	un-English	394.4	schoolmaster's
220.24	death-beds	397.22	cobwebs
271.16	home-feeling	398.10	parti-colored
278.18	book-worms	399.23	whipcord
290.10	half-hanged	403.28	townspeople
290.21	pre-supposed	404.14	schoolmaster's
300.9	state-necessity	406.25	schoolmaster
308.33	half-awake	411.18	winter-day
343.21	tombstone	418.5	grave-diggers
344.25	church-towers	480.7	grave-yard
347.21	ill-lighted	480.21	sprite-like
380.34	brandy-bottle	481.25	ivy-grown
382.19	townspeople		

3. Special Cases

The following possible compounds are hyphenated at the ends of lines in both copy-text and Centenary Edition. Words appear here in the adopted Centenary form which is obscured by line-end hyphenation.

10.31	Footstep	68.33	manor-house
17.5	wonder-stricken	185.12	hearth-smokes
37.8	county-history	339.3	noon-day

ALTERATIONS IN THE MANUSCRIPTS

Hawthorne's practice in making deletions was to wipe out wet ink with a finger or to cancel with pen strokes. Additions he interlined or inscribed over the wiped-out original; now and then he heavily superimposed new language upon the dried original inscription.

In addition to revisions carried out, Hawthorne left evidence of further changes he intended in these unfinished drafts. He added one parenthetical note to himself in the "Ancestral Footstep" sketch (74.10); dozens of such reminders appear in the "Etherege" and "Grimshawe" manuscripts, tucked into paragraph ends or written in margins or interlined. Each of these notes, marked off by angle brackets in the Centenary text, occasions an Alterations entry that describes its location in the manuscript. Hawthorne's resort to any available space inevitably places some notes where they may not seem immediately pertinent; these are inserted in Centenary at the point dictated by the logic of the context.

To indicate repositioning of paragraphs, Hawthorne usually wrote out directions; for smaller units he marked the limits of affected passages with arrowhead pointers, a series of diagonal or vertical lines, or carets—often two- or three-tiered. Wherever possible the Centenary text carries out his intention and an Alterations entry describes his directions or signs.

This listing takes account of Hawthorne's alterations except for deletions that have not been deciphered. Simple mending of letters or words without alteration of the original is ignored, as are Sophia Hawthorne's interlinear glosses upon the "Footstep" manuscript, and marks on the "Etherege" and "Grimshawe" drafts in a librarian's hand noting chapter divisions, omissions, and the like that relate to Julian Hawthorne's 1883 edition. Alterations not in Hawthorne's hand are indicated by an asterisk alongside the page-line reference. Empty square brackets signify one or more undeciphered letters; letters within square brackets are conjectural on some evidence although not wholly certain. In the description of manuscript alterations, *above* means "Interlined" and *over* means "in the same space." The presence of a caret is always noted.

THE ANCESTRAL FOOTSTEP

5.5–6	itinerants] second 'i' mended from 't'
6.4–5	heirships] second 'h' over 'p'
7.3	as he] over wiped-out 'pe[rson]'
7.11	one] over 'an'
8.16	before] 'b' over 'f'
9.21–22	doorway] 'or' over 'wa'
9.25	right] 'r' over 'l'
10.8	now] 'n' over wiped-out 'f'
10.26	had] 'h' over 'a'
11.8	one] over 'a'
12.3	mystery,] followed by wiped-out quotation mark
12.7	certainly] 'ce' over 'a'
12.14	I know] 'k' over possible 'e'
13.8	ago] 'a' over 'in'
13.16	mere] followed by cancelled 'pleasure'
13.27	ancient] 'c' over partial 'g'
14.7	developing] second 'e' over 'o'
14.30	cordiality—] dash over wiped-out comma
16.33	whereby] 'wh' over 'of'
17.8	marriage] 'm' over 'cer'
17.9	after] over 'with'

18.3	as] over 'wh'
18.18	murder—] dash cancels comma
19.11	wrath.] followed by wiped-out quotation mark
19.30	hammer] 'hamm' over 'bull'
19.31	sending] 'sen' over 'fir'
20.19	to] over 'him'
20.23	he] over wiped-out 'but'
20.24	great?] question mark mended from semicolon
*20.26	guiltiness] 'ti' mended from 'it' in a hand not NH's
21.2	along] 'a' over 'l'
21.7–8	exclamation—] dash cancels comma
21.15	turning] 't' over 'a'
21.21	ear] over 'hear'
21.24	and] over wiped-out possible 'th'
22.1	one of] over wiped-out possible 'Nation'
22.24	catastrophe] 'tr' over 'ph'
22.31	given] 'g' over wiped-out 'ha'
23.8	do you] 'd' over 'y'
23.15	alone] 'a' over 'h'
24.1	ecstatic] 's' over 'a'
24.9	reconciled] 'recon' mended from 'now'
24.9	to] over 'me'
24.9	now] 'n' over wiped-out 'k'
24.34	in] over a dash
25.7	disregarded] first 'r' over wiped-out 'g'
25.26	scattered] second 'e' over 'd'
25.34	in] over wiped-out 'his'
26.1	acquiring] 'c' over 'cc'
26.3	in] over wiped-out 'E'
26.27	can] over 'were'
26.35	you!"] exclamation over original quotation mark and new quotation mark then added
27.1	mansion] 'm' over 'far'
27.6	recognizing] 'r' over 'to'
27.8	to] 't' over 'f'
27.11–12	He steadied] 'He stea' over wiped-out 'Whither'
27.15	you] over 'led'

28.26	up] originally 'upon', 'on' cancelled
28.31	yet] over possible 'now'
29.15	in which] 'in' over 'w'
29.27	some] 's' over 'g'
31.23	in] over 'and'
31.26	of] 'o' over 'to'
32.7	matters] 'm' over 'wh'
32.9	Their] over 'His'
32.19	complexity] 'com' over 'wad'
32.23	remarks] initial 'r' over 'm'
32.23	imply] over 'indicate'
32.26	this] 't' over 'S'
32.28	two] followed by cancelled 'conditions'
33.14	newest] 'n' over ascender, possibly of 't'
34.7	ivied] 'ivi' mended from 'rui'
34.14	from] over 'at a'
34.20	a] over possible 'no'
34.27	lively] 'v' over 'k'
35.18	was the arms] 'as' over 'ere'
35.25	tall] over wiped-out 'large'
35.28	perhaps] 'h' over 'p'
35.33	within] 'ith' over 'ha'
36.17	among] 'a' cancels comma
36.32	particular] 'p' over 'd'
37.20	is] over 'li'
37.21–22	ownership] 'p' mended to cancel a terminal 's'
37.23	on] over 'it'
37.25	But] preceded by wiped-out quotation mark
37.27	some] over 'the'
37.31	Middleton] over 'Hammond'
38.5	Norman] 'No' over 'Fr'
38.14	replied] 're' over wiped-out 'sa'
38.32	cynical] 'y' over 'in'
39.11	ancestral] 'an' over 'fam'
39.19	on] mended from 'as'
39.23–24	Hammond] 'mond' over 'ilton'
40.4	some day] mended from 'somewhere'
41.13	gentlemen] 'g' over 'm' of original 'Englishm'

41.16	was unmarried] 'w' over 'h'
42.24	sight] 'si' over 'th'
43.13	its] over 'w'
43.20	though] 'ou' over 'ey'
45.1	Middleton] over 'Hammond'
45.5	a] over 'ra'
45.22	Squire] 'Sq' over 'Mr'
45.23	educated] first 'd' over 'q'
45.25	seat] 'a' over 't'
46.8	dying] 'y' mended from 'ie'
47.9	closer] 'cl' over 'be'
47.11	he.] period cancels comma
47.14	of some] over wiped-out possible 'come'
47.19	the key] 'e' of 'the' over 'ey'
47.21	mimic] 'mim' over possible 'cur'
47.22	floor] 'oor' over possible 'oare'
47.25	drawers] 'draw-|' mended from 'drawe'
48.6	father and] 'a' of 'and' over 'h'
48.11	cabinet.] followed by wiped-out quotation mark
48.24	the cold] 'the' over wiped-out 'beef'
50.1	the family] 'the' over 'a'
50.8	posterity] over 'children'
50.12	had] mended from 'were'
50.25	away] initial 'a' over 'h'
50.26	elder] 'el' over 'se'
51.7	relating] 'r' over 'te'
51.12	to give] 'to' over 'if'
51.12	to the] 'to' over 'of'
51.30	politics] over wiped-out 'Congress, b', the 'b' unfinished
52.16	institutions] 'tut' over 'ion'
52.17	his] 'h' over 'f'
52.26	and] 'a' over 'ta'
52.34	(from] parenthesis cancels comma
53.14	blood] second 'o' over 'd'
54.9	Middleton] 'Mid' over 'Ham'
57.12	engages] initial 'e' over 'p'
57.17	devil] over 'angel'

57.31	encouraged] final 'e' over 'g'
57.32	a] over 'on'
58.6	round] 'ro' over 'aro'
58.24	Introduction] 'I' over 'i'
58.33	nucleus] 'le' mended from 'leo'
59.27	his] over 'de'
61.16	life] 'l' over 'f'
62.18	(airy] parenthesis cancels comma
62.25	saw] over wiped-out 'heard'
62.31	clump] over wiped-out possible 'bush'
63.7	Middleton] above uncancelled 'Eldredge'
63.21	neighborhood] 'ne' over wiped-out 'hi'
64.2	disappearance] 'dis' squeezed in after 'appearance' had been inscribed
64.22	plead] 'a' over 'd'
64.23	gentlemen] last 'e' over 'a'
64.25	stranger's] 'stra' over 'tas'
65.1	kindness] 'd' over long 's'
65.8	rugged] 'rug' over wiped-out 'Nat'
65.13	grounds] over wiped-out 'park'
65.18	We] 'W' over wiped-out 'Y'
65.25	a] over wiped-out 'be'
66.2	a lonely] 'a' over 'l'
66.26	and he] 'and' over wiped-out 'then'
67.8	wildly] first 'l' over 'd'
67.9	made] 'de' over wiped-out 'y a'
67.21	It was a] originally 'I am sure'; 'was a' over wiped-out 'am sure' and 'I' mended to 'It'
68.13	apprehend] 'ap' over 'no'
68.17	have] 've' over 'd'
68.33	in] over 'to'
69.28	and] 'an' over wiped-out 'th'
70.9–10	unapproachableness] first 'n' over wiped-out 'p'
70.15	in] 'i' over 'o'
70.73	rank] 'r' over 'st'
71.1	in] 'i' over 't'
72.6	geography] 'gr' over 'ph'
72.27	even] 'ev' over 'for'

73.18	Eldredge] 'r' over 'g'
73.22	appearance] first 'e' over 'a'
73.23	Eldredge] second 'd' over 'g'
73.28	owner] 'o' over 'l'
73.32	coldness] 'l' over 'o'
74.1	and] followed by wiped-out comma
74.10	(There . . . table)] added in space at end of paragraph
74.14	and enjoyment] 'a' over 'f'; 'en' over 'k'
76.6	Eldredge] second 'd' over 'g'
76.17	Eldredge?] question mark cancels comma
76.27	was] 'w' over 'of'
77.4	at] 'a' over possible 't'
77.9	half] 'f' over 'e'
78.11	magnitude] 'm' over 'pr'
78.18	kept] 'ke' over wiped-out 'fix'
78.32	by] over wiped-out 'and'
78.34	with] over wiped-out 'sealed'
79.1	glance] 'n' over wiped-out long 's'
79.14	authorized] 'autho' over wiped-out 'witness'
79.17	and to] 'to' over wiped-out 'wh'
79.33	regards] interlined with a caret
80.9	in enmity] 'in' over 'as'
80.16	Eldredge] 'r' over 'g'
80.19	had] 'd' over 's'
80.20	out] interlined with a caret
80.26	or] 'o' over 'f'
81.11	character] 'cha' over wiped-out 'light'
81.20	of] 'f' over 'v'
82.3–4	Hospitaller] followed by cancelled 'was'
83.5	his] 'h' over 'l'
83.15	dagger that] followed by cancelled 'is'
83.20	requirements] 'req' over possible 'nee'
83.22	Eldredge] 'Eld' over 'him'
83.32	decide] 'ide' mended from 'de'
83.33	Eldredge] first 'd' over 'l'
83.35	adapted] first 'd' over 'p'
84.12	moat.] period mended from semicolon

84.35	Middleton] 'n' mended from 'n's'
85.8	a] interlined with a caret
85.15	wit] 't' over wiped-out 'th'
85.24	Eldredge's] second 'd' over 'g'
87.3	being] 'b' over 'a'
87.10	Mr] over 'the'
87.10	Eldredge] terminal 'e' over 'es'
87.18	(though] parenthesis cancels comma
87.21	Romance] 'Rom' over wiped-out 'bob[ ]'
88.1	explain] over wiped-out possible 'what'
88.7	Middleton] 'M' over wiped-out 'H'
88.16	find] 'fi' over 'a'
88.26	appeared] initial 'a' over 'b'

ETHEREGE

90.6–12	Give. . . . anybody.] added in top margin of MS page
90.13–14	(The . . . web.)] added in space at end of first paragraph
90.23	a rich] over wiped-out 'Indian'
91.9	slate] interlined with a caret
91.29	of] over wiped-out 'the'
92.12	high] interlined with a caret
92.18–19	But . . . haunted.] interlined with a caret before paragraph beginning 'It did'
92.24–25	with . . . side] interlined with a caret
*92.30	merited it.] 'it' added in pencil above period by SH
93.7	Philosophical] 'Phil' over 'tra'
93.17	journals] 'als' over 'eys'
93.17	of the] 'o' over 't'
93.20–21	housemaid's] 'm' over 'h'
*93.29	been] interlined with a caret by SH
94.13	as] over 'in'

94.18	leaf] over 'page'
94.25	some] over 'stra'
95.11	seem] terminal 'ed' cancelled
95.12	eyes] initial 'e' over 'l'
95.29	fitted] first 't' over 'f'
96.1	but] interlined with a caret
*96.13	though] terminal 't' cancelled in pencil, probably by SH
96.29	gown] 'go' over wiped-out 'scarf'
96.33	unmistressed] interlined with a caret
97.4	the lack of] interlined with a caret
97.7	a genealogist] the article over 'an'
97.8	a collector] 'a coll' over 'an an'
97.22	Growing] 'G' over 'Th', the 'h' incomplete
97.27	imaginative] 'imag' over wiped-out 'pi[ ]li', and the preceding article 'a' changed to 'an'
98.17–99.7	A race . . . appertaining to him.] the passage enclosed by inked lines above, below, and along left margin
98.31	found] above cancelled 'left'
99.17–18	to talk] 'to' above cancelled 'in'
99.20–21	(He . . . not.] added at end of preceding paragraph
99.27	Yes] 'Y' over possible 'I'
99.28	loyal] MS 'loyual', 'a' over 'l'
*100.3	like] cancelled in pencil, perhaps by SH
100.13	some] above cancelled 'many'
*100.15	successfully] 'ly' added in pencil by SH
100.16	Mr.] over wiped-out 'the'
100.32	It] over 'H'
101.1	one] 'o' over 'of'
101.2	whom] 'om' over 'en'
101.5	out] over 'of t', the original 't' incomplete
101.7	prisoners] 'pri' over 'men'
101.16	person—] dash concels comma
101.21–22	It . . . find out] over wiped-out 'But either there were some [di]f'
101.29	stranger] over wiped-out 'Doctor,'

102.2	perhaps,] over wiped-out 'those secret'
102.5	lay—] dash cancels comma
102.22	the good] 'the' followed by terminal wiped-out 'y'
102.25	had been on] over wiped-out ', above a sco'
102.27	at which] 'at w' over wiped-out 'with'
103.2	study] over wiped-out 'bedroo'
103.6	at] 'a' over 'th', the 'h' incomplete
103.13	The] preceded by wiped-out quotation mark
103.16	such] over wiped-out 'of'
104.4	young] interlined with a caret
104.12	is] over wiped-out 'can'
104.16	That] over wiped-out 'Nay'
104.19	likeness] 'lik' over wiped-out 'very'
104.20	you] over 'we'
104.21	we are] over wiped-out 'you'
104.26	present] 'r' over 'u'
104.30	to the] 'to' squeezed in between 'go' and 'the'
104.35	paces] 'p' cancels initial 's'
105.3	spot] over wiped-out 'grave'
105.4	on] over wiped-out 'when'
105.14	I know] preceded by wiped-out double quotation mark
105.15	in] over wiped-out 'it'
105.19	character] 'char' over 'man'
105.32	She . . . you.] added above 'her in it' at end of paragraph
106.6	When] 'If' of original 'If the sn' cancelled and 'When' inscribed over 'the sn'
106.9	doing] 'doi' over wiped-out 'feel'
106.10	But] preceded by cancelled 'It'
106.27	I] over left parenthesis
106.27–28	I . . . day.] added in space at end of paragraph
107.5	(The . . . visit.)] added between paragraphs; centered above is a short wavy line to indicate beginning of passage, 107.6–

108.26, to be inserted before 99.8

107.13	brilliant] 'go' cancelled above 'll'
107.15	purple] second 'p' mended from 'b'
107.17	the ivy] 'the' over wiped-out 'epo'
107.18	little] initial 'l' over 'E'
*108.6	in my] 'in' above 'my' in the hand of JH
108.20	like] 'li' over wiped-out 'th'
108.27	(Insert . . . comes)] added in space after the paragraph, following three dashes indicating end of passage to be inserted before 99.8
108.30	in every word] over wiped-out 'a great interest'
109.9	strikes] over 'seems'
110.26	broom] second 'o' over possible 's'
110.35	to whom] 'to w' over wiped-out 'whom'
111.8	march] 'ma' over 'cre'
111.12	life] 'l' over 'f'
111.34	vilis] over 'be a'
112.21	resulted] 're' over 'ca'
112.28	—the] dash cancels parenthesis
113.2	when a] 'a' above cancelled 'the'
113.15	their] over 'its' and terminal 's' added to preceding 'spider'
113.21	up] 'u' over 'th'
113.24	the fate] 'fa' over wiped-out 'se'
113.26	either] 'i' over 'e'
113.28	dowager] 'dow' over 'or c'
113.30	bed] 'd' over 'q'
114.34	her] 'h' over 't'
115.1	goes to] over wiped-out 'rel[ ]'
115.18	sits] over wiped-out 'comes'
115.30	Uncle?"] question mark cancels comma and double quotation mark
116.29	granddaughter.] period cancels comma
117.11	brother] over wiped-out 'Doctor's'
118.15	at] 'a' over 'l'
118.29	anxious] 'an' over 'ey', the 'y' incomplete
118.31	melancholy] 'm' over 's'

119.11	of what] 'of' over 'as'
119.24	children—] dash cancels comma
120.5	crabbed] 'rab' over wiped-out possible '[ ]gy'
120.17	darling—] dash cancels exclamation point
120.29	make] over 'broa'
121.16	of legs] 'of' over 'and'
121.19	spider] above uncancelled 'monster'
121.29	devised] 'vis' over wiped-out 'scri'
122.9	Doctor] 'D' over 'd'
122.10	old-fashioned] preceded by 'prim', the word cancelled but not the comma
122.16	Then] over 'Here'
122.33	position] 'posi' over wiped-out 'hig'
123.3	ineffectiveness] 'ecti' over 'icac'
123.5–6	an enormous] 'n en' over wiped-out 'mon'
123.31	The] over wiped-out 'At s'
124.26	Having] 'Ha' over 'On', the 'n' incomplete
124.28	likewise] first 'i' over partial 'k'
124.29	born] over 'by'
125.4	residence] 'resid' over wiped-out 'depa'
125.30	or] over 'as'
126.15	among] 'am' over wiped-out 'by'
126.18	Etherege] 'Et' over 'the'
126.19	or] over 'of'
126.31	would] 'w' over wiped-out possible 'sho'
127.2	he] over 'she'
127.4	as if] interlined with a caret
127.11	in an] 'in' over 'an'
127.18	akin] 'a' over 'k'
127.23	year] 'ye' over 'da'
127.33	death] 'd' over 'h'
128.8	(Slightly . . . first)] added in top margin of MS page over '13', above 'It was a day . . . '; '13' added in right top corner
128.30	just] over 'along'
129.12	age-long] 'g' of 'age' over 'lo'
129.13	green] over wiped-out 'clo[ ]'
129.13	in many] 'in m' over wiped-out 'all t'

129.18	A little further] interlined above uncancelled underscored 'Ever and anon'
129.21	passers] 'pass' over wiped-out 'child'
129.26	broken] over wiped-out possible 'waf'
129.31	Cuckoo,—and] 'oo' mended from 'ooo'
129.32	but] over wiped-out 'fi'
130.10	no] over wiped-out 'of'
130.13	he could] 'h' over 's'
130.30	finding] over wiped-out 'while'
130.32	will] 'w' over 'tra', the 't' uncrossed
130.34	is a] 'a' over 'an'
131.11	athwart] first 't' over 'cr'
131.14–15	Throw . . . characteristics] added across top margin of MS page over '14', and above 'That day . . .'
131.17	had been subjected to] over wiped-out 'was violently bea[ ] su'
131.24	to be] 'to' over 'in'
131.27	We] over wiped-out 'we'
131.31	him. His wits] paragraph originally ended 'him.'; new paragraph beginning 'It was' on next line wiped out, and the preceding paragraph continued with 'His wits'
132.1–2	(Make . . . scene)] added in space at end of paragraph
132.3	found] over wiped-out 'saw him'
132.14–16	Around . . . Head."] an amplification of the heraldic description, inscribed following 'Over . . . thereabouts.' (132.16–19), preceded and followed by several vertical lines; its transposition point was marked by a two-tiered caret added before 'Over . . .'
132.22–23	a curtained . . . them] above 'but . . . itself'
132.27	glass.] period cancels semicolon
132.28	narrow] 'na' over 'win'
132.29	through . . . embrasure] interlined with

a caret inadvertently placed before instead of
after preceding comma

132.30   in] over 'on'

132.32   smouldering] 'smou' over 'burn'

133.13   twisting] initial 't' over 's'

133.17   a deep niche] over wiped-out 'the window'; preceded by cancelled 'the embrasure of'

133.24–25   shoulders, and . . . palmer] 'shoulders' was originally end of sentence; a caret was inscribed over the period and 'and . . . palmer' was interlined above the following sentence beginning 'His dress'

133.29   breeches described] above 'were embroidered'

134.6   thinking] above uncancelled underscored 'not knowing', the underscore inadvertently not including 'but'

134.9   help] 'l' over 'p'

135.2   His] 'H' over wiped-out 'c'

135.9   was] over wiped-out 'had'

135.10   left him] over wiped-out 'retired h'

135.17–18   less, he was] over wiped-out 'more[ ] h'

135.34   of] over 'th'

136.6   You] 'Yo' over 'Thi'

136.8   am I?] 'a' over 'I'; question mark over double quotation mark

136.9   one, where] 'w' over wiped-out question mark; comma added and sentence continued

136.14   help] 'l' over 'p'

136.33–34   (There . . . hereafter.] added in space at end of paragraph

137.23   recollections] 'r' over 'd'

137.26   (All . . . name.)] added in space at end of paragraph

138.5   by the] 'the' over 'sur'

139.10   face, when] 'when' over wiped-out 'in his'

140.1   as kind] 'k' of original 'a k' wiped out and 'a' mended to 'as' before inscription of 'kind'

140.5   haughtiness] 'ess' over 'g'

140.11	and it] 'an' over 'as'
140.13	was favorably] over wiped-out 'began to suspect'
140.20	unsatisfactory] 'un' interlined with a caret
140.21	"Being a stranger] interlined with a caret inadvertently placed before preceding period; 'ger' cancels double quotation mark before following 'I'
140.23	Hall] 'H' mended from 'h'
140.29	"You] over wiped-out ' "Had'
140.29–30	but probably] 'But I suppose' over wiped-out 'that is to say'; 'probably' above underscored uncancelled 'I suppose'
141.1	Pearson] over wiped-out 'Mr. P'
141.1	reverend] initial 'r' over wiped-out 'R'
141.2	were] over wiped-out 'did'
141.7	natural] above 'a dignity'
141.7	figure] 'figu' over wiped-out 'and [ ]t'
141.9	This] 'is' over 'ese'
141.11	is a] over 'were'
141.14	were] above cancelled 'are'
141.18	Edward] preceded by cancelled 'The Honorable'
141.20	American?] question mark cancels comma
141.31	bound] 'bou' over wiped-out 'af[raid]'
141.33	I was] over wiped-out 'When'
141.35	for] 'or' over wiped-out 'rom'
142.24	it."]followed by wiped-out 'It' and an ascending stroke
143.1	am young] 'am y' over wiped-out 'can c[on]'
143.2	illusions] 'illu' over 'des'
143.15	friend.] period added after originally inscribed comma and quotation mark were wiped out
143.23	false!] exclamation point cancels comma
143.28	for the] over wiped-out 'and Ethere'
144.5	some luggage] 'some l' over wiped-out 'a packa'
144.19–20	his friend] 'his' over 'its'
144.20	the Doctor] 'the' over wiped-out 'Dr.'
144.23	rich] 'ri' over 'gr'

144.29	these] over wiped-out 'it ha'
145.2	great] 'g' over 'of' and 'reat' over wiped-out 'the tr'
145.4	in a livery] 'in a l' above cancelled 'not in any' ('any' over 'the'); 'l' not cancelled but followed by 'livery'
145.20	blood I had] over wiped-out 'English blood'
145.24	we] over wiped-out 'you'
146.14	right] over 'cor'
146.22	are] 'a' over 'ha'
146.26	when] above cancelled 'if'
146.29	thoroughly] interlined with a caret
147.3	right] over 'write'
147.4	thought] 'g' squeezed in after original inscription
147.11	biennial] mended from 'biannual'
147.12	in the] over 'as a'
147.13	his] 'hi' over 'M'
147.19	freed] 'd' over 'r'
147.32	to which] over wiped-out 'from w'
148.2	latent] interlined with a caret
148.32	the more] 'the' over partially wiped-out 'more'
149.7	could] over wiped-out 'but'
149.10	a] over 'to'
149.11	birth] over wiped-out 'origin'
149.15	very] interlined with a caret
149.19	have been poor] 'have' over 'was'; 'been' interlined with a caret
149.20	Well] over ' "It'
149.20	quite] interlined with a caret
149.31	very] interlined with a caret
149.35	which] 'w' over 'in'
150.3	male or female] interlined with a caret
150.4	which] over wiped-out 'the'
150.8	bound] over wiped-out 'in leat'
150.10	a cathedral] 'a ca' over wiped-out 'the lo'
150.10	seats] terminal 's' over 'ing'

150.10–12	Roman . . . &c] interlined above 'and gentry . . . for the'
150.19	and] over wiped-out 'having'
150.23	learned] 'lea' over wiped-out 'aut'
151.13	of a] 'a' over wiped-out 'of'
151.15	out] 'o' over 'b'
151.16	still] over wiped-out 'anoth', the 'h' unfinished
151.21	however] above uncancelled 'too'
151.21	another] 'an' over 'at'
152.5	cross-legged] 'c' over 'a'
152.10	of early] 'of e' over 'seem'
152.24	vanishing] 'va' over wiped-out 'fr'
152.25	supposed] above uncancelled 'hoped'
152.26	man—] dash cancels comma
152.27	to] over 'on'
152.28	Englishman;—] dash cancels a following 'a'
153.5	to] over 'it'
153.27	stone] interlined with a caret
153.30	clasped] 'cla' over wiped-out 'boo'
153.30	hand. The] 'The' over wiped-out 'an' and original semicolon mended to period
154.15	holds] 's' over 'es'
154.24–25	There . . . existence.] interlined with a caret
154.33	God] 'G' over 'g'
155.10	subtile] 'subt' over 'craft'
155.11	at] 'a' over 'th'
155.15	interior] over wiped-out 'front of'
155.18	lest—] dash cancels comma
155.27	here] 'h' over 't'
156.22	or messes] 'or' over 'of'
156.25	a sufficient] 'a' over 's'
157.1	influence] 'in' over wiped-out 'my'
158.1	past—as] over wiped-out possible 'by the just'
158.23	coming] 'co' over wiped-out 'ap'
158.25	young] over wiped-out 'face of a'
158.35	periods] 's' added to original inscription

159.25	old] interlined with a caret
159.28	the] over 'Pea'
160.28	discovery of] over wiped-out 'naming of a'
161.3	have] over wiped-out possible 'save h', the 'h' unfinished
161.20	under] over wiped-out 'when'
161.24	I do] over wiped-out 'Nay'
161.31	this] over wiped-out 'one'
161.32	if your] 'y' over 's'
161.33	in a] 'a' over wiped-out 'q'
162.1	you] interlined with a caret
162.2	loyal] 'loy' over wiped-out 'you'
162.12	not] over wiped-out 'don'
162.13	any] over wiped-out 'many'
162.19	with . . . feeling] above 'Englishmen . . . Etherege'
163.1–2	race; and] 'a' of 'and' over wiped-out 'A' and original period mended to semicolon
163.3	of men] above 'classes'
163.33	origin] 'ori' over wiped-out 'd[ ]'
164.4	avail] above cancelled 'accept'
164.5	old dwelling] 'old' interlined with a caret
165.5	anywhere.] followed by curving line as though to mark off the following sentence
165.10	there] over wiped-out 'and a'
165.11	another] over wiped-out 'one that'
165.14	who] over 'up'
165.15	almost] over wiped-out 'plotted'
165.19	Is there] 's ther' over wiped-out 'coul'
165.19	one?"] question mark over original comma and quotation mark, followed by new quotation mark
165.21	I] over wiped-out quotation mark
166.32	might] over wiped-out 'seemed'
167.14	own] 'o' over 'b'
167.20	the] over 'he'
168.10	over] over 'to'
168.25	agreeable] 'ag' over 'ge'

168.25   kind] 'k' over 'p'

168.26   Englishman,] comma supersedes exclamation point

169.10   (whose] over wiped-out 'could'; parenthesis cancels comma

169.13   a] over 'some'

169.19   natural] 'nat' over wiped-out 'sensi'

169.20   men] 'm' over wiped-out 'h'

169.22   an Englishman] the article over 'E'

169.34   often] interlined with a caret

170.3   a plebeian Englishman] 'plebeian' above 'Englishman', the article over 'an'

170.8   developed] 'v' over 'l'

170.23   do] preceded by cancelled 'and'

171.7   approbation] initial 'a' over vertical stroke, probably of 'p'

171.7   or] over wiped-out 'of'

171.21–22   even if] over wiped-out 'between'

172.9   even] 'ev' over 'ov'

172.16   yourself] 'y' over wiped-out ascender, possibly of 'b'

172.28   leaf] 'f' over 've'

172.33   hard and] 'a' of 'and' over '&'

172.33   dry.] followed by wiped-out 'They'

173.24   observe] 'o' over 'b'

173.27   nor . . . religion] interlined with a caret

174.29–30   (Etherege . . . cross)] added in space after paragraph

174.31   a family] interlined with a caret

175.3   tower] 'tow' over wiped-out 'gra'

175.11   citizen] over wiped-out 'subject'

175.21   peacocks] 'o' over 'k'

175.28   miniature] over wiped-out 'cannon'

176.1   flattened] over wiped-out '[ ]d a'

176.5   moving] over wiped-out 'moved'

176.8   pavement] 'p' over 's'

176.10   enough.] originally 'enough, and'; comma and 'and' cancelled and period inserted

176.15   fallen] above cancelled 'extinct'
176.18   agreeable] 'ag' over wiped-out 'la'
176.33   them] over 'names'
177.16   of the tower of] interlined with a caret
177.24   the old] over wiped-out 'these old'
178.8   (A . . . tree.] added after preceding para-
                graph
178.16   antiquity] 'an' over wiped-out 'thing'
178.20–21   Some . . . archers.] above 'in what
                . . . connection with'
178.24   surely.] period mended from comma and 'It
                was in comp' of next sentence inscribed over
                wiped-out 'and mere imaging'
179.5   rubbish] above 'a chamber'
179.11   They] preceded by 'Passing round the huge
                rotundity of the yew-tree, they came unex-
                pectedly on a young woman, who sat on the
                bench, and seemed to be sketching the pretty
                scene of the church ['church' above cancelled
                'village green'], and such ['such' over 'those']
                of the houses as ['as' over 'th'] could ['co'
                over 'be'] be brought [MS 'broght'] into the
                same point of view.', uncancelled but marked
                by a curve in left margin encompassing the
                lines of the sentence, plus two diagonal lines
                and a large v-check at its close; these signals
                convey sufficient authorization to delete inas-
                much as Hawthorne has rewritten the sen-
                tence at 180.23–28
179.16   had] over 'were'
180.14–15   the village] 'the' over 'it'
181.1   Warden] 'Wa' over 'gi'
181.25   Etherege] 'Ether-|' over 'They'
181.31–33   their . . . daisies] above 'of a humble
                . . . monument'
182.20   like] 'ke' over 'ttle'
182.24   strewn] 'str' over 'gr'
182.27   we] above cancelled 'you may'

183.5	and] over wiped-out 'flo'
183.8	simple] interlined with a caret
183.22	name,] followed by wiped-out quotation mark
184.11	two] over wiped-out 'frien'
184.30	race] 'r' over possible 's'
185.22	enriched] initial 'e' over 'r'
185.27	though among the noble] over wiped-out 'the clumps of trees there we'
185.29	houses] 'h' over 'of'
187.2	he] followed by wiped-out comma
187.20	letter] 'le' over 'se'
188.29	above the level of] 'above' above cancelled 'on' but original 'level with' unaltered
190.4–5	—the dinner . . . think—] interlined between paragraphs
190.17	banquet] over wiped-out 'dinner'
190.24	hereditary] 'her' over 'fe'
191.33	a part] 'a pa' over wiped-out 'whi'
192.4	wolf's] 'f' over 'l'
193.3	antiquarian] initial 'an' over wiped-out 'and'
194.3	gave] 'g' over 'h'
194.29	whoever] 'w' over 'h'
194.29	inherited] 'inher' over 'succ'
194.32	he] mended from 'le'
195.7	brother's race] 'race' interlined with a caret and terminal 's' added to 'brother'; apostrophe is CENTENARY emendation
195.8	his] over 'this'
195.12	and by] 'and' over wiped-out 'by'
195.13	an] 'a' over upstroke, probably of 't'
195.14	on] over 'as'
196.4	up] 'u' over 'a'
196.10	he] 'h' over wiped-out upstroke of 't'
196.15	he has the] over wiped-out 'gives him the'
196.17	go back] over wiped-out 'come d'
196.18	compared] 'com' over wiped-out 'by c'
196.30	a] over wiped-out 'the'
196.33	hold the] 'e' over 'is'

197.16	They] original 'sh' of 'The sh' wiped out and 'y' added to 'The'
197.18	who] 'o' over 'om'
198.11	An] 'n' over 'nac'
198.31	a treasure] preceded by cancelled 'but'
199.6	were.] period cancels comma
199.30	peace] 'ea' over 'ie'
200.14–15	Bloody Footstep] 'B' and 'F' over 'b' and 'f'
200.28	peaceful] 'pea' over 'gui'
201.10	oysters?] question mark cancels quotation mark
201.16	him] interlined with a caret
201.20	all] followed by cancelled 'but'
202.25	too] second 'o' subsequently squeezed in
202.30	King] 'K' mended from 'k'
202.30	believe] 'be' over 'thi'
202.34	unrefuted] 'un' over wiped-out 'dou'
203.14–15	and friend] 'a' over 'of'
203.15	George] first 'e' over 'o'
203.27	its] over 'his'
203.33	in fields] 'in fi' over wiped 'often'
204.33	character;] semicolon supersedes original period
205.16	but] 'b' over partial 'w'
205.22	his] 'h' over wiped-out 'th'
205.26	appears] 'ap' over 'rea'
206.16	he] over possible 'so'
206.16	sometimes] 'om' over wiped-out 'al'
206.25	Popishified] 'P' mended from 'p'
207.1	or] over 'as'
208.16	an] mended from 'and'
208.20	family.] period over wiped-out semicolon
209.1	morbid] followed by large wiped-out caret
209.3	but by] followed by two partially wiped vertical lines
209.8	lily] mended from 'lilly'
211.4–5	valuable] 'va' over 'w'
211.9	in the] over wiped-out 'where'
211.21	alone] 'a' over 'l'
211.23	party] 'par' over wiped-out 'half'

211.32	again] initial 'a' over wiped-out possible 'q'
212.5	See . . . paragraph] added in top margin of MS page above 'Meanwhile . . . '; see 212.25 below
212.11	several] 'sev' over 'bro'
212.22–23	and . . . breastplates] interlined with a caret
212.24	(This comes first)] interlined with a caret above 'High up in the old'; see 212.5 above
212.25	High] a preceding half-bracket indicates intended new beginning when paragraph is recopied; because rewriting would be needed to adjust the connectives "Meanwhile' and 'to be sure' to a transposed ordering, Hawthorne's directions are not carried out here
*212.29	in] obscured by superimposed 'X', probably not Hawthorne's
212.31	would] over wiped-out 'which'
213.2	strong] 'tr' over 'pr'
213.3	abroad] 'br' over 'bo'
214.15	the image] 'the' over 'his'
215.32	in] preceded by uncancelled 's'
216.14	better—] dash cancels comma
217.31	decay—] dash cancels comma
218.13	hall,] comma cancels original period; following quotation marks wiped out
218.31–32	probabilities] first 'b' over 'p'
218.32	the heir] 'the' over possible 'es'
219.19	in] interlined with a caret
219.25	and] 'a' over 'ha'
220.2	the silver] 'th' over 'w'
220.2	in] 'i' over 'o'
220.16	make] 'm' over 'h'
220.18	one only] mended from 'only'
221.1	nature.] followed by three vertical lines to mark future revision or shift of sentences
221.2	moors] 'mo' over 'co'
222.1	(The family . . . America)] added in top

	margin of MS page above the paragraph 'Take the . . . '
222.9	bloody] 'bl' over 'fo'z
222.11–12	Others . . . time.] above 'paternal . . . race'
222.17	keep] mended from 'hand'
222.28–29	grandfather] 'grand' interlined
222.31	adopted] 'a' over 'in'
223.10	&c) and] MS '&c, and'; 'a' over wiped-out parenthesis
224.24	this—] dash cancels period
225.4	ages;] semicolon cancels period
225.30	estate.] period cancels comma
226.1	claim] followed by three vertical lines to mark future revision
226.3	outside] 'd' mended from 'll'
226.4	may] 'm' over 'sh'
226.17	(being] parenthesis cancels comma
226.21	she] above space between 'Shall' and 'also'
226.22	grand] 'gr' over 'dau'
227.1	of a] over 'a mo'
227.8	them—] dash cancels period
227.11	mystery] final 'y' over 'ous'
227.15	contained] 'conta' over wiped-out 'had a'
228.8	dead] final 'd' over 't'
229.24	teaching.] period cancels semicolon
230.11	queer] over 'be'
230.15	man] 'm' over 'a'; preceding 'an' unchanged
230.30	a] over 'an'
231.22	proofs] 'pr' over wiped-out possible 'cop', the 'p' unfinished
231.28	died] over 'el'
232.11	antiquarian] 'ian' over 'y'
233.15	admitted—] dash cancels comma
233.22	rights] 'rig' over 'en'
233.23	be] 'e' over 'b'
234.12	according] 'accor' over wiped-out 'with'
234.21	covers] 'cov' over wiped-out 'parks'

235.27	three] over wiped-out 'days'
235.30	banquet] above uncancelled 'dinner'
236.28	as . . . diplomatist] interlined with a caret following 'to' but intended to precede 'to'
236.32	which] over wiped-out 'the'
237.21	his father] 'h' of 'his' over 'f'
237.29	(Etherege's . . . table.)] added in space at end of paragraph
238.3	(Dwell . . . somewhat)] added in space at end of paragraph
238.30	A] over 'It'
238.33	the Mayor . . . town] above uncancelled 'the gentleman'
238.34	twice.] period cancels comma
239.3	the sole] 'the so' wiped-out 'and di'
239.23	(The rose-water . . . toasts)] added in space at end of paragraph
239.25	regarded] initial 'r' over 'g'
239.29	interrogative] 'in' over beginning of 'd'; preceding article not mended from 'a' to 'an'
239.29	bows] over 'bough'
239.30	decanters] 'deca' over wiped-out 'wine'
240.18	with.] originally 'with it'; 'it' wiped out and period added
241.13	The . . . nothing] added in top margin of MS page above 'After this ensued . . .'
241.17	Loving] 'L' over 'l'
241.25–26	One . . . drinks] above 'of ceremony; being pretty much'
241.27	covered] 'cove' over 'from'
241.27	took from] above cancelled 'placed on'
241.30	covered] 'cov' over 'pro'
241.31	guest] over 'next'
242.2–3	or . . . taster] above 'drinking with you. The cup . . . ancient'
242.10–11	(Mention . . . dinner.] added in space after paragraph
242.21	hostility] 'ity' over 'y'

242.22   courteous] 'ous' over 'es'
242.23   own] 'ow' over 'ga'
242.27   chose] over wiped-out 'chose to'
242.32   Lord] 'Lo' over 'he'
243.2   has] over 'an'
243.12–13   or . . . poison] above 'withdrew . . .
                    breast'
243.17   poison.] period mended from semicolon; fol-
                    lowed by cancelled 'but possibly we kill as
                    well even'
243.21   honor] over wiped-out '[   ]lt'
244.6   the] over wiped-out 'any'
244.19–20   and . . . one."] above 'am . . .
                    country,'
244.22   gravely] over wiped-out 'quietly'
244.33   honored] followed by cancelled 'English', which
                    was written over 'name'
245.1   from his friend] above 'understood that the'
245.10   The] over 'Our'
245.14   and our] over wiped-out 'then our'
245.19   be a] 'a' over 'an'
245.21   not seem] 'n' over 's'
245.22   ambition] 'am' over 'ab'
245.22   was] over 'were'
247.5   retire.] followed by wiped-out 'B'
247.15–17   Besides . . . it."] added in space after
                    paragraph; 'B' over original closing quotation
                    mark
247.27   accept] 'ac' over 'ex'
247.28   hostility] second 'i' over 'y'
248.9   longer] interlined with a caret
248.11   would gladly spend] 'would gladly spe' over
                    wiped-out 'could spend it'
248.31   centuries] 'cen' over wiped-out 'fift'
249.5   midnight] 'm' over 's'
249.8   water] over wiped-out 'toast and'
249.15   Etheredge . . . wine] interlined between
                    paragraphs

249.19–21	while . . . soda-water] interlined above 'worthy . . . degree that'
249.23	great] 'g' over wiped-out ascender, perhaps of 'k'
249.24	already] 'alr' over wiped-out 'that'
250.1	irresistibly] 'irr' over wiped-out ' "th'
250.8	Is] followed by wiped-out 't'
250.12	as you intimate,] interlined with a caret
250.12	be] over 'any'
250.21	almost the] 'th' over wiped-out 'al'
250.22	his] over 'the'
250.23	he] 'h' over 'f'
250.23	had been found] 'h' over 'a'
250.31	it by] 'i' over 'b'
251.6	an] over wiped-out 'I'
251.12	He] over 'Has'
251.26–27	of family] above inadvertently uncancelled 'of' and cancelled 'this house of Braithwaite'
252.2	selling] 'se' over wiped-out 'te'
253.13	were] first 'e' over 'h'
253.20	sixteen times transmitted] above 'baron of three or four'
253.30	seems—] dash cancels comma
254.14	a person] 'a' mended from 'an'
254.16	replied] 'repl' over wiped-out 'and if'
254.29	would] 'w' over 's'
255.12	we] over possible 'it's no'
256.10	it that] 'i' over 't'
256.11	a] over 'the'
257.18	& I] over wiped-out 'I w'
257.20	on] 'o' over 'w'
258.11	dry] 'd' over 'b'
259.14	himself] 'h' over 'a'
260.11	way] over 'vein'
262.3	What . . . nonsense?] added in space after paragraph
262.15–19	Elsie. . . . time.] preceded by two vertical strokes as a signal for future revision
262.25	(whether] parenthesis cancels comma

263.4	legend] 'leg' over 'sto'
263.5	buried] 'b' over 'so'
263.8	adopted] over wiped-out 'left by'
264.14	Etherege] 'E' over 'him'
264.32	Thug] 'T' over 't'
265.6	A Mahometan] 'A' over 'a'
266.30	an ice-cold] original 'a c' mended to 'an'
267.3	betoken?] question mark mended from exclamation
267.10	having] 'h' over 'a'
267.28	offals.] period cancels comma
270.9	nevertheless] MS 'neverthels' interlined above 'was yet' and 'yet' cancelled
271.2	apartment] 'ap' over 'ho'
271.9	Bloody] 'l' over 'o'
271.20	he] over 'was'
271.33	designs—] dash cancels comma
271.34	ages] over wiped-out 'diff'
272.29	black.] period cancels comma
273.6	show] over wiped-out 'lead'
273.9	public] 'c' over 'ke'
273.21	premises] 'pre' over 'roo'
273.23	some] above uncancelled 'many'
273.23	folios] interlined with a caret
273.27	a rather] the article over 'in'
273.33	diplomatic] over wiped-out 'gentleman from'
273.34	whom . . . been] originally 'whom he has been'; 'lordship' inscribed above 'has been' and 'he' mended to 'his'
*274.2	"I . . . priest.] a dot within a circle in left margin beside this sentence; not necessarily NH's mark
274.9	any] over wiped-out 'men'
275.5	sort] 's' over 'of'
275.8	The] over 'He'
275.22	came] over 'was'
276.15	it was] 't' over 'n'
276.30	do] 'o' over 'es'

277.7	During] follows cancelled quotation mark
277.33	see] 's' over wiped-out 'sp'
278.16	The] over 'Mr'
278.25	into] 'in' squeezed into space preceding initially inscribed 'to'
278.29	boyhood] 'boy' over wiped-out 'youth'
279.15	There] 'Th' over 'H'
279.23	Englishman] 'En' over wiped-out 'thing'
280.1	made] over wiped-out 'tha'
280.11	descendants] 'd' over 'p'
280.15	out] over 'of'
282.5	could] over wiped-out 'there'
282.10	be] followed by a second 'e' wiped out
282.13	that] 'tha' over wiped-out 'all'
283.24	The foot] over wiped-out 'Etherege'
283.32	he] over wiped-out 'the'
284.11	out] 'o' over 'it'
284.12	prophetic] 'e' over 'he' of original 'phrophetic'
284.14	that] over wiped-out possible 'was'
284.19	not] 'n' over 'it'
285.6	spoke] over wiped-out 'asser'
285.17	as] 'a' over 'h'
286.9	in] 'i' over 'o'
286.10	or] over wiped-out 'but'
287.24	idea] 'id' over 'w'
288.12	Yet it] over wiped-out 'Perhaps'
290.12	as] 'a' over 'if'
290.32	arranged.] period cancels semicolon
290.34	habits] over wiped-out 'undoubt'
292.5	supposititious] 'su' over wiped-out 'sp'
292.21	agent—] dash cancels comma
293.16	so] over wiped-out 'as'
294.16	Doctor's] 'D' over 'd'
294.17	nine and twenty] above uncancelled 'thirty five'
294.18	days."] period replaces wiped-out comma, followed by wiped-out 'said' and the left arm of 'H'
294.28	days] over wiped-out 'years'

295.6	Etherege] 'Et' over 'wa'
295.27	recluse] 'rec' over wiped-out 'diss'
295.35	Palsy] 'a' over 'l'
296.4	did] over 'his'
296.22	darkened] 'n' over 'd'
296.27	witchcraft] first 'c' over 'h'
297.6	be] over 'to'
297.29	alacrity] initial 'a' over 'l'
298.2	never] 'n' over 'h'
298.26	victory] 'vic' over wiped-out 'fall'
299.4	it] over 'the'
299.10	fortunes] over wiped-out 're[ ]'
299.22	here—] dash cancels comma
300.2	interest] 'in' over wiped-out 'it'
300.8	death] over wiped-out 'life th'
300.10	Poor victim] underscored and lightly cancelled, but no alternative wording entered
300.19	man] 'm' over 'h'
301.6–8	Whoever . . . ill-feeling] added in top margin of MS page above 'suspicion . . . came.'
302.10	days] over wiped-out 'hours'
302.13	we] over 'h'
302.17	day] over wiped-out 'even'
302.19	sideboard. It] 'It' over wiped-out 'an'; the preceding period over wiped-out comma
303.29	Etherege] 'Et' over wiped-out 'he'
303.34	Left] 'eft' over 'iving'
304.9	It will] 'It w' over wiped-out 'You'
304.16	replied] 'rep' over wiped-out 'ans'
304.28	main line] 'main' over 'branch'; 'line' over wiped-out 'had'
305.9	hither] 'hi' over 'to'
305.30	far] over 'mo'
306.7	In . . . chair.] added in space at end of paragraph
306.16	live long] over wiped-out 'a safe'
307.2	however] 'ho' over 'f'

307.9	active] 'act' over wiped-out ', effe'
307.22	finding] above cancelled 'reading'
307.27	deep ancestral] 'deep an' over wiped-out 'deep chair'
307.30–32	(Etherege. . . . a maze.] The first sentence added in space at end of paragraph, and the second added below first line of paragraph beginning 'When he awoke, or began to awake'
307.33	or] over 'in'
308.2	pre-Adamite] 'pre' over 'ad'
308.13	of] over 'to'
309.6–7	and . . . round.] crossed by a few diagonal lines as if in intention to delete or change
309.14	and] 'a' over wiped-out 'w'; preceding semicolon subsequently inserted
309.16	sleep.] period mended from comma
309.25	neglected] interlined with a caret
309.27	nameless—] dash cancels comma
310.7	of] interlined with a caret
310.9	us—] dash cancels comma
310.16	were?] question mark cancels exclamation point
310.19–22	He . . . while)] added in space at end of paragraph
310.27	did] mended from 'had'
310.30	high] followed by wiped-out 't'
310.34– 311.1	And . . . terror;] crossed by wavy and diagonal lines as if in intention to delete or change
311.6	"It . . . he.] added in top margin of MS page, subsequent to inscription of what follows
311.7–8	"Where . . . voice.] crossed by diagonal strokes as if in intention to cancel or revise
311.9	old . . . answer] underlined to imply need for revision if preceding sentence is deleted
311.25	least] 'lea' over wiped-out 'wo'
312.3	fly] 'y' over 'ie'
312.25	desperately] 'd' over 'f'

314.7   rage] over wiped-out 'aff'
314.8   his] 'h' over 't'
315.1   Bubbleandsqueak.] added in space at end of paragraph
315.33   fascinating] over wiped-out possible 'fashion-able'
316.19   soul] followed by wiped-out 'W'
316.21   Etheredge] 'Ether' over wiped-out 'Brath'
316.23   The] over 'He'
316.26–27 Gone," and] over wiped-out ', it is almo' and period added after preceding 'good-bye'
317.5   the house] 'the' mended from 'his'
317.24   he] over 'the'
318.5   He] over 'They'
318.20   They . . . out.] added in space at end of paragraph
318.25   Mr.] 'M' cancels quotation mark
318.27   Hammond] 'Ha' over 'Mr.'
318.30   the pensioner] 'the' over 'he'
320.1   the secret] 'the' over wiped-out 'his'
320.1–2   of which] 'o' over wiped-out 'w'
320.8   Mr.] 'M' cancels quotation mark
320.16   the Warden] 'the W' over 'Mr. B'
320.27   To] over wiped-out 'Mr'
321.24   at the pressure] 'at the p' over wiped-out 'by one b'
321.29   "Follow!"] exclamation point replaces comma
322.5   Etherege] 'E' over 'h'
323.8   day.] this word ends fol. 67^v, marked '68' by Hawthorne; no fol. 69 is known to have survived
323.27   boy's] 'bo' over 'wa'
323.27   alms-house] 'a' over partial 'w'
323.28   insensed] first 's' over 'n'
325.14   turns] 'ur' over wiped-out 'ak', the 'k' unfinished
325.29   or] 'o' cancels comma
326.4   impossible] 'e' over wiped-out 'y'

327.7	Bottler] 'o' over 'u'
327.24	absurdity.] period cancels semicolon
328.17–18	the Doctor] 'the' over 'his'
329.17	Doctor] 'D' over 'a'
329.19	for] over 'from'
330.4	(His death . . . suggested)] interlined with a caret
331.15	servant.] period cancels comma
332.7	with] 'w' over 'h'
332.23	quickened] 'c' altered to 'i' in another ink and hand, probably JH's
333.28	On] over 'The'
333.28	unreliability] MS 'unreliabilty' mended from 'unreliable'
334.26	In] 'n' over 't'
334.30	forefather had] 'fore' interlined
334.30–31	forefather was] 'fore' interlined
335.23	Brathwaite] 'Br' over 'the'
335.25	villain] second 'l' over 'a'
335.29	to] interlined with a caret
335.33	There] short horizontal lines between this paragraph and the preceding one indicate a break
335.33	many] over wiped-out 'a gr'
335.33–34	and a few . . . extant] interlined, with the exception of the article, with a caret; 'a' then interlined above, with a caret
336.4	life.] followed by cancelled 'Not that it was a picturesque cham'
336.7–8	(Compare . . . there.)] added in space at end of paragraph
336.10	so dim] 'm' over wiped-out 'd'
336.17	Nevertheless] 'N' over 'It'
336.30–31	(to . . . world)] above 'Looking . . . discover'
336.32	Yes] over wiped-out 'Where'
336.33	one] 'o' over 'w'
337.1	antique] above cancelled 'old'
337.14	him.] followed by wiped-out 'As'

337.15	here] 'h' over question mark
337.24	would] 'l' over partial 'd'
337.28	we seem] over wiped-out 'he has'
337.29	old—] dash cancels comma
337.31	stifled] mended from 'stiflfed'
338.10	manner] over wiped-out possible 'prefer'
338.13	been] over wiped-out '[ ] b'
338.15–17	(Once . . . lichens)] added in space beside two preceding sentences
338.18	Again] broken lines between this paragraph and the preceding one indicate a break
338.18–19	let us] over wiped-out 'yet h', the 'h' unfinished
338.22	ever—] dash cancels comma
338.32	no] over 'su'
339.5	were] 'w' over wiped-out 'of'
339.14	There] 'The' over wiped-out 'Pe'
339.30	(Describe . . . things)] added in space at end of paragraph
339.33	has] 'h' over 'th'
340.2	there . . . noosed] above 'as if . . . meditated'
340.2	else] initial 'e' over 'th'
340.11	dressing-gown] 'd' over 'g'
340.30	seem] 's' over 'a'
341.8	apothecary] 'apo' over 'ma'
341.13	mention] over wiped-out 'to-day'
341.25	to do] 't' over 'd'
341.28	individual] 'ivi' mended from 'ua'
341.34	some] above uncancelled 'the'

Grimshawe

343.1	Early . . . century] originally 'Many years ago'; 'Many years' cancelled and 'A long time' added above; 'Soon after the Revolution'

interlined between the alteration and the cancel, and finally 'Early in this present century' added above all the preceding phrases; 'ago' left uncancelled, along with 'A long time' and 'Soon . . . Revolution'

343.3   of grim aspect] interlined with a caret placed inadvertently after instead of before a preceding comma

343.5   remarkably . . . vivacious] above cancelled 'bright little'

343.5–6   perfect . . . blonde] MS 'perfect rosebud of blonde' above cancelled 'pretty little'

343.6   two . . . he] interlined with a caret

343.7   maid] followed by cancelled 'servant of crusty temper'

343.9   (though] parenthesis cancels dash

343.9   though, primarily, no doubt] interlined above 'Doctor's antipathy to broom'; previous alterations, abandoned, include 'though more probably' above original 'or possibly', both uncancelled; and 'primarily', cancelled above 'the grim'

343.13   in . . . card] interlined with a caret

343.14   with] over wiped-out 'upon the'

343.14   forefinger] 'fore' above 'finger'

343.14   and so] over wiped-out possible 'in the dust of'

343.16–17   reader's disagreeable] 'read' over wiped-out 'gloo' and 'disagreeable' added above uncancelled underlined 'gloomy' following 'reader's'

343.21   threshold] 'thes' of MS 'theshold' over wiped-out 'door'

343.22   dismal] above 'cemetery'

343.23   spelled] 'led' over wiped-out 'the'

343.24   learned by heart] interlined with a caret

344.2–3   dandelions . . . seek] 'dandelions' above cancelled 'flowers', itself followed by cancelled 'or ran to fling things at the slate stones, and the slabs of marble which'

344.3   slate and] over wiped-out 'grave of'

344.3–4   and running . . . laughing] above cancelled 'rolling over the grave mound'

344.4   tumbled] 'tu' over wiped-out 'roll'

344.4   grassy] over possible 'grave'

344.6   legitimate] above 'inmates'

344.7   slept] above uncancelled 'were'

344.7   gambols] above cancelled 'laughing'

344.8   merriment] interlined with a caret above cancelled 'voices'

344.9   (Insert . . . paragraph.)] interlined beneath the paragraph just ended

344.10–15   Crusty . . . Doctor.] added in top margin of first MS page

344.11   Monkey,] followed by parenthesis-like mark setting off from MS page number '1'

344.16–17   The spiders . . . barometers.] added along left margin of first MS page

344.18   shall] over wiped-out 'must'

344.22–24   whose . . . daisies] originally 'whose immediate ancestors had had flourished forth with grass and daisy'; 'the substance' added above 'whose immediate' and 'planted' above cancelled 'flourished'; 'succulent' interlined with a caret and 'daisy' mended to 'daisies'

344.24–25   around the low battlemented] originally 'in this churchyard, about the low Norman'; 'in this churchyard,' cancelled; 'country around' cancelled above 'this churchyard'; 'around' above faintly cancelled 'about'; 'battl' over wiped-out 'Norman'

344.27   wild forest] 'wild for' over wiped-out 'a[   ] land'

345.1   both] above 'characteristic of'

345.2   vegetable] above 'other growth,', of which 'other' cancelled; 'growth,' uncancelled though superseded by following 'productions'

345.4	could . . . unless] above 'garden flowers, which perhaps'
345.8	and cause] over wiped-out 'after the po'
345.11	to] interlined with a caret
345.12	that] preceded by uncancelled 'th'
345.13	at] over wiped-out 'that'
345.13	great] interlined with a caret
345.18	successive] over wiped-out possible 'one le[ ]'
345.24	had elapsed] above 'since'
345.24	first] followed by cancelled 'little hillock was piled up among the'
345.29	one or two] interlined with a caret
346.3–4	Describe . . . naughty &c &c] added in top margin of MS page, which begins 'turned up . . . ' (345.20)
346.5–6	The . . . way.] added in space at end of paragraph
346.7	rippled] over wiped-out '[ ] of the'
346.8	old grave] over wiped-out possible 'ancient'
346.9	both . . . nightfal] above original 'street gloomy, so that people'
346.12	buried] 'ied' over 'y'
346.20	material] above cancelled 'clay'
346.23	the] over 'after'
346.27	both] over possible 'reader'
346.29	wearisome] above uncancelled 'nauseous'
346.29	familiar] over wiped-out 'tune of b'
347.1–2	prominent] 'promin' over wiped-out possible 'eminent'
347.2–3	perhaps . . . old] interlined with a caret
347.3	standing right] above original 'front, upon the'
347.4–5	containing . . . entrance] interlined with a caret
347.11	on the] followed by cancelled 'very edge of a grave'
347.14–15	deceased people] above cancelled 'they'
347.15	at . . . exclusive] interlined with a caret

347.17	for . . . need it] interlined with a caret
347.18	merits and] horizontal lines above and below may be a revision signal
347.19	house] above uncancelled 'abode'
347.20	been] over wiped-out 'taken'
347.20	lay out] above uncancelled 'plan'
347.20	and] above cancelled 'of'
347.21	not unsusceptible of] interlined with a caret above cancelled 'capable of comfort'
347.25	a] above cancelled 'his'
347.26	and various] 'and' followed by uncancelled 'a' interlined with a caret
347.26	and contrivances,] interlined with a caret
347.28–29	the grim Doctor's] above cancelled 'his'
347.30–33	which . . . quantity, by . . . class] MS 'by . . . class which . . . quantity' here reordered in conformity with NH transposition signs of a caret preceding 'by' and following 'class' and 'quantity'; the first and third carets conceal commas now restored as emendations
347.31	was able to] interlined with a caret
347.34–348.1	It . . . mankind] over 'Had he learned some of worldly P[ ]ness, he'
348.3	by . . . title] interlined with a caret
348.4	spider's] above 'his'
348.4–5	and suck . . . substance] interlined with a caret
348.5	as he sat] interlined with a caret
348.7	grim] interlined with a caret
348.8	singularly] above uncancelled 'entirely'
348.9	even] initial 'e' over 'h'
348.10	indeed] interlined with a caret
348.10	conscientious] interlined with a caret
348.16	generally] above 'not acknowledged'
348.19	medical] interlined with a caret
348.19–20	His professional] 'His profess' over wiped-out 'The Doctor'

348.21	partly] interlined with a caret
348.29–30	evidently not] over wiped-out 'not a New Engl'
348.31	apt . . . oddly] above cancelled 'strangely'
348.33	came] 'e' over possible 'y'
349.1	did] initial 'd' over partial 'w'
349.2	projecting forehead] interlined with a caret
349.3	eyes] 'ey' over 'o'
349.3	dull] followed by wiped-out 'e'
349.8	and altogether] 'and alto' over wiped-out 'very diff'
349.9	reddish] interlined with a caret
349.16	the] followed by cancelled 'value of' and inadvertently uncancelled 'his'
349.17	and furrows . . . corrugations] above 'wrinkles, whether as indicating'
349.19	such] interlined with a caret
349.20	occasion] terminal 'ally' wiped out
349.22–23	so incrusted . . . traditions] above original 'fluid, that . . . his'
349.25–26	The . . . instruction.] added along left margin of MS page
349.28	strange] followed by cancelled 'stories'
349.31	disagreeable] 'd' over possible 'baf'
349.32	almost] over wiped-out 'f[dd]le'
349.34	crusty] over wiped-out 'c[ ] Ha'
349.34–350.1	the handmaiden] above 'Hannah, but the'
350.1–2	carefully . . . preserved] above 'material, each . . . more'
350.3	so much] interlined with a caret
350.3	wire. Of] period mended from comma; 'Of' over wiped-out 'or the'
350.3	haunts] above cancelled 'houses'
350.7–8	wherever . . . end] above 'point, across . . . panes'
350.8	across] over possible 'over'
350.11–25	Spiders . . . spider-life. What . . . regions.] MS 'What . . . regions. Spiders . . . spider-life.' now reordered in con-

formity with NH transposition signs of four
vertical lines preceding 'What' and following
'regions.', three vertical lines after 'spider-life.'

350.11   Spiders . . . towards] over wiped-out 'You
had an intolerable sense of a spider'

350.11–12   and walked leisurely] interlined with a caret
following cancelled 'ran'

350.14   odious] above uncancelled 'disagreeable'; the
preceding article mended from 'a' to 'an'

350.17   (for] over wiped-out 'was'

350.20–21   of the] followed by cancelled 'sea-captains'

350.26–27   It . . . credulous.] added in space at end
of paragraph

350.28   All] followed by cancelled 'this disagreeable'

350.29   preliminary] followed by wiped-out comma

350.30   biggest] 'big' over wiped-out 'ugliest'

351.4   is found] over wiped-out 'comes f'

351.5   most] over 'length', itself over wiped-out 'd[ ]y';
preceding 'it' mended to 'its'

351.8   poison, which] 'whi' over wiped-out 'ready'

351.10   in a] over wiped-out 'with'

351.13   foul] followed by wiped-out 'd'

351.14   the crushed] over wiped-out 'which would'

351.15   casual] 'c' over 's'

351.31   (Read . . . it.)] added in top margin of
MS page, above 'Considering that'

351.32–33   when . . . him] interlined with a caret

352.3–4   it might be] over wiped-out '[ ] would ha'

352.5   spider-silk] over wiped-out 'g[ti] silk'

352.6   with] followed by cancelled 'parchment-covered
or black leather'

352.6   volumes,] followed by cancelled 'that closed
down'

352.10   powerful] interlined with a caret

352.11   fragrant] followed by cancelled 'afar when he
walked the'

352.12   went.] followed by three vertical lines, the first
of seven such transposition signs in the para-

	graph, the exact intentions of which are too unclear to justify rearrangement here
352.13	who] over wiped-out 'eith'
352.13	hope,] followed by cancelled 'substitute a fixed and dogged'
352.15–16	crystallizes.] followed by three vertical lines
352.16	dim through] over wiped-out 'through the two'
352.17	an old] over wiped-out 'aged'
352.18–19	that . . . tarnished.] interlined with a caret
352.19	The smoke] over wiped-out possible 'that belonged to'; preceding period cancels comma
352.20	stale.] followed by four vertical lines
352.21–22	—if they ran] over wiped-out 'or if you p'; dash cancels comma
352.22	a door] 'a' followed by cancelled 'the'
352.23	bannisters—] dash cancels comma
352.23	sordid] followed by cancelled 'gloom'
352.23	and] 'a' over 'of'
352.24	away.] followed by three vertical lines
352.26	tarnished.] followed by three vertical lines
352.27	fragrance] horizontal lines above and below the word
352.29	in any] over wiped-out 'and sweet'
352.30	fall.] followed by four vertical lines
352.33	there.] followed by three vertical lines
353.3	none] over 'of'
353.4	dainty] horizontal lines above and below the word
353.12	Little] over wiped-out 'It'
353.16	indicating] over wiped-out 'as much'
353.18	Elsie did] 'Elsie' over wiped-out 'I h'
353.25	disobedience] 'diso' over 'mis'
353.30	me;] 'me' followed by cancelled '; perhaps from the little boy' and semicolon inserted after the cancel
353.31	from some] over wiped-out '(since boys h' and a preceding left parenthesis not cancelled
353.33	boy.] followed by two vertical lines

353.33	Persian] interlined with a caret
354.1–2	Crusty . . . &c] added in space at end of paragraph
354.6	more] over wiped-out 'hear'
354.7	about] 'a' over 'h'
354.9	quite] above 'conscious'
354.16	in] over wiped-out 'of'
354.20	at other] 'at o' over 'and t'
354.21	ventured] 'vent' over wiped-out possible 'made'
354.24	Once] preceded by cancelled 'But,'; 'O' over 'o'
354.25	sitting] over wiped-out 'seated'
354.27	chair] 'c' over possible 'l'
354.29	moment] followed by wiped-out comma
354.32–33	Describe . . . &c] added in space at end of paragraph
354.34–35	made up] above cancelled 'combined'
355.1	more] 'm' over wiped-out 'f'
355.2	beautiful] 'b' over 'p'
355.2	of a brown cast] interlined with a caret
355.4	prettiest] over 'little girl,'
355.4	girl] over 'roun'
355.4	a blond] above 'girl'
355.5–6	unconsciously] initial 'u' over ascender, perhaps of 't'
355.8	red-eyed] interlined with a caret
355.9	out] 'o' over wiped-out 'h'
355.9	volumes] 'vol' over wiped-out 'clo'
355.10	vapor from] over wiped-out 'smoky vapor'
355.13	neighboring] interlined with a caret
355.14	bottle.] followed by cancelled 'The grim Doctor's blood, to say the truth'; 'Doctor's blood' originally 'Doctor, in truth'
355.17	utterance] 'utt' over wiped-out 'wi'
355.18	perceptibly] interlined with a caret
355.19	It is true, when] over wiped-out 'When once, it is true'
355.21	observed] 'obse' over 'seen'
355.22	than] 'th' over possible 'as'

355.26–27	(The . . . cupboard)] added in space at end of paragraph
355.29	looking] 'look' over wiped-out possible 'over'
356.10	and as truly] above 'much, as may'
356.16	at my] 'at' over wiped-out 'my'
356.21	how you] over 'you came'
356.22	The] 'he' over wiped-out 'hat'
357.5–7	He . . . understood.] added in space at end of paragraph
357.8	Elsie] over wiped-out 'little'
357.8	You] over wiped-out 'Elsie'
357.10	laugh] above 'peculiar'
357.10	peculiar] over wiped-out 'loud laugh'
357.14	bright] over wiped-out 'little'
357.17	His] above cancelled 'whose'
357.18	childish] 'ish' squeezed in after inscription of 'child'
357.20	follow up] above cancelled 'enforce'
357.24	a display] the article over 'any'
357.24	even in a child] above 'spirit was apt'
357.28	an] interlined with a caret
357.28	you shall] quotation mark wiped out before 'y'
357.29	, boy] interlined with a caret
357.30	alms-house] originally followed by period and quotation mark; the latter left uncancelled, period mended to semicolon
357.31	may] mended from 'must'
357.33	brow] above cancelled 'face' which was written over wiped-out 'brow'
357.35	violent] above cancelled 'long'
358.2	his brow] ''his' mended from 'him' but following comma uncancelled
358.2	brow . . . that] above cancelled 'and crying with him, but Ned turned away'
358.7	cruel] interlined with a caret
358.11	arm-chair] 'arm-ch' over wiped-out 'straight-b'
358.13	caught . . . threshold] interlined with a caret

358.15	down] over wiped-out 'him'
358.15	again] initial 'a' over comma
358.17–18	so infantile] 'so infa' over wiped-out 'looking'
358.19	sense] 'sen' over wiped-out 'dis'
358.21	traits] 't' over 'c'
358.23	from the chance] over wiped-out 'by the dusty wayside,'
358.27	ever] over wiped-out 'betr'
359.1–2	The . . . sad.] added in space at end of paragraph
359.10	fashion,] followed by cancelled 'and round his neck was a noose'
359.11	a noose] 'a' over wiped-out 'th', the 'h' unfinished
359.14–15	sensibility] 'lity' over wiped-out 'ty'
359.17	go] over wiped-out 'drea'
359.18	dream that] over wiped-out 'go on dreaming'
359.21	must] 'm' over possible 'r'
359.27–28	the filaments] 'the' over 'which'
359.32	both of the] over wiped-out 'of the [wea]'
360.1	him] interlined with a caret
360.4	went] 'w' over possible 's'
360.9	Doctor Grimshawe] originally 'After the foregone scene, Doctor Grimshawe'; 'Doctor Grimshawe' cancelled and the words interlined with a caret preceding 'After'
360.11	discourse] 'd' over 'c'
360.12	and demonstrative] interlined with a caret
360.18	to conceal] 'to' over wiped-out 'not'
360.18	Whatever] over partially wiped-out 'The children'
360.27	world] over wiped-out possible 'tribe of'
360.28	he was] 'w' over 'th'
361.15	a . . . house] above original 'abode, there . . . wretched'
361.20–21	a . . . structure] above original 'spoke of, there . . . aged'
361.23	yet stately] interlined with a caret

361.25   died hundreds] 'hundreds' over wiped-out 'centuries'

361.27   a great] over wiped-out 'into h'

361.30–31   and . . . would] interlined with a caret

361.32   Doctor Grim] cancelled, but also circled as if to countermand cancel

362.2–3   as . . . him] above original 'a scowl into vacancy, and . . . merriment'

362.10   It] over wiped-out 'Th'

362.13   "After . . . Doctor.] added in space at end of paragraph

362.13   in] squeezed in after original inscription

362.15   indeed] over wiped-out 'as if' and the preceding comma then inserted

362.19   available] 'e' over 'y'

362.21   natural] over wiped-out 'perception'

362.34   might] 'm' over wiped-out 'h'

363.3–4   A grown-up . . . all.] inserted with caret at end of paragraph

363.11   a Saxon] over wiped-out 'the Saxons'

363.16   and heiress] 'a' over wiped-out 'of'

363.21   himself] 'h' over 'i'

363.21   thinking] 'th' over 'w'

363.22   any] 'a' over 'th'

363.27–   For . . . ugly.] preceded by two vertical
364.3   lines; along left margin 'Insert before.' directs that the passage be moved up to follow the paragraph 'After . . . added.' (on the preceding MS page), along left margin of which is the direction 'See on next page'

363.30   to keep] 'to' over wiped-out 'for'

363.34   its] 'i' over wiped-out 't'

364.4–5   "One . . . triumph,] MS ' "One . . . triumph, was &c.' is a new beginning of the sentence which originally followed the paragraph 'After . . . added.'; now superseded is ' "and," said the Doctor, with a mysterious look of triumph,'; the remainder of the

	original sentence makes irrelevant the 'was &c.' in revised beginning cited above
364.4	One curious] over wiped-out 'And they b'
364.4–5	lowering . . . yet] interlined with a caret
364.8	Who] over wiped-out 'what'; preceding period replaces wiped-out comma
364.15	leaned] above cancelled 'lay'
364.16	long] over wiped-out 'his'
364.18	it seemed] 'it' over wiped-out 'the'
364.18	by the] over wiped-out 'looking'
364.21	weird] 'w' over wiped-out 's'
364.23	returning] second 'r' over 't'
364.26	tale] 'a' over 'l'
365.5	perhap] initial 'p' over wiped-out 'P'; preceded by left parenthesis also wiped out
365.9–11	(Put . . . application.)] added in available space after the paragraph above the two foregoing sentences of dialogue
365.15	print] over wiped-out 'tread'
365.15	a] over 'one'
365.17	no sunshine . . . fade] above original 'years . . . since, no'
365.27	innocent] 'inn' over wiped-out 'foo'
365.31	tradition] 'traditi' over wiped-out 'legend,'
365.33	afterwards] 'aft' over wiped-out 'by t'; a preceding comma wiped out
366.1	how] followed by wiped-out comma
366.3	two] over 'one'
366.5	and then] 'and' over wiped-out 'and'; a preceding comma mended to semicolon
366.14	one of them] 'one of t' over wiped-out 'to return'
366.18	but do it] over wiped-out 'stain its theshol'; 'step' wiped out above 'theshol'
366.33	put] over wiped-out 'hugge'
367.1–2	They . . . it.] interlined between paragraphs
367.7	gleaming] followed by wiped-out comma
367.7	themselves.] followed by cancelled 'In the grave-yard, which was their playground, they ar-

ranged the scenery of the story, making an
ancient square brick tomb to represent the
family mansion'

367.8   Ned, forgetting] 'Ned, forg' over wiped-out possible 'under which'

367.12   he] over 'and'

368.3   intense] interlined with a caret

368.9–10   the awe . . . individually] above 'spoken
. . . might'

368.18   nature] over wiped-out 'gifted'; a preceding
comma not cancelled

368.21   as a] the article over 's'

368.22   sixpence] over wiped-out possible 'shilling'

369.10   one] over 'his'

369.10   and . . . other] above original 'knee, he
would become'

369.12   his character] 'his cha' over wiped-out possible
'ev[   ]te'

369.16   that drew them] over wiped-out '(his affection'

369.18   thing] over wiped-out 'mighty'

369.26   household] 'house' over wiped-out possible 'only'

369.27   strongly] over wiped-out 'people'

369.28   As] between this paragraph and the preceding,
three horizontal dashes indicate a break

370.3   the coarser needlework] interlined with a caret

370.19   mastering] 'master' over wiped-out 'possessing'

370.24   his origin] over wiped-out 'its origin'

370.28   person] over wiped-out 'face and'

370.32   -worm] 'w' over 'of'

371.4   would give him] 'him' over 'them'

371.6   budding] marked off by horizontal lines above
and below

371.8   in . . . mathematics] interlined with a caret

371.11   not . . . boyhood] marked off by horizontal lines above and below

371.15–16   or he . . . youth.] 'or . . . domestic'
above original 'was incapable of polish. It
. . . gem '; 'life . . . youth.' above

'just hewn out An American', the first three words cancelled

371.19   gained a] over wiped-out 'come fine' of original 'be-|come fine'

371.23   another ploughman] 'nother plou' over wiped-out 'ploughman'

371.25   one, might be] 'provided the fem' added above, then wiped out

371.29   out] interlined with a caret

371.29   this] followed by cancelled 'rough', inscribed over wiped-out 'block,'

371.29   ponderous] 'ponderous and' interlined with a caret above 'wood block'; 'wood' cancelled; 'and' left uncancelled

371.32   learning] above cancelled 'knowledge'

371.33   critical] interlined with a caret

371.33   poets and] over wiped-out 'writers of'

372.1   an able tutor] MS 'an abable tutor' over wiped-out 'an able tutor'

372.2   showing] over 'giving'

372.8   the grim Doctor's] interlined with a caret above uncancelled 'his'

372.11   life,] followed by cancelled 'will'

372.14–16   Perhaps . . . themselves.] above 'gentleman . . . thrust themselves.'

372.20–21   the boy] over wiped-out 'the scholar'

*372.28   beautiful and] 'and' cancelled in different ink, probably by JH; not accepted as valid

372.28   noble] followed by cancelled 'manners'

372.29   them,] followed by cancelled 'little Ned'

373.13   afford] above cancelled 'give'

373.15   positive] interlined with a caret

373.16   , being] over wiped-out 'could'

373.17   There] 'Th' over 'A'

373.18   an M. de Grand but] above 'in the town—secretly'

373.18   secretly] over wiped-out 'calling'

373.18   Count—] dash cancels comma

373.27   requirement] 'req' over 'dep'
373.28   absolutely] over possible 'rough'
373.30–31   He . . . too] added in top margin of MS
                page above 'teaching him cudgel-playing'
374.4–7   nor . . . him.] added in space at end of
                preceding paragraph, a caret after 'pupil' indi-
                cating place for insertion
374.14   sometimes] 'so' over wiped-out 'his'
374.18   life] over wiped-out 'th[ ]'
374.21   were] followed by cancelled 'shared'
374.31   the boy] 'the' over 'him'
375.18–19   (It . . . devotion)] added in space at end
                of paragraph
375.26   unusual] over wiped-out 'loudness and'
315.28   spider] 'd' over 'p'
375.28–29   in . . . circles] above original 'head, and
                clutching'
375.35   after] followed by wiped-out comma
375.35   touched] over wiped-out possible 'moved'
376.1   there] 'th' over 'no'
376.6   awakened] followed by wiped-out comma
376.15–   It was . . . Grim. ¶ One . . . mo-
377.12   tive.] The order of these two paragraphs is
                here transposed in accordance with NH's di-
                rections: '(See end of next paragraph.)' inter-
                lined before paragraph beginning 'One' along
                with three pointer signs in left margin and
                two in right; '(Insert the following paragraph
                at the end of the one next preceding)' added
                in space before 'It was . . . Grim.' para-
                graph, along with three pointer signs in left
                margin; and '(See paragraph next but one
                above.)' added in the line beginning the para-
                graph 'But . . . ' along with two pointer
                signs in left margin; these several directions
                were determined before the inscription of the
                latter paragraph
376.18   matter] over wiped-out possible 'eruption'

376.20–21	They remembered] 'They remem' over wiped-out possible 'Those that'
376.26	afterwards] 'af' over possible 'fo'
376.31–32	and heroic saints] interlined with a caret
377.12	motive.] followed by cancelled letter or letters
377.24	wild] 'w' over 's'
377.29	poignancy] over wiped-out possible 'sighs and'
378.17	was] over wiped-out 'seemed'
378.19	certain] over wiped-out 'doubtf'
378.20	mingled] over '[ ]he[ ]'
378.33–34	Make . . . dissenter.] added between diagonals in top margin of MS page above 'Doctor . . . acquaintance'
379.7	both] 'b' over wiped-out 'he'
379.25	Old Spider] 'O' over 'o' and 'S' over 's'
379.27	poor] above cancelled 'blessed'
380.3	him!] exclamation over question mark
380.7	them] 'the' followed by wiped-out 'like'; 'm' subsequently added
380.9	befals] over wiped-out 'many'
380.17	in] over wiped-out 'these'
381.11	as] 'a' over 'he'
381.23–24	the two . . . graveyard] above 'Doctor to give . . . advice'
381.25–31	perhaps . . . entering. But . . . courteous.] MS 'but . . . courteous; perhaps . . . entering.'; now rearranged in conformity with NH transposition signs: two vertical lines preceding 'but' and following 'courteous' and a single vertical line after 'entering.'
381.33	over] 'o' over wiped-out 'ob'
381.34	growling] above 'rough'
381.34	an] 'bru' of original 'abru' wiped out and 'a' mended to 'an'
382.1	reply] above cancelled 'remark'
382.4	part of the] above 'this story'; 'this' cancelled
382.5	story] followed by cancelled 'in view of the qu'

382.5   was] 'w' over 'and'

382.7   emissary] 'e' over 'm'; the word underlined

382.8   who . . . patient] interlined with a caret

382.15   need] 'n' over 'k'

382.20   idle] 'e' over wiped-out 'd'

382.22–   the horrid . . . yesterday; misconceptions
383.1   . . . walked.] MS 'misconceptions . . .
             walked. The . . . yesterday. &c &' now
             rearranged in conformity with NH transposi-
             tion signs: two-tiered carets precede 'miscon-
             ceptions' and follow 'walked.' and two diag-
             onal lines follow '&'

382.22   horrid] 'hor' over wiped-out 'guess'

382.24   free] followed by cancelled 'with'

382.31   witchcraft] 'h' and 'r' over wiped-out 't' and 'f'

383.14   He . . . street.] added in space at end of
             paragraph

383.20   as if] 'a' over 'if'

383.25   stiff . . . off] above 'abroad, his red . . .
             fire'

383.26   belaboring] 'bela' over wiped-out 'poo'

383.27   paying off] over wiped-out possible 'making
             an e'

383.29–31   town; giving . . . received.] 'giving . . .
             received.', preceded by a two-tiered caret, in-
             serted at end of paragraph; its proper place-
             ment indicated by a two-tiered caret following
             MS 'town.'

384.4   One . . . mad.] added in space at end of
             paragraph

384.15   there] over wiped-out 'their'; a preceding comma
             mended to ;

384.16   staggering] above cancelled 'rushing'

384.19   street-bred] above 'progeny'

384.25   multitude] 'tu' over 'de'

384.26   two . . . of] over wiped-out 'the others
             tumbled over'

384.30   it was exercised] 'it was ex' over wiped-out 'he must ha'

384.31	little] initial 'l' over 'f'
384.34– 385.1	Meanwhile . . . ferocity.] added in space at end of paragraph
385.5	(A . . . tickled.] added in space at end of paragraph
385.8	at least] over wiped-out 'and let'; the preceding comma subsequently inserted
385.13	Quack] MS 'Quak' above 'Doctor'
385.13	—a quack—] above 'Grimshawe'
385.14	intemperate] interlined with a caret
385.15	comes a] over 'are sev'
385.19	meeting] above uncancelled underscored 'church'
385.29–30	(Yankee . . . manners)] added in space at end of paragraph
386.2	person] over wiped-out 'man'
386.5–6	His well-intended] over wiped-out 'This so little effect had'
386.10	making] 'ma' over wiped-out 'ass'
386.15	merely] over wiped-out 'a means'
386.23	as suited] 'as s' over wiped-out 'that'
386.23	even] follows cancelled 'as'
386.32	there] first 'e' over 'y'
386.32–33	lay . . . prepared] above uncancelled 'sat in the Doctor's great arm-chair, in the study'
386.33	impressive presence] horizontal lines above and below
387.5	aspect,] followed by cancelled 'as if'
387.8	looked] above cancelled 'was'
387.12	fellow?"] question mark cancels comma
387.16–18	He . . . blow.] added in space at end of paragraph
387.22–23	a . . . members] above 'mistiness in my sensations'
388.5	it . . . supposed] interlined with a caret
388.15–16	what . . . been] interlined with a caret
388.16	but] interlined with a caret
388.26	are . . . and] above original 'unless you

	dropt'
388.32	for the] above cancelled 'at'
389.1	children] over wiped-out 'p[ ]t'
389.6–7	The . . . till] above 'course of the day, Crusty Hannah had'; the partial underscoring of original 'In the course of the day' suggests that it is to be replaced by the interlined wording
389.18	sense] over wiped-out 'feeling'
389.19	His] over wiped-out 'There'
389.22	a little] over wiped-out 'to g[ ]t'
390.3–4	Ned; perhaps . . . addressed.] semicolon replaces original period; 'perhaps . . . addressed.' added after the inscription of the next paragraph had proceeded
390.7	and . . . horror] interlined with a caret
390.13	observing] 'observ' over wiped-out 'watch'
390.28	not] interlined with a caret
390.29	crush] 'c' over 'b'
390.30	as] over wiped-out 'this'
390.30	—not much unkindly] over wiped-out possible 'and [ ]qu[t] breath'; dash cancels comma
391.6–8	Jokes . . . &c.] added in space at end of paragraph
391.12	lives] over wiped-out possible '[ ]ofi[ ]'
391.13	with . . . them] interlined with a caret
391.25	is] over 'are'
391.25	this] mended from 'these'
391.25	boy] above cancelled 'two children'
391.26	of] over 'to'
391.26	teaching] 'tea' over 'tutor'
392.16	so . . . hater] above 'one another's society'
392.16	so . . . impulsive] above 'crude, animal'
392.18	so . . . crooked] above original 'was, so obstructed'
392.21	grasp] 's' over 'p'
392.25	had been] interlined with a caret above cancelled 'was'
392.26	the disgust] 'the' over wiped-out 'a d'

392.31–32   (The . . . England)] added in space at
end of paragraph
392.33   a good deal] above cancelled 'much'
393.13   only] 'o' over 'of'
393.18   by] over wiped-out 'been'
393.33   any excellence] over wiped-out possible 'The
instruction'
394.3   what] 'w' over wiped-out 'th'
394.10–11   like . . . Africa] above original 'if indeed
he required anything more dense'
394.13   performance] 'perform' over wiped-out 'appear'
394.20   once pretty] over wiped-out 'they seemed'
394.23   (The . . . yard)] added in space at end of
paragraph
394.25   specimen] followed by wiped-out terminal 't'
394.27   ale] above uncancelled 'brandy'
395.6   be] 'e' over 'y'
395.12–13   (He . . . there)] added in space at end of
paragraph
395.15   his] interlined with a caret
395.15–16   Pah . . . pipe.] above original 'it. "A very
strange story that!'
395.18   (Perhaps . . . spoken.)] interlined between
paragraphs
395.20   were] above uncancelled 'are'
395.25   four sons] over wiped-out 'five sons'
395.26   all of whom] over wiped-out 'of whom the
secon'
395.26   one] over wiped-out 'all'
395.26–27   —the] over wiped-out 'were'
395.30–31   converted . . . Fox] above 'been . . .
Quakers'
395.32   a] over wiped-out 'one'
396.5   Our legend] 'Our leg' over wiped-out 'They say'
396.8–12   He . . . kidnapped] in space after short
lines ending two preceding paragraphs
396.14   with] 'w' over wiped-out 'th'
396.27   and much] over wiped-out 'to New Engl'

396.29	They . . . married.] added in space at end of paragraph
396.33	Schoolmaster.] followed by cancelled 'But her love for him never ceased;'
396.34	before] over 'after'
397.3	But . . . key.] above 'in . . . up a'
397.11	never] 'ne' over wiped-out 'hea'
397.18–19	It . . . older.] added in space at end of paragraph
397.20	He got up and] over wiped-out possible 'Ned long feared'
399.4	how] 'h' over 'or'
399.18–19	Old . . . existed.] added in space at end of paragraph
399.25	certified] 'cer' over wiped-out 'cop'
399.34	ago] followed by cancelled 'there was a communication of some kind or other'
400.4	that] 'tha' over 'I ha'
401.11	Ay] 'y' over 'h'
402.6	shuddering] 'dde' over 'ing'
402.10	inordinate] 'inor' over wiped-out 'quan'
402.27	him] 'h' over 'D'
402.29	midnight] preceded by cancelled 'summer'
402.32–33	behind . . . night] above original 'of the study, in his old dressing-gown'
403.2	ever] 'ev' over wiped-out 'sh'
403.9	character] 'char' over wiped-out possible 'nature'
403.16– 404.12	It . . . wickedness. Dreading . . . anathema.] MS 'Dreading . . . anathema. It . . . wickedness.' now rearranged in conformity with NH transposition signs: before 'Dreading' are two groups of short vertical lines, five above four, and a caret below 'D' is followed by interlined 'below'; 'anathema.' is followed by five short vertical lines and 'wickedness.' by three
403.20	so] over 'and'
403.23	from] 'f' over partial 'w'

403.24	in] over 'abo'
403.32	If] over wiped-out 'The'
404.2	April came on] over wiped-out possible 'the first warmth'
404.8	and made . . . coffins] above 'it . . . down'
404.13–15	(There . . . scene)] added in space at end of paragraph
404.23	creatures] over cancelled 'soms' of 'blos-|soms'; 'blos-' left uncancelled
404.26	little] over wiped-out possible 'table'
404.27–28	they . . . morning] MS 'They . . . morning.' above 'a-trundling . . . cups' but placement determined by caret following 'table'
404.28	expecting] 'ex' over 'ho'
405.1–2	pausing . . . seat.] enclosed by pen stroke
406.4–5	or . . . round,] above 'Doctor . . . idea'
406.6	thin] over uncancelled 'lank'
406.10	way] 'w' over wiped-out 't'
406.26	catch] 'ca' over wiped-out 'ge'
406.31	very] over wiped-out possible 'grea'
407.10	had] followed by cancelled 'much'
407.16	themselves] 'v' over 'f'
407.20	neglected] 'n' over 'f'
407.24	with] 'w' over wiped-out 'th'
407.32	cut] over wiped-out 'gra'
408.12	"Why?" said Ned again.] added in space after paragraph
408.16	worn out] interlined with a caret
408.17	corner] over wiped-out 'edge of'
408.20	setting doggedly] interlined with a caret after cancelled 'straying'
408.26	fragrant] above 'magnolias'
408.26	the seeds] 'the' over wiped-out 'flow'
408.27–28	leaving . . . them] above 'been . . . happy'
409.15	quarrel] above cancelled 'difference'
409.15	the boy] 'the' over wiped-out 'their'

409.16	whole day] above cancelled 'day or two'
409.16	sometimes] above 'of silent'
409.16	and stately] 'and st' over wiped-out 'displea'
409.20	as naturally] over wiped-out 'the quantity'
409.21	no advantage] 'no adv' over wiped-out 'the ad'
409.34	the rudiments] 'the ru' over wiped-out 'Latin'
411.1–2	(The . . . Hospital)] added in top margin of MS page, above 'and unattainable . . . of', (411.4–5)
411.7	the grim] 'the' over wiped-out 'grim'
411.15	him a] 'a' over 'an'
411.17	him] over wiped-out 'the man'
411.18	Describe . . . day—] added in space at end of paragraph
411.19	rather young] interlined with a caret; preceded by wiped-out interlined 'you'
411.19	person] above uncancelled 'man'
411.20	rather] 'rat' over wiped-out 'fre'
411.20	cold] above cancelled 'shy'
411.20	ungraceful] over wiped-out 'wh[ ]'
411.20–21	(describe . . . clerical)] above 'genial-looking enough'
411.24	would] over wiped-out 'have'
411.26–30	one . . . companions] underscored, possibly to signal an intended revision
411.28	the spider] 't' over wiped-out 'f'
412.3–4	Represent . . . manners—] added in space at end of paragraph
412.3	him] interlined with a caret
412.6	see] above uncancelled 'perceive'
412.9	briefless] interlined with a caret
412.9	barrister] interlined above is 'a clergyman,' but the sense of this and the following sentence requires the original reading
412.11	detain him at] interlined above is 'a curate', related to 'a clergyman' above
412.14	Doctor] 'D' over 'the'
412.21	that he was] over wiped-out ', how rude he'
412.26	had] over wiped-out 'brought'

412.26	entrusted to me] above original 'errand, and of'
412.29	by your townspeople] interlined with a caret
412.29	not] over wiped-out 'who s'
412.30	me] over wiped-out 'you'
412.31	you] 'y' over wiped-out 'I'
413.1–2	still . . . courtesy] originally 'said the stranger, with imperturbable courtesy'; then 'still with mild courtesy' interlined above 'said the stranger' but leaving 'with imperturbable courtesy' uncancelled
413.3	in search of a] above original 'here to find', but 'to find a' left uncancelled
413.17	a grave] the article 'a' over wiped-out 'the g'
413.30	a wilderness] interlined with a caret
413.31–32	He . . . family.] above 'believe . . . deeds'
413.33	titular] over wiped-out 'proofs'
414.13	grave] interlined with a caret
414.17	what marks] over wiped-out 'had, [ ]'
414.27	take the hereditary] 'take' over wiped-out 'remove' and 'her' over wiped-out 'poss'
414.31	thing] over wiped-out 'affair'
415.4	very probably] 'very' above cancelled 'was'; 'probably' followed by cancelled 'buried'
415.4	be] above wiped-out possible 'in'
415.12	traced out] above 'the impress'
415.17	Elsie] followed by cancelled ', having bestowed sufficient attention on the stranger'
415.17	withdrawn] followed by cancelled 'themselves'
415.23	whispered] over wiped-out 'said Ned'
415.24	Doctor] 'D' over 'the'
415.27	not] originally 'no des'; 'des' wiped out and 't' added to 'no'
415.31	requisite] 'qu' over wiped-out 'ady'
416.2	eyes] over wiped-out 'bright'
416.2	glance] 'glan' over wiped-out 'look'
416.10	answered.] followed by cancelled 'Ned, what do you know of this grave-stone?'

416.20	bloody] interlined with a caret
416.22	at] 'a' over 'i'
416.24	The grave-stone] over wiped-out 'It is a fresh grave'
416.31	their] over wiped-out 'great'
416.34	except . . . hand] above 'lay . . . oblivion'
417.26	old] 'o' over 'g'
417.28–29	Make . . . customs.] added in space at end of paragraph
417.30	at] over 'in'
417.31	the old one] over wiped-out 'we had made'
418.1	person had] over partially wiped-out 'gentleman'
418.4	one] above 'of'
418.9	with a] above cancelled 'looking around'
418.11	was never] above cancelled 'is not one whom'
418.12	No] over wiped-out possible 'True'
418.12	Doctor] 'D' over 'the'
418.15	you] 'yo' over 'ha'
418.34	thousand] a terminal 's' cancelled
419.3	who . . . me] interlined with a caret
419.4	says] mended from 'said'
419.5	in] over wiped-out 'here'
419.6	ground] followed by a comma and cancelled 'save and excepting the family lots, where'
419.14	our] horizontal lines added above and below
419.14–19	An . . . up. Stop . . . again.] MS 'Stop . . . again. An . . . up.' re-ordered in conformity with NH transposition signs of a caret preceding 'Stop' and 'An'
419.23	a] over 'an'
419.24	about graves especially] above 'buried . . . yonder'
419.26	But . . . suppose.] above 'People . . . graves'
419.27–28	They . . . mind."] added in space at end of paragraph
419.33	I] over wiped-out 'it'

420.5	proved to] over 'showed its'
420.6	in bas-relief] above 'carving around'
420.9	this] over wiped-out 'inter'
420.12	over] above uncancelled 'into'
420.15	Part] 'P' over 'of'
420.15–16	an . . . and devout soul] interlined with a caret, 'and devout' added with a caret below remainder of phrase
420.17	1687] '8' over '6'
420.22	a] over 'an'
420.31	my father] 'm' over wiped-out 'I'
421.5	aside] 'a' over 's'
421.14	do] interlined with a caret
421.18	dine] above cancelled 'pass the night'
421.19	accepted] 'ac' over 'was'
421.20	probably] 'pr' over 'app'
422.2	estate] 'esta' over wiped-out 'fam'
422.6	unexpected] 'x' over 'p'
422.18	warmly] 'w' over 's'
422.27	After] 'A' over possible 'W'
422.29	home-feeling here] over possible 'inclination to find'
422.33	was] 'w' over 'h'
423.2	even] over wiped-out 'Elsie'
423.22	Are] 'Ar' over wiped-out 'are'
423.27	the grim] 'the g' over wiped-out 'from t'
423.30	ancient] interlined with a caret
423.32	spot] over 'grave,'
423.33	with] mended from 'which'
424.1	a few] above cancelled 'some'
424.3	be] over 'have'
424.3	appertaining] initial 'a' over 'st'
424.24	Little] a series of dashes between this paragraph and the preceding indicates a break
424.24	fatal] above uncancelled 'strange'
424.24	habit] above cancelled 'process'
424.26	little] initial 'l' over 'L'
424.28	life] 'l' over 'f'

424.28	was growing] originally 'had grown'; 'had' cancelled, 'was' interlined, and 'grown' altered to 'growing'
424.29	sunshine] 'shine' subsequently squeezed in
425.4	letter] interlined with a caret placed after rather than before an already inscribed comma
425.5	onward] above 'marching'
425.7	them] interlined with a caret
425.8	they told] 'they to' over wiped-out 'he could'
425.9	echoes, and] comma and 'an' over wiped-out 'of'
425.12	and singular] interlined with a caret
425.12	mind] over wiped-out 'within'
425.16	after] over wiped-out 'they'
425.17–18	became . . . affect] interlined with a caret above 'might affect other minds', of which 'might affect' was superseded but inadvertently not cancelled
425.23	castle in the] over wiped-out 'visionary castle'
425.32	even] initial 'e' over 'th'
426.9	high] over possible 'own'
426.12	all] over wiped-out 'the'
426.19	make you] 'you' interlined with a caret
427.5	eyes, in] over wiped-out ', deep eyes,'
427.9–10	"There . . . aspect.] added in space at end of paragraph
427.12–14	He . . . off] above 'me. It . . . house'
427.15	ever] over wiped-out 'eat a'
427.26	blockhead] interlined with a caret above underscored but uncancelled 'booby'
427.33	to] over wiped-out 'gush' and a comma inserted before 'to'
428.1	hugged] 'hug' over wiped-out ' "[Ned]'
428.5	so.] period cancels comma
428.10	a man whom] article over 'I'
428.11	of my] 'of' over 'my'
428.16	ever] over wiped-out 'I de'
429.6	inevitable] 'in' over 'lo'
429.24	been only] 'been on' over wiped-out 'only be'

429.31	stuff—] dash cancels comma
430.3	venerable] above 'stately'
430.4	there was] originally 'the prolonging'; then 're was' inscribed over wiped-out 'prolonging'
430.11	a man] the article over 'not'
430.23	an Academy] over wiped-out 'a school'
430.27	in a] over wiped-out 'and w'
430.29	saw] 's' over wiped-out 'ca'
430.30	modest] 'm' over wiped-out 'b'
430.33	great] over wiped-out 'school'
430.33	boyhood] 'bo' over wiped-out 'yo'
431.4	beside the] over wiped-out 'the threshold'
431.6	to him—] dash cancels comma
431.13	good] 'g' over 'f'
431.14	heartily] 'h' over 'y'
431.17	singular] '|gular' over wiped-out '¶ "The'
431.18	looking] 'k' over 'f'
431.19	Doctor] 'Doct' over 'Litt'
431.30–31	feminine . . . home] above original 'herself, had . . . was'
431.32–33	(because . . . barrel;)] parentheses added after inscription
431.32	own love] 'e' over 'ed'
432.5	gentle] above 'old'
432.8	home. Was] originally 'home such,'; then 'Was' written over 'such,'; the period is a CENTENARY emendation
432.13	made all] over 'her [ ]t'
432.18	a] interlined with a caret
432.21	Nor] over 'It'
432.24	child)] parenthesis cancels 'in'
432.24–25	no . . . Ned.] above 'business . . . child) instead'
433.2	the Doctor] 'the' over wiped-out 'they'
433.6	hear] over wiped-out 'notice'
433.21–22	referring . . . sometimes] above 'but . . . start'

433.22   &c &c &c &c] below 'but . . . start'
433.28–30   Talks . . . &c] added in space at ends of
                three preceding sentences
434.7   great] over wiped-out 'huge'
434.11   nothing] 'not' over wiped-out 'very'
434.11   filling] over wiped-out 'half-fill'
434.33   Ned . . . too] over wiped-out 'there is
                nothing left'
435.1   nothing] 'noth' over wiped-out 'done'
435.19   —and] over wiped-out 'and a'
435.27   Doctor] 'D' over 'f'
435.30   odorous] initial 'o' over 't'
435.31   re-baptizing . . . with] above original 'man,
                and a half-emptied tumbler'
435.32   and water] 'and w' over wiped-out 'send'
436.4   our old] 'our' added above 'man, old', the 'old'
                inscribed over original 'our'
436.7–8   Indeed . . . succeeded.] interlined with a
                caret
436.10   Hannah] 'Ha' over 'was'
436.13   and the lawyer] 'and the la' over wiped-out
                'Doctor Grim'
436.21   tears, and] 'a' of 'and' over 'f'
436.22   lingering] above cancelled 'crying'
436.22–   Seeing . . . things.] preceded by a wavy
437.7   line between paragraphs and six diagonal
                lines in the indention space, and followed by
                three diagonal lines; this passage and the
                paragraph 'And, finally . . . no.' trans-
                posed in accordance with the seven arrow-
                head pointers and the direction '(See end of
                next paragraph.)' which follow the paragraph
                beginning 'This, however . . . ', from
                the conclusion of which is deleted the un-
                cancelled language 'and kissed his hand to
                her, and laughed [MS laghed] feebly; and
                that was the last that she or any body, the

	last glimpse they had of Doctor Grimshawe alive.' displaced by the interpolation following MS 'chamber;'
436.24	cry] over 'you'
436.26	kiss] followed by wiped-out quotation mark
436.27	think no] 'and let no o' interlined and wiped out
436.28	Old] 'O' over 'o'
436.28	Bloody] 'B' over 'b'
436.30–31	Then . . . morning.] interlined below the preceding sentence after the next paragraph had been inscribed
437.5	it—drop] dash cancels comma
437.7	by the] 'by the' over wiped-out 'of the'
437.9	a] over 'Ned'
437.19	the poor] 'the' over 'poor', which was written over original 'Ned'
437.19–20	still further] interlined with a caret above cancelled 'greater'
437.25	could] 'cou' over wiped-out 'not'
437.26	had] over 'been'
437.32	him] 'hi' over 'th'
437.33	that] followed by cancelled 'it' inscribed over 'of this'
438.18– 439.12	tumbles . . . anxiety,] from *Grimshawe*, 1883, pp. 127–28; the bottom third of MS ²35 has been cut away
439.26	and the] 'the' over wiped-out 'not'
439.27	as] over 'his'
440.3	that] 'th' over 'ar'
440.4	Notes.] preceded by two diagonal marks; a wavy line separates this paragraph from the preceding
441.7	possessed] above uncancelled 'had'
441.9–12	The Doctor . . . memory.] from *Grimshawe*, 1883, p. 354; the bottom third of MS 36 has been cut away
441.13	comes] followed by cancelled 'along a well-

	trodden though solitary path, throwing his shadow before him'
441.14	of vague] encircled by a line; followed by cancelled 'and'
441.17	spring,] comma cancels semicolon
441.19–20	contrived . . . qualities] above uncancelled 'done their utmost'
441.25	influences] 'influ' over 'a[ ]ble'
441.26	void] over 'purified'
441.30	be] over 'the'
441.30	transparent] above 'clear morning'
441.33	now] above 'some'
441.33	some] originally 'something'; 'thing' cancelled
441.33	veil] above cancelled 'invisible'
442.1	sky] above uncancelled 'sun'
442.1	and absorbed] 'and' above original 'absorbing'; 'ed' interlined above 'ing'
442.4	half suspected] interlined with a caret
442.7	good] over wiped-out 'which'; a preceding comma mended to semicolon
442.8	and richness] above 'depth of verdure'
442.11	on] above uncancelled 'along' written over wiped-out 'on which'
442.11	was] over wiped-out 'had'
442.11	moving] above uncancelled 'passing'
442.13	footpath] over wiped-out 'and broa'
442.15	within] 'with' squeezed in after 'in' was inscribed
442.16	thickly] 'ly' added to original inscription
442.16	luxuriant] above 'was it'
442.19	labyrinth of] over wiped-out possible 'not [ ]y and'; preceding article mended from 'an' to 'a'
442.19	little] initial 'l' over wiped-out 'b'
442.24	and twining] interlined with a caret
442.29	whether elms or] over wiped-out 'grew in the line of'
442.31	naked] 'nak' over 'bare,'

442.32	verdant] over wiped-out 'green with'
442.32	or,] over wiped-out 'and'
443.2	tree] 'tr' over possible 'sh'
443.3	leaf] followed by cancelled 'and historic interest, the misletoe'
443.3	instinct, and] followed by cancelled 'thought of the Druids and of Christmas kisses,'
443.7	as it was,] over wiped-out 'though it'
443.8	was] over wiped-out 'from an' and preceding comma then inserted
443.9	than the oak] 'n' over wiped-out 't'
443.10	perhaps] interlined with a caret
443.14	still] above 'retains'
443.23	poorest] 'est' over 'ma'
443.25	road] followed by cancelled terminal 's'
443.30	stone] 'e' over wiped-out 'es'
443.30	by the] 'by t' over 'hob'
444.8	rose] followed by cancelled 'up'
444.9	aloft] above cancelled 'upward'
444.9	made a cheery] above cancelled 'burst into a'
444.10	melody] followed by cancelled 'that was like a sweet, audible spire of flame'
444.10	music] followed by cancelled 'vanishing skyward' which was written over wiped-out 'as if this substance'
444.10	whole] over wiped-out 'substan'
444.16	bird] above cancelled 'voice'
444.16	audible] interlined with a caret above uncancelled 'heard'
444.16	the] above uncancelled 'some'
444.17	shadow] 'sha' over wiped-out 'hid'
444.17	two] above uncancelled 'a'
444.17	trees] above uncancelled 'wood'
444.17	or some] over wiped-out 'or other'
444.18	in a flute-like] over partially wiped ' "Cuckoo, cuckoo" '
444.18	blown] over wiped-out possible 'now'
444.24–25	and rather] interlined with a caret

444.26	thought] over wiped-out 'struggle'
444.26	even of] interlined with a caret
444.27	pale] followed by cancelled 'countenance'
444.27	but] 'b' over wiped-out possible 'as'
444.28	youth] originally 'young man'; 'youth' interlined above uncancelled 'young', and 'man' left uncancelled
444.29	lithe] 'l' over 'a'
444.31– 445.11	enabling . . . clover-blossoms. It could . . . was.] MS 'It could . . . was—enabling . . . clover-blossoms.' reordered in conformity with transposition signs of three-tiered caret preceding 'It' and two-tiered carets before 'enabling' and after 'clover-blossoms.'
444.32	as we] over wiped-out 'in f' and preceding comma inserted
444.32	in] 'i' over 'b'
444.33	rustic] 'ru' over wiped-out possible 'p'
445.1–2	have been] interlined with a caret
445.4	not] over wpied-out 'so'
445.6–7	life, his] followed by cancelled 'dress hung on'
445.7	being worn thin] interlined with a caret
445.8	was such] over wiped-out 'seemed'
445.12	within] above cancelled 'among'
445.13	busy] 'b' over 'a'
445.13	allowed] above uncancelled 'given'
445.17	many of the] above 'observant of trifling'
445.19	overarched,] over wiped-out 'more infringed'
445.20–21	he . . . and] above original 'shrubbery; in . . . board'
445.21	nailed] 'na' over wiped-out 'had'
445.22	notice,] followed by cancelled 'intimating that intruders'
445.22–23	inhospitable] interlined with a caret
445.23	prosecution. He] 'He' follows wiped-out 'and' and period cancels comma which preceded 'and'
445.24	over] above cancelled 'through'

445.32	knew] over wiped-out 'had'
445.33	far] interlined with a caret
446.4	approaching] above 'at the traveller'
446.7	brush] above uncancelled 'shrubbery'
446.11	shyness] 'sh' over wiped-out 'and'
446.11	an instinct that] over 'a kindred shy m[ ]'
446.12	mimicked] second 'm' over wiped-out 'k'
446.13	tamed the] over wiped-out 'called'
446.15	fancied] 'fan' over wiped-out possible 'was'
446.16	freer life,] above 'to want'
446.20	with] over 'the l' and preceding comma then inserted
446.22	precipices, swamps, potholes,] above original 'beasts, leaving nature'
446.23	disarmed] above uncancelled 'deprived'
446.23	deadlier] second 'd' over 'l'
446.26	we sit down] 'we sit' above uncancelled ', sitting' and 'down' above 'on'
446.31	were it] interlined with a caret
446.31	instead of noontime] above original 'nightfall, a will-'
446.31	the] over 'of'
446.33	in this solitude] MS 'in this solitued' interlined with a caret
446.33	some] above uncancelled 'a'
447.2	loud,] followed by cancelled 'and then left a stillness'
447.3	hares and] interlined with a caret
447.6	situation] 's' over wiped-out 'p'
447.6	very] interlined with a caret
447.9	same] over 'long'
447.13	the more] over wiped-out 'pertaining'
447.16	sober] above uncancelled 'waking'
447.20	room] above uncancelled 'chamber'
447.24	bearded] interlined with a caret
447.28–29	Was . . . footstool!] above 'earnestness . . . opened'
447.34	of whose] 'of w' over wiped-out 'visib'

447.34	visible] above 'whose portraits'
448.5	arm] 'a' over 'h'
448.7	read its] over wiped-out 'assigned it'
448.8	natural] 'nat' over wiped-out 'his'
448.11	childhood.] followed by inverted caret which cancels original semicolon; period then inserted
448.11–20	There . . . sunshine.] in MS inserted between 'benign,' and 'saint-like' (451.18), preceded by the direction '(See last page)' and marked off by left margin lines above and below the passage; the point of insert determined by inverted caret and the interlined direction '—see bottom of next page' following 'childhood.'; 'See bottom of next page' also added above three-tiered caret erroneously inserted after 'distinctly.'
448.18	thus] mended from 'now'
448.24	legend] above uncancelled 'motto'
448.27–28	one circumstance] above 'these details were', mended to 'this . . . was' but 'details' not cancelled
448.30	small chest] above 'standing'; follows uncancelled 'table'
448.31	the top of] interlined with a caret
449.1	engraving] 'engr' over wiped-out 'rud'; a preceding comma cancelled
449.7	made] above cancelled 'gave', which was written over wiped-out 'roused'
449.8	intending] 'intend' over 'with'
449.11	(Let . . . costume.)] added in space at the end of paragraph
449.13	watcher] above uncancelled 'figure'
449.14	once] interlined with a caret
449.14	in ancient times] underscored, possibly to call attention to repetition of 'ancient times' later in the sentence; possibly by hand other than Hawthorne's

449.15	might] over wiped-out 'had'
449.15	devout] over wiped-out 'religious'
449.16	those] above cancelled 'such'
449.17	thin] over wiped-out 'and th' and preceding comma then inserted
449.22	good will and] interlined with a caret
449.23	the latter] 'the' mended from 'he'; 'latter' interlined
449.29	Compare him to a palmer] added in space at end of paragraph
450.4	figure] over wiped-out 'seemed to en'; previously inscribed 'man' mended to 'man's'
450.8	hair] over 'silver'
450.11	arm] over wiped-out possible 'head'
450.12	room.] period mended from semicolon
450.13	under] over wiped-out 'by'
450.14	thus vividly] interlined with a caret
450.19	saw] above cancelled 'felt'
450.22	the] followed by cancelled 'old man'
450.24	palm] 'p' over wiped-out 'on'
450.27–28	"a spirit . . . fantasy] interlined with a caret
450.31	close] over partially wiped 's[ ]p'
450.34	an image] 'an' over wiped-out 'the'
451.3	cup] over 'mug'
451.22	But] 'Bu' over wiped-out 'Wh'
451.27–28	Describe . . . delirium] added in top margin of MS page
451.30	still . . . and] interlined with a caret
451.31–32	which . . . fever] interlined with a caret
451.32	day] interlined with a caret
451.32–33	as it were] interlined with a caret
452.6	listening] over wiped-out 'the next'; a preceding semicolon mended to comma
452.7	in the] 'the' over 'an'
452.11	(Make . . . feverish.)] added in space at end of paragraph
452.31	still] interlined with a caret

453.2   in deep] over wiped-out 'deeply'

453.11   manipulations] 'manip' over wiped-out 'profes-
             sion'

453.12   touch] 'to' over wiped-out 'of'

453.14   surgeon.] followed by wiped-out ', who thru';
             period added

453.15–16   in . . . eye] interlined with a caret that
             obscures comma following 'patient'

453.16   slight] interlined with a caret

453.18   has] over wiped-out 'knew how'

453.21   4 or 5] '4' above 'three' and '5' above 'four'

453.23–28   There . . . it. ¶ "It . . . hereafter."]
             the scene was inscribed through 'took his
             leave.' (454.12) when NH became dissatis-
             fied with his original ' "It was an Indian bul-
             let," murmured the patient.' after 'I doubt." ';
             he put four arrowhead pointers in a line be-
             low 'took his leave.' and added the note 'There
             . . . it.' and revised ' "It . . . here-
             after." '; three arrowhead pointers mark trans-
             position point after original; in addition, in
             available space after the paragraph ending
             'then they.' (453.5) NH added five large
             arrowhead pointers and 'See below.' to call
             his attention in future revision; the paragraph
             separation at ' "It' is a CENTENARY emenda-
             tion retaining format of the dialogue

453.29   Indies] interlined after original 'East" ', the 'I'
             obscuring the double quotation mark

453.33   involved] followed by cancelled 'in further ex-
             planation,'

454.6   the young fellow] above cancelled 'patient'

454.11   had . . . art] horizontal lines drawn above
             and below

454.13   half] over 'ora'

454.27   Weakness] 'We' over 'It'

454.27   the . . . nerves] above 'and . . . de-
             pendence'

454.31   in the other] above 'kindness, a'
455.1–2   Notice . . . sickness.] added in space at
           end of paragraph
455.4   perhaps] interlined with a caret
455.5   entirely] above 'not that'
455.6   and be the stronger for it] above 'said . . .
           with a'; 'and' obscures preceding quotation
           mark; 'stronger' over original 'better for' and
           'for it' added after original uncancelled 'it,"'
455.8   stronger] above uncancelled 'wisest'
455.13   "And] added before original ' "Since'
455.17   the] over 'his'
455.17   old] over wiped-out 'man'
455.22   bringing] 'br' over 'as'
455.24–25   At . . . intervals] over wiped-out 'When
           he awoke [ ]p[ ]f'
455.25   his mother] 'his' over 'its'
455.26   his bed] 'his' over 'its'
455.28   kindly] over wiped-out 'saintly'
456.5–8   Perhaps . . . it.] added in space at end of
           paragraph
456.6–7   as in . . . without] 'as' added above 'with-
           out' then wiped out and added before 'in'
456.8   quite] 'q' over 'a'
456.13–   "Ah . . . it?"] the passage marked across
457.11   by a few diagonal pen strokes as though to
           be revised or deleted
456.16   is] over 'was'
456.20   ago] 'a' over 'f'
456.22   The old man smiled] interlined between para-
           graphs
456.22   a] followed by cancelled 'bright and'
456.22   very bright] over wiped-out 'shiny [ ]lf a'
456.24   stranger] followed by cancelled ', earnestly'
456.26   now] above 'you'
456.34   interval] 'inter' over possible 'time'
457.4–7   (The . . . &c)] added in space beside two
           short dialogue paragraphs

457.12	know] over wiped-out possible 'do," '
457.13	Doctor] over wiped-out 'the grim'
457.13	whispered] 'whis' over 'said'
457.17	ought] above cancelled 'will'
457.19	imbecility] 'im' over wiped-out 'of'
457.22	undistinguished] 'un' over 'di'
457.27	or two] above original 'day found'
457.29	his] over 'moo'
457.29	present] interlined with a caret
457.29	spirit] 'sp' over 'hi'
458.2	cares] over wiped-out possible 'ways'
458.4	connected] followed by cancelled 'with'
458.5	battery] 'b' over wiped-out possible 'hi'
458.5	and] 'a' over 'h'
458.9	some] over wiped-out 'twinges'
458.17–18	to listen . . . wind] above original 'his mind, and look . . . at the'
458.19	glimmering] over wiped-out 'shining th'
458.20	illuminating] 'illumin' over wiped-out 'making'
458.21	dim] over 'lam'
458.23	that the] followed by cancelled 'sweet'
458.23	song] interlined with a caret
458.29	prolong] above uncancelled 'promote'
458.30	also] over wiped-out possible ', who'
459.6	organization] 'iza' over 'ati', the 'ti' wiped out
459.9	else] 'el' over 'go'
459.10–13	(When . . . up.)] added in space at end of paragraph
459.12	again] 'ag' over wiped-out 'go'
459.23	throughout] 'thr' over wiped-out 'one'
459.28	Tomorrow] 'To' over wiped-out 'It'
459.28	hope] above cancelled 'purpose'
459.29–30	palmer, "and very . . . go.] 'palmer' followed by two-tiered caret as insertion point for 'and very . . . go.' which, preceded by a similar caret, was added after 'long." ' (459.32); the comma and double quotation mark are CENTENARY emends

459.34	benevolence] 'benev' over 'char'
460.4	serves] over 'is the', the article wiped out
460.4	him who was] over wiped-out 'beneficiaries'
460.7	ponderous] above cancelled 'spacious'
460.10	was] 'w' over wiped-out ', a'
460.14	twelve men,] over wiped-out 'twenty people'
460.16	a sick] 'a s' over wiped-out 'pass'
460.18	moved by] over wiped-out 'although'
460.31–32	the establishment] 'the' mended from 'then'; initial 'e' of 'establishment' over wiped-out ', au'
461.11	people] over wiped-out 'many pe'
461.14	causes] over 'reasons'
461.15	particular] 'parti' over wiped-out 'night'
461.19	had] over wiped-out 'was'
461.19–20	knowledge . . . was] above cancelled 'communication with me'
461.26	childish] 'c' over 'b'
461.28	the secret] 'the' over 'secr'
462.8	be dressed] 'be dre' over wiped-out 'dress him'
462.9	a great] the article over 'gr'
462.10	not much except] above 'with only his', the 'only' uncancelled
462.10	his pale] 'his' over 'a'
462.10	thoughtful] interlined with a caret
462.14	corridor leading] 'corridor le' over wiped-out 'gallery leading'
462.15	(so] parenthesis cancels comma; MS 'so the' over wiped-out 'the one'; the superseding article uncancelled
462.15	Redclyffe's] 'Red' over 'per'
463.5	Redclyffe's] 'Red' over 'tone'
463.5	finely] 'f' over 't'
463.6	and thence] 'and' mended from 'an' and 'th' over wiped-out 'then'
463.10	greater] 'grea' over wiped-out 'a f'
463.12	owing . . . absence] interlined with a caret
463.13	attending] over wiped-out 'attending y'

463.14	I . . . recovered] above original 'in attending you. Do . . . yourself'
463.15	in a] over wiped-out 'able'
463.16	befallen you] 'y' over question and quotation marks
463.18–19	reminiscences. "I am] 'reminiscences' originally followed by 'of [ ]ou[ ]'; quotation mark mark written over 'of' and period inserted; 'I am' over wiped-out '[ ]ou[ ]'
463.22	being told that] above cancelled ', which, I was told'
463.25	indistinct] initial 'i' over wiped-out 'b'
463.26	had just] over possible 'came a'
463.28	had] above cancelled 'were'
463.28	fallen] interlined with an imperfect caret
463.30	come] interlined with a caret
463.31–32	much . . . poachers] interlined with a caret
463.32	exposed] over wiped-out possible 'brought your'
464.3–4	(who . . . woods)] above original 'for . . . here, when . . . drew'
464.7	entirely] over wiped-out 'to it in a'
464.9	suspicion] above cancelled 'conclusion'
464.15	and] 'n' over 'd'
464.16	far] interlined with a caret
464.16	moderate] 'letters' interlined above and then wiped out
464.17	a . . . credit] above 'sum of money'
464.18	feel] followed by cancelled 'justified'
464.21–22	I . . . day."] added in space after paragraph; preceding double quotation mark uncanceled
464.23	probable] 'a' over 'b'
464.24	is strong] over wiped-out 'in itself'
464.34	stranger] 'str' over 'for'
465.1	and parks] interlined with a caret
465.2–3	us. May] over wiped-out possible 'our count'; possible 'ph' over 'ou' of pronoun

465.5	considered] 'co' over 'as'
465.5	as decisive] 'de' of original 'a de' wiped out; 'a' mended to 'as' and 'd' written over wiped-out 'de'
465.5–6	as most] 'as' over 'mo'
465.6	modes] 'mo' over wiped-out 'int'
465.6	observing] above uncancelled 'feeling'
465.7	of] over 'k'
465.8	feeling] second 'e' over 'l'
465.11	and glanced] over wiped-out 'with a sligh'
465.11	it over with] over wiped-out 'over the paper'
465.12	it was] above 'bow; a'
465.13	favor] 'fa' over wiped-out 'Ed'
465.13	Honorable] 'H' over 'h'
465.14	his] over wiped-out 'the b'
465.16	Republic] 'R' over wiped-out 'f'
465.19	held . . . denoted in] above uncancelled 'acquired a title of honor in the such'
465.21	Mr. Redclyffe] interlined with a caret
465.22	hereabouts?] question mark cancels comma
465.29	such] over 'too slight'
465.32	laughing] above 'frankly'
465.33	a long] 'a lo' over wiped-out 'while'
466.2	at pleasure] original 'apt' mended to 'at'
466.8	small] 's' over wiped-out 'p'
466.13	Edward] 'E' over partial 'R'
466.13	had] over wiped-out possible 'could'
466.19	of] over 'be'
466.27	in it] 'in' over wiped-out 'it'
466.31	myself] over wiped-out 'himself'
467.1–10	Redclyffe . . . personage.] an irregular line leads from paragraph indention to the beginning of originally cancelled second sentence 'That . . . London.'; below that sentence is interlined '1' and below the first sentence '2', suggesting a revised plan to reorder rather than cancel; the entire paragraph appears to be supplanted by what follows

467.1	Redclyffe] 'R' over 'Th'
467.2	the next day] above cancelled 'that afternoon'
467.4	comfort. That] originally 'comfort; and that'; 'and' cancelled and initial 't' of 'that' mended to capital but the semicolon left uncancelled
467.5	for] above 'which'
467.8	being] over wiped-out 'being of'
467.12	narrow] over wiped-out possible 'narrow q'
467.12	far ampler] 'far am' over wiped-out 'Warden's'
467.13	was] above cancelled 'had'
467.15–16	new . . . see] above original 'where he found some luggage', but 'found' left uncancelled
467.17	Edward] 'Ed' over wiped-out 'he'
467.18	part] above cancelled 'exact'
467.18	much] above 'to be'
467.18	than] over wiped-out 'had'
467.24	Hospital] above uncancelled "establishment'
467.24	nearly an] above cancelled 'one'
467.24–25	which the] over wiped-out ', about which'
467.25	the establishment] 'the' over 'a'; 'establ' over wiped-out 'bachelor'
467.26	(such] parenthesis cancels comma
467.28	chamber] 'cham' over wiped-out 'room,'
468.1	life] over wiped-out 'and'
468.4	antique] 'a' over 'q'
468.7	such] 's' over 'as'
468.15	circumspect] interlined with a caret
468.16	soon] followed by cancelled 'again'
468.20–21	lighted . . . windows &] above 'spacious apartment, surrounded with'
468.23	rich old bindings] added in top margin of MS page above 'his life a genuine'
469.8	At an] over wiped-out 'But in one'
469.8	one embowed] 'one emb' over wiped-out 'a slight'
469.15	recess] above uncancelled but underscored 'nook'

469.15	study] over wiped-out 'chamber'
469.18	a study] 'a' over wiped-out 'lux'
469.19	inkstand] MS 'instand'; second 'n' over 'd'
469.20	thought] 'tho' over wiped-out 'repo'
469.23	in consultation] 'in' over 'on'
469.25	volume] followed by partially wiped caret, superseded by caret following 'Latin'
469.26–27	printed . . . title-page] interlined with a caret
469.27	with] over wiped-out 'titled'
469.28–29	Lillibulero . . . ballads] above original 'preceding day; and . . . Redclyffe'
469.30	the three volumes] 'the three vol-|' over wiped- 'a novel from a'
469.30	circulating] over wiped-out 'London circu'
469.31	Redclyffe] 'Re' over wiped-out 'Ed'
469.32	educated] interlined with a caret
469.33	are] over wiped-out 'are b'
469.33	and all] 'nd' over wiped-out 'll'
470.8	on] above cancelled 'over'
470.9	German] 'Ger' over wiped-out 'pipe'
470.13	and up] 'and' over wiped-out 'been'
470.14	a feverishly] 'a' over 'an'
470.20	perhaps] 'h' over 'p'
470.29	Edward] 'Ed' over 'Red'
471.10	as I saw them] interlined with a caret

ANCILLARY DOCUMENTS

474.2	anyone] followed by wiped-out 'I'
475.21	system] 'sys' over wiped-out 'by de'
476.10	all] 'a' over upstroke of probable 'h'
476.16	ancestors'] 'an' over 'hav'
477.2	title] initial 't' over wiped-out 'f'
477.6	an] followed by wiped-out 'er'

477.9	romance] 'roma' over wiped-out possible 'color'
477.9	sombre] 's' over 'd'
477.16	one] over 'a l'
477.18	He] over wiped-out 'So'
477.32	at] 'a' over 'l'
478.25	discovers a secret] 'a' over possible 'E'; second 'e' of 'secret' over 't'
478.27	it has] 'it h' over wiped-out 'it sha'
479.8	ancestor] 'a' over 'c'
479.14	while] 'whi' over wiped-out possible 'come'
480.6	Charter-] 'C' over 'c'
480.12	attention] 'a' over 'h'
480.17	vivid] initial 'v' over 'w'
480.18	in] 'i' over 't'
480.26	anon] 'a' over 'i'
480.28	gentleman] second 'e' over 'l'
480.30	A] over 'T'
481.4	for] 'f' over 'of'
481.15	also] 'lso' over 'so'
481.16	tincture] 'c' over 't'
481.26	her] 'h' over 'th', the original 'h' unfinished
481.31	latter] 'l' mended from 'f'
482.9	rambling] 'ra' over 'tra'
482.14	adventurer] terminal 'r' over 'd'
482.24	abode.] period cancels semicolon
482.24	rein] 're' over 'ba'
483.21	splendidly] first 'l' over 'e'
484.9	on] 'n' over 'f'